FRANKLIN D. ROOSEVELT

Recent Titles in
Contributions in Political Science
Series Editor: Bernard K. Johnpoll

FRANKLIN D. ROOSEVELT

The Man, the Myth, the Era, 1882–1945

Edited by Herbert D. Rosenbaum and Elizabeth Bartelme

Prepared under the auspices of Hofstra University

Contributions in Political Science, Number 189

Greenwood Press
New York • Westport, Connecticut • London

Library of Congress Cataloging-in-Publication Data

Franklin D. Roosevelt : the man, the myth, the era,
   1882–1945.

   (Contributions in political science, ISSN 0147–1066 ;
no. 189)
   Papers presented at a Presidential conference
sponsored by Hofstra University.
   Includes bibliographies and index.
   1. Roosevelt, Franklin D. (Franklin Delano),
1882–1945—Congresses.   2. Presidents—United States—
Biography—Congresses.   3. United States—History—
1933–1945—Congresses.   I. Rosenbaum, Herbert D.
II. Bartelme, Elizabeth.   III. Hofstra University.
IV. Series.
E807.F693   1987   973.917′092′4   [B]   87–8456

ISBN 0–313–25949–6 (lib. bdg. : alk. paper)

British Library Cataloguing in Publication Data is available.

Library of Congress Catalog Card Number: 87–8456
ISBN: 0–313–25949–6
ISSN: 0147–1066

First published in 1987

Greenwood Press, Inc.
88 Post Road West, Westport, Connecticut 06881

Printed in the United States of America

The paper used in this book complies with the
Permanent Paper Standard issued by the National
Information Standards Organization (Z39.48–1984).

10   9   8   7   6   5   4   3   2   1

Contents

Preface

To encompass the life of Franklin D. Roosevelt on the occasion of his one hundredth birthday requires that one assess tumultuous times and monumental leaders. Roosevelt was so public a person and affected his times so thoroughly that one cannot account for the times without explaining him as well. Conversely, one cannot account for him by wrenching him from the stream of events of which he was a part and which made him the man he was and the figure he came to be.

He was engaged deeply in the politics of his town, his state, his country and, finally, the entire world, but the bond between him and these arenas is as mysterious as that between other leaders and their spheres. Powerful men and fateful times have found each other throughout history. We look into the secret recesses of their private lives for the mainsprings of their motive power, as if to say that the history books have not told us enough of what we need to understand.

Franklin Roosevelt presents us with a whole host of paradoxes: a young man reared in a setting of Victorian sensibilities who became a daring innovator; a patrician as the leader of the plebs; a playfully ebullient man of great gravity; a fountain of energy in a crippled body; the cautious, wily politician who shrinks from small risks but sets in motion ventures so great as to assure victory, not to himself, but to his antagonists; a man thought not capable of great ideas or of a lively imagination who has left a rich legacy of words and phrases with which to frame political discourse and action down to this very time; the warm, direct, attentive humanitarian who shrinks from giving aid in situations which even now wring our consciences; a man in a political world dominated by men who accepted the scope and weight of the unprecedented and effective participation of his wife, Eleanor. The list seems endless.

That portion of the commemoration that turns upon the examination of the times of Roosevelt is vastly more complex than this complex man. Yet these times seem more comprehensible because they represent the shared experiences of hundreds of millions of people.

Was there ever a thirty-five-year period of history more crowded with cataclysmic change than that between 1910, when Roosevelt entered politics, and 1945, when, exhausted from his long struggle, he died? The fall of the "proud tower" of nineteenth-century tranquility nearly coincided with Roosevelt's political beginnings. Only the most exaggerated terminology can describe the extremes of suffering, degradation, cruelty, and destruction witnessed by the world since then. Extremes of hope, achievement, and optimism for human possibilities matched the suffering. The contradictions defy the imagination; extraordinary organizational efforts and discipline were harnessed to the creation of the greatest chaos; the grandest promises became the handmaidens of the greatest depravities.

The leaders and their times were also matched; those who released the spirits of political evil from its vast reservoir were giants, as were those who sought to build and to harness social forces for the better. Some gave the appearance of heroism and some of the comic opera. Many, perhaps most, fell somewhere in between the grand and the petty. It is undeniable that among the giants of that time was Franklin Roosevelt, and that in the final twelve years of his life he was transformed by the chaotic conditions of his own country and of the world beyond into the man upon whose shoulders could fall the most crushing burdens. While he did not bear these burdens alone, and while the discharge of his duties did not leave his reputation without flaw or tarnish, neither did he flee from them, nor shrink from the most excruciating choices and the most momentous decisions. Throughout, he hewed to the main lines of his political heritage, articulated clearly his humane and generous purposes, enlisted the constructive efforts of millions everywhere, and lifted their hearts with buoyant hope.

The great war which he led did not result in the peace he thought would come and for which his valiant widow expended her physical and moral energy to the last. But the possibilities for peace, the process of it, its future shape and likely content would be familiar to Franklin Roosevelt. Generosity in peacemaking, negotiated settlements, and the provision of aid to relieve suffering were Rooseveltian to the core.

If, at the end, he left much undone, as all such leaders seem fated to do, it was his humanity, and not his neglect or irresponsibility, that accounts for it. The "rendezvous with destiny" to which he called his generation continues to our own time.

As we examine the evidence of his life and of the life of his most faithful and spirited partner and follower, we may be able to sense the way this fateful couple kept their rendezvous. As we reflect on that evidence it ought to occur to us that as a nation and as individuals, even as inhabitants of our globe, we were singularly blessed by him and by her.

This volume is the written record, nearly complete, of the first of Hofstra University's presidential conferences. At the time of its publication, delayed for a variety of reasons, our presidential conferences have become noted events in the life of our institution and in the world of scholarship centering on the U.S. presidency.

The provenance of the presidential series was fortuitous and accidental, though contextual to Hofstra. Scholarly conferences had, by 1981, become a practiced art among us. A broad range of topics and individuals had already been the subject of discussions for some years, when, in the spring of 1981, a customary meeting over morning coffee produced the proposal for a conference on FDR. Harold Klein, the director of University Relations, Professor Paul Harper, the chairman of the Political Science Department, and the undersigned were the trio in question. It was Harold Klein who reminded us of the forthcoming centenary of FDR's birth and the semicentenary of his election to the presidency, adding, "What do you think of an FDR conference?"

In the days and weeks after that first meeting we found to our gratification that the idea enjoyed the support of all of those elements of the university whose ultimate participation would be needed to assure its success.

The late Professor Joseph G. Astman, the founder and director of the University Center for Cultural and Intercultural Studies, was enthusiastic from the start. His two major assistants, Dr. Alexej Ugrinsky and Natalie Datlof, our conference coordinators par excellence, were nothing short of excited by the prospect; the faculty members of the advisory committee proved thoughtful in advice-giving and in the reading of papers. President Shuart's support and that of his staff and his major aides were at all times indispensable and complete.

These conditions greatly eased the concern one might have had about under-taking the task of organizing this effort, and added zest and interest to its management. The realization that, in order to do justice to Roosevelt's life, one would have to think big indeed, came early to us; we realized that no three-day conference could expect to satisfy to the fullest measure the many varied demands placed upon scholarly assessment of that life and those times.

Nor could we choose, given our limited resources, to attract all of the leading scholars who might help to throw light on the most salient aspects of the pres-ident's era. Neither would it have been workable to provide our intended guests with a preformed pattern to which their invited works would have to conform. That imposition would have been difficult to live up to, given the scope of the life and the times to be examined.

Beyond these concerns was the university's need to provide a conference where not only would scholars gather and talk to each other, but which was public in the sense of being accessible and interesting to the immediate com-munity of which Hofstra is a part. And so we devised a formula which would, we thought, strike an intelligent balance between the needs, conditions, and constraints that faced us.

To begin with, the widely disseminated call for papers served as the provider

of the fundamentals of our meeting: scholars looking at FDR through the per-
spectives of their own creation, along lines of method and logic dictated by the
rigor of their own disciplines.

Second, we sought to provide two kinds of leavening for that loaf. We set
about deliberately to attract known leaders of FDR scholarship by extending
invitations to several to bless our event by their participation. Thus we were
able to attract such renowned scholars as Professors Frank Freidel and Arthur
M. Schlesinger, Jr., together with Louis Koenig. In that framework we also
internationalized the event by broadcasting our gathering overseas and, in one
case, by calling it to the attention of the USSR's Institute for American and
Canadian Studies.

Third, we looked for and found survivors of the era of the New Deal and
World War II who were among the movers and makers of these events. In that
way we were able to draw upon these voices from the past. Their presence lent
vividness and immediacy to the conference, and more than a little nostalgic
humor. We were exceedingly proud to have contributed to their pleasure in being
together to recall great and dangerous times.

Fourth, we aimed at providing as much physical evidence of the Roosevelt
era as our quarters would hold. Several private collectors aided us in that, but
none as much as the Roosevelt Library and Museum at Hyde Park, with its
generous cooperation.

As our discerning readers will no doubt note, our call for papers had the happy
result of attracting a stellar cast of contributors and participants. The members
of the community of scholars whose attention is focused on the lives of Franklin
D. Roosevelt and his partner Eleanor, on their times and the rich legacy of
institutional and policy initiatives, was well represented at Hofstra. Their efforts
are eminently worthy of inclusion in this volume.

With these guidelines in hand we assembled a series of events notable for
their weightiness, interest, variety, and liveliness. Regrettably, this volume, in
restricting itself to the bulk of the written record, cannot reflect the entirety of
the conference. In particular, these proceedings omit the rousing banquet address
of the Hon. Jennings Randolph, U.S. Senator from West Virginia, and the lively
contributions of the New Dealers' Roundtable, graced by such luminaries as
Leon Keyserling and the late James Rowe, or Professor Thomas Emerson. Absent
also is the graceful address of Dr. William R. Emerson, the director of the
Roosevelt Library and Museum at Hyde Park, who, by his presence and generosity, brought many events to life by sharing documents, books, exhibits, and
works of art with us. Absent also are the many thoughtful comments of the
chairmen and women of the eight panels, and the many fruitful questions and
interventions of the audiences.

To create the scholarly panels we made two sets of decisions. The first was
to acknowledge the vital role of Eleanor Roosevelt in the life and work of her
husband by specifically inviting papers devoted to her. It was most gratifying
to have received sufficient work to organize two panels, though, in compiling

this volume, some of these had to be sacrificed to the limitations of space. The remaining papers represent, nevertheless, suitable recognition of the many-faceted partnership of Franklin and Eleanor.

The second decision met the contingency of time and the open-endedness of our call for papers. Of the first commodity there is only so much between Thursday morning and Saturday afternoon; thus the number of panels would be limited. The second matter concerned the proper division of subject matter. Our worries on that score eased more than a bit when we discovered the relative ease of the topical fit of the entire collection of accepted papers.

The Keynote Panel offered by Professors Freidel and Schlesinger and presided over by Professor Koenig, sponsored by Hofstra's Student Senate and Political Affairs Club, placed the role of the Roosevelt presidency in the broad sweep of American history and provided a lively comparison with presidential predecessors and successors.

FDR as politician, the topic of Part I of this volume, groups together papers throwing light on Roosevelt the manager of the intricacies of partisan politics, including the notable essay on the Rooseveltian changes in the class composition of the Democratic party during the Great Depression submitted by V. O. Pechatnov of Moscow.

Criticism of FDR's measures dealing with refugees from Nazism is the focus of Part II, which also contains a paper on the assessment of Hitler by FDR and one dealing with early assessment of Palestine by means of "special agents."

The New Deal's proper ideological location is assessed in Part III, titled "The New Deal Re-examined." Here, too, the issue of success or failure is dealt with, at its origin in the Brain Trust.

Foreign policy, in particular the end of isolationism, is the focus of Part IV, where rearmament and Roosevelt's anticolonialism are also discoursed upon.

Roosevelt's contributions to the American presidency are considered in Part V, including administrative innovations and the interesting controversy dealing with Justice Brandeis and Felix Frankfurter.

Parts VI and VII focus on Eleanor Roosevelt, and feature three interesting aspects of the life of the First Lady: her role as columnist, as feminist, and as social worker.

Finally, Part VIII gathers a diverse set of papers under the heading "Institutions and Policies of the New Deal"; Social Security and the OPA are discussed, as is the Roosevelt relation to the press and the interesting role of Frances Perkins in the Roosevelt administration.

It gives us pride to have been the managers and hosts for an assembly such as this, and we are no less delighted to share the conference with the wider public whose interests will be both gratified and stimulated by the contents of this volume. We trust that those readers will share our view that, within these pages, justice was done to truth and a sound basis was provided for conferences yet to come.

Herbert D. Rosenbaum

FRANKLIN D. ROOSEVELT

Introduction: The Legacy of FDR

Frank Freidel

A hundred years after his birth, Franklin D. Roosevelt possesses one of the towering reputations in the nation's history. His zestful, optimistic, humane leadership toward great goals has secured him a leading place in the pantheon of presidents and world leaders. It has not always been thus. Roosevelt during his rise to the presidency, his many years in office, and in the decades since has had various reputations, not all of them complimentary.

Few Americans viewed Roosevelt calmly during his long tenure in the White House. Like most presidents, his reputation waned and waxed, but, even more than that of the controversial Theodore Roosevelt, it polarized. To a considerable portion of the electorate he seemed little short of a savior; to a vehement minority he was the embodiment of Satan. Echoes of these views still persist, although following generations, not having been directly attracted or repelled by his dynamic presence, have come to view him more dispassionately.

There is no massive memorial to Roosevelt in Washington, only a simple tablet, but that is as he wished it. A far more significant monument is the vast number of books and articles devoted to him; more has been written about Roosevelt than even Lincoln. Historians have several times, in polls, ranked him as one of the most outstanding of U.S. presidents, and even his denigrators grant his significance. Political leaders of both major parties court voters by invoking his name.

The reputation of Roosevelt reached two peaks, one at the beginning of his more than three terms as president, and the other at the end. He began by giving the nation firm, optimistic leadership at the nadir of the depression crisis; he died as head of the great coalition of United Nations forces just as they were on the brink of victory in Europe and tightening the ring around Japan. Scant wonder that in 1933 he seemed a miracle worker, and in 1945 was mourned as a war hero. Yet, to a vehement minority, both during his years in office and long thereafter, he appeared the betrayer of the values they held dear both in domestic and foreign policy.

Many historians and contemporaries, agreeing that Roosevelt was a mover and shaker, have differed in their evaluations. At the time, to many relatively sophisticated intimates and observers, he was a complexity of pluses and minuses, both attractive and repellent; on some occasions they cheered him and on others were in opposition. There were those like William Allen White, the Kansas editor who frequently extolled him yet suffered periodic political misgivings. Roosevelt once joked that Bill White supported him three years out of four—the fourth being the election year. There were others who ardently favored his domestic programs, as had the great progressive historian, Charles A. Beard, and the legendary progressive senator, Hiram Johnson, and then broke with him bitterly over interventionist foreign policy. And there were the reverse, in figures like Hoover's one-time secretary of state, Henry L. Stimson, who in 1940 became Roosevelt's secretary of war. Too, there were those close to him, of whom Eleanor Roosevelt was the most notable, who could recognize his talents, yet were not blind to his shortcomings.

The roots of Roosevelt's reputation—both legend and reality—are in his youth. Detractors when he was president painted a dark portrait of an inconsequential weakling, a mama's boy, even something of a wastrel whom his mother would not entrust with money. (That was the anti-Roosevelt explanation for the chronic deficit spending of the New Deal era.) Then there were those who floated even more sinister rumors of untrustworthiness during his years at Groton School and Harvard University.

The truth, as those who knew Roosevelt frequently testified, was quite different, then and in later life. He was not unduly tied to his mother, although he was an affectionate, dutiful son. As a young man of some wealth, he had, like those of his social circle, a good deal to spend, but then and throughout the rest of his life could demonstrate a remarkable personal frugality. When he was assistant secretary of the navy he seldom dined in restaurants and frequently brought associates home in order to save money. As president he bought his shirts from a bargain mail-order firm; when his pajamas wore out at the elbows, rather than discard them he had the sleeves cut off short. In public as in personal life his ideal always was the balanced budget.

Nor was there any apparent basis for rumors of youthful misdeeds. He had entered Groton as a sheltered teenager who had spent so much time abroad that his accent and tastes seemed strange to the other boys. His favorite magazine was the British *Punch*. Scant wonder that he devoted himself to becoming accepted—staying out of trouble except for the superficial amount necessary to make him seem regular.

In 1936, when a fellow Grotonian questioned Roosevelt's sincerity, the forthright headmaster, Endicott Peabody, replied, ''So far as I can remember there was no suspicion of untruthfulness or insincerity during his entire course nor did I hear of anything against his reputation at the University.''

As Roosevelt, becoming secure, began to assert leadership, he became known for characteristics that those disliking him could interpret as an independent, cocky, insincere manner: ''In an argument he always liked to take the side opposite to that maintained by those with whom he was talking. This irritated the other boys considerably.'' It was a lifelong trait and a valuable means of coming to important decisions when he was president. Those who liked Roosevelt, as did the artist George Biddle, remembered how warm and friendly, as well as self-possessed, he could be.

The most telling accusation that opponents of Roosevelt could make concerning his earlier years was that he had given little evidence that he would someday be a person of consequence. As a Harvard undergraduate he was too slight to make a name for himself in sports and strenuous activities, as had Theodore Roosevelt, whom he deeply admired. Instead he served as cheerleader for the football team and as editor of the Harvard *Crimson* exhorted athletes to do their utmost. In his later years as a politician he sometimes referred to his allegedly spectacular reform efforts as editor of the *Crimson,* seeking to give a more significant tinge to his reputation as a youth. As it was, he was considered a charming, jaunty, handsome socialite of no great seriousness of purpose. It was an impression that continued into his early years as a clerk for a Wall Street law firm. Perhaps even this early, as Alice Roosevelt Longworth used to recall, people joked that his initials F.D. stood for ''Feather Duster''—always moving dust around without really changing anything.

A few of those close to Roosevelt saw seriousness of purpose in him even when he worked as a law clerk. A fellow clerk, Grenville Clark, who himself became one of the most distinguished lawyers of his generation, has left the most telling reminiscence:

I remember him saying with engaging frankness that he wasn't going to practice law forever, that he intended to run for office at the first opportunity, and they wanted him to be, and thought he had a very real chance to be President.

I do not recall that even then, in 1907, any of us deprecated his ambition or even smiled at it as we might perhaps have done. It seemed proper and sincere; and moreover, as he put it, entirely reasonable.

Quite soon Roosevelt proved that his aspirations were indeed plausible. Early in 1911, newly a member of the New York State Senate, he almost instantly acquired an impressive public reputation. He no longer seemed merely an amiable young socialite, but rather an indefatigable rising politician, cast in the model of his spectacular distant relative, TR. Like TR he made headlines, first as a reform leader in the legislature at Albany, then in Washington as assistant secretary of the navy. There were still those who scoffed that he was a ''Feather Duster,'' or who dismissed him as a toplofty socialite, but he managed during

World War I to win widespread respect as indeed a leader in the Theodore Roosevelt tradition, a dynamic young man who could get things done. His was not one of the legendary reputations that came out of the war, like those of Herbert Hoover, Bernard Baruch, or Newton D. Baker, but was sufficient to get him the Democratic vice presidential nomination when he was only thirty-eight. The fledgling *Time* in a 1923 cover story reported that "See young Roosevelt about it" had been a byword in wartime Washington. To his standing as an effective, efficient administrator, Roosevelt added a new dimension in 1920 by campaigning for U.S. membership in the League of Nations. The Democrats lost abysmally, but Roosevelt emerged as a national figure, one of the conspicuous heirs of Wilsonian liberalism.

Roosevelt's severe polio attack a year later, which nearly ended his life and would have terminated the political career of any ordinary person, has come to give him a lasting legendary quality. He demonstrated not only his courage in refusing to capitulate to adversity but, as is not as often recognized, exercised the political talent to turn adversity to his advantage. By appearing unable or unwilling to seek office until he had regained the use of his legs, he was able in his early forties to function as a prematurely "elder statesman" in the Democratic party. He sought to mediate between its two conflicting wings, torn hopelessly in the years of Prohibition and the Ku Klux Klan between big city Catholic wets and rural, small town Protestant dries. At the riven Democratic convention of 1924, his eloquent pleas for unity when he appeared on crutches made him a most appealing man for the future. During the years of the bleakest fortunes for the Democratic party, he built for himself a reputation which could be the foundation for a serious try for the presidency.

The candidacy came sooner than Roosevelt had expected. In 1928, still unable to walk without braces or assistance, he agreed to run for governor of New York to bring strength to Al Smith's presidential ticket. Then, as later, opponents brought up the issue of his health; Smith squashed it during the campaign with his gibe that one did not have to be an acrobat to function as governor. While Smith suffered a crushing defeat, even in New York, Roosevelt won by a narrow margin and instantly became one of the most talked about of the Democratic presidential possibilities for 1932. With the enormous rise in his political fortunes, the health issue revived. Roosevelt sought to end it through publicizing his success in obtaining a large insurance policy after a thorough physical examination. Overall, he succeeded. As he firmly grasped the arm of a son and walked, slowly swinging his hips to bring his brace-locked legs forward, he created the impression that he was somewhat lame rather than a paraplegic. Reporters and photographers cooperated in furthering the illusion, so that few people at the time realized that his customary mode of locomotion was a wheelchair.

Nonetheless, the dark counterpart of the image of Roosevelt triumphing over polio spread throughout the remainder of his lifetime. Mean-minded opponents spread stories alleging his physical and, consequently, mental and moral disabilities. Some cursed him as a cripple, and others pointed to his frequent hearty laughter as proof of his growing insanity. A few even alleged that the sums raised through Birthday Balls for the treatment of polio actually went into Roosevelt's personal coffers. None of this whispering made a serious dent in Roosevelt's rising fortunes.

In the years after 1929, as the nation sank into depression, Roosevelt more and more came to appear as a man whom the Democrats not only might nominate in 1932, but could elect. Although in party matters he still functioned as a conciliatory moderate, within New York and nationally he became a resourceful innovator, ready to abandon traditional ways to bring aid to those suffering from the collapsing economy. Nationally, his fame was still minor compared with that of the Republican Roosevelt, but in times of trouble there was a growing appeal in the thought of putting another Roosevelt into the White House. None of TR's family shared the enthusiasm.

As Roosevelt shrewdly and rapidly gained support for the presidential nomination, eastern machine and conservative Democrats were his most formidable opponents. But the most effective attack upon his name came from reformers and intellectuals, disappointed that he refused to make an all-out assault on the Tammany machine to clean up corruption in New York City. To have done so might have cost him the presidential nomination, which would have well suited the reformers. Both reform and conservative Democrats in the East agreed that Roosevelt was a lightweight. A liberal columnist, Heywood Broun, using words he later regretted, labeled him "the cork-screw candidate." Walter Lippmann, in words far more damaging, called him a master of the straddle, "a highly impressionable person, without firm grasp of public affairs and without very strong convictions":

Franklin D. Roosevelt is no crusader. He is no tribune of the people. He is no enemy of entrenched privilege. He is a pleasant man who, without any important qualifications for office, would like very much to be President.

For some historians, Lippmann's evaluation of Roosevelt has seemed to be on target. Much of the electorate in 1932, listening to Roosevelt's cautious campaign speeches after he had won the nomination, would have agreed with Lippmann. They voted against Hoover rather than positively for Roosevelt—but that was what Roosevelt, the careful politician, intended. He wanted to mend party divisions, avoid needless controversies, and obtain the substantial votes from the Republican majority that were essential if he were to win, for at that time only one-third of the registered voters were Democrats. Even after the campaign, during the long interregnum from November to March before he took office, Roosevelt appeared weak and malleable, apparently ready to let the cautious Democratic leaders in Congress set policy. The only exception was in February 1933. He buoyed the public by his coolness when an assassin attempted to kill him. Overall, public expectations were not high when Roosevelt took office; the consensus (in which Lippmann shared) was that at any rate a fresh president would be better than the repudiated Hoover.

When Roosevelt became president the nation was in the throes of an appalling crisis that had closed most of the banks; he had refused to accept responsibility to act before he took office and enjoyed the full presidential power. The more the surprise when Roosevelt in his inaugural address urged the nation to put its fears behind it and confidently promised to act as dynamically as might be necessary. Both Roosevelt's firm, self-assured air and his immediate steps to end the banking crisis won him almost hysterical acclaim. The sportswriter John Tunis, who had been a Republican up to this time, once recalled the mood of the moment and his own feeling:

That March 4 of 1933 Lucy had gone to South Norwalk to cash our usual weekly check of $25 for food and expenses. The doors of the South Norwalk Trust Company were shut politely in her face. We had $3.50 in the house.

Then we turned to the radio and Franklin D. Roosevelt's inaugural address. It was a talk the nation had not heard in my lifetime. . . . I felt not merely the words—arousing, challenging, unexpected—but the tone and the great courage and the strength of the man behind them. How fortunate are those of us who lived at that time and were touched, ever so lightly, by this gigantic force in our history.

Suddenly, Roosevelt appeared to the American people in almost superhuman dimensions and won overwhelming acclaim. It was one of those rare times when a president received such strong national backing that he could breach the formidable bulwarks of Congress and obtain a comprehensive new program overturning previously revered precedents. In the process, even during the first hundred days when the New Deal was new and full of promise, Roosevelt had to marshal his consummate political talents to maneuver his program through Congress. Overall, few members of Congress dared thwart the president, and many, as Senator Hiram Johnson noted, went along with Roosevelt even though they did not understand or trust what he was trying to do. They simply hoped the new measures would work. Yet it was no "rubber stamp" Congress, as a few die-hard members charged, and made significant, often constructive, modifications in the president's proposals. Basically, the dynamic that brought enactment of the first New Deal measures was the public perception of Roosevelt as the miracle worker who could bring quick recovery for everyone and a better life for the dispossessed. The perception became the lasting view of Roosevelt that millions of people, including some farmers, most laborers, and almost all of the dispossessed, continue to hold.

For many others, dazzled with Roosevelt in the spring of 1933, disenchantment ensued, and the hero reverted to villian. Quick recovery did not follow. For several months, as there was some rise in economic indices, financiers and businessmen, not believing in the New Deal, did not want to disturb the precarious recovery process by criticizing the president. But in the fall of 1933 conditions deteriorated, reinforcing their earlier orthodox views, and they began to proclaim their alarm. Financiers across the Atlantic shared the consternation. As Roosevelt, to counter the acute deflation of the time, gingerly moved toward inflation through tinkering with the gold content of the dollar, one British economic observer reported the misgivings of Wall Street being bruited about the city of London: "Roosevelt is mad and is led by madder professors."

As recovery slowly came in fits and starts, well-developed pros and cons began to be heard. Not long before the campaign of 1936, Arthur Krock of the *New York Times,* one of the most respected columnists of his day, and himself a conservative Democrat, summed up the less emotional conflicting estimates:

The Republicans say officially that the President is an impulsive, uninformed opportunist, lacking policy or stability, wasteful, reckless, unreliable in act and contract. . . . Mr. Roosevelt seeks to supervene the constitutional processes of government, dominate Congress and the Supreme Court by illegal means and regiment the country to his shifting and current ideas—a perilous egomaniac.

The Democrats say officially that the President is the greatest practical humanitarian who ever averted social upheaval, the wisest economic mechanician who ever modernized a government, . . . savior and protector of the American way—including the capitalist system—and rebuilder of the nation, . . . Mr. Roosevelt has constructed, with daring and fortitude, a sound bridge from the perilous past to the secure future.

Then Krock added his own moderate view:

"He is not wholly either, and he is certainly something of both. In the opinion of this writer he is much more of the latter than the former."

To a considerable extent this sort of pro-and-con debate has gone on even during the centennial celebration. Some extreme voices have been heard, suggesting that Roosevelt was (to exaggerate only a bit) on the one hand the savior of Western civilization or on the other hand its most persistent, malevolent enemy. On the negative side the respected financial journal, *Barron's,* summed up its distaste for Roosevelt and the New Deal, comprehensively if not tastefully, by faulting the first family for "irregular and curious sexual liaisons during three terms and more in the White House." It blamed Roosevelt in foreign policy for "ghastly diplomatic mistakes at Yalta, which . . . sentimentally and for no quid pro quo, allowed the whole of Eastern Europe, including Poland, to fall into the clutches of the Russian bear."

As for New Deal domestic policy, in it *Barron's* saw "a cynical statist thrust— 'We shall tax and tax, spend and spend, elect and elect'—that was doomed to failure." And *Barron's* goes on to damn everything from the Federal Deposit Insurance program through Social Security, "the biggest New Deal scam of all":

The landscape is littered with legislative and bureaucratic debris. Thus, the glittering promise of TVA had led directly to the dismal showing of the Washington Public Power

Supply System, which has seen two out of five nuclear projects—Whoops!—run out of money and shut down long before completion.

The genius of the editorial writer in blaming FDR for ''Whoops'' is awesome indeed. His final touch was to hail Roosevelt as another P. T. Barnum. But to many of us the Barnum touch seems rather to be *Barron's*.

The fact that a respected journal will print such a thoroughgoing damnation of Roosevelt and his works indicates that there is still need for the more dispassionate appraisal of present-day historians. Overall, two recent polls have ranked Roosevelt third among all presidents, following only Lincoln and Washington. Whether he rates precisely that high need not concern us. My own inclination is to place him with Theodore Roosevelt and Woodrow Wilson as one of the three most notable of twentieth century presidents. All three made significant contributions; all had great strengths and serious weaknesses.

In the case of Franklin D. Roosevelt, on domestic policy most historians give him high marks for the very achievements that *Barron's* finds so noxious. It is exceedingly easy to carp at our federal government today, to ascribe all of its ills to the New Deal origins, and to suggest that rooting out of the Roosevelt programs would restore all for which the nation longs.

It is hard for us to conceive the federal government as it was when Roosevelt took office at a time of depression and despair. We were a nation with no Social Security, no minimum wage or maximum hours protection for workers, no collective bargaining guarantee for union members, no federal prohibition of child labor, no viable program to put a floor under agricultural prices or to prevent farmers from being dispossessed through foreclosures, and no control over the top-heavy public utility empires exploiting consumers and stockholders alike. The relief system had been modernized only partly from the fundamentals of the poor law of the reign of Queen Elizabeth I. The Federal Reserve system was in need of overhaul, and the nation was in the straitjacket of the gold standard. As for TVA, at the time of its creation unutilized water was roaring over the spillway at Wilson Dam on the Tennessee River, and within sound of it farmers were lighting their houses with kerosene lamps. Commenting on Roosevelt on a centennial television program, President Jimmy Carter reminisced that he himself was fourteen when electricity finally came to his relatively affluent farm in Georgia.

The federal government in 1933 took only a very limited responsibility for the well-being of the American economy and of the American people. Roosevelt, with his keen concern for the reducing of the inequities of the American system, sought to create a more just and prosperous society.

Roosevelt's contributions were notable. He did not consider them perfect. Indeed, he assumed that they were only first attempts which would need continued revision. He had no expectation that Social Security as it came into being in 1936 would serve indefinitely without periodic improvement. Indeed, he expressed his concern that there would after many years be financing problems, and, interestingly enough, the date he mentioned when trouble could come was 1980.

Roosevelt was able to marshal the forces for change among his advisors, the media, Congress, and the public because the private sector and much of government within the nation had failed. In the prosperous 1920s he was, as his critics have frequently pointed out, the advocate of state and local initiative; what they less often note is that he decried the growth of government in the Washington of Harding and Coolidge on the grounds that it was Hamiltonian, concentrating power in federal agencies for the benefit of the wealthy. He had been energetic as governor of New York, and was ready when he became president to be a powerful chief executive in the mold of TR and Wilson. He continued to believe that it was the role of the federal government to undertake what individual initiative or state and local action would not achieve, and because of their relative bankruptcy both in funds and ideas, federal initiatives grew enormously.

Historians measuring Roosevelt against the backdrop of popular politics and the restraining and modifying force of Congress emphasize the great limitations upon him. Even in the first hundred days he could operate only within fairly narrow bounds, and the restraints grew increasingly through successive years. Nor was there the slightest likelihood that he would stray from his own firm faith in the American democratic tradition or the free enterprise system—any more than there was any possibility that the Congress and public would allow him to do so. Socialism, fascism—totalitarianism in any form—were all alike abhorrent and unthinkable to him. Rather, like the progressives who had molded his fundamental political thinking, he was insistent that there be a greater sharing of responsibilities and benefits in the American system.

During his many years in office, he made various serious political errors and miscalculations. In domestic policy, there was the fiasco of the plan to pack the Supreme Court. Instead of presenting it to the nation as essential to preserve New Deal reforms like the National Labor Relations Act and Social Security, he described it as a scheme to bring greater efficiency in the handling of cases. He appeared deceitful, and cries of "dictatorship" went up. But the Court did shift toward the New Deal and upheld both the National Labor Relations Act and Social Security. Roosevelt lost his struggle to add justices to the court, for which we can be thankful, and lost much of his political clout. On the other hand, from this point on the Supreme Court has upheld most federal (and state) regulation of the economy as being within the scope of the Constitution. Too, there was the abortive effort to "purge" conservatives in the Democratic primaries of 1938, as well as other failures. Much of the time, he did not, in the mundane, day-by-day functioning as chief executive, appear to be either infallible or great—yet the great changes in domestic policy are still with us.

As for foreign policy, the pattern there is much the same. By 1938, when the aggressions of Hitler in Europe and of Japanese militarists in East Asia were foreshadowing World War II, the debate over Roosevelt's program and character switched to foreign affairs. He already was seeking to establish himself as a symbol of democracy in a world threatened by dictatorship. Immediately after his overwhelming reelection in 1936, he visited Brazil, Argentina, and Uruguay, and came back impressed by the crowds that had hailed him with cries of "Viva la democracia." He sought, further, to rally the American people into a collective security alliance to protect the Western Hemisphere. While many who had opposed his domestic programs became his supporters, many others bitterly charged that he was treacherously intriguing to embroil the nation in war.

It was a debate that ended temporarily with Pearl Harbor and that was renewed after the war, after Roosevelt's death, by those who claimed that he maneuvered the Japanese into the attack as a means of getting the nation into the war against Hitler through the back door. Postwar revisionists added the charge that he had betrayed U.S. interests to the Soviet Union at the Yalta Conference of 1945. "The myth of the Savior is fading," Charles Beard wrote a fellow-revisionist early in 1948. "The country seems to be in a mood to consider the question of how we were secretly governed by our great *Fuehrer!*" There is an enormous literature both pro and con concerning Pearl Harbor and Yalta. In a book just published, a popular historical writer again implicates Roosevelt, although some of the most authoritative scholars have assembled weighty evidence to the contrary. Much the same can be said concerning Yalta, where *Barron's,* as I have said, makes the old familiar charge.

What is perhaps most to the point is that the nation continued to adhere to the collective security foreign policy and the principles of international aid which Roosevelt had helped establish. He has endured as the symbol of the massive American effort to seek a better, safer world.

In the evaluations of historians, Roosevelt has fared well, despite the fervent attacks of revisionists and those of the new left. There are few now who feel bitter, as did Beard. Nor, on the other hand, are many as eulogistic as were the mourners at the time of his death. Rather, they see in Roosevelt a man of both strengths and weaknesses, of nobleness and some conduct short of ideal. They hail him as did Senator George Norris, for his vision of the future. It was one reason why he could inspire so large and enduring a following. He was a president no more contradictory than the times in which he grew up—part Victorian, even more progressive—with the romantic enthusiasm for dreaming great dreams. Added to that was a dash of venturesomeness that impelled him occasionally to abandon his fundamental prudence and experiment with the unknown. In part he led his generation so well because he was so basically of it both in its limitations and its aspirations. He called it to a "rendezvous with destiny," and he himself kept that rendezvous.

I

THE POLITICIAN

1

Frank Hague and Franklin Roosevelt: The Hudson Dictator and the Country Democrat

John Kincaid

The era of Franklin Delano Roosevelt was one of political titans. Abroad, the president contended with Winston Churchill, Joseph Stalin, Adolf Hitler, Benito Mussolini, and other powerful leaders who mobilized vast populations and transformed modern history. At home, the president contended with littler titans who had carved up the American political landscape like so many feudal baronies. Harry F. Byrd of Virginia, Joseph B. Ely and David Walsh of Massachusetts, Huey Long of Louisiana, Eugene Talmadge of Georgia, and other state leaders were continual embarrassments and occasional threats to Roosevelt and his New Deal.

Even more intractable, at times, were the city bosses whose behavior frequently embarrassed and exasperated Roosevelt: Ed Crump in Memphis, James Michael Curley of Boston, Farley in Atlantic City, Ed Flynn of New York, Garfinkel in Nashville, Frank Hague in Jersey City, Edward J. Kelly and Patrick A. Nash of Chicago, Tom McFeeley of Hoboken, Dan O'Connell in Albany, George Parr in Duval, Thomas J. Pendergast in Kansas City, and the like. These were among the men who continued to make city government, in the words of Lord Bryce, "the one conspicuous failure of the United States."[1] Yet they held the votes that were crucial to Roosevelt's political success.

In many ways, Roosevelt prevailed against the leaders of foreign governments more easily than he did against the leaders of American state and local governments who belonged to his own party. Unlike Roosevelt, the bosses were not transformational leaders. They were brokers or transactional leaders who approached "followers with an eye to exchanging one thing for another: jobs for votes, or subsidies for campaign contributions."[2] The bosses could be counted on to the extent that they were party loyalists and national patriots; but they cared little for the New Deal philosophy. Despite substantial federal aid, the policies of local recovery did little to stem, and often hastened, the decline of their loyalties, which eventually resulted in the "urban crisis" of the postwar era. Instead of rebuilding their cities in anticipation of the next frontier, the bosses used the New Deal to buttress their political organizations. As Harold Gosnell concluded with regard to Chicago, the crisis of the 1930s resulted in "the establishment of a political machine of unprecedented power."[3]

Roosevelt is occasionally criticized for not extending the sweep of New Deal reform into local arenas so as to clean out these malodorous titans. Yet they were extraordinarily powerful and, given the constitutional and political realities of the time, Roosevelt had to transact business with them in order to implement his transformational policies. In the process, he tamed the local bosses to a degree; but he could not defeat them, in large part, because the federal system—established to inhibit centralized tyranny—made it difficult for the president to eradicate localized tyrannies, at least overtly.

Although the presidency is the country's only nearly national institution, the office lacks truly national power in the traditional sense. Elected by an often transient assemblage of minorities every four years through the Electoral College mechanism of dispersed state pluralities, the president must enlist the cooperation of the strangest of bedfellows and appease their demands as well. Since the party system was exceptionally strong in Roosevelt's day, the bosses of local organizations were the single most important element in his electoral formula. Roosevelt could not readily move against the bosses because he needed them to win elections and mobilize public opinion support for his programs, just as they needed him to mobilize federal financial support for their localities during the Depression.

Roosevelt was also restrained by the tradition of local autonomy in the United States. As Alexis de Tocqueville observed in 1831, the sphere of local government "is indeed small and limited, but within that sphere its action is unrestrained; and its independence gives to it a real importance."[4] Strong political machines jealously reinforced that independence. Indeed, the machine as a political-governmental form reached its peak of power and prevalence between the two world wars.

Very early in the Depression, mayors began to petition the Congress and the president for federal aid; but at the same time, they expected Washington to facilitate local recovery without impeding local autonomy.[5] The weight of public opinion was still on the side of localism, and fears of centralized tyranny arising from federal activity remained fairly strong throughout the New Deal period, compelling Roosevelt to tread softly in local areas. Overt intervention to unseat even the most unsavory bosses would have also threatened the principles of territorial democracy which reserve to local voters the right, to paraphrase Alexander Hamilton, to elect whomever they wish, even bums.[6] In this, the president was no different from the Congress, which also prefers to let local constituents remove unsavory members.[7]

It may have been all the more imperative for Roosevelt to work with local bosses in promoting electoral support because many of his reform and recovery programs seemed to run against the grain of other American traditions. Active intervention in the economy, deficit spending, federal relief, sizeable grants-in-aid, support for labor unions, and expanded federal activity, all seemed, to certain powerful publics, to undermine the cherished values of free enterprise, self-reliance, and limited government. The public image problem was further aggravated by some of Roosevelt's own New Dealers who were openly critical of business, bosses, and constitutional restraints and who applauded the "obsolescence of federalism."[8] For Roosevelt himself to have posed a serious threat to localism as well might have destroyed the New Deal and possibly his administration. Instead, by substantially respecting localism, the president maintained a climate and framework within which citizens and leaders could perhaps more readily accept and adapt the New Deal thrusts which were, in the long run, more important to national recovery than the immediate elimination of local corruption.

Generally, the administration of domestic affairs in the United States is in the hands of state and local officials. Direct federal administration is minimal, even today. Roosevelt could not expect to override this system without intense state and local resistance, and without unduly increasing the size of the federal bureaucracy as well. Although he battled and circumvented state and local administration when he felt it necessary, in the main Roosevelt worked through, rather than against, the intergovernmental system, occasionally soliciting ideas and taking policy cues from state and local initiatives.[9]

Roosevelt also had to cope with other realities of bossism. Many notable state and local bosses had supported Al Smith for the 1932 Democratic presidential nomination. Furthermore, the Democratic bosses often cooperated with each other and periodically colluded with Republican bosses. Being primarily interested in maintaining their organizations and territorial prerogatives, they were not averse to undermining candidates of their own party, especially reformers and other dissidents who challenged their hegemony.[10]

The power of most local bosses also extended beyond city lines to include counties, metropolitan and rural regions, and sometimes states. Ed Crump controlled Memphis, Shelby County, and most of Tennessee. Frank Hague ruled Jersey City and Hudson County while also dominating New Jersey. Furthermore, most of the city bosses resided in states that had voted Republican in the four previous presidential elections. Even Tennessee had gone Republican in 1920 and 1928. To win these states in 1932, it must have seemed imperative to enlist the support of local bosses. Even if their power had been confined to city limits, the bosses would still have been highly influential because big city population growth reached its historic peak in the 1930s. Given the structure of presidential elections, large city votes can be crucial to winning a state's electoral votes.

Roosevelt's apparent patrician background, reform connections, and early New Deal proposals did not especially endear him to city interests. Regarding himself as "a child of the country," somewhat in the Jeffersonian mold, Roosevelt worried about his ability to attract the urban vote. "Al Smith knows these city people better,'' he told Raymond Moley. ''He can move them. I can't.''[11] As he wrote to a newspaper editor in South Dakota in 1931, ''I am not, as you say, an 'urban leader' for I was born and brought up and have always made my home on a farm in Dutchess County.''[12] Instead of making cities the primary targets of federal aid, Roosevelt's early programs favored rural assistance. He himself encouraged urbanites to trade their ''speculative living in the city for one of stabilized living in a real home in the country.''[13] In 1937 the National Resources Committee of the Department of the Interior issued a report entitled *Our Cities: Their Role in the National Economy,* which listed thirty-six urban problems and as many policy recommendations. Roosevelt paid little attention to it.[14]

In effect, if he could not defeat the bosses directly, Roosevelt could erode their power by persuading their constituents to leave town. This was probably not a conscious strategy, though it may have been a subconscious one insofar as Roosevelt apparently believed that agrarianism is more hospitable to democracy than urban industrialism. Indeed, by trying to remedy what he regarded as an ''overbalance of population in our industrial centers,'' Roosevelt inadvertently anticipated the suburban revolution which did much to undermine the power of the great bosses by the 1960s. At the time, however, the effort was fruitless, and his praise for ''the good earth'' and dislike for ''overcrowded industrial cities and towns'' certainly did not sit well with the urban leaders whose fiscal straits were becoming more urgent.

Roosevelt did not begin aiding cities specifically or countering the bosses in any overt fashion until his second administration. Buoyed by his greatest electoral victory and having no precedent for expecting another term, he was in a position to act boldly. Yet on both counts he was extremely cautious and not very successful, in part because he quickly dissipated energy and popularity on the 1937 Supreme Court fight. Then the famous congressional ''purge'' of 1938, which was not even directed against the loathsome local bosses, was a ''bust,'' in Jim Farley's words. Not only that, the Democrats lost seventy House seats and seven Senate seats.

In 1939 Roosevelt's new attorney general, Frank Murphy, announced that the administration would ''strike hard'' against municipal corruption and ''purge'' unsavory bosses ''if city governments'' did not ''clean up of their own accord.''[15] Yet the only purges were those of Thomas J. Pendergast and James Michael Curley. Roosevelt had already undermined Curley during his first administration by denying him access to federal patronage in Boston. Curley never had a strong organization anyway, and Roosevelt could bypass him by working with the more powerful, statewide, Walsh-Ely machine. Nevertheless, Curley bounced back by winning a U.S. House seat in 1942 and 1944 from which he verbally assailed the president. Roosevelt apparently helped to engineer an indictment of Curley in 1943, which resulted in his conviction for mail fraud in 1946; but President Truman, a product of the Pendergast machine, commuted Curley's prison sentence and then pardoned him.[16] In Kansas City, Roosevelt attacked Pendergast only after the boss had already been wounded by losing a primary election. This defeat at the hands of local constituents allowed Roosevelt safely to court the new Democratic faction and prosecute Pendergast for income tax evasion in 1939.[17]

Roosevelt made other pronouncements against bossism and corruption, trying to some extent to swing public opinion against them; but, like Woodrow Wilson before him, his political behavior was cooperative, and he was reluctant to assault duly elected local officials. "A little patronage, a lot of pleasure, and public signs of friendship and prestige," he told Frances Perkins, "that's what makes a political leader secure with his people and that is what he wants anyhow."[18] Roosevelt despised many of the bosses and disliked socializing with most of them; yet he regarded their support as being necessary to resolve the crisis of the Depression and, then, to unite the country in war. "You have to get the votes first," he argued, "then you can do the good work."[19]

This rule applied even to Frank Hague, perhaps especially to him, because of his immense and longstanding power in a state which had gone Republican in all but one presidential election since 1892 and which would later vote Republican in all but two elections from 1948 through 1980 (see figure). Roosevelt therefore had no reason to believe that New Jersey would support him. He needed powerful local allies, and indeed, would not have carried New Jersey in his first and last elections if Frank Hague had not mobilized and manufactured huge Hudson County pluralities for him in 1932 and 1944.

This electoral connection was about the only common bond between these otherwise markedly different men: Roosevelt, the upper-Hudson Episcopalian aristocrat, and Hague, the lower-Hudson Catholic plebeian. Democrat and demagogue, they were natural opposites. Where Roosevelt was born in the rural setting of Hyde Park Township in January 1882, Hague was born in the Horseshoe in January 1876. The Horseshoe was a gerrymandered slum district in downtown Jersey City which had been created by a Republican state legislature in 1871 in an effort to squeeze the political power of Irish Catholics into a single district and thereby insure native Protestant control of the city government.

Ironically, Roosevelt came precisely from that Anglo-Dutch class that Jersey City's Irish and German Catholics had come to dislike and distrust during their bitter struggle against the local Anglo-Dutch regime that ruled Jersey City for more than a century. Furthermore, Roosevelt was from New York, a state that continually overshadowed and dominated much of the development of northern New Jersey. Jersey City is little more than a doormat for Manhattan and, therefore, a very poor sister and a victim of New York City's aggrandizement. Even the Statue of Liberty is universally associated with New York, although technically it resides in Jersey City.

Roosevelt also came out of that Protestant tradition that had tried to convert the Irish Catholics from "rum, romanism, and rebellion." Soon after arriving in Jersey City in 1847, the Irish Catholics were proselytized and pressured to become "better." Their every electoral effort to gain a proportionate share of city offices was strongly countered by native Protestants who called upon the

Democratic Presidential Vote in New Jersey, 1824–1976

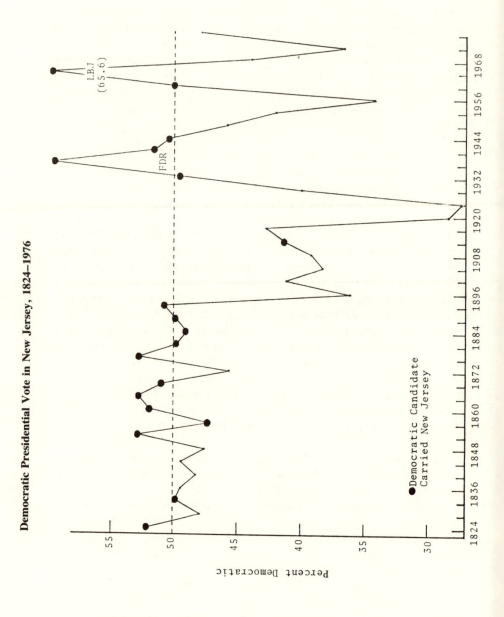

outside county and state governments for assistance whenever necessary. When Catholic Democrats first gained majority representation in city government, local Protestants—Republicans and Democrats—convinced the state legislature, in the name of reform, to take over the city in 1871. The legislature reduced the elected officials to mere figureheads and installed five appointed commissions to run the government. The commissioners were, of course, local Protestants. Instead of "reforming" the city, they promptly plundered it and escalated municipal debt. Among other things, the city treasurer, Alexander Hamilton, fled to Mexico with $87,000 of city funds. With the assistance of a county grand jury, the state Supreme Court, a state constitutional amendment, and a new Democratic legislature, Jersey City's Catholic Democrats finally began to regain control of the city in 1877. In the main, they have held it ever since.[20]

It is often said that the Irish Catholics had a natural penchant for machine politics.[21] While this may be partly true, in Jersey City, at least, they learned much of the trade from Protestant mentors. The native Protestants who originally controlled the local Democratic party openly used the Irish Catholic immigrants as a voting bloc against native Republican Protestants. They encouraged the Catholics to mobilize neighborhood voters, falsify election returns, and distribute patronage. Given the corrupt and unfair practices of the Protestants, Irish Catholics had little choice but to adopt these same measures. In the process, the Protestants taught the Catholics that "reform" was often a code word for Protestant hegemony and Catholic disenfranchisement.

Even after the Catholic victory of 1877, local Protestants continued to press for "reform" and to threaten the Catholic position. To maintain majority control, the Irish Catholics rallied around Robert "Little Bob" Davis, who organized a Catholic machine which nominated Protestant mayoral candidates, invented election returns, and exchanged "floaters" with Tammany's Richard Croker. When Davis died in 1911, there was a tremendous political struggle which concluded six years later when Frank Hague became mayor and began to consolidate his virtually dictatorial control of Jersey City.[22]

The Irish Catholics also learned the importance of having friends in "high places," especially since those places were usually occupied by Protestants and, very often in New Jersey, Republican Protestants. To control Jersey City, it was essential to control Hudson County. This was relatively easy because Jersey City far outranks the county's eleven other municipalities in population. Control of Hudson County was also vital to developing a strong voice in state affairs in order to secure state benefits, thwart hostile intrusions and, especially, to shield local corruption from state prosecution. Consequently, Hague exerted considerable energy in his largely successful efforts to control New Jersey. Although Hudson County was only the state's second largest county, Hague could dominate the state by having a well-organized machine capable of mobilizing huge Democratic pluralities. Fortunately for Hague, the larger city of Newark in Essex County never assembled a comparable machine.

In turn, by dominating the state, Hague controlled congressional seats and extended his influence into the White House. This enabled him to secure federal benefits, control federal patronage and appointments—especially judicial appointments—and block unfriendly federal intrusions. As his principal electoral ambassador to the larger WASP worlds of state and national politics, Hague chose A. Harry Moore—a Mason, Presbyterian, Sunday school teacher, and social notable. Moore was elected to the U.S. Senate in 1934 and was the only three-term governor in New Jersey history (1926–1929, 1932–1935, 1938–1941).

Thus, Hague had come a long way from Cork Row, where he grew up near what is now the entrance to the Holland Tunnel. Tall, thin, and red-headed, Hague was a classic "street kid." Expelled from school at fourteen, he took odd jobs, ran with the neighborhood gangs, managed a lightweight prizefighter, and loitered about neighborhood clubs and saloons. One of these, the Greenwood Social Club, was owned by "Nat" Kenny, Hague's first political mentor. In 1896, a year before Hague was old enough to vote, Kenny gave him $75 to run for constable. Hague won, in part, by fraud. In 1898 Hague was also appointed a deputy sheriff. He later lost that job when he failed to answer a subpoena; but in 1908 he was appointed custodian of City Hall. This gave him $2,000 a year plus some twenty-five patronage jobs, which he began to multiply as quickly as possible.

Hague began to build an organization through hard work, patronage, constituent service, political contacts, voter mobilization, fraud, and violence. As a newspaper reported in 1910, a number of men who opposed Hague were seen leaving a political meeting "with blood streaming down their heads."[23] Hague also opposed Woodrow Wilson, as he would later oppose Roosevelt, and withheld four New Jersey votes from Wilson through all forty-six ballots at the Democratic National Convention in 1912. This, however, caused him some embarrassment. In 1913, when factional conflict and a surge of local reform threatened to destroy his career, Hague suddenly blossomed as a Progressive. He supported a charter reform movement to create a commission form of government which he had helped to defeat in 1911. When Jersey City's voters approved the new charter in 1913, Hauge ran for one of the commission's five seats. Portraying himself as an ardent enemy of bossism, crime, corruption, big corporations, and utility trusts, he won a seat, coming in fourth in a field of ninety-one candidates. Whether by design or accident, Hague was appointed director of public safety, while a more genuine reformer, Mark Fagen, was appointed mayor, an ineffectual post. That same year, Hague joined forces with Fagen and the newly elected president, Woodrow Wilson, to elect the Progressive reformer, James F. Fielder, as Wilson's gubernatorial successor.[24]

As director of public safety, Hague—who would later boast that "Jersey City is the most moralest city in America"—launched a campaign to "clean up" the corrupt police and fire departments. As he pummeled, fined, suspended, and fired drunken and derelict officers, and demanded "discipline" and "results," the local press praised him as "a man of action." In the process, he filled the departments with his own men and broke the back of the Patrolmen's Benevolent

Association, which had become an independent municipal power. Hague also campaigned against prostitution, pornography, burlesque, litter, communism, moviehouse "firetraps," the Ku Klux Klan, and corner stores allegedly selling poisoned candy to children. He banned dancing in places that sold liquor, prohibited saloons from serving women, and apparently halted cocaine trafficking in the city by suspending the jail sentences of all users willing to turn state's evidence against pushers. In attacking the rackets and gambling, however, he eventually brought them under his own control. Occasionally taking a personal hand in law enforcement, he also won public affection by arresting a notorious murderer in hand-to-hand combat with guns drawn.

As a result, Hague became quite popular and was soon able to mobilize more than 2,000 workers for elections. Through the police and fire departments, he set up a network of spies and undercover agents called "zeppelins" and began to use the police to break up opposition political meetings. Meanwhile, his loyal firemen closed down the businesses and meeting halls of dissident citizens for alleged fire-code violations. Hague also organized ward clubs throughout Hudson County and, through them, delivered more personalized services to constituents. He cultivated and received the endorsement of the local Catholic Church hierarchy as well.

In the 1917 municipal election, Hague fielded an "Unbossed" ticket that won all five commission seats, which his organization held until 1949. Appointed mayor, Hague kept that position until he voluntarily "retired" in 1947. Very quickly he also secured control of Hudson County and, thereby, its state legislative and U.S. congressional delegations. He cultivated statewide friends and wisely gave a patronage position to the son of the chairman of the New Jersey Civil Service Commission.

By 1919 Hague was ready to "take Trenton." He did so by electing his friend, Edward I. Edwards, to the governorship. In 1923 he moved Edwards to the U.S. Senate and gave the governorship to George Silzer. For all intents and purposes, Hague governed New Jersey from 1920 to 1941. In 1922 he appointed the chairman of the state Democratic party and secured his own election as New Jersey national committeeman. At the Democratic National Convention in 1924, he was elected a vice chairman of the national committee. Thus, a decade before Roosevelt arrived on the national scene, Frank Hague was a fixed and influential figure in national party politics.

His organization was probably the most powerful political machine in U.S. history. As Dayton McKean wrote in 1940, "Many political machines flourish—and have flourished—in America, but none has approached the perfection of the Hague organization in the completeness of its control over the society in which it exists."[25] There was no effective opposition to Hague between 1921 and 1941. His machine controlled virtually every aspect of the city's life. When Princeton students came to observe an election in 1921, Hague had them arrested, beaten up, and removed from the county. When asked for an explanation, he attributed the incident to "animal spirits. I guess my boys couldn't resist the temptation to have a little fun.'' It was, of course, Hague who once declared: ''I am the law.''

Hague controlled all public sector jobs in Hudson County as well as many in the private sector. In most cases, in order to obtain employment in private industry, one had to obtain a job card from City Hall through a ward leader. Hague also forced large industrial plants to hire his own men as personnel officers and shop foremen. To have any hope of success in the courts, one had to retain a ''Hague lawyer,'' and in a local hospital one was likely to be treated by a ''political doctor,'' since Hague controlled personnel appointments to all public and most private medical institutions. So extensive was his power that he even influenced clergy appointments in the county's religious institutions.

Dissidents were simply arrested, beaten up, fired from their jobs, or ridiculed in public. Recalcitrants who owned homes received increased property tax assessments. Those who owned businesses were boycotted, harassed, and sometimes shut down by fire or health inspectors. When a disaffected dentist wrote too many critical letters to a local newspaper about ''City Haul,'' Hague sent a prostitute into his office where she ripped off her clothes and cried rape. Police, waiting outside the office, promptly arrested the startled dentist. When ''communists'' attempted to organize labor in the 1930s, they were driven out of town, and police were occasionally stationed at the Holland Tunnel exit to turn back automobiles from New York whose passengers looked ''radical'' or whose trunks contained labor leaflets. It was not without reason, therefore, that Hague became known as a dictator and as the ''Hitler-on-the-Hudson.''[26]

It is precisely this image that made it so difficult for liberals then and now to accept Roosevelt's cooperation with Hague. As Willard Wiener wrote in the *New Republic:*

President Roosevelt, by a nod of the head, can break Hagueism. Such a gesture, coming at a time when the free peoples of the world are united against fascism, would make the Four Freedoms . . . a reality for the oppressed people of one section of the USA who have been deprived of them for more than a quarter of a century.[27]

A number of Roosevelt's aides were also troubled by this relationship, though most resigned themselves to it. Harold Ickes loathed Hague and labeled him a reactionary. Tugwell ruefully observed that by 1940 Roosevelt had become ''the prisoner'' of the Democratic party's ''worst element—the big-city bosses.''[28] Needless to say, many Republicans in New Jersey and elsewhere capitalized on this alliance as another example of New Deal perfidy.

Plainly, Hague was not a New Dealer; yet, ironically, his well-deserved reputation as a ''fascist dictator'' made it impossible to ignore him and extremely risky to fight him. Even if such a battle could have been won, from Roosevelt's point of view it might only have brought the Republicans back into power in New Jersey. After the failure of the ''purge'' of 1938, Roosevelt was even more reluctant to tangle with the likes of Frank Hague. By perceptions of necessity, then, the two men became close in certain political respects but remained distant socially, with neither really liking or apparently trusting the other. Although Hague visited the White House on a number of occasions and reviewed the fleet with Roosevelt and other political leaders, he visited Hyde Park only once. This is a telling measure of social distance, since Hyde Park is only a short drive from Jersey City.

Prior to Roosevelt's first nomination, however, Hague was vehemently opposed to FDR. When it became clear that Roosevelt was a viable candidate, Hague set out to line up anti-Roosevelt delegates in the Middle Atlantic states, and then went to the Chicago convention early to marshal the opposition. Like a number of other bosses, Hague supported Al Smith. As leader of the New Jersey delegation and floor manager for the Happy Warrior, Hague pulled out all the stops to block Roosevelt and confidently warned the delegates before the opening of the convention that FDR would be a disastrous candidate:

I deem it my duty as the vice-chairman of the Democratic National Committee and the leader of the Democracy of the State of New Jersey to call to the attention of the delegations and of the leaders of the Democracy in the different states and counties of the country who are gathering here in Chicago that Governor Franklin D. Roosevelt, if nominated, has no chance of winning at the election in November. I have felt out public sentiment, not alone here but in practically every state in the union, particularly those states east of the Mississippi, and I am brought to the conclusion that he cannot carry a single state east of the Mississippi and very few in the Far West . . .

I am genuinely interested because the tendency of the people of New Jersey has been to support the Republican national ticket in Presidential years. It is only fair as the leader of the party in New Jersey to predict that if Governor Roosevelt is nominated our state will be in the Republican column. . . . Why consider the one man who is weakest in the eyes of the rank and file?[29]

In response, James A. Farley issued a terse statement on behalf of FDR: "Governor Roosevelt's friends have not come to Chicago to criticize, cry down, or defame any Democrat from any part of the country. This, I believe, is sufficient answer to Mr. Hague's statement."[30]

Hague, of course, later regretted and recanted his speech, not only because he was wrong and lost, but because many delegates believed it improper for Hague to use his party position to single out one candidate for attack. Nevertheless, Hague did highlight a troublesome aspect of Roosevelt's candidacy that would have to be remedied if Roosevelt were to be successful, namely, his poor showing in big cities during the primaries.

As Al Smith's star began to fall, Hague tried desperately to find another candidate. "At one time Hague offered to switch his thirty-six votes to Garner to form an anti-Roosevelt coalition."[31] Even earlier, Hague had flirted with Newton D. Baker of Ohio, brother of Frank Baker, a prominent New Jersey politician. Believing that Baker rather than Roosevelt would be able to carry New Jersey, Hague encouraged his candidacy so long as Baker expressed willingness to "cooperate with . . . the Party organization." On April 1, 1932, Hague met with Baker's representative, Ralph Hayes, at the Biltmore Hotel in New York City. There he expressed his concerns.

The feelings of X. [Hague] against R. [Roosevelt] are very strong and he is deeply distressed by the strength that Albany is showing. He is entirely convinced that a situation has been reached in which you [Baker] are the only person in the Party who can save it from having R. as the candidate and from the defeat that . . . the election of either R. or Hoover would constitute.[32]

Hague conceded even then that Smith had little chance of winning the nomination. At best, he believed that Smith's bloc of delegates could veto a Roosevelt draft. Consequently, he kept the New Jersey delegation in line for Smith until the bitter end. Roosevelt's troops knew of Hague's machinations and apparently believed that Newton was "the most likely dark horse in the event of a deadlock"[33] but Roosevelt won the nomination anyway, and Hague took an early train back home in a huff. His only Pyrrhic victory was to deprive Roosevelt of a unanimous nomination.

Very quickly, however, Hague realized that he had little choice but to break with Smith and support Roosevelt. A Hoover victory would be disastrous. Furthermore, if Roosevelt were to win without Hague's support, Hague would be subject to the wrath of a Democratic president during a depression. As Dayton McKean noted, "What might a hostile attorney-general find, nosing about Hudson County?"[34]

So, shortly after the convention, Hague telephoned Jim Farley, who was vacationing in Atlantic City. Apologetically, he made peace with Farley and requested that Roosevelt open his campaign with a political rally in New Jersey. On July 11, Hague formally announced his support for Roosevelt to the Hudson County Democratic Committee: "I have no apologies to make for the battle conducted at the Democratic Convention in Chicago. . . . Disregarding words uttered in the white heat of political conflict out of loyalty to a cause espoused, let us consider the actual facts of the situation that now confront us."[35] As he said to Congresswoman Mary Norton, who accompanied him to the Biltmore Hotel in August to smooth things over with FDR: "Al was our man, and we put up a good fight for him. But that's over now. Roosevelt is our candidate, and we're going to do everything we can to elect him." On July 22, Hague and Farley spoke to the New Jersey Democratic Committee, where they put on a show of friendly solidarity.

Hague contributed $8,562.50 to the Democratic National Committee, which was more than his mayoral salary, and urged Roosevelt to make Prohibition his major campaign issue. Promoting his own slogan for FDR, "Hoover fed the Belgians and starved the Americans," Hague mounted a spectacular campaign in New Jersey. The high point was a gigantic August rally for Roosevelt at the New Jersey governor's vacation home in Sea Girt, known locally as "The Little

White House." Hiring cars, busses, and trains, Hague brought nearly 150,000 people—his chief of police claimed 250,000—out to Sea Girt to hear Roosevelt. This was an incredible feat in 1932. Roosevelt was properly impressed and reportedly said, "Only my old friend, Mayor Hague, could have done it."[36] Farley was apparently ecstatic: "If it wasn't the biggest rally in history up to that time, it must have been close to it."[37] In November the Hudson County organization carried New Jersey for Roosevelt. In Jersey City alone, the vote was 93,286 for Roosevelt and 29,868 for Hoover.

Hague immediately warmed up to the new man in the White House, even addressing some early correspondence to "His Excellency." At Sea Girt, Hague's brother had "confided to Roosevelt that Hague's full first name, like Roosevelt's, was Franklin. 'It is a conicidence,' James Hague added, 'that you both were called for the finest character in American history.' "[38] Hague was still concerned, though, about the durability of his tie with FDR. Trying to cultivate Roosevelt's friends, he repeatedly asked if there was "anything else" he could do for them. At one point, the entertainer Eddie Dowling suggested that if Hague would permit the Chicago mobster Edward O'Hare to open a dog racing track in New Jersey, O'Hare would make a large contribution to the Democratic party on Hague's behalf. Hague declined the offer despite his desire to ingratiate himself with Roosevelt by helping with the party's debts. Already having had enough trouble keeping the New York mob out of Hudson County, he wished to avoid penetration by the Chicago mob and possible competition with his own gambling operations.

By January of 1933, however, it became clear that Roosevelt would recognize Hague as New Jersey's chief of federal patronage. While opposing bossism generally and singling out Tammany Hall for attack, Roosevelt began to establish relations with most of the bosses. At a party rally in August in Asbury Park, Farley returned "to thank Frank Hague for the wonderful work he and his organization performed last November."[39] Three months later, Hague wrote to thank Roosevelt: "Your recognition of our State Organization has been substantially manifested and in return I feel we owe you this pledge of loyalty. Should the occasion ever arise when New Jersey need be counted, I am yours to command."[40]

Hague's behavior stemmed not only from greed, power, and pragmatism, but also loyalty. He had a fetish about organizational loyalty as he did about order, discipline, and cleanliness. When being chauffeured about in his bullet-proof limousine, Hague kept the windows closed to protect himself from drafts, dirt, and germs. He demanded loyalty from his subordinates and, in turn, gave it to others. This is one reason why he had not abandoned Smith at the nominating convention. As long as Roosevelt now remained the party's choice, Hague would back him. According to McKean, Hague never criticized the New Deal publicly. Instead, he referred to the president as "that great humanitarian" and often campaigned as though he were the most devoted New Dealer.[41]

Occasionally, some of Hague's officials strayed from the path. The worst offenders were "excommunicated," while others were punished or moved to different posts. When New Jersey's "Hague Republican" governor, Harold G. Hoffman (1935–1938), proved to be an obstruction to certain New Deal programs, Hague clamped down on him. Senator A. Harry Moore voted to override Roosevelt's veto of the Patman Bonus bill in 1935 and then complained that the president's Social Security proposal "would take all the romance out of life. We might as well take a child from the nursery, give him a nurse, and protect him from every experience that life affords."[42] In 1937 Moore embarrassed his boss by criticizing FDR's Supreme Court plan. Hague asked Moore to resign from the Senate that year so as to bring him home for a third term as governor.

Generally, however, Hague's congressional delegates supported the president's initiatives. Most notable was Mary T. Norton, who served in the House from 1925 to 1951. She became one of Roosevelt's best congressional friends. Hague and Norton did ask Roosevelt to veto the Hatch Act, but otherwise they backed him, and Norton was instrumental in moving such legislation as the Wages and Hours bill when she assumed the chair of the House Labor Committee in 1938. When Roosevelt needed help in defeating the Ludlow Resolution that same year, he asked Farley to "call Hague and Kelly and get their delegations lined up."[43] The Hague delegation was most obliging. As a hawk, super patriot, and militant anticommunist, Hague invariably supported Roosevelt's foreign policy thrusts. As war approached and then commenced, Hague organized huge Americanism rallies in Hudson County and recruited soldiers, in part, by promising that the organization would put bonus money away for them during their length of service. Apparently, not a single veteran ever received such a bonus.

Hague may have been a scoundrel, but, as Roosevelt was reported to have said, "Yes, but he's our son of a bitch." Therefore, he showered Hague with federal aid, for which Hague was duly appreciative:

You want to know what the President has done for Jersey City? The President has dumped millions into Jersey City for relief. We have had $500,000 a month to give food to our hungry and work for our idle.

The millions he has dumped into Jersey City have helped us improve our hospital facilities, have improved the general health of the city, and saved many homes. . . .

To property owners who think taxes are high, I say this: If it weren't for Roosevelt I don't know what would have happened to your property.

He is opposed by the moneyed groups, but not by the common people.[44]

In this way, Hague was able to don the cloak of reform and give the appearance of championing the common man even though his city's taxes were not only among the highest in the nation, but increasing regularly to feed his organization.

Hague also derived other benefits from the New Deal. One was federal patronage in New Jersey, where he was especially concerned to control judges, law enforcement personnel, and the Internal Revenue Service (IRS). In 1933 he arranged the appointment of a former Hudson County Freeholder as head of the

North Jersey division of the IRS. Hague had had considerable trouble with the IRS in 1929–1930, which resulted in a $60,000 settlement. The assessment was apparently paid for him by Jersey City's leading building contractor.[45] In 1938 his taxes were again found in arrears, and he settled on a $10,000 payment. But by this time Hague had become something of a national ogre because of his anti-union activities. The hint of possible scandal compelled Treasury Secretary Henry Morgenthau to demand the resignation of Hague's IRS man. However, nothing more was done to investigate Hague's taxes or to explain how he lived as a millionaire on a mayoral salary of less than $10,000 a year.

At the same time, soon after U.S. District Judge William C. Clark ruled against Hague in his famous battle with the Congress of Industrial Organizations (CIO), Hague apparently had a hand in having Clark elevated to the U.S. Court of Appeals and, thereby, out of his immediate bailiwick. Hague recommended that Roosevelt appoint Thomas G. Walker to replace Clark. FDR had to maneuver this through the Senate, but he secured confirmation by December 1939. Happily for Hague, Walker's appointment left a seat vacant on New Jersey's highest court, the Court of Errors and Appeals. Hague convinced the state legislature to appoint his son to the seat even though Frank Hague, Jr., had no college or law degree, despite numerous attempts to earn one or the other.

The net effect of federal patronage was twofold. It gave Hague more jobs with which to reward his friends and strengthen his machine. It also allowed him to build a defensive perimeter around his organization to ward off federal intrusions. Despite his well-known lawlessness, Hague was never indicted and, except for income tax incidents and a few half-hearted investigations, never really pressured to clean up by the Roosevelt administration.

To make matters worse, Hague regularly extracted "contributions" from all persons on public payrolls. They were required to donate 3 percent of their annual income to the organization's Rice Pudding Fund. Likewise, businesses were required to pay "fees" for contracts let by the city and county. But when Attorney General Frank Murphy went to Jersey City during his campaign against municipal corruption, "he was taken in hand by the authorities, wined, dined, given an honorary degree by the John Marshall Law School of Jersey City, and told that there was 'no vice, no crime, no racketeering' in Jersey City."[46]

The greatest New Deal benefits came from federal funds and employment programs. Hague's machine and lifestyle were costly and dependent upon an army of patronage workers. With the deepening Depression, virtually all sources of funds were becoming scarce. In 1932 and 1933 Hague required all city and county employees earning less than $4,000 a year to absorb a 46 percent cut in salary; those earning $4,000 and above had to accept a 52 percent reduction. With rising unemployment, most public employees not only resigned themselves to the situation, but many seemed to become even more loyal to Hague for allowing them to keep their jobs. Hague also created more part-time public jobs and refused to mechanize city operations in order to absorb some of the idle labor from private industry.

The arrival of the New Deal, therefore, did much to oil and rescue the machine. In 1934 Harry Hopkins placed more than 18,000 Civil Works Administration (CWA) jobs in Hague's hands. Hopkins also appointed Hague's friend, William H.J. Ely, to direct the New Jersey Works Progress Administration (WPA) office even though Ely had just lost a state senate election owing to certain scandals. Subsequently, the WPA employed some 76–97,000 individuals a year in New Jersey. By April 1935, there were over 100,000 persons on relief in Hudson County, with eligibility being determined by the Hague organization. From July 1935 through December 1939, the WPA spent $47,003,759 in Hudson County.[47] Additional grants and loans, of course, were received through other New Deal programs. Although Hudson County did not receive appreciably more than other counties, virtually all federal aid to the county was funneled through Hague's machine such that it "became a vast employment and relief agency."[48]

As Richard Connors observed, these resources allowed Hague "to press the button labeled 'fear,' as well as that labeled 'gratitude,' in order to minimize challenges to his hegemony. Fear of economic reprisal motivated families, dependent upon the machine's largesse, to continue trading their votes for its favors."[49] Indeed, both the economic and political powers of the Hague machine reached their peaks by 1936. In addition, Hague usually determined the disposition of federal funds and appointments allotted to New Jersey. The governor routinely referred job seekers to Hague. Other county machines made their requests for shares of the patronage through Hague as well.

Irregularities in Hague's handling of New Deal programs were so routine that administration officials seemed to believe that they could do little more than shrug their shoulders and even play along. Farley and Hopkins were almost always cooperative, Ickes a little less so, and used their influence to secure jobs for Hague's friends and to rescue Hague from administrative difficulties. On one occasion, Hague had to leave a White House dinner early when officials informed him that he needed to correct a problem involving some 2,000 people who were on his WPA payroll without certification. Anxious to avoid discovery by the press, officials asked Hague to get on the telephone and straighten it out immediately.

Another problem arose with Hague's use of WPA funds for capital projects, including a baseball stadium which ultimately cost the WPA about $1.7 million. Hopkins balked at Hague's plan to use funds earmarked for labor to buy seats and plumbing fixtures. But when he called Hague to ask him to use city funds for these items, Hague complained that the city had no money for them. He convinced Hopkins that the stadium would be a great tribute to the administration and very popular with constituents. Hague named it Roosevelt Stadium and wanted FDR to attend the grand opening. Roosevelt did not attend, but Hague made sure that he received recognition: "A major portion of credit for the erection of this new stadium . . . should go to President Roosevelt and the New Deal policies."[50]

The single greatest boondoggle was Hague's use of federal funds to expand the Jersey City Medical Center into one of the largest medical complexes in the world, complete with a penthouse for Hague. The facility had 2,000 beds on "Ninety-Nine Floors of Hospitalization," according to a publicity pamphlet; "medical attention, at any hour, whether you can afford it or not, is as close as your telephone" was the mayor's motto. Hague deployed a fleet of white Cadillac ambulances, emblazoned with large red crosses, driven by uniformed police and staffed by interns wearing white robes. The costs were exorbitant. Facilities were rich and ornate; physicians were given luxury apartments; materials were apparently diverted to build private homes; and funds were used to enrich Hague's friends. Later it was discovered that many floors were vacant and that Hague and his successor, John V. Kenny, had simply "written off" at least $3,684,695 in medical bills as political favors between 1945 and 1951.[51] By the mid-1950s the complex was a decaying white elephant and a drain on city revenues. By 1977 the city had forced the state to assume most of its costs.

Yet Roosevelt came to lay the cornerstone of one of the new buildings on October 2, 1936. Here Hague put on his greatest public performance. Schools were closed and public employees were given a holiday so that nearly 250,000 people could greet the president. As Marquis Child wrote:

Mayor Hague had turned out the town and half the state in an imitation of a Roman triumph. From the moment that the procession of cars rolled out of the Holland Tunnel the thunder of bombs assaulted the ear, and the whole city under a cloudless blue sky seemed one mass of flag-waving humanity. Hague, an iron-jawed master of ceremonies, rode in the presidential car . . . to Hague's great public hospital and clinic in the center of the city.[52]

The president was duly appreciative:

The Mayor has been kind enough to say that this Medical Center would not have been possible without financial help from the Federal Government. But, my friends, remember that it was not just financial help that created this Medical Center. It was something more important than dollars and cents. It was a dream of your mayor dating back many years.

A great many years ago I discovered something, and so did Mayor Hague. We discovered a common bond . . . in the cause of the crippled child. That common bond has persisted through the years. I have tried to help in my limited way. Frank Hague has done a great service not only to you good people who are alive today in Jersey City and Hudson County, but a service that is going to last for many, many generations to come. . . . Mayor Hague, his associates, and the people of this city have pointed the way for many other communities in the Nation. May they see and emulate the fruition of this splendid dream.[53]

Roosevelt also made a point of remarking that "the overwhelming majority of the doctors of the nation want medicine kept out of politics. On occasions in the past, attempts have been made to put medicine into politics. Such attempts have always failed and always will fail." Hague, however, administered the medical center personally, appointing all personnel, supervising operations, and even making case assignments and decisions about medical treatment. He made frequent inspection "raids" and occasionally punched recalcitrant physicians.

Nevertheless, a month later, Hague, at the high point of his power, helped to turn out the largest Democratic presidential vote yet recorded in New Jersey history. He seemed invincible, and the president was in no mood to attack him. Hague had campaigned vigorously for Roosevelt, even to the point of excoriating his old friend, Al Smith, as a traitor. At the same time, Hague never tired of informing the administration of his electoral feats and other services. His requests for aid and service were often accompanied by political notes. In return, the administration generally accorded him substantial recognition. As Roosevelt wrote to Charles Edison, assistant secretary of the navy, in 1938; "The noble State of Woodrow Wilson, Charles Edison and Frank Hague will get a battleship just as soon as the dates allow it."[54] The administration also overlooked serious infractions of the law. When Postmaster General Farley discovered that Hague's Jersey City postmaster was opening the mail of some of Hague's political enemies, he stormed into Roosevelt's office and recommended that the administration prosecute the boss and his postmaster. Roosevelt vetoed the idea, according to Farley: "Forget prosecution. You go tell Frank to knock it off. We can't have this kind of thing going on. But keep this quiet. We need Hague's support if we want New Jersey."[55]

Postal infringements were only one of many growing violations of civil liberties that made the Hague machine an increasing embarrassment for Roosevelt. Hague urged the administration to ship "radicals" off to concentration camps in Alaska and to clean them out of government. He held huge Americanization rallies and parades in Hudson County. At one, in 1938, for example, large posters of himself were plastered about the county with a caption reading: "Stand Shoulder to Shoulder with Mayor Hague and Keep the Communists Out." As his reputation for fascism grew, he simply became more truculent. "As soon as they begin to shout about 'free speech' and 'free press' and 'civil rights,' I know they are Communists," said Hague. "They are not really fighting for rights, but raising this cry as a subterfuge."[56] One will always find an advocate "of civil rights . . . and the rights of the Constitution . . . with a Russian flag under his coat; you never miss," claimed Hague.[57]

The principal objects of his animus were union organizers who, according to Hague, "invaded" Hudson County in 1937. Hague was virulently anti-union and horrified by the efforts of the Congress of Industrial Organizations to organize labor in the New York metropolitan area. From the very beginning he had co-opted or destroyed labor associations, receiving some national attention for these activities as early as 1934. In that year, four miners driving to a union meeting in New York City became lost while looking for the Holland Tunnel. When they asked a policeman for directions, he arrested them. Hague had them charged with "being in an auto and having no legitimate business in Jersey City"[58] and sentenced to ninety days in jail. When the CIO began its drive to organize labor in Hudson County in 1937, Hague's police crashed union meetings, arrested organizers, beat them up, and pushed them onto ferries and trains back to New York or Newark. Even seemingly innocuous "outsiders" were treated harshly. When the National Municipal League sent two people to interview residents in 1938, they were arrested for soliciting without a permit. Told that they would receive permits after an investigation, they were escorted out of town, never to receive permits. The most famous incident occurred when Norman Thomas was pelted with eggs while trying to speak in Jersey City and then driven out of town by Hague's zeppelins.

Nationwide, many newspapers and commentators excoriated Hague as the Hudson County Hitler. The White House received a great many pleas to carry the battle against fascism into Jersey City. As Hague escalated his police-state activities, Roosevelt came under increasing criticism for not squashing the dictator. A federal grand jury investigated Hague's deportation of Norman Thomas, but it voted 14–8 in November 1938 not to indict Hague for kidnapping. During the 1939 visit to Jersey City, Frank Murphy criticized Hague indirectly:

We hear of arbitrary ordinances and arbitrary police action that deny workmen the right of peaceful picketing, even though our courts have recognized that peaceful picketing is a just and proper right of working people. . . . We hear of groups arbitrarily denied the right to distribute literature, even though the Bill of Rights leaves no doubt that freedom of speech and of the press are fundamental to our political system.[59]

But no action was taken against Hague.

Roosevelt also limited himself to indirect verbal reprimands. In his fireside chat of June 24, 1938, he said:

And I am concerned about the attitude of a candidate or his sponsors with respect to the rights of American citizens to assemble peaceably and to express publicly their views and opinions on important social and economic issues. There can be no constitutional democracy in any community which denies to the individual his freedom to speak and worship as he wishes. The American people will not be deceived by anyone who attempts to suppress individual liberty under the pretense of patriotism.

This speech and similar ones were part of Roosevelt's campaign "as leader of the Democratic party . . . to interest himself in primary contests between liberals and reactionaries," as Harold Ickes put it.[60] Ickes was pleased that FDR had taken "a terrific wallop at Frank Hague" even though he did not mention him by name. "But speeches alone will not win this fight," admitted Ickes. "We have to organize to nominate and elect liberals enough to give the President control of Congress and thus serve notice on the reactionaries that they cannot hope to win in 1940."[61]

It was, after all, appropriate that Roosevelt focus on members of Congress (as federal officers) rather than local officials for his first party purge. It is quite possible that he would have initiated a purge of local "reactionaries" had the congressional purge succeeded. Other observers also hoped that Roosevelt's verbal wallops at Hague presaged a real attack on the boss; but the "wretched failure"[62] of 1938 convinced Roosevelt more than ever of the danger of entering local politics. If the congressional battle failed, how could he expect to win a purely local fight in Hudson County? As it was, Roosevelt believed that Hague had been "slapped down in New Jersey"[63] along with some other state and local bosses in the 1938 elections. On the other hand, he attributed the failure to win in New Jersey to Frank Hague.[64]

Roosevelt readily concluded that it was not the prerogative of the president to intervene directly in local governmental affairs unless absolutely necessary. Instead, local voters had to decide the fates of local officials. Representative Jerry J. O'Connell of Montana wrote FDR in May 1938, asking him to do "something definite" about Hague's "fascist regime." At least make him resign as vice chairman of the Democratic National Committee, said O'Connell. After referring the request to Attorney General Homer Cummings, Roosevelt asked his secretary, Marvin McIntyre, to reply. McIntyre wrote: "I just want to drop you a little note acknowledging your letter to the President of May ninth. Some time when it is convenient, I wish you would drop in and have a little talk with me about this."[65] The talk never occurred; ironically, O'Connell was defeated by a Republican in November.

On another occasion, Frank Kingdon and a group of friends also urged Roosevelt to do something about Hague by manipulating federal patronage. "So you think I ought to take a stand against Hague?" replied Roosevelt.

He cocked his cigarette holder and without a smile, asked: "If there were a completely free election in Jersey City tomorrow, without any undue pressure, so that the people could elect for mayor anybody they wished, who would get it?" We [Kingdon] could answer nothing but "Frank would." "Then," said the President, "I suggest that you go back and educate the people of Jersey City to get rid of him."[66]

Roosevelt may have also realized that it would have been virtually impossible to locate another elected official to handle patronage and oversee New Deal programs in New Jersey. Those who were not Hague's minions were anti–New Deal Republicans. Furthermore, A. Harry Moore began his third term as governor in 1938. Roosevelt could have given the patronage to WPA director William Ely, but he could not win elections and was no less a scoundrel than Hague, just less skillful. Indeed, Ely did make several attempts to build his own organization through the WPA. To have suspended federal aid might have been disastrous for citizens dependent on it. Such action would also have opened FDR to even more charges of "playing politics" with the New Deal. In effect, Roosevelt would have had to nationalize the New Deal in New Jersey and appoint his own people to run the programs throughout the state.

The only decisive federal action came from the courts. In 1939 the U.S. Supreme Court upheld lower court rulings enjoining "Mayor Hague and other

Jersey City officials from refusing permits to the CIO and the American Civil Liberties Union to hold meetings in public parks."[67] Roosevelt stayed abreast of the case and received a brief from Grenville Clark prepared in support of the CIO by the civil rights committee of the American Bar Association (ABA). He approved of it and thanked Clark for the ABA's "proper promptitude" in the case.[68] However, the Department of Justice concluded that prosecution of Hague was not warranted and terminated its investigation. No report was issued to the public.

But, publicly chastened by the court rulings, Hague generally complied with them. To an extent, he became a fast friend of labor. Instead of punching union leaders, he purchased their goodwill, and within a year the local CIO affiliates were largely under his control. In subsequent municipal elections, most unions in the city endorsed his ticket.

As war broke out in Europe and Roosevelt anticipated a third term, he seemed less concerned about the antics of local bosses and more concerned about party unity. There was also some fear that Hopkins had become too friendly with Hague and other bosses. Together they might represent a threat to Roosevelt. As Rexford Tugwell noted: "Harry Hopkins, the former social worker, and Corcoran, the White House fixer, were now the intimates of Flynn, Hague, Kelly, Pendergast, and the rest. And these hard bargainers would expect to be paid off."[69] However, Hague and most of the other bosses were solidly behind Roosevelt. Hague wanted FDR to run again and thought that his candidacy would help local tickets, especially after the setbacks of 1938. Thus, they engineered the "draft" for Roosevelt at the 1940 convention. As Farley described it, the bosses met in the Byrnes-Hopkins suite, which

had once before made political history. It was the "smoke-filled room" in which the deal that brought Warren Gamaliel Harding to the White House had been consummated on June 12, 1920. In July 1940, Democratic bosses succeeded the Republican bosses of the twenties in writing history. Here Ed Kelly of Chicago and Frank Hague of Jersey City and Ed Flynn of New York City's Bronx rubbed shoulders with one hundred percent New Dealers like Leon Henderson and Claude Pepper and David K. Niles.[70]

Farley later complained that the bosses had turned the convention into a circus. "It was just too silly for words the way Kelly and Hague acted," said Farley. "The performance of 'the voice of the sewers' was beyond all decency."[71] Yet these voices carried FDR into his unprecedented third term. After expressing strong opposition, the bosses also accepted Henry Wallace as FDR's running mate. When Farley informed Roosevelt that Hague was trying to get to know Wallace and was suggesting that Wallace consult Hague and Kelly for political advice, FDR laughed: "Frank is muscling right in as usual."[72] In 1944, however, Hague helped to convince Roosevelt to drop Wallace.

Hague's organization soon received another boost when the United States entered World War II. Movements of troops and material through Hudson County and the New York–Newark port provided ample opportunities for graft and patronage. The war also relieved some pressure from the machine because, by 1940, Hague's organization had become a kakistocracy with little room for younger members. Sending them off to war was just another form of public employment in Hague's eyes, albeit more patriotic. By controlling the county's draft boards, Hague could also arrange inductions for political dissidents. If this proved difficult, he accused opponents of draft evasion. In one publicized case, Hague convinced the U.S. attorney to arrest Leo Rosenblum, a militant anti-Hagueite, for draft evasion. Although the charge was untrue and the U.S. attorney dropped it, the incident severely damaged Rosenblum's reputation.

Inadvertently, Roosevelt's preparations for war and a third campaign precipitated Hague's eventual decline and fall. Pursuant to these preparations, FDR decided before the 1940 convention that a bipartisan cabinet would be advantageous. The death of the secretary of the navy opened an ideal spot for a Republican; however, Charles Edison, the assistant secretary, was rightfully in line for it. Roosevelt concluded that "the best way to handle it would be to have Frank Hague name him as a candidate for Senator or Governor and he'd resign to run for office."[73] FDR's reason for removing Edison was a difficulty in working with him "because he's so hard of hearing."

Roosevelt may also have believed that Edison's candidacy would be a stronger, more "independent" barrier against a tide of Republicanism that was rising in New Jersey, in part due to anti-Hague reform sentiment. Hague's "fascist" image had begun to undermine his position, even among some New Jersey Democrats. Furthermore, his personal behavior increasingly outraged voters because he spent most of his time at his vacation homes in Florida and on the Jersey shore, from which he governed New Jersey by telephone. Even when he returned to Jersey City, he made few public appearances, preferring to conduct business by phone from a luxury apartment.

Jim Farley balked at the idea of removing Edison and appointing Republicans to the cabinet, but he called Hague for Roosevelt, noting later that he "had a little trouble reaching Hague" because he was out of town.[74] Hague also disliked FDR's idea and its preconvention timing. Hague felt that Roosevelt was insufficiently sensitive to important party matters. Nonetheless, he agreed to nominate Edison for governor. Farley assured him that Edison would be congenial. At the same time, Farley feared for Edison's welfare. "Hague is a hard taskmaster," he told Roosevelt, "and he might want Charley to keep certain obligations that Charley wouldn't want to fulfill. I don't think it would be fair to Charley to get him involved. He's an honorable fellow." "Well, we'll see," said Roosevelt.[75]

Much to Hague's surprise, Edison proved to be the hard taskmaster. One of his first actions was to disconnect Hague's direct phone line to the governor's office. Then he announced that he would appoint "a judge, not a political stooge," to the state's high court. Hague responded angrily, "I'm gonna break you, Charley, if it's the last thing I do, because you're a damned ingrate."[76] Hague maintained a steadily vicious campaign against Edison during his entire term. Calling Hague a "ruthless boss," Edison appealed to Roosevelt for support; but FDR remained silent. Even so, Edison succeeded in trimming Hague's sails a bit. Fortunately for Hague, Edison could not succeed himself; but after a hard, mudslinging campaign, an anti-Hague Republican won the 1943 gubernatorial election. Republicans subsequently held the governorship until 1954.

Why did Roosevelt not aid his friend Charley? Edison seemed to feel personally betrayed, and many others regarded FDR's silence as a cruel disappointment. Perhaps the pressures of war and FDR's reluctance to enter state and local conflicts kept him silent. The growing Republican strength in New Jersey may have also affected his decision. He knew that Hague would still be in power long after Edison left the scene. Hague would be needed to maintain a strong Democratic party in the state and, indeed, Roosevelt would not have carried New Jersey in 1944 had it not been for Hague's large Hudson County plurality.

So Roosevelt continued to cooperate with Hague and placated him with a federal judgeship. This appointment of a Hague "henchman," Thomas F. Meaney, aroused considerable controversy. Senator George Norris of Nebraska made one of his last great speeches in the Senate against this nomination in which he wondered whether "one of the most disreputable and demagogic organizations that ever existed will go beyond New Jersey and take in the whole Federal Government."[77] Governor Edison opposed the nomination as well, viewing it as tantamount to "putting Frank Hague on the federal bench." Mary Norton called Edison "the most arrant hypocrite in the world" for opposing Meaney after Edison had sought Hague's assistance in his own election. Edison dismissed the allegation; but FDR sent Norton a brief congratulatory note on June 1, 1942. It read: "Dear Mary: You are a grand girl!"[78]

This was Roosevelt's last great favor for Hague. Naturally, his death three years later came as a blow to Hague, whose power was already being eroded by a variety of political and socioeconomic forces, some of them set in motion by the New Deal and the war. His relations with Truman were not nearly as smooth and, again, as he had done with Wilson in 1912 and Roosevelt in 1932, Hague opposed Truman's nomination in 1948, predicting that Truman could not possibly win the election.

Instead, Hague's organization lost the wild municipal election of 1949 to a coalitional "Freedom For All" ticket. Ironically, the Freedomites evoked the spirits of Roosevelt, the New Deal, and especially the "Four Freedoms" as their primary appeal for victory. Hagueism was compared to Stalinism in this election, and Hague was accused of having betrayed the ideals of FDR, the great freedom fighter. Subsequently, Hague lost the county elections, and his public employees began to "flip over" to the Freedomites. Angry and bitter, Hague retreated to his luxury apartment in New York City, where he died in 1956.

There can, of course, be no answer to the question of whether Roosevelt should or could have squashed Hague in the 1930s. Roosevelt's restraint certainly derived from a large measure of political expediency and personal ambition. Yet, it was also a matter of principle. Larger issues were at stake: the Great

Depression and World War II. Hague was as much of a dictator as one can be in the United States; but the readiness of some to equate Hague with Hitler was a gross rhetorical exaggeration. There was also the principle of local autonomy and the right of local voters to elect their own officials. This cannot be an unrestricted right; but it must be an expansive one if the principles of federal democracy are to be protected from national overreach. This is an especially important issue with regard to presidential prerogatives in a federal system. Perhaps, as his comments to Kingdon implied, FDR believed that the citizens of Jersey City had the democracy they deserved and, therefore, had only themselves to look to for a remedy.

Most likely a direct assault on Hague would have had three outcomes. The Democrats would have been thrown into disarray; the Republicans would have gained greater strength in New Jersey at an earlier date; and a new machine would have emerged in Hudson County, however weakened and confined to the county by statewide Republicans. The latter is suggested by subsequent developments. The "Freedom For All" leader, John V. Kenny, became a new boss and erected an organization which survived until 1971, when most of its leaders were imprisoned by the Nixon administration for crimes which involved spectacular corruption. A reform administration, elected in a special election that year, was soundly defeated by old-line politicians in 1977.

Indirectly, Roosevelt did undermine Hague by urging him to elect Edison to the governorship, by supporting the rights of unions, by promoting freedom, however rhetorically, and by implementing new socioeconomic policies that moved the United States onto a new frontier where there is little room for bosses. The war also undermined Hague. When the veterans returned from fighting fascism abroad, they opposed Hague and resented the fact that he had spent the war in Florida. What may have been most important in the long run, however, was not so much the immediate substance of Roosevelt's administration, but its image, energy, and rhetoric.

As a result, when Roosevelt died, millions of people mourned, and millions still remember him as one of the greatest presidents. Few Americans even know of Frank Hague. When Hague died, his funeral was sparsely attended. A small, mostly hostile, crowd assembled outside the funeral home in Jersey City. An elderly woman raised an American flag with placard reading: "God have mercy on his sinful, greedy soul." When asked why there were so few flowers, a funeral aide said, "When the big boy goes, it means he can no longer do anything for anybody."[79]

NOTES

   1. James Bryce, *The American Commonwealth*, 2 vols. (New York: Macmillan, 1907), 1:637.

   2. James MacGregor Burns, *Leadership* (New York: Harper and Row, 1978), p. 4.

   3. Harold F. Gosnell, *Machine Politics: Chicago Model*, 2nd ed. (Chicago: University

of Chicago Press, 1968), p. 8. See also Lyle W. Dorsett, *Franklin D. Roosevelt and the City Bosses* (Port Washington, N.Y.: Kennikat Press, 1977); Bruce M. Stave, *The New Deal and the Last Hurrah: Pittsburgh Machine Politics* (Pittsburgh: University of Pittsburgh Press, 1970).

4. Alexis de Tocqueville, *Democracy in America,* 2 vols., trans. Henry Reeve (New York: Schocken Books, 1961), 1:62.

5. Mark I. Gelfand, *A Nation of Cities: The Federal Government and Urban America, 1933–1965* (New York: Oxford University Press, 1975).

6. Russell Kirk, "The Prospects for Territorial Democracy in America," in *A Nation of States: Essays on the American Federal System,* ed. Robert A. Goldwin, 2nd ed. (Chicago: Rand McNally, 1974), pp. 43–66.

7. Edmund Beard and Stephen Horn, *Congressional Ethics: The View from the House* (Washington, D.C.: Brookings Institution, 1975).

8. Harold J. Laski, "The Obsolescence of Federalism," *The New Republic* 98 (May 1939): 362–69. See also Rexford Guy Tugwell, *A Model Constitution for a United Republic of America* (Santa Barbara, Calif.: Center for the Study of Democratic Institutions, 1970).

9. William M. Leiter, "The Presidency and Non-federal Government: FDR and the Promotion of State Legislative Action," *Presidential Studies Quarterly* 9 (Spring 1979): 101–21; James T. Patterson, *The New Deal and the States: Federalism in Transition* (Princeton, N.J.: Princeton University Press, 1969); Daniel J. Elazar, *American Federalism: A View from the States* (New York: Thomas Y. Crowell, 1972).

10. H.R. Shapiro, *The Bureaucratic State: Party Bureaucracy and the Decline of Democracy in America* (New York: Samizdat Press, 1975).

11. Raymond Moley, *The First New Deal* (New York: Harcourt, Brace, 1966), p. 9.

12. Quoted in Bernard Bellush, *Franklin D. Roosevelt as Governor of New York* (New York: Columbia University Press, 1955), p. 76.

13. *The Public Papers of Governor Franklin D. Roosevelt,* 4 vols. (Albany: J. B. Lyon Co., 1930–1939), 1931:757.

14. Gelfand, *A Nation of Cities,* pp. 90–98.

15. Quoted in Harold Zink, *Government of Cities in the United States* (New York: Macmillan, 1948), p. 84.

16. Dorsett, *Franklin D. Roosevelt and the City Bosses,* pp. 33–34; James Michael Curley, *I'd Do It Again* (Englewood Cliffs, N.J.: Prentice-Hall, 1957).

17. Lyle W. Dorsett, *The Pendergast Machine* (New York: Oxford University Press, 1968).

18. Frances Perkins, *The Roosevelt I Knew* (New York: Viking Press, 1946), p. 194.

19. Rexford G. Tugwell, *The Democratic Roosevelt: A Biography of Franklin D. Roosevelt* (Garden City, N.Y.: Doubleday, 1957), p. 151.

20. See especially Douglas Vincent Shaw, "The Making of an Immigrant City: Ethnic and Cultural Conflict in Jersey City, New Jersey, 1850–1877," Ph.D. dissertation, University of Rochester, 1973; Owen Grundy, *The History of Jersey City* (Jersey City: Chamber of Commerce, 1976); Daniel Van Winkle, ed., *History of the Municipalities of Hudson County New Jersey, 1630–1923,* 3 vols. (New York: Lewis Historical Publishing Co., 1924); Alexander McLean, *History of Jersey City, New Jersey* (Jersey City, N.J.: Press of the Jersey City Printing Co., 1895).

21. Edward M. Levine, *The Irish and Irish Politicians: A Study of Cultural and Social Alienation* (Notre Dame, Ind.: University of Notre Dame Press, 1966).

22. See also John Morton Blum, *Joe Tumulty and the Wilson Era* (Boston: Houghton Mifflin, 1951); Ransome Noble, Jr., *New Jersey Progressivism Before Wilson* (Princeton, N.J.: Princeton University Press, 1946).

23. *Jersey Journal,* September 14, 1910.

24. Mark S. Foster, "Frank Hague of Jersey City: 'The Boss' as Reformer," *New Jersey History* 86 (Summer 1968): 103–112.

25. Dayton David McKean, *The Boss: The Hague Machine in Action* (Boston: Houghton Mifflin, 1940), p. xv.

26. McKean, *The Boss;* Richard J. Connors, *A Cycle of Power: The Career of Jersey City Mayor Frank Hague* (Metuchen, N.J.: Scarecrow Press, 1971); Thomas J. Fleming, "There Is No Mafia in Jersey City," *Scanlon's Monthly* 1 (April 1970): 63–69.

27. Willard Weiner, "Hague Is the law," *The New Republic,* 110 (January 31, 1944): 17.

28. Tugwell, *The Democratic Roosevelt,* p. 526.

29. McKean, *The Boss,* pp. 95–96.

30. James A. Farley, *Jim Farley's Story: The Roosevelt Years* (New York: McGraw-Hill, 1948), pp. 14–15.

31. McKean, *The Boss,* p. 96.

32. Elliot A. Rosen, *Hoover, Roosevelt and the Brains Trust: From Depression to New Deal* (New York: Columbia University Press, 1972), p. 224.

33. Farley, *Jim Farley's Story,* p. 19.

34. McKean, *The Boss,* p. 97.

35. Ibid.

36. Ibid., p. 133.

37. James A. Farley, *Behind the Ballots* (New York: Harcourt, Brace, 1938), p. 158.

38. Frank Freidel, *Franklin D. Roosevelt: The Triumph* (Boston: Little, Brown, 1956), p. 330.

39. *The Hudson Dispatch,* August 22, 1933, p. 9.

40. Dorsett, *Franklin D. Roosevelt and the City Bosses,* p. 102.

41. McKean, *The Boss,* p. 99.

42. William E. Leuchtenburg, *Franklin D. Roosevelt and the New Deal, 1932–1940* (New York: Harper Torchbooks, 1963), p. 131.

43. Farley, *Jim Farley's Story,* p. 118.

44. *New York Times,* November 2, 1936, p. 9.

45. *Time,* 16 (September 8, 1930): 18.

46. McKean, *The Boss,* p. 103.

47. Ibid., p. 104.

48. Connors, *A Cycle of Power,* p. 88.

49. Ibid.

50. *New York Times,* December 12, 1935, p. 33.

51. Superior Court of New Jersey, *Final Report of Samuel A. Larner, as Expert Appointed by Hon. Hayden Proctor, Judge of Superior Court of N.J.* (L-3973–52), pp. 155–60.

52. Marquis W. Child, *I Write from Washington* (New York: Harper and Brothers, 1942), pp. 113–14.

53. Samuel I. Rosenman, ed., *The Public Papers and Addresses of Franklin D. Roosevelt,* 13 vols. (New York: Random House, 1938–1950), 5:408–10.

54. Elliott Roosevelt, ed., *FDR: His Personal Letters, 1928–1945* (New York: Duell, Sloan and Pearce, 1950), Part II, p. 804.

55. Dorsett, *Franklin D. Roosevelt and the City Bosses,* p. 103.

56. Leuchtenburg, *Franklin D. Roosevelt and the New Deal,* pp. 275–76.

57. McKean, *The Boss,* p. 228.

58. Alfred D. Hirsch, "Scab City, New Jersey," *The Nation,* vol. 139 (November 7, 1934): 539.

59. *New York Times,* June 22, 1939, p. 14.

60. Harold L. Ickes, *The Secret Diary of Harold L. Ickes: The Inside Struggle, 1936–1939,* 3 vols. (New York: Simon and Schuster, 1954), 2:414.

61. Ibid., 2:417.

62. Louis W. Koenig, *The Chief Executive,* 4th ed. (New York: Harcourt Brace Jovanovich, 1981), p. 140.

63. Roosevelt, *FDR: His Personal Letters,* Part II, p. 827.

64. Farley, *Jim Farley's Story,* p. 149.

65. Thomas H. Green, *What Roosevelt Thought: The Social and Political Ideas of Franklin D. Roosevelt* (East Lansing: Michigan State University, 1958), p. 118.

66. Frank Kingdon, *Architects of the Republic* (New York: Alliance Publishing Co., 1947), pp. 224–25.

67. *Newark Evening News,* October 27, 1938, p. 1; *Hague* v. *C.I.O.,* 307 U.S. 496 (1939).

68. Roosevelt, *FDR: His Personal Letters,* Part II, p. 864.

69. Tugwell, *The Democratic Roosevelt,* p. 526.

70. Farley, *Jim Farley's Story,* p. 261.

71. Ibid., p. 309.

72. Ibid.

73. Ibid., p. 212.

74. Ibid., p. 213.

75. Ibid., pp. 213–14.

76. Ralph G. Martin, *The Bosses* (New York: G. P. Putnam's Sons, 1964), p. 203.

77. James MacGregor Burns, *Roosevelt: The Soldier of Freedom* (New York: Harcourt Brace Jovanovich, 1970), pp. 276–77.

78. Roosevelt, *FDR: His Personal Letters,* Part II, p. 1328.

79. *Time,* vol. 67 (January 16, 1956): 19.

2

FDR's First Hurrah: The "Blue-Eyed Billy" Sheehan Affair

Nathan Miller

Franklin D. Roosevelt was just shy of twenty-nine when he made his debut as a state senator in Albany in January 1911. Freshmen legislators traditionally ranked "somewhere between . . . a janitor and a committee clerk," according to a sardonic newsman named Louis McHenry Howe,[1] but the "second coming" of a Roosevelt to a stage from which Theodore Roosevelt had leaped to fame thirty years before was hardly to be ignored. Reporters hastened to file feature stories about the intense young aristocrat in high collar and gold-bowed pince-nez, and he was immediately elevated above the common herd of neophyte politicians.

"With his handsome face and his form of supple strength he could make a fortune on the stage and set the matinee girl's heart throbbing with subtle and happy emotion," wrote a veteran *New York Times* reporter.[2] But Big Tim Sullivan, the boss of the Bowery, cast a much less admiring glance his way. "Well, if we've caught a Roosevelt, we'd better take him down and drop him off the dock," he told Charles F. Murphy, grand sachem of Tammany Hall. "The Roosevelts runs true to form, and this kid is likely to do for us what the Colonel is going to do for the Republican party—split it wide open."[3] Not long afterward, both Murphy and Sullivan had cause to wish they had given this suggestion serious consideration.

Inspired by the example of the Colonel—his wife's Uncle Ted—Roosevelt had entered politics the year before. To the surprise of political observers, he had won an upset victory in the solidly Republican Twenty-sixth District, which had not sent a Democrat to Albany in decades. The young man had already mapped out a political path for himself that paralleled that of his distinguished relative. Grenville Clark, one of Roosevelt's fellow law clerks in the Wall Street firm of Carter, Ledyard & Milburn, later remembered him saying "with engaging

frankness that he wasn't going to practice law forever, that he intended to run
for office at the first opportunity, and that he wanted to be and thought he had
a real chance to be President."[4] First, however, he would win a seat in the state
legislature, secure an appointment as assistant secretary of the navy, and be
elected governor of New York. "Anyone who is Governor of New York has a
good chance to be President with any luck," Roosevelt had said. No one considered this an idle daydream, Clark noted. "It seemed proper and sincere; and
moreover, as he put it, entirely reasonable."

Roosevelt had campaigned on a vaguely progressive platform and, reflecting
the views of his largely rural district, opposed the attempts of Tammany to
extend its power beyond the confines of New York City. The first business of
the legislature—the election of a U.S. senator—put him on a collision course
with Boss Murphy. Before the ratification of the Seventeenth Amendment to the
Constitution in 1913, the legislatures rather than the voters chose the two senators
allotted to each state. The term of Senator Chauncey M. Depew, a Republican
and a mouthpiece for the Vanderbilt railroad interests, was to end on March 4,
1911, and Murphy had handpicked William F. Sheehan to replace him.

"Blue-eyed Billy" Sheehan had gotten his start as a machine politico in
Buffalo, but he had risen in the world. Working with Thomas Fortune Ryan, a
notorious Wall Street operator, he had become a millionaire in traction and utility
speculation, and a law partner of Alton B. Parker, the unsuccessful Democratic
nominee for president in 1904. He was a member of the city's best clubs and
resided at East 65th Street, not far from the Roosevelt townhouse.

Once Murphy had bestowed his blessing on Sheehan, his election seemed
assured. The U.S. senator would be chosen by a simple majority of the 200
members of both houses of the legislature, in which the Democrats controlled
114 seats, 13 more than needed to win. In reality, the choice could be made by
as few as 58 members—a bare majority of the Democratic caucus. Murphy had,
in effect, the power to personally appoint the senator, for he had more than a
majority of the Democratic legislators in his pocket.

Sheehan had been generous with funds during the previous campaign and, as
a *Times* correspondent noted, "at least a half a dozen Democratic legislators
have drifted into the capital bubbling over with gratitude."[5] No worse than the
average politico of the period, Sheehan wished to crown his career with a U.S.
senatorship, but other Democrats were less enchanted with him. Most supported
Edward M. Shepard, former mayor of Brooklyn, legal counsel for the Pennsylvania Railroad, and a moderate progressive. Franklin Roosevelt was among
them. "Shepard is without question the most competent to fill the position, but
the Tammany crowd seems unable to forgive him for his occasional independence
and Sheehan looks like their choice at this stage of the game," he noted in his
diary shortly after arriving in Albany. "May the result prove that I am wrong!
There is no question in my mind that the Democratic party is on trial"[6]

Roosevelt's decision to resist Sheehan's election was based upon several factors. Although Franklin found him "delightful personally," he was angered by

the undemocratic fashion in which Murphy's choice was to be rammed down the throats of legislative Democrats. Friends like the upstate progressives William Osborn, Thomas Osborne, and John Mack, who had given him his start in politics, were all unhappy with the choice of Sheehan. Family tradition also played a role in his decision because Sheehan had been anathema to Cleveland Democrats like his father. And there was the example of Theodore Roosevelt. Fully realizing that his election in a predominantly Republican district was something of a fluke, the younger Roosevelt understood that if he wished to remain in politics he would have to make a reputation that would guarantee his reelection in 1912. Uncle Ted had vaulted into prominence three decades before by defying party discipline in order to delve into a shady traction deal that made his reputation as a reformer.

Having no wish to make an open break with the party, Roosevelt went to Al Smith, the newly installed Assembly leader, informed him of his opposition to Sheehan and, along with some other insurgents, sought guidance on procedure. With a candor that Franklin remembered many years later, Smith told them: "Boys, I want you to go into the caucus, and if you go in, you're bound by the action of the majority. That's party law. But if you're serious about this fight, keep your hands clean and stay out. Then you're free agents."[7]

Despite these distant rumblings, Sheehan was brimming with confidence on the evening of January 16 as the Democrats began filtering into the Assembly chamber for their caucus. Reporters crowded about, asking him for his views on the issues that would come before him as a senator. "Not now," he confidently replied. "If you call on me tomorrow I may talk."[8] But at nine o'clock, when the caucus was to be gaveled into session, it was discovered that a number of legislators were absent. The meeting was postponed for an hour to allow the party whips to dragoon in the missing members.

Meanwhile, the insurgents gathered in a hotel room under the leadership of Edward R. Terry, a Brooklyn assemblyman and Yale classmate of President Taft, with the intention of preventing Sheehan from receiving enough votes for election. Roosevelt and Terry had arrived first to find themselves alone. "For ten long minutes that seemed like hours," Terry said, "we assured each other that there was no doubt of the speedy arrival of the other eighteen."[9] When the latecomers finally appeared amid sighs of relief, Roosevelt was elected chairman, and they awaited the outcome of the caucus up on Capitol Hill. Sheehan received sixty-two votes, Shepard eighteen, and there were a few scattered ballots for other candidates. All those who voted were bound to Sheehan, but they totaled only ninety-one members—ten fewer than needed for endorsement by the caucus.

Roosevelt issued a manifesto in the name of the insurgents, explaining that they had refused to attend the party gathering because "they believed the votes of those who represented the people should not be smothered in the caucus; . . . the people should know just how their representatives vote . . . and that any majority secured for any candidate should be credited to the representatives in Legislature and not some one outside the body."[10] This last statement was a direct slap at Boss Murphy. The manifesto made headlines, and Roosevelt's name figured prominently in the newspapers the next day. Some of the insurgents supported Shepard, while others backed a variety of candidates, Roosevelt explained, but all "have decided to stand to a man and to the end against William F. Sheehan." They were "fighting against the boss rule system" and would never yield.

All legislative business ground to a halt, and the deadlock lasted for ten weeks. Murphy did not at first appear to take the insurgency seriously. While Sheehan threatened revenge in a private meeting with Roosevelt, the Boss was affability itself when they got together. Roosevelt said they had talked about the weather for five or ten minutes, and he quoted Murphy as saying he was "entirely convinced" that the opposition to Sheehan was "a perfectly honest one." Most party leaders took the position that when suitable enticements were dangled in front of this band of upstarts, the ten or so votes needed for Sheehan's election would be forthcoming. As soon as they had received enough publicity, they would return to the fold.

Roosevelt, the guiding spirit behind the revolt if not its leader, was contemptuously described as a "college kid" and "a calf still wet behind the ears." Some of the old guard even claimed that he was a Trojan horse, bent on splitting the party under instructions from Theodore Roosevelt. But the young man was elated by the slash and parry of political combat. "There is nothing I love as a good fight," he told a reporter with evident glee. "I never had as much fun in my life as I am having right now."[11]

As the struggle wore on, Roosevelt received national attention, for progressives in all parts of the nation were demanding direct election of U.S. senators and an end to bossism. In New Jersey, the newly elected governor, Woodrow Wilson, was waging a similar fight to prevent James Smith, Jr., boss of the Newark-Essex County machine from being appointed to the Senate. Wilson's victory established him as one of the country's major progressive leaders and put him on the road to the White House. "I am delighted with your action & told Woodrow Wilson today of how he & you are serving the nation," William Grosvenor, a prominent clergyman, wrote Roosevelt.[12] From Sagamore Hill, he received a hastily scrawled note: "Just a line to say we are all really proud of the way you handled yourself. Good luck to you! Give my love to dear Eleanor."[13]

The New York Times listed the names of the insurgents on a "roll of honor" on its editorial page, placing young Roosevelt's name at the top.[14] And the Cleveland Plain Dealer commented: "Theodore Roosevelt as a young man merely took advantage of all opportunities to keep himself in the public eye, and to strengthen the impression that he was a fighter . . . Franklin D. Roosevelt is beginning his public career fully as auspiciously. If none of the colonel's sons turn out to be fit objects for public adoration, may not it be possible that this rising star may continue the Roosevelt dynasty?"[15]

Although many observers regarded him as the "head and shoulders" of the revolt, in the words of the New York *Sun*,[16] Roosevelt was more chairman of the board than actual leader of the insurgency. In the beginning, the insurgents met at a hotel, but later moved to the house on State Street that Roosevelt had rented for the session and which served as a combined headquarters and social club. Routine quickly replaced the excitement of the opening stages of the battle. Day after day, week after week, between twenty and thirty men gathered at the Roosevelt house each morning and at 10 A.M. marched up to the capitol, where they went through the futile gesture of casting ballots for a U.S. senator. At 5 o'clock, they returned to gather around the crackling fire in the large library. These meetings were more hand-holding sessions than strategy meetings. "There is very little business done at our councils of War," Roosevelt said. "We just sit around and swap stories like soldiers at the bivouac fire."[17]

Reporters also dropped in to pick up tidbits of news, of which Roosevelt seemed to have an inexhaustible supply. Among them was Louis Howe, the gnarled little Albany correspondent of the New York *Herald*. Howe took particular notice of a coat-of-arms carved over the blazing hearth—a hand holding a club—and thought at once of Teddy Roosevelt's Big Stick. At first, he sized up the younger Roosevelt as "a spoiled, silk-pants sort of a guy," but later admired his spirit. "Mein Gawd!" he declared in the mock German he affected.[18] "The boy's got courage!"

These meetings also marked the beginning of Eleanor Roosevelt's political education. For her, the move to Albany had provided an escape from the domination of Sara Roosevelt, and she indulged her lively intellectual curiosity. As the wife of the most talked about young political figure in Albany, she met people of diverse backgrounds and learned to accept the unexpected without becoming flustered. "The rights and wrongs of the fight" against Sheehan's election "meant very little to me" at first, she said, but soon she began to hover in the background as the insurgents gathered at her home, and she learned how politics really worked.[19] When she thought the time for departure had come, she brought out beer, cheese, and crackers as the signal for everyone to eat, drink, and go home.

Perhaps the most trying time for Eleanor came early in February, when Franklin suddenly announced that Sheehan and his wife were coming to State Street the next day. "Lunch was not so bad for I had my husband to carry the burden of the conversation," she said. "But after lunch we two women sat and talked about the weather and anything else inconsequential that we could think of, while both of us knew quite well that behind the door of my husband's study a really important fight was going on." Finally, the antagonists emerged, both looking grim. After the Sheehans were gone, the greatly relieved Eleanor asked if any agreement had been reached. "Certainly not," Franklin replied.[20] And the battle went on.

Remaining in session while accomplishing nothing was costly to the legislature, and pressure was stepped up on the insurgents.[21] Patronage was denied them, and Roosevelt, who had been appointed chairman of the Forest, Fish, and Game Committee, saw his choice as clerk discharged. The new law firm which he had formed with Langdon Marvin and Henry Hooker after leaving Carter, Ledyard & Milburn lost a client. Even more damaging was the charge circulated by Sheehan's friends that he was anti-Irish and anti-Catholic. The Catholic bishop of Syracuse claimed that the insurgents had revived "the old spirit of Know-nothingism," and in a much quoted statement declared, "You are an Irishman and that's agin you; you are a Catholic and that's agin you." Alarmed, Roosevelt and several of his associates hastily denied any taint of anti-Catholicism and emphasized that some of the insurgents were Irish Catholics and a few were even members of the Knights of Columbus.

Other rebels, more vulnerable financially than Roosevelt, were severely clawed by the angry Tammany tiger. Hints were dropped of called loans and mortgage foreclosures. The owner of a rural newspaper who depended upon printing state materials was warned that if he did not fall into line he would lose the contract when it came up for renewal. Some of the little group were told that their political careers were over, for they would not be renominated. Resolutions from their constituents fomented by Sheehan's partisans around the state piled up on the desks of the recalcitrants. Ed Perkins, the Democratic state committeeman in Poughkeepsie, always antagonistic to Roosevelt, circulated a petition demanding that he follow the wishes of the caucus. Recognizing that some of the 265 names were in the same handwriting, Roosevelt dismissed it as "a fizzle."[22] And he found that his stand against Tammany was popular with the heavily Republican voters of his district. But the situation was not so easy for many of the insurgents, and several times it appeared as if the coalition would break up. "They say that the road of the transgressor is hard," declared a weary Edward Terry. "The transgressor's path is pleasant compared to that of a legislator trying to do what he regards as his duty. His way is beset with temptations on every side."[23]

Politicians abhor a vacancy in any office. As soon as it was evident that Sheehan could not be elected to the Senate, Murphy, reasoning that he had paid his debt to "Blue-eyed Billy," advised him to withdraw gracefully. He quietly began to line up support for Daniel F. Cahalan, his chief lieutenant and son-in-law, who had been his secret choice for the post all along. The Boss apparently believed that the opposition to both Sheehan and Shephard would be so violent that Cahalan would be acceptable to all parties as a compromise candidate. Inscrutability had always been Murphy's stock-in-trade. Upon one occasion, a reporter asked an aide why the Boss had not joined the crowd at a political rally in singing "The Star Spangled Banner." "Perhaps he didn't want to commit himself," was the reply.[24] Shepard's candidacy had also long since vanished, and in his desperation to prevent a collapse of the insurgency, Roosevelt turned to the Republicans for help.

He sought to strike a deal with William Barnes, the Republican boss, by proposing that the Democratic rebels and the Republicans agree on a candidate acceptable to both sides. Barnes rejected this proposal, deciding that it was good politics to let the Democrats fight it out among themselves. Roosevelt next tried to use the conservative Cleveland Democrats to reach the Republicans. The intermediary chosen was a strange one for a reformer: Francis Lynde Stetson, attorney for J. P. Morgan and an organizer of U.S. Steel. The price of this assistance was too high, however. Stetson's group stipulated that in exchange for their help, the insurgents should remain together after the election to block legislative ratification of the income tax amendment to the Constitution and to support pro-business legislation. Roosevelt flatly rejected such a commitment. Nevertheless, when Samuel Untermeyer was proposed as a compromise candidate he opposed the choice. Untermeyer, a brilliant lawyer with nominal ties to Tammany, was widely known for his opposition to the trusts and was disliked by the Morgan interests. Turning this incident against the insurgents, Murphy charged that they were tools of the House of Morgan—reinforcing the charge that the struggle merely masked a conflict between rival groups of Wall Street insiders for control of a Senate seat.

It took a fire that gutted the capitol to break the deadlock. On the night of March 29, the legislative chambers were seriously damaged, forcing the members to meet in the cramped Albany City Hall across the way. Tempers worn raw by the long, drawn-out struggle finally snapped under the physical discomfort. Wagner and Smith anxiously informed Murphy that unless a solution was found quickly they would be unable to hold their forces in Albany. They were ready to vote for anything or anyone so that they could get out of town. Already worried that Roosevelt's maneuverings with the Republicans might produce an alliance, the Boss grabbed the first train to Albany—a milk train which crept up along the Hudson—arriving early the next morning, exhausted and with eyes bloodshot. He put forward the name of Justice Victor J. Dowling, of the State Supreme Court, as a compromise candidate. Two days of sparring followed before a majority of the insurgents, personally promised by Wagner and Smith that there would be no reprisals for their defection, reluctantly agreed to accept Dowling.

Just as they were preparing to leave the Roosevelt house for the caucus, the insurgents learned that they had been soundly outgeneraled. Dowling had declined the nomination, and in his place Murphy had submitted the name of Justice James A. O'Gorman, a former grand sachem of Tammany Hall. This not only filled the Senate seat with someone more to his liking than Sheehan but also opened a vacancy on the State Supreme Court for Dan Cahalan. Angrily denouncing the move, Roosevelt wanted to continue the siege, but it was a futile gesture. The insurgents could not afford to reject O'Gorman. Since his elevation to the bench, he had kept out of politics and enjoyed a good reputation as a jurist. Even more important, in view of the charge that the insurgents had been motivated by anti-Catholicism in opposing Sheehan, he was not only Irish and a Catholic but a former president of the Friendly Sons of St. Patrick. With reports filtering in that Boss Barnes was about to make a deal with Murphy to elect Sheehan if O'Gorman was rejected, a majority of the rebels decided to end their fight. The rest, including Roosevelt, agreed to vote for O'Gorman in the legislative session but declined to take part in the caucus.

A cacaphony of cheers and hoots greeted Roosevelt and the other holdouts as they filed into the Council Chamber on the evening of March 31 to cast their ballots. Someone started to sing the Tammany victory song—"Tammanee . . . Tammanee . . . Swamp 'em, Swamp 'em . . . Get the wampum"—and it was taken up by the rollicking crowd. Legislators and spectators milled about, shouting and hugging each other and paying no attention to the frantic pounding of the gavel. When the speaker managed at last to create a semblance of order, Edgar Brackett, the Republican minority leader, taunted the insurgents. "God moves in a mysterious way," he observed. "Far be it from me to add to the humiliation of the Democrats if I could. They have now accepted a man infinitely more potent in the councils of Tammany Hall than the man they rejected."[25] Taking the floor amid groans and hisses, Roosevelt attempted to salvage a few shreds of dignity from the debacle. "Two months ago a number of Democrats felt that it was our duty to dissent from certain of our party associates in the matter of selecting a United States Senator," he declared. " . . . We have followed the dictates of our consciences and have done our duty as we saw it. I believe that as a result the Democratic party has taken an upward step. We are Democrats—not irregulars, but regulars. I take pleasure in casting my vote for the Hon. James A. O'Gorman."[26]

Everyone agreed that the scalps of Roosevelt and his fellow insurgents dangled from the belts of the Tammany braves as they happily returned to New York City for a brief recess. An "exultant" Murphy hailed the election of O'Gorman as a triumph for majority rule and the party caucus. Roosevelt put up a bold front, however, telling newsmen that the rebels had not been trying to elect a senator of their own but to prevent Sheehan from going to Washington. "The minority never assumed to dictate the choice of the majority," he said.[27] Once the Sheehan express had been derailed, the insurgents were solely interested in electing "a suitable man" so "the only credit Charles F. Murphy can claim in ending the senatorial deadlock" is that he eventually put forward the name of such a man. If the Boss had suggested O'Gorman's name in the beginning, Roosevelt claimed, the insurgents would have accepted him. "We all believe him to be a man of absolute independence." But at their annual dinner a few weeks later, the legislative correspondents mercilessly lampooned him: "What's the matter with Roosevelt and his Plan? All the other reformers have them on the pan. Fattened them up with printer's ink. Then handed them the rinky dink. What's the matter with Roosevelt? Got the can."[28] Nevertheless, the deadlock had mixed results. The insurgents were forced to swallow O'Gorman, but they had prevented the election of Sheehan. Although Murphy had triumphed in the end, he had been bloodied in the struggle. And the cause of direct election of U.S. senators had been dramatized and advanced. As for Roosevelt, the "Sheehan business," as he called it, provided him with a short course in practical politics. In this rough school, he had learned to intrigue and maneuver, to balance conflicting ambitions and intricate relationships and to turn the insatiable need of journalists for colorful copy to his own advantage.

Worried about the effect of O'Gorman's victory on his constituents, Roosevelt hurried down to Hyde Park. The voters had supported his role in the insurgency, but he was concerned that they might view the outcome as a capitulation to Tammany. He was delighted to find that there was little grumbling, and his constituents did not feel that Murphy had won. Thus armed, he transformed a humiliating defeat into victory with a masterful exhibition of political sleight-of-hand. Shrewdly emphasizing that the dragon of corruption and bossism had been dealt a serious blow, Roosevelt claimed a personal victory before a public that wished to believe him. Before long, the details of the "Sheehan business" were forgotten, and all that could be readily recalled of the episode was that Roosevelt had twisted the tail of the Tammany tiger. Six months after he had entered politics, Franklin Roosevelt was already a figure to be reckoned with, and his name was being linked to that of Woodrow Wilson, the progressive choice for the Democratic presidential nomination in 1912.

NOTES

1. Louis M. Howe, "The Winner," *Saturday Evening Post,* February 25, 1933.

2. *New York Times,* January 22, 1911.

3. Ernest K. Lindley, *Franklin D. Roosevelt* (New York: Blue Ribbon Books, 1934), p. 78.

4. *Harvard Alumni Bulletin,* April 28, 1945.

5. Lindley, *Franklin D. Roosevelt,* p. 80.

6. FDR Diary, January 1, 1911 (Line-A-Day), Franklin D. Roosevelt Library, Hyde Park, N.Y.

7. Franklin D. Roosevelt, *The Happy Warrior* (Boston: Houghton Mifflin, 1928), p. 4.

8. Lindley, *Franklin D. Roosevelt,* p. 82.

9. Edward R. Terry, "The Insurgents at Albany," *The Independent,* September 7, 1911.

10. *New York Times,* January 11, 1911.

11. *New York Times,* January 22, 1911.

12. Frank Freidel, *Franklin D. Roosevelt: The Apprenticeship* (Boston: Little, Brown, 1952), p. 103.

13. Letter from TR to FDR, January 29, 1911, Franklin D. Roosevelt Library.

14. *New York Times,* January 19, 1911.

15. Cleveland *Plain Dealer,* January 23, 1911.

16. New York *Sun,* January 20, 1911.

17. *New York Times,* January 22, 1911.

18. Lela Stiles, *The Man Behind Roosevelt* (New York: World Publishing Co., 1954), pp. 25–27.

19. Eleanor Roosevelt, *This Is My Story* (New York: Harper and Bros., 1937), pp. 173–75.

20. Ibid.

21. One of the insurgents went home for a weekend and while there began to look through the newspapers, according to a story told by Louis Howe. "Suddenly he blanched with horror at the front page streamer headline, 'Eight insurgents killed.' He was wondering whether to flee the country while the whole thing blew over when he noticed that the date line was a town in Mexico where a revolution was taking place."

22. Freidel, *Franklin D. Roosevelt,* p. 108.

23. Terry, "Insurgents at Albany."

24. M. R. Werner, *Tammany Hall* (Garden City, N.Y.: Doubleday Doran, 1928), p. 564.

25. *New York Times* and New York *Herald,* April 1, 1911.

26. *Franklin D. Roosevelt,* pp. 114–15.

27. Lindley, *Franklin D. Roosevelt,* p. 97.

28. Alfred B. Rollins, Jr., *Roosevelt and Howe* (New York: Alfred A. Knopf, 1962), p. 31.

3

Franklin D. Roosevelt and the Democratic Party

Vladimir O. Pechatnov

Franklin Roosevelt and the Democratic party have become almost inseparable in American history. And this is no accident, for Roosevelt not only presided over the creation of a modern Democratic party, but was also a moving spirit of this transformation. His role as a party leader, Roosevelt's strategy and tactics in "fighting for the masses" (to use an appropriate Marxist term) are the main subject of this chapter. Though FDR, acting in this capacity, left very few direct traces behind, it is still possible, if only in a sketchy way, to reconstruct a general thrust and evolution of his party policy design.

Basically it was subordinated to and constituted a major element of Roosevelt's overall political strategy, which during the first New Deal sought to preserve the very heterogeneous coalition of all major sociopolitical groups of the country that had voted the Democrats into power in 1932. Hence the appeal of the "party of the whole people," the deliberate playing down of all class and partisan themes, while emphasizing national interests and national unity, which, as the president instructed his cabinet on the eve of 1934 campaign, would be the most productive course also from the "vote-catching" perspective.[1]

But already at that stage Roosevelt and his associates paid special attention to retaining the most dynamic and increasingly turbulent left flank of that coalition. The major instrument, of course, was the reforms of 1933–1934, but political maneuvering also played its role. Roosevelt's support of and effective electoral campaign agreements with the progressives of Minnesota, Wisconsin, and New York, in spite of the local Democrats' opposition, revealed an emerging pattern of forging a liberal alliance across the regular party borders. This pattern, especially in the beginning of the New Deal, was neither universal nor absolute.

The president's natural desire to support those party factions adhering to the New Deal often had to compromise with local conservatism, corrupt city machines (as in Massachusetts, New Jersey, Indiana, and Illinois), or got lost in the chaos of interfaction fighting, often deprived of any policy substance. On the other hand, there were clear limits to Roosevelt's tolerance of the left radicalism within the party, as was demonstrated by the EPIC (End Poverty in California) story in 1934.

By the end of 1934, however, this initial compromise course was running against growing class struggle and political polarization, with the national unity coalition of 1932 being increasingly eroded from opposite sides, right and left. Roosevelt was particularly concerned with the growing attempts of his progressive allies to achieve political independence in 1936, which, as he wrote to Colonel E. House, "would defeat us, elect a conservative Republican and cause a complete swing far to the left before 1940."[2] The mass movement for a new antimonopolistic party of the farmer-labor type by that time reached a really unprecedented level, as is thoroughly documented by Soviet historians N. V. Sivachev and V. L. Malkov.[3]

In short, the Roosevelt Democrats were faced with an imperative of choosing a more selective and bolder party line. It was in those autumn days of October 1934 that Roosevelt received a letter from a fellow Democrat, liberal businessman K. Fulton, suggesting a plan to remove a third-party threat. "Your line, therefore," he wrote,

is to divide, to circumvent, to squash, to remove the need for this growing third party tendency. Failure to do so . . . is sure to ultimately defeat the party in power. The best way to circumvent the third party is to go to the left, to make the Democratic party itself, "the third party." While this will drive out some of our reactionary elements, such a course will be positively good for us. It is time for us again to be able to see some real differences between the two old parties.[4]

Whether this layman's advice reached the president or not, it is hard to think of a more apt description of the tactics Roosevelt was soon to follow.

It was a renewed political orientation deliberately aimed at the maximum feasible expansion of the party's working-class base as the only real counterweight to the reactionaries' growing resistance to the New Deal. Realizing that his main leverage in so doing was not the party's popularity as such, but rather the practical policy of his administration, Roosevelt did his best to avoid the appearance of a routine duel between the two parties, submerging his party, so to speak, into the overall liberal-progressive alliance. This liberal-progressive bloc became a tactical side of the second New Deal. As the president himself outlined his strategy for the 1936 election before the Democratic National Committee's Women's Division, this was to be a New Deal, not a Democratic party appeal, with a special effort made to reach the new groups which had a stake in the continuance of the Roosevelt policies—workers, farmers, Negroes, young people, women, independents.[5]

In electoral terms this was a course of mobilization of the "party of the non-voters" of the twenties and early thirties largely based upon the masses of the great northern cities, which by that time, as convincingly shown by K. Anderson and some others, constituted an unprecedently large pool of uncommitted potential voters available for mobilization.[6]

The main target of these "engagement tactics" became the labor movement. The administration not only established direct contact with the unions' leadership, but also encouraged the formation and made a good use of the Labor Non-Partisan League, which became a major political apparatus for getting out the labor vote for Roosevelt and other Democrats. The story of the American Labor party (ALP) of the state of New York remains the most vivid and politically salient example of this new type of cooperation. From the very start it had the blessing and constant support of Roosevelt, who instantly recognized a chance of winning over to the Democrats' side the socialist-oriented New York labor unions' membership, inclined to vote for FDR, but traditionally hostile to Tammany Hall. Later on, A. Berle, Jr., recalling FDR's lessons to Adlai Stevenson, confirmed that "separate organization of what is now the Liberal Party, was, of course, his idea; he never trusted the city Democratic party organization . . . to carry the state."[7]

This relationship was also satisfactory for Sidney Hillman and David Dubinsky, who were quite comfortable with their status as "junior partners" of Roosevelt Democrats. "I cannot make my people who have always voted for socialists, all of a sudden to vote for the democrats," explained Dubinsky, as a rationale for the new party to Frances Perkins, "so we must have them voting under something which has 'labor' on it. To them it seems almost the same."[8] The Democratic party bosses in Washington and New York were far less enthusiastic, but even they realized the tangible benefits of such an alliance in the election year. "The movement around the Labor party, supported by Hillman and others," calculated James Farley in a letter to Eleanor Roosevelt, "will bring us more than 150 thousand votes."[9] Irritated by these unorthodox leftist allies, Farley underestimated the ALP's potential. Until the late forties the latter served as a crucial balance weight in the state, securing electoral victories for Roosevelt and other liberal Democrats. Actually, it became for him a convenient instrument of indirect control over the radical New York unionists, keeping them within political liberalism.

One more important voting group to be incorporated was that of progressive independents and Republicans. Roosevelt attached great importance to the conversion of this group, which was of vital significance for the future of the formerly minority Democratic party.[10] Hence his active encouragement of and cooperation with the National Progressive Committee and Good Neighbor League, which, as D. McCoy was the first to emphasize, became a sort of "half-way house for those political independents and liberal Republicans who were making their way to the ranks of the Democratic Party."[11] Building up such bridges, or shall I

call them "transmission belts," facilitating the influx of the new political forces
to the Democrats, was the special technique which, as recalled by Henry Wallace,
Roosevelt and his friends "were expert at."[12]

Another method of the kind was to use the left-wing factions within the
Democratic party itself for the same purpose. Very characteristic in this respect
were the not too well known ties between Roosevelt and Culbert Olson, who as
a state Democratic chairman headed a liberal-progressive faction of California
Democrats. Olson's special value for Roosevelt was his influence among the
former EPIC constituency and at the same time his reliability as compared with
Upton Sinclair. Local Democrats reported to Roosevelt and Farley that Sinclair's
withdrawal enhanced the opportunities for a consolidation of his former followers
behind the Democrats. Since 1935 Roosevelt maintained behind-the-scene contacts with Olson, working against a possible third-party threat in California.[13]
By the 1936 presidential campaign Olson and his partners had managed to channel
the radicals' energy into liberalization of the state party organization and support
of FDR's candidacy. Born-again "loyal democrats" did their utmost for the co-
optation of the left-wing voters, including an infiltration into the latter's organizations. They saw their mission (as Olson wrote to Farley) as the "keeping
of extreme left voters within our ranks."[14] The only reward asked for, but not
always forthcoming, was patronage and symbolic gestures of attention from the
national party leadership.

The results of the 1936 election signaled a formation of the New Deal political
coalition which transcended the Democratic party as such, although remaining
under the general guidance of Roosevelt's liberals. The future of this still uneasy
alliance was far from certain and, with it, the fate of the New Deal itself. So
the already tested tactics of the liberal-progressive bloc were preserved and
developed by the president. As R. Nye put it, "What Roosevelt was doing, it
became increasingly clear, was creating within the framework of the Democratic
Party a third party of his own, an alliance of New Dealers, independents, progressives and unions, making the Democratic party itself nationally available to
them as a political tool. Third parties were needed only in those states where
Democratic organization was controlled by conservatives."[15]

Here should be added an important amendment clarifying the essence of
Roosevelt's course of intercepting the masses' political initiative: while temporarily dissolving his own party in the overall stream of progressive forces and
making it "unavailable to them as a political tool," the president in reality was
moving toward an eventual absorption of this stream by his party, viewing this
as the only guarantee against a disruption of the two-party system and the political
system as a whole. The roots of liberal political maneuvering of this kind were
long ago identified by V. I. Lenin, who emphasized that "a liberal needs a voter,
liberals need a crowd which trusts and follows them (in order to push [rightest
deceivers of Leftist causes] *Pourishkeviches* aside) but a liberal is ever afraid of
a crowd's political independence."[16] An opposition from the left might have
been acceptable and even useful as a counterweight to the conservatives and

reactionaries, but only within certain limits of loyalty, without seriously challenging the leadership of the ruling liberal Democrats and FDR himself. Witness
Roosevelt's sharp overreaction to an abortive attempt by Philip La Follette to
launch a national Progressive party, and compare it with the president's ready
acceptance of the more influential but also more controllable and locally confined
American Labor party and Minnesota's Farmer Laborites. An ideal version of
such a "directed opposition" for the president, as he once told Henry Wallace,
would have been to gather all that was to the left of the Democrats into a single
organization and to have it "constantly criticizing us because we were not going
far enough left and then at the last minute come out in support of us."[17]

This curious episode sheds light on the manipulative instincts of Roosevelt,
who was deeply convinced that any political ferment under the surface was more
dangerous than a "legitimate" movement led by a loyal opposition. But his
ultimate goal in dealing with the independent political groupings was their eventual co-optation by his own party. Satisfied with the demise of Wisconsin progressives, he emphasized in a November 14, 1938, letter to Josephus Daniels,
"We have on the positive side eliminated Phil La Follette and the Farmer-Labor
people in the Northwest as a standing Third Party threat. They must and will
come to us if we remain definitely the liberal party."[18]

The president, as evidenced in the Democratic National Committee's Wisconsin correspondence, quietly and discreetly pushed Wisconsin's liberal Democrats toward a fusion with local progressives under Democratic auspices.[19] He
was also the major, if a very discreet, architect of a merger between Minnesota's
Farmer-Labor party and local Democrats which was successfully completed in
1944 to his great satisfaction.[20]

Ever mindful of the balance of political forces, Roosevelt clearly realized the
continuous imperative of keeping the Democratic party left of center, where the
actual political center of gravity was at that time, by means of preserving and
cultivating its newly acquired liberal image as the main guarantee against losing
control over the radicalized masses. This consideration, coupled with the receding
tidal wave of protest by the late 1930s and the growing strength of the conservative opposition, explains, in my view, Roosevelt's new emphasis on the liberalization of his party as distinct from the accentuated nonpartisan appeal of
the mid-thirties. "The Democratic Party," he increasingly began to stress, "will
live and continue to receive the support of the majority of Americans just so
long as it remains a liberal party."[21] The growing conservative opposition to
the New Deal within the party itself now turned into a major threat to this delicate
balancing operation. Hence the famous "purge," dictated in part by FDR's
concern with the preservation of the new Democrats' popular image. In his own
words, the president thus tried to see "to it that the two parties should not be
merely Tweedledum and Tweedledee to each other."[22]

The "purge" might have been a culmination of this liberalization policy, but
definitely not the end of it. Although in 1939–1940 Roosevelt had to pacify the
conservatives trying to consolidate the party and expressed his desire to have

"the factions of our party come together under a common banner,"[23] a union "under a common banner" remained elusive, for each side viewed it quite differently. The Roosevelt Democrats fully realized that the restoration of the pre–New Deal Democratic party would be, as FDR stressed both publicly and privately, "a suicide" for the Democrats both in terms of "preserving the system" as well as retaining their electoral gains of the 1930s.[24]

Such a formula of consolidation was at great odds with the conservatives' lingering hope of "turning back the New Deal tide" and recapturing the party for themselves. The anti-third term campaign became for them a last decisive chance "to save the party from radicalism," as Senator J. Bailey wrote to Farley.[25] But the election's results, and particularly the outcome of the Democratic convention, clearly demonstrated the irreversible character of the deep changes within the party during the 1930s. It was in the convention's decision that the overwhelming majority of James Farley's conservative correspondents finally recognized "the complete breakdown of the old regime," "the end and betrayal of the Democratic party," its complete degeneration into a "New Deal radical party."[26] On the other side, FDR, in a letter written to George Norris after the convention, recorded with satisfaction the failure of the conservatives, who "were greatly heartened by 1938 elections and thought that this would give them a fighting chance to put the control of the Democratic party back to where it was in 1920, 1924 and 1928."[27]

FDR's further plans for his party remain more obscure, both in history and historiography. The long-standing ghost of the great realignment allegedly conceived by FDR in the 1940s has been neither decisively proved nor dispelled, and the question itself awaits further extensive research. But, tentatively speaking from my own perspective, this great-design version does not square too well with FDR's philosophy and tactics as a party leader, nor, no less important, with his ever-present sense of realism. A realignment of the already established political parties within the liberal-conservative cleavage would have seemed to him a more logical and feasible perspective than setting up a new political party with all the immense problems involved.

To sum up: Out of the politics of the New Deal upheaval there emerged a new Democratic party which, naturally, was mostly a product of large impersonal forces of history. Still, it is hard to overestimate FDR's personal contribution to this gradual transformation of the New Deal (or Roosevelt's) coalition into the Democratic party coalition. Here, with all due respect to James MacGregor Burns' admirable pioneering work on FDR as a party leader, I cannot agree with his description of Roosevelt as a mere "brilliant tactician" and "skillful manipulator," rather than "a creative leader" or "political strategist."[28] If by strategy we mean the fine art of using all proper means to achieve a basic goal, in FDR's case, channeling the huge energy of social protest into the legitimate political structures (his own party in particular) for the sake of preserving the existing sociopolitical system of capitalism, then Franklin D. Roosevelt is indeed an outstanding political leader, having very few, if any, peers in American history.

NOTES

1. L. Seligman and E. Lornwell, eds., *New Deal Mosaic: Roosevelt Confers with His National Emergency Council, 1933–1936* (Eugene, Ore. 1965), p. 231.

2. Elliott Roosevelt, ed., *F.D.R.: His Personal Letters*, 4 vols. (New York, 1947–1950), 1:452.

3. N. V. Sivachev, *Politicheskaya borba v SShA v seredine 1930kh godov*. Moscow, 1966, p. 122; V. L. Malkov, Novyi Koors v SShA. Sotsialnye dvizhenia i sotsialnaja politika. Moscow, 1973, p. 215.

4. K. Fulton to F. Roosevelt, October 28, 1934. Franklin D. Roosevelt Library, (hereafter cited as FDRL) Hyde Park, N.Y. Official File (OF) 300, California 1933–1945.

5. Joseph P. Lash, *Eleanor and Franklin* (New York, 1973), p. 578.

6. Kristi Anderson, *The Creation of a Democratic Majority, 1928–1936* (Chicago, 1979), pp. 63, 105.

7. Adolph A. Berle, Jr., to Adlai Stevenson, October 1, 1952. Princeton University Library, Adlai Stevenson Papers, Selected Correspondence.

8. Oral History Collection, Columbia University Library, Frances Perkins, p. 511.

9. James Farley to Eleanor Roosevelt, July 25, 1936. Library of Congress, Washington, D.C., James Farley Papers, General Correspondence, Box 4.

10. James MacGregor Burns, *Roosevelt: The Lion and the Fox* (New York, 1956), p. 28.

11. Donald R. McCoy, "The Good Neighbor League and the Presidential Campaign of 1936," *Western Political Quarterly* vol. 13, (December 1960), 1011–1021.

12. Oral History Collection, Columbia University Library, Henry A. Wallace, p. 744.

13. William Dern to F. Roosevelt, September 6, 1935. FDRL, OF 300, California, 1933–1945.

14. Culbert Olson to J. Farley, July 28, 1936. FDRL, OF 300, Farley's Correspondence, 1936, Political Trends.

15. Russel B. Nye, *Midwestern Progressive Politics: A Historical Study of Its Origins and Development, 1870–1950* (Michigan, 1951), p. 371.

16. V. I. Lenin, *Polnoje sobranie sochineni*, 4th ed., vol. 21, p. 239.

17. Oral History Collection, Columbia University Library, Henry Wallace, p. 2173.

18. *F.D.R.: His Personal Letters*, 2:827.

19. T. O'Malley to F. Roosevelt, November 25, 1938. FDRL, OF 300 (Wisconsin).

20. Oral History Collection, Harry S. Truman Library, Independence, Missouri, O. Ewing, pp. 99, 102; O. Ewing to E. Benson, May 4, 1944. FDRL, The Records of Democratic National Committee 1928–1948, Correspondence with State leaders (Minnesota).

21. S.I. Rosenman, comp., *The Public Papers and Addresses of Franklin D. Roosevelt*, 13 vols. (New York, 1969), 7:517.

22. *Public Papers and Addresses*, 7:xxxii.

23. F. Roosevelt to L. Jiggits, November 20, 1939. FDRL, President's Personal File (PPF) 2405.

24. *Public Papers and Addresses,* 7:517; F. Roosevelt to R. Manner, August 8, 1939. FDRL, PPF 236; F. Roosevelt to S. Nettles, January 29, 1940. FDRL, PPF 6460.

25. J. Bailey to J. Farley, October 17, 1940. Library of Congress, J. Farley Papers, Box 7.

26. J. Wolfe to Farley, August 7, 1940; R. Smith to C. Glass, August 8, 1940; J. Hansen to Farley, July 29, 1940. Library of Congress, J. Farley Papers, Box 9,2.

27. *F.D.R.: His Personal Letters,* 2:1047.

28. Burns. *Roosevelt,* p. 401.

II

RESPONSES TO HITLER AND THE REFUGEE PROBLEM

4

FDR and Palestine: The Role of Special Agents

Matthew W. Coulter

Robert Dallek has written that personal ideas, domestic considerations, and foreign events, "either individually or in various combinations," determined Franklin D. Roosevelt's behavior in foreign affairs.[1] The importance of these factors in the formation of Roosevelt's policy toward Palestine has been documented.[2] The significance of special agents and the role of the Office of Strategic Services (OSS) in providing information and recommendations about Palestine to the president have received less attention, however, and consideration of these is needed.

Franklin Roosevelt's public statements indicated support for the goals of Zionism, but the records of the Roosevelt administration reveal a more ambiguous attitude on the part of the president. Roosevelt's public support for Zionism reflected political reality. There were many more Jewish citizens than there were Arab citizens in the United States. Furthermore, American Jews made up important minorities in three states critical to an Electoral College victory: New York, Pennsylvania, and Illinois. Roosevelt during his 1932 campaign for president had endorsed the Zionist program for a Jewish national home in Palestine.[3] Roosevelt continued his public support, again endorsing a Jewish state in Palestine during the 1944 presidential campaign.[4]

Pearl Harbor forced Roosevelt to adopt a more cautious stance toward Palestine. When FDR made a public statement supporting the Zionists he often subsequently authorized the State Department to send reassuring messages to Arab leaders. World War II had drawn the United States into a more active role in the Middle East, making the threat of Arab-Jewish warfare in Palestine a direct threat to U.S. military, economic, and political interests. Outright and unbalanced U.S. support for Zionism might have touched off Arab-Jewish fighting. Such an outbreak would surely have involved the British and could have pushed the Arabs closer to the Axis. Fighting World War II was FDR's first priority, and he did not want a regional problem to threaten wartime unity. Thus a cautious, ambiguous approach which deferred an ultimate decision on Palestine served wartime needs, as well as Roosevelt's own personal characteristic of avoiding final decisions.[5]

Prior to World War II, the president received official information and policy recommendations concerning Palestine and the Middle East primarily from the State Department. The Near Eastern Affairs (NEA) branch had departmental responsibility for Palestine, and many NEA personnel did not favor the establishment of a Zionist entity in Palestine. Believing that the Zionists had no valid claim in Palestine, these officials thought that long-term U.S. interests in the Middle East lay with the Arabs because of Arab oil reserves.[6] Roosevelt, however, distrusted the judgment of State Department officials, which perhaps partially explains why he discounted the NEA position.[7]

The U.S. entry into World War II opened up new sources of information for Roosevelt. The president had established the Office of Coordinator of Information in July 1941, and in May 1942 the agency became the OSS. The OSS, utilizing civilian experts temporarily serving in the military, provided research and analysis reports on the Middle East for the Roosevelt administration, as well as field reports from agents sent into the area. FDR also appointed Patrick J. Hurley to be a special representative to report on Middle Eastern affairs, and in 1943 Roosevelt encouraged efforts to establish a special fact-finding mission led by Lieutenant Colonel Harold B. Hoskins. Thus the groundwork was laid for the role played by the OSS, Hurley, and Hoskins in supplying information and policy recommendations concerning Palestine to Roosevelt.

OSS Chief William Donovan, whom Roosevelt appointed in 1941, had toured the Middle East in 1940. After visiting Jerusalem, Donovan reported seeing "battalions of Arabs and Jews serving together, their political differences submerged in the need of common defense."[8] This perceived cooperation ended quickly, partly owing to Axis propaganda, which attempted to curry favor with the Arabs. In April 1941 a pro-Axis coup in Iraq required British intervention to maintain a government favorable to the Allies.

Before the United States entered the war, the Roosevelt administration accepted a secondary role to Britain on issues concerning Palestine and the Middle East.[9] Britain controlled Palestine through a League of Nations mandate established after World War I. While the mandate carried with it a commitment to the establishment of a Jewish national home in Palestine, the British had in 1939 issued a White Paper that restricted Jewish immigration to Palestine and included a provision for ending Jewish immigration altogether after five years.[10] Zionists opposed the White Paper, as did FDR, and the confrontation between the British and the Zionists could not help but involve the United States and its large Jewish population.

An OSS report of March 1942 dramatized the situation. Donovan forwarded to Roosevelt a copy of a handbill, printed in Yiddish, which the OSS believed had received wide distribution in New York City. The handbill called for Jews to join the "Zionist-Revolutionist Party which advocates an uprising against England to liberate the Jewish Homeland and Transjordania, and establish a Jewish commonwealth!" Donovan thought Nazi agents had probably distributed the handbill.[11]

In April the OSS suggested that the United States side with the Arabs concerning Palestine. A report titled "Zionism—Aims and Prospects" noted that the Jews immigrating to Palestine from Europe, in contrast to the Arabs, were not culturally united. "Fortunately, the United States is not yet identified in Arab eyes with support of Zionism," the OSS concluded while recommending U.S. support for an Arab federation in which "Zionist immigration into Palestine would have to cease entirely for a period sufficiently long to convince reasonable Arabs that they would not be swamped by Jews." The report, in siding with the Arabs, contradicted Roosevelt's support for Zionism and his opposition to the 1939 British White Paper.[12]

It did not take long for the Arabs to identify the United States with support for Zionism. OSS agents reported anti-American outbreaks in Beirut and Damascus starting in December 1942. "Evidence of the stirring of Arab opinion on the part of the Axis against America because of her apparent support of the Zionist cause in Palestine is plentiful and the situation is definitely dangerous," read an OSS Trend Memorandum received by the White House Map Room in late spring 1943.[13] However, it was not only Axis propaganda that had led the Arabs to identify the United States with Zionism.

An OSS agent reported from Beirut in mid-January 1943 that the Vichy French were acquiescing in and perhaps assisting the Nazi propaganda effort. The French hoped to "make the United States and Great Britain more unpopular than France" so that after the war "the Near East will want French supervision rather than that of [the] pro-Jewish United States or Great Britain."[14]

The same agent reported one month later that the British were also attempting to use the Zionism question "to bolster their position vis a vis the Americans." British censors suppressed pro-Jewish news from England, but "published and even emphasized" such reports from the United States, thereby convincing the Arabs that America was extremely pro-Jewish. To counter the swelling of Arab opinion against the United States, the Psychological Warfare Staff prepared a plan for presentation to the Joint Chiefs of Staff.[15] The idea to increase the U.S. presence in the Middle East was not entirely new. Secretary of State Cordell Hull had in summer 1942 told the U.S. ambassador to Great Britain of a planned military and economic mission to the Middle East which included proposals for strengthening United States propaganda efforts in the region.[16]

A second OSS Trend Memorandum from April 1943 reported on "Growing Zionist Pressures." Citing evidence of escalating Zionist propaganda efforts in the United States and Palestine, the report concluded that the Zionists had redirected their energy away from Great Britain. Stepped-up Zionist efforts in the

Middle East created a dangerous situation. Non-Zionist Jews in Palestine were being subjected to terrorism from pro-Zionist groups, including Menachem Begin's Irgun Zvai Leumi. David Ben-Gurion had reportedly stated that all able-bodied Jews should join the British Armed Forces "to secure military training and arms for the eventual defense of the Zionist state." The Zionists were preparing to fight the Arabs after the world war, and the OSS reported that Zionists were attempting to gain as an ally the Maronite Christians of Lebanon. Zionist efforts went beyond mere preparation. Looking ahead to the postwar peace conference, the Zionists were alarmed when Iraq declared war against the Axis because the act would "secure Arab representation at the peace table." To counter the Iraqi move, the Zionists began broadcasting in Kurdish to Iraq, "seeking to foment a Kurdish separatist movement which will embarrass the Iraq government, and discredit it in the eyes of the other United Nations."[17] A war of subversion had started between the Zionists and the Arab governments as early as 1943.

The two Trend Memorandums were sent to the White House Map Room on May 6, 1943, by the deputy director of the OSS. Reports from Patrick J. Hurley and Harold B. Hoskins arrived in the White House around the same time. Hurley had been appointed by FDR to be a personal representative and report directly to the president on conditions in Palestine and six other Middle Eastern countries.

Hurley's report, dated May 5, stated that the Arabs of the Middle East were not seriously opposed to the "concept of a Jewish National Home," but were hostile to continued Jewish immigration to Palestine, which might bring about a Jewish majority in the country and lead to the establishment of a Jewish state. Many Arab leaders believed that a Jewish state would be a means to continue imperialism in the Middle East. Of special significance was Hurley's finding that the Arabs believed the United States, and not Great Britain, was "insisting on establishing a sovereign Jewish State in Palestine." In talks with David Ben-Gurion, the Zionist leader had indicated that the United States stood committed to a Jewish state, but Hurley had asserted that the United States had made no promises. The Hurley report concluded that Britain could no longer settle the Palestine question "and kindred problems in the Middle East." He recommended that the United States and Britain reach a decision for or against a Jewish state and "share also the responsibility for the consequences of such a decision."[18]

President Roosevelt received additional information on the Middle East from Lieutenant Colonel Hoskins. Hoskins' report resulted from his mission to the region in spring 1943. The Hoskins mission had grown out of Hull's proposals in summer 1942, which had later received Roosevelt's backing.[19] Taken together with the Hurley report and OSS reports detailing deteriorating conditions in Palestine and the Middle East, the Hoskins report made evident the dilemma that Palestine posed for Roosevelt.

Hoskins listed the danger of renewed fighting between the Arabs and Jews as the most outstanding fact discovered during his tour of the Middle East. The interests of Jews and Moslems worldwide made a local settlement of the Palestine question impossible. Regarding Jewish immigration to Palestine, Hoskins noted that Palestine was about the size of New Hampshire but had four times the population. "It is not an unpopulated area into which an indefinite additional number can immediately be poured," he wrote. Public pro-Zionist statements in the United States had in at least one instance touched off anti-American demonstrations, and further outbreaks could threaten U.S. military personnel stationed in North African Arab territories. Hoskins concluded his presentation of the facts with a short paragraph which asserted that Arabs would no doubt fight against a Jewish state in Palestine. "It should therefore be very clear that a Zionist State in Palestine can only be imposed upon the Arabs by military force."

Part II of the Hoskins report, titled "The United States and the Palestine Problem," offered a less positive view of the Zionist program than did Part I:

When American citizens or members of Congress sign petitions advocating the establishment of a Jewish State in Palestine, they should realize that, for all practical purposes, they are asking the American Government to commit itself to the use of American armed force in the Near East after the war. Based on British experience this means that American soldiers will be killed in Palestine in the enforcement of such policy. Whether the American people, if they realized more fully this implication, would still favor its adoption may be a matter for debate. At least, however, they should be clearly informed that only by force can a political Zionist policy in Palestine be made effective.

In Part III, titled "Winning Wartime Support of [the] Arab World for the United Nations' Cause," Hoskins suggested that the Allies publicly state that "no final decisions regarding Palestine will be taken until after the war and then only after full consultation with both Arabs and Jews." Roosevelt on May 26 made such a commitment to Ibn Saud, the King of Saudi Arabia.[20]

In the final section of his report, Hoskins offered a plan for peace in the Middle East. He called for a federation of Arab states to include Lebanon, Syria, Trans-Jordan, and Palestine. Palestine would become a binational state with Jewish immigration allowed "up to but not to exceed parity in numbers with the Arabs." A Jewish state would be formed, but not in Palestine. Hoskins recommended that the Jews be given Cyrenaica, a section of Libya which had been colonized and then abandoned by the Italians. He predicted that the Arabs would acquiesce to the plan if they were guaranteed that Palestine would never become a Jewish state.[21]

The reports from Roosevelt's special agents revealed a grim situation. Hurley had concluded that the United States must share responsibility for a decision on a Jewish Palestine. Hoskins concluded that responsibility for a decision favoring a Jewish Palestine would cost American lives. Yet FDR had publicly endorsed Zionist goals in Palestine.

In mid-June Roosevelt had the opportunity to act upon the information supplied by his special agents. The president met with Zionist leader Chaim Weizmann on June 11. According to Weizmann, the president remarked "(a) that the Arabs have done very badly in this war; (b) that although the Arabs have vast countries at their disposal, they have done very little towards their development; (c) that possibly the Jews might help with the development, just as the United Nations would. He then said that he believes that the Arabs are purchasable."[22] In an effort to establish a rapport between the Zionists and the Arabs, FDR directed Hoskins to contact Ibn Saud concerning a possible meeting with Weizmann. Ibn Saud refused to meet with Weizmann.[23]

Hoskins' role in supplying the president with information on the Middle East diminished after the Ibn Saud mission. Hurley continued to act as Roosevelt's personal representative and met with Zionist leaders in early 1944, but after summer 1943, the role of special agents in supplying the White House with information about Palestine and the Middle East rested essentially with the OSS.[24]

OSS capabilities increased to meet the demand for special information created by the growing U.S. presence in the Middle East. Two representatives from the Research and Analysis Division arrived in Cairo in June 1943 and established contact with the Jewish Agency, a group which represented Zionists in Palestine. The Research and Analysis personnel supplemented OSS Cairo operations, which had started in April 1942. Six OSS agents operated in Palestine and Trans-Jordan, two of whom set up long-term contacts with both Arab and Jewish political leaders.[25] OSS reports of November 1943 contained two significant pieces of information. First, a split had occurred in the top ranks of the Zionist leadership. David Ben-Gurion and Chaim Weizmann were in disagreement over the issue of a Jewish state. Ben-Gurion wished to press publicly for it, while Weizmann wanted to be less vocal. Ben-Gurion served as chairman and Weizmann as president of the Jewish Agency. In late October Ben-Gurion offered his resignation to the Jewish Agency, but it was rejected.[26]

The strains in the Zionist movement were perhaps more important than realized at the time, and might have allowed Roosevelt an opening through which to pursue a more vigorous policy toward Palestine. However, it is important to remember that during the same time period Roosevelt was grappling with the overall war effort, which had brought U.S. troops to the European theater by fall 1943. The events of Stalingrad and Kursk and the upcoming Anglo-American landings in Europe demanded the president's attention.

A second November 1943 OSS report made evident the deepening U.S. involvement in Palestine. U.S. soldiers in Palestine were dating Jewish women, an activity that angered certain Jewish youth groups. On September 3 some U.S. soldiers were attacked and injured, and on the following night "loosely organized groups of soldiers began to march down two of the main streets. They assaulted anyone they met." Thirty-three citizens and six U.S. soldiers were injured. The United States began to feel some of the violence that had been directed against the British in Palestine for so many years.[27]

In 1944 OSS reporting from the Middle East increased. In January the agency reported that the Husseini family, considered to be the most powerful Arab family in Palestine, had contacted the Saudi Arabians.[28] The following month the OSS concluded that the "Palestinian Arabs do not count for much in Ibn Saud's opinion," and reported that the desert king had encouraged the Palestinians to rely on the British for help with the Zionism problem.[29] The OSS predicted that Saudi Arabia would become important to the United States because of its huge oil reserves. American oil reserves would provide "scarcely a score of years' supply at the present rate of consumption."[30]

In spring 1944 two congressional resolutions favoring the Zionist aims in Palestine were introduced into the U.S. House of Representatives. OSS reports on the Arab opposition to the proposed resolutions reaffirmed similar observations by State Department officials in the Middle East.[31] The congressional resolutions were, in part, efforts to influence the British concerning a decision on the 1939 White Paper. It will be remembered that the White Paper provided for Jewish immigration for a five-year period due to end on March 31, 1944. President Roosevelt on March 9 authorized a statement that promised "full justice" to supporters of the Jewish National Home and said that the United States had "never given its approval to the White Paper of 1939."[32]

An OSS report from Cairo found "surprisingly little comment" on Roosevelt's statement in the Egyptian capital. Perhaps the muted response of the Egyptians can be partly attributed to messages given to Arab leaders by the State Department which said that "while it is true that the American Government has never given its approval to the White Paper of 1939, it is also true that this Government has never taken a position with regard to the White Paper."[33]

While such a policy stand might have helped to avoid offending either the Arabs or the Jews, it also contributed to "the loss of hope in any aggressive U.S. foreign policy," according to an OSS agent reporting from Iraq in June 1944. The agent sensed a shift in Iraqi public opinion away from the United States and toward the Soviet Union caused by American support for Zionism. The OSS information affirmed similar State Department reports.[34]

If the Arabs were turning toward the Soviet Union for support, it made more urgent the forming of a joint Anglo-American policy on Palestine. Negotiations to effect a joint policy were carried on at various times throughout the war and are reported in the *Foreign Relations of the United States*.[35] In June the OSS asserted that the Arab world would be important to the United States "chiefly because of American oil interests and potential post-war markets." OSS Research and Analysis officials concluded that "the Anglo-American problem regarding Palestine does not arise from a head-on conflict of mutually irreconcilable interests, but is rather a tangential issue in which a vocal and influential segment of U.S. public opinion is pitted against British official policy in the Near East."[36] A memorandum which Donovan sent to FDR on October 13, 1944, underscored the Anglo-American problem in Palestine. The memorandum cited a report from Iraq which said that the Arabs were becoming more violent toward the "Anglo-Americans for continuing . . . favored treatment of the Jews."[37]

While the incoming OSS reports suggested that a continuation of the cautious approach to Palestine would be beneficial, the upcoming presidential election called for a different course. FDR's Republican opponent, Thomas E. Dewey, pledged support for a Jewish Palestine. Roosevelt followed with an endorsement of the Democratic party platform plank which supported a Jewish Commonwealth in Palestine.[38] The Arab world responded with a wave of protests and a boycott of American goods.[39]

Roosevelt's backing for a Jewish Commonwealth went beyond his previous support of Zionist goals, but it did not end FDR's efforts to reassure the Arabs about Palestine. He attempted to resolve the problem during a meeting with Ibn Saud which followed the Yalta Conference in February 1945. The president acted as his own "special agent," but did not succeed in his mission. Ibn Saud refused to change his position in opposing a Jewish Palestine and received an assurance from Roosevelt of no action "to assist the Jews against the Arabs" and "no move hostile to the Arab people."[40]

In early March 1945 Roosevelt and Hoskins discussed the Palestine issue. FDR said that "there were 15,000,000 or 20,000,000 Arabs in and around Palestine and that, in the long run . . . these numbers would win out." Hoskins asked if the president agreed with his 1943 report that concluded a Jewish state could only be established and maintained by force. Roosevelt indicated agreement with Hoskins' conclusion.[41]

By spring 1945 Roosevelt's policy of caution and assurance to both the Zionists and the Arabs had become exceedingly difficult to administer. The Axis was all but beaten in Europe, and Arabs and Zionists looked to the United States for a favorable decision in Palestine. The postponement of a decision caused unrest in the Middle East. An NEA official wrote in April 1945 that "the lack of any clearcut policy toward Palestine on the part of the United States has contributed materially to the instability of the political situation in the Near East and in particular to the continuance of friction between Arabs and Jews."[42]

President Roosevelt died the following week.

From the foregoing analysis, it is clear that special agents played a role in determining Roosevelt's behavior toward the question of Palestine. President Roosevelt wanted information and policy recommendations concerning Palestine from outside the normal State Department channels, and the OSS, Hurley, and Hoskins filled that role. FDR's special agents urged a more active U.S. part in resolving the Palestine controversy, and, in addition, the OSS Research and Analysis Division and Hoskins suggested that limits be placed on Jewish immigration to Palestine. While not supporting restrictions on Jewish immigration, FDR did take steps to increase the U.S. role in resolving the Palestine problem. He endorsed a Jewish state in 1944 and met with Ibn Saud in 1945 to discuss Palestine. Even so, the evidence indicates that Roosevelt had still not made up his mind about the future of Palestine at the time of his death.

NOTES

The author would like to thank Southern Illinois University for financial support of this research.

1. Robert Dallek, *Franklin D. Roosevelt and American Foreign Policy, 1932–1945* (New York: Oxford University Press, 1979), p. vii.

2. U.S. Department of State, *Foreign Relations of the United States, 1943* (Washington, D.C.: GPO, 1964), 4:813. (Hereafter the collection will be cited as FRUS, followed by year, volume, and page. The present citation would appear as FRUS 1943, 4:813.) FRUS 1944, 5:624; FRUS 1943, 4:786–87.

3. Edgar B. Nixon, ed., *Franklin D. Roosevelt and Foreign Affairs,* 1st ser., 3 vols. (Cambridge, Mass.: Belknap Press of Harvard University Press, 1969), 1:393.

4. FRUS 1944, 5:615–16.

5. James MacGregor Burns, *Roosevelt: The Lion and the Fox* (New York: Harcourt, Brace, 1956), pp. 43–44.

6. National Archives, Washington, D.C., Record Group 59, 867N.01, 1940–1944, no. 7–644, Gordon P. Merriam to Paul H. Alling and Wallace Murray, July 6, 1944. (Hereafter the collection will be cited as R.G. 59, followed by identifying information.) FRUS 1944, 5:624–26, 631, 633.

7. Burns, *Roosevelt,* p. 247.

8. Corey Ford, *Donovan of OSS* (Boston: Little, Brown 1970), p. 103.

9. William R. Polk, *The Arab World,* American Foreign Policy Library, Edwin O. Reischauer, ed. (Cambridge, Mass.: Harvard University Press, 1980), pp. 316–17.

10. FRUS 1939, 4:751–58.

11. Franklin D. Roosevelt Library, Hyde Park, N.Y., President's Secretary's File, Box 165, William J. Donovan to Roosevelt, March 14, 1942. (Hereafter the collection will be cited as FDR Library, followed by identifying information.)

12. National Archives, Washington, D.C., Record Group 226, OSS Research and Analysis report no. 185, "Zionism—Aims and Prospects," April 1942. (Hereafter the collection will be cited as R.G. 226, followed by identifying information.)

13. FDR Library, Map Room File, Box 72, John Magruder (Deputy Director of OSS) to Colonel Chester Hammond (White House Map Room), May 6, 1943, OSS A 4271.

14. Ibid.

15. Ibid.

16. FRUS 1942, 4:26–29.

17. FDR Library, Map Room File, Box 72, Magruder to Hammond, May 6, 1943, OSS A 4271a.

18. FRUS 1943, 4:776–80.

19. FRUS 1942, 4:34–36.

20. FRUS 1943, 4:786–87.

21. R.G. 59, 867N.01, no. 1857 1/2, Colonel Harold B. Hoskins, "The Present Situation in the Near East," April 20, 1943. A summary of the report appears in FRUS 1943, 4:781–85.

22. R.G. 59, 867N.01, no. 1993 1/2, Weizmann memorandum dated June 12, 1943. An edited version of Weizmann's memorandum appears in FRUS 1943, 4:792–94, and Roosevelt's comments on the Arabs have been deleted.

23. FRUS 1943, 4:794, 808.

24. R.G. 226, OSS G 1545, February 3, 1944.

25. History Project, Strategic Services Unit, Office of the Assistant Secretary of War, *The Overseas Targets: War Report of the OSS*, 2 vols. (New York: Walker and Co., 1976), 2:48–49.

26. R.G. 226, Box 409, OSS field report no. 49749, November 15, 1943.

27. R.G. 226, Box 413, OSS field report no. 50200, November 15, 1943.

28. R.G. 226, Box 448, OSS field report no. 54614, January 6, 1944.

29. R.G. 226, OSS Research and Analysis report no. 1652, "The Position of Saudi Arabia Within the Arab World," February 4, 1944.

30. R.G. 226, OSS Research and Analysis report no. 1897, "The Arabian Oil Agreement," February 12, 1944.

31. FDR Library, Map Room File, Box 73, Magruder to Colonel L. Mathewson (White House Map Room), March 29, 1944; FRUS 1944, 5:568.

32. Cordell Hull, *The Memoirs of Cordell Hull*, 2 vols. (New York: Macmillan, 1948), p. 1536.

33. FRUS 1944, 5:591; FDR Library, Map Room File, Box 73, Magruder to Mathewson, March 17, 1944.

34. FDR Library, Map Room File, Box 73, Oliver Jackson Sands, Jr. (Acting Assistant Deputy Director OSS), to Colonel Richard Park, Jr. (White House Map Room), June 13, 1944; FRUS 1944, 5:632, 641.

35. FRUS, "Conferences at Washington and Quebec, 1943," 918–19, 932; FRUS 1944, 3:28; FRUS 1944, 5:600–603.

36. R.G. 226, OSS Research and Analysis report no. 2263, "The Anglo-American Problem in Palestine," June 20, 1944.

37. FDR Library, President's Secretary's File, Box 169, Donovan to Roosevelt, October 13, 1944.

38. FRUS 1944, 5:615–17.

39. FRUS 1944, 5:619; R.G. 59, 867N.01, no. 10–3144, L. C. Pinkerton (Counsul-General, Jerusalem) to Hull, October 31, 1944.

40. FRUS 1945, 8:2.

41. FRUS 1945, 8:691.

42. FRUS 1945, 8:699.

Selected Bibliography

Burns, James MacGregor. *Roosevelt: The Lion and the Fox*. New York: Harcourt, Brace, 1956.

Dallek, Robert. *Franklin D. Roosevelt and American Foreign Policy, 1932–1945*.New York: Oxford University Press, 1979.

Ford, Corey. *Donovan of OSS.*. Boston: Little, Brown, 1970.

Franklin D. Roosevelt Library, Hyde Park, N.Y. President's Secretary's File, Boxes 165 and 169. Map Room File, Boxes 72 and 73.

History Project, Strategic Services Unit, Office of the Assistant Secretary of War. *The Overseas Targets: War Report of the OSS*. 2 vols. Introduction by Kermit Roosevelt. New York: Walker and Co., 1976.

Hull, Cordell. *The Memoirs of Cordell Hull*. 2 vols. New York: Macmillan, 1948.

National Archives, Washington, D.C., State Department Records. Record Group 59, 1940–1949. 867N.00 and 867N.01 (Palestine).

National Archives, Washington, D.C., Modern Military Branch. Record Group 226. Office of Strategic Services.

Nixon, Edgar B., ed. *Franklin D. Roosevelt and Foreign Affairs*. 1st ser. 3 vols. Cambridge, Mass.: Belknap Press of Harvard University Press, 1969.

Polk, William R. *The Arab World*. American Foreign Policy Library, Edwin O. Reischauer, ed. Foreword by Edwin O. Reischauer. Cambridge, Mass.: Harvard University Press, 1980.

U.S. Department of State. *Foreign Relations of the United States, 1939*. Vol. 4. Washington, D.C.: GPO, 1955.

———, *1942*. Vol. 4. Washington, D.C.: GPO, 1963.

———, *1943*. Vol. 4. Washington, D.C.: GPO, 1964.

———, *Conferences at Washington and Quebec, 1943*. Washington, D.C.: GPO, 1970.

U.S. Department of State. *Foreign Relations of the United States, 1944*. Vol. 3. Washington, D.C.: GPO, 1965.

———, *1944*. Vol. 5. Washington, D.C.: GPO, 1965.

———, *1945*. Vol. 8. Washington, D.C.: GPO, 1969.

5

The Prescience of a Statesman: FDR's Assessment of Adolf Hitler before the World War, 1933–1941

William E. Kinsella, Jr.

In December 1932, William Bullitt, then special assistant to Secretary of State Cordell Hull, assured Franklin D. Roosevelt that Adolf Hitler was finished as a possible dictator and that Germany's president, Paul von Hindenburg, absolutely refused to have Hitler as chancellor. The German government, wrote Bullitt, was no longer afraid of the Nazi movement. On January 30, 1933, Adolf Hitler was appointed chancellor. Ambassador John Cudahy, writing from Warsaw several months later, told President Roosevelt that there was no cause for alarm. Rumors that Germany was preparing for war were described as entirely baseless. The Germans, he noted, simply love display and pageantry. This blatant exhibition of militarism, he continued, was merely an expression of a uniquely German gregarious instinct, much like that of the Elks, Eagles, and Woodmen. Such misconceptions soon would be dispelled as the world watched with growing alarm a nation's march to war.[1]

FDR had no illusions concerning the threat posed by Adolf Hitler's Germany. Rexford Tugwell recalled that the president's initial impressions were marked by detestation, dread, and implacable hostility. Roosevelt viewed the Fuhrer as insensitive, overbearing, gross, and aggressively German. He foresaw, asserts Tugwell, that an encounter with Germany might be inevitable. This description of Roosevelt's views, although written in retrospect, seems credible. The course of future events would confirm FDR's intuitive prescience, and strengthen a statesman's prophetic realization that a war of primitive barbarism soon would confront the proponents of peace and civility.[2]

Perhaps a more accurate phrase to describe Franklin Roosevelt's predictive assessment of the German threat would be an informed prescience. Diplomatic reports to the White House, more often than not, were remarkably correct in their analyses of Germany's intentions. The ambassadors who were particularly

expansive in their evaluations of the evolving war situation included William
Dodd (Germany); William Bullitt (Soviet Union and France); Breckinridge Long
and William Phillips (Italy); Robert Bingham, Joseph Kennedy, and John Winant
(United Kingdom); Joseph Davies (Soviet Union and Belgium); Herbert Pell
(Portugal and Hungary); Claude Bowers (Spain and Chile); Josephus Daniels
(Mexico); Lincoln MacVeagh (Greece); John Cudahy (Poland); George Earle
(Austria); and Joseph Grew (Japan). The Departments of State, War and Navy,
and the personal acquaintances of FDR reporting on overseas developments
provided extensive and accurate coverage of foreign affairs. The focus of their
attention was Hitler's Germany.

Initial appraisals of Adolf Hitler's regime in 1933 were not at all sanguine
concerning the future. William Dodd, writing from Berlin, repeatedly warned
of war. More men had been trained, uniformed, and armed in Germany, wrote
the ambassador one year after Hitler's accession to power, than in 1914. He
added that this military might was solely for war. George Earle, minister to
Austria, depicted the Fuhrer as a paranoiac who had made the militaristic spirit
the most intense in Germany history. Austria, predicted Earle, would be the first
nation to fall. Samuel Fuller, president of the American Bemberg Corporation,
reported to the president in May 1933 that Hitler was a successful dictator who
was fully organized, absolutely self-confident, and in complete power. The
Germans view him almost as a god, he continued, and trust him implicitly. His
regime, concluded Fuller, feeds on intense nationalism and pride of race. He
predicted that war would be the end result. Felix Frankfurter, New Deal economic
advisor and personal friend of FDR, wrote to the president stating that the
significance of Hitlerism far transcended ferocious anti-Semitism and fanatical
racism. The attack against the Jews, he said, was merely an index to the gospel
of force espoused by the rulers of Germany. He warned Roosevelt that the
violence and chauvinism of the Hitler regime would be intensified, and that the
air was charged with the kind of feeling preceding 1914.[3]

Similar viewpoints were sent to the president from other diplomatic posts,
and each conveyed the impression that Germany contemplated aggressive expansion. Franklin Roosevelt's press conference remarks in September 1934 reflect the fear of Germany which his correspondents had expressed to him. The
president described the German preparation for war. Factory workers had gas
masks at their side. School children were learning the particular smells of poi-
sonous gases. Bomb shelters were being built everywhere, and with the aid of
a government deduction. Roosevelt told reporters of the little German boy who
prayed each night that God would permit him to die with a French bullet in his
heart. The president intimated that this war psychosis was being created deliberately by the German government in anticipation of eventual aggressive action.[4]

Preparations for conflict were made official soon after these remarks. During
the month of March 1935, Adolf Hitler announced the formation of the German
air force, proclaimed universal military service, called for an increase in the size
of the German army, and initiated a program of naval rearmament. Germany's

first move had been peaceful. The Saar plebiscite transferred control of that territory to Germany. Breckinridge Long, ambassador to Italy, expressed his belief that this event would serve as a big drink of schnapps to the Germans and that Hitler would be emboldened to pursue his Pan-Germanic ideas. Germany, he confided to the president, was still suspected like a wolf, and her intentions were about as peaceful as were those of Attila.[5]

The Attila analogy was shared by other observers of the international scene in 1935. Edward House wrote to Roosevelt saying that war was much more probable now that Germany intended to rearm. Hitler's madness, confessed House, was impossible to understand. Lincoln MacVeagh described the growing anxiety of many in the Balkans, the tinder box of Europe. John Cudahy said that Hitler's military preparations would be complete by 1938, and any eventuality might occur then. General John J. Pershing told the president that Germany would be prepared militarily for any action within the ten-year period in which that nation pledged to keep the peace. Reporter Charles Sherrill, after an interview with Hitler, informed FDR that Germany would march when its army was ready. In the words of Samuel Fuller, Germany was a day-to-day menace to the peace of all nations.[6]

Franklin Roosevelt shared these views, and the collapse of the Geneva Disarmament Conference (in spite of FDR's promise to presidential envoy Norman Davis that he would be accorded burial in Arlington National Cemetery if the talks succeeded) prompted the president to find a means to constrain Germany. During conversations with Henry Morgenthau and Edward House in 1935, Roosevelt proposed a complete blockade of Germany on the Polish, Czecho-Slovak, Austrian, Swiss, French, Belgian, Dutch, and Danish borders. Access to German ports would be closed by the British navy. The United States would participate in what was a blockade of Germany, not a boycott or sanction. Congressional action would not be needed, thought the president, because recognition of a blockade would fall under the executive's power. These proposals of the president remained momentarily private because of domestic political pressures and the appeasement policies of Great Britain and France. They do reveal, however, his serious concern over the future course of German foreign policy under Hitler.[7]

In early February 1936, Norman Davis described for the president the crisis atmosphere prevailing in Europe. All of the political leaders, he wrote, are thinking of how best to prepare for the war which they think Germany is going to force upon them. It was feared that Italy's recent success in Ethiopia would serve as a catalyst for aggressive acts by other nations. Roosevelt, in a letter to Ambassador Long, said that he was watching the daily news from Europe with the feeling each day that the next would bring a major explosion. The president added that he did not share the optimistic view that each recurring crisis would iron itself out and that nothing really serious would happen. This mood of anticipation was heightened when on March 7, 1936, German troops moved into the once demilitarized Rhineland. FDR confided to Ambassador Dodd that in July 1914 the experts had predicted that there would be no war. Today, the president continued, he had his tongue in cheek and, like a fire department, would be ready for any eventuality. William Dodd described the situation as clearly one of dictator Europe against Western Europe. Hitler's plan, he noted, was to extend Germany's power from the Danube to the Black Sea. Germany, in exchange, would support Italy's quest for a renewed Roman Empire. The ambassador's prediction that Germany and Italy would unite in their quest for European dominance appeared to Roosevelt as entirely accurate, especially in view of the developing situation in Spain. The crisis atmosphere of the spring months had barely subsided when on July 17, 1936, civil war erupted in that country.[8]

The U.S. ambassador to Spain, Claude Bowers, provided the president with detailed accounts of what he would describe repeatedly as a war against democracy. His letters to FDR were replete with references to a worldwide fascist conspiracy for which Spain was simply a testing ground. The sublimated gunmen and gangsters of Rome and Berlin, wrote Bowers, had just begun their conquests. He warned the president that with every victory, beginning with China, followed by Ethiopia and then Spain, the fascist powers, with vanity inflamed, would turn without delay to some other country, such as Czechoslovakia, and that with every surrender the prospects of a European war would grow darker. The pitiful policy of retreating before the gesture of bullies, he told Roosevelt, simply would make stronger the fascist internationale. Indeed, Germany, Italy, and Japan had signed formal agreements pledging associative action. Unbridled in their ambitions, they had unharnessed their machines of war. The Spanish interlude was but a prelude to other undeclared wars against the democracies of Europe.[9]

Numerous other reports sent to President Roosevelt by friends and official representatives reflected this atmosphere of impending crisis. Emil Ludwig predicted that Germany's militant character, its longing for revenge, its inferiority complex, and race theory eventually would make a major war inevitable. William Dodd forecast a German thrust toward Austria, Hungary, Rumania, and Czechoslovakia. William Bullitt depicted the Austrian position as that of an apple left hanging on the bough to be plucked at an appropriate moment by Hitler. Roosevelt hoped that it would have the effect of a green apple. Nigel Law told FDR that it was useless to negotiate for peace with such people as the leaders of Germany. Herbert Pell, ambassador to Portugal, warned Roosevelt in September 1937 that the fascist movement was approaching the status of a new religion that would produce fanatics, hypocrites, martyrs, and human sacrifices.[10]

These are but a few of the many despatches similar in content which persuaded the president to make a major policy statement on foreign affairs. The Chicago quarantine address (October 5, 1937) set forth a possible solution to stop the epidemic of world lawlessness. The 10 percent who were threatening the security of peace-loving nations should be quarantined to protect the health of the civilized community. His words revealed the gravity of the moment. He described the situation as most dangerous, adding that neither isolation nor neutrality assured an escape from future conflict. FDR earnestly hoped that these remarks would serve as a tonic toward a realistic appraisal of the grave threat to the security of free peoples and their governments. Roosevelt realized that, as William Bullitt had said, the deluge was fast approaching.[11]

The storm would break over Austria during the night of March 11, 1938, as German troops marched into that nation. There were few who believed that the violence would subside in the near future. Arthur Sweetzer, director of the United States Information Section at the League of Nations, had an interview with FDR soon after the Anschluss. His alarming report to the chief executive indicated that nothing in Central Europe could stop Hitler. During the conversation, Roosevelt mentioned that he had just received a letter describing Austrian Chancellor Kurt von Schuschnigg's meeting with the Fuhrer at Berchtesgaden. The chancellor, said the president, apparently had never dreamt of anything like it. Hitler had been unbelievable, repeatedly invoking the names of Julius Caesar and Jesus Christ during his long tirades. Sweetzer recounted that Roosevelt seemed to think you could do very little with such a man. John Cudahy told the president succintly that all states east and south of Germany were living in constant apprehension as to which might be the next victim of Hitler's expansionist program. The intended victim was identified immediately, for reports that Hitler was planning to seize the Sudetenland in Czechoslovakia were numerous throughout the summer months of 1938. Ambassador Hugh Wilson predicted from Berlin that the Fuhrer would not hesitate to use force to achieve his ambitions in Czechoslavakia. FDR, fully cognizant of Hitler's resolve, decided to intervene to prevent what he foresaw as an inevitable military debacle for the democracies in this approaching confrontation with Germany.[12]

The fear of Germany's military superiority over Great Britain and France convinced Franklin Roosevelt of the necessity for action. All incoming correspondence to the White House had been discouraging. Hugh Wilson had testified repeatedly on the strength and readiness of the German army and air force. From Rome, Ambassador William Phillips expressed no doubts about Mussolini's decision to enter the war as a full-fledged Axis partner. Joseph Kennedy, from his vantage point in London, was certain that Great Britain lacked the preparedness necessary to defeat Hitler. "If war comes they are going to get hell," said Kennedy, "but they are now reconciled." William Bullitt's letters from Paris contained predictions of catastrophic destruction in France should Germany decide on an air attack. It was apparent too that the chief executive took very seriously the Fuhrer's statements concerning the willingness to precipitate a major conflict. He urged that plans be made ready to evacuate Americans from Europe, and later renewed his request for more evacuation ships. Roosevelt expressed his concern to the chief of naval operations, William Leahy, about the need to determine the location of all German warships. He fully expected the worst possible consequences. FDR's plea for a negotiated settlement prevented the expected conflict. The leaders of France, Great Britain, Italy, and Germany agreed to a peaceful solution. The Sudetenland was ceded to Germany.[13]

During a discussion with Josephus Daniels the president explained his actions, acknowledging that if he had been in Neville Chamberlain's place he would have felt constrained to have made terms to prevent a war for which Germany was fully prepared. The chief executive was convinced, he told Daniels, of the great military superiority of the totalitarian countries, and was most concerned with a threatened German air attack on London before the Munich meeting. Roosevelt was certain of a German victory over the prospective British and French allies in September 1938, and this was the major consideration in his decision to attempt to delay the inevitable encounter. These thoughts were in the president's mind when he told a reporter, "It was, as we all know, a very definite crisis and though there are many things which are called crisis which are not, this one was."[14]

President Roosevelt saw no lasting value in any agreement of appeasement with Germany. He told Sir Ronald Lindsay, British ambassador in Washington, that in all probability Hitler would overrun all of Czechoslovakia, and German expansion toward Denmark, the Polish Corridor, and Rumania would follow this success. The Western powers, predicted the president, soon would find themselves at war with Germany and Italy. He then offered a possible response to Axis aggression, telling Ambassador Lindsay to keep secret all aspects of his proposal. Roosevelt renewed his call for a blockade of Germany with the participation of the United States. The blockade line, said FDR, should be drawn down the middle of the North Sea, through the English Channel to Gibraltar and the Mediterranean, including closure of the Suez Canal. Lindsay noted that the president realized that the United States might become involved directly in the European war, although he doubted that U.S. troops could be sent to fight unless Britian was invaded by Germany. FDR later informed Neville Chamberlain, through his personal friend Arthur Murray, that Great Britain would have all the industrial resources of the United States behind it in the event of future hostilities.[15]

Diplomatic despatches relayed to the White House, in addition to the numerous letters sent privately to the president, were in agreement with the view that Germany's drive for European hegemony had only been appeased momentarily. Anthony Biddle told Roosevelt that he was inclined to feel that Hitler's voracious appetite had been whetted by his recent gains. Lincoln MacVeagh warned the president that the shadow of Germany was creeping toward the Balkans, and that fear had become the order of the day everywhere. Claude Bowers continued his reporting of German and Italian atrocities in Spain. John Cudahy described the Fuhrer as intent on building not a ramshackle road like Napoleon once constructed, but one which would not crumble. He believed that Germany intended to have no undigested portions along the way toward its eastward goal. Hitler's program, wrote Josephus Daniels, envisaged control of all territory from Berlin to Baghdad. Joseph Davies was of the opinion that the Fuhrer had crossed the Rubicon and could not stop. Germany was guided by a will for conquest, he observed, not a will for peace. Dictators ride bicycles, he concluded, and are unable to stand still. George Messersmith, assistant secretary of state, was certain that Germany would continue to expand, and he claimed that even the Monroe Doctrine was as much an irritant to the present German government as was the presence of the Czechoslovak state. Breckinridge Long's report to the president of observations he made while touring South America tended to support Messersmith's claims during these immediate post-Munich months. In Brazil, Long told Roosevelt, the whole German population of that nation was part of an organized propaganda network; and in Argentina too, Italy and Germany were sending agents to organize their nationality groups for political activities.[16]

In a speech delivered on October 26, 1938, Franklin Roosevelt made clear his personal interpretation of the real meaning of Munich. Peace by fear, he began, could have no higher or more enduring quality than peace by the sword. The recurrent sanctification of sheer force does not mean peace, he admonished. Americans must be prepared to meet with success any application of force against the United States. It is evident that the president shared the views of his diplomats. The critical point of encounter was fast approaching. He wrote Herbert Pell saying that his British friends must begin to fish or cut bait, and that the dictator threat from Europe was now much closer to the United States.[17]

The international scene after Munich was marked by the triumph of German blitzkrieg aggression. The seizure of Czechoslovakia confirmed Franklin Roosevelt's prophetic understanding of Adolf Hitler's ultimate ambitions. FDR announced during a press conference on March 31, 1939, that the Fuhrer's policy was not limited to bringing contiguous German people into the Reich. There appeared to be no apparent limit to Germany's aims, said Roosevelt. German domination, he explained, could be expected to extend not only to the small nations of Europe, but to other continents. He expressed the general fear that the German nation was attempting to attain world dominance.

The struggle for empire began formally in September 1939, as German forces crushed Poland. Denmark, Norway, Belgium, Luxemburg, the Netherlands, and France fell in rapid succession. Great Britain stood alone, the last of Europe's Western democracies, confronting a triumphant German war machine. The dire assessments of diplomatic observers such as Ambassador John Winant in London portrayed a beleaguered ally whose future existence seemed to be in grave doubt. FDR's frustration in his efforts to provide a means to halt a presumed invincible Axis war machine surfaced in a brief conversation with Henry Morgenthau. The secretary of the treasury recounted that Roosevelt had told him, "If you have to decide along the lines that will not get us into war You decide, but if there is any decision which you think might get us into war, come and see me about it." Morgenthau added in his diary, "He left me with the distinct feeling that he might want to make decisions which might get us into war. I was terribly disappointed and evidently showed it."[18]

Roosevelt's perspective concerning the ultimate ambitions of Hitler was not limited to Europe. Reports that agents of the Axis nations were active in several Latin American countries became more numerous throughout these years. Claude Bowers, then ambassador to Chile, warned that the German population in that country was militantly Nazi. Roosevelt urged Bowers to send him all information of a disquieting character, adding that German agents in many of the Latin American countries would undertake immediate activities with a view of over-throwing existing governments. Edwin Wilson, minister to Uruguay, reported an increase in Nazi activities in that nation with serious possibilities for the future. A memorandum from the chief of naval operations alerted the White House to the possibility of fifth column activities in all the Latin American countries. Argentina, Brazil, Chile, Uruguay, Ecuador, and Costa Rica were considered to have the most numerous espionage groups, and urgent action was suggested in the latter two nations to halt fascist influence. Cornelius Vanderbilt, after a trip through Mexico and the Central and South American countries, told the president that Hitler's agents were preparing for active intervention in Colombia, Costa Rica, and Mexico.[19]

What were Franklin Roosevelt's personal views concerning the fascist threat to the United States? During a press conference on April 18, 1940, Roosevelt offered the following psychological appraisal on the Fuhrer. What would you do, he asked, if your name happened to be Hitler? Victorious Hitlers, he answered, would want to extend their power. Napoleon and Alexander did not think in terms of world domination at first; the thing tended to grow, he said. If the Fuhrer were to achieve control over Europe, why should he wish to leave an entire continent, North, Central, and South America, alone? World domination would be an enticing objective to the mass Hitler mind, asserted Roosevelt. The theme of the compulsive conqueror was reiterated later before an audience of newsmen. Hitler would say to himself, assumed the president, "I have got a third of the world and I have fixed up relations with another third of the world, the Far East. Why should I stop? How about this American third?" Speaking to an American Youth Congress one month later, the chief executive asked his listeners to imagine themselves as victorious Hitlers. Would you go back and paint pictures as some say the Fuhrer will do, he asked them? He may do it, mused Roosevelt, or he might do as other successful conquerors have done and strive for world domination.[20]

The second conviction accepted by Roosevelt was that Germany's planned conquest of the United States would come by invasion and bombing from strategic contiguous territories which would gradually fall under its control either by military occupation or economic blackmail. His geography lessons were numerous and explicit. He urged listeners on many occasions to look at a map and check the proximity of Greenland, Alaska, Canada, Costa Rica, Colombia, Mexico, Venezuela, Brazil, Bermuda, and the West Indies. He replied to those who had accepted Hitler's pledge that he had no intention of invading America by saying simply that it brought back memories and recollections. Why should we accept assurances that we are immune, he asked? Such assurances had been given previously to other nations. Americans, Roosevelt emphasized, must begin to think about the prospects of war in relation to the United States.[21]

Economic blackmail of the Latin American nations by a victorious Germany, in Franklin Roosevelt's opinion, might also enable that country to prepare for an eventual attack on the United States. Argentina, he speculated, would be told by the Germania Corporation that it could not sell its cattle, mutton, or sheep anywhere except through the Germania Corporation. Similar coerced arrangements would be made with other small countries. Political domination would follow closely on the heels of economic subjection. Roosevelt believed that an actual invasion of America might not be necessary once economic dominance had been attained by Germany. He described imposed economic isolation as the "helpless nightmare of a people without freedom—the nightmare of a people lodged in prison, handcuffed, hungry, and fed through the bars from day-to-day by the contemptuous, unpitying masters of other continents." The advance of Hilterism had to be checked forcibly or else the Western Hemisphere soon would be within range of Germany's weapons of destruction. Some people, FDR charged, mistakenly believe that we are not attacked until bombs drop in Chicago, New York, San Francisco, or New Orleans. Czechoslovakia began with Austria, he continued, Norway began with Denmark, and Greece began with Albania and Bulgaria. Roosevelt thought that it would be suicide to wait until Germany was in America's front yard. The Bunker Hill of tomorrow might be several thousand miles from Boston.[22]

In numerous public addresses he conveyed a crisis mood of war expectation. He instructed a gathering of magazine and newspaper editors to give to the reading public an accurate presentation of the terrible seriousness of the Axis threat. He told his listeners that America had to quit all this silly business of "business as usual." The nation must be made to realize that if the fascist powers win, the United States would be put in a vice, a straitjacket, from which it would not recover for one hundred years. The media, Roosevelt demanded, must be frank with the public. Aid to Britain was not of itself a wise slogan, for more might be demanded of Americans who must arm themselves for the future. The seriousness of the situation, he suggested, should be played up all the time. We've got to buckle down to the determination to fight the war through, said Roosevelt. Against naked force, he reasoned, the only possible defense was naked force. The United States, he emphasized, could not escape its collective responsibility for the kind of life that would emerge from the present ordeal.[23]

The first encounter came on May 21, 1941, when the merchant ship *Robin Moor* was sunk by a German submarine. Roosevelt declared that this brutal act revealed that Germany intended to pursue a policy of intimidation, terror, and cruelty in its effort to drive U.S. commerce from the oceans. The United States destroyer *Greer* was sunk on September 4, 1941, and FDR again assessed the action bluntly, saying that the Nazi design was to acquire absolute control of the oceans surrounding the Western Hemisphere. The next step, asserted Roosevelt, would be to use the German bridgeheads in Uruguay, Argentina, Bolivia, and Colombia for a concerted attack on U.S. possessions. The sinking of the USS *Kearney* on October 17, 1941, and the loss of the *Reuben James* two weeks later served to further dramatize the chief executive's earlier warnings.[24]

America's Bunker Hill proved to be several thousand miles away. Japan's attack on Pearl Harbor brought a united and angry nation into the war against the fascist powers. Germany and Italy, as had been expected by the president, also declared a state of war with the United States. FDR had foreseen clearly the inevitability of this conflict. A man of peace and civility, he watched the war preparations of the fascist triumvirate with agonizing concern. He urged the democratic countries to abandon the enticing, but disastrous, policies of appeasement. They responded negatively, as did the American public, until the struggle became one of self-preservation. Franklin D. Roosevelt was a prescient statesman whose vision of the terrifying apocalypse was proven tragically correct.

NOTES

1. William Bullitt to FDR, dated only December 1932, in Orville Bullitt, ed., *For the President Personal and Secret: Correspondence between Franklin D. Roosevelt and William Bullitt* (Boston: Houghton Mifflin Co., 1972), p. 23; John Cudahy to FDR, December 27, 1933, FDR Papers, President's Personal File, No. 1193, Franklin D. Roosevelt Library, Hyde Park, N.Y. (hereafter cited as PPF and FDRL).

2. Rexford Tugwell, *In Search of Roosevelt* (Cambridge, Mass: Harvard University Press, 1972), pp. 251, 253–54; idem, *The Democratic Roosevelt* (Garden City, N.Y.: Doubleday and Co., 1957), p. 439.

3. William Dodd to FDR, July 30, 1933, August 12, 1933, October 13, 1933, Box 42, William Dodd Papers, Library of Congress, Washington, D.C.; George Earle to FDR, November 27, 1933, FDR Papers, President's Secretary's File, Diplomatic Correspondence, Austria, FDRL (hereafter cited as PSF, DC); Samuel Fuller to FDR, May 11, 1933, FDR Papers, PPF, No. 2616, FDRL; Felix Frankfurter to FDR, October 17, 1933, Box 97, Felix Frankfurter Papers, Library of Congress, Washington, D.C.

4. Press Conference No. 142, September 7, 1934, *Complete Press Conferences of Franklin D. Roosevelt*, 25 vols. (New York: Da Capo Press, 1972), 3:58–61.

5. Breckinridge Long to FDR, February 8, 1935, FDR Papers, PSF, DC, Italy, FDRL.

6. Edward House to FDR, April 20, 1935, FDR Papers, PPF, No. 222, FDRL; Lincoln MacVeagh to FDR, May 4, 1935, FDR Papers, PSF, DC, Greece, FDRL; John Cudahy to FDR, October 11, 1935, FDR Papers, PSF, DC, Poland, FDRL; John J. Pershing to Marvin McIntyre, September 6, 1935, FDR Papers, PPF, No. 1179, FDRL; C. H. Sherrill, Memorandum, August 24, 1935, FDR Papers, PSF, DC, Germany, FDRL; Samuel Fuller to FDR, October 11, 1935, FDR Papers, PPF, No. 2616, FDRL.

7. FDR to Norman Davis, August 30, 1933, Box 51, Norman Davis Papers, Library of Congress; Henry Morgenthau, Jr., Diary Entry, March 18, 1935, Book 4, p. 112, Henry Morgenthau Papers, FDRL; and FDR to Edward House, April 10, 1935, FDR Papers, PPF, No. 222, FDRL.

8. Norman Davis to FDR, February 18, 1936, Box 37, Davis Papers, Library of Congress; FDR to Breckinridge Long, February 22, 1936, Box 117, Breckinridge Long Papers, Library of Congress; William Dodd to FDR, April 1, 1936, Box 49, William Dodd Papers, Library of Congress.

9. Claude Bowers to FDR, August 26, 1936, September 9, 1936, September 16, 1936, December 16, 1936, February 16, 1937, March 31, 1937, July 21, 1937, August 11, 1937, October 11, 1937, FDR Papers, PSF, DC, Spain, FDRL. Agreements of

associative action refer to the German and Italian Communiqué of October 1936, and the Anti-Comintern Pact of November 1936.

10. Emil Ludwig to FDR, August 15, 1936, FDR Papers, PPF, No. 3884, FDRL; William Dodd to FDR, September 21, 1936, Box 49, Dodd Papers, Library of Congress; William Bullitt to FDR, January 10, 1937, April 12, 1937, and FDR to Bullitt, April 21, 1937, FDR Papers, PSF, DC, France, FDRL; Nigel Law to FDR, November 26, 1936, FDR Papers, PPF, No. 6032, FDRL; Herbert Pell to FDR, September 11, 1937, Box 12, Herbert Pell Papers, FDRL.

11. Samuel Rosenman, ed., *The Public Papers and Addresses of Franklin D. Roosevelt*, 13 vols. (New York: Random House, 1938–1950), 6:406–11. Discussions of a possible quarantine of Japan may be found in William Leahy to FDR, November 8, 1937, FDR Papers, PSF, Departmental Correspondence, Navy, FDRL. See also William Leahy, Diary Entry, Diary 3, Box 1, William Leahy Papers, Library of Congress; and William Bullitt to FDR, January 10, 1937, and April 12, 1937, FDR Papers, PSF, DC, France, FDRL.

12. Arthur Sweetzer, Memorandum of April 4, 1938, Interview with FDR, Box 34, Arthur Sweetzer Papers, Library of Congress; John Cudahy to FDR, April 10, 1938, FDR Papers, PSF, DC, Poland, FDRL.

13. Hugh Wilson to Cordell Hull, September 8, 1938, 760F.62/701, No. 425, FDR Papers, PSF, Confidential File, Germany, FDRL (hereafter cited as CF); for reports of expected German military action see idem, September 13, 1938, 760F.62/785, No. 436; idem, September 25, 1938, 760F.62/1090, No. 493; idem, September 26, 1938, 760F.62/1089, No. 492, and 760F.62/1106, No. 495, FDR Papers, PSF, CF, Germany, FDRL; William Phillips to FDR, September 29, 1938, FDR Papers, PSF, DC, Italy, FDRL (herein Phillips wrote that Mussolini's recital about going to war with France and Great Britain "left me literally gasping for air"); see also Phillips to Cordell Hull, September 19, 1938, 760F.62/910, No. 254; idem, September 24, 1938, 760F.62/1070, No. 258; idem, September 26, 1938, 760F.62/1120, No. 261; idem, September 27, 1938, 760F.62/1177, No. 263; William Bullitt to FDR, May 12, 1938, May 20, 1938, June 13, 1938, September 28, 1938, FDR Papers, PSF, DC, France, FDRL. See also William Leahy, Diary Entry, September 17, 1938, September 19, 1938, September 26, 1938, September 27, 1938, Diary 4, Box 2, Leahy Papers, Library of Congress.

14. Josephus Daniels, Record of a conversation with FDR, January 16, 1939, Box 7, Josephus Daniels Papers, Library of Congress; Press Conference No. 487, September 30, 1938, *Complete Press Conferences,* 12:117.

15. E. Woodward and R. Butler, eds., *Documents on British Foreign Policy 1919–1939,* 3rd series, 9 vols. (London: His Majesty's Stationery Office, 1946–1965), 7:627–29; Arthur Murray to FDR, December 15, 1938, FDR Papers, PSF, DC, Arthur Murray, FDRL.

16. Anthony Biddle to FDR, October 6, 1938, FDR Papers, PSF, DC, Germany, FDRL; Lincoln MacVeagh to FDR, November 22, 1938, FDR Papers, PSF, DC, Greece, FDRL; Claude Bowers to FDR, March 7, 1938, April 11, 1938, and FDR to Bowers, August 31, 1938, FDR Papers, PSF, DC, Spain, FDRL; John Cudahy to FDR, November 17, 1938, PSF, DC, Poland, FDRL; Josephus Daniels to FDR, October 3, 1938, Box 16, Daniels Papers, Library of Congress; Joseph Davies to Steve Early, October 7, 1938, Box 9, Joseph Davies Papers, Library of Congress; Cordell Hull to FDR, October 1, 1938, U.S., Department of State, in *Foreign Relations of the United States 1938,* 5 vols. (Washington, D.C.: Government Printing Office, 1955), 1:704–6; Breckinridge Long to

FDR, November 18, 1938, FDR Papers, PSF, DC, South America and Central America, FDRL.

17. Rosenman, *Public Papers FDR*, 7:564–65; FDR to Herbert Pell, November 12, 1938, Elliott Roosevelt, ed., *FDR: His Personal Letters*, 4 vols. (New York: Duell, Sloan and Pearce, 1947–1950), 4:826.

18. Press Conference No. 534, March 31, 1939, *Complete Press Conferences*, 13:237–38; John Winant to FDR and Cordell Hull, April 3, 1941, No. 1309, FDR Papers, PSF, Subject File, John Winant, FDRL; see also FDR to Winant, February 8, 1941, enclosing report of Herschel Johnson, February 7, 1941, No. 470, FDR Papers, PSF, DC, Great Britain, FDRL, and Herschel Johnson to Hull, enclosing James Wilkinson, "Bomb Damage in English Cities," January 8, 1941, FDR Papers, PSF, DC, Great Britain, FDRL. Henry Morgenthau, Jr., Diary Entry, December 9, 1939, Book 2, Presidential Diaries, FDRL.

19. Claude Bowers to FDR, May 14, 1940, enclosing Bowers to Cordell Hull, May 14, 1940; idem, May 25, 1940, and Bowers to Sumner Welles, May 25, 1940, also FDR to Bowers, May 24, 1940, FDR Papers, PSF, DC, Chile, FDRL; Edwin Wilson to Cordell Hull, May 15, 1940, and FDR to Sumner Welles, May 20, 1940, U.S., Department of State, *Foreign Relations of the United States 1940*, 5 vols. (Washington, D.C.: Government Printing Office, 1959–1961), 5:1147; Memorandum to the Chief of Naval Operations, July 10, 1940, FDR Papers, PSF, Departmental Correspondence, Navy, FDRL; Cornelius Vanderbilt to Miss LeHand, August 27, 1940, FDR Papers, PPF, No. 104, FDRL.

20. Press Conferences Nos. 636A, 647A, 649A, April 18, 1940, May 30, 1940, June 5, 1940, *Complete Press Conferences*, 15:281–82, 414–15, 501–2.

21. Press Conferences Nos. 635, 636A, 643, 645A, 652A, April 9, 12, 18, 1940, May 23, 1940, June 14, 1940, *Complete Press Conferences*, 15:241–42, 251, 272–78, 361, 570.

22. Press Conference No. 636A, April 18, 1940, *Complete Press Conferences*, 15:282; Rosenman, *Public Papers FDR*, 10:189. On FDR's Bunker Hill comment see Samuel Rosenman, *Working with Roosevelt* (New York: Harper and Bros., 1952), p. 286.

23. Press Conferences Nos. 733, 762, May 23, 1941, August 19, 1941, *Complete Press Conferences*, 17:350–52, 18:92.

24. Rosenman, *Public Papers FDR*, 10:227–30, 385–90, 438–40; Press Conference No. 767, September 5, 1941, *Complete Press Conferences*, 18:140–54.

6

Franklin D. Roosevelt and Refuge for Victims of Nazism, 1933–1941

Sheldon Neuringer

Much of the image of Franklin D. Roosevelt we carry in our minds today consists of memories of the humanitarianism of the thirty-second president. We remember him as the champion of the "forgotten man" and that "one-third of a nation ill-housed, ill-clad, and ill-nourished." Moving beyond the New Deal, many of us can recall the Franklin Roosevelt of the Four Freedoms outlining, in his State of the Union address of 1941, a postwar world that would guarantee to mankind such blessings as "freedom of speech and expression," "freedom of every person to worship God in his own way," "freedom from want," and "freedom from fear."

Encompassing a devastating depression at home followed by an awesome global conflict abroad, the years 1933 to 1945 would afford opportunities for humanitarian endeavor ample enough for any president. In addition to depression and war, the Roosevelt administration and the American people were destined to witness the most massive violation of human rights in recorded history—the onslaught upon European Jewry that would culminate in the genocide of the Final Solution.

Marking the period before Hitler's adoption of the Final Solution, the eight years prior to that grim decision witnessed the unfolding of the Nazi policy to get rid of Jews through means other than mass extermination. Largely because of this, the period from 1933 to 1941 would offer the United States and other non-fascist countries the best opportunity to save Jews either by providing refuge within their own borders or by developing sites for mass resettlement elsewhere. How did the Roosevelt administration respond to this opportunity?

The long agony of the Jews in Europe began in March 1933, within weeks after Hitler's rise to power. The earliest manifestations of the anti-Semitic campaign of the Nazis came in the form of sporadic acts of violence by jackbooted storm troopers, economic boycotts, wholesale dismissals of Jews from civil service posts, and the forced closings of Jewish-owned stores and businesses.

For Jews the world over the events in Germany in the spring of 1933 were painful to behold. In the United States members of the Jewish community, numbering about 4.8 million people, mobilized to counteract the Nazi assault upon their half-million German coreligionists. Appeals went out to the Roosevelt administration for a formal diplomatic protest to the Reich, while the militant American Jewish Congress organized numerous mass rallies and spearheaded a boycott of German imports.

In addition to acting on the diplomatic and economic fronts, Jewish leaders sought to expand immigration opportunities to the United States. To enlarge upon their initial misfortune, Jews in Germany would learn that the 1930s was a particularly inopportune time for finding refuge in that traditional land of asylum. The main barrier was not so much the quota law of 1924, which had placed an upper limit of 25,957 immigrants from Germany each year, but the restrictionist mood of Congress and the American people. This desire to keep the gates of the United States tightly shut stemmed from a nativism that had peaked in the 1920s, strongly reinforced by a fear that any newcomers would aggravate an already severe unemployment problem.

To limit the entry of aliens to an absolute minimum, President Hoover in 1930 had issued an executive order to consular officials abroad calling for the utmost strictness in the interpretation of the "likely to become a public charge" clause of the Immigration Act of 1917. The new regulations, in effect, required not only that a prospective immigrant be of sound physical and moral character, but that he arrive with enough money to keep himself and any dependents off the relief roles for an indefinite period. While a great many German Jews in pre-Hitler times had been fairly prosperous business and professional people, it was clear that because of Nazi expropriations, job dismissals, and currency regulations, only a small handful of them would have been able to pass the "public charge" barrier unless there occurred some easing in State Department policy.

Between 1933 and 1936 American Jewish groups, in cooperation with non-sectarian and church organizations with ties to Hitler's non-Jewish victims, waged a campaign to ease immigration restrictions. Cautious and low-keyed, the effort aimed at admitting a moderate number of refugees so as not to arouse congressional restrictionists. The first victory for the pro-refugee forces came in January 1934 when the State Department allowed American relatives of German emigrants to put up bonds as security against their becoming a public charge. This meant that an empty purse would no longer automatically constitute grounds for denial of a visa.[1]

In September 1935 the situation for German Jewry deteriorated further when the Reich imposed the infamous Nuremberg laws. These decrees stripped all Jews of their citizenship and civil rights, prohibited them from all economic activity except that involving coreligionists, excluded Jewish children from "Aryan'' schools, and sought to confine Jewish inhabitants of major cities in residential ghettoes. These latest outrages prompted pro-refugee groups to intensify pressure on the administration to ease immigration regulations. The result was that in late 1936 Washington ordered consular officials in the Reich to deny visas only if it seemed "probable" rather than merely "possible" that an applicant would become a public charge. This, in effect, meant that bonds would be acceptable from friends and distant relatives in addition to close relatives of refugees.

The salutary impact of the new regulations was striking. In 1937 the total number of Jews admitted to the United States increased to 11,352 as compared to the 6,252 of the previous year.[2] In his annual message for 1937, the president of the Hebrew Immigrant Aid Society (HIAS) expressed his appreciation to State Department officials for "their sympathetic understanding . . . in considering applications for visas by victims of oppression." This statement belied a widespread belief in Jewish circles that department officialdom was heavily infected with anti-Semitism. This belief, which lasted through the war years, in time came to be shared by non-Jewish refugee advocates as well.[3]

Maintaining a long public silence on the matter which lasted until 1938, Franklin D. Roosevelt appeared to have paid little personal attention to the persecutions in Germany. The lone indication of the president's reaction to developments in the Reich comes from an entry in the diary of William E. Dodd, dated June 16, 1933, shortly before his departure for Berlin as the new U.S. ambassador. According to Dodd, Roosevelt delivered the following comments: "The German authorities are treating the Jews shamefully, and the Jews in this country are greatly excited. But this is not . . . a governmental affair. We can do nothing except for American citizens who happen to be victims. We must protect them, and whatever we can do to moderate the general persecutions by unofficial and personal influence ought to be done."[4]

As Arthur D. Morse so forcefully and indignantly reported in *While Six Million Died,* administration action from the outset of the persecutions was limited chiefly to informal admonitions to German diplomats delivered in private talks by Secretary of State Cordell Hull. Morse further lamented that the administration never saw fit to send off an official protest to the Hitler regime, even though similar action had enanated from Britain and France and ample precedent existed for U.S. diplomatic intercession from past instances of minority persecutions abroad.[5]

One must agree with Arthur Morse insofar as it would be impossible to condone the unwillingness of the administration to issue a formal protest. But it is equally impossible to believe that the Nazi regime would have been deterred by such action. Even the imposition of sanctions would not have proven efficacious, except for the kind that could have contributed to the collapse of National Socialism. Few people anywhere during the early 1930s understood the depth of Nazi anti-Semitism. As Lucy Dawidowicz pointed out with chilling detail in *The War Against the Jews,* Jew-hatred was neither susceptible to moderation nor merely an opportunistic ploy for economic and political advantage. It was, instead, something at the very core of an ideology whose true believers had become masters of the German nation and whose unswerving objective was to rid that country of a class of despised outcasts.

In retrospect, Roosevelt's proposal to "moderate the general persecutions by unofficial and personal influence" appears not only paltry but naive. At the time, however, the president's response seemed understandable if not condonable, for few people, even among the victims themselves, could know what lay in store for Germany's Jews. Other considerations within the broader sphere of German-American relations no doubt entered into the administration's decision-making on how to respond to what was happening to Jews. Early New Deal diplomacy with the Reich involved international disarmament as well as efforts to prevent the Hitler regime from defaulting on debts owed to American investors. Thus, it is not surprising that Roosevelt, in the same meeting mentioned above, instructed Ambassador Dodd to "do all you can to prevent a moratorium. It would tend to retard recovery."[6]

In regard to immigration policy, the president again revealed the impact of the Depression on his thinking by showing little inclination to tamper with the Hoover executive order of 1930. The fullest account of Roosevelt's views on this matter is contained in an exchange of correspondence with Governor Herbert Lehman of New York carried on between November 1935 and July 1936. In his initial letter, Lehman petitioned his predecessor at Albany for a modest increase in the admission of refugees, pointing to the stringency of existing State Department regulations. In his reply, Roosevelt expressed sympathy for Hitler's victims, noting that they were already being accorded "the most considerate attention and the most generous and favorable treatment possible under the law of this country."[7] The president made this assessment toward the end of a year in which the German quota would remain more than 75 percent underfilled. As far as allowing the further easing of restrictions, Roosevelt said nothing, either in his first letter to Lehman or in a later one dated July 2, 1936.[8] Whether the president had initiated or merely rubber-stamped the liberalized visa policy put into effect at the end of that year cannot be determined by the available evidence.

Between 1933 and 1937 the United States had accepted some 30,000 refugees, a number exceeded only by Palestine, which admitted about 42,000. The policy of the Roosevelt administration cannot, however, be considered a generous one, if for no other reason than that the aggregate German quota would have allowed entry to nearly 130,000 persons.

If, on the other hand, we view administration policy from a perspective that embraces more than immigration statistics, we may find less basis for criticism. It should be noted that few, if any, Jewish spokesmen before 1938 advocated utilizing the German quota to its limit. Not only fearful about the reaction of congressional restrictionists, Jews in the United States worried that a sizable influx of coreligionists would overtax their charitable resources and aggravate an already ominous anti-Semitism in the United States. Moreover, it was hardly a secret that prior to the Nuremberg laws a large number of German Jews had no intention of leaving their homeland for the United States or anywhere else. Not fully appreciating the depth of Nazi hatred for them, many German Jews for a time lived under the illusion that official anti-Semitism was but a passing phase in the consummation of the new order in the "Thousand Year" Reich.[9]

Until the spring of 1938 there had been grounds for optimism on the part of refugee advocates, even though there could no longer exist any doubt that anti-Semitism was a permanent and integral feature of National Socialism. Over a five-year period notable progress in resettlement had been made through the efforts of the League of Nations and a multitude of refugee-aid societies combined with the sometimes grudging cooperation of various countries in the Western Hemisphere and Western Europe. Between March 1933 and March 1938 approximately 140,000 German Jews had found havens in other lands.

During the second week of March 1938 the fragile optimism about the manageability of the refugee problem was rudely shattered by the violent events in Austria accompanying the Anschluss. The consummation of political union with the Reich comprised the signal for Austria's Nazis to perpetrate the most appalling pogrom on the European continent since the days of the czars. In addition to imposing the Nuremberg decrees, the Nazis in Vienna closed the city's synagogues, engaged in widespread violence against people and property, and imprisoned some 12,000 persons, including many of Austria's Jewish leaders. In short, the refugee problem in Greater Germany was now aggravated by the inclusion of Austria's 180,000 Jews in the sad ranks of the persecuted.

In the United States, the unhappy events in Central Europe set the stage for the Roosevelt administration to end its five-year passivity on the refugee issue. At a press conference held on March 24, President Roosevelt announced that the United States would call a special international conclave aimed at "facilitating the emigration from Austria and Germany of political refugees." An official of the HIAS, upon returning from a tour of the Reich in the autumn of 1933, had commented with gloomy perception that "the book of Israel in Germany is closed." The Roosevelt administration, it seemed clear, had now reached the same conclusion, although in his announcement the president had deliberately used the word "political" to attract wider domestic and international support for this proposal.

Roosevelt knew that his move on behalf of refugees was being taken at some political risk, since it was sure to arouse congressional restrictionists whose support he needed to keep alive his weakened New Deal coalition. By way of reassuring his would-be critics, the president also announced at his press conference that "no country would be expected or asked to receive a greater number of immigrants than is permitted by its existing legislation."[10] The fact that Roosevelt had not ruled out the possibility of filling the German quota to its limit for the first time since the onset of the Depression did not go unnoticed by some restrictionists. On the floor of the House of Representatives, Thomas Jenkins of Ohio chided the president for having gone "on a visionary excursion into the warm fields of altruism. He forgets the "one third' of our people who are "ill-clothed, ill-housed, and ill-fed.' ''[11]

Writers on the Roosevelt administration's response to the Holocaust have expressed a measure of uncertainty about the president's motives in calling an international conference on refugees in 1938. Davis S. Wyman, in *Paper Walls,* observed cautiously that "a humanitarian motive on Roosevelt's part may not be ruled out."[12] Wyman and others also pointed to the strong possibility that the president acted out of political expediency. Following the Anschluss pro-refugee spokesmen, most of them ardent New Deal supporters, had raised a clamor for a bold initiative by the administration. State Department officials, led by Secretary Hull and Undersecretary Sumner Welles, reacted by advising the president to call the international conference as a means of silencing the clamor and forestalling potentially embarrassing efforts by the pro-refugee forces to liberalize the immigration laws.[13]

Whatever the nature of Roosevelt's motives in calling the refugee conference, thirty-two nations responded with varying degress of enthusiasm. Held at the pleasant French Alpine town of Evian-les-Bains between July 6 and 15, the meeting drew delegates from the United States, France, the Low Countries, Britain, the Commonwealth nations, and most of the Latin American republics, in addition to representatives from about forty private rescue and relief agencies. The chief aims of the conference were to sound out delegates about immigration opportunities in their own countries, to explore the possibility of mass resettle-ment in sparsely populated territories, and to establish an Intergovernmental Committee on Political Refugees to coordinate rescue efforts with the League of Nations and to approach Germany with an offer to negotiate an orderly migration of its unwanted people. The latter objective was necessitated by the fact that Hitler had steadfastly boycotted the League ever since the Reich's withdrawal in October 1933.

In a prevailing mood of wary national self-interest, the Evian conference produced but meager results. Most delegates expressed unwillingness to widen the portals of their countries on such grounds as depressed economic conditions and the alleged unsuitability of most refugees for agricultural labor. Many also claimed that their governments had already accepted their fair share of Nazism's victims and could absorb no more. Some of the participants even foresaw the possibility that success in dealing with the German-Austrian problem would induce other countries such as Poland and Rumania to dump their own Jewish populations and other unwanted minorities into the international no-man's-land inhabited by refugees. In addition, Zionist representatives left the conference bitterly disappointed that Britain would not allow discussion of Palestine as a site for mass resettlement. The Roosevelt administration had decided not to challenge the Bristish on Palestine for fear of jeopardizing London's participation at Evian. The only hopeful signs in an otherwise gloomy outcome were the consideration for further study of mass resettlement possibilities other than Pal-estine and the preparations for pursuit of negotiations with Berlin.[14]

A few months after the Evian conference, the plight of Jews in Germany worsened once again, this time as a result of a fierce pogrom known as *Kristallnacht* ("Night of Broken Glass"). Engineered by Dr. Goebbels following the assassination in Paris of a German diplomat by a young Polish Jew, the pogrom of November 8–9 produced tens of thousands of arrests and an orgy of burning, looting, and beatings all across the Reich. The Hitler government also used the assassination in Paris as a pretext for levying a massive atonement fine on the Jewish community and vastly accelerated its program of expropriating Jewish-owned property.

The latest Nazi onslaught sparked headlines throughout the world, including the United States, where President Roosevelt recalled Ambassador Hugh Wilson to show the nation's displeasure. A more propitious, if less dramatic, move by the president in the wake of *Kristallnacht* was his order to extend the visitor's visas of some 12,000 to 15,000 refugees residing in the United States on a temporary basis.[15]

If Roosevelt had any thoughts that this latest action on behalf of refugees would head off efforts to further liberalize immigration policy, he was mistaken. By December 1938 a movement had taken shape aimed at admitting 20,000 refugee children on a quota-exempt basis. Endorsed by Labor Secretary Frances L. Perkins, the bill was formally introduced in January 1939 as a bipartisan measure by Senator Robert Wagner of New York and Representative Edith Nourse Rogers of Massachusetts.

Well aware of the strength of restrictionist sentiment in Congress and in the nation at large, the backers of the child refugee bill had laid their plans carefully. They played down the Jewish aspect of their endeavor by naming their organization the Non-Sectarian Committee for German Refugee Children and selected a prominent Quaker, Clarence E. Pickett, to act as its director. The Non-Sectarian Committee also chose its witnesses for the congressional hearings judiciously by tapping a large number of Southerners and representatives of social welfare agencies in order to impress congressmen from the most restrictionist section of the country and to accentuate the humanitarian nature of the child refugee bill. The backers of the measure even went so far as to enlist the glamor of Hollywood and Broadway to their cause by getting the well-known actors Joe E. Brown and Helen Hayes to testify.

All this was to no avail. Majorities in the Senate and House immigration committees would agree to nothing more than allowing the 20,000 children preference under the German-Austrian quota. Senator Wagner and other backers of the original bill found this unacceptable, with the result that the measure died in committee without ever reaching the floor of Congress for a vote.

Prior to the congressional hearings, the Non-Sectarian Committee had tried to persuade President Roosevelt to issue a public endorsement of their measure. He would not respond.[16] Presumably sympathetic to the Wagner-Rogers bill, the president would do nothing more than tell Eleanor Roosevelt that "it is all right for you to support . . . the bill. But it is best for me to say nothing."[17] It is unlikely that White House backing would have affected the outcome. The president could have spoken out on the bill's behalf as a humanitarian gesture and as a needed reminder to the American people about the nation's proud, if checkered, tradition as a land of asylum for the oppressed. On the other hand, early 1939 was a period during which Roosevelt's influence in Congress had fallen to an all-time low, owing to such missteps as the court-packing scheme and the "Roosevelt purge" in the 1938 midterm elections. The president very likely thought that the risk of further eroding his influence on Capitol Hill would be too great a price to pay for embracing the cause of 20,000 foreign children for whom the United States held no legal responsibility.

Meanwhile, important rescue developments were taking place in the international arena. In February 1939, after months of delicate and protracted negotiations with the Reich, George Rublee, an American lawyer who had agreed to head up the Intergovernmental Committee established at Evian, announced the adoption of a plan that would have allowed the orderly emigration of some 400,000 persons. The would-be beneficiaries of the Rublee plan, as it was called, consisted not only of self-identified Jews but a large number of Jewish converts to Christianity who had failed the "Aryanization" tests decreed by the Nuremberg laws.

Receiving an enthusiastic endorsement from Roosevelt and the State Department, the Rublee plan would have permitted Germany's "non-Aryans" to leave the Reich in exchange for a requirement by the emigrants to purchase German goods once they became established in their new homelands. These purchases were to be financed through a trust fund administered by the German government. Another feature of the plan involved a commitment by the United States, Britain, and France to seek out and develop resettlement sites. To assume the costs of relocation, the plan further envisioned the establishment of a corporation financed by private Jewish and Christian agencies. As for those too old to emigrate, the Reich agreed to allow such persons to live out their remaining years unmolested.

The vast amount of effort involved in putting together the Rublee plan came to naught, for within six weeks after the completion of final arrangements World War II broke out. The British and French, who now faced the problem of national survival, would expend no further effort on behalf of German Jews. Present also in the thinking of British and French leaders was the possibility that the Reich would use the refugee exodus to infiltrate spies and saboteurs.

Even if implementation of the Rublee plan could have begun earlier, there is considerable doubt that it would have amounted to anything like the panacea that some supporters envisioned. Few countries, including the United States, as the fate of the child refugee bill had revealed, seemed willing to let down their immigration barriers. In addition, mass resettlement proposals, as numerous preliminary investigations had indicated, involved almost insuperable difficulties in the form of financing, site selection, vocational retraining, and disease control.[18]

Not least in importance was the question of the sincerity of the Reich in holding to its part of the bargain. Never enthusiastically supported by the more radical Nazis, the negotiations with the Intergovernmental Committee had been handled by one of the moderates, Dr. Hjalmar Schacht, the head of the Reichsbank. During the period of the Schacht-Rublee talks, the Gestapo had shown that it could dispose of outcasts in other ways, such as the rounding up and dumping of Polish-born Jews across the German-Polish frontier and the encouragement of the sale of often fraudulent Latin American visas to terrified persons threatened by internment in concentration camps. The latter practice led to the much-publicized and ill-fated voyage of the *St. Louis* in May 1939.[19]

The outbreak of World War II aggravated the plight of Jews on the European continent. The swift German conquest of western Poland placed at least half of that country's 3 million Jews within the Nazi orbit by the end of September. Also, the annexation of the Sudetenland and the military occupation of Prague prior to the onset of war had swept most of Czechoslovakia's 350,000 Jews into the clutches of the Nazis. The start of hostilities, however, did not mean that the Hitlerites had yet decided to implement the Final Solution. That grim decision was not to be made until January 1942. For the time being, the Nazi approach to making the Reich and its dominions *judenrein* (free of Jews) was through expulsion, as it had been since the latter part of 1938, if not earlier.

In the United States the first months of war found Franklin D. Roosevelt with an undiminished interest in mass resettlement possibilities. Such a solution to the refugee problem would stand as a viable option just as long as the Hitler regime allowed Jews to depart, ports remained open, and oceangoing vessels were available for transportation. Mass resettlement, moreover, now seemed the only option, for Britain and France could no longer be expected to take in as many refugees as before. Briefly considering the United States as a possibility for filling this void, the president in late 1939 instructed his commissioner of immigration, James L. Houghteling, to investigate the mood of Congress on easing immigration barriers. Houghteling could report only that "the chances of liberalizing legislation seemed negligible."[20]

Roosevelt had foreseen as early as October 1939 that the war could produce as many as 20 million refugees. (What he could not foresee, of course, was that by the war's end relatively few of these would be Jews.) Given the anticipated scope of the postwar refugee problem, the president viewed the establishment of one large haven, as distinguished from a series of smaller ones, as the most propitious approach to resettlement. The preferred site for the fulfillment of Roosevelt's grandiose vision was Africa, where he thought a new republic called the "United States of Africa" could be established, preferably in the Portuguese colony of Angola. Although the Africa proposal had enlisted support from some prominent British Jews as well as from the financier Bernard Baruch, the scheme fell through for a number of reasons, not least of which in importance were the lack of interest on the part of most Zionists and the resistance of the British and Portuguese governments.

Despite this failure literally dozens of other, more modest, ventures were proposed, studied, and discarded between mid-1938 and mid-1940. The only enterprise that actually went so far as to produce settlers was the one set up at Sosua in the Dominican Republic. With the help of the administration, the American Jewish Joint Distribution Committee founded an agricultural colony in January 1940 that ultimately envisioned the resettlement of 28,000 refugees. Owing to a number of difficulties the Sosua venture proved a near-failure, and in the end would provide asylum for fewer than 500 persons.[21]

Although the president was markedly willing to back resettlement projects in foreign territories, he offered no public support for such ventures on soil controlled by the United States. In March 1940 two Democratic members of Congress, Senator William King of Utah and Representative Frank Havenner of California, introduced an Alaska development bill that would have created a refugee haven in the territory and at the same time would have provided the capital and skilled manpower to develop its rich natural resources. Strongly backed by Interior Secretary Harold Ickes, the King-Havenner bill met with predictable hostility from restrictionists, who saw the measure as providing an opportunity for backdoor entry by refugees to the United States proper. Surprisingly, the bill also met with staunch opposition from the Alaskan press and officials of the territorial government. Already suspicious of Secretary Ickes, Alaskan spokesmen also showed that they were not immune to nativist and anti-Semitic thinking. One official, Ernest Gruening, pointing to a provision in the bill that would have required refugees to remain in the territory for at least five years, feared that the measure would convert Alaska into a concentration camp. Lacking support even from most Alaskans, the King-Havenner bill died in committee.[22]

Whether a timely endorsement from President Roosevelt would have saved the King-Havenner bill is a moot question. According to Harold Ickes, the president had studied and seemed favorably disposed toward the Alaska proposal when it was submitted to him as a report for the Interior Department in late 1939. During the following year, however, Roosevelt would remain publicly silent. The State Department opposed the measure and warned that a White House endorsement would antagonize congressional restrictionists whose support was needed for defense appropriations. The president in 1939 had also raised the objection that the Alaska proposal failed to place a numerical limit on the entry of refugee Jews. Henry Feingold, in *The Politics of Rescue,* conjectured that Roosevelt may have later withheld support from the bill in order to put some distance between himself and the American Jewish community in order to silence certain critics of the administration.[23]

In mid-1940 another resettlement scheme on United States territory came to the fore. This time the site was the Virgin Islands, where Secretary Ickes hoped to admit up to 2,000 refugees on temporary visas. The Interior Department intended to allow the refugees to use the Islands as a way-station until they could qualify for entry to the mainland as permanent immigrants. Receiving the support of the territorial governor and its legislature, the Ickes proposal also envisioned the presence of the newcomers as a stimulus to the depressed Islands' economy.[24]

Apparently impressed, however, with the argument of an important hotel operator in the Islands, who warned that an influx of refugees would ruin the Islands' tourist industry, the president wrote Ickes late in 1940 that "I yield to no person in . . . my deepseated desire to help the hundreds of thousands of foreign refugees. The Virgin Islands, however, present a very serious economic problem yet not solved."[25]

Far more damaging was the State Department argument that the entry of refugees to the Islands could seriously breach the security of the United States by affording the Reich an opportunity to infiltrate Nazi agents. Dubbed the "security gambit" by Henry Feingold, the fear of German spies and saboteurs would, by mid-1940, replace the "Jobs for Americans" slogan as the major rallying cry for those who would lock the country's gates against refugees.[26] The underlying reason for the emergence of the security gambit was not hard to find. By the spring of 1940 the period of "phony war" had ended and Americans now witnessed a seemingly unstoppable Nazi juggernaut overrun the Low Countries and France. As administration policy on the war moved from neutrality to nonbelligerent intervention, many Americans would feel for the first time the threat posed by Nazi Germany to national security. Abetted by a spate of magazine articles and motion pictures, the fear of infiltrators and fifth columnists would reach levels of near-hysteria by 1941.[27]

The nation's chief guardian against infiltration of Nazi agents in the guise of refugees was Breckinridge Long, a friend and political ally of Roosevelt since the Woodrow Wilson days. In January 1940 Roosevelt had appointed Long to the newly created post of assistant secretary of state for the Special War Problems Division, under which the department's visa division was placed. Long could be best characterized as a determined bureaucrat possessed of an anti-Semitism enmeshed in a generalized xenophobia.[28] He began his quiet crusade to guard the nation's ramparts in the late spring of 1940. Temporarily lacking congressional authorization to initiate more stringent procedures, the assistant secretary took matters into his own hands by sending revised directives to consular officials abroad. In an interdepartmental memo dated June 26, 1940, Long revealed what he was up to: "We can," he wrote, "delay and effectively stop . . . the number of immigrants into the United States. We could do this by simply advising our consuls to put every obstacle in the way and . . . resort to various administrative advices [devices?] which would postpone and postpone and postpone the granting of visas."[29]

One particularly flagrant example of Long's handiwork was an order issued in June 1941 that temporarily barred all refugees with relatives remaining in Germany and its occupied territories. The directive stemmed from a fear that such newcomers could be blackmailed into engaging in subversive activities.[30]

The "administrative advices" of Breckinridge Long and the Special War

Problems Division laid the foundation for large-scale tragedy. Cold statistics can convey the essentials of the story. In fiscal year 1941 (July 1, 1940, to June 30, 1941) the combined quotas for Germany and other refugee-producing countries revealed a shortfall of over 50 percent. In comparison, the quotas for Germany and Austria for FY 1939 and FY 1940 had been almost fully subscribed for the first time since 1930. Had the 1941 quota been completely filled, an additional 20,000–25,000 persons could have found asylum in the United States. Many of those stranded on the Continent were either malnourished and terrified children or anti-Nazi activists sought by the Gestapo in Vichy France.[31] Undoubtedly, an unknown number of people unsuccessful in obtaining U.S. visas found refuge elsewhere. We can only guess how many others perished in the death camps.

As one might surmise by now, Franklin Roosevelt was not immune to the security gambit. In fact, he abetted it. Jarred by the advance of the German blitzkrieg in Western Europe, Roosevelt in May 1940 delivered a fireside chat in which he alerted the American people that "today's threat to our national security is not a matter of military weapons alone. We know of new weapons of attack, the Trojan horse, the fifth column that betrays a nation unprepared for treachery. Spies, saboteurs, and traitors are the actors in this new strategy. With all that we must and will deal vigorously."[32]

Painfully aware of the potentially tragic effects of the security gambit, pro-refugee groups, in the months ahead, tried to sensitize the president to their point of view. They would remind him that human lives were at stake and that the nation should not abandon its tradition of asylum at such a desperate hour. Pointing to the fact that such important refugee havens as France and the Low Countries had fallen to the Germans, they also tried to convince the administration that fears about the infiltration of Nazi agents in the guise of refugees were greatly exaggerated, if not totally unfounded.

The only victory of any consequence that refugee advocates would achieve came in June 1940, when the president agreed to a program that ultimately extended temporary visas to 3,268 carefully selected persons, mostly from the small-quota countries of Central and Eastern Europe. The beneficiaries of the temporary visa program consisted mainly of prominent antifascist political leaders and persons who had distinguished themselves in the arts and sciences. The program envisioned that once the quotas of their countries of origin became vacant, the newcomers would be allowed to remain on a permanent basis.[33]

Other than this, the president's conduct revealed essential agreement with Breckinridge Long and the State Department. Henry Feingold and, in less emphatic fashion, David Wyman have questioned the likelihood of an influx of German agents disguised as refugees.[34] It cannot, however, be conclusively demonstrated that Assistant Secretary Long and the security hounds were mistaken, for the stringent visa procedures initiated in mid-1940 did in the end prove effective in screening out Nazi infiltrators. Without questioning Roosevelt's stated sympathy for the plight of refugees, one can conclude that in the charged atmosphere of 1940–1941 the political costs of a major breach in national security would have been far greater for the president than the political rewards of a bold commitment to the nation's tradition of asylum.

During the second half of 1941 the plight of those who sought to escape the clutches of the Hitlerites would grow even more desperate. In July the United States closed its consular offices in the Reich and Nazi-occupied Europe. In the following month Germany ceased issuing exit permits. Departure from the Reich and its dominions could no longer be undertaken through legal means.[35] By then hundreds of thousands of Polish Jews, along with countless Gentile compatriots, had died as a result of disease, starvation, murder, and physical abuse in forced labor camps. During the second half of 1941, hundreds of thousands more Jews would die in the wake of Hitler's invasion of the Soviet Union. Executed by special killing squads trailing the German army, most of these later victims could not have escaped their fate even if asylum awaited them in the United States or anywhere else. Finally, on January 20, 1942, a number of Hitler's chief cohorts, meeting secretly at the Berlin suburb of Wannsee, agreed to set in motion the ultimate horror of the Final Solution.[36]

Robert A. Divine, in a history of American immigration policy published in 1957, concluded that "considering that throughout this period [1933–1941], the United States was engulfed in the worst depression in its history, the relief given to refugees was a major humanitarian achievement."[37] There is much truth in Divine's assessment. During this period close to 250,000 refugees found a haven in the United States. No other country, including Palestine, received more. A closer look at immigration statistics for 1938–1941 alone would reveal, however, a shortfall representing about 50,000 persons if one includes the quotas of twelve European refugee-producing countries other than Germany.[38] Thus, from the standpoint of numbers alone, the United States was not as generous as it could have been.

As demonstrated here, whatever willingness was shown to extend a welcoming hand to refugees came not from an unyieldingly restrictionist Congress but from the Roosevelt administration. From the White House emerged the initiative for the 1938 international conference at Evian. In the same year Roosevelt allowed up to 15,000 persons on temporary visas to remain in the country and suspended the executive order of 1930, a move that permitted the German-Austrian quota to be filled in the next two fiscal years for the first time since the onset of the Depression. In 1940 Roosevelt took further action by allowing over 3,200 persons to enter under a special visa arrangement that would ultimately entitle them to remain on a permanent basis.

The president took these steps at a time when the political environment in the United States was extremely hostile to the entry of immigrants of any kind. Given this fact, could the president have done more? The answer appears to be yes. Roosevelt would never use the White House as a forum to remind the American people about the nation's tradition of asylum or to offset the negative image of refugees fixed in the minds of many citizens. He would not even endorse the admission of 20,000 refugee children, even though it was abundantly clear that the youngsters could not compete for scarce jobs. Most likely such conduct on Roosevelt's part would have been futile. Moreover, the president, by 1938, felt his influence in Congress slipping and perhaps had become overly sensitive to a characterization of the New Deal as the "Jew Deal." Small in numbers and already committed to New Deal liberalism, American Jews and other pro-refugee elements could not exert enough political pressure to offset the negative influences affecting the president's thinking and conduct.

Where Roosevelt lay more clearly vulnerable to criticism was in his response to developments from mid-1940 to the end of 1941 when the plight of would-be escapees from Nazism became more urgent than ever before. During this period the nation was engulfed in a wave of hysteria over national security that would, ironically, further victimize those in flight from persecution. Himself under the influence of the security gambit, Roosevelt allowed a zealous State Department officialdom to erect administrative barriers aimed at reducing the entry of refugees to minimal levels. In view of the tragic results described earlier, the president, at the very least, could have pursued the possibility of internment for refugees whose loyalty was in doubt. Such a proposal might have raised an outcry from pro-refugee spokesmen in the United States, but it also could have led to an acceptable quid pro quo between those primarily concerned with the nation's security and those whose foremost concern lay in offering asylum to those in need.

In the years between 1942 and 1945 the problem of finding havens for Hitler's victims would become overshadowed by the more fundamental problem of saving them from the gas chambers. For two critical years, 1942 and 1943, the president followed a pattern of conduct on the matter of rescue that had emerged earlier during the refugee phase of 1938–1941. This pattern was marked by a disinclination to challenge congressional restrictionists, a continued susceptibility to the security gambit, and an inclination to defer to the State Department, whose Special War Problems Division was to be headed by Breckinridge Long until the end of 1943. As Henry Feingold pointed out in gripping and saddening detail, the president, as did most of his advisors, would justify a policy of inaction upon the catchy slogan of "rescue through victory." Not until 1944, as a result of intensified pressure from outside and within the administration, did the president alter his behavior in a meaningful way. In January of that year Roosevelt ordered the establishment of a War Refugee Board whose activities, as Arthur Morse and Henry Feingold reported, would save many lives, especially from among the Jews of Hungary, Rumania, and Bulgaria.

How many victims of the Holocaust could have been saved had a more forceful policy been pursued by the Roosevelt administration is a moot question. Indeed, rescue from the death camps, as distinguished from providing a haven in the United States, was task formidable enough for any U.S. president, even for one who headed an awesome world power. Such an undertaking would have required dedicated cooperation not only from within Congress and the administration, but also from the Allies, the neutral countries of Europe, the Vatican, and the International Red Cross. As it turned out, each of these parties would show a degree of determination to rescue Jews that would scarcely match the determination of the Nazis to destroy them.[39]

In once offering an assessment of Franklin D. Roosevelt, Tom Corcoran, a former aide of his, concluded by making the comment that "a great man cannot be a good man."[40] One can either agree or disagree with this overall appraisal. But in regard to the president and refuge for victims of Nazism, one may safely reverse the components of Corcoran's judgment and conclude that, at most, Franklin Roosevelt was a good man who could not be a great man.

NOTES

1. Sheldon M. Neuringer, *American Jewry and United States Immigration Policy, 1881–1953* (New York, 1980), pp. 205, 214–215, 219.

2. Ibid., pp. 221, 226; Arthur D. Morse, *While Six Million Died: A Chronicle of American Apathy* (New York, 1967), pp. 197–198.

3. Neuringer, p. 218; Hebrew Immigrant Aid Society, *Twenty-ninth Annual Report* (New York, 1937), p. 11.

4. Quoted in Morse, p. 120. See also William E. Dodd, Jr., *Ambassador Dodd's Diary* (New York, 1941), p. 5.

5. Morse, pp. 107, 117–129.

6. Dodd, pp. 4–5; Lucy S. Dawidowicz, *The War Against the Jews, 1933–1945* (New York, 1975), esp. pp. 3–28, 77–92, 112–116.

7. Herbert Lehman to Franklin D. Roosevelt, November 1, 1935; Franklin D. Roosevelt to Herbert Lehman, November 13, 1935, Herbert Lehman Papers, Reel 82, Columbia University, New York, N.Y.

8. Franklin D. Roosevelt to Herbert Lehman, July 2, 1936, Franklin D. Roosevelt Papers, File 133, Franklin D. Roosevelt Library, Hyde Park, N.Y.

9. Neuringer, pp. 216, 220–222, 236–237; Mark Wischnitzer, *To Dwell in Safety: The Story of Jewish Immigration since 1800* (Philadelphia, 1948), pp. 174–179.

10. Neuringer, pp. 226–228; Samuel I. Rosenman, ed., *The Public Papers and Addresses of Franklin D. Roosevelt*, 13 vols. (New York, 1938–1950), 7:169; *B'nai B'rith Magazine* 48 (November 1933): 49.

11. Quoted in Henry L. Feingold, *The Politics of Rescue: The Roosevelt Administration and the Holocaust, 1938–1945* (New Brunswick, N.J.), p. 24.

12. David S. Wyman, *Paper Walls: America and the Refugee Crisis, 1938–1941* (Amherst, Mass., 1968), pp. 44–45.

13. In addition to Wyman, see Morse, pp. 203–4; Feingold, pp. 22–24.

14. Feingold, pp. 26–36; Wyman, pp. 48–51.

15. Neuringer, pp. 241–242; Feingold, pp. 42–44.

16. Neuringer, pp. 243–47.

17. Telegram from Franklin D. Roosevelt to Eleanor Roosevelt, February 22, 1939, FDR Papers, File 200, Franklin D. Roosevelt Library.

18. Feingold, pp. 37–66, 69–78; Wyman, pp. 51–56.

19. Feingold, pp. 65–68, 81–88.

20. Memorandum from James L. Houghteling to Franklin D. Roosevelt, January 5, 1940, FDR Papers, File 133, Franklin D. Roosevelt Library.

21. Feingold, pp. 82–86, 90–94, 99–117, 120–123.

22. Wyman, pp. 99–112.

23. Feingold, p. 97. If indeed it was Roosevelt's intention to placate his critics, he apparently chose an issue that would not offend Jewish sensibilities, for there appeared to be little or no interest on the part of Jewish organizations in Alaska as a refugee haven. As late as the early summer of 1940, the HIAS, for example, had not even taken up the King-Havenner bill for study and discussion. See Hebrew Immigrant Aid Society, ''Minutes of a Meeting of the Committee on the Work in Foreign Countries,'' July 2, 1940, p. 2 (New York: Archives of the Yiddish Scientific Institute—YIVO).

24. Wyman, pp. 112–113.

25. Memorandum from Franklin D. Roosevelt to the Secretary of the Interior, December 18, 1940, FDR Papers, File 3186, Franklin D. Roosevelt Library.

26. Feingold, pp. 128, 155–157.

27. Ibid., p. 128; Wyman, pp. 184–190.

28. Feingold, pp. 131–137, 159. For other unfavorable characterizations of Breckinridge Long, see Morse, pp. 38–42, and Wyman, p. 212.

29. Quoted in Wyman, p. 173.

30. For accounts of State Department activity regarding the issuance of refugee visas during 1940–1941, see Wyman, pp. 142–147, 174–178, 191–204, and Feingold, pp. 143–148, 157–164.

31. Wyman, pp. 128–134, 137–138, 209, 211–12, 221.

32. Quoted in Feingold, p. 128.

33. Wyman, pp. 138–142, 148–149, 191, 199–203; Feingold, pp. 137–143.

34. Feingold, pp. 129–131; Wyman, p. 189.

35. Feingold, p. 161.

36. Dawidowicz, pp. 182–185, 533–37, 540–41.

37. Robert A. Divine, *American Immigration Policy, 1924–1952* (New Haven, 1957), p. 104.

38. Wyman, pp. 209, 217–19.

39. For accounts of rescue developments from 1942 to 1945, see Feingold, pp. 167–307, and Morse, pp. 3–99, 313–384.

40. Quoted in Arthur M. Schlesinger, Jr., *The Coming of the New Deal* (Boston, 1958), p. 584.

III

THE NEW DEAL
REEXAMINED

7

The New Deal and the Vital Center: A Continuing Struggle for Liberalism

David K. Adams

What the New Deal was is still a matter of debate, and even to many contemporaries its meaning was unclear. What could be made of a movement of which Senator Henry Hatfield of West Virginia said, that "while it sings the praises of Jefferson and Jackson, it is more in keeping with the preachings of Norman Thomas, Stalin, Mussolini, and Hitler''? This group, had they read the senator's words in the *Congressional Record,* would have found themselves strange bedfellows indeed! It was Norman Thomas himself who accused the New Deal of "trying to cure tuberculosis with cough drops"; the Communists who referred derogatively to FDR as a "smiling India rubber liberal in the White House''; and from a position of initial sympathy Hitler came to view Roosevelt with increasing contempt as a capitalist imperialist in the hands of the Jews.[1]

In political affairs, the most difficult path to tread is the middle road between the political extremes of right and left. This is the ground commonly occupied by "liberalism." But liberalism, like all isms, is capable of many varied definitions according to the particular time and place. In Western European democratic societies it does perhaps have a generally assumed meaning and a rightful place in the political spectrum, with a political definition that embraces analysis of means as well as ends. But in the United States established meanings are elusive, and in New Deal historiography the profile is confused. The few synthetic interpretations are not particularly persuasive. Some of them, like that of Barton Bernstein, seem to judge the New Deal by the presuppositions of a later time and to measure its achievements and failures according to the perceived state of society at the writer's time, attributing to the New Deal of the 1930s full responsibility for the imperfections of the 1960s. New Deal historiography has also been shaped by continued acceptance of the view, first projected by Basil Rauch in 1944, that the New Deal period can be divided into two distinct parts that embodied radically different approaches to the problems of social and economic reform.[2]

My argument is that the New Deal can best be seen as a whole, and that Franklin Roosevelt was deeply committed to a philosophical tradition that was recognizably "liberal." I am aware of the problems of definition, what Louis Hartz calls "the useless argument" that develops with the attempt to affirm "the liberalness of a liberal society in absolute mathematical fashion," but I do not share his belief that " 'liberalism' is a stranger in the land of its greatest realization and fulfillment," nor that there was an irrationality in the "sublimated 'Americanism' " of FDR. I would suggest that FDR was not just a pragmatic politician but a more substantial thinker; that the New Deal embodied a set of coherent philosophical and ethical values "more noble than mere monetary profit"; and that it sought to work toward the fulfillment of these through policies and programs generally directed to the establishment of a mixed political culture, in which government fully participated in creative partnership with the private sectors of the economy. The unpredictability of human affairs, the constraints imposed by the political environment, and the burden of what John Kenneth Galbraith has called "the poor state of economic intelligence" meant that policies did not become blueprints and that development was not linear. Roosevelt himself used a football metaphor: "If the play makes ten yards, the succeeding play will be different from what it would have been if they had been thrown for a loss. I think that is the easiest way to explain it."[3]

In general, I am sympathetic to Roosevelt's own claim in the fireside chat of July 24, 1933, that the legislation of the hundred days was not "just a collection of haphazard schemes, but rather the orderly component parts of a connected and logical whole." He had already indicated in the preconvention address at Oglethorpe University the previous summer that clarity of aim should not inhibit experimentation, that objectives should not be confused with methods, and had also offered the simple metaphor of the tree which, as it grows, continually produces dead wood: "The radical says: 'Cut it down.' The conservative says: 'Don't touch it.' The liberal compromises: 'Let's prune, so that we lose neither the old trunk nor the new branches.' This campaign is waged to teach the country to march upon its appointed course, the way of change, in an orderly march, avoiding alike the revolution of radicalism and the revolution of conservatism." Donald Richberg was expressing similar thoughts when he summarized the objectives of the National Recovery Administration (NRA) as "seeking to establish a half-way house of democratic cooperation for the common good, midway between the anarchy of unplanned unregulated industrialism and the tyranny of State control of industry."[4]

A correspondent wrote to FDR in December 1934 that the Democratic party should lose no time in making clear to all its position in the liberal center, and the New Deal was, in fact, committed to what the *New Republic* in 1935 declared to be "no longer a feasible middle course" between unregulated capitalism and socialism. Ideological liberals, for whom the designation "radical" is perhaps more appropriate, were always skeptical about FDR. The League for Independent Political Action, which in 1931 denied that he was a "real liberal," supported Norman Thomas, the Socialist party candidate, in 1932. Their ambition for a "co-operative Commonwealth with a scientifically planned economic system, based on social control of the means of production" was shared by the Farmer-Labor governor of Minnesota, Floyd Olson, who declared forcefully in 1934 that he was not a liberal but a radical, and that his ultimate aim was the establishment of the cooperative commonwealth. This sort of radicalism found expression in the Farmer-Labor Political Federation and the American Commonwealth Political Federation. In their rejection of the New Deal they saw more clearly what it was about than did the Republican presidential candidate in 1936. Alf Landon believed that it represented total regulation and the antithesis of free competitive enterprise. There was, he declared, "no halfway house between these two systems." Roosevelt believed that there was, and continued to stand on the position he had stated in 1924, that "the Democratic party is the Progressive party of the country, but it is not and I hope never will be the radical party of the country which is a very different thing."[5]

The New Deal developed out of the tremendous economic collaspe and attendant social problems of the Great Depression. It sought to work itself out during years of continuing social and economic disturbance. A generation later, at another time of crisis, although differently created and differently perceived, a historian who had grown up during the Roosevelt period, and who was himself to become one of its leading analysts, sought to define the halfway house that he and many others believed the United States should build to protect itself at a time of Cold War. Arthur M. Schlesinger, Jr., sought to redefine liberalism so that at the heart of the nation could be a self-sustaining faith—a commitment and an energizing force that would allow the United States to regain confidence in its destiny and resist the dangers inherent in the interaction of foreign challenge and domestic fear. After World War II many Americans increasingly felt that the United States was threatened by internal weakness as well as external threat. Schlesinger was a man for whom, in his own words, "American liberalism has had a positive and confident ring. It has stood for responsibility and achievement, not for frustration and sentimentalism; it has been the instrument of social change, not of private neurosis."[6]

To assist in the process of reclaiming democratic ideas, and the recharging of faith, Schlesinger published *The Vital Center: The Politics of Freedom*. Schlesinger described and analyzed the nature of the challenges from left and right, discussed the innate fallibility of each alternative, and reemphasized the need to revive American liberalism and reconstruct techniques of freedom so as to make freedom once again a fighting faith. He argued, in ways that are helpful to the study of the New Deal, that the problem of "democracy," which *is* liberalism, is that by its very nature it

dissipates rather than concentrates its internal moral force. The thrust of the democratic faith is away from fanaticism; it is toward compromise, persuasion and consent in politics, toward tolerance and diversity in society; its economic foundation lies in the easily frightened middle class. Its love of variety discourages dogmatism, and its love of skepticism discourages hero-worship. In place of theology and ritual, of hierarchy and demonology, it sets up a belief in intellectual freedom and unrestricted inquiry. The advocate of a free society defines himself by telling what he is against: what he is for turns out to be certain *means* and he leaves other people to charge the means with content.[7]

The New Dealers had not, he suggested, been required to give precise definition to their philosophical position, for the combined threats of National Socialism in Germany and communism in the USSR had established, *prima facie,* their liberal tenets. Fascist totalitarianism was ipso facto to these men unacceptable, while the "unearthly radiance" of the communist left had been dimmed both by Soviet failures and by the fact that the New Deal itself filled the "vacuum of faith" inherited from the material cynicism and complacency of the 1920s.[8]

For Schlesinger the liberal stresses were, above all, the "ultimate integrity" of the individual, but in the context of a social structure that can contain the increasing velocity of the life of mankind; a velocity powered by science and technology, which stimulate and enforce change and can destroy as well as advance civilization. Loss of innocence, doubts about the inexorability of progress, force on the individual a self interested devotion to wider social needs and community concerns. The depersonalizing pressures of urban-industrial societies that challenge traditional individualism also ensure the failure of solutions inspired by romantic utopianism.[9]

Schlesinger firmly believed, and it is difficult to quarrel with his premise, that the strength of American capitalism and deep-seated commitment to it as a form of economic organization imposed their own perimeters on the liberal debate. Although the evolution of American capitalism had led to the divorce of ownership and control of property, and although it had been shown in many ways to have become socially irresponsible, nonetheless invention of a type of responsible capitalist order remained the dream. It certainly seemed preferable to the adoption of what was generally regarded as the alien creed of socialism.[10]

Whether or not New Deal liberalism belonged to the progressive tradition has been an additional matter of debate, and Schlesinger, like others, believing that progressivism was a movement based on "a sentimental belief in progress," sees the New Deal as something different. But his own statement that "the history of governmental intervention has been the history of the growing ineffectiveness of the private conscience as a means of social control . . . and that, therefore, the only alternative is the growth of the public conscience, whose natural expression is the democratic government," elegantly expresses what was an integral part of the progressive approach to reform. The centrality of Hartz's form of mainstream American liberalism is perhaps to be found in general subscription to the principles of regulation advocated by James Madison. With the rejection of radical extremes, a vital center, if it did not exist, would have to be reinvented out of Madison's *Federalist* No. 10.[11]

Franklin Roosevelt certainly understood, instinctively and intellectually, that the role of the state was to help create a cooperative environment within which decisions on economic and social policies could be made. He recognized that the state, through the government, had to be part designer, part umpire, but also part player; for the government was not a separate mechanism within society but rather the representative of all interests, checking, challenging, guiding, and influencing all innate forces but not directing them like some *deus ex machina* with an objective and superior and independent existence.[12]

Before he became president, Roosevelt had, after all, himself questioned the fundamental nature of the state, and had given a classically democratic answer at a time when other countries were denying the Western tradition of individualism and the dignity of man. In a speech to the New York State legislature in August 1931 he asked: "What is the State?" Imagine the scene: a hot, humid August day in Albany; the part-time legislators decked informally about the chamber as usual; the rather high-pitched voice of the governor suddenly throwing to them a philosophical challenge: What is the State? They must have been astonished, those who even heard. He answered his own rhetorical question in the following way: The state

is the duly constituted representative of an organized society of human beings, created by them for their mutual protection and well being. "The State" or "The Government" is but the machinery through which such mutual aid and protection are achieved. Our Government is not the master but the creature of the people. The duty of the State towards the citizens is the duty of the servant to its master. The people have created it; the people, by common consent, permit its continual existence.[13]

The individual, then, finds his place in an organized society of human beings, and this restatement of Locke can be traced back to Roosevelt's first career in politics. As a senator in the New York State Assembly, he had spoken in 1912 to the People's Forum at Troy, New York, and offered his version of progressivism. Always fond of making historical excursions, he claimed that the history of the Western world, at least since the Renaissance, had been a struggle for representative government, and that in most Western countries that freedom had been largely assured. But men had not then reached utopia: "During the past century we have acquired a new set of conditions which we must seek to solve. To put it in the simplest and fewest words I have called this new theory the struggle for liberty of the community rather than liberty of the individual." He went on to say that American society had passed beyond the stage when the individual should do as he pleased with his own property, and had moved into a phase when it was necessary to check this liberty for the benefit of the freedom of the whole people; i.e., as the individual's use of his property affects the whole community, then he must accept regulation of that property by the community in the greater interest. This type of communitarianism became integral to Roosevelt's thinking but, as he was later to reemphasize frequently, it did not mean total governmental control. Rather, it did mean limited government intervention to provide minimum security and "to restrain the kind of individual action which in the past has been detrimental to the community."[14]

Aware of the processes of socioeconomic change, he believed that the problem was that "we have today side by side an old political order fashioned by a pastoral civilization and a new social order fashioned by a technical civilization. The two are maladjusted. Their creative interrelation is one of the big tasks ahead of American leadership." The issue had become one of preserving "under the changing conditions of each generation a people's government for the people's good."[15]

And, of course, in the attempt to create this new interrelationship, men should not be inhibited by old shibboleths. Economic laws are not made by nature, they are made by human beings. He was therefore prepared to try "bold, persistent experimentation." The purpose of politics was not to make men and women serve some system of government and economics but to ensure that the system of government and economics served the people, hence the stress on enlightened administration and, throughout the New Deal, on the general welfare. This is in no way surprising; Franklin Roosevelt had grown up during the progressive years, admiring his cousin, Theodore, and had dreamed of carving out his own career on similar paths. Theodore Roosevelt's speech at Osawatomie, Kansas, in 1910, in which the former president declared that "every man holds his property subject to the general right of the community to regulate its use to whatever degree the public welfare may require it," must have been familiar to him.[16]

It has sometimes been suggested that Theodore Roosevelt's new nationalism, consolidating the policies and rhetoric of his presidency, was influenced by Herbert Croly. Croly argued for uniting "the Hamiltonian principle of national political responsibility and efficiency with a frank democratic purpose . . . [that] will give . . . new power to democracy." Unrestrained liberty necessarily led to inequality, and simple Jeffersonian slogans were precisely those deployed by robber barons in their own defense. Jeffersonian ends, therefore, had to be pursued by Hamiltonian means. National regulators, applied by a government firmly representative of a national consensus, must be used to restrain individual liberty in the interest of the entire national community.

In the face of great concentrations of economic power Croly advocated what Galbraith was later, in another context, to call countervailing power. The people could only control big business by the deployment of big government, in a national situation that also posited the existence of strong labor unions; hence there had to be an assertion of federal authority and policies of "constructive discrimination" to favor the weak against the strong in the interest of national harmony and democratic development. But Croly's regulatory state was again not an abstract entity to be worshipped, but rather something that resulted from the actions of a strong, active, national democracy. His assertion that "the state lives, and grows by what it does rather than by what it is" suggests the influence of the philosophical pragmatists whom he had studied at Harvard.[17]

The New Deal has often been called pragmatic, meaning expedient. Its methods have led to a considerable amount of analytic confusion among historians who find it difficult to reconcile the corporativism of the NRA and the Agricultural Adjustment Administration (AAA) with the individual emphasis of the Works Progress Administration (WPA), the failure to nationalize the banks with the establishment of the Federal Deposit Insurance Corporation (FDIC) and the Securities and Exchange Commission (SEC). They stress FDR's emphasis on action now, as if action was an end in itself, detached from ultimate purpose.

Pragmatic philosophers, however, generally believed that meanings and values must be referred to specific contexts; there are no objectively perceived absolutes, and so risks must be taken in an experimental way to try to attain specific goals. There is no determinism, for individuals make decisions, and individuality is denied if they are reduced to material for social engineering. The basic instruments for change are ideas, and in the process of change improvements are looked for, but not utopia: the best can therefore only be the enemy of the better. The means employed inescapably influence the ends sought, and how we go about the process of social change determines what changes are brought about, just as the changes sought determine how we go about changing things.[18]

For the academic pragmatists the individual, although the ultimate locus of value, was not the lonely individual of nineteenth-century rugged individualism but the individual in society. And increasingly, as the social order became more complex, the individual had to seek self-improvement through collective means. Societal ends only acquired their value insofar as they were embodied in the lives of individuals, and so no state is strong if its individual citizens are weak; no state is rich if its individual citizens are poor. FDR was saying the same thing when he said that "a nation cannot function as a healthy democracy with part of its citizens living under good conditions and part forced to live under circumstances inimical to the general welfare." He denied that individualism could solve problems with no help from government. Justice meant freedom from exploitation "on the part of those who do not care much for the lives, the happiness and the prosperity of their neighbors." Such had been the themes of the Commonwealth Club speech of 1932, subtitled "Campaign Address on Progressive Government." He approved of a Jefferson for whom government was not an end in itself but a means to an end, a Jefferson who accepted the validity of government intervention to protect individualism, not to destroy it. Society necessarily had to impose restraints on property rights because "we know that individual liberty and individual happiness mean nothing unless both are ordered in the sense that one man's meat is another man's poison."[19]

Were not such concepts implicit, even where not explicit, in the New Deal? There were of course many other antecedents. In his first presidential message to Congress in 1825 John Quincy Adams had stated, "The great object of the institution of civil government is the improvement of the conditions of those who are parties to the social compact.'' But it was not until the twentieth century that government threw its weight behind social reforms in a coherent attempt to rid the country of excessive laissez-faire practices in the interest of the wider community of citizens.[20]

Before political government took this road with a convinced and determined sense of direction, clear markers were being implanted by members of the judiciary and others. Oliver Wendell Holmes had been a member of the Harvard Metaphysical Club with Peirce and James. His legal realism was founded on the belief that ''our Constitution . . . is an experiment, as all life is an experiment.'' The sociological jurisprudence of Roscoe Pound and the social statistics of Louis Brandeis emphasized that the lawyer should not simply study the law, but also economics, sociology, and politics, since these ''embody the facts and present problems of today.'' Here also lie some of the pieces out of which the New Deal was made, and according to which it tried to define its middle way. The state had a role to play, a clear and coherent role. But the state existed through its component parts. It worked, therefore, through these parts and in cooperation with them. All New Deal programs, AAA and NRA, TVA, public works and Social Security, placed a premium on cooperation rather than coercion. The New Deal experimented in its attempt to attain general goals. It was not visionary but practical. It sought to meliorate conditions by consent, not to transform them by imposition. It accepted democracy both as a method of political organization and as an end to be pursued. Men had certain inalienable rights to health, work, and shelter plus the freedoms of the Bill of Rights: but a government that sought to impose policies to bring about such conditions would be destroying its own mandate. Sovereignty, after all, in the United States resides in the people. The vital center is one which only they, assisted by their government, can define. Hence the compromises of the New Deal, its apparent vagaries, its perpetual appeal to the interest groups and the institutional structures that gave form to the American democratic system. Without their support, or acquiescence, the New Deal could only have moved away from the vital center toward abstract models that bore little relation to FDR's democratic humanism.[21]

At the same time, however, in providing efficient government to serve the interests of the people and fulfill electoral mandates, the president came to believe that he should not shrink from the challenges of national leadership. He should be prepared to modify the instruments of political control if, by persuasion and the continuing process of education, he could bring about changes that would ensure the success of legislative policies in accordance with the mandate of the ballot box.

Whether or not Roosevelt was personally committed to transforming the American system into one more nearly akin to Westminster, in which majority will would prevail; whether or not, as the Supreme Court fight suggested, he was prepared to challenge the traditional relationship between the judiciary and the other two branches of the federal government—to emphasize the national at the expense of the federal—he certainly believed that it was his responsibility to advance the cause of liberal democracy. This is the theme of the 1938 volume of the *Public Papers,* which is subtitled "The Continuing Struggle for Liberalism." Rejecting the third-party approach of the radicals of 1934 that had been flirted with even by liberal Republicans, he sought to strengthen the liberal elements within his own party by throwing his weight in the primary elections of 1938 against candidates whom he believed had demonstrated their lack of support for the New Deal.[22]

Governor Philip La Follette's open opposition to the New Deal from April 1938, followed by the formation of the National Progressives of America, demonstrated the strength of left-of-center opposition, even though the *New Republic, Common Sense*, and *Christian Century* were doubtful of the value of third-party movements. They chose to regard the NPA as a challenge to the Democratic party to reinvigorate its own liberal philosophy. And Roosevelt later argued that this was essentially what he had been trying to do. He developed the theme of liberal democracy, explicitly rejected what later came to be known as the theory of the New Deals, and claimed that since 1933 the task of government had been not only to save the economic system but to purify it from the abuses that had brought it near to collapse. This meant restraint of the powerful minorities of concentrated power that, by 1938, had once again become uncooperative and represented a renewed threat to liberalism. He justified the bills introduced into the Seventy-fifth Congress as necessary acts to continue the work done by his first administration, designed to bring about a new equipoise between the component parts of American society, with governmental power used to restrain the powerful and uplift the weak. He explained his intervention in the 1938 primaries as a necessary function of his duty "to see to it that my party remains the truly liberal party in the political life of America," and justified his actions by the fact that a number of Democratic members of Congress had shown themselves to be out of step with the public mandate of the New Deal.[23]

The distinction he made between liberal and conservative parties was that whereas the conservative believes in private enterprise, individual initiative, and private philanthropy, the "liberal party is a party which believes that, as new conditions and problems arise beyond the power of men and women to meet as individuals, it becomes the duty of Government itself to find new remedies with which to meet them. The liberal party insists that the Government has the definite duty to use all its power and resources to meet new social problems with new social controls—to insure to the average person the right to his own economic and political life, liberty, and the pursuit of happiness." He quoted with approval Abraham Lincoln's dictum that "the legitimate object of government is to do for a community of people whatever they need to have done, but cannot do at all, or cannot do so well, for themselves, in their separate and individual capacities."[24]

He went on to articulate a theory of party duty and solidarity, emphasizing that persons elected on a liberal platform should act as liberals after election, and this led him to an apparent commitment to a new concept of ideologically based political parties: they "should not be merely Tweedledum and Tweedledee to each other." This was a view that apparently rejected the traditional American concept of party as broad-based coalitions of interests without rigorous ideological definition. In so doing he was perhaps venturing into what might have become the only truly revolutionary phase of his presidency, and was driven to suggest that restoration of "the moral integrity of democracy" against the selfish pressures of entrenched minorities required the acceptance of majority rule.[25]

At a press conference on April 21, 1938, in response to a question as to whether the South would stay "solid" very long, Roosevelt said that he thought it would but it would be a "more intelligent form of democracy." In a fireside chat on June 24 to mark the end of the Seventy-fifth Congress, he reviewed its accomplishments against the fact that it had been elected on a platform which he called "uncompromisingly liberal." Congress had in general, he believed, responded to "the devotion of the American people to a course of sane consistent liberalism" but nonetheless there was an increasing volume of interest group opposition that sought to exploit some of the mistakes made by government. Defining liberalism as belief in progressive principles of democratic and representative government, he developed an ideological view of the American two-party system, suggesting that elections could not give the country a firm sense of direction if the national parties "merely have different names but are as alike in their principles and aims as peas in the same pod." He asserted that as president he would not take part in Democratic primaries, but that as head of the Democratic party, charged with the responsibility of carrying out the platform pledges, he had "every right to speak . . . where there may be a clear issue between candidates for a Democratic nomination involving those principles, or involving a clear misuse" of his own name.[26]

In July 1938 he journeyed through Kentucky, Arkansas, Oklahoma, Texas, Colorado, and Nevada to join the USS *Houston* at San Diego for a cruise through the Panama Canal to Pensacola, Florida. This trip was used to reiterate his consistent call for a "government of constant progress along liberal lines . . . government with a soul." In Kentucky he had insisted that he had not gone to the state on a political mission, that he could only get to Oklahoma by crossing Kentucky. But, as in the forthcoming primary, Senator Alben Barkley was to be challenged by Governor Albert B., "Happy," Chandler, the president took the opportunity to refer to Barkley's devoted service to the New Deal. Support, although less enthusiastic, was given in Oklahoma to Senator Elmer Thomas. Outright electioneering on behalf of liberal candidates began at the end of his cruise. He spoke at Barnesville, Georgia, on August 11, 1938, in the presence of senators Walter George and Richard B. Russell and Governor Ed Rivers. Basing his remarks on the recent report of the Committee on Economic Conditions in the South, he insisted that action had to be taken by the federal government, and that therefore it was in the interest of the South to send legislators to Washington who accepted this. The difference between the political situation in

Kentucky and Georgia was that, whereas in the former state the senator offering himself for reelection was a committed supporter of the New Deal, in Georgia the senior senator, Walter George, could not "possibly be classified as belonging to the liberal school of thought." While emphasizing his personal friendship with George and his appreciation of the senator's sterling qualities as a man, he did not think that his voting record showed him to be someone in sympathy with the objectives of the administration. One of the other candidates, former Governor Talmadge, was also clearly opposed to many of the administration's objectives. The third candidate, U.S. Attorney Lawrence Camp, however, was a fighting liberal and therefore would have the president's vote were he entitled to vote in the state of Georgia.[27]

FDR returned to Washington and on August 16 issued a statement at his biweekly press conference, headed "Why the President "Interferes' " He was playing his customary games with his friends of the press, but the statement was seriously meant, ending with reference to Congressman John J. O'Connor of New York, a leading opponent in the House of Representatives: "Week in and week out O'Connor labors to tear down New Deal strength, pickle New Deal legislation. Why shouldn't the responsible head of the New Deal tell the people just that?" The primaries came up again in the Hyde Park press conference on August 23. On Labor Day he was speaking at Denton, Maryland, on the Eastern Shore. The themes were familiar: emphasis on community consciousness, attack on prejudice and privilege, analysis of conservativism and liberalism, reiteration of his commitment to keeping the Democratic party liberal.[28]

In an interesting and little noticed address on Constitution Day, FDR drew parallels between the antifederalists of 1788 and those with whom he was out of favor in 1938. He called the greatest men those "who have sought to make the Constitution workable in the face of the new problems and conditions that have faced the American Nation from year to year."[29]

There was certainly nothing covert about the president's position. He was fully prepared to state his views before the widest possible audience and devoted the whole of his fireside chat of November 4 to the issue, later giving it the title "The Fight for Social Justice and Economic Democracy . . . Is a Long, Weary, Uphill Struggle." Speaking from Hyde Park, where he had gone to await the election returns, he reminded people of the need for "continuous liberal government to provide a system that would efficiently and smoothly provide for the distribution of national resources and serve the welfare and happiness of the American people" in a community that was interdependent. Committing himself to a continuing fight for social justice and economic democracy, he called for the election of experienced liberals. He had only limited success within his own party and, furthermore, the 1938 elections marked a resurgence for the Republicans; the GOP picked up eighty-one seats in the House, eight in the Senate, and a net total of thirteen governorships.[30]

This man, whom Rosenman had called in 1932 a "confirmed and relentless liberal," who had boasted to Rexford Guy Tugwell that by the end of his period in office he would leave behind, if not a Democratic party then at least a progressive party, had not been successful in making his party truly the "party of liberal thought" that he had dreamed of in his 1932 acceptance speech. Its achievements had been substantial, and its legislative record had transformed the nature of the American polity for decades to come, but the strength of traditional forces within the Democratic party and the historic nature of the federal system had defeated his attempt to reconstruct party politics. There was, however, something splendid in his attempt to redefine the center of the American political spectrum, to produce a political philosophy that would serve the needs of the nation and generate a body of legislation that would guarantee individual human rights in the context of an interdependent society. It was no bad thing to be a "doctrinaire of the center" in a world that was experiencing the rise of Stalinism, fascism, and military totalitarianism.[31]

NOTES

1. Quotations from George Wolfskill and John A. Hudson, *All but the People: Franklin D. Roosevelt and His Critics 1933–39* (New York, 1969). See also George Wolfskill, *Happy Days Are Here Again* (Hinsdale, Ill. 1974), pp. 81ff.; James V. Compton, *The Swastika and the Eagle* (Boston, 1969).

2. Barton J. Bernstein, "The New Deal, the Conservative Achievements of Liberal Reform," in Barton J. Bernstein, ed., *Towards a New Past* (New York, 1967); Basil Rauch, *The History of the New Deal 1933–1938* (New York, 1944). See also, e.g., James MacGregor Burns, *Roosevelt: The Lion and the Fox* (New York, 1956); Arthur M. Schlesinger, Jr., *The Age of Roosevelt*, 3 vols. (Boston, 1957–1960); Frank Freidel, *The New Deal in Historical Perspective* (Washington, D.C., 1965); Richard Kirkendall, "The New Deal as Watershed: The Recent Literature," *Journal of American History* 54 (March 1968); William H. Wilson, "The Two New Deals: A Valid Concept?" *The Historian* 28 (February 1966); Otis L. Graham, Jr., "Historians and the New Deals, 1944–1960," *Social Studies* 54 (April 1963); William E. Leuchtenburg, *Franklin D. Roosevelt and the New Deal 1932–1940* (New York, 1963).

3. Louis Hartz, *The Liberal Tradition in American* (New York, 1955), pp. 7–8, 11, 265; FDR First Inaugural Address, in Samuel I. Rosenman, comp., *The Public Papers and Addresses of Franklin D. Roosevelt*, 13 vols. (New York, 1941–1948) (hereafter cited as PPA), 1933, p. 12; John Kenneth Galbraith, *The Great Crash* (New York, 1954); FDR Press Conference, April 19, 1933, *PPA 1933*, p. 139; see the discussion in Arthur M. Schlesinger, Jr., *The Coming of the New Deal* (Boston, 1959), pp. 193–94. Frances Perkins records that "Roosevelt's mentality was not intellectual in the sense in which the word is ordinarily used. He was a man of high intelligence, but he used *all* his faculties when he was thinking about a subject. He did not enjoy the intellectual process for its own sake as many educated, and perhaps overeducated, men do." Frances Perkins; *The Roosevelt I Knew* (New York, 1946), p. 153.

4. *PPA 1933*, p. 295; "The Country Needs, the Country Demands Bold, Persistent Experimentation," address at Oglethorpe University, May 22, 1932, *PPA 1928–1932*, p. 646. FDR reiterates his belief in the coherence of the one hundred days in *On Our Way* (New York, 1934), pp. 34–36; see D. K. Adams, *Franklin D. Roosevelt and the*

New Deal (London, 1979), pp. 34–35; Richberg is cited in James Holt, "The New Deal and the Anti-Statist Tradition," in John Braeman, Robert H. Bremner, and David Brody, eds., *The New Deal*, 2 vols. (Columbus, Ohio, 1975), 1:28.

5. W. C. Benton to FDR, December 10, 1934, OF1663, FDR Library, Hyde Park, N.Y.; Donald R. McCoy, *Angry Voices: Left of Center Politics in the New Deal Era* (Lawrence, Kans., 1958), pp. 15, 37–38, 55, 60, 80–81. See FDR's comments on the direction of the New Deal in Roosevelt, *On Our Way;* Landon's statement is cited in Holt, "The New Deal," p. 28; FDR to James A. Edgerton, December 12, 1924, cited in Frank Freidel, *Franklin D. Roosevelt; The Ordeal* (Boston, 1954), p. 204. Frisch also believes that the New Deal assumed the viability of a middle course; see Morton J. Frisch; *Franklin D. Roosevelt: The Contribution of the New Deal to American Political Thought and Practice* (Boston, 1975), p. 45. On the defection of many intellectuals, who wanted a pervasive commitment to ideological reform, see Arthur M. Schlesinger, Jr., "Sources of the New Deal," in Schlesinger and Morton White, eds., *Paths of American Thought* (New York, 1963). John Dewey's disquiet was expressed in *Liberalism and Social Action* (New York, 1935).

6. Arthur M. Schlesinger, Jr., *The Vital Center: The Politics of Freedom* (Boston, 1949), pp. vii–viii.

7. Ibid., p. 245. Schlesinger's assertion that democracy *is* liberalism raises profound questions beyond the scope of this chapter, for it seems to suggest an emphasis on political mechanisms rather than political values, and to dilute the role of leadership. When, in *The Good Society* (New York 1937), Walter Lippmann expressed concern about some of the directions of the New Deal, Max Lerner pointed to the difficulty of equating liberalism with democracy, and suggested that Lippmann and others subscribed to "minority-rights liberalism" rather than political democracy and majoritarian rule. See Arthur A. Ekirch, *Ideologies and Utopias: The Impact of the New Deal on American Thought* (Chicago, 1969), pp. 203–4.

8. Schlesinger, *The Vital Center*, p. viii.

9. See the foreword to the revised English edition (London, 1970).

10. Schlesinger, *The Vital Center* (Boston ed.), pp. 26–34. See also Joseph A. Schumpeter, *Capitalism, Socialism and Democracy* (New York, 1947); A. A. Berle and G. C. Means, *The Modern Corporation and Private Property* (New York, 1932); C. R. Van Hise, *Concentration and Control* (New York, 1912).

11. Schlesinger, *The Vital Center*, pp. 38, 171, 176. For the debate on the New Deal and progressivism see Richard Hofstadter, *The Age of Reform* (New York, 1955), and Hofstadter, *The American Political Tradition* (New York, 1948); Otis L. Graham, *Encore for Reform* (New York 1967). Frisch discusses Hofstadter's views in *Franklin D. Roosevelt*, Appendix One; see also FDR's Jefferson Day Dinner address, St. Paul, Minn., April 18, 1932: "A Concert of Action, Based on a Fair and Just Concert of Interests," *PPA 1928–1932*, pp. 627–39.

12. Daniel Roper, secretary of commerce, reflected similar views when he said that the role of the federal government was not one of dictation, but of coordinating, guiding, and stimulating "all to wisely help themselves"; cited by Holt, "The New Deal," p.34.

13. FDR message of August 31, 1931, *PPA 1928–1932*, pp. 457–58. Morton Frisch aptly cites Locke's words in the *Second Treatise on Government*, Chapter 6, para. 57: "Freedom is not, as we are told, a liberty for every man to do what he lists (for who could be free when every other man's humour might domineer over him?), but a liberty to dispose, and order as he lists, his person, actions, possessions, and his whole property,

within the allowance of those laws under which he is, and therein not to be subject to the arbitrary will of another, but freely follow his own," Quoted in Frisch, *Franklin D. Roosevelt*, p. 30.

14. FDR speech to the People's Forum, Troy, N.Y., March 3, 1912, in Basil Rauch, ed., *Franklin D. Roosevelt, Selected Speeches, Messages, Press Conferences and Letters* (New York, 1957), pp. 12–16. Freidel comments that this speech was "almost a unique effort and it is of particular interest because it sums up his thinking as a progressive before the First World War," Frank Freidel, *Franklin D. Roosevelt: The Apprenticeship* (Boston, 1952), p. 132. FDR frequently reverted to this theme; see Radio Address to the Young Democratic Clubs of America, August 24, 1935, *PPA 1935*, pp. 336–44. In *The Promise of American Life* (New York, 1909; repr. 1963) Herbert Croly phrased similar thoughts, for example, "the interest of the community should be dominant," p. 202; and also: "society is organized politically for the benefit of all the people," p. 180.

15. FDR speech of July 28, 1928; see Adams, *Franklin D. Roosevelt*, p. 15; "Memorandum on Leadership," July 6, 1928, FDR Papers Relating to Family Business and Personal Affairs, Gp. 14, Box 110, FDR Library. Roper phrased a similar thought in 1935 when he referred to adjustment "from the individualistic era of the past to the interrelated, coordinated era in which we are now living"; cited in Holt, "The New Deal," p. 36.

16. FDR acceptance speech, July 2, 1932, *PPA 1928–1932*, p. 657; FDR Oglethorpe University speech, May 22, 1932, *PPA 1928–1932*, p. 646; see also the address on progressive government, Commonwealth Club of San Francisco, September 23, 1932, *PPA 1928–1932*, pp. 742–56; Theodore Roosevelt, *Works*, National ed., 20 vols. (New York, 1920), 17:22.

17. Croly, *The Promise of American Life*, pp. 22, 154, 167–171, 180–85, 257–64 275.

18. Henry Steele Commager, *The American Mind* (New Haven, 1950), p. 208, cites Lester Ward's address to the International Congress of Sociology, in which he stated that collectivism and individualism "are not opposites but concomitants. . . . Every step in the direction of a true collectivism has been and must be a step in the direction of true individualism." See also William James, *Pragmatism: A New Name for Some Old Ways of Thinking* (New York, 1907); Commager, *The American Mind*, pp. 91–97; Merle Curti, *The Growth of American Thought* (New York, 1943), pp. 560–66.

19. John Dewey; *Human Nature and Conduct: An Introduction to Social Psychology* (New York, 1922). FDR messages of January 14, 1937, *PPA 1936*, p. 685; address on receiving an award for Distinguished Service in the Interest of Agriculture, December 9, 1935, *PPA 1935*, p. 490; Commonwealth Club speech, *PPA 1928–1932*, p. 755.

20. James D. Richardson, *A Compilation of the Messages and Papers of the Presidents, 1789–1897*, 10 vols. (Washington, D.C., 1896–1899), 2:311.

21. Commager, *The American Mind*, pp. 374–390.

22. *PPA 1938, Introduction*, pp. xxi–xxxiii. Senator Lynn J. Frazier of North Dakota, a Republican, had stated in a speech in October 1934 that "a third party in America is not only necessary, it is inevitable, if the Republican and Democratic parties continue to be dominated by reactionaries," a view that was echoed by Fiorello LaGuardia. See McCoy, *Angry Voices*, p. 52.

23. McCoy, *Angry Voices*, 158–83; *PPA 1938, Introduction*, pp. xxi–xxxiii.

24. *PPA 1938, Introduction*, pp. xxix–xxx; at San Diego, in October 1935, FDR had recognized the need for government to adapt to changing conditions: "Democracy is not

a static thing. It is an everlasting march,'' *PPA 1935*, p. 405. He had used the Lincoln quotation in an address at Marietta, Ohio, July 8, 1938, *PPA 1938*, p. 429.

25. *PPA 1938, Introduction*, p. xxxii; "We in Turn Are Striving to Uphold the Integrity of the Morals of Our Democracy," Jackson Day Dinner address, Washington, D.C., January 8, 1938, *PPA 1938*, pp. 37–45. It is clear that FDR always had faith in the innate common sense of the electorate if choices were clearly presented to it, and believed that the general welfare could best be sustained by democratic processes. This did not absolve national leaders from the obligation to lead, and he was prepared to accept it, just as he tried to educate the people through his fireside chats. A major theme of the annual address of 1936 had been the concern of democratic nations to prevent the rise of autocratic institutions and keep power within the control of the people. The government was both "the representative and the trustee of the public interest." As such it intended "to build upon essentially democratic institutions, seeking all the while the adjustment of burdens, the help of the needy, the protection of the weak, the liberation of the exploited and the genuine protection of the people's property . . . [public power] in the hands of a people's Government . . . is wholesome and proper. But in the hands of political puppets of an economic autocracy such power would provide shackles for the liberties of the people."*PPA 1936*, pp. 13, 16. Cf. FDR, *Looking Forward* (New York, 1953): "perhaps the greatest duty of statesmanship is to educate," cited in Tugwell, *In Search of Roosevelt* (Cambridge, Mass., 1972), p. 115.

26. *PPA 1938*, pp. 264, 391–400.

27. Address at Oklahoma City, July 9, 1938, *PPA 1938*, p. 445; address at Covington, Kentucky, July 8, 1938, ibid., pp. 423–29; address at Barnesville, Georgia, August 11, 1938, ibid., pp. 463–71. See also FDR's remarks at Greenville, South Carolina, August 11, 1938, ibid., pp. 476–77.

28. Ibid., pp. 487–90, 499–501, 512–20.

29. Ibid., pp. 527–28.

30. Ibid., pp. 584–93. A few days earlier FDR had commented on "Liberalism and Reaction in the California Political Campaign," letter to George Creel, October 31, 1938, ibid., pp. 570–72. See also Leuchtenburg, *Franklin D. Roosevelt*, p. 271.

31. Samuel I. Rosenman, *Working with Roosevelt* (New York, 1952), p. 49; Rexford Guy Tugwell, *The Brains Trust* (New York, 1962), p. 411; *PPA 1928–1932*, p. 650; Bernstein, "The New Deal," p. 276. Adolph Berle commented that "in a world in which revolutions just now are coming easily the New Deal chose the more difficult course of moderation and rebuilding." Cited in Schlesinger, "Sources of the New Deal," p. 389. John Dizikes concludes his study of *Britain, Roosevelt and the New Deal: British Opinion 1932–38* (New York, 1979), p. 310, with the comment: "Franklin Roosevelt possessed to a supreme degree the quality Dr. Johnson admired in Chatham: 'the faculty of putting the State in motion.' " For a contemporary New Deal attempt to distinguish between individualism and rugged individualism, and to analyze concepts of liberty in the context of an evolving democratic system, see Harold L. Ickes, *The New Democrary* (New York, 1934).

8

The Paradox of the New Deal: Political Success and Economic Failure

Raymond S. Franklin

INTRODUCTION

The basic question that I seek to answer in this chapter is why the New Deal was an economic failure. While some would disagree with that view,[1] I mean by this that the New Deal never achieved the level of employment implicitly and explicitly sought in its full recovery goals. By 1939 the "army of unemployed people stood around 9 million, . . . taking about one victim of five who were willing to work."[2] As a matter of fact, the unemployment rate remained above 10 percent up to 1941.[3] My explanation for its failure is developed in the form of a paradox: the New Deal's economic failure was related to its political success—winning elections, establishing and maintaining a coalition of divergent and incompatible interest groups, and preserving the social order at a time when many were questioning its efficacy. The elaboration of this paradox serves to cast light on the democratic capitalist state's inability to innovate effective economic policies in periods of profound crisis.

THE NEW DEAL

For the purposes of establishing a common frame of reference, a brief sketch of what is generally meant by the New Deal is in order. In most general terms, the coming of the New Deal subsumes those categories of change in which the laissez-faire state gave way to the fiscal state on the one hand, and the regulatory state on the other. The former involved compensatory government spending on an accelerated scale, and the latter involved legislative efforts to control or harness privately owned industries for the purpose of achieving some politically conceived notion of national well-being. The New Deal also involved steps to establish the security state, which led to a variety of collective insurance schemes for farmers, workers, and the aged.

These new functions (fiscal, regulatory, and security) in retrospect represented efforts to develop a more centralized state bureaucracy, an administrative infrastructure with national economic pretensions and functions more appropriate to a modern, industrially concentrated twentieth-century economy. It meant, conversely, a decline in local administrative power which proved increasingly inadequate relative to the scale of modern industry. In view of the fact that a significant portion of the contours of the 1930 economy had been established by the 1890s, the New Deal was a political development long overdue. But it is sometimes forgotten that this development, which was born in the 1930s and spread dramatically during and after World War II, was received with trepidation, partly because it was not succeeding in economic terms and partly because it was perceived even by some Keynesians themselves as a state of affairs that would terminate "political democracy" and its assumed prerequisite, "the automatic price system."[4]

As the decade of the 1930s came to an end, a fear emerged that only a war-oriented economy could bring about full recovery. This predisposition was articulated by none other than J. M. Keynes when he wrote in 1940: "It seems politically impossible for a capitalist democracy to organize expenditures on a scale necessary to make the grand experiment which would prove my case—except in war conditions."[5] In this instance, we know that Keynes was right. It was warfare expenditures—not welfare ones—that succeeded in accomplishing in a few years what the New Deal had failed to achieve in a period of seven. Planned war deficits were generated to the tune of nearly $50 billion annually. Such deficits, however, did not prove the logic of Keynesian policies, as many Keynesians have suggested, even though the deficits achieved full employment. Given the size of the undertaking, what the huge deficits proved was that they could do the job if they were accompanied by bureaucratic price and wage controls, rationing, and other planning devices, in order to prevent runaway inflation. To these planning mechanisms must be added the ideological and political hegemony achieved through wartime patriotism necessary to fight against the external enemies of democracy. Such developments are not, of course, the same as the pure Keynesian peacetime vision of deficits that "automatically" liquidated themselves through the creation of budgetary surpluses as recoveries reached their peak. The Keynesian strategies, when applied with a vengeance, tend to require a degree of state intervention, control, and consensus that is far removed from illustrations that appeared in many textbooks in the fifties and early sixties.

THEORIES OF THE NEW DEAL'S ECONOMIC FAILURE

Since the general validity of my thesis, i.e., that political success is critical to the understanding of the New Deal's inability to forge viable full employment policies, acquires its coherence through a contrast with the more limited causal analyses developed by others, I have chosen first to discuss a number of other explanations that have been put forward to account for the New Deal's economic failure. This is further necessitated by the fact that aspects of these more limited explanations represent evidence that supports my more encompassing political reasoning, especially as it relates to the incapacity of the democratic state to overcome forces unleashed in the Depression with viable rescue policies.

1. Almost all major works on the New Deal devote, to one degree or another, attention to Roosevelt's personality, his style, his orchestration of the political process. For example, Paul K. Conkin argues that the

New Deal was an exceedingly personal enterprise. Its disparate programs were unified only by the personality of Franklin D. Roosevelt. Every characterization, every evaluation of the governmental innovations from 1933 to 1938 terminates and often flounders in this personality. . . . Roosevelt's vague goals restricted the possible and excluded many expedients. . . . He never had the ability to bring unity or rational order to his own actions or to governmental programs. . . . The end result was to be a failure to attain . . . recovery.[6]

2. From the perspective of some leftists, the New Deal is seen as a demagogic movement that sought primarily to rescue capitalism as it simultaneously appealed to dissident groups. This twin process involved making deals with the vital elements of a faltering business class, while generating reformlike proposals that derailed the energies of the working class from concerning itself with more basic changes.[7] A less complex variation of the left position argues that the New Deal was simply one possible form of "capitalist domination."[8] In the final analysis, the New Deal was constrained by the business company with which it was associated.

3. Assimilating what was viewed as "typical" of business fears about the New Deal,[9] Joseph Schumpeter, a conservative, argued along lines almost opposite to those of leftists. The New Deal policies, given their reform tone and vacillating character, negatively affected the investment climate. New Deal meddling in general, and its specific intrusions into the domain of private utility operations in the form of the TVA and the Public Utilities Holding Company Act, further demoralized an already uncertain and pessimistic business class. In other words, the New Deal generally discouraged private investment and thereby contributed to stagnation.[10] Implicit in Schumpeter's view, a *do nothing* policy would have stimulated the economy sooner than adding uncertainty via governmental policies of a reform nature.

4. Conservative businessmen worried that the New Deal was taking the country down the road to socialism. Roosevelt's oft-cited antibusiness rhetoric, especially with the launching of the Second New Deal in 1935, appeared to confirm their consternation. The New Deal's alleged confiscatory implications had to be fought because they stifled or smothered business energy. More sober businessmen expressed something that probably came closer to the truth. The business community did not want the government to be responsible for achieving and

maintaining full employment through *useful* and needed job development programs. The New Deal had to be restricted in this respect. "Relief" programs were another matter and were in fact preferred.[11]

The business view, when reinterpreted for our immediate purposes, implies that the New Deal failed because the business community severely limited the expansion of *productive* governmental activity. This interpretation, it should be noted, is consistent with the general Marxian position, as well as with that of the conservative Herbert Stein, who observed that business did not oppose deficits when they involved decreasing taxes, but only when they involved increasing government spending.[12]

5. Kenneth Boulding, a highly respected maverick of the economic profession, picked up some of the reasoning characteristic of many trust-busters in the New Deal. The basic argument here is that the New Deal could not get the country out of the Depression because it could not overcome the rigidity in the price system associated with concentrated economic power. The market structure, dominated by large-scale organizations, "makes prices and money wages more 'sticky' and less flexible than they otherwise [would] have been." This means that decreases in national money income necessarily will "be taken out in the form of reductions in output and employment."[13] The New Dealers put the case in slightly different terms. Since price "stickiness" tends to be in the downward direction but not in the upward one, it undermines purchasing power, and therefore effective demand for goods and services relative to the potential supply; price rigidity produces a permanent imbalance between consumption and production.[14] Unlike the New Deal trust-busting types, Boulding argued that "organization-busting is neither practicable nor desirable."[15] His main "solution" in retrospect revolved about Keynesian monetary expansion through governmental deficits.

6. Keynes himself put a great deal of emphasis on the inability of state officials to understand his views about fiscal and monetary management. What was lacking was Keynesian knowledge. Basically, his argument was that the system needed big fiscal deficits and the willingness of monetary authorities to push down the long-term interest rate so that it remained below the marginal efficiency of investment. Keynes shied away from attacking the institutional fabric of private markets or business enterprises, although on occasion he belatedly contemplated the value of socializing the investment decision. More generally, Keynes viewed businessmen as fragile souls; too much tinkering with their interests would change their confidence and therefore negatively affect their investment schedules. Most Keynesians put a great deal of stress on the absence of Keynesian wisdom in interpreting the New Deal's failure. As a matter of fact, the nature of the New Deal's economic ignorance to explain its failure is employed almost as an axiom that requires little elaboration.[16] The same Rooseveltian quotes about the virtues of balancing the budget are employed repetitiously to "prove" that Roosevelt did not understand deficit spending.

While each of the above interpretations may have some validity in specific terms, they do not add up to a meaningful whole or catch the spirit of the New Deal's evolution. The left position suggests that the state was so closely tied to the business system that it proved incapable of transcending the very crisis which was inherent in that system itself. The state was therefore used by the capitalist class to mollify working-class antagonism until the crisis was over.

In contrast, Schumpeter's position tended to emphasize the "success" of the New Deal in actually using the state against the business system's interests. Thus, the New Deal managers of the state tended to prevent business energy from working or recovering sufficiently to bring the country out of the doldrums.

The business view of its own failure is a peculiar "synthesis" of both the left and Schumpeter's position. On the one hand, the successful reform capacities of the New Deal worsened business confidence; on the other, the business class "admittedly" proved sufficiently powerful to prevent the state from being used productively and in excessively threatening ways. This kept the state from achieving a recovery that would have bypassed the business system and its interests.

Using Roosevelt's personality as a limiting factor seems to avoid some serious questions. It avoids coping with the structural boundaries, especially in the political arena, which operated to limit Roosevelt's understanding of what had to be done. In my view, Roosevelt's requirements for political success were not consonant with effective economic policies.

The New Deal's inability to overcome the pricing policies of oligopolies, either through regulation (which some New Dealers advocated) or through trust-busting (which others wanted), is consistent with the left position. In the latter perspective, the New Deal was viewed as an instrument, in one form or another, of private enterprise. Its limits were the limits inherent in the system. In the price-rigidity barrier argument, the New Deal was an insufficiently strong protagonist of the giant corporations that dominated the business system. The New Dealers tried but failed.

Finally, the lack-of-knowledge assumption implies that the state was potentially capable of rational actions if only its administrators had listened to Keynesian advisors; if they had Keynesian intelligence. The limitations of putting the failure question in this form are illustrated by the opposing statements made by two relatively conservative economists in their reflections on the knowledge that prevailed among New Dealers. One cynically suggested that the Depression "would not have been so severe as it was, or lasted as long as it did, if there had been no economists around at all. The problem was so clear-cut, the solution so apparent that one had to be [an academic economist] not to see it."[17] The other, in a more serious vein, suggested that knowledge would have made a difference but Roosevelt unfortunately "did not consult the most eminent economic specialists, . . . nor did he directly use the main orthodox means of influencing the general level of business."[18] In substance, one professional reflection about the New Deal's economic failure suggests that it was tragic to have used the knowledge possessed by experts; the other suggests that the available experts with the most knowledge were not consulted, thereby needlessly prolonging the Depression. The knowledge emphasis, in my judgment, is simply an unproductive line of inquiry.

In sum, none of the above positions does justice to the complex and contradictory reasons why the New Deal was an economic failure. Each explanation contains an element of truth; none stands as a reasonably valid generalization. The main reason for this, in my judgment, has to do with an inadequate understanding of how the democratic political processes that determine the functioning of the state diverge from the private market processes that determine the functioning of the economy. Political success does not necessarily require or presume comparable accomplishments in the economic sphere. This dichotomy represents, in different forms, the core of our success/failure paradox.

FAILURE AS FUNCTION OF SUCCESS

Political success required achieving a considerable degree of consensus about the Democratic party as an instrument of salvation. This is not to be confused with achieving general agreement about specific programs and general goals. Consensus and the means employed to achieve it forced continuous compromises in economic policies that made them relatively ineffective. The political genius that is identified with Roosevelt was not related to his thought, his vision, or his substantive understanding of the world; it concerned his ability to orchestrate a discordant collage of interests in the political arena.[19] Thus, insofar as Roosevelt's personality was important, it was his ability to keep people of divergent interests and persuasions attached to the political system, involved in its operation and modification. He managed to build up trust through personal charm, wit, candidness, and warmth among a variety of publics, even among those with whom he fought. His personality emerged as an important social symbol.[20]

The American "climate of opinion" reflected conditions that involved many contradictions: it accepted big business for its alleged efficiency and wanted it controlled for its abuses. By developing unenforceable codes of regulation and agencies involving indirect controls where interstate commerce was the concern, the Roosevelt administration preserved bigness and convinced the public that it was checking big business's abuses. Regulation, which many Americans wanted, required a more centralized state bureaucracy, but aroused trepidation because it carried with it a possible loss of personal freedom and liberty. Centralization of government also involved bypassing local government, an institutional arrangement that likewise was cherished.[21] Thus Roosevelt advocated competition, and not infrequently sang the praises of the forgotten man and the little farmer; he also provided reasonable degrees of political autonomy to "local" politicians who needed to deviate from the national "line" in order to win elections. In essence, Roosevelt adroitly managed and orchestrated the symbols that reflected the above contradictions in ways that were consonant with the moods of the time, in ways that had precedent and were intimate and seemingly fair to a wide cross-section of the public. By dispensing a flow of marginal innovations in divergent directions that appeared just, the process sustained a broad coalition of interest groups in the political sphere without paying the price of the contradictions taking place in economic policies.

In more organizational terms, the New Deal, functioning through the Democratic party, gave enhanced political opportunities to organized labor, intellectuals, and professionals—groups that would have become more radicalized in the absence of such opportunities. This was accomplished partly by widening the party's appeal so as to reach hitherto unsolicited portions of the population (e.g., the acquisition of the black vote) and partly through the proliferation of agencies created by the New Deal to meet its diverse and contradictory purposes. With respect to this latter process, it has been observed:

Roosevelt's very failure to pursue one coherent program allowed a greater variety of fascinating people to enter the government service. Among them were the social workers and do-gooders, a few from the academies, but most from labor unions, welfare agencies, newspapers, and architectural firms.[22]

Moreover, the heads of these agencies were given considerable freedom to fashion their own particular plans.[23]

Thus the Democratic party through a variety of means became a populist party led by a populist leader who had patrician origins. People had a feeling that they could get Roosevelt's ear if they got enough petitions signed or organized a sufficiently large demonstration or argued well for a good cause. When the dust finally settled, the Democratic party not only brought new groups into its fold, but managed to extend its reach to include farmers, southern bourbons, liberal reformers, and white ethnics. It was not even void of some big business supporters, business press rhetoric to the contrary. While this coalition of unnatural allies involved much political cockfighting and petty jealousy, Roosevelt and his New Deal cohorts managed to keep it together and "working as a team . . . [making] everyone [feel] at the very center of things."[24] The heterogeneity of this political coalition and the processes that determined its influence had their economic drawbacks. When it came time to forge decisive economic measures, delays, compromises, and contradictory policies prevented the development of a coherent economic package in aggregate terms.

LEGISLATIVE EVIDENCE

A brief examination of some specific legislative acts may serve to illustrate the way by which the economic teeth of policies were blunted or neutralized because of political considerations.

1. The Fair Labor Standards Act of 1938 (Wages and Hours Act) illustrates how the necessity of achieving political compromises completely diluted the

bill's intended economic consequences. The Wages and Hours Act was aimed at establishing a floor for wages and a ceiling on the maximum hours that could be worked per week. The minimum wage was to begin at twenty-five cents per hour and be increased ultimately to forty cents per hour over the next seven years. Maximum hours per week were scheduled to decrease from forty-four to forty over a three-year period. Other matters involving child labor and who was to be covered by the act were specified. The passage of this piece of legislation involved a bitter fight within labor and between labor and capital, between regions and within regions. "In effect, Northern urban liberals, . . . reformers and large, mature corporations 'favored the bill.' Entrenched labor unions, struggling small business, farmers, and the South opposed it,"[25] although southerners like Hugo Black and Claude Pepper supported the bill.[26] It was finally passed in June 1938, but "was trimmed by amendment or limited by the necessity of basing it on the interstate commerce clause. The very laborers who most needed its protection— local extractors, agriculture, domestic, small retail—were excluded. The largest beneficiaries . . . were Southern factory workers."[27]

The act in general has been judged as being highly unsatisfactory. "So many exemptions had been written into the measure that at one point Representative Martin Dies filed a satirical amendment: 'Within 90 days after appointment of the administrator, she shall report to Congress whether anyone is subject to this bill.' "[28] In addition to the exemption question, there is the fact that the marginal uplift the bill may have given to some was probably offset by producing unemployment for others.

2. Not all the New Deal legislation necessarily was confronted to the same degree by conflicting political forces. But even when it was not, safeguard measures were not infrequently built into the legislation to mollify potential opposition. The Social Security Act of 1935 is a good example of this phenomenon. First, it should be noted, the Social Security Act was part of a cluster of legislative proposals that marked, as we have suggested, the beginning of the Second New Deal. Second, the memory of the disastrous NRA, which had been destroyed by the Supreme Court, was still fresh in the minds of many New Dealers. When the Social Security Act was thus proposed, in no small part to derail the followers of Dr. Francis Townsend,[29] the act had built into it a regressive payroll tax which has been interpreted as one of the main reasons for the 1937 downturn. The law also, it should be noted parenthetically, "denied coverage to numerous classes of workers, including those who needed security most: notably farm laborers and domestics. Sickness, in normal times the main cause of joblessness, was disregarded. . . . In many respects, the law was an astonishingly inept and conservative piece of legislation."[30] In any event, to return to our main concern, why was this landmark piece of legislation which established social rights for the individual so poorly designed with regard to the nature of its funding? Was it ignorance or a case of insufficient economic advice?

Frances Perkins (secretary of labor) and Rexford Tugwell (an important advisor) both argued at the time that a regressive payroll tax was not a good method to finance Social Security for the aged. Some time later, Roosevelt remarked that he knew it was bad economics, but that such economics is often necessary to safeguard reforms in the political arena:

Those [Social Security taxes], were never a problem of economics. They are politics all the way through. We put those payroll contributions there so as to give the contributors a legal, moral and political right to collect their pensions and unemployment benefits. With those taxes in there, no damn politician can ever scrap my social security program.[31]

3. In response to demagogic movements advocating wealth-sharing, led by Senator Huey Long and Father Charles E. Coughlin, the revenue acts of 1935 and 1936 were passed. While motivated to redistribute income, discourage corporate saving, increase consumer demand, and decrease the power of large corporations, they accomplished little, if anything, in these directions.[32] From the initial proposals to their final passage, the acts were so emasculated that one might conclude that the American people had little interest in more equity, increasing aggregate demand, or "soaking" the rich.

4. The Muscle Shoals–Tennessee Valley Development Act (1933), which created the Tennessee Valley Authority, again suggests how the necessity of political mollification weakened the hopes of the regional planning that was part of the act's original design. The TVA had a combination of objectives: cheap power, flood control, economic development, rehabilitation of dying communities, experiment in public planning to enhance competition with the private power trust, and the establishment of self-sufficient rural-based communities.[33] The TVA was supported by farmers and small businesses in the Mississippi Valley, and, of course, by left-wing New Dealers who saw it as the first major experiment in social planning. It was bitterly opposed by large corporations and by private utility companies that argued from the beginning that the market was already saturated with an adequate supply of power. Initially, some politicians attacked it as being "patterned closely after one of the Soviet dreams," and the *New York Times* viewed it as a "Congressional folly."[34]

In the course of its history, it ran into many barriers. As a result of a suit brought against it by the Commonwealth of Southern Corporation, "the TVA found itself stymied in efforts to acquire distribution facilities and expand operations. Efforts to exclude TVA-type activities from expanding into other regions met a complete impasse and were eventually dropped."[35]

Perhaps more important, the TVA was forced to retreat from a number of its earlier goals as a result of political pressures and the need to compromise. The efforts to widen the base of its planning processes, for example, created the need for a political bargain that David Lilienthal had to make with Harcourt Morgan, the TVA's first director. In order to "neutralize opposition to public power, TVA's farm program had to acquiesce to the interests of the more prosperous white planters."[36] Reflecting on the TVA years later, Rexford Tugwell stated,

"The TVA is more an example of democracy in retreat than democracy on the march."[37]

5. The New Deal's economic policies not only zig-zagged over time as a result of changes in political moods, but particular policies had built into them conflicting interests at specific moments in time. Dominant and subordinate themes, regardless of logic, were necessitated in order to placate or nurture cooperation among hostile segments of the public.

The NRA, for example, was generally conceived as an instrument for planning and establishing collusive industry arrangements to contrive scarcity and stabilize prices (stop the forces of deflation). It was supported by big business, which favored the NRA's objective to promote a "cartelized, risk-free economic order."[38] Some saw in the NRA a humanizing design to prevent "cut-throat" competition that "resulted in drastic wage reductions, declining quality, reckless waste of natural resources."[39] To labor, it appeared as a "means of raising wage rates, spreading work, abolishing child labor, and promoting trade unions."[40] The NRA enabled independent retailers to peg prices so as to "remove the competitive advantages of the chain stores."[41] In general, the NRA found favor among workers and national economic planners.[42] Lastly, it had the formal support of such organizations as the Chamber of Commerce, the National Association of Manufacturers, and the American Bar Association—all of which favored the relaxation of the antitrust laws "so as to allow employers to enter into voluntary trade association agreements."[43]

While the supporters of the NRA represented a broad spectrum, there was opposition. It mainly came from "antitrusters and small business liberals, men who stressed the evils of monopoly and were reluctant to abandon the competitive tradition [and some consumer groups]."[44]

The economic success of the NRA required the cooperation of numerous groups that lacked common interests. Once the crisis dimensions that appeared to generate the necessity of the NRA passed, "some business leaders began to have serious misgivings; and there was a noticeable decline in their willingness to cooperate, either with the government, the unions, or their business colleagues."[45] The final demise of the NRA was, as we have noted, declared by the Supreme Court in 1935. Its malfunctioning was observed long before. No doubt its failure was related to a number of factors; not least was the one of internal conflict, which was inevitable because of the *political need to include the participants of incongruous interest groups*. Each group initially sensed that the NRA provided an immediate change for economic betterment. While the NRA may have temporarily served a salutory political function, it was an economic disaster.

6. Finally, as the New Deal was approaching its final hour, its directors could not make up their minds whether to accelerate its antitrust policies, return to its early planning and regulation policies, devise more intermediate efforts at control, or pursue compensatory spending. Under circumstances of a stalemate, the

proper "solution" is to establish an "expert commission, which studies the question and often ends by representing the same internal conflicts that led to its creation."[46] The Temporary National Economic Committee (TNEC) was such a commission; and as Senator William Borah predicted at the time, it would "string along and finally reach the dust of the upper shelf in the form of ten or twenty volumes which few will ever consult."[47] The battle over the composition of the TNEC reflected many of the issues that led to its establishment.

Summarizing the contradictory tendencies: "The New Deal began with government sponsorship of cartels and business planning; it ended with the antitrust campaign and the attack on rigid prices; and along the way, it engaged in minor excursions into socialism, public utility regulation, and the establishment of 'government yardsticks.' "[48] In another sphere, "Roosevelt's . . . friendly attitude toward consumer cooperatives was . . . largely cancelled out by his sensitivity to protests from independent retailers."[49] The Depression produced demands to stem the ruinous tide of deflation; this led to demands for "planning, rationalization, and the creation of market controls."[50] The Depression also brought the problem of monopoly and sticky prices to the forefront; this "intensified anti-monopoly sentiment, destroyed confidence in business leadership, and produced equally insistent demands that big business be punished and competitive ideas be made good."[51] As the demand for more competition emerged, there developed a demand for more exemptions from applying the competitive rules to allegedly "sick" industries. Thus industry pleas and pressures emanating from oil, railroads, coal, and the motor carriers made their mark and avoided prosecution from the government's antitrust division.[52] Politically, all these conflicting demands had to be met. Given this fact, the New Deal "could hardly be expected to come up with an intellectually coherent and logically consistent set of business policies."[53]

The political processing of the above developments reflected struggles and pressures from a large variety of specific economic interest groups, factions within strata, as well as a more general conflict between capital and labor. If a laboratory prevailed to test the pluralistic thesis (classically defined as "the existence of multiple centers of power . . . [for the purpose of taming] power, securing the consent of all, [and settling] conflicts peacefully"),[54] the New Deal was such a laboratory. As a political formation, it reflected the circulation of many centers of power and vested interests; no particular constellation of forces appeared to dominate excessively. The power centers, moreover, changed over the decade, and therefore the New Deal served as a dynamic illustration of the entry-exit process in the political arena of what allegedly operates in more competitively structured markets. The New Deal, however exemplary of a state influenced by the processes of political pluralism, had one main shortcoming: it failed to resolve the economic crisis of the decade. The dire circumstances that mobilized the various and sundry conflicting groups into the political arena tended to undermine the political sphere's effectiveness to alter the dire economic circumstances.

When one examines the common denominator of much New Deal legislation, it illustrates how proposals, ideas, spending efforts, and policies were delayed and screened by a fractionated political network of divergent interests that sought to use the political system to meet short-run economic needs. The result was that democratic political pluralism worked to keep all kinds of groups engaged inside the Democratic party, but it diffused efforts at mobilizing the aggregate forces of the economy. For this reason, the New Deal managed to save capitalism because it failed. Its economic failure was related to its political success.

The great confusion and variety of interpretations about the meaning of the New Deal fit within the above paradigm of its dilemma. Businessmen who saw the New Deal as socialistic in direction were partially correct in the sense that the New Deal translated into political rights ("social entitlements" if you will) certain economic matters that were previously determined by market relations alone. Those Marxists and socialists who viewed the New Deal managers of the state as saviors of the system were also correct; the capitalist system was propped up and subsidized by the New Deal. The system's unfortunate rejects were supplied with economic dole rather than new avenues of reconstruction. And, finally, the majority of active New Dealers, who viewed themselves as having participated in a grand social experiment, were not totally wrong. They did have a sense of participation in a large variety of new projects which were experimental in nature and humanistic in objectives. But the quantitative dimensions of such projects were minuscule relative to the magnitude necessary to revive the economy. Their participation was real, but they inflated its consequences.

By relating the New Deal's economic failure to its political success, the complex, contradictory character of the New Deal's meandering throughout the decade is explained in a generalized way. It is a generalization, moreover, that incorporates or locates the alternative explanations.

Some social scientists have understood aspects of the meandering New Deal policies. Paul K. Conkin astutely observes:

Every New Deal reform . . . was usually a confused compromise by . . . good and bad men of power. When an ambiguous, potentially radical program did survive, or was sneaked in by executive order, it was neutralized by administrators, . . . frustrated in its day-by-day operation, or eventually destroyed or emasculated for political reasons.[55]

Ellis Hawley comes even closer to describing the conflict between economic rationality and political expediency when he states:

To condemn these policies for their inconsistency was to miss the point. From an economic standpoint, condemnation might very well be to the point. They were inconsistent. One line of action tended to cancel the other, with the result that little was accomplished. Yet from the political standpoint, this very inconsistency, so long as the dilemma persisted, was the safest method of retaining political power. President Roosevelt, it seems, never suffered politically from his reluctance to choose between planning and antitrust action. His mixed emotions so closely reflected the popular mind that they were a political asset rather than a liability.[56]

What is lacking in these interpretations is a statement in conceptual terms about the state in relation to the economy that enables "good" politics to become "bad" economics. What follows is a brief depiction of a unique aspect of the democratic capitalist society that embraces various kinds of connections between politics and the state, and between the state and the economy. The depiction will serve to define the institutional context in which the New Deal's economic failure was related to its political success.

INSTITUTIONAL WEAKNESS OF THE DEMOCRATIC CAPITALIST STATE

Lester Thurow, the well-known MIT economist, argues that the American people must acquire political consensus on the distribution of the burdens entailed in the proposed solutions to the current array of problems (energy costs, inflation, unemployment, environmental decay, and the general decline of U.S. productivity since 1965).[57] But since American society is divided into numerous interest groups, each of which already feels overburdened with its share of the costs associated with the ailing U.S. economy, the "solutions" sought are always aimed at making some other group pay. The result is a social and political stalemate, and therefore policies forthcoming through the political route are not presently possible. Yet a political solution cannot be bypassed, since the sum of the uncoordinated, short-run microeconomic decisions do not aggregate to an acceptable pattern, level, and rate of economic activity.

The 1930s and the 1980s, of course, represent decades with very different objective circumstances. Nevertheless, they both point to an institutional weakness of the democratic capitalist state which makes it more than fortuitous that coherent and consistent economic policies cannot be innovated to alter the drift of the economy. While my concern about the state is aimed at the problem raised by the economic failure of the New Deal, it is not without relevance for the present.

The theory of the state is in a mess. It is not uncommon to find reputable scholars lamenting over the fact that no school of thought has an adequate theory of state behavior.[58] Thus it would be pretentious to suggest that my efforts in this sphere can do more than raise some provocative issues and questions for the specific purposes of adding to the understanding of how the New Deal's economic failure related to its political success.

In the debate between Marxists and pluralists, the Marxists repetitiously make the point that the state is biased in favor of the dominant class or various factions of it. Or, if it is preferred, it can be said that the state functions to reproduce the stratification of class relations in a capitalist society. In addition to such general propositions, there is a lively debate among contemporary Marxists that delves into many details concerning how the state functions to maintain itself and perpetuates dominant/subordinate relations required by the system.[59] Be that as it may, the Marxian view, while an effective counterpoint to versions of the pluralist one for some purposes, fails to cast light on noncapitalist and even "socialist" states that manifest similar efforts to reproduce their social stratification and employ mechanisms similar to those used by the capitalist states. In other words, many of the attributes that Marxists designate as endemic to the capitalist state turn out, upon inspection, to be endemic to a variety of states with different modes of production. Marxists, contrary to their claims, have a general theory of the state but not one specific to democratic capitalist social orders.

To get at the structural dimension of the democratic-capitalist state that relates to our New Deal thesis, it is well to remember that

[the struggle of economic liberalism] took the form of an unremitting effort on the part of the bourgeoisie to enforce a clear-cut distinction between private and public spheres in life. The economy was assigned to the private sphere, the state to the public sphere. . . . Success in their struggle may be said to have marked the triumph of capitalism.[60]

Or as Karl Polanyi has argued in his effort at pinpointing the unique quality of the nineteenth-century self-regulating market system: capitalism requires that the economy be institutionally disembedded from the state that reflects the larger society's interests. In the process the state and the politics affecting it are reduced to a subordinate sphere relative to the economy, which is propelled by a purely economic motive.[61]

The essence of my argument revolves about the separation of those who govern in the political sphere and those who command a disproportionate amount of power in the economic one. The origin of the capitalist state, when thinking about it in conceptual terms, involves understanding the difference between a governing "class" on the one hand and a ruling "class" on the other. The former—which administrates, legislates, and adjudicates through the apparatuses of the state in behalf of society—involves *public* officials who "claim to be guardians of what is public" and have "unique access to the use of legal coercive power . . . within a given territory."[62] The ruling class in a capitalist society is in the private domain and is outside the direct public purview. Since it owns much of the means of production and is an appropriator, accumulator, and prime allocator of much of society's surplus, it possesses an inordinate amount of power that is not directly accessible to public authorities. Whatever the nature of the interaction between the public domain and the private one, there is an institutional weakness built into the capitalist state. It was precisely this weakness that was idealized by classical liberal economists in the nineteenth century and is lamented by present-day conservatives as having passed. It should be emphasized, moreover, that the more pluralistic the distribution of political power in such a state relative to private economic power, the weaker is the state's capacity to govern in the public interest relative to the business system's capacity to rule in the private one. This is, of course, the main institutional basis upon which Marxists criticize pluralists.[63]

In the course of capitalist society's evolution, especially from its heyday in the nineteenth century, the state—as a result of class and group struggles in the political sphere—has become increasingly democratized, while the economic order has remained more or less hierarchical.[64] As a result, governing power has come to reflect over the long haul—not of course without ebbs and flows—a large variety of groups other than those who represent the propertied classes. The state increasingly functions to embrace and reproduce—through its formal entitlement programs and special subsidies, as well as through the political party system that controls the state apparatus—a larger spectrum of divergent interest and status groups. But because there is a significant bifurcation between the political exigencies required of those who govern and the economic ones required of those who command the economy, the governing job of holding together its array of interest groups in the state and political sphere becomes incompatible with the kinds of policies required in the economic one, especially when the economy is in serious difficulty. The state must simultaneously yield to the democratic pressures that have widened over the years, and at the same time cater to the immediate economic needs of the business system, which involve policies competitive with maintaining political legitimacy. This is the main reason why, in a period of crisis like that of the 1930s, the state, driven by the need to sustain and enlarge its political legitimacy, can be ineffective in the economic sphere.

The New Deal represented a meandering political reform performance in the political sphere. It succeeded in democratizing national politics and enhancing the number and quality of social entitlements to the poor and less privileged classes. But the New Deal lacked a consistent majoritarian mandate; it sustained majority support by increasing political space for a large variety of particular interest groups and factions within classes, and therefore lacked the ability to develop a coherent vision and political will to affect the private economic sector, much of which was out of its control and institutionally separated from the state apparatuses. While this separation is conducive to sustaining civil rights, political freedom, and the right to dissent, since political control even by the "enemies" of capitalism does not directly threaten the position of those who command the economy, it does not serve well in periods of an economic crisis when consistent and dramatic economic policies need forging. In a bifurcated social order, what happens in the White House does not readily affect who minds the store and how it is managed. As the New Deal's House became more democratic and successful, its economic programs were not only more inconsistent, but they were often unenforceable and inconsequential in the economic sphere.

NOTES

I want to express my appreciation to Lloyd Raines, Solomon Resnik, Carl Riskin, Mark Rosenblum, Bertram Silverman, and Frank Warren for their comments on an early draft of this chapter.

1. See Carl Degler, *Out of Our Past* (New York: Harper and Row, 1959), p. 416.

2. Hans Apel, *Scenes from Our Economic Past* (Westport, Conn.: Calvin K. Kazanjian Economic Foundation, 1956), p. 43.

3. R. A. Gordon, *Economic Instability and Growth: The American Record* (New York: Harper and Row, 1974), p. 77.

4. Alvin Hansen, "Economic Progress and Declining Population," in American Economic Association, *Readings in Business Cycle Theory* (Philadelphia: Blakiston Co., 1944), p. 387.

5. J. M. Keynes, "The United States and the Keynes Plan," *The New Republic,* vol. 103 (July 29, 1940): 158.

6. Paul K. Conkin, *The New Deal* (New York: Thomas Y. Crowell Co., 1967), pp. 1, 14, 23.

7. See Rick Hurd, "New Deal Policy and the Containment of Radical Union Activity," *Review of Radical Political Economics* 8, No. 3 (Fall 1976): 32, 38.

8. Maurizio Vandagna, "The New Deal and Corporativism in Italy," *Radical History Review* 4, No. 203 (Spring-Summer 1977): 27.

9. For what constitutes "typical" of business reaction to the New Deal, see W. M. Kiplinger, "Why Business Men Fear Washington," *Scribner* (October 1934); cited by Frank Friedel, ed., *The New Deal and the American People* (Englewood Cliffs, N.J.: Prentice-Hall, 1964), p. 95.

10. Joseph Schumpeter, *Capitalism, Socialism and Democracy* (New York: Harper Torchbook, 1953), pp. 64–65.

11. See Sidney S. Alexander, "Opposition to Deficit Spending for the Prevention of Unemployment," in Lloyd A. Meltzer [and others, 1st ed.], *Income, Employment and Public Policy: Essays in Honor of Alvin Hansen* (New York: W. W. Norton & Co., 1948), p. 197.

12. Herbert Stein, *The Fiscal Revolution in America* (Chicago: University of Chicago Press, 1969), p. 74.

13. Kenneth Boulding, *The Organizational Revolution* (New York: Quadrangle Books, 1968), pp. 208, 210, 211.

14. Ellis W. Hawley, *The New Deal and the Problem of Monopoly* (Princeton, N.J.: Princeton University Press, 1966), p. 390.

15. Boulding, op. cit., p. 210.

16. See Charles P. Kindleberger, *The World in Depression: 1929–1939* (Berkeley: University of California Press, 1973), p. 276.

17. Irving Kristol, "Ten Years in a Tunnel: Reflections on the Thirties," in Morton J. Frisch and Martin Diamond, eds., *The Thirties: A Reconsideration in the Light of the American Political Tradition* (DeKalb: Northern Illinois University Press, 1968), pp. 15–16.

18. Frank H. Knight, "The Economic Principles of the New Deal," in Frisch and Diamond, op. cit., p. 95.

19. This is an important ability in periods of considerable economic stress and conflict

because at such times impersonal rules become less reliable as instruments of coordinating organizational life. The price system cannot accomplish through the process of exchange such important externalities as "trust among people, . . . loyalty or truth telling." Yet these have "a very important pragmatic value. . . . [they are] important lubricant[s] of a social system." Kenneth Arrow, *The Limits of Organization* (New York: W. W. Norton & Co., 1974), pp. 74, 23.

20. William E. Leuchtenburg, *Franklin D. Roosevelt and the New Deal: 1932–1940* (New York: Harper and Row, 1963), pp. 330–31.

21. See Hawley, op. cit., pp. 472–94.

22. Conkin, op. cit., p. 51.

23. Ibid., p. 52.

24. Ibid., p. 90.

25. Ibid., p. 10.

26. Leuchtenburg, op. cit., p. 262.

27. Conkin, op. cit., p. 10.

28. Cited by Leuchtenburg, op. cit., p. 263.

29. See Basil Rauch, *The History of the New Deal* (New York: Capricorn Books, 1963), pp. 161–62.

30. Leuchtenburg, op. cit., p. 132.

31. Arthur M. Schlesinger, Jr., *The Coming of the New Deal* (Boston: Houghton Mifflin Co., 1958), pp. 308–9.

32. Harry N. Scheiber, Harold G. Vitter, and Harold U. Faulkner, *American Economic History* (New York: Harper and Row, 1976), pp. 338–89.

33. Hawley, op. cit., p. 328.

34. Leuchtenburg, op. cit., p. 55.

35. Hawley, op. cit., p. 339.

36. Leuchtenburg, op. cit., p. 87.

37. R. G. Tugwell and E. C. Banfield, "Grass Roots Democracy—Myth or Reality?" *Public Administration Review* 10 (1950): 47–55; cited by Leuchtenburg, op. cit., p. 87.

38. Hawley, op. cit., p. 20.

39. Ibid.

40. Ibid.

41. Ibid., p. 28.

42. Ibid.

43. Ibid., p. 23.

44. Ibid., pp. 29, 75.

45. Ibid., p. 69.

46. Ibid., p. 404.

47. Cited in ibid., pp. 412–13.

48. Ibid., p. 15.

49. Ibid., p. 201.

50. Ibid., p. 14.

51. Ibid.

52. Ibid., pp. 205–25.

53. Ibid., p. 14.

54. Robert A. Dahl, *Pluralist Democracy in the United States: Conflict and Consent* (Chicago: Rand McNally and Co., 1967), p. 24.

55. Conkin, op. cit., pp. 72–73.

56. Hawley, op. cit., p. 476.

57. Lester Thurow, *The Zero-Sum Society: Distribution and the Possibilities for Economic Change* (New York: Basic Books), 1980.

58. See Robert Solo, "Theory of the State," *Journal of Economic Issues* 11, No. 2 (June 1977): pp. 379–85.

59. For summaries of this literature, see David A. Gold, Clarence Y.H. Lo, and Erik Olin Wright, "Recent Development in Marxist Theories of the Capitalist State," Part I, *Monthly Review*, 27 (October 1975): 29–43; Part II, *Monthly Review* (November 1975): 36–51; and Bob Jessop, "Recent Theories of the Capitalist State," *Cambridge Journal of Economics* 1, No. 4 (December 1977): 353–73.

60. Paul Sweezy and Leo Huberman, eds., "Is Socialism Really Necessary?" *Monthly Review* 10 (January 1959): 340.

61. Karl Polanyi, *The Great Transformation* (New York: Rinehart and Co., 1944).

62. Peter T. Manicus, *The Death of the State* (New York: Putnam's Sons, 1974), p. 31.

63. See Ralph Miliband, *The State in Capitalist Society* (New York: Basic Books, 1969), p. 146.

64. See Samuel Bowles and Herbert Gintis, "The Invisible Fist: Have Capitalism and Democracy Reached a Parting of the Ways?" *American Economic Review, Papers and Proceedings* 68, No. 2 (May 1968): 358–68.

This, of course, is not meant to deny that the internal prerogatives of managers in enterprises have not become increasingly circumscribed over the years with regard to working conditions, wages, and employment.

9

The New Deal and the Corporate State

Daniel R. Fusfeld

Franklin D. Roosevelt's New Deal is usually interpreted in terms of recovery and reform: measures to promote recovery from the Great Depression of the 1930s, and reform designed, first, to reduce the likelihood of or prevent another depression, and second, to benefit the weak, the poor, the less fortunate. The world was to be made into a better place for the underdog. In this respect the New Deal is viewed as the successor of earlier reform movements in the United States, especially the Populists and Progressives.

But while interpretation of the New Deal often looks backward to its antecedents, there is a curious reluctance to evaluate the New Deal in terms of subsequent events. History unfolds continuously. The events of one period lead into those that follow. Historical time proceeds from the past to the present and into the future. Any event has both antecedents and consequences. With respect to the New Deal, our understanding must consider what followed as well as what preceded it.

That the objectives of the New Deal were centered on economic recovery and reform cannot be doubted. But its policies developed in the context of powerful economic forces, rooted in the processes of capital accumulation, technological change, and organizational development in a private enterprise economy, which were transforming both the economy and the structure of power within the United States. These forces were operating before, during, and after the New Deal years and helped to determine the alternatives open to policy makers in government.

Nor can the international context be ignored. An international struggle for world political and economic hegemony was going on during the New Deal era. It led up to World War II, from which the United States emerged as the dominant world power. Simultaneously, a struggle for ideological hegemony between world communism, socialism, and private enterprise capitalism was going on both within individual countries and on the world stage.

The New Deal was caught up in all of these crosscurrents and trends, and was one factor in the historical outcome. For by the end of World War II the United States had moved to a political system characterized by centralized federal powers, presidential authority, and bureaucratic control; an economy strongly dominated by big business and finance and controlled by a self-selecting economic elite; and policies oriented toward international economic expansion and world hegemony, supported by a strong military position. Big government, big business, and military power were united in a system run by a relatively few political, economic, and military leaders. This developing corporate state was legitimized by traditional democratic political processes and supported by psychological appeals to traditional American values and the material benefits of an expanding economy.

The New Deal years, in peace and war, were the formation period of the postwar American corporate state. A political movement rooted in older American traditions of social reform instituted most of the changes that led to the negation of those very ideas of reform. "Men make their own history, but they do not make it just as they please."

ECONOMIC BACKGROUND OF THE NEW DEAL

The New Deal came to power at the depths of the Great Depression of the 1930s, and coping with that crisis was the chief problem of the first years of the Roosevelt administration. But the economic crisis of the 1930s came at a particular stage in the development of American capitalism. The process of capital accumulation and economic development, of technological change and organizational transformation, brings about changes in the business and financial sectors of the economy, in the relationships of authority in the workplace, in the labor sector, in the relationships between consumers and producers and between buyers and sellers. These economic changes are reflected in the extent to which economic interest groups and social classes have access to the sources and structure of power. The political process reflects these changes in the underlying economic and political structure. The New Deal, in this context, should be seen as an effort to deal with the crisis brought on by the Depression, within the context of the changing political economy of the time.

The political economy of the 1930s was created by deep-seated forces for change in the development of U.S. capitalism. In the business sector a continuing process of economic concentration was at work. By 1930 it had brought about an oligopolistic organization of basic industry in which a few large firms dominated the leading manufacturing sectors. A similar trend was at work in finance, transportation, and public utilities. The chain store was developing in retail distribution. Yet the spread of big business and its penetration more and more deeply into the economic fabric of the nation had by no means gone as far as it has today. What we would call the small business or "competitive" sector was relatively more important then than now. Nevertheless, it faced a continuing war of attrition from the big business sector even in the best of times, and its problems were multiplied by the Depression. Roosevelt and the Democratic party found substantial political support from small business and commercial interests seeking relief and protection from the twin threats of economic crisis and big business.

In the labor sector, manufacturing was well into the mass production era. This meant production line technology, division of jobs into routine components, and control of the workplace by engineering requirements and the discipline of the assembly line. In basic manufacturing industries such as steel, electrical equipment, automobiles, and rubber, the new technology and organization of the workplace had brought large increases in productivity and high wages, but it also created a mass of discontented and dissatisfied workers who had been subjected to years of rigorous discipline imposed by an unyielding and uncompromising machine technology. Workers were ready for change.

Regional changes in the distribution of industry also contributed to discontent and conflicting interests. The 1920s saw a tremendous burst of industrial development in the Midwest, keyed by the automobile industry, steel, rubber, and chemicals. The Southwest and California had oil and related industries. But the South was depressed as a result of the boll weevil and stagnation in textiles manufacturing, and New England had begun its long economic decline. Just as today the frostbelt is discontented, by the late 1920s a similar malaise affected the South and New England.

In agriculture the family farm, based on a labor intensive technology, was giving way to the larger and more capital intensive farm, and in some agricultural areas such as California and Florida to large-scale corporate farming. The changing technology and organization of agriculture in the 1920s, as well as hard times for farmers in the 1920s, contributed to substantial discontent in rural America. Many farmers were ready for a political shift to the Democratic party.

The Depression intensified these deep-seated problems in business, regional development, labor, and agriculture. A process of unequal development, both intensive and extensive, had created large groups in American society who were left behind, excluded from the benefits that others obtained—benefits that proved to be transitory for many of the beneficiaries during the Depression. The Great Depression of the 1930s was indeed a crisis of capitalism in the United States, but it was a crisis that had been building for many years in the basic structure of economic relationships.

The crisis had international aspects as well, and not only in the dislocations that brought on the financial collapse of 1933. Germany and Japan were moving to challenge for world hegemony. The first German challenge had been turned back in World War I. But German and Japanese economic development, coupled with French and British stagnation, brought another confrontation that escalated in the 1930s toward World War II. The United States in the 1930s clearly had the economic muscle to contest for supremacy, but was held back by concentration on domestic affairs, traditional isolationism, and opposition to war that was related to the experience of World War I. Germany and Japan, on the other hand, were both willing and able to challenge Britain, taking advantage of U.S. preoccupation with its own affairs and the political isolation of the Soviet Union. Yet by the late 1930s the Roosevelt administration was already turning its attention to the looming conflict. World politics then began to transform the New Deal as the United States moved toward the center of the struggle for world hegemony.

The threat of international communism to international capitalism was also lurking in the background. The Soviet Union in the early 1930s did not have either the military strength or the economic base to threaten the existing structure of international economic and political power. The Soviet challenge for world hegemony was still in the future. The ideological challenge was present, however, as it had been ever since the Russian revolutions of 1917. Here the New Deal reacted in two ways. The leading New Deal leaders saw their economic reforms as an answer to socialism, both democratic and authoritarian. And the New Deal made no serious effort to halt harassment of the left by Congress, the Federal Bureau of Investigation, and other government agencies, although Roosevelt and other administration leaders tried not to associate themselves directly with the continuing drive against the left. Recognition of the Soviet Union in 1933 made little difference. It was done largely in anticipation of large increases in trade that did not materialize, and it was accompanied by an intensified drive against the domestic left by the FBI. The shift in Soviet policy in the mid-1930s to a "united front" against fascism brought another intensification of the drive against the domestic left, culminating in passage of the Alien Registration (Smith) Act in 1940. The contest between capitalism and communism for ideological hegemony continued during the New Deal years and was destined to become a major preoccupation of the U.S. government in the years to come.

The international struggle for power came increasingly to absorb the attention of the Roosevelt administration in the late 1930s, as the Japanese and German threat to the international structure of power escalated. The New Deal followed a policy of alliance with the opponents of Germany and Japan that ultimately took the nation into World War II in alliance with Britain and the USSR. But the fight against communism made a peacetime rapprochement with the Soviet Union impossible, not only in the United States, but in England and France as well. Politically isolated, the Soviet Union made its peace with Germany, and World War II began. But first things first: once the war was on, U.S. policy centered on defeating the more immediate threat of Germany and Japan. The contest between capitalism and communism could be resumed later, as indeed it was.

In the late 1930s the chief policy concerns of the New Deal gradually shifted from economic recovery and reform to the struggle for world power. In the course of this shift the New Deal forged an alliance between big government and big business that moved the United States to world hegemony and the Cold War—and toward an emerging corporate state in which the concentrated economic power of big business was allied with the centralized political power of big government and a massive concentration of military power. This was not the goal of the New Deal, but it was one of its important outcomes.

ROOSEVELT'S PHILOSOPHY OF THE STATE

Franklin D. Roosevelt brought to the presidency a philosophy of politics that envisaged a unified, holistic society. It was rooted in the *noblesse oblige* attitude of the Hudson River elite from which he came. In this view, the nation was seen as a larger version of the local community, in which each individual participated in the life of the whole and took responsibility for his or her role. In return, the community was responsible for the welfare of the individual during times of storm and stress. For example, during Roosevelt's two terms as governor of New York he promoted state development of electric power, not only to provide fuller service at lower rates—the traditional argument of the reformist liberal—but as part of a regional plan for the entire state that included land use planning and development, transportation, and integration of urban and rural interests. The New Deal's Tennessee Valley Authority was founded on a similar ideal.

This social philosophy required an expanded role for government. The laissez-faire ideal of government limited to providing a framework within which individual action in the market would determine what happened to people as individuals and to the community as a whole was rejected in favor of an interventionist philosophy. The community had a responsibility for the individuals who comprised the community, and those individuals should be able to use the community's governmental institutions to that end.

In many respects the Rooseveltian social philosophy was an extension of Benthamite liberalism. Jeremy Bentham had argued that individuals should be free to maximize their net satisfactions, just as did the laissez-faire liberals. But Bentham also understood that social institutions were man-made, and not ordained by natural law. They could, and should, be transformed in order to enable people to develop and use their freedom of choice. A democratic government was the instrument that freely acting individuals could use, through political action, to establish an institutional environment within which individual happiness could be pursued.

Roosevelt's interventionist liberalism was reinforced by the idea that social change was inevitable. Economic development and technological change brought new problems and new situations within which problems had to be met. The laissez-faire position was either that individual adjustment to new situations was all that was needed (the pure laissez-faire position) or that the institutional structure would be fitted to the welfare maximizing needs of individuals (Social Darwinism). Interventionist liberalism rejected both of those positions. It held that the institutional environment had to be deliberately molded to meet the needs and desires of people, because vested interests and the power structure would otherwise prevent it, or conscious planning was more efficient than unplanned evolution, or simply because the will of the people called for it. At one time or another Franklin Roosevelt took all of these interventionist positions.

Finally, Roosevelt's social philosophy comprised a curious blend of egalitarian belief in the value of ordinary people with a belief in elite leadership. In one sense, everyone in the community had value as an individual member of the community on a basis of equality with everyone else. In another sense, people were not equal. Some had greater intelligence, leadership ability, or insight than others. But those qualities were the result of natural endowments, not individual choice, and should be used for the benefit of the community as a whole and the less fortunate members of the community. In this way, individual differences would be used to bring social unity rather than distinctions and conflict. Perhaps Roosevelt's disagreement with laissez-faire liberalism rested most fundamentally on this point: laissez-faire tended to bring conflicts that weakened and potentially could destroy the social fabric. The basic role of government was to hold the social fabric together.

This social philosophy had a strong appeal to those groups in American society that had been victims of the unbalanced development of the American economy—industrial workers, small farmers, owners of small businesses, and Southerners. To these were added the traditional Democratic strongholds in the eastern cities, nationality groups, and the older progressive reformers. The Great Depression made Roosevelt's victory in 1932 a landslide, but the New Deal coalition was built from deeper and more durable material than merely an economic crisis.

THE CHANGING ROLE OF GOVERNMENT

Two basic changes occurred in American political-economic relationships during the 1930s. One was a fundamental shift in the role of government. The second was a new relationship between labor and capital. Both of those developments had been gathering force for years. They matured and were institutionalized under the New Deal.

Quantitatively, in terms of spending, employment, and functions, the role of government had been growing in the United States for thirty years or more. Relatively, however, when measured against the rate of growth of gross national product, there had been little change until the early 1930s. World War I had brought a large relative expansion of government spending and employment, followed by a partial pullback after the war that left government with a larger role than before the war. Aside from that episode, the growth of government was not significantly greater than expansion of economic activity from the turn of the century to 1930.

The Great Depression changed that. The role of government began to grow in the Hoover administration. but the relative expansion owed more to the decline of the private sector than to governmental growth. With the Roosevelt administration, however, a rapid growth of federal spending and employment, only partially counterbalanced by reductions at local and state levels, brought a quantitatively significant upsurge in government spending and employment, and a widening of governmental functions.

Qualitatively, governmental powers shifted significantly from local and state governments to the national government. This shift was foreshadowed by adoption of the income tax as a major source of federal revenues in 1914 and the adoption of graduated rates during World War I. Reductions in 1926 still left the federal government with a large and flexible source of income which became the financial basis of the shift in the locus of governmental power during the 1930s.

Within the federal government political power shifted significantly from Congress to the executive branch. In part this shift came about because of the charismatic nature of presidential leadership, which could mean the difference between victory or defeat in close races for individual congressmen and senators. But much more important was the growth of the federal bureaucracy. It could influence the spending of funds and, backed by the constituents who benefited from the various programs, bring pressure to bear on Congress. Simultaneously, the bureaucracy could partially neutralize presidential control by developing alliances with congressmen and senators sensitive in their home districts to the politics of special interest groups. Several branches of the federal bureaucracy became very adept at using this political *zugzwang* to gain considerable degrees of independence, particularly the military, the Department of Agriculture, the Veterans Administration, and the Federal Bureau of Investigation. The locus of governmental power did indeed shift strongly toward the federal government during the 1930s, and in Washington toward the executive branch. But within the executive branch a fourth arm of government, the federal bureaucracy, expanded and gained a significant degree of independence.

These changes in the role of government and the locus of governmental power were accompanied by a fundamental shift in constitutional law. Prior to the New Deal legislation of the mid-1930s the powers of the federal government were, for the most part, limited to those powers specifically granted to the federal government by the Constitution. That fundamental proposition had been eroded somewhat in the years before the New Deal, but the erosion had largely taken the form of broader definition of the specific powers stated in the Constitution. The accepted interpretation was that the Constitution limited the powers of the federal government to those specifically designated.

On the basis of that "strict" interpretation of the Constitution, the Supreme Court struck down several key pieces of New Deal legislation and brought on Roosevelt's efforts to enlarge the court. Roosevelt lost that battle but won the war. Under pressure from the administration, and with its eye on the ballot box, the Court decided a number of cases in 1937 that upheld New Deal legislation. In doing so it shifted the justification for federal action from the specific powers granted by Article I, Section 8, of the Constitution to the phrase in the Preamble "to . . . promote the general Welfare." This change in the legal interpretation of the Constitution replaced a government with limited and specific powers with one with general and, in some respects, unlimited powers. (We should note that almost simultaneously with the extension of federal powers the Court began that long series of decisions protecting individuals from arbitrary action by both federal and state governments and greatly extending the constitutional Bill of Rights.)

Perhaps the most important single change in American political economy brought about by the New Deal was the institutionalization of the positive state, complete with centralization of powers in the federal government, presidential leadership, a quasi-independent bureaucracy, and constitutional legitimacy.

THE LABOR-CAPITAL RELATIONSHIP

The relationship between capital and labor was also profoundly changed under the New Deal. Nothing less than a comprehensive accomodation between those two great social classes was developed, which stabilized and narrowed the conflict between them, institutionalized a system of conflict resolution and management, and helped set the stage for both wartime cooperation and the surge of economic growth after World War II. The accomodation between capital and labor had been developing for half a century around the concept of collective bargaining. But the accomodation involved other actions by government as well.

Restrictions on immigration, which began in 1882 with legislation to limit immigration of Chinese laborers, culminated in the quota acts of 1921 and 1924 (which went into effect in 1929). This legislation was strongly supported by labor unions as a means of reducing competition from immigrants willing to work for low wages. It was the first important building block of the capital-labor accomodation, and it reflected the growing political clout of the industrial labor force.

A network of legislation protecting workers against economic risks was filled out. The Social Security Act of 1935 provided for both unemployment insurance and old age and survivors' benefits. It placed part of the burden of workers' benefits on employers. This legislation was supplemented by state laws providing compensation for injured workers that began in 1902 in Maryland, had spread to forty-two states by 1920, and was completed by passage of a Mississippi law in 1948.

A third building block of the capital-labor accomodation involved a commitment by the federal government to assure high levels of employment. The New Deal followed a program of promoting high levels of aggregate demand in an effort to promote recovery in the private sector of the economy. This policy, which was not formalized until passage of the Employment Act of 1946, was unsuccessful until World War II brought very large increases in government spending. But the policy was also implemented by direct provision of jobs in federal job creation programs. These included the Civilian Conservation Corps, Public Works Administration, Works Progress Administration (later the Work Projects Administration), and the National Youth Administration. Unemployment persisted at high levels throughout the 1930s, in spite of the New Deal policies, but the federal commitment to high levels of employment as a major element in national economic policy, and perhaps the most important element, was firmly established.

Federal legislation to place a floor on wages and a cap on hours worked was also important. Under the Public Contracts Act of 1936 firms making contracts with the federal government were required to pay "prevailing wages" as determined by the U.S. Department of Labor, provide an eight-hour day and forty-hour week, and employ only workers over the age of sixteen. This was followed by the Fair Labor Standards Act of 1938, which established minimum wages and maximum hours for all firms engaged in interstate commerce and prohibited shipment of goods made by child labor. Agriculture was exempted, along with a number of other sectors of the economy.

This legislation reflected the rise of the industrial labor force as a major element in the American economy. The New Deal brought that group into the political coalition that controlled the levers of power. The legislation that resulted met some of the needs and goals of industrial labor, those that were largely related to macroeconomic problems and the functioning of national and regional labor markets. Government responsibility for those aspects of labor problems made it possible for collective bargaining to focus on the microeconomic issues of wages, hours, working conditions, and related matters in individual plants, firms, and industries. One reason for the success of collective bargaining was the opportunity for both labor and management to set aside some of the larger problems as the responsibility of government and concentrate on the more immediate issues arising from the workplace.

Legislation establishing a legal framework for collective bargaining completed the New Deal's accomodation between capital and labor. Embodied first in Section 7A of the National Industrial Recovery Act (NIRA) of 1933, and later in the National Labor Relations Act (NLRA) of 1935, workers were guaranteed the right of collective bargaining through unions of their own choice. Employers were forbidden to interfere with the effort to organize, to discriminate against union members, or to support company unions. Paralyzed for over two years by injunctions and court challenges, the NLRA was upheld by the Supreme Court in 1937 and 1938. A mechanism was in place for settlement of differences between capital and labor.

The accomodation between capital and labor was completed by an informal and unwritten agreement by the two parties on the issues on which collective bargaining focused. The approach adopted was that of the American Federation of Labor, in the tradition of Samuel Gompers' "pure and simple" unionism. This meant emphasis on wages, hours, working conditions, and union membership for workers. This "business unionism" rejected political radicalism and efforts to replace capitalism with some form of socialism or worker control. It left property relations untouched and accepted management authority over the organization of work, technological change, and the process of capital accumulation. This aspect of the accomodation led to an internal struggle in some unions that ended with defeat and expulsion of radical leaders. The quid pro quo on the part of employers was acceptance of the union and the process of collective bargaining to determine the division of the economic surplus between the employer and the work force. In essence, each side recognized the continuing right of the other to exist within the private enterprise economy, while antagonisms between the two were settled by negotiation.

The accomodation between labor and capital that emerged during the New Deal years was a complex mixture of state legislation (workers' compensation), national legislation (immigration laws, unemployment insurance, old age and survivors' benefits, wage and hour legislation, collective bargaining), and a tacit agreement on the issues to be settled by collective bargaining on the part of labor and management. Various elements in the accomodation developed prior to the New Deal, and it was modified somewhat after World War II, but its basic components became a key element in the political economy of the United States during the New Deal years.

THE BUSINESS-GOVERNMENT RELATIONSHIP

The relationship between government and business changed substantially during the Roosevelt administrations. In the early years an effort was made by the New Deal leadership to promote cooperation among business enterprises to stabilize prices and control markets as a means of promoting economic recovery under the National Industrial Recovery Act. The failure of the program, and invalidation of the act in 1935, brought a shift to a policy of enforcement of the antitrust laws and opposition to private market control. With the outbreak of World War II, however, the administration shifted again, to a policy of cooperation with big business that has prevailed, with some ebb and flow, to the present.

The shifts of policy with respect to business enterprise reflected a division of opinion within the New Deal leadership. Franklin Roosevelt shared the traditional belief in the benefits of competition and the desirability of small enterprise. Dispersal of economic power was necessary for a viable political democracy. On the other hand, he had participated in the trade association movement of the 1920s, out of which came the idea of business cooperation for mutual benefit that led to NIRA. Among administration economists there was a similar split. One group advocated measures to stabilize and "reflate" prices in order to return business enterprises to profitability and to ease the burden of debt. A second group thought that prices should be reduced in order to stimulate purchasing power. This group made common cause with a third group that felt that high prices imposed by monopolistic market control practices constituted a basic weakness of the economic system.

Roosevelt, however, had already committed himself during the 1932 campaign to a program of business cooperation under government direction, in his speech to the Commonwealth Club in San Francisco on September 23. NIRA was the legislative outcome of this effort to include business enterprise in the national community of interest—and to build political support for the New Deal coalition among business interests.

The National Recovery Administration (NRA) floundered, however, because of lack of cooperation on the part of both big business and small enterprise. Big business interests disliked those portions of the program that required minimum wages and collective bargaining. Even more, however, large firms balked at the market-sharing provisions of the industry codes that protected the smaller firms. Large firms in an oligopoly are quite willing to share markets with other large firms, even during hard times, in order to avoid costly retaliation from large and powerful rivals. But smaller firms are considered fair game, particularly when times are hard, and the codes protected the smaller ones against predation by the big firms. The small firms also disliked the codes, because their chief defensive weapon, even with the partial protection of the codes, was price cutting to obtain sales. Thus, big firms opposed the codes because their aggrandizement was slowed, while small firms broke the price lines and the employment rules in order to survive. Many of the industry codes were becoming unenforceable before NIRA was declared unconstitutional by the Court.

The labor provisions of NIRA were soon reinstituted by the National Labor Relations Act and the Fair Labor Standards Act. Nor did the idea of business cooperation under government direction die completely. In the oil industry a system of production planning, price fixing, and market sharing was established through a complex system of cooperation among the federal government, state governments in the chief oil-producing states, and the major oil companies. This system remained in effect until 1973, when the Organization of Oil Exporting Countries (OPEC), in cooperation with the major international oil companies, took over supervision of the industry. Likewise, in the bituminous coal industry the federal government sought to establish a system of price, output, and marketing controls after the demise of NIRA. Several efforts failed, until the United Mine Workers Union was able to establish an informal system of price and output controls in 1946—supported, of course, by the large coal mining firms—which lasted until the expansion of western coal production in the 1970s. Planning of prices and market sharing by a combination of business cooperation and government regulation was also developed in the transportation industries, including railroads, motor bus and trucking services, and air transport. The New Deal never abandoned its support of business cooperation in schemes of price fixing and market control.

Another approach to business-government relations developed in the electric power industry, which was restructured in a mixed public-private-cooperative framework. The Public Utility Holding Company Act of 1935 broke up the three great corporate networks into which the industry had formed in the 1920s, although their financial collapse was causing them to break up anyway. Regional firms were established that had effective monopoly positions, but were expected to be regulated by state regulatory agencies and to have their geographical expansion limited by the Federal Power Commission. At the distribution level, the Public Works Administration provided funds for construction of municipal power plants, and the Rural Electrification Administration promoted distribution by consumer cooperatives. The most spectacular ventures were in production of hydroelectric power by the federal government: the Tennessee Valley Authority; Boulder Dam on the Colorado River; Grand Coulee and Bonneville dams on the Columbia River; and Fort Peck Dam on the upper Missouri. This restructuring of the electric power industry departed from both the policy of fostering a competitive economy and the idea of business self-regulation under government supervision.

The third approach—antitrust enforcement to preserve a competitive economy—was revived after the demise of NIRA. The Department of Justice and the Federal Trade Commission expanded their antitrust work. In addition, the investigations and publications of the Temporary National Economic Committee were intended as documentation of the continuing growth of economic concentration and of the need for a strong antitrust policy. By 1938, however, national policy concerns were turning toward the rapidly accelerating international crisis. The military needs of the national government were soon to create a growing dependence on the kinds of goods produced by the big business sector. So before it could fairly get started the new antitrust policy was first weakened and then abandoned. That interlude, from 1936 to 1939, was the last time a serious effort was made to arrest the growing concentration of economic power and wealth in the American economy.

The outbreak of World War II brought a fundamental shift in the relationship between big business and the federal government, moving toward the symbiosis between those centers of power that characterized the postwar years. The shift began in 1940, with establishment of the National Defense Advisory Committee (NDAC) during the German blitzkrieg against France. The committee's task was to prepare the American economy for war. It was headed by liberal New Dealer Leon Henderson, with six other members, one each from General Motors, U.S. Steel, the Burlington Railway, labor, agriculture, and academia. Business representatives were a minority. That quickly changed. The NDAC was soon replaced by the Office of Production Management (OPM), headed by William Knudsen of General Motors. Business leadership was now in charge of the defense effort. OPM gave way in turn to the War Production Board in January 1942, headed by Donald Nelson, and a stream of business executives converged on Washington. They were largely second-ranking executives from relatively large firms who were appointed to oversee war production in the industries from which they came. They were aware, of course, that they would be returning to the industries and/or large firms from which they came, and their decisions reflected big business interests.

Contract procedures favored relatively large firms. Contracts were let to large "prime contractors," which then subcontracted portions of the contract to suppliers and smaller firms. Contract specifications were often set in ways that precluded bidding by small firms, or that required use of processes or products protected by patent rights held by large firms.

Allocation of raw materials, supplies, and skilled labor was controlled by a subsidiary agency of the War Production Board, the Supply Priorities and Allocations Board. The work of this agency was structured in large part by the contracts for war production, and was also run by business executives drawn from large firms. In addition, by the end of 1942 special boards had been established for allocation of rubber, oil, and solid fuels. Although located within existing departments for administrative purposes, these boards were also run by executives from the industries they supervised.

One of the few exceptions to the emphasis on big business was the Smaller War Plants Corporation, which provided loans and guarantees to small business between 1942 and 1945. It had much less impact than the Reconstruction Finance Corporation, which provided funds for large enterprises. In leadership, contract procedures, allocations, and finance, the war production process gave a favored position to big business under the protective umbrella of the federal government.

This policy shift was perhaps inevitable. Big business had the technology, organization, and expertise to produce the goods on which national military power rested. Any government aspiring to victory in war and military power would have to come to terms with the established business leadership. The New Deal chose a policy of government management of procurement, production by private firms motivated by profits, and executives from big business in charge of the government agencies involved.

This accommodation between big government and big business set the style for the continuing relationship of these two centers of political and economic power after World War II. The United States emerged from the war as the leading military power in the world, challenged potentially only by the Soviet Union, and there only in land warfare. The United States also entered the postwar years with its great production capacity and financial resources intact, modernized, and expanded. With the fascist nations defeated, the only significant enemy was world communism, and U.S. foreign economic, political, and military policy quickly turned to that conflict. Big business was a natural ally, for its interests lay in economic penetration of the noncommunist, nonsocialist sectors of the world. Big business needed big government as a wedge and a shield—just as big government needed the weapons produced in the big business sector to validate its claim to world hegemony. The basic outlines of this symbiosis had their origins in the government-business relationships established under the New Deal in oil, coal, and transportation, and were firmly established during World War II under the New Deal at war.

The New Deal was many things. It was a response to the economic crisis of the Great Depression, which was itself one aspect of the development of capitalism in the twentieth century. The New Deal response was to move strongly toward a much enlarged economic role for government and increased power for the executive and the bureaucracy. In this respect, the New Deal's response was similar to that of governments in other nations, and was part of a longer run trend toward expansion of government action and powers when faced with problems generated in the private sector of the economy.

The New Deal was also a movement for reform within the framework of a private enterprise economy. It was the successor of earlier and similar reform movements. In political philosophy the New Deal was in direct descent from the interventionist liberalism of Jeremy Bentham and John Stuart Mill, within a holistic view of the social order as an integrated community of responsible individuals. It sought to apply that philosophy to the modern industrial age.

One outcome of that philosophy was a peculiarly American accommodation between capital and labor that brought the class conflict of modern capitalism under control. A framework of national protective legislation, plus limited intervention in labor markets, enabled labor and management to settle other disputes through collective bargaining. This mutuality of interest among labor, capital, and government lasted into the 1970s, a period of over forty years.

The New Deal also came to terms with the growth of big business, economic concentration, and the rise of a business elite. A symbiotic relationship between big government and big business developed during the 1930s and particularly during World War II. The mutuality of interests was based, in part, on domestic economic needs of the two parties, but was related primarily to the U.S. drive for world power and economic hegemony that was taken up during World War II. The New Deal made no serious effort to arrest the growth of big business and the process of economic concentration, despite the antitrust interlude of the late 1930s. Its commitment to private enterprise capitalism foreclosed any significant interference with private accumulation of capital by big business. The capital-labor accommodation also accepted business control over the economic surplus, subject to the divisions arranged through collective bargaining. And inclusion of business and farm interests in the political coalition put together by the New Deal precluded any significant modification of property rights. Indeed, major elements of the coalition, including organized labor, strongly supported the drive against domestic radicalism that was part of the ideological battle against socialism and communism that went on in the 1930s and was taken up on a world scale as a central element in national policy after the New Deal and World War II.

Seen from the perspective of a half century, the New Deal was indeed a turning point in the history of twentieth-century America. But the turn was only temporarily toward the goals of liberal reform in the interests of the common man. Those goals were quickly transformed by the administration's efforts to come to terms with big business and concentrated economic power, in the context of the struggle for world power and the ideological conflict between capitalism and communism. In the long run the turn was toward centralized political power, centralized economic power, militarism, and control by an economic-political-military elite. It was reform and change, but not the sort envisaged by New Deal liberals. In the words of Robert Burns:

> The best-laid schemes o' mice an' men
>   Gang aft agley,
> An' lea'e us nought but grief an' pain,
>   For promis'd joy!

10

Roosevelt, the Brain Trust, and the Origins of the New Deal

Elliot A. Rosen

History is replete with paradox and improbabilities. According to economists of the New Era, the Great Depression could not possibly occur. Wesley Clair Mitchell at Columbia University and other members of the economic establishment believed that they knew the pattern and causation of business cycles, with their automatic, built-in correctives. The Great Engineer in the White House symbolized this confidence in the genius of our business system. Together, the business community, with Hoover at Commerce from 1921 through 1928, had mastered the problems of mass production through scientific management and modernized labor relations. "Unemployment," he explained, in acceptance of his party's 1928 nomination, "in the sense of distress is widely disappearing." Within two or three years the improbable had occurred.[1]

We need to consider a second paradox. There is little to suggest that a man at age fifty, namely, Franklin D. Roosevelt, is amenable to conjecture, essentially a capacity to reject received dogma as unworkable in an altered set of circumstances. Whereas Roosevelt turned to a Brain Trust for radical departures to reverse the course of depression, Hoover insisted on adherence to the American system. For Herbert Clark Hoover, no new set of facts dictated alteration of the fundamental values of our society, values he traced to the Founding Fathers and especially Thomas Jefferson. Outlined as a set of homilies in his *American Individualism,* published in 1922, they transcended immediate economic circumstance. Hoover extolled individualism maintained in a framework of voluntary, associational activity; the efficacy of the emery wheel of competition; the superiority of a society that nurtured the efforts of the self-made man and resolved its problems at the community and state levels.

Hoover reiterated these principles in his Madison Square Garden speech of October 31, 1932, in *The Challenge to Liberty* (published in 1934), and again in his *Memoirs* in the 1950s. The American system, he explained in the 1932 campaign, "had been builded up by 150 years of the toil of our fathers." It was the unique accomplishment of our race and experience. In a rejection of conjuncture, he explained the Depression as fleeting, nearly ended, readily resolved by the restoration of business confidence, maintenance of the United States on the gold standard, and community-based relief. Roosevelt's New Deal portended the enlargement of federal bureaucracy, its power and budget, at the people's expense and to the detriment of state and local government. Tyranny would ensue. Free speech would die and with it free enterprise.[2]

Defeated at the polls in 1932, Herbert Hoover devoted the balance of his years to a struggle to undo the centralizing tendencies of the New Deal. And his philosophy, anchored in nineteenth-century values, served as the basis for the modern conservative coalition. Yet contemporary Hoover scholarship, revisionist in nature, represents him as the progenitor of the interventionist state when, in reality, Hoover and his treasury secretary, Ogden L. Mills, insisted on budget retrenchment and adherence to the gold standard, a policy that contributed to the final collapse of late 1932 through early 1933. The resulting deflation was of such magnitude that it wiped out millions of jobs and threatened the closure of major banks, the freezing of credit, and the pricing of commodities below the cost of production.[3]

ORIGINS OF THE BRAIN TRUST

To return to the problem of conjuncture, Samuel I. Rosenman and Roosevelt surmised that they required an economic expertise unavailable in the statehouse at Albany. The Albany experience bore scant relation to the national and international crisis. Raymond Moley argued, in *After Seven Years,* that it was natural for Roosevelt to assemble a group of academic experts—a Brain Trust—in March 1932, given the governor's frequent reliance on university expertise for the solution of state problems. But it was one thing, as Rosenman explained, to entrust technical problems such as water power development or judicial reform to college professors—a notoriously impractical lot—another to rely on them for formulation of ideas in a political campaign, given the inevitable compromises.

When Rosenman proposed the recruitment of Moley and other academics to forge a new relationship between government and society, Roosevelt hesitated. Professors talked too much on the outside, he demurred. Rosenman surmised, however, that FDR's thoughts turned to a heavy schedule of speeches. One might add that other considerations entered the governor's mind. The team of James A. Farley, Louis M. Howe, and Edward M. House, the balance of the Albany advisors, had faltered in the political arena. A conservative coalition, funded by the Du Ponts and Bernard M. Baruch, demonstrated a growing capacity to check Roosevelt's progress toward the nomination, then substitute Newton D. Baker as party nominee. Moreover, none of Roosevelt's advisors could offer a clear rationale of depression causation and cure. As the (March) evening ended, the governor relented. "Well," alluding to the volubility and vanity of academics, "we'll just have to take our chances on that."[4]

The creation of intellectuals, the New Deal was barely comprehended by its principal beneficiary, the forgotten man. Scarcely the outpouring of a popular movement, the New Deal emerged as the conception of an elite, three uncommonly brilliant scholars, members of the Columbia University faculty. And it was orchestrated by a patrician politician, characterized by Walter Lippmann as temperamentally and intellectually unfit for the task of social and economic reconstruction.

Curiously, for a generation, the richest source on the New Deal's origination remained in Raymond Moley's possession, untapped by liberal historians repelled by his reactionary views. Moley, in turn, convinced that he had ushered in a behemoth, in time a friend and admirer of Hoover, supported the notion that Roosevelt's failure to cooperate in the 1932–1933 interregnum caused the Depression to reach bottom with the bank crisis. Like Lippmann, who made the argument in *The Yale Review* in 1935, and recent Hoover revisionists, Moley credited much of the New Deal program to the Great Engineer. In fact, Ogden Mills and Arthur Ballantine at Treasury *had* developed mechanisms to assure bank liquidity in the 1932–1933 crisis. But Hoover rejected them on the ground of dubious federal authority under the World War I Trading with the Enemy Act and left to Roosevelt the opportunity for a display of resolution and the origination of the interventionist state.[5]

Hoover feared the dread hand of government, saw the federal government as facilitator, the free enterprise system as auto-regenerative. Conversely, Roosevelt possessed an activist view of government in an advanced society and, to use his own football metaphor, considered only the choice of plays. Put another way, the New Deal was not an ad hoc creation. Though experimental in its techniques, Franklin D. Roosevelt and the Brain Trust shaped its objectives in 1932.

MOLEY'S OUTLINE OF THE NEW DEAL

Raymond Moley introduced the term "New Deal" in his memorandum of May 19, 1932, prepared at Roosevelt's request. It had two dimensions, suggested in their initial major collaborative effort, the Forgotten Man speech, delivered on the radio. A political scientist, Moley viewed the two major parties as Tweedledum and Tweedledee. Both had grown conservative and stultified in the face of growing social and economic problems. "What do men want?" Moley inquired. His reply, "Work and security." It constituted the essence of the New Deal program.[6]

Sensing Roosevelt's new direction, the Albany advisors, particularly Louis Howe and Edward House, objected, urged caution, fiscal restraint, above all no experimentation with political nostrums. House especially invoked his connections with the party's conservative business supporters. For a major speech at

St. Paul, Woodrow Wilson's former advisor urged: "I shall not favor the rich as such, nor shall I favor the poor. . . . What this country needs, what humanity in general needs, is equality for all and special privilege for none." This was the essence of Herbert Hoover's ideology.[7]

The Forgotten Man speech objected to trickle-down theory, called attention to the impoverished agrarian and urban unemployed, offered the theory that this nation could not endure half boom, half broke. At St. Paul, Roosevelt and Moley broke with the conservatives of their party in their affirmation of a "concert of interests," the notion that sectors of society are interlocked and ultimately cannot prosper unless all prosper.[8] The Moley memorandum of May 19 delineated a specific program requiring expanded federal functions. These included the following:

1. Corporate surpluses, or excess profits, should be taxed. The memorandum assumed that extraordinary gains in industrial output, a product of improved machinery, materials, and processes, including greater managerial and labor efficiency, facilitated a 50 percent increase in labor productivity in the 1920s. Instead of provision of higher dividends and wages, enlarged profits were retained as corporate surpluses. These made their way into foreign loans and the call money market for speculation in corporate securities, hence the speculative frenzy that led to the collapse of the stock market. Moley urged, therefore, heavy taxation of inheritance, income, and corporate profits, intended to divert national income to social programs.

2. The May memorandum also indicated the future direction of emergency programs by proposing a relief–public works package of $2.6 billion, intended to carry the unemployed through the Depression. It suggested immediate federal relief amounting to $500 million. It would subsume the maximum allowed by Hoover, some $1.1 billion in self-liquidating public works such as bridges, tunnels, and government buildings. It extended the relief concept to include $500 million for rural projects and $500 million for an urban emergency housing corporation. Since budget balance achieved by regressive taxation in the form of John N. Garner's sales tax proposal was unacceptable, Moley proposed the use of an emergency budget for relief or extraordinary outlays. This enabled Roosevelt to portray himself as a fiscal conservative and satisfy thereby supporters such as Bernard Baruch. Until pressed by expenditures for war, Roosevelt could claim that his ordinary budget was in balance.

3. Work relief could tide people over until the industrial system recovered sufficiently to offer adequate employment. But even in normal times, the business system proved subject to seasonal swings and discarded those too old to work. The answer lay in provision for the social minimal: old age pensions and unemployment insurance. These served humane ends and cushioned the system against future depressions.

4. Collapse of security values, held by individuals and fiduciary institutions,

and market manipulation—for example, the utility and railroad holding companies built upon small investments and huge flotations of worthless paper; market rigging by pools; the sale of stock by securities affiliates of commercial banks, which in turn loaned depositors' funds to clients for the purchase of such securities, often speculative in quality—led to the divorcement of commercial from investment banking, regulation of securities issuance through the SEC, and regulation of stock exchange practices.

5. Beginning at St. Paul, later during the campaign and interregnum, Roosevelt proposed the development of public power as a yardstick for measurement of utilities' rates, considered indecently high, especially in rural areas. By February 1933, Roosevelt, going beyond the Moley memorandum, expanded the concept to include federal multipurpose development of the impoverished Tennessee Valley. The concept, which evolved as a collaboration with George W. Norris of Nebraska, included generation of cheap electricity, improvement of river transportation, production of fertilizer, education of poor farmers toward more productive techniques and soil conservation, construction of health and educational facilities, better housing, even the sale of electric appliances. Roosevelt hoped to extend the idea to other river valleys, such as the Missouri and Columbia, only to be checked eventually by a growing coalition of conservative opponents of the New Deal.

6. In foreign affairs, Moley urged the concept of intranationalism. However desirable international cooperation appeared in theory, economic nationalism or autarchy had taken hold in the era following World War I. The debts-reparations tangle, Great Britain's inability to maintain the international gold standard, the imperial preference system, import quotas and exchange controls, and a high tariff system had created an environment inhospitable to international trade. Then, too, if recovery was to be achieved by creation of artificially high price levels, especially for agricultural commodities, the nation's economy, remarkably self-sufficient, required insulation from international economic tides. "Foreign trade," Moley noted, "only 1/10 of the problem," meaning 10 percent of gross national product. "The solution is to get hold of the two ends of the equation. But you cannot if one end is abroad." Given the promise of the Hundred Days program for reflation of prices and wages, Roosevelt rejected currency stabilization at the World Monetary and Economic Conference of 1933. Intranationalism gave priority to domestic requirements, a course changed only in the 1940s.[9]

NEW DEAL AGRICULTURAL POLICY

Roosevelt and Moley regarded the Depression's principal cause as the collapse worldwide of commodity prices following World War I. Eventually (by 1931–1932) prices for staples such as corn, wheat, cotton, hogs, and tobacco fell below their cost of production. Demand had been stimulated in the United States during the war by record civilian consumption and the requirements of European nations overrun by armies and short of manpower. Urged on by Hoover's Food Administration, agrarians borrowed to the hilt for land and machinery. Farmers were in trouble as early as 1921, when Woodrow Wilson withdrew wheat price supports of $2.25 a bushel. Within months wheat fell to $1 a bushel, then less. As soldiers returned to their farms in Europe and placed them in production, then demanded subsidies for protection from U.S. imports, later as Canada and Australia demanded special protection for commodities within the Empire, American farmers found themselves excluded from traditional European markets. Unable to repay wartime loans, millions of farmers worked for the bankers who owned their mortgaged farms. As prices continued to plummet, farms were abandoned altogether; agrarians drifted to the cities, and country banks collapsed.

Roosevelt and his advisors judged that some 40 percent of the population was depressed long before the Wall Street crash, and thus eventually pulled down other sectors of the economy. Farmers simply could not consume the products of American industry, hence the priority given to agriculture in the Roosevelt era. The New Deal agricultural program, its most successful and consistent economic venture, intended, through production controls and a policy of income redistribution, a shift in purchasing power away from the eastern-industrial-financial sector toward the South and the West. Hence, the loyalty of James Byrnes, Pat Harrison, and Joe Robinson to Roosevelt despite strong ideological differences.

Roosevelt and Moley knew that agrarian economists at the Bureau of Agricultural Economics, at midwestern state universities, and in the Rockefeller Foundation had been tackling the problem of rural depression for a decade. It was common knowledge that Hoover had rejected radical solutions such as acreage control, introduced into the Congress in 1932, as unwarranted federal interference in a market economy. Moley knew further that a colleague at Columbia, a young economist, Rexford Tugwell, had presented a version of acreage allotment to Alfred E. Smith and Belle Moscowitz in 1928, only to meet rejection. Tugwell introduced an air of intellectual excitement into the deliberations at Albany and Hyde Park. A product of Simon Patten at the University of Pennsylvania, who as a young man had broken with the laissez-faire doctrine of his profession, Tugwell moved toward institutionalism and experimentalism. Influenced by John A. Hobson's underconsumptionist views, also by Thorstein Veblen's anthropological approach to current economic practice, Tugwell broached the concept of a concert of interests, an organic economy of interrelated parts, one which required overhead management or planning. And he conceived the notion of conjuncture, the abandonment of received dogma in the face of new realities. If business could plan its production in anticipation of market demand, through oligopoly, government could apply the same principles to millions of small farmers.

Under the direction of John D. Rockefeller, natural resource industries, such as petroleum, had long since become profitable by balancing supply with demand.

Government needed to do the same for agriculture: gauge market demand in advance, tailor production to that demand, and in the process shift income from the urban consumer to the agrarian sector. Tugwell lacked the mechanisms, but learned these from M. L. Wilson in June 1932, then introduced Wilson to Roosevelt. It was Wilson, Tugwell, Mordecai Ezekiel, and Henry A. Wallace who developed the' New Deal agricultural program. That program included acreage allotment, a processing tax supplanted later by subvention and crop loans, the ever normal granary, and other short-range solutions. Long range, it intended the removal of marginal land from production as well as reforestation, soil conservation, scientific farming, and the resettlement of the rural poor into more productive environments. In the process—and this was typical of the New Deal—several programs could be dovetailed. Civilian Conservation Corps (CCC) work provided useful employment for urban youths, reforestation, national park trails for recreation, income for the parents of these youths, and the removal of marginal land from production.

Tugwell wanted more: the abandonment of a market economy and introduction of planning for the industrial and financial sectors, including price fixing, allocation of resources and capital, and the direction of production toward socially useful purposes. The notion was rejected by Roosevelt, on the advice of Adolf A. Berle, in August 1932. As Moley later put it—initially he was amenable— "planning ran against the nature of the American people. We used it for agriculture where it was necessary. Business could plan for itself." It was required, however, to divert the income stream from speculative activity and the hoarding of profits to wages and social purposes.[10]

THE BUSINESS-GOVERNMENT RELATIONSHIP

By 1932, with the failure of the Creditanstalt, the German banks, then thousands of banks in the United States, fiduciary institutions, pressed by depositors, liquidated equities for cash. Now legitimate values were in jeopardy, speculative situations long since liquidated. With the nation's financial system very nearly at a halt, Moley, at Roosevelt's request, turned for technical expertise to a brilliant colleague on the Columbia Law School faculty, Adolf A. Berle, Jr. A child prodigy at Harvard, Berle, through his publication with Gardiner C. Means, in 1932, of *The Modern Corporation and Private Property,* brought a new dimension to our understanding of corporate aggregates. When Moley approached this colleague, he met a jarring reply. Berle favored Newton D. Baker as Democratic nominee and in fact would campaign for Baker's nomination at the 1932 convention. Like Lippmann, he regarded FDR as a lightweight. "It was not his vote we required," Moley countered. "It was his technical expertise." That Berle gave as he joined the Brain Trust. Roosevelt's upbringing supported the notion of Christian capitalism—fair wages, fair prices, reasonable profits, overall an ethical marketplace; Berle's sophistication and background furnished an additional dimension to the academic group around the candidate and meshed with

Roosevelt's instincts. Berle's father, Adolf Augustus, had been a minister of the social gospel and a teacher of Christian ethics at Tufts University. In his reminiscences Adolf, Jr., recalled his experience as a boy in Chicago, as he trudged to school in the winter past corpses dead of hunger and exposure; and the visits of Jane Addams and Louis Brandeis, progressive reformers, to his father's home. The poverty of abundance seemed a paradox in the age of iron and steel, when some had too much, others too little to sustain themselves.

Berle's conclusions in *The Modern Corporation* and his memorandum on economic restoration reflected three currents: the social gospel; the new jurisprudence that had taken hold at Harvard Law School under Oliver Wendell Holmes, Roscoe Pound, Louis Brandeis, and Felix Frankfurter, which treated the law as an instrument of social action; and institutionalism, with its faith in human intelligence as opposed to laissez-faire determinism, in other words, the application of technical expertise to economic and social problems. In *The Modern Corporation* Berle and Means demonstrated the concentration of power in the industrial sector in 200 large corporations managed by some 1,800 individuals. Put simply, the age of Rockefeller and Carnegie is gone. Owners are now stockholders interested only in profits and dividends and do not effectively manage their property in the modern economy. The resultant creation is the large corporation with a life of its own operated by a small managerial class. "The problem is therefore," Berle asks, whether the corporation "will dominate the state or whether the two will coexist with relatively little connection? . . . This is a question which must remain unanswered for a long time to come."

As he concluded his opus, Berle hoped for the evolution of business statesmanship responsive to community pressures. "Control of the great corporations should develop into a purely neutral technocracy, balancing a variety of claims by various groups in the community and assigning to each a portion of the income stream on the basis of public policy rather than private cupidity." Corporate managers needed to set forth a program comprising fair wages, security to employees, reasonable service to the public, and stabilization of business, the essence of the later National Industrial Recovery Administration. When, in fact, business-government cooperation failed, government assumed an enlarged role, as in the Wagner Act, with its creation of a powerful National Labor Relations Board, and the later Fair Labor Standards Act.

At Moley's request, Berle contributed a lengthy memorandum in May 1932 on possible avenues of economic restoration. It contained an analysis of the financial origins of the Depression, short-range solutions, and long-range remedies. Depression causation and economic stagnation were attributed to a collapse of values, caused initially by speculation, then the liquidation of legitimate investments. Sterilization of money and credit followed, with the hoarding of cash by banks and individuals, resulting in an absence of demand.

Short-term recovery depended upon the restoration of liquidity and therefore confidence in the normal workings of the financial system. Since banks feared for their own liquidity, the credit of the United States government would serve

as a basis for the salvage of certain securities. Other securities would be liquidated. As an example, speculators in vacant real estate or the stock market could
not be bailed out. But homeowners and mortgages on urban dwellings held by
banks needed to be salvaged, and were, by the Home Owners Loan Corporation
(HOLC). The same principle would be applied to agriculture through the Farm
Credit Administration headed by Henry Morgenthau, Jr., and in the bank crisis,
with the federal government providing liquidity and turning the situation around.
This process, incidentally, came to Berle through his study of Alexander Hamilton's Assumption Act.

Based on his study of the modern corporation, Berle proceeded to long-range
solutions, although now, in 1932, he was less sanguine regarding corporate or
financial statesmanship. With utility and railroad pyramids in collapse and the
practices of financiers in question, Berle insisted on exposure of business decisions in the form quarterly reports, publicity of transactions in securities by
corporate officers, creation of a Capital Issues Board (the later Securities and
Exchange Commission), the divorcement of commercial and investment banking,
encouragement of chain banking for greater stability, and repeal of antitrust in
favor of federal oversight and regulation in the event especially of 50 percent
domination of an industry by one or two firms.

Concentration of control in the hands of a few also necessitated a federally
mandated system of insurance against illness, unemployment, and old age for
the many. The individual was at the mercy of powerful economic aggregates.
Hoover's American system, based on individualism and voluntary, charitable
rescue activity in depression, had become a fiction.

Roosevelt's Commonwealth Club speech, delivered in San Francisco on September 23, 1932, constituted his most significant statement on business-government relations. As the campaign train headed south from Portland, Moley,
working with Berle's speech draft, sensed the chance for a historic statement.
Jefferson's Declaration of Independence counseled restraint on excesses of government. Now it seemed time to suggest limitations on the private sector, that
the age of laissez-faire had ended. As FDR put it, "I feel that we are coming
to a view . . . that private economic power is . . . a public trust." Private advantage must give way, where required, to public advantage, to a new constitutional
order consisting of a better economic balance, better distribution of purchasing
power, restoration of wages, the end of unemployment, and a return to agricultural prosperity. Roosevelt hoped that business would put its own house in
order (NIRA); otherwise government would intervene for the protection of the
public interest (Section 7a, the Wagner Act, Social Security, the Fair Labor
Standards Act).[11]

In conclusion, the bank crisis simply highlighted the collapse of the nation's
credit system, long in the works. Its resolution rested not on FDR's speechmaking
abilities, but on his willingness to use the credit of the United States to afford
liquidity. In time, through the Reconstruction Finance Corporation (RFC), the

federal government financed business expansion; and through mechanisms such as the HOLC and Farm Credit Administration, millions of homeowners and farmers, as well as thousands of banks that held their paper, were salvaged.

Second, Roosevelt and the Brain Trust aimed at parity between the agrarian and urban sectors. Currency debasement was avoided as the solution, since it would simply restore old disparities and inequities. Parity was achieved through management of production, soil conservation, and major economic transfers effected by taxation and expenditures.

Emergency relief through Public Works Administration (PWA), WPA, and similar mechanisms would tide people over until the economy recovered. With recovery, the social minimum would carry people through future economic downturns and old age.

Essentially, the New Deal aimed at a new economic equilibrium as a replacement for the disequilibrium of the 1920s. "We wanted recovery," Rexford Tugwell explained. "We wanted a balanced economy, we wanted to institutionalize the balance, and prevent future depressions." After seven years, in 1939, Raymond Moley conceded, "The harvest is past, the summer is ended, and we are not saved. Vastly important reforms remain to be achieved." Yet, in the last analysis, Roosevelt and the Brain Trust had met the test of conjuncture, the use of creative intelligence in a time of crisis. This was their lasting contribution.[12]

NOTES

1. Herbert Hoover, *The New Day: Campaign Speeches of Herbert Clark Hoover, 1928* (Stanford, Calif.: Stanford University Press, [1929]), p. 15.

2. Herbert Hoover, *American Individualism* (Garden City, N.Y.: Doubleday, Page, 1922); "Campaign Speech at Madison Square Garden, New York City, October 31, 1932. The Campaign a Contrast Between Two Philosophies of Government (Analysis of Democratic Proposals as Dangerous to the Foundations of American National Life)," in William Starr Myers, ed., *The State Papers and Other Public Writings of Herbert Hoover*, 2 vols. (Garden City, N.Y.: Doubleday, Doran, 1934), 2: 408–28.

3. For a more complete discussion of Hoover's Depression program, see Elliot A. Rosen, *Hoover, Roosevelt and the Brain Trust: From Depression to New Deal* (New York: Columbia University Press, 1977), Chapter 11.

4. Ibid., pp. 113–14; Raymond Moley interviews, 1963–64, tape recorded, in author's possession; Samuel I. Rosenman, *Working with Roosevelt* (New York: Harper, 1952), pp. 56–58.

5. Raymond Moley, with the assistance of Elliot A. Rosen, *The First New Deal* (New York: Harcourt, Brace and World, 1966), pp. 208–20.

6. Raymond Moley to Franklin D. Roosevelt, May 19, 1932, and memorandum attached, Moley Papers. The Moley papers were researched when they were in his possession. They are currently deposited with the Hoover Institution on War, Revolution, and Peace, Stanford, California.

7. Edward M. House to Franklin D. Roosevelt, April 14, 1932, Box 95, folder 3287, ser. 1, Selected Correspondence, House Papers, Yale University Library, New Haven,

Conn. See also Memorandum, "Dictated by Mr. Howe . . . Regarding Water Power—Interest," n.d., Moley Papers.

8. For a fuller discussion of the drafting and implications of the Forgotten Man and St. Paul addresses, see Rosen, *Hoover, Roosevelt and the Brain Trust,* pp. 130–40.

9. The concept is described more fully in Rosen, "Intranationalism vs. Internationalism: The Interregnum Struggle for the Sanctity of the New Deal," *Political Science Quarterly,* vol. 81 (June 1966).

10. The discussion of Tugwell and agriculture is based on a reading of the following collections: Raymond Moley (Hoover Institution); Rexford G. Tugwell (FDR Library, Hyde Park, N.Y.); Adolf A. Berle, Jr. (FDR Library); M. L. Wilson (State University of Montana, Bozeman); and Henry A. Wallace (University of Iowa, Iowa City). I have relied also on tape recorded discussions with Raymond Moley, 1963–1964, in my possession, and on Bernard Sternsher, *Rexford G. Tugwell and the New Deal* (New Brunswick, N.J.: Rutgers University Press, 1964).

11. See Rosen, *Hoover, Roosevelt, and the Brain Trust,* pp. 195–211, 356–60.

12. Rexford G. Tugwell to Elliot A. Rosen, May 5, 1964.

IV

FOREIGN POLICY: THE BREAK WITH ISOLATIONISM

11

The First Link: Toward the End of Isolation

Joseph Cardello

The study of U.S. foreign policy during World War II has suffered from a preoccupation with the origins of the Cold War. This impulse is natural and understandable—to explain the failure of yet another massive war to establish a stable structure of world peace. The participants had a clear vision of this burden: "I shudder to think of what will happen to humanity," Roosevelt declared in his 1943 State of the Union message, "... if this war ends in an inconclusive peace." And one week before his death he wrote to Stalin, "It would be one of the great tragedies of history if at the very moment of victory, now within our grasp, such distrust, such lack of faith should prejudice the entire undertaking after the colossal losses of life, material, and treasure involved."[1]

The unfolding of this postwar tragedy has been a compelling topic for those living with the consequences of that inconclusive peace. But this focus on the origins of the Cold War has seriously distorted the realities of U.S. policymaking during the war. Franklin Roosevelt, as much as anyone, understood the importance of Soviet-American relations in determining the nature of the postwar world. Survival of the wartime coalition was indeed his central objective. But one cannot focus exclusively on this effort without misunderstanding the context of decision making that Roosevelt had to face. One critical issue in particular— the continuing struggle against isolationism—has been neglected by those seeking to trace the beginnings of cold war, rather than understanding the war years in their own context and from their own past. Even for understanding its legacy today, we need to grasp the past as it was lived, in relation to its own past, rather than searching through it too exclusively for its future.

It has become commonplace in writing of Franklin Roosevelt and World War II to speak of the ghostly influence of Woodrow Wilson, the League of Nations, and the memory of 1919. The implication is most often negative: that misjudgments and miscalculations resulted from an obsession with past mistakes, from an attempt to avoid repeating Wilson's errors nearly a quarter-century after the fact. Many see Roosevelt, Cordell Hull, and others preparing to fight old battles rather than responding to contemporary circumstances. But the circumstances of 1944 were not so different on the domestic front from those of 1918. The tradition of nonentanglement dating back to George Washington's day had actually reached its peak in the 1930s. World War II could easily appear as merely another brief interruption in the long-standing policy of noninvolvement in overseas political affairs, especially those of Europe. The memory of isolation was necessarily fresh and vital in the minds of those destined to cope with the dilemmas of total global war.

Too often the end of isolationism and the "triumph of internationalism," as one writer describes it, have been assumed as inevitable results of the cataclysm of World War II.[2] But the leaders of government could not take for granted the end of an attitude so deeply entrenched in American life and, more important, in many of their own personal experiences. They could not assume its demise— they had to work to end it. And to many of that generation, even with the countless new and complex international problems thrust upon Americans for the first time, it was that battle to end isolationism that had to be won before the United States could deal effectively with the world's more specific and mounting crises.

Roosevelt had no reason to assume that the threads of the past would be severed by a single blow, no matter how sharp. Traditional isolationism was too deeply woven for such a neat, abrupt discontinuity. Yet too many writers discuss the war as if Pearl Harbor marked a clean break with history; as if the long decades of fundamental belief and the most recent conflicts and tensions of the 1930s had been swept away; as if this struggle for survival which was World War II was merely a prelude to cold war rather than an uncertain epilogue to 150 years of noninvolvement. Roosevelt, Hull, Henry Stimson, and many others in the administration were keenly aware of the realities and continuities of traditional American values in foreign affairs. They were ever sensitive, but not overly sensitive, to public responses that might jeopardize the long-range aim of securing a permanent U.S. involvement in world politics.

The deep flows of the past did not stop suddenly in December 1941; the currents remained, and the need to shape them, to redirect them, fell to harried men in the midst of total war—men faced with a unique, perplexing set of circumstances—men challenged by an unfamiliar world power, both their own and that of the Soviet Union.

ISOLATIONISM BEFORE PEARL HARBOR

Throughout Franklin Roosevelt's public life a single, overriding issue dominated the debate on foreign policy: How much overseas political activity would the American people tolerate? Roosevelt had played a direct role in each of the peaks in this controversy between isolationism and internationalism. In 1914 he had followed the example of his "Uncle Teddy," advocating an early U.S. intervention in World War I. As a member of Wilson's cabinet—he was assistant secretary of the navy—he supported the movement toward internationalism, becoming its principal spokesman as Democratic vice presidential candidate in 1920. His experience of the events of 1919 was unusually personal. He sailed to Europe on January 2 aboard the USS *George Washington,* the same liner on which President Wilson had departed for preliminary peace talks only a month earlier. After completing his Navy Department business, Roosevelt returned to the United States on February 15. This time Wilson was also aboard the *George Washington.* Only the day before, the signing of a covenant for a new League of Nations had been announced. The aloof Wilson kept to himself through most of the return journey, but surprisingly took time for a personal chat with his young assistant secretary. Wilson spoke with great fervor of his hopes for establishing the new league as the basis for future peace. Roosevelt never forgot this surprising personal attention. When he returned to the United States, he actively supported the League of Nations and the Versailles Treaty. He had reservations, he admitted in many of his speeches, but he warned that America could never "go backwards toward an old Chinese wall policy of isolation." The treaty was far from perfect, he said, but retreat into isolation would be a "grievous wrong."[3]

In 1921, after the resounding defeat of the Democratic national ticket, Roosevelt became chairman of a committee to establish the Woodrow Wilson Foundation, a pro–League of Nations organization which awarded cash prizes to individuals and organizations working for peace and the ideals of the ex-president. In 1930 Roosevelt also helped to establish the Walter Hines Page School of International Relations at the Johns Hopkins University. By 1928, however, he no longer advocated U.S. entry into the League. He still supported an international organization and believed that the United States should cooperate with it—but short of full membership. During the campaign of 1932 he even made a speech opposing U.S. entry. The Democratic platform on which he ran did not even mention the League of Nations.[4]

The tragedy of the Great Depression had overwhelmed all other issues. It preoccupied the minds of all Western democratic leaders, and Roosevelt was no exception. In such a domestic emergency the American people had even less tolerance for international affairs. And Roosevelt did not challenge this pervasive mood. He was never one to crusade against overwhelming public opposition.

As president during the 1930s, perhaps the most isolationist of decades, Roosevelt felt the severe restrictions of a series of neutrality acts—laws designed to guarantee that the United States would not be drawn once again into European quarrels. The president accepted isolationist neutrality laws; whether he did this reluctantly or out of genuine agreement has been the subject of some debate. Given his earlier internationalist views, and his later interventionism, and given the public's near-unanimity on staying clear of the dangers of world affairs, there may have been a certain reluctance in the president's following along after the Congress and the people in their pursuit of perfect isolation. His desire to keep the United States out of war was sincere. But when the nature and scope of the Axis threat became clearer, Roosevelt late in 1937 began a cautious, gradual shift away from strict neutrality.

For the next four years he worked at the fearful task of convincing the public that U.S. security was in danger. This was the most difficult and frustrating struggle of his presidential career. Late in 1939, after the war in Europe had begun, he described the prospect for William Allen White:

Things move with such terrific speed, these days, that it really is essential to us to think in broader terms and, in effect, to warn the American people that they, too, should think of possible ultimate results in Europe. . . . Therefore, my sage old friend, my problem is to get the American people to think of conceivable consequences without scaring the American people into thinking that they are going to be dragged into this war.

Whatever his views had been in the mid-1930s, by June 1940 he came to denounce the policy of isolation as a "delusion."[5]

The president's remarkable patience was well suited to this delicate task, but he was only partially successful. The American public was willing to take certain steps to support the British, but too few would contemplate any direct participation in the fighting. In the end, Pearl Harbor forced a still reluctant, divided people into war.

Roosevelt could hardly forget these long, frustrating, divisive years. These decades of experience with isolationism placed great demands on his political abilities. He learned to approach this issue slowly, tentatively, with extreme caution, always probing carefully ahead, always one step at a time. The League and Wilson, the neutrality acts, and particularly the struggle to get the United States into the war, all developed in him a heightened concern for both congressional and public opinion. He learned a degree of caution even beyond his already highly developed sensitivity to public moods. And this intensified wariness on the issue of internationalism continued after December 7, 1941.

From the president's point of view the battle against isolationism was in no sense resolved by the attack on Pearl Harbor. On the contrary, the need to commit the United States to a permanent responsibility in world affairs continued as the principal goal of policymaking during the war. The fear of a resurgent isolationism continued to affect Roosevelt's decisions—and in this fear, this active concern to thwart the reactionary forces of isolation, lay some of the more effective limits on U.S. policy in the war years. Isolationism, counted out by some, continued to operate as a pervasive restraint on Roosevelt's conduct of diplomacy.

WARTIME PERSISTENCE OF ISOLATIONISM

In a campaign speech at the Foreign Policy Association in New York on October 21, 1944, Roosevelt stressed the issue of internationalism and the lessons of World War I. He warned of the return of the "heavy hand of isolationism" if Republicans should dominate the national government:

Now, the question of the men who will formulate and carry out the foreign policy of this country is in issue . . . very much in issue. It is in issue not in terms of partisan application, but in terms of sober, solemn facts—the facts that are on the record.

If the Republicans were to win control of the Congress in this election . . . inveterate isolationists would occupy positions of commanding influence and power.[6]

Tracing "Old Guard" policies from Versailles to Pearl Harbor, the president went on to catalogue a pattern of Republican errors: opposition to League membership, refusal to join the World Court, passage of high tariff walls blocking international trade, opposition to recognition of the Soviet Union, resistance to overhauling the neutrality acts in 1939, among others. He continued in his conversational style:

Let us analyze it a little more. The majority of the Republican members of the Congress voted—I am just giving you a few figures, not many—against the Selective Service Law in 1940; they voted against repeal of the Arms Embargo in 1939; they voted against the Lend-Lease Law in 1941; and they voted in August 1941, against extension of the Selective Service—which meant voting against keeping our Army together—four months before Pearl Harbor.[7]

That last vote had extended Selective Service by a margin of one vote. That was not a memory calculated to inspire faith in public or congressional enlightenment.

Roosevelt clearly linked the compelling logic of World War I experience with the need to bury permanently the policy of isolation—an obvious, time-worn connection, but one with which the president retained a strong personal identification. In the same New York speech he said:

When the first World War was ended—it seems like a long time ago—I believed—I believe now—that enduring peace in the world has not a chance unless this Nation—our America—is willing to cooperate in winning it and maintaining it. I thought back in those days of 1918 and 1919—and I know now—that we have to back our American words with American deeds.

A quarter of a century ago we helped to save freedom, but we failed to organize the kind of world in which future generations could live—with freedom. Opportunity knocks again. There is no guarantee that opportunity will knock a third time.[8]

On this subject he grew indignant: "Never again, after cooperating with other Nations in a world war to save our way of life, can we wash our hands of maintaining the peace for which we fought." This generation, he concluded, had to act not only for itself and for the future, "but as a trustee for all those who fell in the last war—a part of their mission unfulfilled."[9]

For Franklin Roosevelt, these memories of the last three decades of foreign affairs were intense and personal. His New York speech carried warnings, remembrances, satire—and was saturated with references to isolationists. His principal theme called upon an inexperienced American public to take up the burden of world responsibility. As late as October 1944, then, this message held a forward place in the president's thinking. After years of personal frustration it remained the broadest goal of his policy.

Throughout the war public opinion polls showed a majority in favor of U.S. membership in an international organization. These reports were somewhat encouraging, but, as will be seen, they failed to measure the quality or intensity of this seeming change in the public mind. Roosevelt, for one, was not convinced. To the end of his life he remained uncertain of either the depth or permanence of this commitment. During the campaign of 1944 an editorial appeared in *Life* magazine arguing that, in attacking the Republicans for being isolationist, Roosevelt was beating a dead horse—that the issue was as dead as "locofocoism." The president did not agree. He commented: "Anybody who thinks that isolationism is dead in this country is crazy. As soon as this war is over, it may well be stronger than ever."[10] Late in October 1944 Robert Sherwood suggested that for an upcoming address in Philadelphia the president use an excerpt from a recent speech by Winston Churchill to dramatize the fact that the United States was at "the highest pinnacle of her power and fame." Roosevelt responded with great seriousness: "What Winston says may be true at the moment, but I'd hate to say it. Because we may be heading before very long for the pinnacle of our weakness." Sherwood was shocked and intrigued by this reaction. Roosevelt's words, he wrote, "were burned into my memory, and my curiosity. . . . I've always assumed that he was looking forward to the approaching moment when the reaction might set in, and isolationism again be rampant, and the American people might again tell the rest of the world to stew in its own juice."[11]

Concern over the ancient question of nonentanglement was not confined to the presidential campaign, although it may have reached its greatest intensity at that time owing to the genuine anxieties Roosevelt felt about his opposition. The lesson of responsibility—of the "family of mankind," of global good neighborliness, as he characteristically phrased it—was one of his most deeply felt convictions, one going beyond political considerations. In a Christmas Eve fireside chat in 1943 he spoke of the "ill-fated experiments of former years" and pledged to do all in his power "to see to it that these tragic mistakes shall not be made again." He went on:

There have always been cheerful idiots in this country who believed that there would be no more wars for us if everybody in America would only return into their homes and lock their front doors behind them. Assuming that their motives were of the highest, events have shown how unwilling they were to face the facts.[12]

The president's address in March 1945 after the Yalta Conference also made clear his continuing worry over isolationism. While less general than his campaign speeches and more concerned with particular contemporary problems, that persistent worry over American "responsibility" revealed much about Roosevelt's thinking. His basic theme in approaching the public on foreign affairs remained the same: "Responsibility for political conditions thousands of miles away can no longer be avoided by this great Nation." The United States would need to exert its influence for peace and "to share in the responsibility for keeping the peace. It will be our own tragic loss, I think, if we were to shirk that responsibility." Roosevelt did not share the confidence of Henry Luce, publisher of *Life,* that a policy of international involvement had already been decided. His tone remained insistent, educative, admonitory: "There can be no middle ground here. We shall have to take the responsibility for world collaboration, or we shall have to bear the responsibility for another world conflict." Again he drew on what he called the "tragic sequence of events" over the last twenty-five years:

For the second time in the lives of most of us this generation is face to face with the objective of preventing wars. . . .

Twenty-five years ago, American fighting men looked to the statesmen of the world to finish the work of peace for which they fought and suffered. We failed them then. We cannot fail them again, and expect the world again to survive.[13]

Even after the Yalta Conference, Roosevelt believed that the public had to be convinced.

POSTWAR INFLUENCE OF ISOLATIONISM

The president was not the only member of his administration who was disturbed over the survival of isolationist sentiment. Secretary of State Cordell Hull kept the elements of public opinion constantly in mind. On numerous occasions he spoke of his fears about the future of U.S. policy. After substantial gains by the Republicans in the 1942 congressional elections, Henry Wallace spoke with the secretary: "Hull seemed to think the country was going in exactly the same steps it followed in 1918. He thought it was utterly important to keep the sequence of events from following the 1919–1921 pattern because he felt if we went into isolationism this time, the world was lost forever." Henry Stimson recalled how Hull "again and again" emphasized that the overriding issue still was "whether or not the United States would truly become a participating and effective member of the world community." Stimson shared Hull's fear that the United States might again "slump into isolationism" after the war: he placed permanent involvement in world affairs on the top of his list of priorities. The two men spent many hours discussing the problems of educating the public about the place of the United States in the world, dividing their epithets among isolationists and "fuzzy-minded idealists."[14]

Recognition of Soviet sovereignty in the Baltic States touched a particularly sensitive nerve in Hull's political concern. Estonia, Latvia, and Lithuania, parts of Imperial Russia thirty years before, had been independent entities since World War I. In 1939 and 1940 the Soviet Union had annexed them and during the war demanded that they be accepted as part of postwar Soviet territory. From the first suggestions in June 1941 of an Anglo-Soviet treaty recognizing these expanded Russian boundaries, Hull sought to avoid any agreement on this issue for fear of violating American principles of self-determination and rekindling isolationist disgust over secret agreements and international politics-as-usual.

In December 1943 he urged Ambassador Averell Harriman to get the Soviets to quiet the Baltic issue. He feared its negative effect on the movement toward international cooperation: it would "play into the hands of the trouble-makers in this country. . . . If you can tactfully get this view before the Soviet Government, it would be calculated to avoid what may soon become serious crimination and recrimination among irresponsible elements in this country."[15] But the Baltic issue was not the only one to rouse Hull's fear of controversy. He also wished to avoid having the European Advisory Commission as a major decision maker on future policy. He wrote to Ambassador John G. Winant in England on January 9, 1944: "I believe that you will appreciate the possible long-term repercussions on American public opinion should the impression be gained that this Commission . . . is secretly building the new world." For this and other reasons, the commission, established after the Teheran Conference late in 1943 to handle postwar European problems, exercised few important functions.[16]

Hull developed the reasoning behind this cautious approach in a conversation with the British ambassador in August 1942. The secretary stated that, second only to winning the war, the "greatest danger to the whole post-war planning was . . . the question of securing the support of the electorate for our post-war program as it may be made up; that unless the most careful, sound and tactful course is pursued . . . the governments supporting any different plan and program will be completely swamped at first election after the last shot is fired." This slow, careful nurturing of popular support constituted the "all-important phase" which must precede informal talks and, later, more formal meetings. Such an effort was particularly necessary in dealing with the Senate, and Hull consistently stressed the need for a gradual, detailed approach to cooperation with the Congress in developing a consensus on international collaboration.[17]

There were others beside Hull and Stimson who wisely recognized the delicate tensions between foreign policy and domestic opinion. Elbridge Durbrow, assistant chief of the Division of Eastern European Affairs in the State Department, warned of these dangers in Baltic policy. In November 1944 the new secretary of state, Edward Stettinius, had seen Ambassador Andrei Gromyko in New York at a rally celebrating the anniversary of Soviet-U.S. relations. Gromyko had raised the issue of U.S. policy regarding the Baltic states. Stettinius requested a position paper on the subject, and Durbrow drew one up. In it he urged continuing the policy of nonrecognition of changes accomplished through force, and postponement of territorial adjustments until after the war. Public reaction figured prominently in his reasoning:

Certain sections of the American public have received the impression that the United States Government has adopted a policy of "appeasement" toward the Soviet Union and that we have abandoned the principles enunciated in the Atlantic Charter. Therefore, if we should at this time give any indication that we have accepted the absorption of the Baltic States by the U.S.S.R. there might be very grave repercussions which would seriously prejudice the possibility of the American public accepting the Dumbarton Oaks plan.[18]

The plan developed at Dumbarton Oaks in the late summer of 1944 had established the preliminary framework of a new international organization—a successor to the old League of Nations. U.S. officials were clearly determined not to repeat the historic errors of Wilson and the League after Versailles.

This view was not limited to European affairs. Hull's chief political advisor, Stanley Hornbeck, made the link with China policy soon after the attack on Pearl Harbor:

It cannot be too often recalled that the attitude of the American people has as yet by no means become permanently one of willingness to assume responsibilities abroad—one might say that this is especially true with respect to the Far East. There is every reason to assume that at some time in the not too distant future there will be a considerable reaction in American public sentiment from the present position of enthusiastic desire to cooperate with China. We have in the past few days had evidence, in connection with our relations with Great Britain, that even under present conditions there are important elements of public opinion which are reluctant to see the United States undertake necessary cooperation with other countries.[19]

The future of the British Empire presented another problem which might revive the "ostrich isolationism" feared by Roosevelt. Herbert Matthews, chief of the European Affairs Division, had written to Hull in March 1943 that the main concern of the British remained the urgent need to bring the United States into a permanent world commitment. John Davies, a career Foreign Service officer attached to the embassy in China, thought this might prove difficult unless the British softened their imperial views: "In the minds of most Americans a better world is identified with the abolition of imperialism, and there is a very real danger that the United States may again become isolationist after the war as a result of a feeling by the American people that they have been made dupes of British imperialism."[20] There were endless complications here. The most basic principle of U.S. policy lay in continued Anglo-American cooperation and the need to insure England's survival as a first-rate power. But that power depended to a great extent on the British Empire, which many Americans opposed out of concern for a rising Asian nationalism and the Atlantic Charter principle of self-determination. In this, as in many other issues, an already complex question was made even more difficult by the specter of isolationism. As Davies put it, "If Britain does not want the United States to go isolationist, it must be careful to leave us some freedom to state our own case in Asia."[21]

Early in 1944 difficulties between the Soviet government and the Polish government-in-exile in London sharpened U.S. concern for the temper of public opinion. The Poles had asked the president to serve as an intermediary in the dispute. Roosevelt discussed the matter with Hull, and they agreed to a U.S. tender of good offices to get talks started. But Hull was profoundly troubled by the general direction of events. In a long cable to Ambassador Harriman on January 15 he urged a direct approach to the Soviets on the question of arranging Soviet-Polish discussions. Harriman should make it clear to the Russians that continued refusal to meet with Polish leaders would set back the cause of international cooperation. While the U.S. government would take no position on substantive matters of disagreement between the two parties—it merely intended an earnest, friendly effort to help the Soviet Union reach a settlement of the problem—Hull did stress the "far-reaching" effect on the American press and public of recent hostile Soviet propaganda. If the Soviets chose a course of ruthless, unilateral action the repercussions in the United States could be dangerous. Many important individuals viewed the whole Polish-Soviet quarrel "as a test of the reality of international cooperation in its broad future aspects on a basis of friendly accord and respect for the rights of nations." The conferences at Moscow and Teheran late in 1943 had helped in this effort, Hull wrote, but he now pointed out the "danger to the cause of cooperation in an international security system which would result from an arbitrary dealing with the Polish-Soviet differences."[22]

Harriman presented these views to Vyacheslav Molotov, but the Russians were not moved. A week later Hull again warned Harriman of developing impressions that the Soviet Union had embarked on an arbitrary policy in relations with Poland. The effect of such an approach was clear, he argued: the Soviets would open themselves up to critics in this country and thus jeopardize public support for a program of international cooperation. Present Soviet conduct constituted "an approach which American public opinion will not understand." Hull drew out the lesson for Harriman: "As you well know, without the whole-hearted support of public opinion, this great movement toward international cooperation cannot be transformed into a solid practical basis for the establishment of a stable and durable peace." He emphasized how important it was for the Soviets to understand that American public faith in an international security arrangement with the USSR depended upon the willingness of both countries to act reasonably, fairly, openly, and without resort to force. Continuation of present Soviet policies, he feared, "will inevitably be interpreted by a large section of American opinion as as significant step backward in the direction of power politics and spheres of influence. We believe the Soviet Government must realize how serious the effect of this will be upon our public opinion and upon Congress in respect of the cooperation of the country in any international system of world security."[23]

On February 9 Hull again addressed the beleaguered Harriman. The American people were "mystified and alarmed" by a series of recent Soviet acts in foreign relations. The Soviets must soon choose either cooperation or unilateralism:

The American people will be unable to reconcile the contradictions between the two and will not be disposed to favor American participation in a scheme of world organization which will merely be regarded as a cover for another great power to continue to pursue a course of unilateral action in the international sphere based on superior force.[24]

He expressed these views late in March 1944 to Ambassador Gromyko in Washington, warning of a "rising hostility to Russia" which might damage future relations.[25] Again, however, the argument seemed to have little impact on Soviet leaders.

Roosevelt also addressed the issue, echoing Hull's views. On February 7, 1944, he cabled a mild, inoffensive plea to Stalin on the matter of Polish-Soviet differences. He urged some sort of compromise solution. He mentioned the approval of the "overwhelming majority of our people and Congress" for the spirit of cooperation developed at the Moscow and Teheran conferences, and hoped that the inevitable conflicts of international politics would not jeopardize future peaceful relations. The fear of a latent isolationism hovered along the edges of his indirect warning to Stalin:

While public opinion is forming in support of the principle of international collaboration, it is especially incumbent upon us to avoid any action which might appear to counteract the achievement of our long-range objective. I feel that I should ill serve our common interest if I failed to bring these facts to your attention.[26]

The commitment to internationalism, American leaders believed, was by no means assured; and flagrant Soviet behavior, it was feared, might upset the delicate process of bringing along a reluctant, ill-informed, immature American electorate. Harriman continued to impress upon Soviet officials the significance of adverse public reaction in the United States, just as Hull ordered—but he continued to get nowhere.

As the war went on, the pollsters eagerly measured public responses on the question of a new international organization. The results seemed overwhelming:

May 1941: 38% approved a new League after the war, 39% opposed
July 1942: 59% favored membership in a new League, 22% opposed
November 1942: 62% favored joining "some sort of organization of nations after the war." In January 1943, 72% in favor
December 1942: 73% wanted the government to "take steps now, before the end of the war," to establish a new international organization

May 1943: Should the United States participate in "an international police force after
        the war?" 74% yes; 14% no

April 1945: 81% favored a "world organization with police power to maintain world
        peace"[27]

Through the last months of the war, a steady 70–80% approved U.S. entry into
a new peacekeeping body. George Gallup, responsible for many of the surveys,
described the trend as "a profound change in viewpoint on international affairs."
And one historian of the internationalist movement in the United States has
concluded, "Public opinion polls showed that more and more Americans were
moving toward internationalism."[28] Must one conclude, then, that Henry Luce
was right? Were Roosevelt's fears of a surviving isolationism exaggerated? Was
the question of isolationism as dead as "locofocoism," as Luce put it?

There were other polls, and these showed the need for caution in interpreting
the surveys outlined above. In October 1943, for example, Americans were
asked to name the number one problem facing the country after the war. Fifty-
eight percent selected "jobs"; only 13 percent opted for "lasting peace." Another survey discovered that 50 percent of the people expressed greatest concern
about the future of the economy; only 16 percent thought foreign affairs the
most important public concern. Even more revealing, a Gallup poll taken in
1939, when isolationism dominated American thinking, had shown that 46 percent of those asked were in favor of an international police force. In May 1943,
74 percent approved.[29] Clearly, the *New Yorker* concluded, opinion polls could
be misleading: "Asking a man whether he wants an international police force
is like asking him whether he wants the Rockettes." Many professional pollsters
qualified the results of their own surveys. Jerome Bruner, for example, believed
that the public did not fully realize what an "international police force" might
involve: "We are for it in the same way as we are for vaccination. Force stops
aggression. Vaccination stops smallpox. Never mind the niceties."[30]

The State Department conducted its own opinion polls, with the same results
as the private surveys. But government officials remained skeptical of the meaning of these suddenly lopsided percentages: they warned that "thus far opinion
has been elicited and expressed only in vague terms. . . . The public as yet is
generally unaware of the specific implications of international organization and
of the price they will have to pay for such organization."[31] The polls could not
measure the depth of public commitment and could not predict how views might
change under later, perhaps adverse, circumstances. The polls also failed to
distinguish between process and substance in foreign policy—between image
and reality—between simple membership in a new League and a constant, frustrating, costly involvement abroad. In short, the polls could prove dangerously
weak reeds for government leaders to rely on in shaping future policies. Perhaps
the poll-takers should have asked more pointed questions: Would you commit
American troops to maintain the peace in Europe after the war? Would you agree
to spending a substantial percentage of tax dollars for foreign assistance, aid for

reconstruction of devastated countries, and a permanent military establishment in the United States? Of course these, too, would present problems of interpretation—they are leading questions, hypothetical projections into the future coaxing the expected, respectable response. But they might have offered a more precise idea of American thinking on foreign affairs beyond the abstract ideal of membership in a new League of Nations.

In two critical areas the public showed an unwillingness to make serious, substantive, permanent commitments of U.S. power in the world. First, the people insisted on bringing the boys home as soon as possible after the war. No one advocated maintenance of troops abroad, and Roosevelt had to operate on this assumption. The U.S. military would dissolve at war's end—and in 1945 and 1946 it did just that, even in an atmosphere of developing cold war. Second, the Congress struggled in 1945 to reduce taxes by cutting shipments of Lend-Lease aid as soon as the fighting stopped. Many representatives did not trust Roosevelt, and, even though the president since November 1944 had promised to limit Lend-Lease to war use and to stop it completely when the war ended, the Congress sought to rewrite aid authorization bills in order to guarantee that "lend-lease could not be used for reconstruction," relief, or redevelopment overseas. Part of the motive was political, anti-Roosevelt; part of it was fiscal, to reduce federal expenditures as soon as possible and thus provide relief from high taxes. But the impact on U.S. allies was severe. The president had wanted to continue massive aid to Britain after the defeat of Germany and before the defeat of Japan. He had cancelled earlier orders to end assistance after V-E Day, but for months he neglected to issue any new orders to the bureaucracy. Meanwhile, at the Quebec Conference in September 1944, an informal agreement for aid totalling $6.5 billion had been negotiated with the British, who desperately needed it to handle their critical economic problems. The Lend-Lease supplies were to be delivered during Stage II—the period between the defeat of Germany and the defeat of Japan. Later negotiations reduced the figure to $5.4 billion. But in the last weeks of the year, under pressure from some cabinet officials, the president drew back from this commitment, wavering between his fears of a rising Anglophobia in Congress and his sincere desire to help the British. The agreement still had not been formalized when Congress acted in the first months of 1945 to cut Lend-Lease aid.[32] These new pressures came amid mounting public criticism of U.S. allies—both Britain and Russia—and seemed to reflect a growing reaction against world politics—a desire to bring the boys home and get out of Europe as soon as possible.

Popular views on foreign aid were not encouraging. Samuel Rosenman forwarded a report to the president on November 24, 1943, containing the results of a survey conducted by Hadley Cantril, head of the Office of Public Opinion Research at Princeton. According to Cantril, two-thirds of the people thought that "we should not give aid to foreign countries after the war" if this aid "would lower our own standard of living"—and nearly 50 percent believed that it would. Cantril recommended that administration policy "should carefully avoid giving the impression to the nation that foreign affairs will be carried on at the expense of domestic programs."[33]

Early in 1945 the president's relations with Congress reached an all-time low. Among other anti-administration moves, the Congress cut sharply both the British aid agreement and another negotiated with the French. Roosevelt had to give in to an adamant Congress, agreeing in February that Lend-Lease in wartime would not become foreign aid or postwar reconstruction assistance in peacetime.[34] It remained to be seen whether the Congress and the people would approve any independent foreign aid program after the war. But, clearly, the events of early 1945 were not encouraging.

This ongoing concern over isolation did not reflect a foolish obsession with the nation's past. There was enough evidence that isolationism might again obstruct peacemaking efforts. The whole mood of the country during the war showed something less than a mature sense of commitment. In the last years of the war people turned away from an earlier mood of sacrifice and displayed a remarkable self-indulgence—a "carnival of consumption," as one historian has described it.[35] Movie stars and a professional advertising campaign had to be used to meet quotas in the sale of war bonds. Drives to collect paper and other materials slowed. Civil defense programs phased out as enemy planes failed to appear. In domestic politics there was a distinct turn to the right as many New Deal programs were dismantled by a conservative Congress. Advertising looked ahead to when the boys returned and their money could be spent on all the latest in fashions and appliances. The Office of War Information told the president that the vision most Americans had of the postwar world was "compounded largely of 1929 values and the economics of the 1920's."[36] Years of deprivation combined with the new affluence of the war years led people to yearn for the prosperous, fun-filled days before the Depression. For the American people, it appeared, this was very much a foreign war—something to be gotten over with in a hurry so that they could resume their normal and, they hoped, more prosperous lives—without such external disruptions.

As the war dragged on, Americans at home went on an escapist binge. That early spirit of sacrifice, of pulling together in a common cause, seemed lost. On many occasions Roosevelt expressed his concern over this lack of proper wartime spirit. It offended his sense of the common good. "Disunity at home," he said in January 1944, "—bickering, self-seeking partisanship, stoppage of work, inflation, business as usual, politics as usual, luxury as usual—these are the influences which can undermine the morale of the brave men ready to die at the front for us."[37] Roosevelt had reason to be upset. When he proposed tax measures which would more equitably distribute the financial sacrifice of war and limit the accumulation of fortunes while young men died, the Congress scorned him and passed a wholly inadequate tax bill which he angrily denounced as "relief not for the needy but for the greedy."[38] There were other disturbing tendencies in the country at large. In 1942 hotel owners in Miami had to be forced to turn off their lights after dark even though they knew their greed was making it easier for German submarines to sink U.S. merchant ships silhouetted against the night sky. As Samuel Eliot Morison wrote, "Ships were sunk and seamen drowned in order that the citizenry might enjoy business as usual." But even with the limitations of blackouts, and with gasoline rationing and the ban on new car production, tourist business in Miami in 1944 was up more than 20 percent over the previous year. The trains were packed, and scalpers sold tickets at exorbitant rates.[39]

Restaurants boomed. There were few vacancies at country clubs. Retail sales of women's clothing doubled by 1943. On December 7, 1944, Macy's had its biggest sales day in history. " 'People want to spend their money,' one store manager said, 'and if they can't spend it on textiles they'll spend it on furniture; or . . . we'll find something else for them.' " Race tracks also enjoyed banner years—both betting volume and attendance reached record heights in 1944 and 1945, despite a five-month shutdown enforced by the government in the sobering aftermath of the Battle of the Bulge. The movie theater grew as the neighborhood social center. Yearly gross soared to an all-time high, climbing an average of 33 percent a year. By 1944 Hollywood once again served up the usual diet of romances, comedies, and musicals. The public would no longer pay to see war films. Songs about the war also faded after 1942. Sentimental love songs, typically sad and yearning, were most popular—songs such as Irving Berlin's "White Christmas," and "I'll Be Seeing You." Radio carried on much as before. There were some changes to accommodate the war, especially in news reporting, but entertainment still dominated the air waves. Total advertising revenues rose 85 percent in the war years and total profits showed a 120 percent increase since 1940. There were riots at the Paramount theater when Frank Sinatra sang there, and two riots when Harry James appeared. Every form of entertainment boomed: bowling allies, Broadway plays, baseball, nightclubs, roller-skating—despite an increase in federal amusement taxes from 10 percent to 20 percent.[40] All this could be seen as a harmless outlet for war-weariness, an escape from wartime pressures. The president could appreciate this and was fully in favor of maintaining morale on the home front. What concerned him and many others was that this self-indulgence might also reflect a world-weariness whose influence would be felt when peace returned.

When the war ended, the public outcry focused on two demands: bring the boys home, and lift all wartime controls on consumer production and personal activity. As depicted in the movies, one historian writes, "Your ordinary, plain, garden-variety GI-Joe always knew what he was fighting for, although he couldn't define it in fancy words. He was fighting for the smell of fried chicken, or a stack of Dinah Shore records on the phonograph, or the right to throw pop bottles at the umpire at Ebbets Field."[41] The suggestive query, "Don't you know there's a war on?"—half-joking, half-scolding—troubled many who looked to the American people for some sign of a deeper seriousness about matters of war and peace. Phillip Wylie put it most bitterly: "To many it hardly seems worthwile fighting to live until they can be assured that their percolators will live, along with their cars, synthetic roofing, and disposable diapers."[42]

The election of 1942 had already sent up danger signals to all internationalists. The Republicans picked up 44 seats in the House and 9 in the Senate. Out of 115 congressmen considered to have strong isolationist voting records, only 5 were not reelected.[43] The old-line isolationists were a minority, but a very powerful one with legislative influence far beyond their numbers. And involvement in the war had not yet reduced their membership. They remained a potent force in American politics—a force whose appeal had always attracted the public in normal peaceful times. Roosevelt warned of the impact if this trend should be extended in the next election. In an October 1944 speech he described for the public the consequences if there were a Republican victory: Gerald P. Nye, arch-isolationist, would be chairman of the Senate Appropriations Committee; Hiram Johnson, long-time opponent of world involvement, would be chairman of the Senate Foreign Relations Committee; and two of the renowned conservative trio of "Martin, Barton, and Fish" would move up—Joseph W. Martin would most likely be speaker of the House, and Hamilton Fish would become chairman of the House Rules Committee. "Can anyone really suppose," the president asked, "that these isolationists have changed their minds about world affairs? That's a real question. Politicians who embraced the policy of isolationism, and who never raised their voices against it in our days of peril—I don't think they are reliable custodians of the future of America."[44]

This was not just campaign rhetoric. In early June 1944 the president told Florence Harriman, "It should be clear that the Republican leaders, not knowing how to cooperate with the Democrats, know even less how to cooperate with other nations."[45] On at least two occasions Roosevelt expressed to Hull his deep distrust of Republican promises on foreign affairs; the Mackinac Declaration of the summer of 1943, professing a broad Republican internationalism and hailed as a milestone in American political opinion, did not soften his suspicions where this old isolationist party was concerned. The declaration itself, while certainly a step in the right direction, offered only a very lukewarm commitment to internationalism. It pledged the Republican party to support "responsible participation by the United States in postwar cooperative organization among sovereign nations to prevent military aggression and to attain permanent peace with organized justice in a free world." But each new obligation, the statement went on, would have to be considered with "careful regard for its effect upon the vital interests of the nation." The many other qualifications in the declaration led some internationalists to wonder over its precise meaning. One press correspondent wrote that "it apparently required nothing specific and precluded nothing specific for the future." An internationalist publication expressed concern that the Mackinac statement contained such a disturbing number of "mental reservations around which surviving isolationist tendencies might some day cluster.'' The president agreed with this assessment. He had trouble understanding just what the Republicans meant. When asked about his reaction to the declaration, he avoided any specific comment, telling reporters, ''Well, I always have my Thesaurus handy on my desk.''[46]

Roosevelt feared that if the Republicans were victorious in 1944, as many of those closest to the president anticipated, the future course of U.S. foreign policy would be at best uncertain. But the results of the 1944 election were encouraging. While the president's popular margin was smaller than in 1940, he did prevent the Republicans from occupying the White House. Democrats made moderate gains in Congress, although not enough to disturb the dominance of the conservative Democratic-Republican coalition. A number of old isolationists went down to defeat: Stephen Day of Illinois, Bennett Champ Clark of Missouri, Hamilton Fish of New York, and Gerald P. Nye of North Dakota. The future looked brighter for a new, more responsible international policy.

In January 1945 Senator Arthur H. Vandenberg of Michigan, an influential Republican member of the senate Foreign Relations Committee and a former staunch isolationist, dramatically moved toward the center, renouncing American insularity and advocating a hybrid system of general security which would not compromise American sovereignty. Vandenberg's cooperation with the administration in the early months of 1945 was another bright spot for internationalists, even though the senator's recent conversion retained a heavy, protective dose of nationalism.

By late 1944 there was less reason for anxiety over a possible reversion to prewar attitudes. There was less likelihood of a return to the near-total isolation of the 1930s. But uncertainties remained: if membership in a new League seemed more probable, the precise nature and extent of the U.S. role in the postwar world remained unclear. Wartime enthusiasm for an active U.S. foreign policy might evaporate when the fighting ended and the burden of constant responsibility and conflict had to be faced. The famous journalist Walter Lippmann, while hopeful that the United States would reject the discredited policies of the past, still had his doubts. In 1943 he wrote, ''Even now, as we approach the climax of the struggle, it is still by no means certain that a settled American policy can be established against the abiding illusions of more than a century of inexperience in the realities of foreign policy.''[47]

At the end of 1944 the famous pollster Jerome S. Bruner published a volume on the state of American public opinion. ''It is impossible to talk for five minutes,'' he wrote, ''about America's role in international politics after the war without bumping up against the urgent question, 'But what about isolationism? Is America any less isolationist than she was before the war?' '' Bruner concluded that it was, that the strain of ''pure and fervid isolationism'' was weak, and that the great majority of Americans were willing to accept an active postwar role. From his analysis of hundreds of polls taken throughout the war, he believed that the people were ready to assume the real, costly responsibilities of world power. "Opinions about our general role in world affairs are not, contrary to the fears of the faint-hearted, made of straw. People stick to their opinion even when you try to argue them out of it."[48]

Bruner was optimistic about the future of the United States as a participant in international politics. But he tempered his views with a strong dose of caution. Experience and good sense, he argued, precluded any excessive optimism. While he thought that the public would "not be satisfied with a return to classical isolation," there were still many potential dangers which might limit the scope and effectiveness of U.S. postwar involvement. "There is one influential school of thought which holds that American opinion on participation in world affairs can be turned very sour indeed at the first evidence of land-grabbing by a European power." This was particularly relevant to the problem of the Soviet Union and the Baltic States. On this point Bruner expressed uncertainty, but concluded that "no sane observer of the public would doubt that indiscriminate grabbing might turn us away from participation in world councils." Bruner judged that "the Canons of Caution" should still be followed. "The prospects are good now; but the future is not assured."[49]

American leaders during World War II saw themselves involved in a movement toward the end of a century and a half of fundamentalism in foreign affairs. This purpose formed the core of a necessary concern for public opinion and produced a powerful, ever-present restraint on U.S. policy. Its impact can be seen in a number of critical areas:

1. The policy of postponement. Fear of a resurgent isolationism played an important role in the public policy of postponing territorial settlements until after the war. More specifically, it was feared that recognition of Soviet demands for the Baltic States and parts of eastern Poland would cause a reaction in the United States—a revulsion against international politics which could jeopardize acceptance of a role in the world. In the spring of 1942 a proposed Anglo-Soviet treaty recognizing the expanded Russian boundaries of June 1941 particularly troubled U.S. officials. The territories in question had been taken by force and in cooperation with the Nazis in 1939 and 1940. A treaty approving such ill-gotten gains would be hard for the American people to swallow. As we have seen, Hull sought to avoid any secret treaty of this type, hoping to deprive the isolationists of a potential grievance. The U.S. ambassador to the Polish government in London thought that the treaty risked strengthening the isolationists and all other elements hostile to the British and the Russians. Roosevelt also opposed the agreement, but was willing to go along if absolutely compelled. He hoped, if there had to be a treaty, that at least it would have some provision for an exchange of populations. Sumner Welles advised that such a provision would certainly be in closer accord with the Atlantic Charter, perhaps making it easier for Americans to accept the transaction.[50] But it would still be risky. Any agreement reflecting imperialist or expansionist aims was potentially explosive.

Such agreements seemed best avoided—postponed, if possible, until American opinion became more definite, more reliable.

2. Education of the public. As Henry Wallace commented late in 1942, it was the task of government and private organizations to inform the public on international questions: "I too had great faith in democracy but I felt that democracy without education as to the changing nature of the situation could bring about a situation such as existed after the last war."[51] But a necessary sensitivity to opinion led officials to avoid disclosure of any international unpleasantness. With few exceptions, U.S.-Soviet relations were presented in a positive, hopeful light; conflicts and difficulties were seldom discussed where the American people could hear. The result was a public unprepared for a less than harmonious postwar relation between wartime allies. Official public comments were confined to generalized calls for responsibility and peaceful cooperation. Details, specific problems, were usually avoided.

The president did not work forcefully enough to develop a mature public opinion. He did not think it wise to rush the people into unfamiliar territory. Too sudden a shift from prewar isolation to postwar involvement might provoke an unwanted reaction. As a result, the public received few lessons from their government on the realities of international life. At one point Stalin himself complained to the president about this apparent lack of spadework among the people. During the Teheran Conference, in discussions about the future of the Baltic States, Roosevelt commented that Americans "neither knew nor understood" the issues at stake. Stalin responded that, if such were the case, the people should be "informed and some propaganda work should be done."[52] But throughout the war Roosevelt avoided public discussion of specific questions. Only fine-sounding generalities were considered suitable for public consumption. At a press conference on March 24, 1944, in response to criticism that the administration had no discernible foreign policy, he read this statement: "The United Nations are fighting to make a world in which tyranny and aggression can not exist; a world based upon freedom, equality and justice; a world in which all persons regardless of race, color or creed may live in peace, honor and dignity." When he concluded, he turned to the reporters: "Some of you people who are wandering around asking the bellhop whether we have a foreign policy or not, I think that's a pretty good paragraph. We have a foreign policy. Some people may not know it, but we really have." He then went on to mention the problem of Nazi atrocities and promised punishment of Axis criminals. "That is more foreign policy," he remarked. "We are getting a lot today." Only rarely would he go beyond the ideals of the Atlantic Charter when approaching the public on foreign affairs. The Charter, he stated in December 1944, was "just as valid as when it was announced in 1941." It remained as "an objective," something "pretty good to shoot for." Beyond that he feared to go.[53]

3. Secretiveness. On the rare occasions when an unsavory agreement was reached, such as the granting to the Soviet Union of more than one seat in a

new international organization, Roosevelt chose to keep it secret. He wished, as he told Churchill in October 1944, to postpone this issue "so directly related to public opinion" in the United States and Great Britain, and among the smaller countries of the world. All detailed questions of an international organization, in fact, seemed to provoke secretiveness among officials. When contemplating these matters the reaction of the public was never far from their minds. When Harry Hopkins, for example, learned in March 1943 of a British plan for regional security systems, he told Anthony Eden that the president strongly favored a single worldwide organization. Hopkins was most concerned that no separate European council be set up, "for this could give free ammunition to the isolationists, who would jump at the chance of sitting back in a similar regional council for the American continent." Similarly, and typically, Hull approached the issue with great caution. At the Moscow Conference of October 1943 he agreed to a proposal made by Molotov for creation of an international organization. But he requested that there be no public announcement of discussions; he feared that "political groups and other elements in the United States might give undesirable publicity to this commission and stir up agitation in regard to a future world organization."[54] Discussions, he hoped, would remain private.

4. Approaching the Russians. Concern over public reaction led Roosevelt to stress again and again to Stalin the importance of opinion in American policymaking. When Maxim Litvinov was recalled as ambassador to the United States in 1943 he complained to Hull that the Kremlin did not understand the significance of opinion in a representative government.[55] Such ignorance worried U.S. officials. So Roosevelt's many approaches to the Russians on the subject of domestic politics in the United States, some of them seemingly fatuous, showed his interest in making the Soviets aware of this reality, and thus encouraging a fuller understanding between the two countries. But the arguments failed to impress.

5. Rapid demobilization. A lasting U.S. military presence in Europe could not be contemplated. The American people would want their sons home as soon as possible. A European policy had to be developed which took into account this quick withdrawal of U.S. power from a devastated, vulnerable continent. If an international police force were ever deployed in Europe, the president told Stalin late in 1943, the United States might contribute air and naval forces—but the ground troops would have to come from the Soviet Union and Britain. The American people, he stressed, would not approve the commitment of soldiers overseas except in time of war.[56] Roosevelt believed that there was no way to avoid the recall of U.S. troops once the war ended. Americans would only remain in Germany for as long as it took them to carry out their responsibilities as an occupation force.

6. Roosevelt the Wilsonian. As time went on, and especially in the last year of the war, the president placed more and more emphasis on an international organization in his approach to the postwar world. The idea had not seemed so

attractive to him in the first years of the war. As late as his fireside chat on Christmas Eve, 1943, he had made frequent references to keeping the peace "by force." He had preferred a hard-headed program—the "Four Policemen," as he called it—with the Great Powers retaining their military strength, guaranteeing world peace, and punishing any aggression.[57] Perhaps among other reasons for his apparent shift to collective security was his growing realization of the value of a new League—a United Nations—as a vehicle for developing public commitment to internationalism. It was a familiar, idealistic concept which might rally many doubtful individuals who wished not to risk accusations that they were repeating the errors of 1919. Eden had sensed in 1943 that the president was seeking some safe means to bring the public along. But he had thought "that it is through their feeling for China that the President is seeking to lead his people to accept international responsibilities."[58] Perhaps Eden identified the wrong means, but he understood the pressing need to lead the American people away from the evasions of the past.

Three years after Roosevelt's death, former prime minister Winston Churchill wrote this of his wartime friend and ally: "In Roosevelt's life and by his actions he changed, he altered decisively and permanently, the social axis, the moral axis, of mankind by involving the New World inexorably and irrevocably in the fortunes of the Old. His life must therefore be regarded as one of the commanding events in human destiny."[59] Even compensating for Churchillian rhetoric, there is a critical truth here. The issue was a momentous one in American life, and the Roosevelt administration moved cautiously to insure its final resolution. That it was not the only issue of serious import in wartime foreign policy is obvious— but the conflict between what was required to assure the end of isolation, and what was necessary to influence the Soviets and deal effectively with certain other difficult issues, often proved irresolvable. Some measures simply could not be considered because of the domestic risks and the fear of touching off a persistent American irresponsibility. Soviet Ambassador Maxim Litvinov, with an understanding of U.S. politics rare among Soviet officials, worried about how Americans would respond to Soviet territorial demands: "He said he feared there would be difficulties within the United States concerning Russia's need for this territory because of the ideological questions that would be raised. Certain of the reactionary groups in different areas had representatives in the United States who would shriek to high heaven about the Red menace."

In another context, John Davies, one of the China experts at the U.S. embassy in Chungking, wrote of "our unwillingness and inability to engage in realpolitik." He emphasized how this handicapped the United States in its relations with other countries. During the war these perils of making foreign policy in a democracy revolved around the issue of isolationism. "It is difficult," Davies commented, "to escape the conclusion that we are in Russian (and British) eyes the victims of the insularity and international political immaturity of our people and of the unwieldy processes of democracy."[60] This was a part of the reality of decision making as Roosevelt confronted it. The advantage in a violent world clearly went to the ruthless dictatorship over the vacillating, reluctant democracy. And the war years offered little relief from the frustrations and dangers of this unfortunate fact.

The president's instinctive caution after years of isolationist opposition served to deepen this problem of blending what Americans wanted and what Americans needed in foreign affairs. Fear of isolationism did not represent the only limit on American flexibility, but it did exert a severe pressure on Roosevelt's options in world affairs. It was unfortunate that, at the same time a total global war was being waged and the shape of the postwar world was being decided, political leaders had to move so slowly in order to settle an ancient score.

NOTES

1. *The Public Papers and Addresses of Franklin D. Roosevelt*, ed. Samuel I. Rosenman (New York, 1950), 12:32; President Roosevelt to Marshal Stalin, April 5, 1945, *Stalin's Correspondence with Roosevelt and Truman, 1941–1945* (New York, 1965), p. 207.

2. See Robert A. Divine, *Second Chance: The Triumph of Internationalism in America During World War II* (New York, 1971).

3. Kenneth S. Davis, *FDR: The Beckoning of Destiny, 1882–1928* (New York, 1971), p. 573; for details of FDR's contact with Wilson, see pp. 549–561, especially p. 560.

4. Davis, *FDR*, pp. 689, 816–18; Frank Freidel, *Franklin D. Roosevelt: Launching the New Deal* (Boston, 1973), pp. 102–3.

5. Franklin D. Roosevelt, *FDR: His Personal Letters*, ed. Elliott Roosevelt (New York, 1947, 1948, 1950), 2:968; Robert A. Divine, *Roosevelt and World War II* (Baltimore, 1970), p. 31.

6. *Public Papers and Addresses* (New York, 1950), 13:348.

7. Ibid., pp. 344–47.

8. Ibid., pp. 342–43.

9. Ibid., pp. 351, 353.

10. Robert E. Sherwood, *Roosevelt and Hopkins: An Intimate History* (New York, 1948), p. 827.

11. Ibid.

12. *Public Papers and Addresses*, 12:559–60.

13. Ibid., 13:570–86.

14. *Henry A. Wallace, The Price of Vision: The Diary of Henry A. Wallace, 1942–1946*, ed. John Morton Blum (Boston, 1973), p. 129; Henry L. Stimson and McGeorge Bundy, *On Active Service in Peace and War* (New York, 1947), pp. 591, 595–96; Wallace, *The Price of Vision*, p. 202.

15. *Foreign Relations of the United States*, State Department Series, 1943 (Washington, 1963), 3:611–12 (hereafter cited as *FRUS*).

16. *FRUS*, 1944 (Washington, 1966), 1:12.

17. *FRUS*, 1942 (Washington, 1960), 1:197–98.

18. *FRUS*, 1944 (Washington, 1966), 4:932–33, 935.

19. *FRUS*, 1942, China (Washington, 1956), p. 473.

20. *Public Papers and Addresses,* 13:32; *FRUS,* 1943, 3:26–27; *FRUS,* 1943, China (Washington, 1957), pp. 879–80.

21. *FRUS,* 1943, China, pp. 879–80.

22. *FRUS,* 1944 (Washington, 1965), 3:1228–29.

23. Ibid., 3:1234–35.

24. *FRUS,* 1944 (Washington, 1966), 4:824–26.

25. Ibid., 4:854–55.

26. *Stalin's Correspondence with Roosevelt and Truman,* p. 120.

27. Divine, *Second Chance,* pp. 39, 68–69, 85, 110, 134, 252.

28. Ibid., pp. 68–69, 85, 182.

29. Ibid., pp. 110, 135.

30. Ibid., p. 110.

31. Ibid., p. 69.

32. For a discussion of the Lend-Lease problem, see George C. Herring, Jr., *Aid to Russia, 1941–1946: Strategy, Diplomacy, the Origins of the Cold War* (New York, 1973), pp. 174–93. See also John Morton Blum, *V Was for Victory: Politics and American Culture During World War II* (New York, 1976), pp. 302–23.

33. Blum, *V Was for Victory,* p. 255.

34. Samuel I. Rosenman, *Working with Roosevelt* (New York, 1952), pp. 427–49. On this and other "Limits of American Internationalism," see Blum, *V Was for Victory,* pp. 302–23.

35. Blum, *V Was for Victory,* p. 90.

36. Blum, *V Was for Victory,*, p. 104. The home front is discussed in Richard R. Lingeman, *Don't You Know There's a War On? The American Home Front, 1941–1945* (New York, 1970); Geoffrey Perrett, *Days of Sadness, Years of Triumph: The American People, 1939–1945* (New York, 1973); Richard Polenberg, *War and Society: The United States, 1941–1945* (Philadelphia, 1972).

37. *Public Papers and Addresses,* 13:35–36.

38. Blum, *V Was for Victory,* p. 243.

39. Perrett, *Days of Sadness,* p. 211; also see Blum, *V Was for Victory,* pp. 90–105. *Days of Sadness.*

40. Perrett, pp. 237–46, 379–97, Lingeman, *Don't You Know,* pp. 271–322; Blum, *V Was for Victory,* pp. 90–105.

41. Lingeman, *Don't You Know,* p. 208.

42. Blum, *V Was for Victory,* pp. 99–100.

43. Divine, *Second Chance,* p. 73.

44. *Public Papers and Addresses,* 13:348–49.

45. Divine, *Second Chance,* p. 203.

46. For origins of Mackinac Declaration and commentary, see ibid., pp. 130–32.

47. Walter Lippmann, *U.S. Foreign Policy: Shield of the Republic* (Boston, 1943), p. 46.

48. Jerome S. Bruner, *Mandate from the People* (New York, 1944), pp. 31, 34, 35.

49. Ibid., pp. 55, 60, 61, 65.

50. *FRUS,* 1942 (Washington, 1961), 3:140–42, 538–39.

51. Wallace, *The Price of Vision,* p. 148.

52. *FRUS,* Tehran (Washington, 1961), p. 595.

53. *Complete Presidential Press Conferences of Franklin D. Roosevelt* (New York, 1972), 23:112–14; 24:276, 277.

54. Quoted in Winston S. Churchill, *Triumph and Tragedy* (Boston, 1953), pp. 219–20; Anthony Eden, *The Memoirs of Anthony Eden: The Reckoning* (Boston, 1965), pp. 438–39; *FRUS*, 1943 (Washington, 1963), 1:669.

55. *FRUS*, 1943, 3:522–24.

56. *FRUS*, Tehran, p. 531.

57. *Public Papers and Addresses*, 12:559–60.

58. Eden, *Memoirs*, p. 436.

59. Comments made by Churchill in a speech in the United States on April 12, 1948. Quoted in Sherwood, *Roosevelt and Hopkins*, pp. 933–34.

60. *FRUS*, China, 1945 (Washington, 1969), p. 157.

12

The Anticolonial Views of Franklin D. Roosevelt, 1941–1945

John J. Sbrega

Some historians have criticized President Franklin D. Roosevelt for being generally uninterested in postwar planning.[1] Nevertheless, whenever Roosevelt allowed himself to think about the postwar world, he frequently did so in terms of specific conditions which had plagued the prewar world.

According to Roosevelt, colonialism was a major threat to international peace. The president relied on his intuitive conviction that postwar restoration of colonialism would surely lead to more wars. At the Casablanca Conference, he told one of his sons, "Don't think for a moment, Elliott, that Americans would be dying in the Pacific tonight, if it hadn't been for the shortsighted greed of the French and the British and the Dutch. Shall we allow them to do it all, all over again?"[2] Roosevelt rarely revealed his *exact* thoughts to anyone, but whenever he spoke about the postwar era, he spoke of his opposition to colonialism and support for dependent peoples trying to achieve independence.

A projected international organization after the war complemented not only Roosevelt's general scheme of the United States playing a leading role in global affairs, but also his specific ideas about promoting dependent peoples toward the goal of independence. Roosevelt and Prime Minister Winston S. Churchill alluded to the eventual creation of an international organization in the 1941 Atlantic Charter, which called for "the establishment of a wider and permanent system of general security."

It is significant to note that the Atlantic Charter, in Point Three, affirmed "the right of all peoples to choose the form of government under which they will live." It is also significant to note that the language of Point Three would cause much mischief in the Roosevelt-Churchill "special relationship" during World War II. Roosevelt interpreted Point Three as a distinct preliminary phase in the dismantling of colonial empires,[3] but Churchill believed that the language of Point Three was merely compatible with the existing British imperial system.[4]

During the war, numerous episodes disrupted Anglo-American cooperation by feeding American suspicions that narrow imperial interests, not total victory, motivated the British war effort. Two early examples of this underlying Anglo-American friction were (1) the circumstances surrounding the collapse of the ABDA Command[5] and (2) the alleged British seizure at Rangoon of Lend-Lease goods destined for China.[6]

In 1942 another problem involving British colonialism led Roosevelt and his administration to a broad examination of the postwar status of all dependent peoples. Generalissimo Chiang Kai-shek and his wife visited India in February. After talking with Mahatma Gandhi, Chiang tried to enlist the aid of Roosevelt in pressuring the British to grant the demands of Gandhi's Congress Party.[7] Churchill, however, remained obdurate. He sternly informed the Generalissimo that "the best rule for Allies to follow is not to interfere in each other's internal affairs."[8]

Roosevelt clearly sympathized with the approach suggested by Chiang but deferred to the arguments of the State Department against interfering.[9] Although he withdrew from further embroilment over India, Roosevelt nonetheless assured Chiang of "the deep interest of this Government, both under its longstanding policy and especially under the provisions of the Atlantic Charter, in independence for those who aspire to independence."[10]

The fallout from this diplomatic eruption over India carried two important by-products for Roosevelt and his handling of colonial questions. The first revealed the unyielding resolve of Churchill to brook no outside interference in British imperial arrangements. The second came in the form of a warning from Laughlin Currie that the United States was becoming identified in Asian eyes with British imperialism.[11] Currie's report held far-reaching implications for Roosevelt's views about decolonization. The colonial powers were benefiting from apparent U.S. indifference (despite the president's protests to the contrary).

One stumbling block to Roosevelt pursuing a more vigorous internationalist (including anticolonial) diplomacy stemmed from his impression that a sizeable number of Americans still embraced isolationism-noninterventionism. There is a direct connection between the president's support for a postwar world organization and his designs for decolonization. Hoping to avoid the Wilsonian precedent, he cautiously prepared the American people for an active role in international affairs through the projected world organization. In turn, through the international organization Roosevelt expected to facilitate the process of decolonization. Reflecting U.S. predominance, that organization would, he hoped, develop machinery to supervise all dependent areas.

Within the context of this anticolonial impulse, it is possible to identify two main and interrelated threads of presidential action: (1) efforts to create a world organization, and (2) the concept of territorial trusteeship for dependent areas.

To overcome the harsh fact (at least in his mind) that some dependent peoples were simply not ready for independence, Roosevelt proposed an international trusteeship for these areas. Thus, under the supervision of the Big Four, dependent peoples would be guided to eventual independence. Later, however, Roosevelt shifted his concept of trusteeship from the Big Four to the projected international organization. One important reason for his change of mind undoubtedly was the awareness that China could not assume the responsibilities of one of the four global policemen. Another was the opening of Anglo-American conversations in August 1942 to formulate a general policy on dependent areas, either through international trusteeship—as the Americans preferred—or through the British proposals to retain, with slight modifications, the prewar colonial systems. These discussions continued after 1942 and had produced a broad consensus by the time of the Yalta Conference.[12]

Although he allowed Secretary of State Cordell Hull and the State Department to develop the U.S. position in these conversations, Roosevelt emphasized his strong anticolonial feelings on several occasions. For example, during his conversation with Soviet Foreign Minister V. M. Molotov on June 1, 1942, Roosevelt brought up the idea of international trusteeship. The president mentioned Indo-China, the Malay States, Siam (mistakenly, since it was an independent country), and the Dutch East Indies and noted that "a palpable surge toward independence" existed in each of these areas. Invoking one of his favorite anticolonial examples, the Philippines, Roosevelt suggested that "trustees might endeavor to accomplish what we accomplished in the Philippines in 42 years."[13]

At the Casablanca Conference, Roosevelt hinted at the broad implications of his anticolonial attitudes. Emphasizing that all the colonies in Southeast Asia were interrelated, the president declared, "If one gets its freedom, the others will get ideas."[14] Moreover, when Anthony Eden visited the United States in March 1943, Roosevelt mentioned more specific dependent areas that he considered eligible for postwar international trusteeship. These areas included French Indo-China, Portuguese Timor, Korea, the Japanese mandated islands in the Pacific, as well as certain strategic points like Bizerte and Dakar. The president brushed aside Eden's ploy of inviting the United States to take over the Japanese mandated islands and made clear that he did not want an advance commitment that all colonies would be returned to the prewar imperial powers.[15]

It is a measure of the importance the concept of trusteeship had in Roosevelt's postwar thinking that, shortly after talking with Eden, the president confided to a trusted aide, "The policy of policing the world was not insurmountable."[16] At a White House briefing in October 1943, Roosevelt broadened his ideas on trusteeship, which he felt could be applied to "all sorts of situations," telling Hull to stress the concept of international trusteeship at the forthcoming Conference of Foreign Ministers in Moscow.[17] A month later, the president informed the Joint Chiefs of Staff that international trusteeship also represented "a very satisfactory solution of the government of ex-enemy territory."[18]

At the 1943 Cairo and Teheran conferences, Roosevelt exerted U.S. influence concerning the postwar status of dependent territories. To the considerable excitement of the British, the Cairo communiqué mentioned nothing about restoring prewar colonies to their former owners other than returning Manchuria, Formosa, and the Pescadores to China. Churchill confessed to his anxious war cabinet that the wording of the communiqué, while troublesome, was much better than the language in the original U.S. draft.[19]

At Teheran, Roosevelt pressed his anticolonial views on Soviet Premier Joseph Stalin. The president elicited a mild endorsement of trusteeship from Stalin, who most probably had his own ideas about postwar territorial dispositions. Both agreed that Indo-China should not be returned to the French, but when Roosevelt explained his ideas to have an international committee "visit every year the colonies of all nations and through use of instrumentalities of public opinion to correct any abuse that they find," Stalin merely stated that there was "merit" in the proposal. Stalin proved similarly noncommittal when Roosevelt talked of India and the need for "reform from the bottom." The Soviet premier pointed out that India was a complicated subject and that reform from the bottom would mean revolution.[20] During the course of his conversations at Teheran, the president made clear his intentions to propose trusteeship not only for dependent areas (including prewar colonies) but also for ex-enemy territories and certain strategic points around the world. For example, he mentioned Darien, control of islands near Japan, control of the straits in the approach to Vladivostok, and Dakar.[21] Roosevelt subsequently summarized both the territorial discussions at Teheran and his own ideas during a meeting of the Pacific War Council in Washington.[22]

Despite the purported "special relationship" between Britain and the United States, the complex issues touching on the general question of colonialism afflicted the alliance between the two countries.[23] Indeed, the close affinity of the British and the Americans—from the Churchill-Roosevelt relationship on down—simply afforded more opportunities for playful teasing and harsh criticism by Americans about the British Empire. To their credit, the British suffered both the teasing and the abuse, for the most part, in private. Churchill sounded a general warning to the four Dominions in late 1942. He pointed out:

It is clearly important that we should encourage the United States to look outwards rather than inwards and to be a world power rather than a hemispheric power. For this purpose we should do well not to resent but rather to welcome American interest in the British Colonial Empire, and there would be advantages in so arranging our affairs that the United States joins us in public acceptance of a line of policy towards Colonial peoples and their development.[24]

And months before the 1944 election, Victor Cavendish-Bentinck, in the Foreign Office, advised his colleagues not to become too upset with the anticolonial statements of the president, "who, in a year's time, may be merely a historical figure."[25]

Nevertheless, British frustration at U.S. meddling in imperial affairs, even if largely confined to private circles, occasionally revealed its sharp edges. For example, in January 1945 the following exchange took place during a discussion of colonialism between the president and Colonial Secretary Oliver Stanley:

ROOSEVELT: I do not want to be unkind or rude to the British but in 1841, when you acquired Hong Kong, you did not acquire it by purchase.

STANLEY: Let me see, Mr. President, that was about the time of the Mexican War.[26]

Stanley's quick-witted retort not only illustrated His Majesty's Government's determination to resist outside interference in British imperial interests but also reflected, on the eve of the Yalta Conference, the sharp contrast between well-intentioned American generalizations about colonialism and the crisp, specific approach of the British to that subject. Moreover, the British could take comfort from the presence of their ultimate wartime diplomatic weapon: Churchill. Statesmen on both sides of the Atlantic recognized the pervasive influence of the prime minister on the president. One close aide to Churchill has written, "It is fair to say that Churchill felt that he could convince the President of the wisdom of any course he wanted to pursue by written memoranda and by conversation."[27] During his preparations for the Yalta Conference, the prime minister reviewed the progress of the continuing Anglo-American conversations regarding a general colonial policy for the postwar era and noted the U.S. insistence on international trusteeship. Churchill took up the challenge. He told Eden:

How does this matter stand? There must be no question of our being hustled or seduced into declarations affecting British sovereignty in any of the Dominions or the Colonies. Pray remember my declaration against liquidating the British Empire. If the Americans want to take Japanese islands which they have conquered, let them do so with our blessing and any form of words that may be agreeable to them. But "Hands Off the British Empire" is our maxim and it must not be weakened or smirched to please sob-stuff merchants at home or foreigners of any hue.[28]

At Yalta, the issue of international trusteeship, which had seemed a potential powderkeg, sailed to unanimous agreement with surprising ease—save for one brief explosion by the prime minister. The flare-up occurred on February 9 as Secretary of State Stettinius was reading a draft proposal that the Big Five should consult on territorial trusteeships and dependent areas in preparation for the forthcoming United Nations Conference. Churchill interrupted Stettinius to say that he would never consent to "forty or fifty nations thrusting interfering fingers into the life's existence of the British Empire." The prime minister jumped up and shouted that he would never agree to have a British representative placed in the dock to defend the Empire, and he repeated the words: "never, never, never." Harry Hopkins said later that he could hardly follow the excited and rapid speech of the prime minister. Even after sitting down, Churchill continued to mutter "never, never, never." He suddenly turned to Stalin and inquired how the marshal would feel about a suggestion to internationalize the Crimea for use as a summer resort. Stalin immediately responded that he would be delighted to give the Crimea as a place to be used for meetings of the Big Three. Fortunately, there was a recess at this point.

In fact, it was during this intermission that the sweeping idealism of Roosevelt's concept of trusteeship shattered. With Alger Hiss of the State Department playing a leading role, U.S. and British officials reached a compromise which affirmed that trusteeship would be applied only to (1) existing mandates of the League of Nations; (2) any territories detached from the enemy; and (3) "any other territory that may *voluntarily* be placed under trusteeship." The wording of this hastily written compromise was substantially embodied in the final "Protocol of Proceedings."[29]

By acquiescing in the idea of voluntary submission to trusteeship authority, Roosevelt virtually ensured that all colonial powers would retain control over their prewar possessions. Nevertheless, he clearly indicated during the remaining weeks of his life that he confidently expected to win the day over his imperial antagonists. Aboard ship going home from the Crimea, the president, almost paternalistically, told reporters that "dear old Winston will never learn" to understand the political aspirations of dependent peoples.[30] On March 9 he reaffirmed to the cabinet his concept of international trusteeship,[31] and a week later, he insisted to Charles Taussig that "independence" and not "self-government" should remain the ultimate political goal for all dependent peoples.[32] At his last press conference on April 5, the president once again emphasized his support for the concept of international trusteeship. Responding to a specific question about who would govern the Japanese mandated islands, Roosevelt's answer implied the general framework he had in mind for dependent peoples. He said, "I would say the United Nations. Or—it might be called—the world, which has been much abused now, will have a chance to prevent any more abuses."[33]

Roosevelt undoubtedly died believing dependent peoples everywhere were already on the path to independence in the sense that his leadership had marked out the inevitability of that political process for the postwar era. Some historians, too, have reached similar conclusions. For instance, Foster Rhea Dulles and Gerald Ridinger observed in their pioneering study that "an important phase of the foreign policy of Franklin D. Roosevelt was a *vigorous and persistent opposition to colonialism*"[34] (emphasis mine). Yet, the Yalta Protocol marked the virtual demise of any hopes for a progressive postwar readjustment in the treatment of dependent peoples. Presidential procrastination and indecision served to erode liberal and humane aspirations concerning colonialism. Roosevelt pursued what might be called a "nonpolicy of determined drift," and, to the extent he did so, he unwittingly contributed to the gradual bastardization of his original concept of a comprehensive system of international trusteeship to promote independence for all dependent peoples. But what had caused this retreat from high idealism?

Several complicated and interconnected reasons shaped the president's policies regarding postwar treatment of dependent peoples. These ranged from highly personal factors, such as ill health,[35] racism,[36] and a desire not to complicate further the normal turmoil of domestic politics,[37] to conditions beyond Roosevelt's immediate control. For example, D. C. Watt concluded, "Where American policy-makers did not succeed in forcing their views through, it was much less, as some 'revisionist' historians have argued, from their fear of communism and consequent need for the friendship of the European powers, but simply that their power to act turned out in practice to be illusory."[38] Finally, and perhaps most important, Roosevelt nourished a buoyant optimism that led him on occasion not only to an innocent naivete, despite his rigorous experience in the rough-and-tumble world of American politics, but also to an exaggerated self-confidence, which sometimes bordered on the dangerous—*naive,* in expecting the imperial powers to accede to his own impression that the era of colonial systems had ended, *potential danger,* in miscalculating his ability to manage both Stalin and the course of Soviet-U.S. relations.[39] Also, this supreme sense of optimism led him to what Stimson called "an impulsive nature."[40] It led him to overemphasize the personal equation in diplomacy; it led him to substitute idle chatter in place of hard, realistic decision-making; and it led him to a blind faith in the efficacy of international trusteeship to establish stability and equity in postwar relations among the "developed" and the "developing," where formerly instability and exploitation had characterized those relationships. If ever the term "Happy Warrior" described anyone, it described Roosevelt.

To be sure, the president was no caricature of witless joy. Merely to cite his political achievements and the military victory of the United Nations coalition is to indicate his considerable abilities and to deny any intention to oversimplify or distort his personality and record. Roosevelt astutely recognized that world peace and the security of the United States depended in part on the successful resolution of the aspirations of colonial peoples. He also perceived, with slight exaggeration, that certain imperial powers had mishandled some of their dependencies. Above all, in this context, he foresaw—perhaps better than any of his contemporaries—the postwar explosions of nationalism and decolonization that shattered the old order. His earnest anticolonial attitude, in fact, flowed in large part from his determination to defuse those mighty forces.

Roosevelt can be criticized for letting slip from his grasp the chance to use his position and tremendous influence to make qualitative changes in postwar international affairs. By refusing to discuss urgent political problems and detailed postwar arrangements until the last shot was fired, Roosevelt virtually forfeited his powerful diplomatic leverage in a way that others, like Stalin and de Gaulle, did not. For example, Roosevelt insisted: "We expect to be consulted with regard to any arrangements applicable to the future of Southeast Asia."[41] But he took no concrete measures to ensure such consultation—save to repeat vague, almost ritualistic, political incantations about "independence" and "international cooperation" as if his wishes, if expressed often enough, would come true.

Passivity plagued Roosevelt's policy. In the absence of purposeful, clear leadership from the White House, U.S. wartime policy concerning dependent areas floated aimlessly. The original sweeping vision, born of the highest idealism and crippled by the lack of bold formulation, could not long endure—especially after the death of its creator and in the face of resolute action by the colonial powers to protect their imagined imperial interests. Thus, the praiseworthy intentions that marked U.S. postwar planning early in the war drowned in Roosevelt's "nonpolicy of determined drift."

NOTES

1. See, for example, Robert Dallek, *Franklin D. Roosevelt and American Foreign Policy, 1932–1945* (New York: Oxford University Press, 1979), pp. 358–59; William Roger Louis, *Imperialism at Bay* (New York: Oxford University Press, 1978), pp. 439–40; Francis Lowenheim, Harold D. Langley, and Manfred Jonas, eds., *Roosevelt and Churchill: Their Secret Wartime Correspondence* (New York: E. P. Dutton and Co., 1975), p. 75.

2. Elliot Roosevelt, *As He Saw It* (New York: Duell, Sloan and Pearce, 1946), pp. 114–15. It has become mandatory for historians both to warn of the questionable reliability of this source and to give reassurances that the quotations, if not exact, at least capture the spirit of the occasion. Elliott repeats this particular quotation in Elliott Roosevelt and James Brough, *A Rendezvous with Destiny* (New York: G. P. Putnam's Sons, 1975), pp. 332–33.

3. See, for example, E. Roosevelt, *As He Saw It*, p. 38; Christopher Thorne, *Allies of a Kind: The United States, Britain, and the War Against Japan, 1941–1945* (New York: Oxford University Press, 1978), pp. 102–3, 214–15.

4. See the text of Churchill's remarks to the House of Commons on 9 September 1941 in Great Britain, Parliament, *Parliamentary Debates* (House of Commons), 5th ser., vol. 374 (9 September–11 November 1941), cols. 67–74. See also Leo Amery, secretary of state for India and Burma, memorandum, "Interpretation of Point III of Atlantic Declaration in Respect of the British Empire," WP (G) (41)85, 29 August 1941, CAB 67/9, Public Record Office, London (hereafter cited as PRO); Lord Moyne, colonial secretary, memorandum, "Interpretation of Point III of Atlantic Declaration in Respect of the British Colonies," WP (G) (41)89, 2 September 1941, CAB 67/9, PRO.

5. For information on the ill-fated ABDA Command and the alleged refusal of the British commander, General Sir Archibald Wavell, to accept assistance from the Chinese, see Lord Wavell, *Despatch by the Supreme Commander of the ABDA Area to the Combined Chiefs of Staff in the South-West Pacific: 15 January 1942 to 25 February 1942* (London: H.M.S.O., 1948); Department of State, *Foreign Relations of the United States, 1941* (Washington, D.C.: Government Printing Office, 1959), 4:755 (hereafter cited as *FRUS); FRUS, 1941,* 5:531; Foreign Office to Lord Halifax, British ambassador to the United States, 11 July 1942, FO 371.31811, F 4740/4/23, PRO; see the three telegrams dated 12 February 1942: General Sir John Dill, head of British Joint Service Mission in Washington, to Churchill, Churchill to Dill, Churchill to Roosevelt, in General the Lord Ismay Papers, folder "PM's tels.—1942," Basil Liddel Hart Military Centre, King's College, London (hereafter cited as Ismay Papers); Wm(42)130, 28 September 1942, CAB 65/27, PRO; WM(42)136, 8 October 1942, CAB 65/28, PRO; Wavell to British

Chiefs of Staff, 27 October 1942, FO 371.31811, F 7443/4/23, PRO; COS(43)127(0), 17 June 1943, CAB 79/61, PRO.

6. For information on Chinese and U.S. suspicions that the British were confiscating Lend-Lease goods at Rangoon destined for China (especially aboard the USS *Tulsa* in December 1941), see FE(41)125, 25 June 1941, CAB 96/4, PRO; *FRUS, 1941,* 5:729–30, 734–35; Anthony Eden, foreign secretary, to Halifax, 7 January 1942, PREM 3–90/2, PRO; Lord Beaverbrook-Harry Hopkins correspondence in December 1941, Lord Beaverbrook Papers, folder D/28, Beaverbrook Library, London (hereafter cited as Beaverbrook Papers); Governor of Burma to Amery, 29 December 1941, PREM 3–90/2, PRO; Clarence Gauss, U.S. ambassador to China, to Cordell Hull, secretary of state, State Department Files, Record Group 59 (hereafter cited as SD), 893.24/1236, National Archives, Washington, D.C. (hereafter cited as NA); Hull to Gauss, 31 December 1941, SD 893.24/1246, NA; Eden to Halifax, 7 January 1942, PREM 3–90/2, PRO; Maxwell Hamilton, Far Eastern Division, memorandum, 15 January 1942, SD 893.24/1266, NA.

7. Chiang Kai-shek to Roosevelt, 30 July 1942, enclosed in Roosevelt to Churchill, 30 July 1942, PREM 4–45/4, PRO; Chiang Kai-shek to Churchill, 27 February 1942, PREM 3–167/1, PRO; Chiang Kai-shek to T. V. Soong, 19 April 1942, OPD Executive File 10, Item 196, Modern Military Branch, NA.

8. Churchill to Chiang Kai-shek, 26 August 1942, FO 371, F 6122/54/10, PRO.

9. *FRUS, 1941,* 3:179–81.

10. *FRUS, 1942,* 1:715–17.

11. Currie to Roosevelt, 11 August 1942, SD 740.0011PW/2718, NA. Currie was in Asia as Roosevelt's personal advisor.

12. For a convenient summary, see the unsigned State Department memorandum, 25 August 1943, Charles Taussig Papers, file "Trusteeship—Background Material Before San Francisco," Box 59 (hereafter cited as Taussig Papers), Franklin D. Roosevelt Library, Hyde Park, N.Y. (hereafter cited as FDRL); also Louis, *Imperialism at Bay.*

13. *FRUS, 1942,* 3:580–81.

14. E. Roosevelt and J. Brough, *Rendezvous with Destiny,* p. 327.

15. *FRUS, 1943,* 3:28–39; Eden to Churchill, 28 March 1943, PREM 4–42/9, PRO; WM(43)53, SSF, 13 April 1943, CAB 65/38, PRO.

16. William D. Hassett, *Off the Record with F.D.R., 1942–1945* (London: George Allen and Unwin, 1960), pp. 166–67.

17. *FRUS, 1943,* 1:541–43. Some new areas earmarked by Roosevelt for trusteeship included the Baltic passages, Persian Gulf, Hong Kong, and other global security points such as Truk, Bonine Islands, Kurile Islands, Raboul or elsewhere in the Solomons, Ascension Island, and some point in Liberia.

18. *FRUS, The Conference at Cairo and Tehran, 1943* (Washington, D.C.: Government Printing Office, 1961), p. 197. (Hereafter cited to as *FRUS, Cairo and Tehran.*)

19. Churchill to Clement Attlee, deputy prime minister, 30 November 1943, PREM 4–74/2, pt. 2, PRO.

20. See "Memorandum of Conversation," 28 November 1943, Record Group 43, folder "The Tehran Conference," Box 1, NA.

21. *FRUS, Cairo and Tehran,* pp. 376, 509, 532, 567.

22. Ibid., pp. 868–70. See also the report by Halifax of Roosevelt's comments about the postwar status of dependent areas to a group of diplomats on 16 December 1943, in Halifax to Foreign Office, 19 December 1943, FO 371.35921, F 6656/1422/61, PRO.

23. See, for example, OSS public opinion survey, 3 July 1942, OSS 22759–C, Modern

Military Branch, NA; Charles Taussig memorandum of conversation with Roosevelt, 24 June 1943, Taussig Papers, file "Miscellaneous 1939–1944," Box 52, FDRL; Harry Dexter White (Treasury) memorandum, 15 September 1944, SD 711.61/9–13/44, NA.

24. Churchill to Dominion Prime Ministers, 11 December 1942, PREM 4–42/9, PRO.

25. Victor Cavendish-Bentinck memorandum, 22 December 1943, FO 371.35921, F 6656/1422/61, PRO.

26. Charles Taussig memorandum of conversation, 16 January 1945, Taussig Papers, file "1945—January–June," Box 52, FDRL.

27. General Sir E.I.C. Jacob memoir-essay in Sir John Wheeler-Bennett, ed., *Action This Day: Working with Churchill* (London: Macmillan, 1968), pp. 207–08; Jacob interview with the author, 26 June 1973, Woodbridge, Suffolk, England. For more on Churchill's influence over Roosevelt, see diary entry for 4 November 1943 by Henry L. Stimson, secretary of war, in Stimson Papers, Vol. 45, Sterling Library, Yale University, New Haven, Conn. (hereafter cited as Stimson Papers); Sir Llewellyn Woodward, *British Foreign Policy in the Second World War* (London: H.M.S.O., 1962), pp. xxxvi–xxxvii; William D. Leahy, *I Was There* (New York: Whittlesey House, 1950), p. 138.

28. Churchill to Eden, 31 December 1944, PREM 4–31/4, PRO.

29. *FRUS, The Conference at Malta and Yalta* (Washington, D.C.: Government Printing Office, 1955), pp. 844–45, 856, 858–59, 935, 944–47, 977; James F. Byrnes, *Speaking Frankly* (New York: Harper and Brothers, 1947), pp. ix–x; Robert Sherwood, *Roosevelt and Hopkins: An Intimate History* (New York: Harper and Brothers, 1948), pp. 865–66; Lord Moran, *Winston Churchill: The Struggle for Survival, 1940–1965* (London: Constable, 1966), pp. 228–29; Edward R. Stettinius, Jr., *Roosevelt and the Russians* (Garden City, N.Y.: Doubleday and Co., 1949), pp. 238–39; Woodward, *British Foreign Policy*, p. 536; Anthony Eden, Earl of Avon, *The Memoirs of Anthony Eden, Lord of Avon: The Reckoning* (Boston: Houghton Mifflin Co., 1965), 2:595; Louis, *Imperialism at Bay;* Thorne, *Allies of a Kind;* Dallek, *Franklin D. Roosevelt and American Foreign Policy;* Leahy, *I Was There*, p. 313.

30. Samuel I. Rosenman, comp., *The Public Papers and Addresses of Franklin D. Roosevelt* (New York: Macmillan, 1945), 13:563–64.

31. Walter Millis, ed., *The Forrestal Diaries* (New York: Viking, 1951), p. 33.

32. Taussig memorandum of conversation with Roosevelt, Taussig Papers, file "1945—January–June," Box 52, FDRL.

33. Rosenman, *Public Papers and Addresses,* 13:607–11.

34. Foster Rhea Dulles and Gerald Ridinger, "The Anti-colonial Policies of Franklin D. Roosevelt," *Political Science Quarterly* 70 (March 1955): 1.

35. Moran, *Churchill,* pp. 222–23, 226; Herman Bateman, "Observations on President Roosevelt's Health During World War II," *Mississippi Valley Historical Review* 40 (June 1956): 82–102; James McGregor Burns, "FDR: The Untold Story of His Last Year," *Saturday Review* (11 April 1970); Lt. Cmdr. Howard G. Bruenn, *Annals of Internal Medicine* (April 1970).

36. In considering the moral attitude of Roosevelt with regard to decolonization, it might be well to keep in mind his strong racist views. See, for example, his views on racial mixing, described in Sir Ronald I. Campbell (British Embassy in Washington) to Sir Alexander Cadogan, permanent under-secretary of state for foreign affairs, 6 August 1942, PREM 4–42/9, PRO; Christopher Thorne, *Allies of a Kind,* pp. 6, 8–9, 158–59, 167–68, 539, 695; also Roosevelt's remarks throughout the war on racial inferences, as recorded in Hassett, *Off the Record.*

37. See, for example, D. C. Watt, "American Anticolonial Policy and the End of the European Colonial Empires, 1941–1962," in A.N.J. den Hollander, ed., *Contagious Conflict: The Impact of American Dissent on European Life* (Leiden: Brill, 1973), pp. 106–07. Watt pointed out, "It was only after Roosevelt had invoked the extension of the Atlantic Charter to Asia under the needling of his Republican opponent in the 1940 election, Wendell Willkie, that Churchill was driven to his famous public statement, 'I have not become the King's First Minister to preside over the liquidation of the British Empire.' "

38. Ibid., pp. 124–25. Watt added, "Behind all this lay, not an economic imperialism *per se,* as sometimes argued by revisionists of a Marxistic turn of views, but a moral imperialism and an arrogance of power which has done much in its turn to induce the growth in Western Europe of a turn of consciousness of separateness from, and lack of identity between, its own political system and that of the United States."

39. Roosevelt is quoted as saying "Stalin would play ball if approached right" in Charles Taussig's memorandum of conversation with Eleanor Roosevelt, 27 August 1945, Taussig Papers, folder "1945—July to December incl.," Box 52, FDRL; see also Roosevelt's confident air in his ability to handle the Russians in his last telegram to Churchill, 12 April 1945, Roosevelt-Churchill correspondence, FDRL.

40. Stimson diary entry for 4 November 1943, Stimson Papers, Vol. 45, No. 59.

41. Roosevelt to Stettinius, 17 November 1944, Roosevelt Papers, PSF, file "Indo-China," Box 55, FDRL.

13

Franklin D. Roosevelt and Naval Rearmament, 1932–1938

John C. Walter

Nearly all works dealing with the U.S. Navy during the period from 1933 to World War II take the view that Franklin D. Roosevelt, having been assistant secretary of the navy during President Wilson's administration, was predisposed toward a navy "second to none." Consequently, the argument is made that as president, with great powers to influence the direction of funds, he would automatically direct funds to his favorite department. His allocation of $238 million for the navy from the National Industrial Recovery Administration (NIRA) in August 1933 and the passage of the Vinson-Trammell bill in March of the next year have been used as evidence by a large number of historians and other writers as proof of this thesis. To date, no comprehensive history of the relationship between the New Deal, FDR, and the navy has been written, and the erroneous simplification of the relationship between the president and the U.S. Navy continues to dominate the majority of dissertations, articles, and books on the period.[1]

The record, however, does not bear out these points of view. One has only to consider the character of Franklin Delano Roosevelt to understand that he did not possess the temperament that would have predisposed him, except in times of stress, toward the serious and sober long-range planning that was necessary to build up the navy with the speed and efficiency that has been credited to him.[2] The fact is that Roosevelt, by 1932, was no longer the young and unsophisticated assistant secretary of the navy he had been in Woodrow Wilson's administration, and he was not so committed to the swiftest development of a navy "second to none" as most scholars evidently think. No evidence exists to support this popular thesis.

It is now well known that Franklin Roosevelt preferred diplomacy to the use of armed might in the settling of disputes. Any unbiased analysis of the Roosevelt administration prior to World War II indicates that this is the route that he invariably took. It was this approach that caused Hitler's celebrated response to Roosevelt's conciliatory message in April 1939.[3] The evidence is persuasive that Roosevelt, as president, saw the navy as a grand toy, but when the time for play was over, it was the department itself, with the vigorous aid of the Congress, that urgently led the way toward full naval preparedness. This they did, despite Franklin D. Roosevelt.

It must be remembered that Roosevelt took over the presidency during the Great Depression, and, rhetoric aside, he had promised during his campaign to attempt to balance the budget by curtailing government expenditures. If this were to be done, the navy and the War Department, as well as all other government agencies under presidential control, would suffer cutbacks. As Armin Rappaport has noted, "The Depression did not retire with the outgoing Republican administration in March 1933, and considerations of economy precluded lavish appropriations for the fleet."[4] In fact, no lavish appropriation was ever made for the navy during the Roosevelt administration until 1940, when the appropriation exceeded $1 billion. This appropriation was made in the year that war had begun in Europe and the United States had decided to become the arsenal of democracy.

In the first three months of the New Deal, the Navy Department went through a period of deep anxiety because the financial treatment that it had expected from Franklin D. Roosevelt was not forthcoming. Instead, a pay cut was instituted, early retirements were encouraged, and a number of naval officers found themselves working for the Civilian Conservation Corps. By June 15, 1933, conditions were such that Admiral William D. Leahy wrote in his diary, "No administrative office in the Navy Department appears attractive now in view of the certain shortage of funds and retrenchment of activities that the Navy faces in the immediate future."[5] This was the same Leahy, a friend of Roosevelt from the time that FDR was assistant secretary of the navy, who had written in his diary some seven months earlier:

The election of Franklin Roosevelt is pleasing to me because I believe from personal knowledge of the man that he will use his office for the benefit of the United States.... The Country and the Navy undoubtedly face a bad period, but I believe their policies will now be directed by a man whose point of view is wholly American.[6]

On June 16, however, Roosevelt signed into law the NIRA bill from which the navy received $238 million for the building of ships and other facilities, and one may conjecture that Leahy's initial perceptions seemed to hold.

The history of the incorporation of funds for the navy in the NIRA project is credited by some as having come directly from Roosevelt, but it is indeed a fact that the original idea came from Representative Carl Vinson (D., Ga.), with the support of the Navy Department. Before Roosevelt's inauguration, Vinson had already spoken with the president-elect several times about the navy's fortunes and had come to the conclusion that Roosevelt did not seem too very much different from Hoover regarding the navy's future. Vinson was also aware that public opinion was not as strong toward the navy, or rearmament generally, as he, Vinson, would have liked.[7] Consequently, he called upon Nathaniel Mead Hubbard, Jr., then chairman of the Navy League, to attempt to influence public opinion favorably. On April 1, 1933, Hubbard released a document to the press, approved by Admiral Emory S. Land, then chief of the Bureau of Construction, showing that 85 percent of the cost of shipbuilding went to labor. Building a ship utilized 116 distinct trades, the release reminded Americans, and therefore expansion of shipbuilding would be in the interest of national recovery.[8] Roosevelt also responded to this barrage by incorporating into the NIRA budget funds for the navy, using the very same arguments that had been put forth by Carl Vinson and the Navy League.[9]

It should be noted that this $238 million allocated to the navy was merely part of a program of $4.8 billion from which the army also benefited. It is also important to bear in mind that, in this particular instance, no real exception was made for the navy. It is also very doubtful that these funds would have been forthcoming had it not been for the strenuous lobbying of the Navy League under the prodding of Carl Vinson with the vigorous cooperation of the Navy Department.

But if Franklin Roosevelt desired a Navy "second to none," as president of all the people, he had to balance the varied demands made upon the scarce funds available to the government. Only an inept politician would have displayed a marked favoritism toward any one branch of the government. This would have been to court political disaster, and Roosevelt was, if he was anything, an astute politician.

A further point needs to be made in passing regarding this $238 million. This sum was appropriated for a period of several years, and as late as 1939, funds were still being drawn from it. Prorated over a five-year period, it did not amount to very much money. Neither was it particularly significant in terms of the number of ships that it was supposed to buy, since over five years it would be used to build twenty destroyers, five light cruisers, four submarines, and one aircraft carrier.[10] It should be remembered also, that although the $238 million had been allocated in 1933, that same year the regular appropriations fell even lower. These reduced appropriations were not the product of a hostile Congress, but rather the result of a Democratic Congress' desire to cooperate with its popular leader. It therefore gave him the reduced appropriations for which he asked.[11]

These, then, were confusing times for the navy, for though late in 1933 navy officials knew operating funds for 1935 would be curtailed, Representative Carl Vinson and Senator Park Trammell (D., Fla.) were working actively on bills designed to authorize the build-up of the navy to the strength permitted by existing treaties. They also knew that the probability of their passage was good. What was uncertain was what kind of benefits, if any, would accrue to the Navy Department.[12]

The Vinson-Trammell bill passed the Congress in March 1934 with President Roosevelt's firm support. But Roosevelt went to great lengths to let everyone know that this was merely an authorization measure, and that no monies had been appropriated for it. It could be argued that this remark regarding the absence of funding was an attempt to allay the fears of isolationists and the peace lobby, while intending to enlarge the navy. Possibly there is some element of truth in this view, but it soon became clear that the president was not particularly anxious to make significant demands on Congress for this purpose. The eventual demands came not on the initiative of President Roosevelt, but from the Navy Department and Carl Vinson. The bill enhanced the power of Vinson in the House, for despite the opposition of antimilitary people in and out of Congress, the bill passed with surprising ease in both Houses.[13]

Undoubtedly one of the principal reasons for the president's caution in requesting funds was the upcoming London Naval Conference, preliminary talks for which began in late 1934. Roosevelt wished to do nothing during 1934, despite the navy's poor condition, to influence the conference against a proposal that he had formulated regarding naval limitations. This proposal recommended a 20 percent reduction in naval armaments, and his commitment to this idea apparently precluded any attempts to *radically* increase the navy. It was this commitment that in great part dominated Roosevelt's behavior toward the navy between 1933 and 1936.[14]

The awareness of the Japanese intent to withdraw from the treaties and the fear that the treaties might indeed expire in 1936 did have a short-lived effect on the president. On December 17, 1934, he sent a confidential letter to the secretary of the navy, ordering him to see to it that the bureaus concerned immediately begin studies for the development of "new types" of ships. He recommended a pocket battleship larger than the German type and other innovations regarding cruisers and aircraft carriers. He also wanted studied the possibility of two very large air bases in the Philippines and smaller ones at Guam and in the Midway Islands. These studies were to be considered highly confidential.[15] On January 3, 1935, in his budget message, he asked that $180 million additional be allotted to the Navy Department.[16] This public gesture in the budget message has led some historians to argue that the imminent failure of the London Conference made for a dramatic turning point in U.S. naval rearmament.[17] However, the Roosevelt request for added funds should not be misconstrued, for it was no radical departure in policy.

This point is easily proven when one examines the short history of the "new types" of ships and of bases in the Philippines about which FDR had written to Swanson the previous December. The Navy Department had received the president's suggestions with enthusiasm and, indeed, formally recommended them. On May 3, however, Roosevelt wrote to Swanson that he was rejecting the navy's recommendation. After citing as one objection the possibility of the Philippines becoming independent in ten years, he further stated, "To make a move at this time, pending further knowledge on whether the Washington and London Naval Treaties will be extended, is undesirable."[18] This was an astonishing reversal, but Claude Swanson and the Navy Department would soon receive another disconcerting note from the president on the subject of battleships mentioned in the same memo concerning Philippine bases.

On June 29, 1935, the secretary wrote confidentially to the president, reminding him of previous communications regarding battleships, about which Roosevelt had agreed "that it was desirable to be prepared, in the absence of other agreements to the contrary, to undertake the construction of battleships upon the termination of the present treaty agreements on 1 January 1937."[19] The secretary further informed him that the General Board had recommended a building schedule that called for one 35,000–ton battleship, twelve destroyers of 1,500 tons, and six submarines of approximately 1,350 tons. Apparently Swanson expected a positive answer from Roosevelt, for he ended his letter by saying, "Before taking any further steps in this matter, it is desired that you give final approval to this program."[20] Three days later, Roosevelt replied by accepting the proposals concerning the destroyers and submarines, but rejecting the battleship construction proposal except for further design studies. Nothing should be done, he cautioned, "until we are more clear in regard to the Naval Treaty."[21]

This response must have appeared odd indeed to the Navy Department, for Japan had already announced its intention to withdraw from the Naval Treaties, and Britain, two weeks earlier, had publicly abandoned the principle of ratios. But anyone cognizant of Franklin Roosevelt's world view in 1935 would have understood that the president preferred the retention of relatively small "treaty navies" and abhorred the idea of an arms race. Thus, despite a radical change in the attitude of the two major signatories of the Washington and London Naval Treaties, the U.S. Navy, at the end of fiscal year 1935, found itself stymied, and, on the part of some officials, confused by the man who was supposed to be its savior. It was operating with only 81 percent of the complement desired by the department; naval pay was below that of other government agencies; and, as Rear Admiral Norman Smith of the Bureau of Yards and Docks reported; "Due to administrative action restricting obligations during 1935 against naval appropriations for public works construction, the volume of such work was comparatively small."[22] Therefore, even the public works funds (so much talked about as a clever way to build up the naval establishment) would be forthcoming, but only in a "small" and gradual manner.[23]

The case of the Virgin Islands Naval Squadron further illustrates the parsimony that actually characterized Roosevelt's treatment of the navy during the New Deal. A few weeks after the British had announced their abandonment of naval ratios, the energetic assistant secretary of the navy, H. L. Roosevelt, wrote to the president reminding him that he (the president) had wanted to establish a squadron at St. Thomas.[24] Two days later Roosevelt replied, restating that he was still in favor of the idea and that the department should proceed as fast as possible to establish the squadron at St. Thomas.[25] But if the navy had any expectations that it would receive a fully equipped establishment because the British recently had abandoned the principle of ratios, it was soon disappointed.

Responding to the president's directive in November, Secretary Swanson informed Roosevelt, in a very detailed letter, of the base's needs. The secretary wrote that $100,000 was needed for runways, against which FDR promptly penciled in, "Cut to $80,000." Where the secretary required $130,000 for barracks for the enlisted personnel, the president wrote, "Cut to $70,000." Finally, Roosevelt arrived at a grand total of $275,000, a cut of almost $100,000 of which he wrote, "Total of $275,000 will do a complete and good job with it."[26] This was final, for Swanson's letter was forwarded directly to Harold Ickes, who directed his assistant to put the project through "in accordance with the pencil marginal notations of the President."[27]

An argument can be made in this instance that the sum under consideration was not exceedingly large and that, in relative terms, there was nothing drastic about a $95,000 cut by the navy's commander-in-chief. However, the reductions approximated more than 25 percent of the total. It must also have been discouraging to the naval personnel concerned to have had these cuts unceremoniously made, apparently without consultation. But this behavior was not inconsistent with Roosevelt's determination to treat the Navy Department as he would other federal departments, and by this time the Navy Department should not have expected any special consideration. For on the day before he penciled in these cuts, on the occasion of naming the delegates to the London Naval Conference, FDR told the American people that he was opposed to the creation of navies which progressively cost more money.[28]

Furthermore, in 1935 Roosevelt announced that he would ask for 4,000 additional enlisted men to bring the navy up to 100,000 in order to man the new ships to be commissioned in fiscal year 1937. In this same press interview, he informed his listeners that he wished to cut back on relief programs the next year.[29] These relief programs often benefited the navy, and any cutbacks would have a negative effect on naval development. In consequence of the administration's austerity initiatives, in FY 1937 public works expenditure in the naval establishment declined by approximately $76 million from the previous year.[30] The subject of the 4,000–man increase was another matter. In testimony before the House Subcommittee on Appropriations in February 1936, Rear Admiral J. K. Taussig, acting chief of naval operations, reported that the president had directed the Navy Department to reduce its request for 99,000 men to 96,500 for 1937 for "budgetary" reasons. Taussig indicated that this number was inadequate, as well as the number of officers, but that was what he was perforce asked to request.[31] The grand increase of 4,000 would not be forthcoming, but instead, a modest increase of 500 men. Here, again, we find Roosevelt's behavior consistent, for no exception was made for the navy under the administration's austerity initiatives.

Even this modest increase, however, was soon threatened. On June 23, 1936, the president informed all departments, including the navy, that out of their appropriations for 1937, "substantial reserves" should be set aside to effect savings as well as to avoid "the necessity of supplemental appropriations."[32]

The definitive word came on July 11, when the secretary of the navy informed the bureaus that $10 million would be required to be set aside as a reserve fund, the largest cut of $3 million to be made in "Replacement of Naval Vessels, Construction and Machinery."[33] Ironically, this curtailment coincided with the announcement by the British that they would be maintaining 40,000 tons of overage destroyers in excess of the old treaty limits. Japan also announced that it would maintain 15,000 tons in excess of treaty limits in overage submarines as well as 11,000 tons of destroyers. The U.S. Navy Department, despite the $10 million cutback, responded with the announcement that it too would maintain 40,000 tons of overage destroyers.[34]

To the leadership of the navy, the president's behavior at this time must have seemed strange, and on November 5, Admiral William H. Standley, the chief of naval operations, vigorously protested to the Bureau of the Budget. He reminded the administration that "the present moment is not one when the United States can safely reduce its means for national defense without jeopardizing our national security."[35] Perhaps Standley's impassioned advocacy, combined with the earlier announcements of the British and the Japanese, belatedly impressed the president. On January 8, 1937, he announced his intent to order the construction of two new battleships. The president went to great lengths to inform the reporters that this was merely replacement and said he had "hoped that the date of replacement would have been deferred for another term so as to avoid the building of these new ships."[36] Was this a devious way to build up the navy without incurring local wrath and international animus? There is nothing in the record to support such an interpretation. What seems clear instead is that Franklin Roosevelt was sincere, and that he had no intention of swiftly building up the navy to treaty strength. Neither was he anxious, as late as January 1937, to engage in any naval race.[37]

The retirement of Admiral Standley as chief of naval operations at the end of 1936 brought in his place the aggressive and politically active Admiral William D. Leahy. In consort with Representatives Carl Vinson and Edward T. Taylor (chairman of the House Committee on Appropriations) and Senator David I. Walsh, Leahy brought heavy pressure to bear on FDR. Indeed, it was this concerted leadership that greatly assisted in salvaging the navy's fortunes during and after 1937. For congressmen concerned with naval preparedness were far ahead of Roosevelt by this time and were showing signs of impatience with his strange temporizing.[38]

This attitude was apparent in hearings on the appropriations bill for fiscal 1938. Representative William Umstead, chairman of the House Subcommittee on Appropriations, informed the Navy Department that, although the committee had seemed to be harsh in reducing the sum applied for, in fact, the reduction was really a "deferment." This deferment, he noted, was due to administration pressure because no naval building was anticipated next year, and so $27 million had been cut from the naval building request. He said, however, that if the $27 million were really needed later, the navy could come back for it.[39] It seems that the Congress was ready and the president was not, for on April 7, 1937, Roosevelt once more sent a message to all departments asking for reduction in spending. "You will carefully examine the status of appropriations for your activities," he directed, "with a view to making a substantial saving by eliminating or deferring all expenditures which are not necessary at this time." He wanted a report on this by May 1.[40]

In response, the navy was forced to make internal cuts, including prohibition of the ordinary use of vehicles.[41] But FDR was not finished. In early April he rejected a request for additional torpedo manufacturing facilities on the basis of economy,[42] and on the same day rejected a request to build 16–inch guns because, he argued, the United States should not be the first to do so.[43]

April 1937 was not a felicitous month for the navy, for the skirmishing between the department and the president on the question of auxiliary ships came to a head. The navy had been requesting auxiliary ships from the administration since 1934, when it had requested that twenty-three auxiliary ships be laid down over a period of three years.[44] A draft bill was prepared, with Congressmen Vinson and Trammell ready to sponsor, but Roosevelt did not support the bill, and so the venture died in 1935.[45] Attempts by the Navy Department, in cooperation with Vinson and Trammell, to get a bill through Congress in 1936 failed, simply because Roosevelt opposed the attempt.

By early 1937 the situation was getting critical, and so the Navy Department asked for forty-eight vessels, totaling 160,000 tons, instead of the fifty-four aggregating 221,000 tons requested the previous year.[46] The director of the Bureau of the Budget, D. W. Bell, recommended funding for two lesser options: (1) nine vessels at a cost of $49 million, or (2) twelve vessels at a cost of $70 million.[47] FDR was unimpressed even by his budget director's advocacy, usually a certain passport to funds. Instead, he countered with an offer of five ships at a cost of $44,576,300. This was a severe reduction from the forty-eight vessels for which the navy had asked. Roosevelt, therefore, was now in the position of allocating even less than the recommendations of his own Budget Bureau, an office that was not famous for its generosity during the New Deal.[48]

On this matter, the Navy Department was willing to fight fiercely. Knowing of its growing support in Congress, the navy tried to extract a further concession from FDR by asking for at least nine vessels, including three very urgently needed seaplane tenders, costing a mere $3,879,950 more than the president's offer.[49] But Roosevelt was having none of this. He now countered with six vessels, including one seaplane tender. This offer, he indicated, was final.[50] The navy now had no real recourse but to go along, and in July the necessary legislation easily passed both houses.

The history of the fight for the auxiliaries adds to a clear refutation of the thesis that Franklin Roosevelt was pro-navy in any responsible sense of the word. It lends credence to the charge of Admiral J. O. Richardson that Roosevelt occasionally deluded himself into thinking he knew better what was good for the navy than did experienced senior officers.[51] In fact, the very next month, despite a glaring need for more enlisted men, the president turned down a request from Secretary of the Navy Swanson for 9,000 urgently needed additional men for FY 1938, giving instead 7,000.[52] Yet, on April 20, Roosevelt told reporters that he adhered to the principle of a navy "second to none," although admitting that the U.S. Navy was now where it should have been in 1930.[53]

By fall of 1937, world events and pressure at home caused a moderate change in Roosevelt's outlook. In early October he delivered his "Quarantine Speech" and on November 10 he wrote to Leahy ordering the construction of two high-speed motor boats and two sub chasers each year. "I think we should build," he said, ". . . instead of waiting until war breaks out."[54] The chief of naval operations, Admiral William D. Leahy, responded promptly with a proposal that the president incorporate in the yearly appropriations bill a request for four battleships and four light cruisers.[55] Roosevelt, cautious as ever, temporized, stating in a letter to House Appropriations Committee Chairman Edward T. Taylor that he might ask for additional funds for ships early in 1938.[56] This he did on January 28, asking for a 20 percent increase over the existing authorized program. True to form, he did not ask for the four battleships and four cursiers requested by the navy, but for one-half the request.[57] It was vintage Roosevelt, and Leahy should have expected it.

One should not assume that Franklin Roosevelt had committed himself to even this fewer number of ships without prodding. He was pushed by Carl Vinson, Edward Taylor, David I. Walsh (chairman of the Senate Naval Affairs Committee), Admiral Leahy, Sumner Welles (undersecretary of state), and Norman Davis (formerly chief delegate to the London Naval Conference).[58] The vehicle for the president's request was the so-called second Vinson naval bill, introduced in the House on the same day as the president's budget message. It incorporated Roosevelt's 20 percent increase request and happily, for the navy, provided for the remainder of the cherished auxiliaries that Roosevelt had previously proposed. Clearly, in this bill, Vinson was indicating his exasperation with Roosevelt for, in addition, he incorporated into the bill a request to bring the commissioned officers of the line (excluding commissioned warrant officers) to 6 percent of the enlisted personnel. Eventually, however, this section was removed from the bill because Roosevelt got the cooperation of Leahy to have it introduced as a separate bill.[59]

The second Vinson bill finally passed without serious modification on May 13 and, indeed, it can only be properly understood as a final break with the past. Its overwhelmingly easy passage indicated that, despite perceptions to the contrary, the majority of Americans and their representatives in Congress would support a navy "second to none." Furthermore, it must have indicated to the Navy Department that, despite the vacillations of the president, it was now politically safe to press with relative impunity for a truly adequate naval establishment.

The evidence that the Navy Department need no longer fear the excessive caution of the president was highlighted in the fight to increase the number of

commissioned officers. First a part of the second Vinson bill, this proposed
increase eventually became a bill of its own on March 23, 1938.[60] Roosevelt
was thoroughly against it. In April he wrote to the secretary of the navy, voicing
his opposition: "I cannot see the reason for increasing the line strength to six
percent of authorized enlisted strength. It is not clearly shown that the present
percentage is too low."[61] He opposed, too, the proposal for promotion based
partially on seniority that was contained in the bill.[62]

But the Navy Department refused to be drawn into open conflict with the
president. It passively sided with Vinson on the issue, for Vinson was indeed
trying to give the navy what it wanted. And, despite certain "disadvantages,"
Admiral J.O. Richardson, chief of the Bureau of Navigation, also viewed it as
a progressive bill.[63] In an attempt to have the bill modified, Roosevelt requested
that Senator Walsh dissuade Vinson, but Walsh soon reported that he could not
"do anything with Vinson at all."[64] Finally, Vinson agreed to a 5.5 percent
instead of a 6 percent increase as a goodwill gesture to Roosevelt. Six days after
the bill passed both houses of Congress, FDR was still seething. He wrote to
Richardson, "I am very disturbed by it because I think it is going to ball up the
Navy for the next twenty years to come."[65] Richardson's reply was cool, pointing
out strengths and weaknesses, but recommending that the president approve the
bill.[66] This Roosevelt did because a veto would have been politically most
unfortunate for him, and he knew it.[67]

By the fall of 1938, President Roosevelt now appeared convinced that another
world war was probable, and that the United States could become involved.
Suddenly the president executed an about-face and directed urgent memos to
bureau chiefs and secretaries urging the speeding up of ship construction. On
December 1 he inquired of the assistant secretary, "Have you any report on
what would happen if we worked two shifts or three shifts on naval construction
both in Navy yards and private yards?"[68] Similar notes became commonplace
by late December, culminating in the celebrated one of December 28, 1938, in
which he informed the Navy Department that

Navy yards doing construction should be ordered—not requested—to put as many people
to work on new ships as it is possible to use at any given time. . . . We are all of us being
seriously criticized and it is time to get action.[69]

The tone and content of these notes came as balm to the U.S. Navy, for they
were clear signals that events were now proving their long-held contention that
an expanded and improved navy was necessary. It was this precarious milieu
that forced FDR to adopt a more consistent pro-navy posture. By then, any
intelligent naval officer could have perceived that, Roosevelt notwithstanding,
the fortunes of the navy were now firmly set on a progressive course.

The U.S. Navy, at the end of 1938, was certainly a far distance from being
"second to none." It had, indeed, been enlarged and improved since 1933, but
this improvement, despite claims to the contrary, had been very slow. It came

not because of the predisposition of Franklin Roosevelt to a big navy or a navy "second to none," but rather in consequence of the untiring effort of the department itself in persuading persons and institutions concerned with its welfare to support its programs. In this effort, the navy was fortunate to have had allies in the Senate, such as Trammell, Walsh, and Byrnes. It was fortuitous, too, that in the House of Representatives Glover Carey of Kentucky and William Umstead of North Carolina were thoroughly big navy men. But dwarfing all these personalities was the figure of Representative Carl Vinson of Georgia. Without him, it is most unlikely that naval fortunes would have improved as much as they did.

The contention, then, that major credit should be given to Franklin Roosevelt for naval expansion during the New Deal is based on unfounded assumptions. The reality is that, although FDR genuinely cared for the welfare of the navy and assisted in its general improvement during the New Deal, he at no time gave it special preference. It could be argued that until the end of 1938, the president saw the navy as a grand personal plaything, with a mechanism with which, as Admiral J. O. Richardson said, he liked to "tinker." It was not, therefore, until late 1938 that a convergence of domestic, individual, and institutional, as well as international, pressures forced him to adopt a new and radical perspective. As these pressures increased, President Roosevelt had no choice but to recognize the U.S. Navy as a martial instrument and a department of government that needed to be treated with seriousness and discipline.

NOTES

1. See, for example, E. B. Potter and Chester W. Nimitz, *Sea Power* (Englewood Cliffs, N.J.: Prentice-Hall, 1960). Potter and Nimitz argue that Roosevelt "showed a perception of the intimate relation between diplomatic and military strength," that Roosevelt recognized the true seriousness of a deteriorating world situation, and consequently, because of him, American shipbuilding entered a new phase (p. 484). See also Donald W. Mitchell, *History of the Modern American Navy* (New York: Alfred A. Knopf, 1946), in which Mitchell argues that Roosevelt was predisposed toward the navy, and this brought about the appointment of Claude A. Swanson, whom he called "a pronounced exponent of a large Navy," as secretary (p. 347). The implication is that Roosevelt, like Swanson, was an exponent of a large navy and hired Swanson to do work for him. George T. David, in his book, *A Navy Second to None* (New York: Harcourt, Brace and Co., 1940), states: "when Mr. Franklin Delano Roosevelt became President of the United States, he brought to the office ideas which indicated a strong influence of his service under Woodrow Wilson. He found it possible to lead a moral crusade for peace and to advance simultaneously the greatest naval expansion in the history of the country" (p. 356). Samuel W. Bryant's book, *The Sea and the States* (New York: Thomas Y. Crowell Co., 1947), postulates that Roosevelt had favored the navy and consequently expended funds for the navy through public works, as this was politically safe. In addition, he argues that, out of sympathy for Anglo-Saxon democracy, Roosevelt built up the navy (pp. 433–81). Admiral William D. Leahy, in his book, *I Was There* (New York: Wittlesey House, 1950), argues that Roosevelt was indeed opposed to war, but by late 1937 was convinced

that war was unavoidable, and in the winter of 1937 began to wonder if the United States could not be invaded. Because of this, he felt compelled to ask for a 20 percent increase for the navy in January 1938 (p. 304). In *A Time for Decision* (New York: Harper and Rowe, 1944), Sumner Welles recalls that Roosevelt sincerely wanted to reduce armaments because he saw them as reducing living standards for the world, and that he pursued this goal until 1939 (p. 50).

Stephen Roskill, in *Naval Policy Between the Wars* (Washington, D.C.: U.S. Naval Institute Press, 1976), finds Roosevelt's relationship with the navy at times "remarkable" and "astonishing" in its inconsistency, but the book does not explain or resolve this apparently odd behavior (pp. 468–71). Although Patrick Abbazia calls his book *Mr. Roosevelt's Navy* (Washington, D.C.: U.S. Naval Institute Press, 1975), he inadvertently highlights similar contradictions in Roosevelt's behavior toward the navy. For example, he notes that "in the Thirties, Congress carefully watched over the Navy, making certain that new installations were located in appropriate districts and repair work was evenly shared by Depression-ridden districts" (p. 8). Yet, he notes that Roosevelt *created* the Atlantic Squadron in 1938, but by 1939 this squadron's destroyers were extremely undermanned and none of the seventeen destroyers had depth charges (p. 63). Finally, Frank Freidel, in his book, *Franklin D. Roosevelt: Launching the New Deal* (Boston: Little, Brown and Co., 1973), finds President Roosevelt's behavior ambiguous, particularly with respect to war, contending that Roosevelt's tenure as assistant secretary of the navy "led him to speculate on the moves of the United States in case of war with Japan in somewhat the same fashion that others might amuse themselves with the playing of hypothetical bridge hands" (p. 123).

Most journal articles also argue that FDR was an unstinting benefactor of the navy. See, for example, George V. Fagan, "F.D.R. and Naval Limitation," *United States Naval Institute Proceedings*, Vol. 81 (April 1955), in which it is contended that the failure of the Geneva Disarmament Conference (1932–1935) and the London Naval Conference (1934–1936) sparked a naval race beginning in 1936, Roosevelt, of course, being party to this (pp. 411–18). Barbara Bennett Peterson finds Roosevelt more enigmatic, but while citing the "evidence" of the $238 million and the passage of the Vinson-Trammell bill, she is forced to admit that "there appears to be a discrepancy in the early New Deal years between the rhetoric and the intended policies of President Roosevelt in relation to some degree of preparedness" *(Pacific Historian* No. 2 [1977], 17:60). This work is based only on State Department and published papers, and no attempt was made to research the voluminous Navy Department papers.

The most recent pertinent dissertations are Robert H. Levine, "The Politics of American Naval Rearmament, 1932–1938," Harvard University, 1972, and Michael Kedian Doyle, "The U.S. Navy: Strategy, Defense, and Foreign Policy, 1932–1941," University of Washington, 1977. Levine's study sought to "analyze the relationship between American Naval rearmament and domestic social welfare policies between 1930 and 1938" (p. 1). Yet, although he found that the Navy Department was a "major" recipient of public work funds from the NIRA, he found that Harold Ickes, the administrator chiefly concerned with the allocation of the PWA largesse, was "opposed [to] giving PWA allotments to either of the military services" (p. 3). In similar fashion, the Navy Department found itself in conflict with the secretary of labor, Frances Perkins, a Roosevelt favorite. In consequence, Levine notes, "the Department had also fallen into disfavor with the Administration over its attitude toward the New Deal" (p. 5), and "by the end of 1937, the Department was demoralized" (p. 4). It is clear, then, that despite Levine's claim that the Navy Department received "major" funding from the PWA, these funds were not of such magnitude to bring the navy up to treaty strength by 1940, and neither were they available in quantity or kind to prevent departmental demoralization by the end of 1937.

Michael Doyle's work is not concerned with FDR and naval rearmament but with the role the navy played between 1932 and 1941 in the development of foreign policy. Ultimately, however, even in this kind of study, one has to deal with the physical development of the navy and the role of President Roosevelt. Doyle appears no less confused than most researchers on this difficult subject, for on page 557 (of 628 pages of text and notes), he manages to make the usual statement of Roosevelt's predisposition toward the navy, yet notes in the next breath that by 1938 the navy's General Board "began warning that the naval establishment remained unprepared to cope with the national emergency that it foresaw emerging." Within one paragraph, then, Doyle undermines, if not contradicts, his previous statement that "from 1933 on, the Navy's fortunes prospered," and that "despite domestic constraints on his diplomatic and defense policies, Roosevelt proved himself as good as his réputation." If this were so, the U.S. Navy would not have been so woefully deficient in materials and personnel in 1938, and the General Board would not have been so apprehensive.

2. Howard Zinn, "The New Left Views the New Deal," in Alonzo Hamby, *The New Deal* (New York: Weybright and Talley, 1969), p. 235. See also James MacGregor Burns, *Roosevelt: The Lion and the Fox* (New York: Harcourt, Brace and Co., 1956), p. 238. Both of these works cite Roosevelt as an "improvisor," someone not given to long-range planning.

3. William E. Leuchtenburg, *Franklin D. Roosevelt and the New Deal* (New York: Harper Torchbooks, 1963), p. 289.

4. Armin Rappaport, *The Navy League of the United States* (Detroit: Wayne State University Press, 1962), p. 157.

5. William Leahy Diaries, Book 2, p. 37, Manuscript Division, Library of Congress, Washington, D.C.

6. Ibid., p. 34.

7. John C. Walter, "Congressman Carl Vinson and Franklin D. Roosevelt: Naval Preparedness and the Coming of World War II, 1932–1940," *Georgia Historical Quarterly* 64, No. 3 (Fall 1980): 295.

8. Rappaport, *The Navy League,* pp. 157–158.

9. Ibid. See also Carl Vinson's long letter to Roosevelt, dated December 28, 1932, in which he passionately argues against Roosevelt's plan to reduce the size of the navy and in which he stresses the theme of the value of naval shipbuilding to national recovery, since 85 percent of shipbuilding costs go directly to labor. It was in this letter also that Vinson urged the policy of a yearly laying down of a specific number of ships. It was part of the Vinson plan that was incorporated into the NIRA program (Carl Vinson to Franklin Roosevelt, December 28, 1932, President's Personal File 5901, Franklin D. Roosevelt Library, Hyde Park, N.Y. [hereafter cited as PPF, FDRL]).

10. Stephen Roskill notes that the modest beginning in building that came from the $238 million created problems later for the Navy Department because in this program no destroyers or submarines were begun, and it meant that the Japanese, in 1935–1936, would be asked to scrap ships in those categories, and that, of course, would be an "inequitable proposal" (Roskill, *Naval Policy Between the Wars,* 2:161).

11. U.S. Congress, House, *Hearings, Subcommittee on Appropriations,* U.S. House of Representatives, December 6, 1933 (Washington, D.C.: Government Printing Office,

1933), p. 6. At the hearing, Admiral C. C. Bloch, the navy budget officer, read a letter from Assistant Secretary of the Navy H. L. Roosevelt in which Roosevelt reported that $322 million had been appropriated by the Hoover administration for FY 1935, but when FDR took office, he "immediately decided that drastic reductions in public expenditures must be made with a view to balancing the budget" (p. 5). H. L. Roosevelt noted that the department, with President Roosevelt's approval, was requesting $280 million instead.

12. Confidential memorandum of Bureau of Construction and Repair to Chief of Naval Operations, December 19, 1933, in which the Bureau *assumed* funding of $100 million. This memo formed the basis for a letter from the secretary of the navy, December 22, 1933, in which the navy asked for $100 million for building twenty-five vessels. See Bureau of Construction and Repair to Chief of Naval Operations, December 11, 1933, R.G. 80, Box 2A, File Al–3/FS(331219), National Archives (hereafter cited as NA), and letter of H. L. Roosevelt, Acting Secretary of the Navy, to the president, December 22, 1933, R.G. 80, Box 2A, File Al–3(331222), NA.

13. *Congressional Record,* 73rd Congress, 2nd Session, Part 4 (March 5, 1934), 78:3814.

14. It is true that in 1935 the Operating Ships Force carried 306 ships, while in 1936 there were 318, and in 1937, 349. Also in 1935, there were 81,510 enlisted men, while in 1936 and 1937 there were 81,000 and 96,500, respectively. It should be noted, however, that a significant increase came only in 1937, after the failure of the 1935–1936 London Naval Conference, and between 1937 and 1939 the Operating Ships Force was relatively stable, while the number of enlisted men rose very gradually, as did the number of officers. Despite repeated requests for increases by the department through the secretary of the navy, Roosevelt invariably turned these requests down. See *Secretary of the Navy Annual Reports* (Washington, D.C.: Government Printing Office, FY 1933 through 1939).

15. President Roosevelt to Swanson, December 7, 1934, in *F.D.R. and Foreign Affairs,* ed. Edgar B. Nixon (Cambridge, Mass.: Belknap Press, 1969), 2:322–23.

16. President Roosevelt to Admiral Joseph M. Reeves, Commander-in-Chief, United States Fleet, November 8, 1934, in *F.D.R. and Foreign Affairs,* 2:261–62.

17. George V. Fagan, "F.D.R. and Naval Limitation," *United States Naval Institute Proceedings* 81 (April 1955): 411–18.

18. President Roosevelt to Swanson, May 3, 1935, in *F.D.R. and Foreign Affairs,* 2:495–96.

19. Swanson to President Roosevelt, June 29, 1935, President's Secretary File (hereafter cited as PSF), Box 28, FDRL.

20. Ibid.

21. President Roosevelt to Swanson, July 2, 1935, PSF, Box 28, FDRL. See also R.G. 80, Box 109, NA.

22. Rear Admiral Norman Smith to Secretary Swanson, December 4, 1935, R.G. 80, Box 2086, NA.

23. Clipping from the *Nation,* dated January 23, 1935, in which Oswald Garrison Villard accused Roosevelt of trying to build up the navy secretly through the use of Public Works Administration funds, in R.G. 80, Box 12, NA.

24. H. L. Roosevelt to President Roosevelt, August 20, 1935, PSF, Box 28, FDRL.

25. President Roosevelt to H. L. Roosevelt, August 22, 1935, PSF, Box 28, FDRL.

26. President Roosevelt's notations on Swanson's letter to him, November 20, 1935, R.G. 80. Box 11, NA.

27. Memo, Ickes to Shnepfe, November 21, 1935, R.G. 80, Box 11, NA.

28. *New York Times,* November 20, 1935, 1:4.

29. *New York Times,* November 23, 1935, 3:1.

30. *Secretary of the Navy Annual Reports*, 1936 and 1937.

31. U.S. Congress, House, *Hearings, Subcommittee on Appropriations,* U.S. House of Representatives, February 17, 1936 (Washington, D.C.: Government Printing Office, 1936), p. 38.

32. President Roosevelt to all Executive Departments, June 23, 1936, R.G. 51, Box 154, NA.

33. Swanson to all Bureaus and Offices, July 11, 1936, R.G. 51, Box 154, NA.

34. *New York Times,* September 3, 1936, 1:2.

35. Address of Admiral Standley, Chief of Naval Operations, before the Bureau of the Budget, November 5, 1936, R.G. 80, Box 110, NA.

36. Presidential News Conference, January 8, 1937, in *F.D.R. and Foreign Affairs,* 3:573–74.

37. Ibid.

38. House Report No. 349, 75th Congress, 1st Session (Washington, D.C.: Government Printing Office, 1937), pp. 22–23.

39. Ibid.

40. President Roosevelt to Heads of Executive Departments, Independent Agencies, Establishments and Other Government Agencies, April 7, 1937, R.G. 51, Box 190, NA.

41. Leahy to All Bureaus and Officers, April 15, 1937, R.G. 51, Box 190, NA.

42. President Roosevelt to Secretary of the Navy, April 8, 1937, PSF, Box 23, FDRL.

43. President Roosevelt to Secretary of the Navy, April 8, 1937, PSF, Box 25, FDRL.

44. Chief of Naval Operations to Secretary of the Navy, December 19, 1934. Confidential Memo, G.B.F. 420–2 (Washington, D.C.: Classified Operational Archives, Washington Navy Yard [hereafter cited as COA]).

45. President Roosevelt to D. W. Bell, Director, Bureau of the Budget, May 2, 1935, Official File (hereafter cited as OF) 18, Box 2A, FDRL.

46. Acting Director, Bureau of the Budget to President Roosevelt, April 1, 1937, R.G. 51, Box 190, NA.

47. Budget Director to President Roosevelt, April 1, 1937, R.G. 51, Box 190, NA.

48. President Roosevelt to D. W. Bell, April 5, 1937, R.G. 51, Box 190, NA.

49. Bell to President Roosevelt, April 13, 1937, R.G. 51, Box 190, NA.

50. Ibid. On Bell's letter to the president, a penciled-in response.

51. J. O. Richardson, *On the Treadmill to Pearl Harbor* (Washington, D.C.: U.S. Naval History Division, Department of the Navy, 1973), pp. 435–36.

52. Confidential letter of Secretary of the Navy to President Roosevelt, May 21, 1937, Confidential Correspondence, 1927–1939, R.G. 80, NA.

53. *New York Times,* April 21, 1937, 5:1.

54. President Roosevelt to Leahy, November 10, 1937, PSF, Box 25, FDRL.

55. Leahy to President Roosevelt, December 15, 1937, OF 18, Miscellaneous, FDRL.

56. President Roosevelt to Edward T. Taylor, December 28, 1937, OF 18, Miscellaneous, FDRL.

57. U.S. House of Representatives, Document No. 510, 75th Congress, 3rd Session (Washington, D.C.: Government Printing Office, 1938).

58. See, for example, Davis' letter to FDR, July 30, 1937, PSF, Box 25, FDRL; Sumner Welles to President Roosevelt, January 7, 1938, PSF; *Welles,* FDRL; Marvin

McIntyre to President Roosevelt (re: Congressmen Taylor and Umstead's impatience), January 1, 1938, Miscellaneous File, "The Navy," FDRL.

59. H. N. Wiseman to Budget Director Bell, February 9, 1938, R.G. 80, Box 2086, NA.

60. House Report No. 2134, 75th Congress, 3rd Session (Washington, D.C.: Government Printing Office, 1938).

61. President Roosevelt to Secretary of the Navy, April 21, 1938, OF 18, Box 6, FDRL.

62. Ibid.

63. Admiral J. O. Richardson to President Roosevelt, June 22, 1938, OF 18, Box 6, FDRL.

64. Marvin McIntyre to President Roosevelt, June 6, 1938, OF 18, Box 6, FDRL.

65. President Roosevelt to Admiral Joseph Richardson, June 21, 1938, OF 18, Box 6, FDRL.

66. Admiral Richardson to President Roosevelt, June 22, 1938, OF 18, Box 6, FDRL.

67. Stephen Roskill finds it "difficult to understand" why Roosevelt viewed the personnel bill with suspicion, since the president had earlier asked for a 20 percent increase in tonnage of combatant vessels. A better knowledge of the relationship of Roosevelt and the navy since 1932 would have resolved this difficulty, for FDR had consistently refused to provide the navy with the necessary complements of officers and men. By December 1, however, the president could no longer temporize as he had to face squarely increasing evidence that war was likely and imminent.

68. President Roosevelt to Charles Edison, December 1, 1938, OF 18, Box 28, FDRL.

69. President Roosevelt to Secretary of the Navy and the Chief of Operations, December 28, 1938, OF 18, Box 27, FDRL.

V

FDR AND THE MODERN PRESIDENCY

14

The Franklin D. Roosevelt Presidency, Louis D. Brandeis, and Felix Frankfurter

Leonard Baker

Louis Dembitz Brandeis and Felix Frankfurter frequently are pictured as the masterminds behind the Roosevelt administration, stepping beyond the bounds of judicial propriety if necessary to achieve their ends. A popular 1934 book, *The New Dealers,* declared that "the secret of the Administration's tenacity, ingenuity and boldness depends to a great extent on" Brandeis and Frankfurter. Newspaper accounts in those years of the two men's influence are numerous; for example: "the greatest monument to Justice Brandeis's social thought" is the 1933 recovery program; Brandeis is the person of "some deeper and more mature mind" on whom Roosevelt relied; Frankfurter "is the most influential single individual in the United States," and the "Frankfurter influence at Washington is a masterpiece of remote control."[1]

That characterization of the two men—as powers behind the throne—continues today; it is, in fact, an accepted part of the Rooseveltian folklore. For example, of two 1980 books, the first reports that "by 1933, Frankfurter was already acting as mediator between Brandeis and Roosevelt" and "Brandeis and Frankfurter grasped this opportunity to bring competent, dedicated people into the new administration"; and the second that "by the middle of the decade [Frankfurter] was perhaps the single most important nonelected official in national government."[2]

In 1982 a new book asserted that a secret arrangement existed in which "Brandeis enlisted Frankfurter . . . as his paid political lobbyist and lieutenant. Working together over a period of twenty-five years"—that is, until 1939—"they placed a network of disciples in positions of influence, and labored diligently for the enactment of their desired programs."[3]

The problem with this "powers behind the throne" interpretation of history is that it suggests that the programs of the Roosevelt administration were the inspired invention of a relatively small elite bent on manipulating the country to certain liberal practices. My thesis is that Brandeis and Frankfurter were involved but not all that influential, and that we must look elsewhere for the source of the New Deal and the Roosevelt leadership in the war years.

To understand the FDR-Brandeis-Frankfurter relationship two points must be made. First, both Brandeis and Frankfurter came to the Supreme Court, and studied the Court, in a time when extrajudicial activity was common for Supreme Court justices. Oliver Wendell Holmes, Jr., friend and mentor to both men, discussed his decisions at White House dinners and advised presidents on appointments.[4] Associate Justice Willis Van Devanter in 1918 redrafted a bill for an assistant attorney general, and advised him; "If I thought there was any impropriety in this note I would not write it, but I will prefer that you regard it as personal to you." In 1922 Van Devanter also lobbied for the appointment of John W. Davis to a Supreme Court seat.[5]

William Howard Taft was chief justice at the time, and the candidate for whom he lobbied was not Davis but Pierce Butler. Taft, a former president, was so involved in the Harding and Coolidge administrations that his brother, Horace Taft, wrote him, "It seems to me that you and the President are a good deal closer than most Presidents and Chief Justices."[6]

Then there was Harlan Fiske Stone, who served on the Supreme Court with both Brandeis and Frankfurter. In the 1930s he planted articles in the news media, gave tips on the constitutionality of legislation at cocktail parties, and lobbied—all this was while on the bench—for FDR to retain J. Edgar Hoover as head of the Bureau of Investigation.[7]

In the 1940s examples of extrajudicial activities are those of Associate Justice James F. Byrnes and Roosevelt in the months following Pearl Harbor and of Chief Justice Fred Vinson and President Truman.[8]

The second point to understand about Brandeis and Frankfurter is their extreme closeness. One who knew both well said that "their relationship seemed like father and son." Their letters to each other over almost a thirty-year span are warm and glow with admiration. For many years Frankfurter was listed as a beneficiary in the Brandeis will. From 1916 through approximately 1923, Brandeis occasionally assisted with Frankfurter's expenses for Zionist activities that the latter undertook at Brandeis' request. Beginning in 1925 Brandeis provided $3,500 a year for Frankfurter's expenses in connection with the latter's activities for public causes. This arrangement began because Frankfurter needed funds to defray the cost of his wife's illness. We know that the payments continued at least through 1934, but we do not know when they ended. There was nothing secret about this help. In at least four letters to persons other than Frankfurter, Brandeis referred to the financial assistance he was giving Frankfurter, did not describe it as private, nor ask the letters' recipients to refrain from speaking about it to others.[9]

When Roosevelt came to the White House in 1933, Brandeis already was a historical figure. The crusader for social causes in the early years of this century, the controversial Wilson appointee to the Supreme Court, the author of decisions and dissents that made Wall Street shudder, the producer of articles, pamphlets, and books criticizing bankers and trusts—this man obviously had to have an influence. No intellectual, scholar, politician, student of economics could avoid contact with the Brandeis of the previous thirty years—contact and reaction.

Brandeis at first had a positive feeling toward Roosevelt, saying, immediately following the 1932 Democratic convention that nominated him, that "Roosevelt is much underrated by the Liberals." Brandeis, who believed that one could tell a person by his or her enemies, continued, "The opposition of the vested interests, who have opposed [Roosevelt], indicated that they fear him."[10]

He met with Roosevelt in November 1932, in a session arranged by Frankfurter. "Yesterday had [a] 15–20 minute satisfactory interview with F.D.R. at which he did most of the talking," said Brandeis.[11] There were other meetings between Roosevelt and Brandeis in the early years of the New Deal. "I had a most satisfactory talk with Justice Brandeis before he left," wrote FDR to Frankfurter, adding; "He has and is 'a great soul.' "[12]

Frankfurter also was pushing his mentor's ideas into the New Deal melting pot. In 1933 Frankfurter recommended a particular individual for a New Deal job and told FDR that "this morning I had word—which I convey to you for your personal information—that L.D.B. shares these views." Frankfurter also told Raymond Moley that Brandeis was a "mine of wisdom . . . available to the President and ought to be tapped before very long." There were also many notes from Frankfurter pushing a public works plan developed by Brandeis.[13]

With all this, however, there is general agreement that the New Deal did not represent the views of Brandeis. In the early years, at least, the dispute seemed to be between those Roosevelt braintrusters who advocated big government to watch over and counter big industry, and the Brandeis followers, who were alarmed at giantism wherever they saw it.

This view of Brandeis as a White House outsider is strengthened by a letter Frankfurter sent him in 1934 after returning from a year's teaching at Oxford. Frankfurter wrote Brandeis a long account of the visit. He described FDR's appearance, his attitude toward his job, provided some details of developing programs—all the kind of information supplied to an outsider. This particular letter was typical of many Frankfurter wrote to Brandeis beginning about this time.[14]

Brandeis especially was interested in unemployment compensation. He favored a particular plan, called the Wisconsin plan. Basically this plan made each employer responsible for unemployment at his worksite. This approach was a throwback to Brandeis' activities in the first decade of the century when he was able to regularize employment in some Massachusetts shoe factories. He also was interested in the Wisconsin plan because it had been developed in that state by Paul A. Raushenbush and his wife, Elizabeth, who was Brandeis' daughter.

The problem with the Wisconsin plan, however, was that it assumed that unemployment could be successfully tackled by each employer and was not affected by conditions outside the particular employment site. Eventually Brandeis acquiesced in an approach which combined state action with federal encouragement. This allowed the states to run the program under minimum conditions set by the federal government. Probably with no New Deal program had Brandeis worked so hard, lobbied so extensively, advised as many participants, and encouraged so much. The final program enacted, however, did not meet Brandeis' hopes.[15]

Brandeis, nearing the ninth decade of a long and active life, could not understand why there were no results when he pushed the political buttons. By 1934 he was angrily telling his friends that he had gone along with the New Deal to that point but that he believed the trend toward bigness in government and industry would persuade him to hold legislation unconstitutional in the future.[16]

Why then was Brandeis rated so highly as a New Deal power?

One reason is that he was genuinely liked by many of the New Dealers. They would come to his teas, chat with him for a few moments, bask in the glow of a person they understood to be one of the great figures in American history. William O. Douglas, who came to Washington originally as a member of the Securities and Exchange Commission, has talked much of this kind of relationship with Brandeis.[17]

A second reason why Brandeis was rated so highly was that he was an easy target. Because of his activities for the previous thirty years he was well known— to the public perhaps the most well known Supreme Court justice. When Hugh S. Johnson spoke on the radio about his stewardship of the National Recovery Administration and said, "During this whole tense experience, I have been in constant touch with that old counselor, Judge Louis Brandeis"—an exaggeration—everyone knew of whom he was speaking.[18]

Frankfurter was in a different situation than Brandeis during the 1930s. A professor at Harvard Law School, he was free to be as active an advisor as he wished to be and as FDR wished him to be. When FDR offered him the post of solicitor general early in 1933, Frankfurter recalled, "This took me completely off my feet." Frankfurter may have been surprised, but no one else was. Rumors of Frankfurter becoming either attorney general or solicitor general had been circulating in Washington for weeks. Thomas D. Thacher, the solicitor general in the Hoover administration, had written Frankfurter, "I hear you are to succeed me in this office."[19]

Frankfurter chose, instead, to remain outside of the president's official family and to be an active member of his unofficial family. That he was active, there is no question. He recruited many individuals for the new agencies, as he had recruited persons for agencies in the Hoover administration and for leading Wall Street law firms. The New Deal gave him the opportunity to broaden this work, but it was a broadened opportunity, not a new one.[20]

Frankfurter's influence on government through these men has been much written about, typical of the most extreme comment being that Frankfurter had staffed the NRA with "disciples who hoped to turn the cumbersome [agency] into the substructure of an American Socialist regime."[21]

Opinions can vary; so do the facts. Here is one New Dealer's account of Frankfurter's influence:

I don't know that there was any particular discussion about bringing new men into the Department of Agriculture. We had one thing after another that needed to be done and we obviously needed a different kind of people than were there to do it so we looked for them. We got many suggestions, of course, from Frankfurter, particularly about lawyers.

And another account:

Felix Frankfurter did not come into this at all. We never heard of him in Agriculture. He was never much heard of around Washington—that was mostly a fancy.[22]

If Frankfurter did exert an influence on the Roosevelt administration through these persons, it was the influence any good professor exerts. Archibald MacLeish, close to Frankfurter and involved in the New Deal himself as a writer and then a participant, described the "happy hot dog" situation this way:

Anyone who seriously wonders why so many of Mr. Frankfurter's students went to Washington when the world fell apart in the thirties and forties has only to consider what teaching of Frankfurter's kind would mean to a young mind. It was not, as some of Mr. Frankfurter's critics supposed, because he had used the Law School to propagate New Deal philosophy—whatever that may have been. It was because he had used the Law School, as the greatest teachers in the school have always used it, to examine the relation between the law and the living.[23]

Frankfurter was active in the developing of legislation—as a legislative craftsman, not as a philosopher. Early in the New Deal, for example, he was called down from Harvard to work on the Securities Act. Along with James M. Landis and Ben Cohen, he is credited with getting the act into legislative shape so that it could pass Congress and hold up before judicial scrutiny. But if Frankfurter was responsible for the mechanics of the bill, he was not responsible for its philosophy. The concept of bringing the securities market under federal supervision had been broached as far back as 1914 by Representative Sam Rayburn of Texas. It was Rayburn, a Democrat always suspicious of the eastern money interests, who resurrected the bill in 1933 and pushed it through. "I believe we are going to be able to get out a good workable bill," said Rayburn to Frankfurter.[24]

Through the remainder of the 1930s, FDR called on Frankfurter for assistance and advice, as would anyone with a friend as brilliant, knowledgeable, and helpful as was Frankfurter. Often the advice was used; sometimes it was not. One instance when FDR specifically avoided asking Frankfurter's advice was his 1937 proposal to "pack" the Supreme Court. That was unveiled without either Frankfurter's or Brandeis' advance knowledge.[25]

After Frankfurter joined the Supreme Court in 1939, he continued to be a friend of FDR's and to be active in extrajudicial activities. This is a well-known story: Frankfurter bringing Stimson into the cabinet, suggesting that Harlan Fiske Stone become chief justice rather than Robert H. Jackson; Frankfurter checking the constitutionality of the Lend Lease Act, bringing Niels Bohr together with the president; running about Washington solving administrative hassles.[26]

Joseph P. Lash, the editor of the Frankfurter diaries, comments about Frankfurter in the war years, "Never had Frankfurter's 'unimaginable gift of wiggling in wherever he wants to' been exercised more vigorously than during the War."[27]

But even this has been grossly exaggerated. Said one newspaper columnist at the time, "It is a fact that second only to the President himself, Justice Felix Frankfurter has more to do with guiding our destinies of war than anyone in Washington."[28] We tend, in our media, to create fictional characters out of real people and then perpetuate the fiction in our history books.

But if Brandeis and Frankfurter were not the manipulators, the powers behind the throne, the ones who stamped their philosophies on the Roosevelt administration, then who was? I suggest that we look to the individual who manipulated the Frankfurters and Brandeises, the one who pulled the best they had to offer from the Raymond Moleys and Rex Tugwells, the one who cajoled all the energy and the passion from the Harold Ickeses and Henry Hopkinses. I suggest that we acknowledge that the New Deal was not "the greatest monument to Justice Brandeis's social thought," and that Frankfurter was not "the most influential single individual in the United States."

Instead, we should acknowledge that the one who pulled the strings, who used all these people and others, the one to whom the New Deal was the "greatest monument" and the one who indeed was "the most influential single individual" was Franklin Roosevelt himself.

NOTES

1. John Franklin Carter, *The New Dealers* (New York, 1935) p. 307; *New York Times,* January 28, 1934, sec. 5, p. 4; Frank R. Kent, "The Great Game of Politics," clipping in Frankfurter Papers, Manuscript Division, Library of Congress, Washington, D.C.; *Albany Times-Union,* November 1, 1936, p. 4–A; Hugh S. Johnson, "Think Fast, Captain!" *Saturday Evening Post* (October 26, 1935), p. 5.

2. Nelson L. Dawson, *Louis D. Brandeis, Felix Frankfurter, and the New Deal* (Hamden, Conn., 1980), pp. 6, 47; H. N. Hirsch, *The Enigma of Felix Frankfurter* (New York, 1980), p. 99.

3. Bruce Allen Murphy, *The Brandeis/Frankfurter Connection,* (New York, 1982), p. 10.

4. Mark DeWolfe Howe, ed., *Holmes-Pollock Letters,* (Cambridge, Mass., 1941), p. 170; James B. Peabody, ed., *The Holmes-Einstein Letters,* (New York, 1960), p. 279.

5. Willis Van Devanter Papers, Manuscript Division, Library of Congress: W.V.D.

to Huston Thompson, February 16, 1918 (Letterbook 11); W.V.D. to John W. Davies, October 28, 1922 (12); W.V.D. to Walter H. Sanborn, October 11, 1922, and November 2, 1922 (12).

6. C. Herman Pritchett, *The Roosevelt Court* (New York, 1963), p. 18; Alpheus Thomas Mason, *William Howard Taft: Chief Justice* (New York, 1965), pp. 138–42, 145–47, 168–69.

7. Alpheus Thomas Mason, *Harlan Fiske Stone: Pillar of the Law* (New York, 1956), p. 303; Marquis W. Childs, "The Supreme Court Today," *Harper's*, (May 1938); Frances Perkins, *The Roosevelt I Knew* (New York, 1946), pp. 286–87; H. F. Stone to F. Frankfurter, April 14, 1933, and F. Frankfurter to H. F. Stone, April 17, 1933, both in Felix Frankfurter Papers, Harvard Law School Archives; Box 171 (13).

8. James F. Byrnes, *All in One Lifetime* (New York, 1958), pp. 147–48; *New York Times*, September 9, 1953, p. 26.

9. H. J. Friendly Interview, May 7, 1981. Papers dealing with Brandeis' will in L. D. Brandeis Papers, University of Louisville, NMF/Box 20 (20–2b).

The letters dealing with Brandeis' financial assistance are Brandeis to Frankfurter, November 19, 1916:

> You have had considerable expense for travelling, telephoning and similar expenses in public matters undertaken at my request or following up my suggestions & will have more in the future no doubt. These expenses should, of course, be borne by me.
>
> I am sending check for $250 on this account. Let me know when it is exhausted or if it has already been . . .

And when Frankfurter returned the check, Brandeis to Frankfurter, November 25, 1916:

> [Mrs. Brandeis] and I talked over the matter before I sent the check and considered it again carefully on receipt of your letter. We are clearly of opinion that you ought to take the check.
>
> In essence this is nothing different than your taking travelling and incidental expenses from the Consumers League or the New Republic—which I trust you do. You are giving your very valuable time and that is quite enough. It can make no difference that the subject matter in connection with which expense is incurred is more definite in one case than in the other.
>
> I ought to feel free to make suggestions to you, although they involve some incidental expense. And you should feel free to incur expense in the public interest. So I am returning the check.

Both letters are found in Melvin I. Urofsky and David W. Levy, eds., *Letters of Louis D. Brandeis* (Albany, New York, 1971), 4:266–67.

Next is Brandeis to Frankfurter, May 3, 1917 (Brandeis had sent a $1,000 check to a fund for a friend who had died. When the fund was delayed in being set up, Brandeis turned the money over to Frankfurter.):

> I therefore suggest that you deposit that check in a special account & draw against it for your disbursements, past & future, in public matters.

Felix Frankfurter Papers, Manuscript Division, Library of Congress, Box 26.

Next is Brandeis to Jacob deHaas, April 7, 1920:

> I note that the question is undecided whether the Z[ionist] O[rganization] shall pay the expenses to the Conference of delegates other than members of the office force. If the decision

is *not* to do so, I shall be glad to pay Felix's expenses. Of course he must not be permitted to pay his own.

Urofsky and Levy, 4:458.
Next is Brandeis to Julian W. Mack, January 12, 1922:

> . . . I am entirely clear (1) that F.F. ought not to accept anything from either of your funds or from Mrs. Fles—(2) that anything which he should accept from anyone should come from me.
>
> And, of course, anything that I can do for Felix, which is best for him and for the causes he so generously serves, I am more than glad to do.
>
> My doubt is as to what it is best to do. You know my apprehensions of "easier ways" and the removal of financial limitations; also my belief in the saving grace of what many call drudgery.
>
> But I think it may be consistent with what is best to put $1000 into his hands this year to pay expenses incident to his public work, and I shall write him to that effect.

Felix Frankfurter Papers, Manuscript Division, Library of Congress, Box 26.
Brandeis to Frankfurter, January 6, 1923:

> . . . I have had some concern lest your most commendable public services in many causes may involve you quite unconsciously in incidental expenses which in the aggregate are pretty large. And unless you and Marion object, I want to send you on Feb. 1 check for $1000 on this account. I know there can be no better use of the funds.

Felix Frankfurter Papers, Manuscript Division, Library of Congress, Box 26.
Brandeis to Frankfurter, September 24, 1925:

> I am glad you wrote me about the personal needs and I'll send the $1500 now or in instalments as you may prefer. Your public service must not be abridged. Marion knows that [Mrs. Brandeis] and I look upon you as half brother, half son.

Felix Frankfurter Papers, Box 27, Library of Congress.
In Brandeis to Frankfurter, October 3, 1925, Brandeis again refers to the $1,500 figure, and on December 27, 1925, talks about a $2,000 amount (Felix Frankfurter Papers, Manuscript Division, Library of Congress, Box 27).
Brandeis to Frankfurter, June 2, 1927:

> I am deeply chagrined at my oversight in not having [the secretary] make the deposit of $2000 on Jan. 1st/27. I am writing her by this mail & asking her to advise you immediately on making the deposit. Until further notice, it is my intention that $1500 shall be deposited Oct 1 and $2000 Jan. 1 during each year for our joint endeavors through you. If, by any chance, the deposit is not regularly made please enquire of [the secretary] or let me know.

Felix Frankfurter Papers, Manuscript Division, Library of Congress, Box 27.
Brandeis to Edward McClennen, October 30, 1932 (McClennen is working on Brandeis' will, and Brandeis is writing of "commitments, legal or moral"):

> There remains only the $2,000 Jan. 1 and $1,500 Oct. 1 to Felix Frankfurter Special.

L. D. Brandeis Papers, University of Louisville, NMF/Box 20 (20–2a).
Brandeis to Julian W. Mack, March 11, 1934 (Frankfurter at Oxford planned a trip to Palestine and had asked Mack, in his capacity as a Zionist official, to fund the trip. Mack asked Brandeis to supply the funds.):

I assume Felix goes to Palestine in the Zionist interest (had not heard of the project). You may have P.E.F. cable the 250 pounds and I will send Bob a check when I know the exact amount.

I am surprised Felix is short of cash. Of course, he has spent much on cabling, telegraphing and the like—but I have for years made him an allowance of $3,500. a year for public purposes. . . .

L. D. Brandeis Papers, University of Louisville, Z/P-Box 58 (1d).

The four letters to persons other than Frankfurter are cited above: Brandeis to deHaas, April 7, 1920; Brandeis to Mack, January 12, 1922; Brandeis to McClennen, October 30, 1932; and Brandeis to Mack, March 11, 1934.

Although B. A. Murphy writes that the payments continued until 1939 (see note 3 above), he does not cite any letters or other data past 1934.

10. Urofsky and Levy, 5:505.

11. Regarding Frankfurter arranging the meeting, Frankfurter to Marguerite LeHand, November 10, 1932, and Brandeis to Frankfurter, November 17, 1932; Brandeis quote, Brandeis to Frankfurter, November 24, 1932, all letters in Felix Frankfurter Papers, Manuscript Division, Library of Congress/Correspondence File.

12. FDR to Frankfurter, June 11, 1934, Franklin D. Roosevelt Library, PPF 140/ Box 1.

13. Frankfurter to FDR, November 9, 1933, Franklin D. Roosevelt Library, PSF/Box 150; Frankfurter to R. Moley, March 21, 1933, Felix Frankfurter Papers, Manuscript Division, Library of Congress, Box 183 (003517); for example, Frankfurter to Moley, February 9, 1933, Felix Frankfurter Papers, Manuscript Division, Library of Congress/ Correspondence File. The details of the recovery plans—there were two of them—are in H. Shulman memorandum to Frankfurter, in Felix Frankfurter Papers, Manuscript Division, Library of Congress/Correspondence File, and in "Memorandum on Public Works Program," Frankfurter Papers, Manuscript Division, Library of Congress, Box 226 (004135); also Frankfurter diary entry, February 10, 1933, Manuscript Division, Library of Congress.

14. Frankfurter to Brandeis, August 31, 1934, Brandeis Papers, University of Louisville, Box 134 (G-9-2b), and other letters at the same site.

15. For the role of Brandeis in the unemployment compensation struggle, see Paul A. Raushenbush, "Starting Unemployment Compensation in Wisconsin," *Unemployment Insurance Review* (April-May 1967): 21–4; Arthur M. Schlesinger, Jr., *The Coming of the New Deal* (Boston, 1959), pp. 301–6; Charles E. Wyzanski, Jr., "Brandeis," *Atlantic* (November 1956): 69; Paul A. Freund, "Justice Brandeis: A Law Clerk's Remembrance," p. 10 (written for *American Jewish History* and supplied to author by P. A. Freund); Perkins, *Roosevelt I Knew*, pp. 188–89; Brandeis to Jack Gilbert, January 22, 1936, Brandeis Collection, Brandeis University, Box 21; Brandeis to Elizabeth Raushenbush, October 20, 1934, and March 24, 1936, both in Brandeis Papers, University of Louisville, Box 216 (M 2–7); and author's interview with Paul A. Freund, July 17, 1981.

16. Adolf A. Berle, *Navigating the Rapids 1918–1971* (New York, 1973), p. 95.

17. W. O. Douglas, *Go East, Young Man* (New York, 1974), pp. 306–7; also see James F. Simon, *Independent Journey—The Life of William O. Douglas* (New York, 1980), pp. 71, 156–7.

18. For the details of the Brandeis-Johnson brouhaha, see Perkins, *Roosevelt I Knew*, p. 201; F. R. Kent, note 1, above; copy of *New York Herald Tribune* editorial, September 25, 1934; Brandeis to Frankfurter, September 25, 1934; Johnson statement, undated;

Brandeis to Frankfurter, September 22, 1934; H. F. Stone to Frankfurter, October 2, 1934, all in Frankfurter Papers, Manuscript Division, Library of Congress/Correspondence File; and Johnson to Brandeis, June 1, 1935, Brandeis Papers, University of Louisville, Box 230 (M17–1b); and "Conversations between L.D.B. and F.F.," Harvard Law School Archives.

19. Felix Frankfurter, *Felix Frankfurter Reminisces* (New York, 1962), p. 286; T. D. Thacher to Frankfurter, February 25, 1933, Frankfurter Papers, Manuscript Division, Library of Congress, Box 180 (003646). See also *New York Times,* December 23, 1932, p. 8, and February 1, 1933, p. 1.

20. Frankfurter, *Reminisces,* pp. 290–1; Eugene Meyer to Frankfurter, November 24, 1931, Frankfurter Papers, Manuscript Division, Library of Congress/Correspondence File; Frankfurter to Eugene Meyer, April 26, 1932, Frankfurter Papers, Manuscript Division, Library of Congress, Box 181 (003477); E. Meyer to Frankfurter, February 16, 1932, Eugene Meyer Papers, Manuscript Division, Library of Congress, Box 22; Henry L. Stimson and McGeorge Bundy, *On Active Service in Peace and War* (New York, 1948), p. 161.

21. *Albany Times-Union,* November 1, 1936, p. 4–A.

22. Oral History Projects, Columbia University: Rexford G. Tugwell, p. 45, and Paul H. Appleby, pp. 29–30.

23. A. MacLeish, "F. F. Frame for a portrait," vol. 76 *Harvard Law Review* (November 1962), pp. 23–24.

24. Schlesinger, *Coming of the New Deal,* pp. 439–42; C. Dwight Dorough, *Mr. Sam* (New York, 1962), p. 225; in Frankfurter Papers, Manuscript Division, Library of Congress, May 8, 1933, diary entry, and in Folder 003498, Rayburn to Frankfurter, April 18, 1933; Frankfurter to Rayburn, April 24, 1933; and Frankfurter to FDR, May 8, 1933.

25. See Leonard Baker, *Back to Back: The Duel Between FDR and the Supreme Court* (New York, 1967).

26. See, for example, Joseph P. Lash, *From the Diaries of Felix Frankfurter* (New York, 1975), pp. 3–90; Liva Baker, *Felix Frankfurter* (New York, 1969), pp. 212–80; Leonard Baker, *Roosevelt and Pearl Harbor* (New York, 1970), pp. 76–77.

27. Lash, *Diaries,* p. 74.

28. Quoted in L. Baker, *Frankfurter,* p. 253.

15

Franklin D. Roosevelt and the Modern American Presidency

Morton J. Frisch

There is an opinion current that it is not really possible to separate the institution of the presidency from the person who occupies the presidential office and, consequently, that the man corrupts the office or, more generally stated, that the office is continuously shaped and reshaped by the succession of men who occupy that office. But the American presidency, contrary to that understanding, has not been in a state of continuous flux, and while certain American presidents have exerted an influence on the institution, sometimes in rather profound ways, as Franklin D. Roosevelt surely did, the institution is not subject to the whims and caprices of any president who happens willy-nilly to get elected to that office. In fact, I would say that, to some extent, precisely the opposite is the case, that is, that the institution shapes the man, and that it was intended to do just that. Grover Cleveland and Harry S Truman are good examples of ordinary men who became statesmen through their presidential experience.

What is interesting and fascinating about the American presidency is the extent to which this institution was expected to fashion the political behavior of the occupier of that office and thus enable him to rise to statesmanship. Institutional structure was intended to influence political behavior; the system was so structured that the ambition of the man is to attach itself to the ambition for that office. According to the famous argument of *Federalist* number 51: "The great security against a gradual concentration of the several powers in the same department, consists in giving to those who administer each department, the necessary constitutional means and personal motives, to resist encroachments of the other. . . . Ambition must be made to counteract ambition. The interest of the man must be connected with the constitutional rights of the place." Any particular president therefore has the greatest stake in the presidency insofar as his own ambition is concerned. Surely the relationship between the presidency and the

president—how the institution of the presidency has affected certain presidents—
needs very careful analysis.

I am going to discuss the modern American presidency. But the modern
presidency cannot simply be understood in terms of the expansion of presidential
power, for presidential power has been expanding and contracting throughout
the course of American history. All the great crises in American history have
witnessed an enormous expansion in presidential power, not to mention the fact
that this expansion has been the most controversially political subject in the
recent history of American public affairs. That subject was an issue in the debate
over President Roosevelt's recommended reorganization of the executive branch
in 1938; President Truman's seizure of the steel mills in 1952, intended to prevent
a nationwide steel strike, and the Supreme Court's nullification of that decision;
the Bricker Amendment controversy in the mid-1950s over limiting presidential
power to make executive agreements (in the wake of FDR's secret executive
agreement with the Russians at Yalta in 1945); and President Johnson's escalation
of U.S. involvement in the Vietnam War in 1965 on the basis of the controversial
Gulf of Tonkin Resolution. But the modern American presidency must be accounted for in terms of the growth of national government activity rather than
simply in terms of the expansion of presidential power.

The American presidency is one of this country's basic political institutions.
There have been some changes in it in modern times which were instituted as
a result of Franklin Roosevelt and the New Deal. But the modern presidency is
a harmonious development from the original foundations. The framers of the
U.S. Constitution had a view of a strong, independent executive. Alexander
Hamilton, a great theoretician of the presidency,[1] stated: "Energy in the executive
is a leading character in the definition of good government. . . . A feeble executive
implies a feeble execution of the government. A feeble execution is but another
phrase for a bad execution: And a government ill executed, whatever it may be
in theory, must be in practice a bad government."[2] Hamilton is famous for
having presented with great force and clarity the case for a strong presidency.
Moreover, as Washington's secretary of the treasury, he did much to bring about
his activist view of the presidential function which he so forcefully articulated
in *The Federalist*.

The U.S. Constitution, however, outlined a complex governmental structure.
Congress was regarded as the central political institution, but what was also
wanted was a very strong president in competition with Congress, and a presidential office that was to be in a significant sense a political office. The founders
of the American regime perceived the necessity of a delicate balance between
legislative and executive power; neither foreclosing the possibility of statesmanship nor requiring it as an indispensable condition of or requirement for the
conduct of government. They apparently felt that legislative and executive power
must be so moderated and controlled that a competition between them would
not result in a deadlock, but in a delicate but unequal balance. Beyond this
uneven balance of somehow divided power, divided between the legislative and

executive, giving an edge to the legislative, but not complete preponderance, it could be said that the president was expected to exercise some positive political leadership. The Founders moved the emphasis away from the need for statesmanship without ruling out entirely the possibility that such statesmanship might be needed. Franklin Roosevelt, however, tried to create for statesmanship, and presidential statesmanship in particular, a latitude that is not in contradiction with, and even fulfills, the clearest and highest thought of the best thinkers on the subject of the presidency. Accordingly, the growth of the presidency is consistent with the intention of the Constitution.

James MacGregor Burns, a distinguished student of the American presidency, suggests in his recent volume on the wartime Roosevelt that the foundations of modern presidential government were laid during World War II, in the president's third term of office, rather than in the earlier New Deal years. Burns emphasizes the impact of the exercise of FDR's wartime powers on presidential organization, stating that "by the end of 1943 virtually a new system of presidential government had grown out of the makeshift arrangements of old. The foundation had been laid for a powerful Executive Office, a huge war structure, and a vastly-expanded social-welfare organization, which were to characterize the presidency for decades to come. During World War II, indeed, the modern presidency was created."[3] I believe that what Burns says is only superficially the case, for in order to understand the distinctive character of what he refers to as presidential government, a distinction needs to be made between the expansion of presidential power and the growth of national government activity.

Roosevelt's reconstruction of the presidency and hence the creation of the modern American presidency was accomplished, first, by the growth of national government activity, and second, by the presidency engaging in high political education, taking the nation to school, so to speak. The Founding Fathers anticipated and even laid the foundations for the expansion of presidential power. They emphasized the need for vigorous administration and good government. But that which makes the modern American presidency the most important governmental office in the present-day world results from the deep intrusion of the national government into the economic sphere that was instituted in the United States during the period of New Deal reform. That was the qualitative change in our political system which enhances the power and prestige of the American presidency in a way in which the mere expansion of presidential power could never do. I would say, therefore, that the coming into being of the welfare state during the New Deal period, in which government now becomes responsible for the regulation of the national economy, set the stage for the appearance of the modern American presidency.

The New Deal rejected the view that an economic system such as that of the United States would regulate itself automatically by the uncontrolled competition of private enterprise, and therefore it imposed regulations and controls on the economy as a whole. The series of economic measures of the New Deal— including the regulation of agricultural prices, production, and marketing; the protection and support of collective bargaining; Social Security legislation; wages and hours legislation; the regulation of security exchanges; and increased control over money and banking—meant a significant expansion in the functions of government and hence the character of the American presidency. The hostility of the traditional democracy to the regulatory and welfare measures of the New Deal rested on a rather narrow understanding of the functions of government. An important part of that understanding was the simple consideration that all the important things in life are done by society, setting society apart from government, and that the function of government is primarily to secure the conditions of happiness.

The Declaration of Independence defines the function of government in terms of a certain understanding of the relation between happiness and the conditions of happiness. According to that understanding, life, liberty, and the pursuit of happiness constitute the conditions of happiness, and it is the function of government to guarantee those conditions, but not happiness itself. FDR, on the other hand, believed the function of government to be that of achieving the greater happiness of the greater number. He seemed to consider happiness as well-being, and he defined his own understanding of the change in terms of the movement from political to economic rights. It is *this* fundamental change in emphasis which gives the New Deal its distinctive character as a political movement, for from then on, government furnished not only the conditions of happiness, but, to a considerable extent, the enjoyment or possession of material happiness which might properly be called well-being or welfare.

The great contribution that the New Deal made to the American political tradition consisted in its correcting the narrow understanding of the function of government (or of the relationship between government and the economy) that characterized the traditional democratic view, and only in this light can we see the modern American presidency in its clearest dimensions. Fundamental to the New Deal position was FDR's contention that "government has the final responsibility for the well-being of its citizenship," while the traditional democratic view continued to assert that government was necessary only under certain conditions. The beginning of an understanding of the modern presidency, therefore, is to see that only after the coming into being of the welfare state could the presidency move into the center of the American political system.

The second feature of the presidency, as I see it, is the president explicitly taking on the role of high political educator. FDR saw it as part of the proper performance of the presidential function to attend to the guidance and enlightenment of popular opinion (and this innovative practice starts with Theodore Roosevelt and Woodrow Wilson). But that would require that proposals be constantly explained, shaped, and couched in ways which would make them intelligible and understandable to the American people and hence offer them the possibility of deliberating about them. Felix Frankfurter, one of the president's closest advisors, wrote him in May 1934:

No one knows better than you the need and the difficulties of political education. . . . I venture to say, however, that particularly in these restless days, in which foolishness and fanaticism and self-interest are exploited by professional poisoners of the public mind, . . . it becomes even more important than it was in the days of T.R. and Woodrow Wilson for the President to do what you are able to do with such extraordinary effectiveness, namely, to give guidance to the public in order to rally them to the general national interest.[4]

In the political thought of Franklin Roosevelt, the president is under an obligation not only to do things, not only to administer things, not only to propose things, but to explain himself to the American people so as to win their subsequent approval. That means that the American presidency is the greatest educational force in this country, and it makes the president both responsive and educative with regard to public opinion. The language FDR used makes it clear that he had this intention in mind: "Government includes the art of formulating a policy, and using the political technique to attain so much of that policy as will receive general support; persuading, leading, sacrificing, teaching always, because the greatest duty of a statesman is to educate."[5]

The main vehicles for this high political instruction, above and beyond speeches and addresses which presidents traditionally employed, were his fireside chats to the American people and his nearly 1,000 presidential press conferences. Although at the time the president could not be directly quoted, he could be indirectly quoted by the press, and what he said at those press conferences had a way of getting through to the American public. For example, the 1935 conference at which he characterized the Supreme Court justices as operating as if they were living in a "horse and buggy age" was undoubtedly the most famous of all presidential press conferences, going down in history as the "horse and buggy" press conference. No student of the American presidency or of American political thought can disregard the contents of that encounter in which FDR launched his attack on the Nine Old Men for their invalidation of the NRA. The president believed that statesmen have a decisive educational task of seeing more clearly than others the dangers citizens must be attentive to in a democratic regime and communicating that awareness.

The conduct of U.S. foreign policy became the theme of the presidential teaching from 1937 through 1941. The grand theme running through Roosevelt's speeches at that time was the threat to democratic public values and institutions inherent in the rise of fascist dictatorships. Recognizing, for example, that the United States could not safely avoid the hard, politically unpopular decision of involvement in the European war, at least up to a point short of war itself, Roosevelt was always looking for ways of making that policy of intervention more palatable to a broad segment of American public opinion with its strong infusion of isolationist sentiment. Shortly before the signing of the Munich Agreement in September 1938, Roosevelt spoke of "the conflict . . . still sharp ening throughout the world between two political systems. The one system represents government by freedom of choice exercised by the individual citizens. In the other, and opposing system, individual freedom and initiative are all made subordinate to the totalitarian state.'' He continued: ''Democracy cannot succeed unless those who express their choice are prepared to choose wisely. The real safeguard of democracy, therefore, is education. It has well been said that no system of government gives so much to the individual or exacts so much as a democracy. . . . To prepare each citizen to choose wisely and to enable him to choose freely are paramount functions of the schools in a democracy.''[6] There were two points in Roosevelt's political instruction: first, he attempted to define the conflict in terms of opposing systems or ways of life and, second, he took that opportunity for instructing the people as to what a commitment to the principles and objectives of a free society involves, and thus he revealed his conception of the role of political leadership in the formation of enlightened public opinion. The importance of this political teaching can hardly be exaggerated, for a government where all powers are derivative from the popular will necessitates a populace comparatively enlightened through the guidance of statesmanship. As he cautioned the nation in November 1938:

We cannot carelessly assume that a nation is strong and great merely because it has a democratic form of government. . . . Comparisons in this world are unavoidable. To disprove the pretenses of rival systems, democracy must . . . become a positive force in the daily lives of its people. . . . Too many of those who prate about saving democracy are really only interested in saving things as they are. Democracy should concern itself also with things as they ought to be.[7]

The president knew that the success of his interventionist policy required that it be supported by a solid popular agreement on the great issues at stake in the European conflict, for the main attack on interventionism was made in the name of an overpowering absorption in self-interest. Accordingly, he acted in such a way as to counter that habit of mind which insisted that the European conflict was hardly more than a struggle for power and not, as he himself believed, a conflict between different forms of government or different ways of life. In June 1940 Roosevelt had an exchange with representatives of the American Youth Congress, a group whose mind-set had been conditioned to look at the European war from a cynical, power-politics point of view. In the course of that exchange, he asked one of the youths whether he would prefer living in France or Germany, and the youth replied that he would much prefer living in the United States. But the president insisted that the choice, as he had stated it, was between France and Germany, that is, between a cumbersome democracy and an efficiently ordered tyranny. As for himself, the president remarked, he ''would rather live in France than in Germany,'' and that was because the French have ''a pretty free method of life'' and ''a great deal of civil liberty.''[8] In other words, a free way of life and the practice of civil liberties were evidence of the indisputably superior justice of the French form of government to the German form, for there could be no broadly distributed sense of political responsibility without that.

In his address at a Jackson Day dinner in January 1940, Roosevelt said that Alexander Hamilton was a hero to him because he did the job which had to be done, that is, he brought stability out of the chaos of currency and banking difficulties,[9] which is precisely what Roosevelt himself did in his first New Deal administration. Roosevelt is often identified with the Hamiltonian viewpoint, and for good reason. Hamilton was the architect of presidential power. The development of the presidency during the Washington administrations, the role of the presidency that Hamilton, under Washington's aegis, had forged for it at that time, can best be understood with a view to the strengthening of the executive power resulting from the need to administer the new government. Roosevelt, following largely in the tradition of Hamilton, was the architect of the modern American presidency. He resuscitated energetic government in the United States instituted by the Federalists. Although Roosevelt departed somewhat from Hamilton's understanding of limited energetic government, it was a departure, I would argue, which was necessitated by the crisis of the Great Depression, and one which preserved liberal democracy in that crisis.

NOTES

1. See *Federalist*, numbers 70–77.

2. *Federalist*, number 70.

3. James MacGregor Burns, *Roosevelt: The Soldier of Freedom* (New York, 1970), pp. vii, 339–43.

4. Felix Frankfurter to FDR, May 7, 1934, *Roosevelt and Frankfurter, Their Correspondence, 1928–45*, annotated by Max Freedman (Boston, 1967), pp. 213–14. See Samuel I. Rosenman, *Working with Roosevelt* (New York, 1952), p. 171: "One of the outstanding accomplishments of Roosevelt the statesman was his successful course of educating the American people in the uses of democracy, accompanied by practical examples of the doctrines he was teaching. In 1933 there were few books and no national precedents for the philosophy or legislation that came to be known as the New Deal. He had to write his own books in the form of speeches and messages, and then create the precedents himself to carry them out."

5. Franklin D. Roosevelt, "Campaign Address on Progressive Government, September 23, 1932," *The Public Papers and Addresses of Franklin D. Roosevelt*, compiled by Samuel I. Rosenman, 13 vols. (New York, 1938–1950), 1:756. Hereafter cited as *Papers and Addresses*.

6. Roosevelt, "Message on Education for American Education Week, September 27, 1938," *Papers and Addresses*, 7:537–38.

7. Roosevelt, "Address on Electing Liberals to Public Office, November 4, 1938," *Papers and Addresses*, 7:585–86.

8. Roosevelt, Press Conference No. 649A, June 5, 1940, *Press Conferences of Franklin D. Roosevelt* (Hyde Park, N.Y., 1956), 15:488–89.

9. Roosevelt, "Address of the Jackson Day Dinner, January 8, 1940," *Papers and Addresses,* 9:29–30.

16

Franklin D. Roosevelt's Administrative Contributions to the Presidency

A. J. Wann

During Franklin D. Roosevelt's tenure in the White House, there was a tendency on the part of the press and many political observers generally to describe his administrative conduct in predominantly negative terms, to dismiss his administrative record as essentially unsuccessful, and to conclude that his deficiencies in the administrative sphere detracted from his overall presidential performance and his almost universally conceded abilities as a political leader.

A careful survey of the administrative aspects of Roosevelt's twelve years as president, however, reveals that he made a number of important administrative contributions which had significant effects upon the operation of the presidency. In light of these, his administrative performance should be reassessed as mainly one of success rather than of failure.[1]

Perhaps his most obvious long-run contribution was the tremendous expansion that took place in the sheer size of the administrative organization of the executive branch. This, of course, was the inevitable accompaniment of the equally great expansion that Roosevelt called for in the range of activities and functions of the national government. Although this growth took place to some degree throughout his years as president, it was most marked during two particular periods: during his first two years in the White House, when he sharply increased both the number and the functions of administrative agencies in his efforts to combat the Depression; and after 1939, when he did the same thing in developing the national defense system of the country following the outbreak of war in Europe. Between his first inauguration in 1933 and his untimely death, Roosevelt more than doubled the size of the executive branch through the creation of many new agencies, commissions, boards, bureaus, and other miscellaneous forms of administrative organizations.

Roosevelt established the policy of setting up a host of new, specialized agencies, separate from the regular departments, to deal with both the emergency conditions of the Depression and of the national defense and war programs. He seems to have regarded this as an essential mechanism in dealing with emergencies, although he was well aware that so many agencies would complicate his job as the administrative head of the government. Coordinating the activities of the new agencies with those of the established departments, and the added number of administrative subordinates who would have to report directly to him as president, would add to the difficulties of his job. He felt, however, that the advantages outweighed the disadvantages. Among these were setting up an urgent program in a new independent agency to avoid having it compete, probably disadvantageously, for attention and resources with older, already established programs; and the introduction of innovative and dynamic new personnel, as heads of their own new agencies, not as subordinates to the heads of already existing departments. As a result, the number of independent agencies and the overall size of the administrative organization burgeoned by very sizable proportions during his administration.

This expansion was accompanied by a correspondingly large increase in government personnel. When Roosevelt became president in 1933, the national government employed slightly less than 600,000 persons. By 1939 the number had grown to 920,310 as a result of the additions during the New Deal years, and in 1940, as the expansion of the national defense program was getting under way, the number of employees advanced to slightly over 1 million for the first time in the history of the country. By the time Pearl Harbor plunged the country into war in December 1941, the number had increased to over 1.5 million, and by 1943 it had soared to over 3 million. An all-time peak was reached in January 1945, when a total of 3.375 million civilians were employed by the federal government.[2]

This great increase in the size of the government has had a permanent effect upon the presidency and upon the administrative conduct of all of Roosevelt's successors in the White House. Although government employment was curtailed rather sharply after World War II under President Harry S Truman, it never fell to less than 2 million persons under any of the presidents following Roosevelt, in contrast to the less than 600,000 of March 1933 when he took office. After Roosevelt, "big government" was clearly here to stay, with all of its implications for the problems of administrative organization and management. Subsequent presidents without exception have inevitably found it necessary to deal with the administrative tasks of a presidency which has continued on a Rooseveltian scale and with essentially a Rooseveltian organizational model. This has remained true because of the sheer size and complexity of the government and its degree of involvement in all aspects of American life. Despite the expressed intentions of some of the presidents who have followed Roosevelt, the ensuing years since shortly after World War II have not witnessed any appreciable diminution in the size of the administrative organization or the number of government personnel employed, with the latter figure gradually ranging upward from approximately

2.1 to 2.3 million in the period following World War II and the 1950s to the approximately 2.8 to 2.9 million at which it has remained rather remarkably stable for about the past ten years.

A second significant contribution of Roosevelt, but one that is not so readily obvious, was the substantial amount of structural integration he accomplished in the government. In trying to improve the president's administrative management of the executive branch, it is possible to proceed in two ways: either (1) the organizational structure can be better integrated by combining all of the administrative agencies and functions together under relatively few line departments, with the president then dealing directly with the department heads and relying primarily on them to aid him in coordinating all the activities of their subordinate divisions and branches; or (2) specific functions can be placed in specialized individual agencies responsible directly to the president, with improvements being made in the staff facilities and services available to the president to assist him in coordinating the activities of the departments and agencies through his own office. In other words, structural integration and functional coordination may be thought of as alternative possibilities to use in attempting to provide better management of the administrative organization.

Perhaps Roosevelt devoted considerably more attention to trying to improve the coordination of the various parts of the executive branch than he did to integrating it structurally. The important fact should not be overlooked, however, that at different times he tried to do both. In the years 1933 to 1936 he created many agencies to administer the New Deal programs, and he attempted, first through creation of an Executive Council and later through a National Emergency Council, both of which were composed of heads of executive departments and of the major new independent agencies, to provide suitable mechanisms for improved coordination. At the same time he consolidated, transferred, and eliminated a considerable number of agencies and functions under the broad reorganization authority which he had been granted by Congress from 1933 to 1935.

It was during the years from 1936 to 1940, however, that Roosevelt made his main effort to achieve improved structural integration. One of the major recommendations of the President's Committee on Administrative Management, to which Roosevelt had appointed Louis Brownlow, Charles E. Merriam, and Luther Gulick in early 1936, was that all of the more than one hundred governmental agencies then in existence should be integrated into a total of twelve executive departments, to include a new Department of Social Welfare and a new Department of Public Works. Roosevelt supported this proposal wholeheartedly in his recommendations to Congress and in his two-year battle to secure congressional approval for his comprehensive reorganization program.

When Congress finally did enact the Reorganization Act of 1939, it seriously limited what the president could do in the way of integration by excluding twenty-one of the more important agencies from his reorganization authority and providing that he could neither abolish nor establish an executive department.[3] In his Reorganization Plan No. 1, transmitted to Congress on April 25, 1939,

Roosevelt tried, nevertheless, to accomplish what he could along this line by creating three new "superagencies" with almost all of the attributes of regular departments except the name and statutory authorization. These were the Federal Security Agency, the Federal Works Agency, and the Federal Loan Agency, all of which were eventually to be consolidated and integrated into the regular executive department structure. By his five reorganization plans which went into effect in 1939 and 1940 he placed most of the previously independent agencies either in one of the ten regular executive departments or in one of the three new superagencies and thus achieved a considerable degree of structural integration through a large number of consolidations and transfers which reduced very substantially the number of agencies reporting directly to the president. All in all, the number of agencies and functions consolidated, transferred, or abolished during Roosevelt's administration from 1933 to 1945 totaled over 300, almost all of which were accomplished by presidential action under his reorganization authority.[4]

A third significant contribution of Roosevelt was the positive assertion by both word and deed of the president as the "chief administrator" or "general manager" of the entire administrative organization, and the increased general acceptance of this concept. From the day he became president, Roosevelt acted on the assumption that the Constitution made him the responsible head of all the administrative work of the executive branch. It was his view that the president had no more fundamental responsibilities than the operation and direction of the government's administrative machinery and, in the words of Arthur Schlesinger, Jr., "little fascinated Franklin Roosevelt more than the tasks of presidential administration."[5] Certainly he devoted a very great amount of his time and energy to superintending and coordinating the activities of his administrative subordinates, and he tried to keep closely in touch with the details of as many things as possible that were going on throughout the departments and agencies. No other president in the twentieth century, it is safe to say, has matched Roosevelt in the amount of attention given to the administrative work of the executive branch and in the personal knowledge he possessed about the detailed activities of the administrative organization.

In addition to Roosevelt's personal example, the concept of the president as the head of the entire administrative organization was greatly clarified and strengthened by the work of the President's Committee on Administrative Management and by Roosevelt's strong support of that committee's recommendations. Among all the things that the committee did, it is probably true that "its most important effect," as Wayne Coy has written, "was a much clearer conception of the role of the President as the responsible head of the whole administrative establishment."[6]

At the core of the committee's proposals was the basic idea that the president urgently needed help to enable him to fulfill the responsibilities imposed upon him by the Constitution, and that without such increased assistance the president could not exercise adequate direction and control over the functions performed in his name and under his authority throughout the executive branch. To this end, the committee proposed that the president's immediate office should be augmented by the addition of six administrative assistants, that the three fundamental governmental functions of budgeting, planning, and personnel management should be supervised by persons serving directly as administrative arms of the president, and that the entire executive branch should be integrated and streamlined in such a way that the chain of command from the White House down would be tightened and made more responsive to the president's direciton.

The committee strongly urged that the president should be given badly needed help in doing his job instead of trying to devise ways of reducing the size and scope of the job. There was no recommendation at all for the increased delegation of the president's administrative functions. He was to be provided with substantially increased staff assistance to help him in performing his many administrative duties, but there was no provision for the duties to be diminished. The committee accepted the premise as strongly as did Roosevelt that the president should properly serve as the chief executive of the government in fact as well as in name. Although this premise has certainly not lacked influential and vocal critics among political scientists and students of public administration, it has nevertheless remained at the heart of all the later studies that have been made of the administrative aspects of the presidency. Friend and foe alike have to recognize the validity of George Graham's statement that "the Report of the President's Committee on Administrative Management is a landmark from which all subsequent discussions of the Presidency must take their bearings."[7]

A fourth significant contribution Roosevelt made which had great effect on the administrative organization was his creation in 1939 of the Executive Office of the President as an overall umbrella office in which to locate those agencies of most immediate use and service to the president in performing his varied duties. Probably no other single administrative action by Roosevelt has received such widespread approbation as has this one. For example, Executive Order 8248, by which Roosevelt established the Executive Office of the President, prompted Clinton Rossiter to write, "For some years now it has been popular, even among his friends, to write off Mr. Roosevelt as a 'second-rate administrator.' In the light of Executive Order 8248, an accomplishment in public administration superior to that of any other President, this familiar judgment seems a trifle musty and platitudinous."[8] Among other comments of a similar nature that might be cited are statements by Herman Somers: "Establishment of the Executive Office of the President is a grand landmark in the administrative history of our government"; George Graham: "The creation of the Executive Office of the President was a milestone in the history of the Presidency"; and Fritz Morstein Marx: "There is widespread agreement . . . that the formation of the Executive Office of the President under the Reorganization Act of 1939 has been a most constructive move."[9]

Shortly after the Executive Office was set up, the unprecedented burden of national defense and wartime problems placed an exceedingly heavy administrative load upon Roosevelt and the new organization. For the most part, the components of the Executive Office met this severe test quite well, though not always with complete success, and there can be little doubt but that Roosevelt would not have been able to meet nearly so well the extraordinary demands which the war made on him without the assistance of the Executive Office agencies, especially his expanded White House Office, the Bureau of the Budget, and the Office of Emergency Management. In the period since, despite the numerous changes in the composition of the Executive Office as most of the old components have been eliminated and many new ones added, the general acceptance of the need for the Executive Office has been so complete that it is now virtually impossible to conceive of the presidency being able to operate without some sort of institutionalized system of this nature. In fact, it is true to say that whereas the Executive Office was created only to help the president do his various jobs, the presidency itself, as we have thought of it in recent years, could no longer exist without the Executive Office.

Of the original five component parts of the Executive Office of the President as established in 1939—the White House Office, Bureau of the Budget, National Resources Planning Board, Office of Government Reports, and Liaison Office for Personnel Management—only two, the White House Office and the Bureau of the Budget (renamed Office of Management and Budget in 1970), now remain to perform essentially the same basic functions as at the beginning, though both have expanded greatly since 1939 in terms of personnel employed and range of services rendered to aid the president in the execution of his tasks. The other three original agencies have long since either been eliminated or had their functions absorbed into other governmental entities—the National Resources Planning Board in 1943, the Office of Government Reports in 1948, and the Liaison Office for Personnel Management in 1953.

All told, as of 1981 there has been a total of forty-four various organizational units of one sort or another in the Executive Office of the President since its founding in 1939, of which ten are now in operation: the White House Office, Office of Management and Budget, Council of Economic Advisers (established in 1946), National Security Council (1949), Office of the Special Representative for Trade Negotiations (1963), Council on Environmental Quality (1969), Domestic Policy Staff (replacing in 1978 the Domestic Council, which had been established in 1970), Intelligence Oversight Board (1976), Office of Science and Technology Policy (1976), and Office of Administration (1977).[10] In spite of all the organizational changes that have occurred in the Executive Office, the fundamental concept that motivated its creation has not undergone significant alteration. All of the structural changes have conformed to the general purpose first described in the report of the President's Committee: to provide the president with an institutional arm to help him in the performance of the multifaceted obligations of his office.

Since 1939, however, it has always been the Bureau of the Budget/Office of Management and Budget that has continued to be the institutional backbone of the Executive Office of the President. In fact, Roosevelt's transfer of the Bureau of the Budget to the newly established Executive Office of the President in 1939, his increased utilization and expansion of the bureau's services, and the emphasis that he placed on the bureau as the most important single institutional instrument that he had available to help him manage the activities of his administrative subordinates—these combine to form a fifth significant Roosevelt contribution which had a major effect upon the administrative organization of the executive branch.

Roosevelt had already made substantially greater use of the Bureau of the Budget before 1939 than had any of his predecessors, but a combination of factors had tended to prevent him from relying upon it as much as he was to do following its transfer to the Executive Office of the President. One of these factors was the previous location of the bureau in the Department of the Treasury, where it had been placed by the Budget and Accounting Act in 1921. In formulating its recommendations, the President's Committee on Administrative Management had considered the possibility of leaving the bureau in Treasury and proposing to rebuild the department into an institution somewhat more like the British Treasury whereby it would be the agency which would unify the budgetary process with all the other major fiscal functions of the government. Although there might have been some beneficial results from this approach, the committee decided that they were outweighed by other considerations and recommended that the Bureau of the Budget should be taken out of its somewhat anomalous position in Treasury and placed immediately under the president, to whom it had been directly responsible, in fact, since its establishment in 1921.

This decision was based on the view that a national executive budget requires an overall perspective which has to encompass the entire government, and that under the U.S. constitutional system the president is the only one who has to look at the whole administrative organization, above and beyond the particular interests of individual departments and agencies. Because of this, it was thought preferable to strengthen and improve the Bureau of the Budget as a staff agency to assist the president rather than delegating a part of the president's managerial authority to the secretary of the treasury. Also, it was thought that the problems that would be involved in transforming a long-established operating department like the Treasury into an agency with overall management responsibilities would undoubtedly be very substantial. Roosevelt, in supporting the recommendation of the President's Committee, cited particularly that the expanded coordinating functions which he hoped to obtain from the Bureau of the Budget would be facilitated if the bureau was not a part of one of the departments.[11] Consequently, the bureau was placed in the Executive Office of the President, and the concept of the executive budget, prepared and administered by the Bureau of the Budget under the direction and control of the president, became firmly established in the government of the United States.

The sizable increase in the bureau's functions and importance after 1939 is attributable to several factors. First of all, the president was badly in need of the increased help that the bureau could provide. As Roosevelt himself was to write later, "It seemed evident that I had to be provided with expanded staff facilities to assist in the job of administrative management. One obvious move was the strengthening of the Bureau of the Budget."[12] The field for assisting the president in managing and coordinating the executive branch was a relative void, except for what the Bureau of the Budget had already been called upon to do along these lines, for Roosevelt, despite some initial, largely unsuccessful attempts to do so earlier through establishing an Executive Council and, somewhat later, a National Emergency Council, had not developed any effective or lasting institutional machinery for coordination in the years before 1939. The resulting near-vacuum was thus available to be filled by a staff agency whose leadership demonstrated ability, ambition, and imagination.

The second major factor was the new director of the Bureau of the Budget whom Roosevelt appointed in 1939, Harold D. Smith. Smith had all three of the attributes mentioned above in generous amounts. He possessed a broad, dynamic view as to the functions of the bureau and the services that a presidential staff should perform. He wrote, "The main function of the Bureau is to serve as an agent of the President in coordinating operations and in improving the administrative management of the government."[13] This was a quite different conception from that of many of his predecessors who believed that the only function of the bureau was to try to insure a balanced budget. In addition, Smith very quickly established a good personal relationship with Roosevelt. This was especially important as Roosevelt frequently tended to view administration in terms of personalities and relied most on those for whom he felt a close personal affinity.

A third factor was the inevitable relationship and overlapping between the budget function and the other functions involved in administration and coordination. A comprehensive executive budget is in effect a master plan for the administrative activities of the entire government, and the budgeting process must unavoidably impinge to some degree upon how those administrative activities are to be carried out. So, given these three factors, it is not surprising that Roosevelt looked more and more to the Bureau of the Budget, so that it came to occupy an increasingly vital place at the very heart of the president's administrative organization. To some degree this was reflected in the fact that the bureau quadrupled both its funds and its personnel within the first two years after Smith became director.[14] With Roosevelt's encouragement and Smith's leadership, the bureau developed many of the methods of budgeting, managing, and coordinating the administrative organization in the president's behalf to the high level of accomplishment which, for the most part, has characterized its work down to the present day.[15]

Roosevelt's sixth and last contribution to be singled out here was his imaginative establishment and highly innovative utilization of the Office of Emergency Management in conjunction with the national defense and wartime emergency resulting from World War II. Placing a provision in Executive Order 8248 in

September 1939 that authorized the later creation of the Office of Emergency Management in the Executive Office of the President can be characterized as almost a sheer stroke of both administrative and political genius on the part of Roosevelt and Louis Brownlow. Toward the end of a description of the component parts of the Executive Office of the President, Roosevelt and Brownlow had presciently inserted the language that the Executive Office should contain "in the event of a national emergency, or threat of a national emergency, such office for emergency management as the President shall determine."[16] Except for this one vague reference, which Clinton Rossiter aptly referred to as "an office in embryo,"[17] this potential additional agency in the Executive Office was not mentioned in Executive Order 8248.

It is difficult to overstress the importance of this action—which Brownlow has described as "putting a rabbit in the hat" to be pulled out by the president later[18]—as it was a novel and completely unprecedented administrative approach that allowed the president to move ahead in devising new emergency agencies for defense and war in a much easier, much faster, and much more flexible way than would undoubtedly have been the case if he had had to secure approval through the regular processes of congressional action. By using his reorganization power, Roosevelt activated the Office of Emergency Management officially on May 25, 1940.[19] It was to serve as an effective "holding company" for almost all of the new defense and war agencies. These agencies were created with no statutory base or authorization other than the president's reorganization authority as set forth in the Reorganization Act of 1939, in Roosevelt's Reorganization Plan No. 1, and in Executive Order 8248. In this way, Roosevelt, through use of the Office of Emergency Management, was able to eliminate what had often plagued Wilson and earlier wartime presidents—the difficulty of obtaining congressional sanction for each new emergency organization.

It is also of interest to note what Roosevelt did not do with the Office of Emergency Management. At no time did he delegate to it the authority to act as a central coordinating agency in his behalf. This seems unfortunate, as the Office of Emergency Management's location in the Executive Office of the President as the parent body to which almost all of the emergency agencies belonged would have made it eminently suited to serve as a strong coordinative body acting for and with the approval of the president. Roosevelt, however, apparently never intended to use the Office of Emergency Management as a supreme coordinative device other than to provide him with a channel through which he could establish whatever new agencies he deemed necessary, and which he could then coordinate himself.

The Office of Emergency Management did serve as an auxiliary agency with general housekeeping functions for its numerous component parts, and it provided central administrative service and a coordinated information service. However, the liaison officers for emergency management, William H. McReynolds and his successor, Wayne Coy, were never given any power to direct or control the operations of the subordinate organizations. It is interesting to conjecture whether the story would have been different if it had worked out for Roosevelt to appoint Louis Brownlow as his "liaison officer," as he had offered to do in 1939. It seems probable that a person of Brownlow's character and leadership ability might have tried to invest the job with considerably more authority than was true under McReynolds, a longtime career civil servant, although Brownlow was later to write that the agency functioned along the lines he and Roosevelt had envisioned for it:

I had originally conceived of the Office of Emergency Management in the Executive Office of the President as a holding company—an agency which was to do little or nothing on its own but which was to establish continuous lines of instantaneous communication between the President and any of the defense organizations to be set up and which was also to serve as a catalyzer so that the President on his own motion at any time, without having to seek legislation from the Congress, could create, modify, consolidate, or dissolve any particular agency set up for the emergency. In that respect, despite many difficulties, I believe the agency justified itself; and materially advantaged the operations during the years of preparedness. It made possible the greatest effort ever made by any nation through its governmental machinery to equip an army and navy—the army and navy that won World War II.[20]

Almost certainly there would have been a substantial difference in the way the liaison officer for emergency management operated if Roosevelt had followed through on his inclination to appoint Fiorello LaGuardia to the job, as he seriously contemplated doing at the time he was planning to establish the Office of Production Management in December 1940. Secretary of the Interior Harold L. Ickes reported in his diary on December 21, 1940:

The President also indicated that he was going to offer Fiorello LaGuardia one of his Executive Assistantships with the idea of making him liason man between himself and the new setup. . . . I learned later that when the President suggested this to the Stimson, Knox, Knudsen, Hillman group, he met with almost unanimous opposition. The theme was that LaGuardia would not work with the team but would run all over the field with the ball.[21]

In retrospect, it appears to some degree strange that Roosevelt did not see fit to develop the Office of Emergency Management as his top-level coordinative agency. As it was in the Executive Office of the President and was the legal "home" of all the specialized defense and war agencies, it could have been developed into something similar to what the Office of War Mobilization (OWM) ultimately came to be after Roosevelt established it in May 1943, with someone like OWM Director James F. Byrnes, former Supreme Court justice and senator, or another highly respected and capable political leader gifted in the art of compromise and conciliation as its head. This would have allowed him to appoint one important top-level figure in whom he had great confidence to assist him in the White House, as Byrnes was later to do, by heading up the coordination of the activities of the defense agencies and in settling the conflicts and jurisdictional disputes which inevitably would occur.

Such a move might possibly have been made at the time of the establishment of the Office of Emergency Management (OEM) in May 1940, although the time might not have been politically suitable. In any case it could undoubtedly have been done no later than early 1942 when the War Production Board was established shortly after Pearl Harbor. Again, in retrospect, this might have been a better solution than delegating extensive authority for coordination to the chairman of the War Production Board, Donald M. Nelson, who concentrated his attention almost entirely on developing the War Production Board as the major industrial and military production agency, rather than as the top-level coordinating agency which Roosevelt and the war program needed by that time. Such a step could have substantially eased Roosevelt's administrative and co-ordinative burdens, and might have improved the general administration of the war effort by providing faster and, in some cases, possibly better decisions based on more complete information and fuller consideration of the issues involved.

Roosevelt's failure to use the Office of Emergency Management in such a coordinative capacity and his slowness in delegating authority must be reckoned as a deficiency in his administration of the presidency, which may have hindered and delayed to some degree the accomplishment of his defense and war pro-duction programs. Nevertheless, his innovative use of the OEM as the institu-tional mechanism through which he brought into being almost all of the defense and war agencies must be regarded as an administrative contribution of the highest order.

Overall, some other presidents undoubtedly administered the presidential office in a better and more orderly manner than Roosevelt did, if evaluated only as to standards of efficiency and economy. Nevertheless, it is equally true—and more important—that no other president made a greater administrative contribution to the operation of the presidency or had a more significant total effect upon the scope, the structural arrangement, and the functioning of the administrative organization of the executive branch.

That Roosevelt did not achieve all of the administrative changes in the federal government that needed to be made goes almost without saying. The extensive reforms enacted as a result of the recommendations of the two Hoover Com-missions under the administrations of presidents Truman and Eisenhower made this abundantly clear, along with the additional reorganization measures carried out under presidents Kennedy, Johnson, Nixon, and Carter. His failure to ac-complish other worthwhile changes in the administrative system may have been partly owing to deficiencies on his own part. Mostly, however, the limitations and restrictions placed on his reorganization efforts by Congress and by numerous political considerations accounted for this failure. Some of his earlier interest in improving the administrative organization of the government, as expressed over a period of many years before he became president, remained relatively obscured during his first term by his political and legislative activities. To these he gave first priority in order to effect the economic programs and social reforms that he thought necessary to get the country out of the Depression. The same can also be said of the last year of his second term and his entire third term, when he was preoccupied with the national defense emergency and World War II.

Although Roosevelt was interested throughout his career in questions of administration, it is accurate to say that this interest was subordinate to his interest in politics. Perhaps it is really more accurate to say that Roosevelt as president never actually distinguished politics and administration from each other in any clear-cut way. In his thinking, everything he did as president was inevitably political. It seemed almost second nature, or a sort of automatic reflex, for Roosevelt to consider the political consequences of every administrative action and to weigh constantly the implications of all that he did in terms of his leadership of the Democratic party, of Congress, and of the country.

It appears that Roosevelt was particularly concerned about being a good president. Rather than a "great administrator" or a "great politician," he wished history to call him a "great president." He knew from his close study of the lives of many of his predecessors that neither political achievements alone nor administrative achievements alone would be sufficient to secure the mantle of presidential greatness. Instead, a combination of both, in varying amounts with other essential ingredients in some sort of mysterious and elusive formula, was required. He well recognized the truth of what Herman Somers was later to write: "Long experience has demonstrated that a President is likely to succeed in most of his jobs or in none. They are mutually dependent. . . . The President is not politician *and* administrator; he is rather a *political administrator*."[22]

Consequently, in his administrative actions and in the changes he wrought in the administrative organization, Roosevelt was motivated not so much by a desire to be a better administrator but to be a more effective president. Certainly he regarded the creation of the Executive Office of the President as considerably more than a device for enabling him to manage the administrative organization more efficiently and economically. He was interested in designing improved machinery to help him perform his administrative tasks, but he was even more interested in establishing the Executive Office as a means of reducing his administrative burdens to a sufficient degree that he would be helped in performing all of his other duties more effectively. In his administrative methods he was usually concerned most of all, not with whether they were neat and orderly, or whether they were especially efficient or in conformity with a logically designed, elaborate plan, but with the questions of whether or not they worked, and what effect they might have on the overall performance of his presidential obligations. Robert E. Sherwood has discussed this point in the following passage:

Roosevelt's methods of administration . . . were to say the least, unorthodox. They filled some practical-minded observers with apprehension and dismay, and some with disgust; they filled others with awe and wonder . . . but there is one thing that can be said about these methods—whether they were good or bad, sensible or insane, they worked.[23]

In this connection, Sherwood went on to quote from a lengthy interview which he had with Harold Smith, the "modest, methodical, precise man, temperamentally far removed from Roosevelt," who served as Roosevelt's budget director from 1939 to 1945. He quotes Smith as follows:

A few months ago . . . a magazine asked me to write an article on Roosevelt as administrator. I thought it over and decided I was not ready to make such an appraisal. I've been thinking about it ever since. When I worked for Roosevelt—for six years—I thought as did many others that he was a very erratic administrator. But now, when I look back, I can really begin to see the size of his programs. They were by far the largest and most complex programs that any President ever put through. People like me who had the responsibility of watching the pennies could only see the five or six or seven per cent of the programs that went wrong, through inefficient organization or direction. But now I can see in perspective the ninety-three or ninety-four or ninety-five per cent that went right—including the winning of the biggest war in history—because of unbelievably skillful organization and direction. And if I were to write that article now, I think I'd say that Roosevelt must have been one of the greatest geniuses as an administrator that ever lived. What we couldn't appreciate at the time was the fact that he was a real *artist* in government.[24]

There seems to be little doubt on the part of most students of American government and politics but that history will accord Franklin D. Roosevelt a secure place somewhere high among the galaxy of great American presidents, along with Washington and Lincoln, Jefferson and Jackson, Theodore Roosevelt and Wilson. As mentioned earlier, however, to many observers Roosevelt's administrative shortcomings constituted a major detraction from his overall performance as president. "Even his stoutest friends admit that Roosevelt was not much of an administrator," Clinton Rossiter has observed. But then he adds, "It is possible that his friends give away too much to his enemies on this particular count."[25]

Certainly Roosevelt's overall contributions to the role of the president as the administrative head of the executive branch were most significant. All of the presidents since his day have had to operate administratively under the broad shadow that Roosevelt cast after him and have necessarily proceeded along lines that his administrative views and actions clearly foreordained. The work of his successors has been shaped and greatly facilitated by the reorganizations that Roosevelt initiated in his effort to enable the president to manage a vastly expanded executive branch. And they have carried on their work through essentially the same institutionalized administrative framework in the White House Office and Executive Office of the President created by Roosevelt to help the president discharge his responsibilities more effectively.

When viewed now from the perspective of more than fifty years after his election as president and forty years after his death, the opinion that Roosevelt's administrative record was mainly one of failure is believed to have resulted from premature judgements, based upon perceptions much too limited in scope. When one carefully weighs the pros and cons of Roosevelt's administrative contributions to the presidency and his total effects upon the president's administrative role, the balance clearly indicates that his administrative achievements should properly be recognized as contributing most importantly to his overall presidential performance.

NOTES

1. For an earlier and much fuller discussion of some of the views set forth here, see A. J. Wann, *The President as Chief Administrator: A Study of Franklin D. Roosevelt* (Washington, D.C.: Public Affairs Press, 1968).

2. *United States Government Manual, 1945* (Washington, D.C.: Government Printing Office, 1945).

3. *53 Stat.* 561, enacted on April 3, 1939.

4. *United States Government Manual, 1945,* pp. 590–622; Joseph P. Harris, "Wartime Currents and Peacetime Trends," *American Political Science Review* 40 (December, 1946): 1150.

5. Arthur M. Schlesinger, Jr., *The Coming of the New Deal* (Boston: Houghton Mifflin Co., 1959), p. 521.

6. Wayne Coy, "Basic Problems," *American Political Science Review* 40 (December 1946): 1131.

7. George A. Graham, "The Presidency and the Executive Office of the President," *Journal of Politics* 12 (November 1950): 599.

8. Clinton Rossiter, *The American Presidency* (New York: Harcourt, Brace and Co., 1956), p. 101; see also, by the same author, "The Constitutional Significance ʒf the Executive Office of the President," *American Political Science Review* 43 (December 1949):1209.

9. Herman Miles Somers, *Presidential Agency* (Cambridge, Mass.: Harvard University Press, 1950), pp. 208–9; Graham, "The Presidency," p. 603; Fritz Morstein Marx, *The President and His Staff Services* (Chicago: Public Administration Service, 1949), p. 15.

10. John Helmer, "The Presidential Office: Velvet Fist in an Iron Glove," in Hugh Heclo and Lester M. Salamon, eds., *The Illusion of Presidential Government* (Boulder, Colo.: Westview Press, 1981), pp. 58–59.

11. *The Public Papers and Addresses of Franklin D. Roosevelt,* ed. Samuel I. Rosenman (New York: Macmillan, 1941), 1939 vol., p. 250.

12. *Public Papers,* 1939 vol., pp. 498–99.

13. Harold D. Smith, "The Bureau of the Budget," *Public Administration Review* 1 (Winter 1941): 114.

14. Arthur N. Holcombe, "Over-all Financial Planning Through the Bureau of the Budget," *Public Administration Review* 1 (Spring 1941): 225–30; Edward H. Hobbs, *Behind the President* (Washington, D.C.: Public Affairs Press, 1954), p. 29.

15. For an excellent account of the development of the Bureau of the Budget/Office of Management and Budget, see Larry Berman, *The Office of Management and Budget and the Presidency, 1921–1979* (Princeton, N.J.: Princeton University Press, 1979).

16. *Public Papers,* 1939 vol., p. 491.

17. Rossiter, "Constitutional Significance of the Executive Office," p. 1209.

18. Louis Brownlow, *A Passion for Anonymity* (Chicago: University of Chicago Press, 1958), p. 423. Brownlow's account of his own highly important part in this action is related on pp. 423–32.

19. *Public Papers,* 1940 vol., pp. 693–94, 697–98.

20. Brownlow, *Passion for Anonymity,* pp. 426–27.

21. Harold L. Ickes, *The Secret Diary of Harold L. Ickes,* Vol. 3, *The Lowering Clouds, 1939–1941* (New York: Simon and Schuster, 1954), p. 398.

22. Herman Miles Somers, "The President as Administrator," *Annals of the American Academy of Political and Social Science* 283 (September 1952): 111.

23. Robert E. Sherwood, *Roosevelt and Hopkins* (New York: Harper and Brothers, 1948), p. 72.

24. Ibid., pp. 72–73.

25. Rossiter, *American Presidency,* pp. 117–118.

VI

FDR AND ELEANOR ROOSEVELT

17

Eleanor Roosevelt and "My Day": The White House Years

Maurine Beasley

As the year 1936 dawned, a new columnist arrived on the American newspaper scene. She was First Lady Eleanor Roosevelt, whose unprecedented column, "My Day," provided readers from coast to coast, six days a week, with a detailed recital of her activities. Billed as a "diary," the column occupied an unusual niche in American journalism. It gave behind-the-scenes glimpses of White House life and served as a platform from which the First Lady could state her personal views. Part an "inside" look at celebrities, part political oratory, part public relations for the New Deal, part the perceptions of an individual playing a leading role in the drama of her times, "My Day" eluded a definite classification. Frequently criticized for its trivial content and lack of literary style, "My Day" remained a journalistic fixture for over a quarter of a century, continuing after Mrs. Roosevelt left the White House.

Unfortunately, historians have paid little attention to "My Day," except to note its existence among Mrs. Roosevelt's numerous other ventures. It has been written off as shallow and inconsequential, especially during the period when Eleanor Roosevelt was First Lady.[1] A reappraisal is needed, particularly in light of current interest in women's history. Restricted in what she could say as First Lady, Eleanor Roosevelt had to focus on the obvious—herself and her position. Much of what she wrote stressed the commonplace. Still, tens of thousands of readers hung on her every word. No doubt, many sought vicarious satisfaction in following the activities of the president's wife. Another aspect of the column, however, should not be overlooked, the very artlessness sneered at by intellectuals.[2] Eleanor Roosevelt wrote like a grandmother, a favorite aunt, or a friendly neighbor next door. She offered advice and counsel to Americans coping with vast social upheaval—first the Depression, then World War II. She appealed, she urged, she offered herself as a guide for her readers, many of whom were women. "My Day" displayed her own activities as models for her readers to follow.

Mrs. Roosevelt's motivation in beginning the column seems clear. In a letter to her intimate friend, Lorena Hickok, she wrote, "I need the money."[3] She spent large sums annually, sometimes more than the president's $75,000 salary, mainly on philanthropy. By the time she started "My Day," she was no stranger to writing for pay. Under the tutelage of Louis Howe, the newspaperman who had guided Franklin D. Roosevelt's political career, she had become a frequent contributor to magazines before Roosevelt's election as president.[4] Shortly after she moved into the White House, United Features Syndicate asked her to do a daily column, apparently at the suggestion of Gretta Palmer, women's page editor of the *New York World-Telegram*.[5] Mrs. Roosevelt rejected the idea because of other commitments, including a weekly series for the Columbia Syndicate on social customs in Washington and the work of government agencies.[6] This series turned out to be disappointing, in her own words "a very dull affair."[7]

Two years later United Features took over Columbia and pressed her to sign a five-year contract for publication of a daily "diary." She prepared a sample version for December 30, 1935, in competition with another new Washington column, one written by her tart-tongued cousin, Alice Roosevelt Longworth.[8] Mrs. Roosevelt's editor, Monte F. Bourjaily, general manager of United Features, greeted "My Day" with some trepidation as well as delight. Fearing that she might lack ideas, Bourjaily sent her a lengthy list of suggestions: The "high spot" of her day; what the individuals she met "have on their minds"; "things of interest to women in their homes as reflected in White House housekeeping"; her personal interests; "real life stories" taken from her mail or her own experiences; tips on etiquette; "pieces of inspiration"; the "trend of thought in the country" as revealed in her daily mail; and, "most important of all, the day-to-day experiences, interests and observations in which you may share that part of your life which you are willing to make public with newspaper readers."[9] Still uncertain that she would develop a suitable format, Bourjaily enclosed a model—the popular column by Franklin P. Adams titled "Dairy of Our Own Samuel Pepys," which ran in the *New York Herald-Tribune*.[10] Fearful that copy might not flow continuously, Bourjaily tried to enlist the help of "Tommy," Malvina Thompson Scheider, Mrs. Roosevelt's secretary. He asked her to play a "Boswellian role" and jot down comments Mrs. Roosevelt made each day for use if "the regular column fails to reach us on time."[11]

Mrs. Roosevelt had her own doubts about the venture. Realistically, she recognized that her position made her writing saleable. Yet she wanted it to be valued on merit. When a magazine returned an article shortly before she started the column, she wrote Hickok, to whom she frequently sent manuscripts for criticism:

You see I haven't the feeling that the things are good in themselves. I've always felt it was largely name & I'm glad to have it back because it shows they are wanting something besides name. If I can't do this after giving it a good try then I must do something else that is all & one and I can only find out by trying.[12]

Her desire to succeed stemmed from her own psychic tensions in the opinion of family and friends. Her son, Elliott, attributed it to a need for "power and influence, provided it was in her own right and her own name."[13] According to Dr. James A. Halsted, a son-in-law, she needed to work to give herself an identity.[14] In Halsted's view, her pursuit of a career allowed her to handle "wisely and intelligently" emotional problems resulting from disclosure of Franklin D. Roosevelt's infidelity in the World War I era, long before his election as president.[15] To her grandson, John R. Boettiger, her career represented one of the ways "she struggled to be as full a human being as she was."[16] Certainly she received enthusiastic support from Howe, who saw that she could win countless friends for the Roosevelt administration through writing, lecturing, and other public activities.[17]

At first Mrs. Roosevelt thought a daily column would be "the most dreadful chore," but she soon decided otherwise.[18] Asked to submit sample articles to Bourjaily, she tossed them off with ease, telling Hickok, "The writing is easy so far, they must want one incident out of the day & so far I've had no trouble."[19] The pilot column featured an innocuous account of her falling over "gentlemen" waiting to see the president in a dark White House hall.[20] It set a tone of making the White House somewhat analogous to the typical American home where misadventures often occurred. The "gentlemen," however, were not identified.

This tendency to leave out vital information brought forth a delicate admonition from Bourjaily. After she praised the work of a Works Progress Administrator in Arkansas who had been killed in a plane crash, but failed to mention his name, Bourjaily chided gently, "I may be entirely mistaken but it seems to me that such a beautiful tribute would have been heightened and everyone concerned would have been highly pleased if you had mentioned the name of the WPA Administrator involved."[21] When she told her readers of fruitless attempts to obtain a Chuddar shawl for "Colonel Howe" without giving Howe's first name or explaining what a Chuddar shawl was, the syndicate added an editorial note defining Chuddar shawls as large sheets worn by women in India.[22] Editors took pains to save her from embarrassing mistakes, but let her know of their efforts. "I know that nobody enjoys a laugh on herself better than yourself, therefore pour le sport I am taking the liberty of enclosing copy of an editorial memorandum," George Carlin, Bourjaily's successor at United Features, wrote on one occasion.[23] He enclosed his memo from an editor who had corrected some awkward wording:

I note with horror that the First Lady had turned cannibal. The lead sentence in her story is "We had a lunch of some 50–odd ladies yesterday. . . . " and a little further down she goes on with the fearful orgy as evidenced by: "We returned in time for lunch and had a very distinguished group of doctors. . . . " I have carefully changed these 2 sentences lest we lose our vegetarian readers.[24]

During its first year "My Day" touched on humanitarian concerns Mrs. Roosevelt addressed repeatedly during her White House years: unemployment, poverty, youth, women's role, education, rural life, labor, conservation. Yet, much of it could be read as ingenious political propaganda during an election year. The column used various devices to enhance the administration: direct praise of New Deal programs; vignettes of encounters with taxi drivers and other average Americans passionately eager to vote for Roosevelt; and anecdotes picturing Franklin D. Roosevelt as a warm human being reacting gracefully to such political setbacks as the Supreme Court's rejection of the Agricultural Adjustment Administration.[25] Overall it projected her as an incredibly energetic grandmother devoted to family, friends, and worthy causes while presiding at the White House, flying around the country to give speeches, and campaigning for the Democratic party. It showed her as a kind of "superwoman," finding time to read popular books, attend the theater, and partake of numerous cultural events, often mentioned in unsophisticated critiques. For example, she reported *Gone with the Wind* was a "book you would like to read straight through. . . . I can assure you you will find Scarlett O'Hara an interesting character . . . circumstances mold even the little animal she seems to be."[26]

According to Elliott Roosevelt, the column concealed his mother's true identity as a "detached, harried, faultfinding wife and parent."[27] If so, there still were hints of deep-seated emotions that the writer kept to herself. Not surprisingly, these appeared in observations on women in general. Commenting on Nazi Germany, where women were being limited to childbearing, she stated her support for work as a human right: "There are three fundamentals for human happiness—work which will produce at least a minimum of material security, love and faith. These things must be made possible for all human beings, men and women alike."[28] She attacked a claim that "there will never be any really great women writers in the theatre, because women do not know as much as men," replying: "women know not only what men know, but much that men will never know. For, how many men really know the heart and soul of a woman?"[29] She offered consolation for anyone "in the public eye," explaining, "the more you live in a 'goldfish bowl,' the less people really know about you."[30]

The names of many famous women paraded through "My Day," particularly those of New Deal figures—Frances Perkins, Mary W. Dewson, Mary Anderson, Hilda W. Smith, Hollie Flanagan, Caroline G. O'Day—making the column a kind of newsletter for women in politics.[31] Not a feminist, Mrs. Roosevelt used "My Day" as a forum for opposition to the equal rights amendment, contending that laboring women, unlike their professional counterparts, needed protective legislation.[32] Although it exhorted women to enter politics, "My Day" never challenged the conventional wisdom requiring women to be family oriented.[33] Yet the First Lady sometimes alluded to a vague sisterhood of sex in such comments as "There are practical little things in housekeeping which no man really understands."[34]

The column gave the administration a highly flexible weapon in its political arsenal, which may have accounted for its enthusiastic acceptance by Franklin D. Roosevelt.[35] It was the logical place to scotch a silly rumor that the president's mother charged the government rent for the time Roosevelt spent in the family mansion at Hyde Park.[36] When Eleanor Roosevelt became ill in September 1936, the president offered to write the column for her, but she declined, telling her readers, "We refused, courteously and rapidly knowing that if it once became the President's column we would lose our readers and that would be very sad."[37]

No doubt the two conferred on some of the contents. Shortly before the Democratic National Convention in 1936, the president directed Mrs. Roosevelt to print verbatim a report on steel industry automation, which had caused unemployment that he wanted blamed on Republican industralists, not the New Deal.[38] The report appeared without attribution to Hickok, the actual author, then a confidential investigator for Harry Hopkins, Roosevelt's relief czar. Mrs. Roosevelt apologized to Hickok:

Dearest, From your Youngstown letter, taking out the name of place & industry, I've written my Monday piece at Franklin & Roy Howard's [Howard was head of the Scripps Howard newspaper chain] suggestion. If you mind I'm terribly sorry. I wanted to wait for your consent but Franklin won't let me. I think he wants me to be whipping boy & tho' he can't bring the question out he wants it out.[39]

Over the years Mrs. Roosevelt never failed to do the column, covering all the topics Bourjaily outlined in his letter of instruction plus many more. She never ran out of ideas in spite of illness, travel, and vacation, so her secretary never had to assume the "Boswellian role" Bourjaily had envisioned. Mrs. Roosevelt dictated the column to Scheider, frequently under trying circumstances while traveling—during picnic lunches, in automobiles, trains, planes, and ships, and in hotel rooms so cramped that the bed was the only place for a typewriter.[40] Sometimes difficulties arose in filing the copy, carefully marked "Press Rates Collect."[41] The First Lady shared her problems with her readers, telling them when telegraph offices were closed, lines down, and deadlines barely made.[42]

From the first the column proved a financial success. Six months after it began, Bourjaily reported that it had fifty-one clients, the same number it had started with, although several large papers had dropped it and smaller ones picked it up.[43] Depending on the number of subscribers, the column brought Mrs. Roosevelt from $1,100 to $2,000 a month during her White House years. Clients represented a mixed bag of newspaperdom, ranging from the then-mighty Scripps Howard chain to obscure sheets which were given a bargain weekly rate under a dollar.[44] The syndicate kept the initial price low to compete with the Longworth column, which soon vanished from the scene.[45] By 1938 "My Day" appeared in 62 newspapers with a total circulation of 4,034,552, giving Mrs. Roosevelt exposure to more readers than David Lawrence, Raymond Clapper, and Heywood Broun, although she lagged behind Walter Lippmann, who reached

8 million readers in 160 newspapers, and Dorothy Thompson, who reached 7 million in 140.[46]

Critics of "My Day" abounded. Stylists objected to her repeated use of cliches and "persistently sweet tone," marked by numerous references to events as "interesting," "lovely," or "momentous."[47] Some scorned her selection of family anecdotes, which, for example, showed her as a doting grandmother pretending to be a growling lion for a grandson, and a loyal mother, plugging her daughter Anna's book, *Scamper, the Bunny Who Went to the White House.*[48]

Perhaps shrewdly, Mrs. Roosevelt made these complaints the subject of a column, running a letter from a woman complaining of her "inane chatter about your family affairs" and urging her not to "waste your valuable time and the space in the paper with something so worthless . . . when you could so easily write something which might have marvelous results."[49] Mrs. Roosevelt ingenuously answered, "You must occasionally have something lighter to relieve you."[50] Soon she thanked the "many people" who had written to say they enjoyed reading "about the little things."[51] Left unsaid were references to the political goodwill her columns brought the administration. They established Mrs. Roosevelt as a prototypical wife and mother, and they helped defuse criticism of the family divorces and business ventures.

Columnist Westbrook Pegler occupied a special category as critic. Although he first applauded "My Day," Pegler protested when Mrs. Roosevelt joined the American Newspaper Guild, a union of newspaper employees, attacking her credentials as a bona fide journalist. Since United Features syndicated Pegler as well as Mrs. Roosevelt, Carlin came to Mrs. Roosevelt's defense, writing her:

"My Day" goes on and on, not because it is written by the wife of the President of the United States, but because it is an honest projection of one of the great personalities of our own time; a woman great in her own right, and as a newspaper columnist, possibly the best trouper of them all, never known to miss a deadline.[52]

Over the years the column progressed from a simple chronicle to an oblique source of information on administration policy. In 1939 Arthur Krock of *The New York Times* labeled it "required political reading," after Mrs. Roosevelt sat at the president's side during a press conference and prompted him to discuss cutbacks in work relief programs.[53] She covered the same subject in her column and used the same figure of speech as the president.[54] Still, the column remained her personal platform. "My Day," for instance, announced her resignation from the Daughters of the American Revolution when the organization refused to let a Negro, Marian Anderson, sing in its hall.[55]

Sympathy for youth led her to make "My Day" a vehicle for promoting and defending the left-leaning American Youth Congress. Indications of fellow-traveling disturbed her syndicate editors. In a tactful warning, Carlin told her that he "inwardly applauded" a comment that communism was increased by "empty stomachs" but hoped she would never repeat it: "The word Communist is a red flag. It is dangerous, I think, for a column like 'My Day.' "[56] His admonition brought a denial from Scheider that Mrs. Roosevelt had actually written "Communist," although, the secretary agreed, "you were right that it could be interpreted that way."[57] At issue was a column quoting a man who claimed that Congress had made "ten potential Communists for every [actual] one" by cutting out WPA jobs.[58] "Mrs. R. says she will be extremely careful in the future," Scheider promised.[59] Mrs. Roosevelt continued to uphold the Youth Congress in "My Day," however, denying that it was a communist front and reporting her support for the group at congressional hearings investigating it for un-American activities.[60]

As war opened in Europe, Mrs. Roosevelt turned "My Day" into a vehicle to prepare Americans for entry into the conflict. Her accounts of the visits here of the king and queen of England in 1939, which led to the temporary sale of her column abroad, fostered interest in cementing the Anglo-American alliance.[61] Occasionally she became so caught up in European development that she forgot her position as a newspaper columnist. After she referred to gluing herself to the radio for war news, Carlin passed on a letter of complaint from a Memphis editor who objected to the inference that newspapers were secondary news sources. "As you know, radio competition is a very sore point with newspapers," Carlin emphasized.[62] A few days later Mrs. Roosevelt tried to make amends. "Curious how we have settled down again after our first flurry of excitement and now turn to our newspapers for real information," she told her readers.[63]

Even as she foresaw American participation in war, she appealed for peace and creation of a new world where aggressors would be curbed and humanity freed to reach new heights. Long before bombs dropped on Pearl Harbor, Mrs. Roosevelt implied the inevitability of Americans dying in battle. "When force . . . is as menacing to all the world, as it is today, one cannot live in a Utopia which prays for different conditions and ignores those which exist," she wrote.[64] On the eve of the election of 1940, when Franklin D. Roosevelt won an unprecedented third term, she downplayed the certainty of American involvement in war: "The fact is before you that in a world of war we are still at peace."[65] But after the election she returned to the theme: "For most of us, it seems imperative that we meet physical force with physical force," adding, "our endeavor should be to use this physical force to achieve the results in which we believe."[66]

The dream of a better world tomorrow resounded through "My Day" after the United States declared war. In support of the war effort, "My Day" pleaded for increased racial and religious harmony in the United States. To Mrs. Roosevelt, American intervention symbolized a crusade to prove the superiority of democracy. "If we cannot meet the challenge of fairness to our citizens of every nationality . . . if we cannot keep in check anti-semitism, anti-racial feelings as well as anti-religious feelings, then we shall have removed from the world, the one real hope for the future," she stressed.[67]

Mrs. Roosevelt, however, said relatively little about extending the rights of women. Although a ceaseless advocate of women's participation in defense work, "My Day" saw women simply as willing subordinates to military men carrying the burden of saving Western civilization. The First Lady urged women to work in munitions plants, become nurses, volunteer for noncombatant duty, and mobilize in hundreds of different ways, from saving grease to ferrying airplanes, to keep the homefires burning brightly. In common with most of the rest of the population, Mrs. Roosevelt assumed that the war would not bring a permanent change in women's status. Commenting on a "question which surprised and interested me"—whether women should give up jobs to returning servicemen—she replied, "It seems to me to be clear that every serviceman has been promised that he will be restored to his former job."[68]

Dissatisfaction with women's status crept into "My Day," but blame was put on women themselves. Suggesting a national service act, covering women as well as men after the war, Mrs. Roosevelt wrote in 1944:

Women are often attacked because no radical changes have occurred since they obtained their rights as full citizens of this democracy, and now is the time to show they recognize their responsibilities.

I have always contended that women have had a very general influence on the trend of government in the past twenty-five years, but I cannot say that I think they have used their abilities and opportunities to the utmost.[69]

In numerous columns during the war years, Mrs. Roosevelt ignored the diary format, turning to patriotic messages, descriptions of her travels to far-flung war theaters, including the South Pacific, letters from servicemen, and advice from the Office of War Information. A column urging Congress to continue food subsidies to combat wartime inflation prompted a gentle rebuke from Carlin, who enclosed a letter from the editor of the *New York World-Telegram* calling the column a "political speech."[70] With customary diplomacy, Carlin noted: "I am afraid we will both have to agree that the basic diary form of 'My Day' has sometimes been more honored in the breach than in the observance. Personally, I miss the daily regularity of the diary, because, like your 6,000,000 other readers, I enjoy most the notion of a daily visit with Mrs. Roosevelt."[71] Apparently heeding his counsel, Mrs. Roosevelt resumed a more detailed chronicle of her activities.

With concern for women's rights diminished during the war, Mrs. Roosevelt muted protests against discrimination. In one of her last columns written from the White House, she commented, "The need for being a feminist is gradually disappearing in this country," although, she added, "we haven't quite reached the millennium."[72] As an example of the "little ways in which women are discriminated against," she cited the specifying of "men only" for "higher positions" under civil service.[73]

After Franklin D. Roosevelt's death on April 12, 1945, she told readers that she planned to continue "My Day." She wrote that she had always looked upon the column "as a job which I wanted to have considered on its merits," but had been restricted by being the president's wife.[74] "Now I am on my own, and I hope to write as a newspaper woman," she declared.[75] Subsequently the column became more outspoken, figuring in a bitter dispute with the Roman Catholic hierarchy over her position on federal aid for parochial schools.[76] But it still retained its personal flavor of a woman describing her own activities and interests.

It is difficult to assess the impact of "My Day" during Mrs. Roosevelt's White House years. Without doubt, it symbolized the quintessence of political wifehood, promoting the administration through favorable publicity for New Deal programs and personalities. Curiously, the syndicate alluded to this aspect of the column in marketing it. It referred to "My Day" as a "service, although a most pleasant one," offered by Mrs. Roosevelt to the American people, implying that it constituted a special civic bonus presented by the Roosevelt administration.[77]

As a journalistic endeavor, "My Day" remained unique from beginning to end. Her editors took it seriously and so did she, bowing to their directions and meeting their requirements. Beyond its political overtones, "My Day" sent a series of mixed messages regarding the position of women in society. Mixing naivete and shrewdness, Mrs. Roosevelt's candor raised questions that still have not been answered. As she described her hectic schedule, combining ceremonial, political, and family responsibilities along with career interests, she personified the problem of fragmented lives, one faced by many women on a lesser scale. When she wrote, "I wish I could be three people, [one] . . . holding teas, luncheons . . . [one sitting] at a desk eight hours a day . . . [the third] a wife, mother, grandmother and friend," she surely hit a responsive note.[78]

Still, "My Day" failed to offer a role model of much meaning to the average woman. After all, few individuals could realistically hope to follow in her footsteps as First Lady. Nevertheless, the column showed a middle-aged woman continually on the move, literally and figuratively, defining a role for herself outside the customary boundaries of her position. It pictured her trying her hand at the competitive occupation of daily journalism and establishing a place in spite of criticism, ridicule, and obvious inexperience.[79]

As she traded on her role as a wife, she enhanced it, increasingly becoming a public figure in her own right. If not a feminist, she addressed feminist concerns, although she minimized them. In one sense, "My Day" can be viewed as a journalistic way station on the road to women's liberation. Surely it can be seen as the portrait of a woman seeking a personal liberation through highly unusual circumstances. It is possible to say what millions of readers saw in "My Day," but the column's durability testified that substance lay behind its bland exterior.

NOTES

1. James E. Polland, *The Presidents and the Press* (New York: Macmillan, 1947), p. 791. See also Susanna Scuito Dado, "Eleanor Roosevelt as a Columnist," M.A. thesis, California State University, Northridge, 1977.

2. Virginia Pasley, "First Lady to the Common Man," *American Mercury* 58 (March 1944): 275–83.

3. Eleanor Roosevelt to Lorena Hickok, December 13, 1935, Box 2, Hickok Papers, Franklin D. Roosevelt Library, hereafter cited as FDRL.

4. Elliott Roosevelt and James Brough, *An Untold Story: The Roosevelts of Hyde Park* (New York: Putnam, 1973), pp. 267–68. See also Joseph P. Lash, *Eleanor and Franklin* (New York: Norton, 1971), p. 414.

5. James R. Kearney, *Anna Eleanor Roosevelt* (Boston: Houghton Mifflin, 1968), p. 132.

6. Ruby Black, *Eleanor Roosevelt* (New York: Duell, Sloan and Pearce, 1940), p. 113.

7. Anna Eleanor Roosevelt, *This I Remember* (New York: Harper, 1949), p. 177.

8. Kearney, *Anna Eleanor Roosevelt*, p. 132.

9. Monte F. Bourjaily to Eleanor Roosevelt, December 14, 1935, Box 4873, Eleanor Roosevelt Papers, hereafter cited as ERP, FDRL.

10. Enclosure, Bourjaily to Roosevelt, December 14, 1935, Box 4873, ERP, FDRL.

11. Monte F. Bourjaily to Malvina Thompson Scheider, December 14, 1935, Box 4873, ERP, FDRL.

12. Roosevelt to Hickok, September 8, 1935, Box 2, Hickok Papers, FDRL.

13. Elliott Roosevelt and James Brough, *An Untold Story,* p. 299.

14. Interview with James A. Halsted by Emily Williams, May 17, 1979, Hyde Park, N.Y., p. 7, ER Oral History Archives, FDRL.

15. Halsted interview, p. 7, ER Oral History Archives, FDRL.

16. Interview with John R. Boettiger by Emily Williams, August 1, 1979, Northampton, Mass., p. 58, ER Oral History Archives, FDRL.

17. Alfred B. Rollins, Jr., *Roosevelt and Howe* (New York: Knopf, 1962), p. 426.

18. Roosevelt, *This I Remember,* p. 177.

19. Roosevelt to Hickok, December 17, 1935, Box 2, Hickok Papers, FDRL.

20. Eleanor Roosevelt, "My Day," (for) December 30, 1935, Box 3170, ERP, FDRL.

21. Bourjaily to Roosevelt, January 24, 1936, Box 4873, ERP, FDRL.

22. Roosevelt, "My Day," (for) January 15, 1936, Box 3170, ERP, FDRL.

23. George Carlin to Eleanor Roosevelt, April 16, 1937, Box 4873, ERP, FDRL.

24. Memo to George Carlin from JC (unidentified editor), April 8, 1937, Box 4873, ERP, FDRL.

25. Kearney, *Anna Eleanor Roosevelt,* pp. 132–35. See also Lash, *Eleanor and Franklin,* pp. 560–61.

26. Roosevelt, "My Day," (for) August 20, 1936, Box 3170, ERP, FDRL.

27. Elliott Roosevelt and James Brough, *An Untold Story,* p. 268.

28. Roosevelt, "My Day," (for) February 1, 1936, Box 3170, ERP, FDRL.

29. Roosevelt, "My Day," (for) March 6, 1937, Box 3171, ERP, FDRL.

30. Roosevelt, "My Day," (for) January 7, 1936, Box 3170, ERP, FDRL.

31. Susan Ware, *Beyond Suffrage: Women in the New Deal* (Cambridge, Mass.: Harvard University Press, 1981), p. 74.

32. Roosevelt, "My Day," (for) August 12, 1937, Box 3171, ERP, FDRL.

33. Ware, *Beyond Suffrage,* p. 130.

34. Roosevelt, "My Day," (for) December 4, 1937, Box 3171, ERP, FDRL.

35. Roosevelt, *This I Remember,* p. 178.

36. Black, *Eleanor Roosevelt,* p. 115. Also Roosevelt, "My Day," (for) August 8, 1936, Box 3170, ERP, FDRL.

37. Roosevelt, "My Day," (for) September 23, 1936, Box 3170, ERP, FDRL.

38. Doris Faber, *The Life of Lorena Hickok: E.R.'s Friend* (New York: Morrow, 1980), pp. 207–8. Also Roosevelt, "My Day," (for) May 11, 1936, Box 3170, ERP, FDRL.

39. Roosevelt to Hickok, May 7, 1936, Box 2, Hickok Papers, FDRL.

40. Roosevelt, *This I Remember,* p. 178.

41. Lash, *Eleanor and Franklin,* p. 561.

42. Roosevelt, "My Day," (for) March 11, 1937, September 3, 1937, and December 30, 1937, Box 3171, ERP, FDRL.

43. Bourjaily to Roosevelt, June 3, 1936, Box 4873, ERP, FDRL.

44. File financial statements, United Features Syndicate to Eleanor Roosevelt, Box 4873, ERP, FDRL.

45. Bourjaily to Roosevelt, June 3, 1936, Box 4873, ERP, FDRL.

46. Margaret Marshall, "Columnists on Parade," *Nation* 137 (February 26, 1938): 14–15.

47. Kearney, *Anna Eleanor Roosevelt,* pp. 133–34.

48. Roosevelt, "My Day," (for) January 30, 1937, Box 3171, ERP, FDRL.

49. Roosevelt, "My Day," (for) January 26, 1937, Box 3171, ERP, FDRL.

50. Roosevelt, "My Day," (for) January 26, 1937.

51. Roosevelt, "My Day," (for) February 1, 1937, Box 3171, ERP, FDRL.

52. George Carlin to Eleanor Roosevelt, August 17, 1940, as quoted in Lash, *Eleanor and Franklin,* p. 565.

53. " 'My Day,' Dominant Influence," *Saturday Evening Post* 212 (September 9, 1939): 24. Also in "Excerpts Press Conference 570," *The Public Papers and Addresses of Franklin D. Roosevelt* (New York: Macmillan, 1947), 8:432–433. Also Arthur Krock, *New York Times,* August 10, 1939, p. 18.

54. Dorothy Dunbar Bromley, "The Future of Eleanor Roosevelt," *Harper's Magazine* 58 (January 1940): 137. Also Roosevelt, "My Day," (for) August 9, 1939, Box 3145, ERP, FDRL.

55. Roosevelt, "My Day," (for) February 27, 1939, Box 3145, ERP, FDRL.

56. George Carlin to Eleanor Roosevelt, August 8, 1939, Box 4873, ERP, FDRL.

57. Malvina Thompson Scheider to George Carlin, August 13, 1939, Box 4873, ERP, FDRL.

58. Roosevelt, "My Day," (for) August 8, 1939, Box 3145, ERP, FDRL.

59. Scheider to Carlin, August 13, 1939, Box 4873, ERP, FDRL.

60. Roosevelt, "My Day," (for) December 1–2, 1939, Box 3145, ERP, FDRL.

61. Roosevelt, "My Day," (for) June 10–14, 1939, Box 3145, ERP, FDRL.

62. George Carlin to Eleanor Roosevelt, September 8, 1939, Box 3145, ERP, FDRL. Also Roosevelt, "My Day," (for) September 8, 1939, Box 3145, ERP, FDRL.

63. Roosevelt, "My Day," (for) September 13, 1939, Box 3145, ERP, FDRL.

64. Roosevelt, "My Day," (for) May 17, 1940, Box 3146, ERP, FDRL.

65. Roosevelt, "My Day," (for) November 2, 1940, Box 3146, ERP, FDRL.

66. Roosevelt, "My Day," (for) November 12, 1940, Box 3146, ERP, FDRL.

67. Roosevelt, "My Day," (for) December 16, 1941, Box 3175, ERP, FDRL.

68. Roosevelt, "My Day," (for) September 9, 1944, Box 3177, ERP, FDRL.

69. Roosevelt, "My Day," (for) January 14, 1944, Box 3177, ERP, FDRL.

70. Lee B. Wood to George Carlin, November 26, 1943, Box 4873, ERP, FDRL.

71. George Carlin to Eleanor Roosevelt, November 27, 1943, Box 4873, ERP, FDRL.

72. Roosevelt, "My Day," (for) February 23, 1945, Box 3178, ERP, FDRL.

73. Ibid.

74. Roosevelt, "My Day," (for) April 19, 1945, Box 3178, ERP, FDRL.

75. Ibid.

76. Joseph P. Lash, *Eleanor: The Years Alone* (New York: Norton, 1972), pp. 150–53.

77. Promotion copy for series on royal visit, United Feature Syndicate, May 24, 1939, p. 3, Box 4873, ERP, FDRL.

78. Roosevelt, "My Day," (for) December 14, 1936, Box 3170, ERP, FDRL.

79. Dado, "Eleanor Roosevelt as a Columnist," p. 228.

18

Molly Dewson: The Roosevelts' "Aid to the End"

Gloria J. Barron

One of the overriding truisms of the age of the Great Depression, as we have come to realize, is that this national calamity, while reducing many to despair, gave meaning and purpose to the lives of workers within the Roosevelt administration. Franklin Roosevelt's commitment to social justice and his strong faith that something could be done to alleviate suffering and better the lives of the people stirred the enthusiasms of New Deal workers. At the same time both the Roosevelts, Franklin and Eleanor, called for and received the fullest utilization of energy from their own closest associates. Molly Dewson, cherished by the Roosevelts as a personal friend, served the purposes of this administration.

She later attested in the opening lines of her unpublished memoir entitled, "An Aid to the End": "I served Franklin Roosevelt with all that in me lay. I believed in the things that he stood for. Some of them I had worked for with determination, if with small gains, before I knew him. . . . My contribution was in educating voters to the double end of support for his program and his re-election."[1] In her late fifties, after a full career in the field of social welfare, Molly Dewson committed herself to Roosevelt, "signed up for the duration,"[2] and entered "this period which was the most satisfactory and exciting of my life."[3]

Mary Williams Dewson, always "Molly" to her friends and associates, was born in Quincy, Massachusetts, on February 18, 1874. She was the youngest child of a large, middle-class, Unitarian family of four boys and two girls, which traced its ancestors back to earliest New England colonials. Molly's tomboyish childhood with "four brothers and roughly speaking forty boy cousins and comrades" was also filled with a goodly amount of serious reading. Her father, a perennial invalid suffering from neurological and digestive complaints, was the intellectually inclined of her parents. Although he had left school at the age of thirteen to go to work, he was a reader throughout his adult life and shared Molly's own interest in history. As for Molly's reading, she attests to the fact that "long before the normal period I was deep in Cooper's novels and reading heavier works like Motley's Rise of the Dutch Republic and Prescott's Conquest of Peru." At age seventeen she announced to her father that she " 'ached' to know more and wanted to go to college." Her parents granted their able child her wish. Molly was enrolled in the Dana Hall School in Wellesley from 1891 to 1893, and then entered Wellesley College in 1893, at age nineteen. Specializing in history and economics, she received a B.A. degree from Wellesley in 1897, thus becoming one of a tiny group of women college graduates in the late nineteenth century.[4]

While at Wellesley Molly Dewson successfully combined her studies with extracurricular activities. She became president of her class, won tennis tournaments, and managed a sizable course load in economics, history, and sociology, taking all the courses offered in those subjects.[5] In the fall of her senior year Molly applied to Milwaukee Downer College for a teaching position, the expected career choice for Wellesley graduates.[6] Her letters of recommendation at that time attest to early demonstrations of competence by this tall, energetic young woman. She was cited as "a woman of unusual executive ability for her years; a strong and forceful personality," "a clear, independent thinker and an enthusiastic and vigorous worker," and one whose "fine physique and attractive presence contribute not a little to the success of her undertakings."[7] Milwaukee Downer was a little slow in replying.[8] By the time the teaching offer came, Professor Katharine Coman had already recommended Molly to Mrs. Glendower Evans, a wealthy Boston philanthropist and untiring worker in the field of social welfare. Molly became a researcher for Mrs. Evans at the Women's Educational and Industrial Union in Boston and thus began a relationship with the woman who was to play the most significant role in the unfolding of Dewson's career as a social worker.[9]

For the next thirteen years Mrs. Evans both guided the career and utilized the services of the hard-working Molly Dewson for her own social work objectives. From 1897 to 1900 Molly compiled statistics and wrote reports for her on the problems of women in domestic service, an area suggested to Mrs. Evans by her friend Louis Brandeis. In 1900 Mrs. Evans, also a trustee of the Massachusetts Industrial Schools, secured for Molly her second position—superintendent of parole work for girls from the State Industrial School at Lancaster, Massachusetts, a position which she held until 1912.[10] During this time Molly also collaborated with Mrs. Evans on a study of feeble-mindedness and juvenile deliquency.[11] Then, through her friend Florence Kelley, general secretary of the National Consumers League (NCL), Mrs. Evans became interested in minimum wage legislation for women and children, helped to get a commission established in Massachusetts to investigate the idea, got herself appointed to the commission (in reality she "became its driving force"[12]), and then recruited Molly Dewson to be executive secretary of the commission. Molly and her small force, "working like beavers,"[13] managed in a short six-month period to gather and tabulate statistics for Mrs. Evans' report, submitted to the Massachusetts legislature in 1912. As a result of this report and of the report and of the Lawrence textile strike the Massachusetts legislature passed the first minimum wage law in the country in 1912.[14]

Florence Kelley, nationally, and Mrs. Glendower Evans in Massachusetts initiated the battle for the minimum wage. Molly Dewson was not the instigator of this reform, but, when her services were called upon, first by Mrs. Evans and later by Mrs. Kelley, Molly became a hard-working adherent to the cause. With her commonsense practicality ("I always preferred figures to adjectives," she later explained),[15] Molly and her statistical gatherings provided ammunition for the fight.

Periodically Molly Dewson was to complain about being worn out by bouts of strenuous labor. In February 1912 she was at the Chateau Frontenac, Quebec, "recuperating from work as Sec'y of the Commission on Minimum Wages."[16] Her mother, with whom she had been living in the family homestead in Quincy since her graduation from Wellesley, died on December 27, 1912. Molly then resigned her superintendency of the State Parole Department for Girls (she had taken a leave of absence while serving on Mrs. Evans' committee) and with her good friend and henceforth lifelong companion, Mary G. "Polly" Porter, bought a dairy farm in Berlin, Massachusetts. The Misses Dewson and Porter ran the farm from May 1913 to October 1917, at which time they departed for France, where Molly became a zone director for the Bureau of Refugees of the American Red Cross.[17] While in Berlin, Molly had become involved in the women suffrage campaign in Massachusetts. She later reported, "No work I have ever done was more entertaining for women suffrage has nothing to do with economics."[18]

Returning from France after the war, Molly went back to her old work for minimum wage laws. This time it was in answer to an urgent call from Mrs. Kelley. Florence Kelley's National Consumers League had been fighting challenges in the courts to state hours and, sometimes, wages legislation through the famous Brandeis brief. Brandeis acted as unpaid counsel, and his sister-in-law, Josephine Goldmark, research secretary of the National Consumers League, prepared the economic, sociological, and statistical data for the briefs. When Brandeis was appointed to the U.S. Supreme Court, he recommended that the National Consumers League turn to Felix Frankfurter, a young Harvard Law School professor, as counsel. Then Josephine Goldmark resigned. With minimum wage battles looming in the courts, Kelley quickly had to find a replacement for her. In June 1919 she wrote Molly Dewson, still in France, asking her to "take sole charge of our nationwide campaign for minimum wage laws," which meant, Kelley explained, working for the passage of further legislation.[19] Undoubtedly Kelley also had in mind that Molly Dewson, with her proven ability in the gathering of statistics, would be needed to write the factual parts of the briefs for which Frankfurter would be writing the legal argument.

The Frankfurter-Dewson team collaborated in the unsuccessful defense of the

District of Columbia's minimum wage law—the famous case of *Adkins* v. *Children's Hospital*—and in the preparation of a brief in defense of the California minimum wage law. The latter case was dropped after it was discovered that the plaintiff was suing at the direction of her employer.[20] Molly again exhausted herself in the preparation of these briefs. At one point she wrote testily to Frankfurter: "Guess I can't get much further till I know what you want. I must not delay for I can't possibly get caught in a rush as I was last time. My doctor says I would be 57 kinds of a dumbbell if I did."[21] She resigned her position as the NCL's research secretary in 1924 despite a strong effort by Kelley to persuade her to stay. She pleaded fatigue, but there is some indication that Molly, who had strong leadership potential, was chafing at her subaltern status.[22]

Although she could not be considered wealthy, Molly Dewson had an independent income and was free to abandon well-paying regular employment from time to time. She continued to serve the interests of social reform, however, as president of the New York Consumers League and chairman of its committee on labor legislation, "positions entailing more prestige than remuneration."[23] She also volunteered her services to a number of liberal organizations, one of which was the Women's City Club of New York, where she was civic secretary. These organizations, together with the Women's Trade Union League, the League of Women Voters, the industrial board of the YMCA, the American Association for Labor Legislation, the Women's Christian Temperance Union (WCTU), and the New York Child Labor Committee, formed a Joint Legislative Conference which lobbied throughout the 1920s in Albany for protective labor laws. Eleanor Roosevelt, a member of the Women's Trade Union League, influential in the League of Women Voters and in the Women's City Club, and for one year chairman of the Joint Legislative Conference, moved in the same organizational circles as Molly Dewson. Molly came into contact with her at the Women's City Club in the fall of 1924 and was a frequent guest in the Roosevelt home that winter.[24] As a result, the last phase of Molly's active life was about to begin. Eleanor Roosevelt was soon to enlist her services, and for a decade Molly Dewson would be "an aid to the end" for Eleanor's and Franklin's political objectives.

As Molly relates it, Eleanor Roosevelt, who organized women's work for the Democratic National Committee in the 1928 presidential campaign, unexpectedly called for her help. "In late August, 1928," Molly writes in her memoirs,

during the Al Smith presidential campaign, Mrs. Roosevelt telephoned me at my summer home in Castine, Me. saying, "Harry Hawes says the women in the Midwestern Headquarters of the Democratic National Committee are fighting and I must come out, but I cannot possibly leave the headquarters in New York. Will you go in my place? I know only two women whom it would be safe to send and you are one of them."

Evidently she could not refuse, for she continues:

Scattered all over this country are, I imagine, a great many persons who have never been able to say "No" to the Roosevelts or even, "I will think it over and telephone you." I am no exception. That was a Friday. The next morning, Miss Porter and I started on the two day trip by motor to New York. Monday, I reported at the Al Smith Headquarters for instructions, bought some dresses, and, with a newspaper woman, caught the evening train for St. Louis.[25]

Although Molly professes complete surprise at the telephone call from Eleanor Roosevelt, she may have been quietly promoting her own entry into politics. Only a month before she had written to her good friend Lucy Ward Stebbins a very long letter full of praise and enthusiasm for Al Smith. "I could fill a book," her letter began, "with reasons why I am for Smith,"[26] and she practically did. Mrs. Roosevelt may indeed have had some inkling that Molly was ready and willing to engage in this campaign.

In any event, Molly Dewson's memoirs go on to describe proudly the success of her political debut. "Evidently I was a comfort to Sen. Hawes," she writes,

for he begged me to stay through the campaign although as Emily Newell Blair [Vice-Chairman of the Democratic Committee, 1924–28] used to say with amusement, "And she never had any political experience, and never was elected to any office, even precinct leader." In rebuttal I answered that working for twelve years as Superintendent of Parole for Girls in Massachusetts and trying to pass labor legislation there and in New York did not leave me a complete greenhorn.[27]

Molly Dewson had qualities that helped her to succeed in a man's political world. Shrewdness, common sense, directness of manner, and a sense of humor, coupled with breeding and an air of distinction, were all plusses.[28] Lorena Hickok, in an opening chapter on Molly Dewson in her book *Ladies of Courage,* refers to "her solemnly humorous face, rimless glasses perched atop her patrician nose," and goes on to paint her portrait as follows:

She wore homespun suits, the jacket pockets sagging a little because of her habit of thrusting her hands into them. Her rather large feet were comfortably and serviceably shod. A hat to Molly Dewson has always been something you wear for the sole purpose of keeping your head from getting cold. She had probably never owned a lipstick in her life. Yet there is about her an air of distinction. Her casual clothes suit her. . . . She has never been, to use a Dewson adjective, a "buttery-uppery" person. Her forthright manner and her disregard for the more obvious feminine wiles reassured the men. They thought they understood her. Few of them ever realized how well she understood them.[29]

In her memoir Molly gave her own rendition of why she succeeded in politics. "I was going to make the men find working with women easy, pleasant, and profitable—if I could," she explained. "Fortunately, I was old enough to be their aunt, and men are at their best with their mothers and favorite aunts." She also maintained, "I feel at ease with human beings and expect to get on with most of them to our mutual satisfaction.'' She felt ''competent in handling people,'' and ''the men politicians . . . were [not] inclined to push her around.''[30]

In 1930 Eleanor Roosevelt asked for Molly's services in another campaign, this time for her own husband's gubernatorial reelection bid. Molly was brought into the New York State Women's Division where, utilizing a flier prepared by Samuel Rosenman to illustrate the differential in electric rates between New York localities and Canadian cities, she mobilized Democratic women to approach Republican and independent homemakers and explain Roosevelt's program to curb the private utilities. The county organizations of women may have had something to do with the Roosevelt landslide in 1930. His margin was 725,000 votes, and he carried upstate New York, the first Democrat ever to do so, by 167,000 votes. But Molly herself, declaring that ''Mrs. Roosevelt was a very great factor in F.D.R.'s re-election,'' gave the most credit to Eleanor's political activity ''all over Up-State New York'' throughout 1929 and 1930.[31]

The time was now at hand for Molly Dewson's very large political contributions to Roosevelt's first two presidential election victories. Ostensibly she was director of the Women's Division during these years. In truth, she and Eleanor Roosevelt worked as a team. Since the candidate's wife, however, could not take the limelight, Molly, really her deputy,[32] was credited with the whole operation. It was a role that Molly appeared to enjoy, since with it went visibility and recognition.

Her initial involvement with the presidential run began in the spring of 1931 when Eleanor Roosevelt recruited her for FDR's preconvention campaign. Molly's job was to sign form letters to Democratic women, one of which carried the letterhead ''Friends of Franklin Roosevelt.''[33] Her office was at 331 Madison Avenue, while Jim Farley, the contact man with the party bosses, had an office at the Biltmore Hotel. As Molly describes it: ''At first Louie Howe had a room with one window in our suite and Mrs. Roosevelt and I a desk apiece in the second and smaller room, also with one window.''[34] After Roosevelt won the nomination, 331 Madison Avenue became headquarters of the Democratic National Campaign Committee. It was this committee, rather than the Democratic National Committee, that ran the campaign.[35] Louis Howe, Eleanor Roosevelt, and Molly Dewson continued to have their offices at 331 Madison Avenue while Farley was stationed at the Biltmore.

Molly Dewson's second job in the preconvention stage was to make a western tour in the late fall of 1931, following Jim Farley's successful summer tour, in search of delegates. She had interviews with male Democratic leaders as well as ''the few women they produced,''[36] and also got some assurances of delivery of delegates for Roosevelt. On her return, Louis Howe told her ''how satisfied Roosevelt was with this performance.''[37]

By the time of the Democratic national convention, June 1932, Molly again was exhausted. After FDR's fourth-ballot victory, she reports: ''I did not wait for Roosevelt's triumphant entry, but took the first train for my home at Castine, Maine. The Pre-convention Campaign had been long and strenuous and I was tired.''[38] While Molly Dewson was resting, Eleanor Roosevelt at campaign headquarters thoroughly organized the Women's Division. How much of it was Eleanor's doing, rather than Molly's, is revealed in a letter Eleanor sent to Molly in Maine. ''Dear Molly,'' she began:

I sent you a wire last night and now this is to explain the general organization being set up for the campaign.

The Campaign Committee will be quite separate from the National Committee. Mr. Michelson will run publicity generally, half the time in Washington, half the time in New York. A skeleton organization for the National Committee will be kept in Washington but no regular work will be done there until the campaign is over. We will keep in touch with Governor Ross and use her for field work and possibly speeches where we feel her valuable. I want to bring Sue White [Mrs. Ross's assistant][39] over to be Executive Director under you and keep in touch with Governor Ross. Mrs. Whitney will go on with Sue White until you get back, then you and I will work together as much as you want.

Your plan of working in the states is to be carried out and the money will be available, I think, in early August. We are working with the people we are already in touch with except where some change has come about. They are to make out a list and advise us of any changes in men they are looking to in the various states to do work. Our work at Headquarters will be divided into the following sections:

Here Eleanor went on to list clubs, speakers' bureau, field force executive, labor, files, mail, information clerk, advisory council (representatives from regions of the country, on a rotating basis), and publicity. She outlined suggested personnel for each section. ''I will send you a chart of this organization in a few days with names attached,'' she added, ''after I hear from you if you have any further suggestions and what names you sent in.'' In Molly's absence the structure was all but set in place, except for the winding up of details. Eleanor concluded her letter by saying, ''I do not want to make you come down to New York. I am, however, driving to Campobello and wonder if you would be willing to drive down to Maud Gray's for the night to talk things over with me the week after next?''[40]

In her memoirs Molly gives the organizational structure as follows:

The Staff of the Women's Division
Mary W. Dewson, Director
Sue S. White, Executive Secretary
Mary Chamberlain, Director of Publicity
Lavinia Engle, Director, Speakers' Bureau
Mrs. Henry Morgenthau, Jr., Director of Radio
Emily Newell Blair, Director, Bureau of Women's Clubs
Jo Coffin, Director, Bureau of Labor

Advisory Committee
Governor Nellie Tayloe Ross, Vice-Chairman, Democratic National Committee
Senator Hattie E. Caraway

Representative Mary T. Norton
Representative Ruth Bryan Owen
Honorable Frances Perkins

The Advisory Committee, she indicates, were their "top string" speakers, along
with Mrs. Emily Newell Blair, vice chairman of the Democratic National Committee from 1924 to 1928. Molly concludes:

> Mrs. Roosevelt's name is not listed because she was not officially a part of the organi-
> zation, but we continued to have desks back to back in the same little room and she spent
> much time at hers keeping up an enormous personal correspondence. She was satisfied
> with our campaign's nervous system and that it was functioning at top speed and she
> knew we would turn to her if we needed extra pressure on the men at any given moment.
> Having through Mrs. Roosevelt a direct line to the Governor, to Louis, and to Jim, and
> having such a sympathetic operator, was an incalculable timesaver.[41]

Using Molly's plan, aimed at putting in place a thorough organization of workers—state and county vice chairman, town and precinct leaders—and developing
a local army of "grass trampers" to distribute literature to homemakers, the
Women's Division targeted small towns and rural areas. "We were very careful," Molly writes, "to explain [to Farley] that nothing we did would bother the
machines."[42] The literature that Molly devised was the Rainbow Fliers, one-page
leaflets, each a different color, each representing a single subject, for example,
"The Republican Tariff Wall," "Your Electric Bill," "The Forgotten Farmer."
She later declared proudly that the Rainbow Fliers were "the best practical idea I
ever had" and attributed their origin to her experience in using a one-page fact
sheet during the suffragists' campaign in Massachusetts.[43] She had, perhaps, con-
veniently forgotten that the idea was basically Sam Rosenman's in the 1930 gubernatorial campaign.[44] In any event, the fliers were so successful that the men
county chairmen asked for some as well.[45] Six million fliers were distributed.[46]

Zeroing in on Louis Howe's "fighting states," Molly's "indefatigable can-
vassers" were later credited by Howe with "a far greater part in the securing
of women's votes than any of us realize."[47] In her memoirs Molly asserts,
"Roosevelt told me time and again the women's vote elected him," although,
she adds, "Roosevelt's statement to me was not at odds with the repeated thanks
and words of appreciation he gave Farley, because the women's vote would not
have been anywhere near enough without the party stalwarts."[48]

With the Roosevelts fully aware of the importance of the Women's Division,
it was established on a permanent, full-time basis within the Democratic National
Committee and Molly Dewson installed as its director, October 16, 1933. Jim
Farley had not wanted a permanent Women's Division and had to be persuaded
by Eleanor to go along.[49] "He had not thought of me as a part of his future,"
Molly writes querulously.[50] As for Molly, she claims to have accepted the
directorship reluctantly. "In the end," she maintains, "I gave in as I always
did whenever the Roosevelts asked me to do anything, although I stipulated that

I should have an office in Farley's New York headquarters in the Biltmore Hotel and spend only part of each week in Washington,"[51] perhaps because Polly Porter refused to leave New York.[52]

As director, Molly Dewson's first objective was to secure appointments for qualified Democratic women in the new administration. "If I had not done my best to get recognition for women," she later explained, "few would have been interested in any plans of mine to carry through a program that would win support for the New Deal and put ginger into the Democratic women workers."[53] Ostensibly, patronage for women within the Roosevelt administration was the work of Molly Dewson. In truth, Eleanor and Molly worked as a team. Molly drew up lists and hounded department heads, and sometimes even "harried Farley into helping [her]."[54] But the lists were also sent to Eleanor, whom she could count on to exert the needed pressure when the going got tough.[55] Lists were also requested by Mrs. Roosevelt.[56] In later years Molly confessed to Lorena Hickok:

I had next to no "struggle" because FDR backed me. It was the psychological moment for women to get "started." You elevated me above my status [in *Ladies of Courage*]. I'm not particularly modest. I'm just weighing things. . . .

The reason I did not emphasize in my "An Aid to the End" how much Eleanor helped me was because I thought she was in a delicate position, and the less I said about her in connection with my work, the better.[57]

Although Molly Dewson complained at the time that women did not receive as much recognition as they should have—in late 1935 she wrote to Eleanor Roosevelt that if the president were "to go into the states," he could "make the women forget their disappointment over patronage" and "draw out the stored up venom"[58]—in her memoirs she wrote only of women's progress in the thirties. "In Roosevelt's day women were recognized as never before," she asserted. "The change from women's status in government before Roosevelt is unbelievable."[59] "What a leap forward women made under Roosevelt," she wrote to Grace Tully in 1949. "I hold it is a great feather in his cap, even though with such help from ER I do not see how he could have done less for her sex."[60]

Molly's second goal, as director of the Women's Division, was to achieve fifty-fifty representation for women on all party committees, national, state, county, precinct, and program. In this she was not as successful.[61]

Her third goal, which she emphasizes in her memoirs as "my obsession,"[62] was to organize women to spread understanding of the New Deal. The device used was a unique idea of hers, the "Reporter Plan." Twenty-two "reporters" would be developed in each community, each an expert on one of twenty-two New Deal agencies. They would hold discussions among themselves and with interested women, informing Republican and independent women as well as Democrats. By November 1935 there were 15,000 reporters in the field, working between campaigns, when Molly thought elections were truly won. The Women's

Division developed their monthly magazine, the *Democratic Digest,* in part to funnel factual information on governmental programs to their workers. The whole effort was geared toward a campaign based on issues rather than personalities.[63] Eleanor Roosevelt heartily approved. "Molly has had a conception of work for the Women's Division," she wrote Emma Guffey Miller, "which I consider very valuable, namely, she has put education first and I think the women needed that more than anything else."[64]

Molly had resigned the directorship of the Women's Division in June 1934 but was in effect the active coordinator of activities as chairman of its General Advisory Committee, a committee of one.[65] With FDR's backing and Eleanor's persuasiveness with Farley, the Women's Division managed to get monies to publish its magazine and a 1936 budget of $4,000 a month.[66] Concentrating on the pivotal states, utilizing grass trampers with Rainbow Fliers (which the men used also and which constituted 80 percent of the campaign literature),[67] engaging the efforts of volunteer speakers through their Speakers' Bureau, publicizing Republican women who were committed to Roosevelt, the Women's Division ran an effective campaign. Molly went after "the extra 10% to 15% of votes from the independents or from the Democrats unreached by the machine and frequently not bothering to vote."[68] Her emphasis on issues was helped by the fact that Roosevelt now had a New Deal record to run on. Taking pride in her accomplishment, Molly claimed, "We had made the silent voters aware of what they already knew, although somewhat vaguely, and given them confidence in their opinions." She even boasted, "I believe the work of roughly seventy-three thousand Democratic women leaders, begun 'between campaigns' and carried on persistently until voting day, made the difference between an adequate majority for Roosevelt and his landslide of 523 votes to Landon's 8. . . . In addition, I believe the by-product of increased and more specific understanding of what Roosevelt had brought about helped him with his new undertakings during his second term."[69]

Throughout the thirties Molly Dewson had maintained her interest in social legislation and from time to time had prodded the president, in a general way when she thought that he was moving too slowly, or in specific situations when a word from him would be beneficial. She had also played a large part in Frances Perkins' appointment as secretary of labor. Roosevelt was planning to have a woman in his cabinet and was considering his New York industrial commissioner, Frances Perkins.[70] Molly, on her own, had helped the cause along by launching a large letter writing campaign.[71] She later explained her reasons as follows:

This was not an act of friendship on my part. Frances and I were never personal friends. I just believed that here was the golden opportunity for pushing ahead the labor legislation program for which I had worked for so many years. I am convinced that certain women like Frances Perkins, Clara Beyer, now Assistant Director of the U.S. Division of Labor Standards, and Katharine Edson, who was a member of the Industrial Commission of

California, have been more successful in getting progressive labor laws passed and more effective in their administration than any men ever have been or could have been.[72]

When for personal reasons Perkins had hesitated in accepting the appointment, Molly, who was always convinced that women could do a job equal to, if not better than, men, had reminded her that the advance of women would also be served by this appointment. "You owe it to the women," Molly had told her. "You probably will have this chance and you must step forward and do it. You mustn't say no. Too many people count on what you do. Too much hangs on it."[73]

In 1937 the Roosevelts called on the old social worker Molly Dewson for one more service. On August 23 of that year she was appointed to a six-year term on the three-member Social Security Board, becoming the first woman appointee and replacing the ineffectual Vincent M. Miles when his short two-year term expired.[74] Although Molly had had a long career as a social reform advocate and had served on the Advisory Council on Economic Security, a committee which had aided Frances Perkins' Committee on Economic Security in the formulation of the Social Security Act, her role on the Social Security Board, as envisioned by the Roosevelts, was to be of a political rather than a technical nature. As Eleanor Roosevelt wrote to her:

Franklin tells me that he is naming you on the Social Security Board and I am delighted for I know that that is the thing you are really best suited to do, and where they need you most.

That being a permanent set-up, the relationship of the people on the Board with Congress is very important and none of them now seem to have the ability to establish any kind of an understanding. I feel you can do it.[75]

Part of her job was to assuage disgruntled congressmen on the question of patronage.[76] William Mitchell, the Social Security Administration's director of the Bureau of Business Management and later personnel director, has indicated, however, that Roosevelt had an even more specific objective in the Dewson appointment than good relations with Congress. The president was particularly concerned about press criticism that the SSA was staffed primarily by New York Jews and perhaps feared that such criticism would undermine the success of this all-important new agency. Molly Dewson was placed on the board to change the situation. In his oral memoir Mitchell discloses:

She hadn't been there more than a week or two when she called me into her office and said, in confidence I guess although she didn't identify it as such, that one of the things that President Roosevelt had discussed with her before she came over—He wanted her to look into several things that had been subjects of criticism in the press.

One of them was that the Social Security Administration was getting filled up with New York Jews. He wanted to know whether this really was the situation, and if it really was the situation, he wanted it cleaned up forthwith. Miss Dewson passed this dictum along to me as the operating person with that type of responsibility.

Mitchell goes on to say:

It did turn out, upon research, that we were heavily weighted with New Yorkers and people of the Jewish faith. I never felt that was due to any bias, any preferential consideration, but rather that the Civil Service registers were loaded with such people. Not only were they on the registers, but they were the ones with the higher marks and were at the top of the registers. So when you objectively made a choice, many, many times the top three would be all New York Jews, and your choice would be among those three.

Now the Social Security Administration went to a degree of artificial rectification. Mitchell reveals:

We had people from every state in the union, many, many. But there was a disproportionate share from New York. So we did have to institute a very confidential and, I would say, very small program of careful screening thereafter, to see if we couldn't bring these proportions back into a little more equanimity.[77]

Molly Dewson's personal relations with her fellow workers in the Social Security Administration were excellent. In the Columbia University Oral History Collection of their memoirs she comes in for universal praise, being described as practical, a woman of common sense and a sense of humor, with "a twinkle in her eye all the time," a "wonderful old gal," a "grand old trouper," sharp, possessed of "a good mind" that "could cut through to the heart of the matter very quickly."[78] She worked hard to master the technical issues that were dealt with in the lengthy board meetings,[79] but her main service was intended to be political. She was valuable, attests Frank Bane, executive director of the Social Security Board, "from the standpoint of contacts up on the Hill. She knew everybody in town."[80] She also served as troubleshooter and liaison to executive branch agencies and departments.[81] Mitchell surmises that her "initial concern was to carry out the will of the President,"[82] and in her own memoir, generally in reference to her relationship to Roosevelt, Molly contends that he brought her up to be a politician and that "my chief service to F.D.R. was political."[83]

Pleading ill health, Molly Dewson approached FDR in the late spring of 1938 with her intention to resign from the Social Security Board. He persuaded her to take the summer off and come back in the fall in order to be on hand when the board met with the Advisory Council on Social Security, appointed by Congress, to consider drawing up amendments to the Social Security Act. Roosevelt was interested in extending coverage of the act, in part to take care of a large reserve problem, and Molly helped in this endeavor.[84] In her letter of resignation, dated December 10, 1938, she confirmed, "The administration of the law is well in hand and, *following your suggestion,* essential amendments are being prepared for rounding out the act."[85] She was finally free to retire with Miss Porter to their home in Maine, but the Roosevelts did not let her go without first inquiring about her means of support. The president "with the gentlest and most tactful consideration . . . asked how I was situated financially," Molly reports, adding, "As I could get along without working he did not have to make any plans for me, but I have always wondered what his warm, fatherly interest would have led him to do."[86]

Eleanor Roosevelt called her back for a few weeks work in the 1940 campaign, explaining:

I think it would be a tremendous help to Dorothy McAllister [director of the Women's Division] if you would come down around the middle of September to be on hand. We do not want you to do any work that you would not feel able to do, but if you could be at the office to meet people and do some of the work with the men, it would be a great help. That is where Dorothy is weak.[87]

By the time of the 1936 campaign Farley had come to appreciate the value of women's work,[88] but Farley's successor, Ed Flynn, had not yet come around. Dorothy McAllister was on her own, and this situation was too difficult for her because, Molly explains, "Dorothy had not yet learned how to get her way in a bunch of men."[89] So Molly Dewson returned to work for the Roosevelts, briefly, in 1940, and got the money that was necessary to adequately staff the Women's Division.[90]

Retiring for good at the end of the 1940 campaign, Molly Dewson became increasingly isolated in Castine, Maine, where she lived until her death in 1962. She had served the Roosevelts loyally and tirelessly.[91] Earning her title "The General" while director of the Women's Division, she had driven her staff and herself hard. "Molly Dewson is all you say—guide, philosopher, and friend, but even more important than all these, she is a boss, and not always an easy one," Felix Frankfurter once observed.[92] Later in life she admitted to Eleanor Roosevelt: "I no longer have that energy which one day you said made you tired. I think you were in the bath tub and I wanted you to get out and come to the phone."[93] In her sunset days she could now leisurely reflect how in furthering Franklin Roosevelt's political fortunes, and thereby the New Deal, she had advanced her ancient cause of social reform.[94] At age eighty-five she concluded, "Serving the Roosevelts has been the great satisfaction of my life."[95] In turn, she could be perceived as one of the instruments they used to accomplish their political goals. She was indeed their "aid to the end."

NOTES

1. Mary W. Dewson, "An Aid to the End," 2 vols., unpublished memoir, 1949, 1:1, Mary Dewson Papers, Franklin D. Roosevelt Library, Hyde Park, N.Y. (hereafter cited as FDRL).

2. Ibid., 1:10.

3. Mary W. Dewson to Fred Shipman, March 25, 1947, Mary Dewson Papers, Schlesinger Library, Radcliffe College, Cambridge, Mass.

4. Mary Dewson, "As I Remember My Mother," unpublished manuscript, Mary Dewson Papers, Schlesinger Library; Mary Dewson to Lorena Hickok, November 21, 1952, FDRL; Education and experience record of Mary W. Dewson, Mary Dewson Papers, Schlesinger Library; Dewson, "An Aid to the End," 2:206.

5. Education and experience record of Mary W. Dewson, Mary Dewson Papers, Schlesinger Library.

6. Jean Glasscock et al., *Wellesley College 1875–1975: A Century of Women* (Wellesley, Mass., 1975), p. 406.

7. Letters from Katharine Coman and Elizabeth Kendall to Milwaukee Downer College, November 1896, Mary Dewson Papers, FDRL.

8. Charles E.M. Lenegan to Mary Dewson, July 10, 1897, Mary Dewson Papers, Schlesinger Library.

9. Katharine Coman to Mary Dewson (May-June 1897 handwritten by Dewson), Mary Dewson Papers, Schlesinger Library.

10. Molly Dewson to Barbara Solomon, October 20, 1959, Mary Dewson Papers, Schlesinger Library.

11. Education and experience record, Mary Dewson Papers, Schlesinger Library.

12. Mrs. Glendower Evans, speech by Mary Dewson at Memorial Meeting, Ford Hall, Boston, January 28, 1938, Mary Dewson Papers, Schlesinger Library.

13. Ibid.

14. James T. Patterson, "Mary Dewson and the American Minimum Wage Movement," *Labor History* 5 (Spring 1964): 142.

15. Molly Dewson to Lorena Hickok, November 21, 1952, FDRL.

16. Handwritten notation by MWD on letter from Mary W. Dewson to Theodore Roosevelt, February 1912, Mary Dewson Papers, Schlesinger Library.

17. Education and experience record, Mary Dewson Papers, Schlesinger Library.

18. Mary W. Dewson to Herman Kahn, December 4, 1958, Mary Dewson Papers, Schlesinger Library.

19. Josephine Goldmark, *Impatient Crusader: Florence Kelley's Life Story* (Urbana, Ill., 1953), pp. 152–73; Patterson, "Mary Dewson," pp. 144–45; Florence Kelley to Mary Dewson, June 16, 1919, Mary Dewson Papers, Schlesinger Library; Mary Dewson to Herman Kahn, December 4, 1958, Mary Dewson Papers, Schlesinger Library.

20. Patterson, "Mary Dewson," p. 184n; Warren Pillsbury to Felix Frankfurter, January 10, 1925, Felix Frankfurter Papers, Library of Congress, Washington, D.C.

21. Mary W. Dewson to Felix Frankfurter, October 8, 1923, Felix Frankfurter Papers, Library of Congress.

22. Florence Kelley to Sister Dewson, February 17, 1924, Mary Dewson Papers, Schlesinger Library; Elsie L. George, "The Women Appointees of the Roosevelt and Truman Administrations: A Study of Their Impact and Effectiveness," Ph.D. dissertation, American University, 1972, p. 103.

23. George, "Woman Appointees," p. 104.

24. Joseph P. Lash, *Eleanor and Franklin: The Story of Their Relationship, Based on Eleanor Roosevelt's Private Papers* (New York, 1971), pp. 280–81, 310; Ellen Condliffe Lagemann, *A Generation of Women: Education in the Lives of Progressive Reformers* (Cambridge, Mass., 1979), pp. 135–36; Dewson, "An Aid to the End," 1:5, 8–15.

25. Dewson, "An Aid to the End," 1:6.

26. Molly Dewson to Lucy Ward Stebbins, July 22, 1928, Lucy Ward Stebbins Papers, Schlesinger Library.

27. Dewson, "An Aid to the End," 1:6–7.

28. For the last quality, see comments by Frances Perkins, Frances Perkins memoir, Columbia Oral History Collection (hereafter cited as COHC), 7:492.

29. Eleanor Roosevelt and Lorena A. Hickok, *Ladies of Courage* (New York, 1954), pp. 12–13. Although the book carried Roosevelt's name as a coauthor, it was actually written by Hickok. MWD's handwritten notation on a Hickok letter reveals that the book was coauthored "I believe because ER wanted to give Hick publicity." And Molly adds, "Whether this was accomplished or not, it certainly brought very few letters to me." See Lorena Hickok to Molly Dewson, September 24, 1952, Mary Dewson Papers, FDRL.

30. Dewson, "An Aid to the End," 1:46, 83; 2:201.

31. Ibid., 1:11; Scrapbook—Politics, 1932–1933, Mary Dewson Papers, FDRL; Lash, *Eleanor and Franklin,* p. 336.

32. Lash, *Eleanor and Franklin,* p. 338.

33. Molly reports that "the response to these letters was not impressive. Women political leaders at that period had little independence or power. Outside of a few exceptions they were just figureheads, symbols acknowledging that women had the vote. They waited for the go-ahead signal from the man who was responsible for their appointment." "An Aid to the End," 1:21.

34. Ibid., 1:24–25.

35. In her memoir Molly explains that "the ancient and hoary practices of the past were completely upset by Roosevelt. . . . First of all, the campaign was to be conducted, not by the Democratic National Committee, but by a Democratic National Campaign Committee, composed of ardent and energetic supporters of Roosevelt. He took no chances on having his campaign run by any men who had been bitterly opposed to him a few weeks before. As one rotten apple can ruin a barrel full, so one or two outspoken, unimaginative, defeatist men can take the edge off a campaign." Ibid., 1:58.

36. Ibid., 1:27.

37. Ibid., 1:32.

38. Ibid., 1:37.

39. Ibid., 1:123.

40. Eleanor Roosevelt to Molly Dewson, July 16, 1932, Mary Dewson Papers, FDRL.

41. Dewson, "An Aid to the End," 1:67, 69.

42. Ibid., 1:44.

43. A handwritten note, clipped to a group of Rainbow Fliers, Mary Dewson Papers, Schlesinger Library.

44. Ibid., p. 10.

45. Louis Howe, "Women's Way in Politics," n.d., Mary Dewson Papers, Schlesinger Library.

46. Dewson, "An Aid to the End," 1:65.

47. *Boston Globe,* December 25, 1932.

48. Dewson, "An Aid to the End," 1:41.

49. Lash, *Eleanor and Franklin,* p. 387.

50. Dewson, "An Aid to the End," 1:77.

51. Ibid., 1:5.

52. George, "Women Appointees," p. 130.

53. Dewson, "An Aid to the End," 1:124.

54. Ibid., 1:125.

55. See especially Molly Dewson to Eleanor Roosevelt, April 27, 1933, Eleanor Roosevelt Papers, FDRL.

56. George, "Women Appointees," pp. 44–45.

57. Molly Dewson to Lorena Hickok, 1953, Mary Dewson Papers, FDRL.

58. Molly Dewson to Eleanor Roosevelt, November 5, 1935, Eleanor Roosevelt Papers, FDRL.

59. Dewson, "An Aid to the End," 1:135, 139.

60. Molly Dewson to Grace Tully, April 19, 1949, Mary Dewson Papers, Schlesinger Library.

61. Dewson, "An Aid to the End," 2:1–6.

62. Ibid., 2:7.

63. Ibid., 2:7–24, 63–64.

64. Eleanor Roosevelt to Emma Guffey Miller, June 28, 1936, Emma Guffey Miller Papers, Schlesinger Library.

65. Dewson, "An Aid to the End," 2:39–40.

66. Ibid., 2:61–62, 93.

67. Ibid., 2:156. Eighty-three million Rainbow Fliers were distributed in the 1936 campaign. See "Advance of Democratic Women" (1940 reprint from the *Democratic Digest*), p. 26, Mary Dewson Papers, Schlesinger Library.

68. Dewson, "An Aid to the End," 1:43–44.

69. Ibid., 2:163–70, 179.

70. Frank Freidel, *Franklin D. Roosevelt: Launching the New Deal* (Boston, 1973), p. 155; George Martin, *Madam Secretary: Frances Perkins* (Boston, 1976), p. 233.

71. Dewson, "An Aid to the End," 1:78.

72. Ibid., 1:33.

73. Frances Perkins memoir, COHC, 3:525.

74. George, "Women Appointees," p. 114. For comments on Miles see William Mitchell memoir, COHC, p. 17; Lavinia Engle memoir, COHC, pp. 54, 82.

75. Eleanor Roosevelt to Molly Dewson, August 17, 1937, Mary Dewson Papers, FDRL.

76. See Dewson, "An Aid to the End," 1:3–4; George, "Women Appointees," pp. 112–114.

77. William Mitchell memoir, COHC, pp. 17–18.

78. See Jane Hoey memoir, COHC, p. 88; Jack Tate memoir, COHC, pp. 12–13, 18–19; Frank Bane memoir, COHC, p. 101; Gordon Wagenet memoir, COHC, p. 79; Maurine Mulliner memoir, COHC, pp. 128–29.

79. Maurine Mulliner memoir, COHC, p. 128; George, "Women Appointees," p. 118; Lavinia Engle memoir, COHC, pp. 54–55, 83.

80. Frank Bane memoir, COHC, p. 102. See also Dewson, "An Aid to the End," 1:3–4.

81. George, "Women Appointees," p. 121.

82. William Mitchell memoir, COHC, p. 23.

83. Dewson, "An Aid to the End," 2:216, 180.

84. Ibid., 2:224; George, "Women Appointees," pp. 119–20, 133.

85. Mary W. Dewson to Franklin D. Roosevelt, December 10, 1938, Mary Dewson Papers, Schlesinger Library. Emphasis added.

86. Dewson, "An Aid to the End," 2:224.

87. Eleanor Roosevelt to Molly Dewson, August 6, 1940, quoted in Dewson, "An Aid to the End," 2:202.

88. See Dewson, "An Aid to the End," 2:176–77.

89. Ibid., 2:202.

90. Ibid., 2:203–4.

91. Molly Dewson was always angry when any of Roosevelt's official family evidenced disloyalty. Of Jim Farley she wrote in her memoirs, "Congresswoman Mary Norton told me Al Smith said to her, 'Farley betrayed me. Wait and see him betray Roosevelt.' " Molly also "was incensed during the first year of Roosevelt's administration by the way some of the Brain Trust deserted him." See ibid., 1:53; 2:211.

92. Felix Frankfurter to Dorothy Kenyon, November 8, 1934, Mary Dewson Papers, FDRL.

93. Molly Dewson to Eleanor Roosevelt, December 29, 1952, Eleanor Roosevelt Papers, FDRL.

94. "I consider I have done my best work for the objectives of social workers in the six political years under the leadership of the greatest social worker of us all, Franklin D. Roosevelt," Molly Dewson wrote to Jim Farley, August 27, 1937, Mary Dewson Papers, FDRL.

95. Molly Dewson to Chester Bowles, May 1959, Mary Dewson Papers, Schlesinger Library.

19

The Character of Social Feminism in the Thirties: Eleanor Roosevelt and Her Associates in the New Deal

Ann Davis

Feminism in the early twentieth century has been described as existing in two distinct strains, "social" feminism and "hard-core" feminism.[1] The former was "chiefly concerned with problems like child labor and the exploitation of working mothers. This . . . did not unduly strain the feminine image of middle class women."[2] Although some social feminist organizations like the Women's Trade Union League (WTUL) included socialists, the thrust of most groups, such as the National Consumers' League (NCL) and the National Federation of Business and Professional Women's Clubs (GFWC) was toward reform.[3] Most members were well-educated women drawn from elite social classes.[4] "Hard-core" feminists were largely drawn from the same socioeconomic origin, yet were more militant,[5] less compromising,[6] and possibly more interested in challenging the domestic role of women.

Much of the social legislation of the New Deal was initiated and implemented by progressive reformers, who prominently included the social feminists.[7] We would like to explore their self-conception as women and the choice of tactics that tended to characterize the group which was actively involved in the New Deal, and to examine the implications of this tradition for women's advancement during this period.

It seems clear that Eleanor Roosevelt and her "network"[8] were social feminists. Eleanor Roosevelt clearly worked for and achieved a greater role for women in politics and in responsible government positions. She was part of a strong association of women who saw themselves organized vis-à-vis men for advancement of women. Although the women involved in the New Deal were dedicated to social and humanitarian goals, they nonetheless supported each other as women. On the other hand, on most occasions they sought the opportunity to serve as individuals, not to seek redress as a disadvantaged group themselves. They were clearly conscious of setting an example of the role that women could play in responsible public positions, but they did not pursue the implications of this for changing the role of women in the family. They were less interested in the liberation of women per se, but sought to use their own influence to preserve and protect the role of women as mothers, and to protect children and other vulnerable groups in society.

POLITICS, WOMEN, AND THE NEW DEAL

Eleanor Roosevelt herself was the most prominent social feminist in the New Deal. Mrs. Roosevelt held political positions before her husband became president; for example, in 1928 she handled the Democratic National Committee headquarters for the Al Smith campaign,[9] and was a leader in the New York League of Women Voters, the New York Consumers' League, the New York Women's Trade Union League, and the Women's Democratic Committee.[10] As the president's wife, however, she withdrew from formal organizational positions and became more involved in correspondence, press conferences, her nationally syndicated column, consultation with party leaders and government agency heads, White House conferences, and obtaining the ear of the president for selected associates.[11] As Mary (Molly) Dewson said of the 1932 campaign:

Mrs. Roosevelt's name is not listed [on the staff of the Women's Division of the Democratic party] because she was not officially a part of the organization, but we continued to have desks back to back in the same little room and she spent much time at hers keeping up an enormous correspondence. . . . She knew we would turn to her if we needed extra pressure on the men at any given moment. Having through Mrs. Roosevelt a direct line to the Governor, to Louis, and to Jim, and having such a sympathetic operator, was an incalculable timesaver.[12]

Eleanor Roosevelt was a mainstay of the organization of women in the Democratic party by virtue of her growing national following, her formal position as First Lady, and her informal influence with the president. A pattern of cooperation was formed between Mrs. Roosevelt and the formal head of the Women's Division of the Democratic National Committee, beginning with her friend Molly Dewson, with whom the arrangement was developed, and continuing with Molly's hand-picked successor, Dorothy McAllister.[13]

Other women with key positions in government agencies were also aided by the personal support and influence of Eleanor Roosevelt, while at the same time she shared the credit with them for implementation of their initiatives. Since these women as often acted through indirect pressure as from formal authority, and cooperated in most of their activities, we will examine their role through the correspondence between Eleanor Roosevelt and four of her prominent associates, Mary Dewson, Frances Perkins, Rose Schneiderman, and Ellen Woodward.

Because she was a central figure for women in the Democratic party, an examination of the work and relationships of Mary W. Dewson will help indicate the quality of the involvement of women in the party. Eleanor first met Molly at the Women's City Club in 1924 in New York City,[14] and later invited her to join the 1928 campaign for governor. Molly stayed on to play a key role in the Democratic party, first directing women's involvement in the 1932 presidential campaign. After the election, Eleanor persuaded Jim Farley, the chairman of the Democratic National Committee, to make the Women's Division full time because of the importance of the women's vote in the election of FDR.[15] Eleanor and Franklin agreed on the choice of Molly Dewson as the first full-time director of the Women's Division, and Molly was subsequently introduced at Eleanor's January 15, 1934, press conference. Molly and Eleanor shared common views of the potential of women to raise the level of politics and to strengthen the Democratic party, a mixture of idealistic and pragmatic goals.[16]

As director of the Women's Division, Molly Dewson developed the Reporter Plan to involve women in their communities, and the Rainbow Flyers, put out by the Women's Division, which supplied 80 percent of the material distributed in the 1936 campaign.[17] The Women's Division claimed no pride of authorship, however.

Because we feared some men might be prejudiced by material put over the Women's Division name, they carried the label of the Democratic National Committee only. We women made this sacrifice cheerfully because we considered the collapse of the Hoover years an emergency calling for the election of a leader like Roosevelt, and that the recognition women might win by the fliers could be forgone.[18]

Molly W. (who became known as "More Women") Dewson had certain principles about the ways in which women were to be involved in the Democratic party. They were to be educated on the issues, rather than personalities, and the candidate was to run on his record. As Molly put it, "Elections are won between campaigns." This contrasted sharply with the view of old-style politicians such as Jim Farley, chairman of the Democratic National Committee (DNC), who was unfamiliar with the new requirements of coalition politics. Jim felt rather, "Why waste money between campaigns?"[19]

Molly also understood the importance of patronage but felt that it should be used to reward women who were active workers in the campaigns rather than politicians' girlfriends. Only women who were qualified would be appointed to key positions.[20] As to her explicit attitude toward women, she said: "I am not a feminist. I am a practical politician out to build up the Democratic Party where it sorely needs it."[21]

After the 1932 victory, Molly called in her political debts with FDR, much as she had done in the 1928 governor's campaign.[22] Finding jobs for well-deserving women occupied her correspondence with Eleanor Roosevelt almost entirely during the first year. Their success is made evident in the fact that more women were appointed in the New Deal than at any time since World War I.[23] In all agencies combined there were 172,733 women, or 18.9 percent of all employees,[24] up from 15.8 percent in 1923. Yet there were also times of considerable discouragement. Molly wrote to Eleanor: "Our only aim is to get some of the workers instead of the drones. . . . If we were playing personal politics you could see why we might expect resistance and inertia."[25] Apparently they did not articulate their difficulties as resulting from any systematic bias against women.

One of Dewson's prominent successes was the appointment of the first woman cabinet member, Frances Perkins.[26] Molly wrote to FDR half jokingly that the Perkins appointment "was my price for the political work I did."[27] Yet she also gives him credit for a genuine appreciation of women's capabilities, possibly influenced by Eleanor, and an enjoyment of breaking precedent. In 1948 Perkins was to look back on the New Deal with Molly, saying, "With unbridled exaggeration as to my contribution, 'You and I, Mary, made Roosevelt's labor policy.' "[28]

Perkins may have been referring to some of the events that helped sow the seeds for New Deal programs, such as her own beginning with the 54 Hour bill, for which she was an active lobbyist on behalf of the Consumer's League in 1912,[29] in New York; or Molly Dewson's and Perkins' contact with Felix Frankfurter to develop a concept of the minimum wage which would pass the test of constitutionality.[30] Perkins also helped assure that public works be included in the NRA bill.[31] Dewson's letters in May 1933 to Eleanor and Franklin[32] may also have contributed to pressure to include provision for minimum wages in the NRA codes, which in turn helped pave the way for the 1938 Fair Labor Standards Act.[33]

You know my loyalty to you and I don't need to sugar coat my ideas to you so I dare say that when I heard your speech to the Chamber of Commerce I thought one of Hoover's speeches must have been left in your desk drawer and you had put your hand on it by mistake. . . . Any self-governing plan of manufacturers of, for, and by themselves will never result in the legal limitation of hours and wages. Truly, Franklin, I have been close to industry since 1911 and nothing will be achieved for labor in the way of hours and wages except by mandatory law.[34]

Of course one mustn't underestimate the effect of political pressures from other sources,[35] including Senator Robert Wagner of New York with whom Dewson also collaborated.[36]

But Molly Dewson did not always win everything. As director of the Women's Division of the DNC, she and Eleanor were somewhat successful in pressuring Farley regarding jobs for women. But when Molly and Jim disagreed over the division's budget, they decided to go to Franklin to resolve the disagreement over Molly's request for $50,000. The resolution, reflected in correspondence with Eleanor, was a budget of $36,000 and Molly's resignation.[37] Although Eleanor was not directly part of the negotiation between Louis Howe, Farley, Dewson, and FDR, she responded sympathetically to Molly's reports and to her apology for not being able to continue to work for Franklin. In order to save money, Molly offered to work for the Women's Division without pay, an offer which was accepted. In her memoirs, she cheerfully assured Eleanor of her pleasure in working for nothing in pursuit of an ideal.

After her resignation, Dewson became director of the General Advisory Committee of the Women's Division from 1934 to 1936. She planned to have no members of this advisory committee, however, since all the good women were needed locally; she recalls facetiously in her memoirs that experienced women know better than to ask her about the committee's members. She wrote, "Experienced women are astute."[38]

When she resigned as the director of the Women's Division, one of the concessions Molly won was the "50–50 Plan," which would provide women equal representation on all committees. But to back up this demand, in 1936, Molly was unwilling to "stage any pretty revolutions,"[39] but instead sought to work informally through the network. "This would sound spineless to a feminist but I am practical and am concentrated on a Democratic victory this fall."[40] In this particular year, Molly's pragmatic approach won substantial involvement for women on the Platform Committee, where women were allowed to serve as alternates for men. But the impact of women on the 1936 platform was not substantial, for there was no mention of the Child Labor Amendment or Section 213 of the National Economy Act, a law prohibiting married women from holding federal jobs if their husbands were also working for the federal government, which the Republican party platform opposed that year.[41] (In 1940, 50–50 representation for women was achieved on the Platform Committee, and the Democratic party adopted the socialist feminists' position of opposition to the Equal Rights Amendment.)[42]

Molly's service as vice chairman of the DNC from 1936 to 1937 reflects some of the conflict between the Democratic women themselves, who were mostly social feminists, but some of whom were members of the National Women's party, a "hard-core" feminist group. Molly had supported FDR's position on Section 213. That position, also supported by Eleanor Roosevelt in her speeches,[43] was that to prohibit women from holding jobs was wrong in principle, but tolerable as an emergency measure in the Depression, and should be repealed soon after. In March 1937 Molly urged FDR to seek repeal of 213. She confessed:

It is petty of me to dislike having "my nuisance" [Emma Guffey Miller, Democrat and supporter of the National Women's Party] get the credit for this repeal when I have born the burden of holding the girls in conformity with your wishes.[44]

But Franklin "let her down," referring to section 213 as "minor legislation,"[45] even though opposition to 213 "created a unity among women's organizations and institutions unmatched since the passage of the 19th amendment."[46] In messages conveyed to Molly by Eleanor in response to her inquiries, Franklin professed to have other plans in mind, a reorganization rather than a repeal.[47] Molly's role in "holding the girls" back from opposition to 213, in addition to the manner in which she was selected to become vice chairman of the Democratic party, gave grounds to Emma Guffey Miller to lobby for Molly's dismissal.[48] FDR supported Molly, as she wrote to Eleanor:

Jim told Emma that while FDR was the Democratic leader until 1940 he would choose his man and woman leader and it was no use trying to prove I was chosen by Tammany methods or not at all as she claims because Jim did not read my name at the head of the list as reported by the nominating committee.[49]

Molly, however, had already offered to Eleanor to resign.[50] In August Molly was appointed to the Social Security Board,[51] and in September she resigned from the post of vice chairman of the DNC,[52] after Section 213 had been repealed in July;[53] this was once again reflected in her correspondence with Eleanor.

In spite of her disappointment with FDR regarding the handling of Section 213, Molly remained loyal politically. She expressed frustration with FDR's lack of appreciation of his supporters, perhaps especially disappointing for the women among them, yet she sees women per se as less important than the New Deal coalition as a whole.

I was disappointed that Franklin could not see me. . . . The importance of seeing me depends on whether he thinks any real number of votes are gained by anything but great currents of thought started by the acts of the administration and the President's interpretation of them. . . . I am discouraged by my powerlessness. . . . Yet I cannot bear not to do all possible for victory in 1936.

[signed] Your Gloomy Gus[54]

Dewson's own political influence was increased because she had involved women workers in the Democratic party. "No doubt Dewson's political stature was enhanced by the 15,000 Reporters . . . 60,000 Democratic women precinct workers, as well as 10,000 state and county leaders."[55] Yet with all this mobilization, the women had little power. According to Dorothy McAllister, Molly's successor as director of the Women's Division, the "men control the party machinery."[56]

In another context, there was almost no issue of greater or longer standing concern to Molly and the social feminist women reformers of the National Consumers' League than child labor. Yet she wrote again of her loyalty. "This is a critical moment for the Child Labor Amendment and I believe Franklin could save the day if he thinks it wise, but I will accept whatever decision he makes."[57] Her writing to Eleanor on personal matters has a different tone, perhaps indicating that the association with FDR as a political ally was surpassed in depth by the association of women in emotional as well as humanitarian bonds. "Like everyone I think of you as the grandest woman in the country, but more important to me I think of you intimately as a friend."[58]

In so briefly reviewing Molly's role in the period 1933–1940, we may make a few observations. Molly occupied various positions in the hierarchy of the Democratic party. She was instrumental in involving women in the issues of the New Deal through the Reporter Plan. Women were also newly involved in the Platform Committee of the Democratic party. Yet she spent probably the majority of her time in negotiation with male politicians for patronage for women. The women in the network were in the position of asking for political favors and calling in debts in a political machine controlled by others. Their vehicle, the Women's Division, existed at the discretion of the men. Its budget was beyond their control, as was its innovation, the Reporter Plan, which ended in the 1940s,[59] and its very existence as a division, which ended in 1953.[60]

The strength of the women in the network came from their ability to deliver votes, their professional competence in New Deal positions, and the position and role of Eleanor Roosevelt as First Lady. The power of these women in local communities may have come similarly from their elite class positions. Leadership in campaigns was apparently continually referred to the same prominent women appointees,[61] so that the Hatch Act of 1939, which prohibited political activities by civil servants, hampered the functioning of their organization.[62]

Among the women, Eleanor and Molly struggled to keep Emma Guffey Miller from holding either the position of director of the Women's Division or vice chairman of the DNC.[63] Was this because of Miller's penchant for personal advancement, as they claimed, or her overt style of seeking to advance women?[64] In Molly's own words, Miller was a "fighter" as well as a "nuisance."[65] "Practically singlehandedly . . . she convinced the Democratic Party to endorse the ERA in the 1940's."[66] The strength and perhaps unwelcome assertiveness of Miller contrasts with the woman which Eleanor and Molly did choose as Molly's successor as director of the Women's Division. In 1940 Eleanor was to write to Molly for help, saying that Mrs. McAllister was "weak with the men."[67] One might wonder, then, whether Eleanor and Molly simply ignored the problem of training successors,[68] or whether they chose successors who agreed with them about the desirability of not challenging the men, ultimately weakening the Women's Division's ability to survive.

In these incidents it seems that we have a clear contrast in style between the "social" feminism represented by Dewson and Eleanor Roosevelt and the "hardcore" feminism of Emma Guffey Miller. The social feminists were quite willing to compromise their most strongly felt goals, such as employment of married women and opposition to child labor, for the sake of the political coalition. During the New Deal itself, when the coalition was strong, this pragmatism no doubt helped advance their legislative gains within the Roosevelt administration. But in the period of reaction to the New Deal in the late thirties, when FDR reached to cover his right flank in national politics, seeking "rapprochement with big business,"[69] the women were left with no strong leadership or political party of their own with which to pursue their goals. Whether because of the times or the women's choice of political strategy, gains for women ceased during this period.[70] In the forties, when women were essential in factory production for the war, few women had leadership positions in the war agencies, even in matters related to consumers. When the Women's Division was amalgamated into the Democratic Party in 1953, the women were once again "loath to start a public fight."[71]

The same style of social feminism generally characterizes other women in Eleanor Roosevelt's network, such as Frances Perkins, Rose Schneiderman, and Ellen Woodward. Frances Perkins, the first woman cabinet member, was a tribute to Dewson's patronage success and a significant factor in the passage of such social legislation as the Fair Labor Standards Act of 1938 and the Social Security Act of 1935. Perkins has been said to have been ineffectual,[72] perhaps because of the impeachment proceedings against her.[73] Yet she was one of two cabinet members to stay for FDR's entire twelve-year term. Molly, of course, had a sympathetic explanation of Perkins' bad press, such as sour grapes by (male) organized labor, Frances' intellect and her willingness to let it show, her tendency to dominate meetings, and her lack of understanding of people.[74]

Perkins' relationship to Eleanor Roosevelt was cool, reportedly competitive.[75] Files of her correspondence with Eleanor show a distance, without the usual effusive expressions of attachment found in other correspondence with the First Lady.[76] Yet Perkins and Dewson were close. At a 1929 luncheon honoring Perkins, Dewson said, "That luncheon . . . has given me a new insight into the beauty of loyalty and chivalry between women. How fine it is to play the game together all these years, isn't it?" Dewson recalls that, "except for this moment, perhaps, between us two cooperation has been of the head, not of the heart."[77]

We see, then, that Eleanor Roosevelt's involvement with women in the New Deal was not always direct, say between Eleanor and Frances Perkins, but indirect, from Eleanor to Molly to Frances. Nonetheless, they functioned more or less as a unit.

Perkins was fairly typical of New Deal women in her political views regarding labor and women. She was not a rabid anti-communist. For example, she delayed the deportation hearing of Harry Bridges, a labor organizer and suspected communist, for lack of evidence. As a result, impeachment proceedings were begun against her, instigated by the leader of the House Un-American Activities Committee.[78] On the other hand, Perkins did not support labor's most radical gain of the New Deal, the Wagner Act of 1935. Perkins and FDR were critical of certain provisions of this act, such as the use of majority rule to choose the collective bargaining agent, and the National Labor Relations Board made independent of the Department of Labor. Perkins, who had counseled more gradual gains, felt that the reaction against labor represented by the Taft-Hartley Act of 1945 could have been avoided.[79]

Perkins was also not strongly committed to the cause of woman's rights. "So far as I was personally concerned, woman's rights and woman suffrage even were not matters of primary importance. I was much more deeply touched by problems of poverty."[80] Yet in accepting her position as secretary of labor, she did so "for the sake of other women. . . . It might be that the door would close on them and weaker women wouldn't have a chance."[81] Perkins, then, was proud to set an example for other women but did not see herself as leading a woman's movement, by any means.

Eleanor's relationship with Rose Schneiderman, head of the Women's Trade Union League, contrasts with the one with Perkins. Mrs. Roosevelt regularly supported the WTUL with donations, committee service, and speeches.[82] Frances Perkins appointed Rose to the Labor Advisory Council of the NRA, where Rose says she "deems it a great privilege to serve under [General Johnson's] leadership."[83] Eleanor and Rose corresponded about the details of the code for various industries, such as the textile industry, where large numbers of women were employed,[84] sometimes involving Eleanor Roosevelt in negotiations.

Schneiderman was reportedly co-opted by her role in the NRA,[85] and clearly the negotiation of detailed codes for a multiplicity of industries was no mean task, codes which nonetheless allowed for a wage differential between men and women and failed to cover large numbers of women's jobs.[86] Even in relation to Eleanor, Rose upon occasion would express sensitivity to Mrs. Roosevelt's formal public position. For example, when asking Eleanor to be honorary chairman of a "label" campaign to label products produced in decent working conditions, Rose said, "Don't do it, darling, if you think it will get you into 'hot water.' "[87] On another occasion, Rose apologized for Mary Hilyer of the Shirt and Collar Workers Union who had asked Eleanor to speak at a "mass meeting," saying, "Please believe me. I had no share in this at all. I would never encourage her to make any such requests."[88]

It appears, then, that Rose was sensitive regarding her ties to Eleanor, much as the women were careful with their ties with the men. In spite of their personal friendship, there appears to remain an awkwardness of this WTUL coalition between fond women of different social classes.

A prodigious correspondent with Eleanor Roosevelt was Ellen Woodward from Mississippi, one of Molly's 1932 deserving supporters of FDR.[89] As head of the Women's Division of the Work Relief program, her job was to develop specific employment projects for women, to set up the federal-state apparatus to administer the program, and to protect the mandate of employing women. Woodward felt that small-scale projects, rather than mass production settings, were more appropriate for women.[90] She took pains to include job training along with work relief [91] and, in contrast with other New Deal women,[92] believed in setting up nursery schools for women with children under school age.[93] As she believed in setting a good example, all of the state directors under Woodward were women.

Although not an original member of the Roosevelt circle, she became closer to Eleanor as a result of their work together.[94] Ellen relied on the president's wife as a key advocate in tight situations, such as a hostile reorganization,[95] complaints from the private sector regarding stolen business,[96] and meetings with state directors where Eleanor Roosevelt served as keynote speaker and consultant.[97]

At the peak of their correspondence, Mrs. Woodward received an average of 400 letters a month forwarded from Eleanor Roosevelt. She would investigate and answer each, as well as use them to lobby for further support for her programs.[98] The two of them shared the embarrassment of the lack of involvement of Negro women. Mrs. Woodward and Mrs. Roosevelt met with the Council for Negro Women in Washington, but no doubt shared the same reluctance to openly advocate their cause. As Ellen wrote to Eleanor: "It is wisest to work unobtrusively for Negroes since the whole matter is so highly controversial and too much publicity concerning our efforts for this minority group is bound to boomerang."[99] Even in the period of New Deal budget cutting in 1937 and 1938, Ellen Woodward would continue to develop new programs and devise new ways to increase employment without increasing the budget. Both Mrs. Woodward and Mrs. Roosevelt were to testify before Congress opposing the budget cuts.[100] For her efforts, Woodward was appointed to the Social Security Board, where she succeeded Molly Dewson, and shortly thereafter the WPA programs were returned to the states.

In 1940 Woodward wrote to Eleanor, "You always give me a certain 'lift' and a feeling of courage and confidence that no one else could give."[101]

This relationship shows Eleanor's openness, personally as well as formally, to another woman of similar motivation and aims (not to mention background). Yet in their advocacies they were clearly constrained by the political realities regarding both Negro women and budget cuts that threatened their hard-won accomplishments.

WOMEN'S RIGHTS

The positions of these women on such issues as the Equal Rights Amendment (ERA) and women's suffrage is also instructive in ascertaining their role as feminists. In Molly Dewson's files, for example, are some elaborations of the group's position on the ERA. Like many prominent women of her day,[102] Eleanor Roosevelt opposed the ERA on the grounds of the resulting loss of protective legislation for industrial women workers.[103] Yet Molly's files reveal further reasoning among FDR's women supporters when protective legislation was seen as likely to remain constitutional after 1941. Dorothy Strauss, a New York lawyer and Roosevelt supporter, wrote to Molly Dewson: "I am very keen to have other dangerous aspects of the proposed amendment emphasized since the change in attitude of the Supreme Court towards protective measures has made the labor aspect somewhat less important in the future."[104] The "other dangerous aspects" of the legislation, which Molly was to emphasize in a letter to Wagner, included wives responsible for their husbands' support, husbands rendering service in the homes, and differential ages for legal marriage for men and women[105] (although

Molly wanted the *Democratic Digest* to present both sides of the issue). Although less often articulated, the social implications of the ERA seemed to cause as much concern to some of these women as the presumed loss of protective labor legislation. In contrast, the "hard-core feminists" of the National Woman's Party initiated and led the battle for the Equal Rights Amendment.[106]

Mrs. Roosevelt's own statements on the ERA seem quite defensive. In 1938 she wrote in the *Democratic Digest*, "It seems to me that the best way to advance equal rights for women is for every woman to do her job in the best possible way so that gradually the prejudice against her will disappear."[107] At other times she seemed as concerned with women gaining special consideration on the grounds of sex as she was supportive of equal rights.

In the ordinary contacts of life women must learn that if they want equal pay they must give equal work. If they want equal consideration they must prepare themselves to adjust to other people and make no appeals on the grounds of sex. When women take part in the business world or in the political world they should take part as people, not as women.[108]

She goes on in this context to discourage the use of sex appeal as a substitute for competence.

In her "My Day" columns, Eleanor Roosevelt also opposed the ERA, but in 1951 there is a gradual softening.

While women in industry were not very well organized it seemed to me unwise to pass an amendment that might remove some of the protective laws passed for their benefit. Today however women can be as well organized as men and are certainly able to fight for their rights. . . .

I can see that perhaps it does add a little to the position of women to be declared equal before the law and equal politically and in whatever work a woman chooses to undertake. . . .

[But] the people have to accept changes and when you are changing age old customs this is sometimes difficult. . . . People have to be persuaded.[109]

But even in 1963 when the President's Commission on the Status of Women made its report, it said there was no need for the ERA,[110] although this commission was formed at Eleanor Roosevelt's prodding (with some help from Emma Guffey Miller) and was chaired by Eleanor until her death,[111] and both parties had by this time endorsed the ERA.[112]

For a person so active in involving women in politics, Eleanor Roosevelt was also slow to support the Women's Suffrage Amendment, opposing it in 1912 and later supporting it in 1920.[113] She was confident of women's potential, but skeptical of public acceptance of a political role for women. This pragmatism led her to counsel modest goals for women, combined with improved skills and wider experience. In 1934 she wrote:

Time will show, I think, that women are more capable than men . . . but until this has been proved, there is very little use in pushing women into positions which will be made untenable for them by prejudice. . . . I do not want women to take up positions before they are prepared to fill them.[114]

In spite of the special problems of women in politics, Eleanor favored "a complete amalgamation of men and women in public organizations." Her assessment of the impact of women's suffrage was also not "millennial."[115] "Let us acknowledge no really great changes in government since women's suffrage and . . . there is no sign that when moral questions come up women rise in a body and think and act alike to bring about certain reforms."[116] She felt that the achievements of suffrage did not justify its passage, but rather that it is more the right of the individual woman just as for the man.[117]

Like Perkins, Eleanor Roosevelt had a sense of the need for gradual reform. Either because of her position as wife of the president, or because of her own beliefs, or both, she backed away from youth groups who were clearly associated with the Communist party.[118] Mrs. Roosevelt was anxious to end poverty, and at times expressed interest in utopian schemes, but in the end did nothing to embarrass her husband politically.[119] She and Franklin both saw the unity of interests between capital and labor as possible within the capitalist system. She saw problems in the society as resulting from individual behavior rather than from the organization of the system itself. "I see no reason why a private profit system should interfere with peace, if . . . we are fair and just and reasonable. . . . It is not a question of system. It is a question of individual morals and the desire to do the right thing."[120]

In spite of her evident lukewarm response to overtly feminist issues, and her preference for gradual change, Eleanor Roosevelt was praised by the feminists as well. As Sue Shelton White, a NWP supporter, wrote to Molly Dewson:

The intellectuals are simply wild about Mrs. Roosevelt. . . . One of my feminist friends said to me . . . that . . . Mrs. Roosevelt had advanced the cause of women since the election more than 20 years of propaganda. . . . They are eloquent in their praise of her.[121]

And even Eleanor Roosevelt was subject to anger at men upon occasion. She wrote to Molly in 1932: "If Franklin is nominated you will have to go off now and then and speak and I can't. . . . I simply had a bit of rebellion against the male at times. I've had 'em [sic] before but sober sense does come to my rescue."[122] One wonders if, after she had traveled and spoken more widely, her "sober sense" still controlled her "rebellion," and what would have happened if it had not.

CONCLUSION

The women in the New Deal advocated the rights of women in employment, in legislation, and in the development of institutional norms. They shied away from tactics which challenged the decorum of genteel ladies, the institutions of the family, or the structure of the economy. In seeking to reform certain practices with respect to women rather than question the basic assumptions regarding woman's place, these women continued the tradition of social feminism of the twenties.

The so-called hard-core feminists of the National Woman's party provided an alternative in terms of more militant tactics and a less protectionist or "maternalistic" approach to advancing women's rights. By advocating the ERA rather than protective legislation, they may have been more open to fundamental changes in the role of women and to the construction of an alternative legal and political structure through which women can exercise power more equally with men.[123]

Yet neither group of feminists involved working-class women to a substantial degree[124] or advanced the unionization of women in the industrial labor force.[125] Neither challenged the economic structure of capitalism in the United States. In these respects the nature of the feminism of the thirties was most likely structured by historical circumstances in which it was founded, such as the narrowing in focus of the suffrage movement, its predecessor, in the 1890s,[126] the red baiting of social feminism in the 1920s,[127] the indifference or hostility to women by organized labor,[128] the ambivalence of the left to women's issues, and the misfortunes of the socialists and the radical labor movements such as the International Workers of the World in the first decades of the twentieth century.[129] Such a foreshortening of the political spectrum of the United States served to narrow the options available to organized women in the thirties, by and large organized into "clubs" rather than unions or political parties. One must be grateful for their energy and dedication to humanitarian goals at the same time as one must keep in perspective the relatively narrow scope of the gains which they made. Women became active in politics in the thirties within a tradition which would provide little disturbance to the social order,[130] either in terms of women's role in the family or in the economy.

One can only speculate whether a more integrated stance among the "social" and the "hard-core" feminists would have helped make the women's gains during the thirties more enduring. As it was, the "social" feminists tried to isolate the "hard-core" feminists of the National Women's party, opposed their Equal Rights Amendment, and struggled to keep them out of leadership positions in the Democratic party. Perhaps because of these divisions among the feminists, Eleanor Roosevelt and her group made advances for women, but only within male-defined limits that they acknowledged and accepted.

NOTES

1. See J. S. Lemons, *The Woman Citizen* (Urbana: University of Illinois Press, 1973); W. L. O'Neill, *Everyone Was Brave* (Chicago: Quadrangle, 1969).

2. O'Neill, op. cit., p. 51.

3. Ibid., pp. 101, 134.

4. Susan Ware, "Political Sisterhood in the New Deal, 1933–1940," Ph.D. dissertation, Harvard University, Cambridge, Mass., 1978, pp. 37–39, 198. O'Neill, op. cit., p. 141.

5. O'Neill, op. cit., pp. 52, 126–30.

6. Ibid., pp. 125–26; Lois Scharf, *To Work and to Wed* (Westport, Conn.: Greenwood Press, 1980), pp. 21–35.

7. Clarke Chambers, *Seedtime of Reform* (Minneapolis: University of Minnesota Press, 1963), Chap. 3, esp. pp. 82–83; Scharf, op. cit., p. 135; Susan Ware, *Beyond Suffrage* (Cambridge, Mass.: Harvard University Press, 1981).

8. A term defined and developed in Ware, *Beyond Suffrage*.

9. Ware, "Political Sisterhood," p. 64.

10. Joseph P. Lash, *Eleanor and Franklin* (New York: Norton, 1971), p. 374.

11. See Ware, "Political Sisterhood," pp. 77–78, 113, 144, 163; Lash, *Eleanor and Franklin;* Black, *Eleanor Roosevelt: A Biography* (New York: Duell, Sloan and Pearce, 1940); James Kearney, *Anna Eleanor Roosevelt* (Boston: Houghton Mifflin, 1968).

12. Molly W. Dewson, "An Aid to the End," unpublished bound autobiography, 2 vols., 1949, 1:69, Molly Dewson Papers, Franklin D. Roosevelt Library, Hyde Park, N.Y. (FDRL).

13. Dorothy McAllister to Molly Dewson (MWD), 3/15/39, 11/27/39, Box 291, Women's Division of the Democratic National Committee (DNC) Papers, FDRL.

14. Elsie George, "The Women Appointees of the Roosevelt and Truman Administrations," Ph.D. dissertation, American University, 1972, p. 104.

15. Lash, *Eleanor and Franklin*, pp. 387–88. See also pp. 338, 351 regarding Molly's role as Eleanor Roosevelt's "deputy."

16. Ibid., p. 387. Eleanor Roosevelt (ER) speech at Vassar College, 7/31/37.

17. Arthur Schlesinger, *The Age of Roosevelt,* 3 vols. (Boston: Houghton Mifflin, 1957–1960), 3:597, 440. According to Lash, *Eleanor and Franklin*, p. 578, 85 percent of the press was opposed to Roosevelt.

18. Dewson, "An Aid," 1:63–64.

19. Ibid., 2:37–38.

20. Lash, *Eleanor and Franklin*, p. 515; Kearney, op. cit., p. 119; Black, op. cit., p. 148. Molly Dewson (MWD) to ER, 4/27/33; MWD to ER 9/18/33; ER Papers, 100 series, Box 1259, FDRL.

21. MWD to M. A. MacIntyre, FDR Secretary 2/5/34, as quoted in George, op. cit., p. 72.

22. Ware, "Political Sisterhood," p. 120; Lash, *Eleanor and Franklin*, pp. 323–24.

23. Ware, *Beyond Suffrage*, p. 62.

24. Ware, "Political Sisterhood," p. 107.

25. MWD to ER, 9/18/33, handwritten, ER Papers, 100 series, Box 1259, FDRL.

26. Most agree that the Perkins appointment was due to Dewson, not ER. See George Martin, *Madame Secretary: Frances Perkins* (Boston: Houghton Mifflin, 1976), p. 235; Lash, op. cit., p. 464. ER does also mention in her article "What Do Ten Million Women Want" *Home Magazine* (March 1932) that women want a female secretary of labor.

27. Dewson, "An Aid," 1:79.

28. Ibid., Vol. 1:32.

29. Martin, op. cit., Chap. 9, pp. 91–102; Daniel R. Fusfeld, *The Economic Thought of Roosevelt and Origins of the New Deal* (New York: Columbia University Press, 1956),

p. 46. FDR apparently voted for the 54 Hour bill but did not actively support it, in spite of his wife's active involvement.

30. Martin, op. cit., p. 240.

31. Ibid., pp. 260–69.

32. Dewson, "An Aid," 1:104–5.

33. Ware, "Political Sisterhood," p. 143, fn. 17.

34. MWD to FDR, 5/8/33, as quoted in Dewson, "An Aid," 1:111–12.

35. Ware, "Political Sisterhood," pp. 128–135.

36. Dewson, "An Aid," 1:112–13.

37. ER to MWD, 12/20/34, with attached MWD to ER 12/18/34, in ER Papers, Series 100, FDRL. See also "An Aid," 2:37–38.

38. Dewson, "An Aid," 1:39–40.

39. Ware, *Beyond Suffrage,* p. 82.

40. Ibid.

41. Ibid.; Dorothy McAllister to ER, 6/5/40, Box 339, Women's Division of DNC Papers.

42. Dorothy McAllister to Rose Schneiderman (RS), 8/9/40, and RS to McAllister, 7/9/40, Box 316, Women's Division of DNC papers.

43. ER article in *Good Housekeeping,* #3, 1939, Box 3037, ER Papers, and ER speech, "Married Women Working," 1938, Box 3035, ER Papers, speech and article series. In private correspondence, ER said that Section 213 was a "very bad and foolish thing" because it diverted attention from the real causes of the Depression. ER to Secretary of Commerce D. Roper, 5/17/38, as quoted in Ware, "Political Sisterhood," p. 193, fn. 68.

44. MWD to FDR, 3/19/37, Box 3, Dewson Papers, Folder: A. E. Roosevelt, 1937–1958 and undated. Other early MWD letters opposed to Section 213 are MWD to ER, 10/29/35 and 7/25/36, in Box 3, Dewson Papers, E. A. Roosevelt, 1925–1936 folder. Also MWD to ER, 4/7/37, in Box 339 of Women's Division of DNC Papers regarding repeal of Section 213.

45. ER to MWD 4/8/37, and attached 4/7/37 MWD to ER, Box 1420, ER Papers, 100 series, FDRL.

46. Scharf, op. cit., p. 59.

47. ER to MWD 4/20/37, and attached 4/14/37 handwritten MWD to ER, Box 1420, ER Papers, 100 series, FDRL.

48. MWD to ER 6/11/37, Box 3, Dewson Papers, file A. E. Roosevelt, 1937–1958 and undated. See also ER to MWD 6/24/37, Box 1420, ER papers, 100 series, FDRL.

49. ER to MWD 6/24/37, Box 3, Dewson Papers, file A. E. Roosevelt, 1937–1958 and undated and attached MWD to ER, 6/22/37, Box 1420, ER Papers, 100 series, FDRL.

In other correspondence, MWD reveals how much of an issue was the criticism from E. G. Miller. In MWD to ER, 6/11/37, Box 3, Dewson Papers, folder 1937–1958, she wrote, "I do not believe that Emma would stop her campaign against me on anything short of a personal request of the President." In a letter from May Thompson Evans to MWD, 6/10/37, May writes, "She [EGM] is bitterly attacking you" and attaches a memo which elaborates the charges. In a letter from MWD to ER, 4/17/37, also in Box 3, Dewson Papers, Molly writes: "With Emma Guffey Miller on my trail and theirs [the new leaders of the Democratic National Committee] they will be sunk unless *you* help."

See also Ware, *Beyond Suffrage,* p. 189.

50. MWD to ER 6/11/37, Box 3, Dewson Papers, A. E. Roosevelt 1937–1958 and undated. Molly wrote, "I am only too eager to be relieved of the Vice Chairmanship."

51. ER to MWD 8/17/37, Box 3, Dewson Papers, A. E. Roosevelt 1937–1958 and undated.

52. MWD's secretary to ER 9/22/37, with attached, Box 1420, ER Papers, 100 series, FDRL. Molly wrote two letters to Jim Farley, one a formal resignation, the other suggesting that her formal explanation be made available to the press.

53. Section 213 was repealed in July 1937. Scharf, op. cit., p. 53.

54. MWD to ER 11/5/35, Box 1335 (handwritten) in ER Papers, 100 series, FDRL.

55. Ware, *Beyond Suffrage,* p. 80.

56. Ibid.

57. MWD to ER 2/5/34, ER Papers, 100 series, FDRL. See also George, op. cit., pp. 104–5.

58. MWD to ER 10/25/38, Box 1455, ER Papers, 100 series, FDRL.

59. Ware, "Political Sisterhood," pp. 211–12.

60. Ware, *Beyond Suffrage,* p. 134.

61. ER to MWD 5/2/36 and attached MWD to ER 4/20/36 in Box 3, Dewson Papers. A. E. Roosevelt file, 1925–1936, in which MWD recommends McAllister over E. G. Miller for her position as vice chairman of DNC. See also ER to MWD, 2/15/38, and attached letters regarding McAllister's Republican family of origin, Box 3, Dewson Papers, A. E. Roosevelt file, 1937–1958. See also MWD to ER 9/15/36 and attached ER to MWD, 9/21/36, regarding women speakers from the Treasury Department giving up their salary during the campaign. Box 1375, ER Papers, 100 series, FDRL.

62. Ware, *Beyond Suffrage,* p. 121.

63. ER to MWD 5/2/36, Box 3, Dewson Papers, A. E. Roosevelt file, 1925–1936, and MWD's secretary to ER 9/22/37 (see note 52 above).

64. Ware, "Political Sisterhood," pp. 190–92, 205.

65. Molly writes to E. G. Miller, "We need your magnificent speaking ability," in MWD to E. G. Miller, 6/30/36, Box 1375, ER Papers, 100 series, FDRL. MWD to FDR 3/19/37, Box 3, Dewson Papers, folder A. E. Roosevelt, 1937–1958 and undated (see note 44 above).

66. Ware, *Beyond Suffrage,* p. 121.

67. Ibid., p. 126.

68. Ibid., p. 129.

69. Theda Skocpol, "Political Response to Capitalist Crisis . . . New Deal," *Politics and Society* 10, No. 2 (1980): 196–98.

70. Ware, "Political Sisterhood," pp. 212–16.

71. Ware, *Beyond Suffrage,* p. 34.

72. Lash, *Eleanor and Franklin,* p. 463; June Sochen, *Movers and Shakers: American Women Thinkers and Activists 1900–1970* (New York: Quadrangle, 1973), p. 161; William H. Chafe, *The American Woman: Her Changing Social, Economic, and Political Role, 1920–1970* (New York: Oxford University Press, 1972), p. 107; Lois W. Banner, *Women in America: A Brief History* (Harcourt, Brace, Jovanovich, 1974), pp. 180–81.

73. Ware, "Political Sisterhood," p. 208.

74. Dewson, "An Aid," 1:82–87.

75. Martin, op. cit., p. 235; Lash, *Eleanor and Franklin,* p. 464.

76. Perkins to ER 2/8/37, Box 717, ER Papers, 70 series; Perkins to ER 4/27/40, Box 787, ER Papers, 70 series. ER to MWD 4/30/39, Box 1494, ER Papers, 100 series,

where ER requests MWD to speak to Perkins because she is likely to have greater influence.

77. Dewson, "An Aid," 1:89.

78. Ware, *Beyond Suffrage,* p. 124. Martin, Chap. 31, pp. 407–19.

79. Martin, op. cit., pp. 381–86. According to Skocpol, op. cit., p. 179, FDR and Perkins "favored only 'paternalistic' concessions to labor, such as legislative measures to regulated wages, hours, and working conditions. They were not particularly friendly to organized labor; nor would they sponsor government measures to increase its power."

80. Ware, *Beyond Suffrage,* p. 15.

81. Ibid.

82. Rose Schneiderman to ER 11/18/35, Box 1356, ER papers, 100 series. ER papers, Speech and Article series, 11/28/32, Box 3023 and 10/19/37, Box 3034.

83. RS to ER 7/3/33, Box 1277, ER Papers, 100 series, FDRL.

84. ER to RS 3/24/34; RS to ER 3/14/34; RS to ER 2/20/34; RS to ER 4/13/34; all in Box 1319, ER Papers, 100 series, FDRL.

85. Jane Humphreys, *Review for Radical Political Economics* 8, No. 1 (Spring 1976): 106–10, esp. p. 109. See also Meredith Tax, *Rising of the Women* (New York: Monthly Review, 1980), p. 113.

86. Ware, "Political Sisterhood," pp. 140–42.

87. RS to ER 4/24/33, Box 1277, ER Papers, 100 series, FDRL.

88. RS to ER 9/13/34, Box 1319, ER Papers, 100 series, FDRL.

89. George, op. cit., p. 136, vs. Ware, "Political Sisterhood," p. 91.

90. Ellen Sullivan Woodward (ESW) to ER 10/31/35, Box 672, ER Papers, 70 series, FDRL.

91. See ibid., and ESW to ER 2/7/35, Box 672, ER Papers, 70 series, FDRL.

92. According to Martin, op. cit., pp. 457–58, Perkins and Mary Anderson opposed federal programs for child care centers during World War II. See also Scharf, op. cit., p. 17.

93. ESW to ER 3/3/36, with attached paper entitled "Women at Work under WPA," p. 4, in Box 704, ER Papers, 70 series, FDRL. This position on providing nursery schools for children with working mothers is all the more remarkable since there may have been only 400 or so nursery schools in the United States at this time. See paper entitled "Nursery Schools in the U.S.," Box 3027, ER Papers, Speech and Article series, 1933–1934.

94. George, op. cit., pp. 178–80.

95. ESW to ER 12/21/35, Box 96, ER to Harry Hopkins (HH); ER to Harry Hopkins 12/30/35, Box 96 of HH Papers, FDRL.

96. ESW to Scheider 9/17/35, with attached copies of letters from ESW to the National Association of House Dress Manufacturing, Inc., Box 672, ER Papers, 70 series, FDRL.

97. ESW to Scheider 4/22/36, Box 704, ER Papers, 70 series; ESW to ER, 7/29/38, Box 100, Hopkins files; ER to ESW 6/20/39, and attached ESW to ER, 6/23/39, Box 767, ER Papers, 70 series.

98. ER to ESW 4/10/36 and attached; ESW to ER 4/6/36, Box 704, ER Papers, 70 series.

99. ESW to ER 4/4/38, Box 741, ER Papers, 70 series. See also ER to Harry Hopkins 7/16/35. Box 96, Group 24, HH Papers.

100. ER to Harry Hopkins 12/36 regarding careless haste in WPA layoffs, undated Box 96, Group 24, HH Papers.

101. ESW to ER 9/7/40, Box 795, ER Papers, 70 series.

102. Document in MWD files on ERA, 1937–1946, Box 8, from Dorothy McAllister as director of Women's Division. A press release against the ERA was signed by Mary Anderson, Frances Perkins, Susan B. Anthony, ER, Carrie Chapman Catt, and RS.

103. See ER's "My Day" columns, 6/1/46 and 11/18/46, Box 3149, and "My Day" column, 2/2/50, Box 3152, ER Papers, *My Day* Mimeo series.

104. Dorothy Strauss to MWD 1/4/38, Box 8, Dewson Papers, ERA folder, 1937–1946.

105. MWD to Strauss 1/26/38. MWD to Wagner 1/26/38, Box 8, Dewson Papers, ERA file.

106. Chambers, op. cit., pp. 77–78. O'Neill, op. cit., pp. 274–94.

107. *Democratic Digest* (February 1938), Box 3035, ER Papers, speech and article series.

108. ER's third *Good Housekeeping* article draft, 1939, Box 3037, ER Papers, speech and article series.

109. ER's "My Day" column, 5/25/51, Box 3153, ER Papers, *My Day* Mimeo series.

110. "President's Commission on the Status of Women," (Washington, D.C.: Government Printing Office, 1963), p. 45.

111. See Ware, "Political Sisterhood," p. 225; Joseph Lash, *Eleanor: The Years Alone* (New York: W. W. Norton, 1972), p. 317. The following correspondence shows that Emma Guffey Miller had not stopped being active in her efforts to promote women in the Democratic party, in spite of her earlier disagreements with Molly Dewson.

Emma Guffey Miller wrote to ER on 2/24/61: "Since you are a long-time supporter of recognition of women in our party by their appointment to important positions, I believe you will be disturbed, as many of us are, by the new Administration apparently by-passing able women. . . . I do not know whether you will be able to help us women or not, but at any rate, I thought you should be aware of the situation." See Eleanor Roosevelt Papers, General Correspondence, 100 series, 1961 DNC file, Box 4456. ER penciled a response: "I am aware of this but can't think of anything that can be done."

In March, Eleanor visited Kennedy with a three-page list of women nominees (see Lash, *Years Alone*) and in August Emma Guffey Miller wrote to Lyndon Johnson on the same issue (see Ware, "Political Sisterhood"). By 12/05/61, President Kennedy wrote to Eleanor, "I am deeply grateful for you agreeing to serve as Chairman of the President's Commission on the Status of Women." In ER Papers, General Correspondence, 100 series, JFK file, 1961.

112. Barbara Deckard, *The Women's Movement* (New York: Harper and Row, 1975), p. 291; Martin, op. cit., p. 459.

113. Harevan, op. cit., pp. 27–28.

114. ER, *Democratic Digest,* 1933.

115. ER radio speech from Vassar College 7/31/37, Box 3034, ER Papers, speech and articles series.

116. ER, *Good Housekeeping* article #2, 8/39, Box 3037, ER Papers, speech and article series.

117. Ibid.

118. Lash, *Eleanor and Franklin,* Chaps. 48–49.

119. Ibid., pp. 385–87.

120. *Democratic Digest,* 2/38, Box 3035, ER Papers, speech and article series.

121. "Sue" (presumably Sue Shelton White) to MWD 3/21/33, Box 1259, ER Papers, 100 series.

122. ER to MWD 3/11/32, Box 3, Dewson Papers, A. E. Roosevelt file, 1925–1936.

123. Tax, op. cit., pp. 171–78.

124. Freida S. Miller to ER 1/15/46 in ER Papers, UN Correspondence, Box 4562. According to the position articulated by Eleanor Flexner in *Century of Struggle* (New York: Atheneum, 1974), pp. 328–29, laws are ineffectual without unionization to provide the power necessary for enforcement. Clarke Chambers, op. cit., p. 63, argues the opposite position. Meredith Tax, op. cit., pp. 120–22, has pointed out how unresponsive organized labor has been to the needs of working women.

125. Tax, op. cit., pp. 166–68.

126. Minutes of meeting of the National Women's Organizations having a Consultive Role in San Francisco, 3/29/46, Box 4593, ER Papers, UN series.

127. Tax, op. cit., p. 122.

128. Carrie Chapman Catt to ER, 5/7/46, ER Papers, Box 4587, UN: Human Rights Commission, General Correspondence.

129. Harry Truman to ER 9/22/49, ER Papers, Box 4560, Correspondence between ER and Harry Truman, 1945–1960.

130. O'Neill, op. cit., pp. 94–95.

BIBLIOGRAPHY

Published Sources

Banner, Lois W. *Women in America: A Brief History*. New York: Harcourt, Brace, Jovanovich, 1974.

Black, Ruby. *Eleanor Roosevelt: A Biography*. New York: Duell, Sloan, and Pearce, 1940.

Chafe, William H. *The American Woman: Her Changing Social, Economic, and Political Role, 1920–1970*. New York: Oxford University Press, 1972.

Chambers, Clarke. *Seedtime of Reform: American Social Service and Social Action, 1918–1933*. Minneapolis: University of Minnesota Press, 1963.

Deckard, Barbara. *The Women's Movement*. New York: Harper and Row, 1975.

Flexner, Eleanor. *Centuries of Struggle*. New York: Atheneum, 1974.

Freidel, Frank B. *Franklin D. Roosevelt: Launching the New Deal*. Boston: Little, Brown, 1973.

Fusfeld, Daniel R. *The Economic Thought of Roosevelt and Origins of the New Deal*. New York: Columbia University Press, 1956.

Harevan, Tamara. *Eleanor Roosevelt: An American Conscience*. Chicago: Quadrangle, 1968.

Humphreys, Jane. "Women: Scapegoats and Safety Valves in the Great Depression." *Review of Radical Political Economics*, 8, No. 1 (Spring 1976).

Kearney, James. *Anna Eleanor Roosevelt*. Boston: Houghton Mifflin, 1968.

Lash, Joseph P. *Eleanor and Franklin*. New York: Norton, 1971.

Lemons, J. Stanley. *The Woman Citizen: Social Feminism in the 1920's*. Urbana: University of Illinois Press, 1973.

Leuchtenburg, W. E. *Franklin D. Roosevelt and the New Deal, 1932–1940*. New York: Harper Torchbooks, 1963.
Martin, George. *Madame Secretary: Frances Perkins*. Boston: Houghton Mifflin, 1976.
Montgomery, David. *Workers' Control in America*. New York: Cambridge University Press, 1979.
Mower, A. Glenn. *The United States, the United Nations, and Human Rights: The Eleanor Roosevelt and Jimmy Carter Eras*. Westport, Conn.: Greenwood Press, 1979.
O'Neill, William L. *Everyone Was Brave: The Rise and Fall of Feminism in America*. Chicago: Quadrangle, 1969.
Scharf, Lois. *To Work and to Wed*. Westport, Conn.: Greenwood Press, 1980.
Schlesinger, Arthur, Jr. *The Age of Roosevelt*, 3 vols. Boston: Houghton Mifflin, 1957–1960.
Skocpol, Theda. "Political Response to Capitalist Crisis: Neo-Marxist Theories of the State and the Case of the New Deal." *Politics and Society* 10, No. 2 (1980): 155–202.
Tax, Meredith. *The Rising of the Women*. New York: Monthly Review, 1980.
Ware, Susan. *Beyond Suffrage*. Cambridge, Mass.: Harvard University Press, 1981.

Unpublished Sources

Bilsborrow, E. J. "Philosophy of Social Reform in the Speeches of Eleanor Roosevelt." Ph.D. dissertation, University of Denver, 1957.
Dewson, Mary W. "An Aid to the End," 2 vols. An unpublished, bound autobiography, Dewson Papers, FDRL, 1949.
Mary Dewson Papers, FDR Library, Hyde Park, N.Y.
George, Elsie. "The Woman Appointees of the Roosevelt and Truman Administrations." Ph.D. dissertation, American University, 1972.
Johnson, M. Glen. "The Contribution of Eleanor and Franklin D. Roosevelt to the Development of International Human Rights." *Human Rights Quarterly* 9, No. 1 (February 1987): 19–48.
"President's Commission on the Status of Women." Established by Executive Order 10980, December 12, 1961. Washington, D.C.: GPO, 1963.
Eleanor Roosevelt Papers, FDR Library, Hyde Park, N.Y.
Ware, Susan. "Political Sisterhood in the New Deal, 1933–1940." Ph.D. dissertation, Harvard University, 1978.

VII

INSTITUTIONS AND POLICIES OF THE NEW DEAL

20

Roosevelt and the OPA: The Evolution of One War Agency

Geofrey T. Mills

INTRODUCTION

For the most part, the story of economic stabilization in World War II remains untold, although recently some scholars are pointing their efforts in this direction.[1] Most of the literature consists either of the memoirs of the participants or works commissioned by the government at the war's end.[2] While these works are certainly valuable and even contain insights, they lack historical perspective, and much of the economic aspect of the war remains to be unearthed. This essay attempts partially to fill this gap by examining the evolution of the Office of Price Administration (OPA), specifically, in relation to the domestic war effort and Franklin Roosevelt's attitudes toward economic matters. The time span covers 1940–1946 but concentrates on the crucial years of 1942–1945. My intention is to describe the events and personalities that shaped the administration's attitudes toward price control, one piece in the stabilization puzzle.

It would be presumptuous to attempt here to explain the economic stabilization program in its entirety. Therefore, such important economic tools as monetary policy, strategic materials control, agricultural and tax policy, spending plans, and wage controls will be discussed only as they pertain to price policy.[3] They were all important features in the total stabilization picture and certainly helped to shape the role of the OPA, but they are tangential to this discussion.

BEGINNINGS AND SELECTIVE PRICE CONTROL

It is ironic that, after a decade of falling prices and high unemployment, in early 1940 FDR had to retool his thinking and begin to address the inflation issue.[4] Part of this was the natural result of trying to push ahead with a massive war production scheme after a decade of low industrial output. In the vortex of events after Germany invaded Poland, and later France, Roosevelt gave only lip service to inflation control until early 1943. For it was in the winter of 1942–1943 that inflation began to threaten his armaments program, and labor strife increased. Before this time the OPA was only one of many war agencies, some operating at cross purposes, that engaged in the twin goals of raising production and containing prices.

That there would be a price control agency in the event of another war was foreordained by the clumsy method of price control in World War I and the subsequent interwar debate on excess profits and mobilization.[5] By 1940 the specific nature and responsibilities of such an agency were still to be determined, but the army, in its fourth revision of an Industrial Mobilization Plan (IMP), called for one under its direction.[6] The National Defense Act of 1920 called for the convening of a National Defense Advisory Committee (NDAC) in a future war and provided that one of the seven "advisors" should be on price control.[7] Bernard M. Baruch and the Veterans of Foreign Wars were also vociferous advocates of price controls.[8] The foundation for price controls had been laid, but the proximate cause of the OPA proved to be the Temporary National Economic Committee (TNEC) hearings of 1939.[9]

Three months after the invasion of Poland, the TNEC held hearings on war and prices. These hearings were transcribed in Part 21 of the TNEC proceedings and contained considerable discussion of price controls.[10] A consensus of witnesses was that the World War I inflation did little to advance the war effort, was detrimental to the economy, and was unnecessary for higher production levels.[11] Even the businessmen who testified felt price control to be an essential aspect of war mobilization.[12] Therefore, while a particular plan for price controls did not emerge from these hearings, the weight of the testimony, coupled with the institutional momentum of the IMP, the NDAC, and Baruch's influence with FDR, all combined to establish a foundation upon which such an agency would be built. The key element in all of this was the near unanimous agreement that rising prices would hinder war production.

Another crucial development of the TNEC hearings was the emergence of Leon Henderson as the chief spokesman for inflation control. Henderson, a pugnacious and abrasive economist, had served in New Deal agencies since 1934.[13] As the executive secretary of the TNEC, he used the position to gather information and political support for his beliefs. Henderson became convinced in 1939 that the United States could not avoid participation in the European conflict and that the tremendous expansion of production would require government supervision and direction.[14] Furthermore, Henderson was placed in charge of what price controlling activities did exist in 1940 and 1941 and as a result became wedded to the idea that selective control of certain key prices was the proper course.[15] As a result of this thinking, he collected a staff of legal and economic experts who could render expert advice on what prices should be controlled, and when.

Through all of this, FDR maintained his piecemeal and fragmented approach to economic affairs. Businessmen were strengthening attacks on the New Deal as the spending programs of the late 1930s failed to end the Depression. And as the "Phony War" broke out in Europe, this seemed to tranquillize efforts to mobilize the economy on a war footing. All war-related programs were put on hold.[16]

It was not until Germany had conquered most of northern Europe in early 1940 that FDR decided to act. Invoking the 1920 National Defense Act, he gave life to the NDAC and on May 29 appointed the seven advisors.[17] However, Henderson, as chief inflation watcher, found little to watch.[18] Price rises were hardly a problem at that time, and Henderson had little to do. Roosevelt, on the other hand, had a hidden agenda because he was laying the groundwork for war by establishing the basis for strong agencies to control the economy.[19]

Henderson, with two associates, John Hamn and David Ginsberg, set out to create an agency to control industrial prices selectively. This was part of an entire philosophy of "consumption planning" and war mobilization worked out previously. Wages and farm prices were, significantly, not included in this scheme, as the Depression had pushed these prices too low.[20] It was believed that some time would be needed before they reached normal levels again. The staff created by Henderson was a collection of experts who could, it was hoped, select and control only those prices necessary to ensure a stable price level. Having discarded B. M. Baruch's plan for a general freeze on all wages and prices, they encouraged increased production while attempting to limit some prices.[21]

Their efforts at price control were hindered by the lack of legislation enabling such control to occur. The Price Stabilization Division (PSD), the formal name of Henderson's group, therefore began a program of jawboning which continued on into the spring of 1941.[22] While not especially effective, the exercise did afford the PSD the chance to develop and adjust its methods and ideas.[23]

Meanwhile, FDR realized that the NDAC structure was incapable of dealing with a war mobilization. So with the 1940 election safely won, he set out to organize for war in earnest. In January 1940 the Office of Production Management (OPM) was established to oversee industrial production.[24] Henderson asked for, and received, additional authority in the form of an executive order establishing the Office of Price Administration and Civilian Supply (OPACS).[25] The OPACS was the old PSD with the additional responsibility (CS) for rationing civilian goods.[26] But since this agency still was without a legal base, Henderson sat his lawyers down to draft a proposed price control bill.[27]

For a while, the selective control methods without a legal backing worked reasonably well. But by August 1941, there were sufficient bottlenecks in the industrial system that some critical prices shot up alarmingly, and all prices began to advance. Henderson stepped up his issuance of price schedules and the campaign for legislation. In early August Roosevelt sent to the House Banking and Currency Committee Henderson's draft bill, entitled "The Emergency Price

Control Act'' (EPCA), and hearings were scheduled. In December the Senate received the bill, and with the prod of Pearl Harbor they rapidly sent it to the president, who signed it into law in January 1942.[28]

The specific content of this bill proved crucial to the course of price control and the OPA. The farm bloc was against any controls on agricultural prices, believing with some justification that they had not yet recovered from the Depression. As a result, Section 3 of the EPCA prohibited the OPA from controlling farm prices until they reached 110 percent of parity.[29] Labor, using the same argument, was able to exclude wages from control entirely but did agree to a ''no strike'' pledge in mid-December 1941. Therefore, the passage of the bill enabled Henderson to set only industrial prices.

For a few months this looked to be enough. Henderson was fighting for a comprehensive economic stabilization policy from the administration that would do most of the work of containing prices. Such a program would include higher taxes, credit controls, a tight money policy, and a forced saving plan. This would enable the OPA merely to fill in the gaps in a residual fashion.[30] Roosevelt, preoccupied with military and diplomatic affairs, did not encourage such a macroeconomic policy. In its stead he made a number of weak and halting attempts at an overall policy, all of which failed, until the situation deteriorated to the point where he had to take decisive action.

In March there were a number of high-level conferences in an attempt to build an anti-inflation program. Opinions were divided, and tempers flared. By late April a consensus package had been built and on April 27 was unveiled.[31] Of the seven points in the plan, four (tax policy, wages, farm prices, and savings) were extremely weak, amounting only to a request for good behavior. The other three (credit controls, rationing, and a general freeze on prices) were stronger. The General Maximum Price Regulation (GMPR) was thought to be a sort of ultimate weapon against inflation because it froze all prices that the OPA had power over.[32] But even though Henderson vigorously pursued price control with his new powers, the existing legislation only gave him control over roughly 40 percent of all items in the Consumer Price Index (CPI).[33] This, coupled with FDR's nonattempts at stabilization, allowed prices to continue to advance.

Henderson, Galbraith, and others then argued for more power. Their concerns centered on controlling farm prices at parity, and wages. Without these, effective price control would remain a dream. But FDR did not want to agitate either labor or the farmers. Both groups still felt left out of the new prosperity as industrial profits grew, and it seemed that they were being asked to shoulder an unfair part of the burden of controlling prices. This situation came to a head in September with Congress and the president blaming each other for a lack of progress. In this, an election year, emotions were high, and FDR gave Congress his famous inflation ultimatum on September 7.[34] The message contained a request for an Office of Economic Stabilization (OES) to coordinate all the stabilization activities, control of wages by the National War Labor Board (NWLB), and control of farm prices at 100 percent of parity. Congress reluctantly gave Roosevelt his bill, former Supreme Court justice James Byrnes was appointed head of the OES (in effect becoming an economic czar), and everyone thought this would be the end of the inflation.[35] However, it turned out to be only the beginning of the end.

Byrnes' appointment sealed Henderson's fate. No longer could he think of himself as the chief spokesman on price policy. Henderson had also made many enemies in his fight for the OES. He became a political liability and resigned on December 15 as attacks on him came from all quarters. But Byrnes was not able to control prices very effectively either, and the CPI continued to rise.

GENERAL PRICE CONTROL AND ECONOMIC STABILITY

In late 1942 efforts at price control were thwarted by two major flaws in the system of controls. First, the group of experts whom Henderson had assembled were victims of their own expertise. They believed that they had the ability to set individual prices exactly at levels consistent with stability. This involved extensive studies, and one by-product was a great number of "price relief" adjustments to firms pleading economic distress. Because of the belief in scientific price control, too many adjustments were made. Second, and most important, there existed a fundamental disagreement between the major political groups— labor, farmers, and business—on how the domestic costs of the war should be shared. In early 1943 there was still no agreement, and each group was out to get all it could. Business resisted price controls; labor was beginning to chafe under the no-strike pledge, and there was an alarming resort to strike threats;[36] while the farmers fought tooth and nail against anything that would limit their incomes. This all landed on Byrnes' desk, and he had to solve these two problems. As a good friend of Baruch's, he was swayed by the older man's arguments for an overall freeze (with no adjustments), and he was not impressed with the OPA selective control methods.[37] Furthermore, he was enough of a politician to be able to fashion an agreement among labor, the farmers, and business. This bargain became the linchpin that allowed economic stabilization, with no inflation, to endure for the remainder of hostilities.

The major stumbling block to stabilization thus far had been the lack of a political agreement over the division of the domestic costs of price control and the price relief granted certain industries under existing OPA regulations. Each of the three major groups in the stabilization picture felt that it was sacrificing more than the other two. Byrnes set out to correct both problems with a single move.[38]

Up until the previous October, wages and farm prices had not been subject to control. And while industrial prices were contained, the tremendous increase in output allowed business profits to expand greatly. Business was, however, reluctant to expand capacity because of a fear of having excess capacity at the conclusion of the war.[39] As a result, it was reluctant to join in any overarching agreement until its fears could be quieted. An accelerated depreciation provision for new plant and equipment plus a war plants act specifying government re-purchase (at war's end) went a long way in obtaining business' agreement.[40] Furthermore, with wages and farm prices increasing, business did not want to be in a position of giving away too much.

Labor was clamoring, owing to farm price advances and price increases, for a relaxation of the "Little Steel" agreement.[41] This agreement was the basic understanding of how wages should be set during the war, and many unions, notably the United Mine Workers, were advocating a repeal of the no-strike pledge.

Farmers did not want agricultural products under price control because they still felt behind in the income shares they received from GNP. As a result, they wanted all sorts of special treatment under the new guidelines, and were, for the most part, receiving it.[42]

Byrnes reviewed this situation and concluded that it was time for strong leadership. With the blessing of FDR he set out to establish a viable plan for economic stabilization which was to last until V-J Day.

The keystone of stabilization was the Hold-the-Line Order (HTLO) of April 8, 1943.[43] This executive order absolutely prohibited the OPA and the NWLB from increasing prices or wages beyond the minimum amount allowed by law. This took away the OPA's ability to alter prices at its discretion and helped to solve the fears of business and farmers about the course of future wage move-ments. FDR vetoed the Bankhead bill on April 2, denying special treatment of agriculture. On March 16 the NWLB rejected a petition of the American Fed-eration of Labor (AFL) to change the Little Steel formula in its favor.[44] And business received its aforementioned accelerated depreciation and war plants legislation.

This series of agreements which Byrnes arranged established a delicate political balance that yielded a comprehensive program of stabilization, which in turn proved the basis for the remarkable price stability of the next twenty-four months. The CPI (see appendixes) increased roughly 22 percent from January 1941 to April 1943 but only about 4 percent until August 1945. None of the parties in the agreement could afford to disrupt it as long as the war continued.

This agreement is significant when pointing out the political nature of such price control plans. They are heavily dependent upon the voluntary acceptance of all concerned parties and are quite vulnerable to political attack. That the agreement disintegrated immediately after the war is indicative of the special, even peculiar, atmosphere necessary to allow controls to work.[45]

Chester Bowles was appointed to lead the OPA in April 1943, and his ascension symbolized a new era in OPA operations. Severely limited by the provisions of the HTLO, Bowles had to rely on positive public opinion and a large staff of volunteers to keep prices in check.[46] Gone were most of the experts, and in their place was a group of bureaucrats intent upon "holding the line" through public acceptance of the controls. It is quiet testimony to Bowles' efforts and enthusiasm that from April 1943 to August 1945 the United States achieved record levels of production while 12 million men were under arms, and the price level increased about 2 percent per year.

CONCLUSION

What is to be learned from this, the strange case of the OPA? Can we glean anything for current policy from this experience? With its rapid demise at the war's end, the agency has all the appearances of a hothouse flower, able to grow and flourish only in the particular atmosphere of total war. As with all generalizations, this one is partly true and partly false.

Certainly it is true that the OPA was one of the many true World War II agencies. Created in the frightening days of 1941, it grew to become the best known, as well as the most admired and feared, of all the domestic agencies. Originally staffed with a few elite professionals, after April 1943 it was a "people's" agency headed by a former advertising executive, and it democratically controlled all prices. We see in this transformation a shift from selective controls to controls severely limited by law and formula. During the hold-the-line period, in the way of expert opinion and much in the way of mass appeals to public opinion, Bowles made great efforts to get people involved in and knowledgeable about the OPA.[47]

A lesson for today lurks here. First, the success of the OPA in 1943–1945 was based on the political agreement discussed above and a mass appeal for public support of the domestic war effort. In the main the population responded with admirable sacrifice, and the controls were voluntarily obeyed.[48] The theme of patriotism was struck, and the people responded. No price control scheme can ever work without the public willingly obeying the rules. Therefore the population must be convinced that there is a problem serious enough to warrant the effort, and they must be provided with good leadership.

Second—a topic touched on only briefly here—there must be a supporting cast of other economic measures to ensure that the controls will be permitted to function properly. This should include monetary and fiscal policies consistent with price restraint, and might, depending on circumstance, include credit restrictions, high taxes, forced saving plans, rationing, a tight monetary policy, industrial allocation schemes, and subsidies to some producers.[49]

Third, the major economic actors in the political arenas, such as the unions and large corporations, must consent to restrain their usual behavior in favor of the public interest. It was obvious in World War II that any one of the three major groups could have wrecked the price restraint program. They agreed not to do so in early 1943.

NOTES

I would like to thank Dr. David A. Martin, Head of the School of Business, SUNY-Geneseo, and Dr. Paul Uselding, Chairman of the Department of Economics at the

University of Illinois, for their helpful remarks on earlier drafts of this chapter. Both provided the author with advice and encouragement which is most gratefully acknowledged and appreciated. They should not, of course, be implicated for any errors of fact or interpretation that remain.

Please refer to the appendix for details on the WPI and CPI for the years in question as well as the annual unemployment rates and the Federal Reserve production index. These three series are referred to often in the text and, to avoid numerous tables, were placed in the appendix.

1. Hugh Rockoff, "The Response of Giant Corporations to Wage and Price Controls in WWII," *Journal of Economic History* 41, No. 1 (March 1981): 123–28; Rockoff, "Price and Wages Controls in Four Wartime Periods," ibid. 41, No. 2 (June 1981): 381–401; and an untitled manuscript on the history of price controls in the U.S., which he kindly supplied to the author. Mary Yeager, "Bureaucracy," in Glen Porter, ed., *The Encyclopedia of American Economic History* (New York: Charles Scribner and Sons, 1980).

2. U.S. Bureau of the Budget, *The U.S. at War* (Washington, D.C.: Government Printing Office, 1946); U.S. Office of Temporary Controls, *Historical Reports on War Administration: OPA*, vols. 1–15 (Washington, D.C.: Government Printing Office, 1947–1948). J. K. Galbraith, "The Selection and Timing of Inflation Controls," *Review of Economics and Statistics* 23, No. 1 (February 1941): 81–85; and Galbraith, *A Theory of Price Control* (Cambridge, Mass.: Harvard University Press, 1952); Andrew Bartels, "The Politics of Price Control: The OPA and the Dilemma of Economic Stabilization, 1940–1946," Ph.D. dissertation, The Johns Hopkins University, 1980; and Geofrey T. Mills, "The Economics of Price Control: The OPA Experience 1941–1946," Ph.D. dissertation, University of Illinois, 1978.

3. These included the "Controlled Materials Plan" initiated by the War Production Board in 1942; agricultural policy was controlled by many different pieces of legislation but came to be centered on production subsidies and control of farm prices at 100 percent of parity in late 1942; wage controls were established on prevailing wage rates in October 1942 and handed to the National War Labor Board.

4. Prices fell more or less steadily in the entire decade of the 1930s; unemployment peaked in 1933 but was still 14 percent in 1940. An economic interpretation of the New Deal would certainly center on its activities to mitigate the low employment levels and the effect of high unemployment.

5. See Mills, op. cit.; Bartels, op. cit.; Rockoff, passim.

6. Bernard M. Baruch waged a loud and visible campaign between the wars for a system of emergency industrial controls in the event of another war. He testified before congressional committees on the topic almost incessantly and had the ear of most important Democrats (especially FDR) as late as 1960. See his "Taking the Profits out of War," *Atlantic Monthly* (January 1926): 23–29. The U.S. Army also had a price control agency in its Industrial Mobilization Plan, revised four times between 1922 and 1938.

7. NDAC was created as part of the National Defense Act of 1920 and consisted of advisors on industrial materials, industrial production, employment, farm products, transportation, consumer protection, and price stabilization. Most of these so-called advisors were senior executives in major corporations or labor organizations. Thus it seems that FDR, in the event of another war, was willing to turn control of mobilization over to big business. See, for example, Eliot Janeway, *The Struggle for Survival* (New Haven, 1951),

pp. 45–75, and Bruce Catton, *The War Lords of Washington* (New York, 1948), Chapter 4.

8. See note 6 above for citation on B. M. Baruch. The VFW was also quite active in an effort to "take the profits out of war." This developed out of their fear that the common fighting man possibly had to sacrifice his life while industrial labor and big business reaped unconscionable profits as a result of the war.

9. The TNEC was originally formed in 1938 as part of FDR's attempt to limit the concentration of production into a few large firms. He handed this task to Thurman Arnould as the head of the Anti-Trust Division of the Justice Department. It was only later, as war threatened, that TNEC became a forum for the discussion of war-related stabilization issues.

10. Hearings before the TNEC, 76th Congress, 2nd Session, Part 21, *War and Prices*. See especially testimony of Isador Lubin, Willard Throp, and Theodore Kreps, pp. 11021–331.

11. Donald M. Nelson, vice-president, Sears, Roebuck and Co., ibid., pp. 11238–45.

12. Ibid., and D. M. Nelson, *Arsenal of Democracy: The Story of American War Production* (New York, 1946), Chapter 2.

13. Leon Henderson served for most of the New Deal in a number of economic agencies. He held posts in the National Recovery Administration and the Work Projects Administration, was a commissioner on the Securities and Exchange Commission, and became executive director of TNEC.

14. Henderson saw the U.S. entry into the war as inevitable, and therefore he thought it best to gear up war production as rapidly as possible. However, this was not a unanimous view, as many people thought that the United States could avoid the conflict and merely reap the profits from furnishing the Allies with arms. This latter group was labeled the "business as usual" faction, and a loud and acrimonious debate broke out between them on the proper role and course for mobilization.

15. Leon Henderson, "The Consumer and Competition," *Annals of the American Academy of Political and Social Science* 183, No. 1 (January 1936): 263–74; Henderson, "We Only Have Months," *Fortune* 24, No. 1 (July 1941): 68; Henderson and D. Nelson, "Prices, Profits, and Government," *Harvard Business Review* 19, No. 4 (Summer 1941): 389–404.

16. The War Resources Board (WRB) was established in early 1939 as a sort of trial balloon to see how industrial mobilization might be managed and who would run it. The WRB was dominated by business and military personnel, and Roosevelt seems not to have liked it much. During the "Phony War" of late 1939 he allowed it to disintegrate and did not immediately replace it with another body.

17. U.S. Office of Temporary Controls, *The Beginnings of OPA* (Washington, D.C., 1947), pp. 128–40.

18. See the first two tables in the appendix.

19. The course followed by the PSD into the OPACS and eventually the OPA was also followed by other NDAC advisory committees. The industrial production advisor, William Knudsen of General Motors, for example, became head of the Office of Production Management (OPM) in May 1940. The OPM evolved later into the WPB, which directed war production for the duration of the war.

20. Henderson was led quite naturally to a concentration on industrial prices and consumption planning. His entire background, back to World War I, was spent in study

of large concentrations of economic power. His term as executive secretary to TNEC, coupled with his friendship with Thurman Arnould, only reinforced his view that there were two sectors of the economy. One sector was characterized by intense competition, small production units, and little concentration. In this sector prices were naturally held low, and it would not need government control. The other sector held the bulk of the big producing units and had the ability to administer its prices. In this sector, therefore, a system of selective price controls seemed logical and desirable to Henderson.

21. Hearings before the House Banking and Currency Committee, 77th Congress, 1st Session, on the "Emergency Price Control Bill," August–October 1941—hereafter cited as HB&C—Henderson's testimony, pp. 650–1181. *Beginnings of OPA,* p. 72.

22. *Beginnings of OPA,* p. 44.

23. Ibid., Part I.

24. Ibid.

25. Executive Order 8374, April 11, 1941, in Samuel Rosenman, ed., *The Public Papers and Addresses of Franklin D. Roosevelt,* 13 vols. (New York, 1938–1950), 9:99–103. Hereafter cited as *PPP.*

26. There is much confusion over the official title of what I refer somewhat loosely to as the OPA. Originally, in the NDAC, consumer protection was placed under a separate advisor from price stabilization (see note 7 above). This meant that any rationing would be handled there. In April 1941 FDR combined these two functions into the Office of Price Administration and Civilian Supply (OPACS). In August the CS section was moved to the WPB. In January 1942 the CS (rationing) function was transferred back to the OPA, but *not* the CS title.

27. See appendix and OPA *1st Quarterly Report,* April 30, 1942, Washington, D.C., pp. 1–33. J. K. Galbraith was recruited to be head of the Price Division of OPACS. This was basically the old PSD of the NDAC. See also J. K. Galbraith, "The Selection and Timing of Inflation Controls," *Review of Economic Statistics* 23, No. 1 (February 1941): 81–85.

28. This bill was weakened, in the view of many of those in the OPA, in late 1941. Many, including Galbraith, recommended a presidential veto because the lack of control over wages and farm prices would hamper price control. Henderson, however, thought he could live with the bill and urged FDR to sign it. *Beginnings of OPA,* pp. 156–80.

29. Given the low level of farm prices in 1940–1941, it would require large advances for them just to reach parity. The 110 percent of parity restrictions effectively precluded any control of agricultural prices.

30. J. M. Blum, *From the Morgenthau Diaries: Years of War 1941–1945* (Boston, 1967), indicates that the revenue bills of the early war years were much less than FDR wanted and therefore taxes could not provide their full share of the stabilization effort.

31. Rosenman, *PPP,* 11:216–24.

32. OPA, *1st Quarterly Report,* pp. 199–228 for text of the GMPR. This, of course, did not cover the farm prices excluded specifically in Section 3 of the EPCA. Furthermore, it was felt that the use of rollback subsidies would not be helpful. These were not used effectively until early 1943.

33. OPA, *2nd Quarterly Report,* July 31, 1942 (Washington, D.C., 1942), Chapter 1.

34. Rosenman, *PPP,* 11:356–77.

35. FDR gave Congress the choice of being a part of the stabilization process by

passing his bill October 1 or being embarrassed by Roosevelt acting alone under presidential war powers.

36. The United Mine Workers (UMW), led by John L. Lewis, was the most visible and vociferous of the unions. Lewis actually threatened to take the UMW out, but was only the opinion leader for a large body of union feelings.

37. Byrnes was a friend, some say crony, of Baruch and was influenced a great deal by Baruch's ideas for a general overall freeze on all wages and prices.

38. This analysis borrows heavily from John T. Dunlop, "The Decontrol of Wages and Prices," in C. Warne, ed., *Labor in Postwar America* (New York, 1949), pp. 3–25, and "A Review of Wage Price Policy," *Review of Economic Statistics* 29, No. 3 (August 1947): 154–60.

39. This was, with some reservations, the same situation that existed in World War I.

40. Accelerated depreciation was provided by the Revenue Acts of 1942 and 1943. The War Plants Act was passed in late 1942.

41. The Little Steel agreement was the basic understanding under which wage increases were allowed up until April 1943. This formula was developed in settling a wage dispute among some of the smaller steel companies in mid-1942. It allowed wage advances of up to 15 percent above the January 1941 levels on the assumption that the cost of living would be stabilized as of levels prevailing in May 1942. Henderson asked the NWLB to repeal this on the grounds that a large number of the wage increases allowed under this agreement were, while legal, not economically necessary. And they made his job more difficult.

42. The Bankhead bill would have allowed large increases in cotton prices, which would have caused textile prices to advance. It was seen as a sacred cow of the farm bloc. U.S. Office of Temporary Controls, op. cit. pp. 76–81.

43. Executive Order 9328, April 8, 1943. Rosenman, *PPP,* 12:148–53.

44. See explanation in note 41 above.

45. Controls virtually fell apart after V-J Day. They were first relaxed and then emasculated, and by mid-1946 were ineffective. See Dunlop, op. cit., and B. M. Bernstein, "The Truman Administration and Its Reconversion Wage Policy," *Labor History* 6, No. 3 (Fall 1965): 214–31.

46. U.S. Office of Temporary Controls, *Volunteers in OPA* (Washington, D.C., 1946), Chapter 2.

47. Chester Bowles, *Promises to Keep* (New York, 1969), Chapter 7.

48. Marshal Clinard, *The Black Market* (New York, 1952), Chapter 3.

49. In a democracy it is impossible to police an entire control program. Enforcement must rest on voluntary compliance.

APPENDIX

Appendix 1
Retail Prices (CPI), 1935–1939 = 100

	1939	1940	1941	1942	1943	1944	1945	1946	1947
J			100.8	112.0	120.7	124.2	127.1	129.9	153.3
F			100.8	112.9	121.0	123.8	126.9	129.6	153.2
M	99.1	99.8	101.2	114.3	122.8	123.8	126.8	130.2	156.3
A			102.2	115.1	124.1	124.6	127.1	131.1	156.2
M			102.9	116.0	125.1	125.1	128.1	131.7	156.0
J	98.6	100.5	104.6	116.4	124.8	125.4	129.0	133.3	157.1
J			105.3	117.0	123.9	126.1	129.4	141.2	158.4
A			106.2	117.5	123.4	126.4	129.3	144.1	160.3
S	100.1	100.4	108.1	117.8	123.9	126.5	128.9	145.9	163.8
O		100.2	109.3	119.0	124.4	126.5	128.9	148.6	163.8
N		100.1	110.2	119.8	124.1	126.6	129.3	152.2	164.9
D		100.7	110.5	120.4	124.4	127.0	129.9	153.3	167.0

Sources: *Survey of Current Business; Monthly Labor Review; Federal Reserve Bulletin* (various issues).

Appendix 2
Wholesale Prices, Combined Index (all commodities) 1926 = 100

	1939	1940	1941	1942	1943	1944	1945	1946	1947
J		79.4	80.8	96.0	101.9	103.3	104.9	107.1	141.5
F		78.7	80.6	96.7	102.5	103.6	105.2	107.7	144.5
M	76.7	78.4	81.5	97.6	103.4	103.8	105.3	108.9	149.5
A		78.6	83.2	98.7	103.7	103.9	105.7	110.2	147.7
M		78.4	84.9	98.8	104.1	104.0	106.0	111.0	147.1
J	75.6	77.5	87.1	98.6	103.8	104.3	106.1	112.9	148.0
J		77.7	88.8	98.7	103.2	104.1	105.9	124.7	150.6
A		77.4	90.3	99.2	103.1	103.9	105.7	129.1	153.6
S	79.1	78.0	91.8	99.6	103.1	104.0	105.2	124.0	157.4
O		78.7	92.4	100.0	103.0	104.1	105.9	134.1	158.5
N		79.6	92.5	100.3	102.9	104.4	106.8	139.7	159.5
D	79.2	80.0	93.6	101.0	103.2	104.7	107.1	140.9	163.1

Sources: *Survey of Current Business; Monthly Labor Review; Federal Reserve Bulletin* (various issues).

Appendix 3
Total Industrial Production (includes utilities) 1947–1949 = 100

	1938	1939	1940	1941	1942	1943	1944	1945	1946
J	46	54	65	76	95	119	127	123	84
F	45	54	62	78	96	122	128	123	80
M	45	54	61	80	98	123	126	123	88
A	44	52	61	79	99	124	125	120	87
M	43	53	63	84	100	125	123	117	84
J	44	55	65	87	102	124	123	115	89
J	46	56	66	87	103	125	120	110	91
A	49	57	67	88	107	127	122	98	93
S	50	61	69	89	109	128	120	87	95
O	51	65	70	91	113	129	121	85	96
N	53	66	72	92	115	129	121	88	97
D	54	66	74	93	117	126	122	86	96

Source: *Federal Reserve Bulletin*, 45:12 (December 1959), p. 1469.

Appendix 4
Unemployment Rates, Annually (in percent)

1930	8.7	1940	14.6
1931	15.9	1941	9.9
1932	23.6	1942	4.7
1933	24.9	1943	1.9
1934	21.7	1944	1.2
1935	20.1	1945	1.9
1936	16.9	1946	3.9
1937	14.3	1947	3.9
1938	19.0	1948	3.8
1939	17.2	1949	5.9
		1950	5.3

Source: U.S. Department of Commerce, *Long Term Economic Growth, 1860–1970* (Washington, D.C.: USGPO, 1973), pp. 212, 213.

21

An Examination of the Major Influences on the Content and Timing of the Social Security Legislation, 1935

Lottie Tartell

The Great Depression lasting from 1929 to 1940 was an event of such unparalleled and long-lasting economic and social upheaval that it brought under scrutiny traditional attitudes, the responsibilities of government, and the ideology of the capitalist system. The Social Security Act that emerged out of this ferment was limited in scope, conservative in operation, and did not affect the managerial prerogatives of capitalists. This was in no small part owing to President Roosevelt's conservative bias and political acumen.

The intention here is to address the conditions, economic and political, that led to the acceptance of a program for Social Security in the United States; to the suggestions and options explored at the time and advocated by different groups; and to the role that Roosevelt played in determining its context and emphasis.

The centerpiece of the Social Security legislation is insurance to cover periods of unemployment and benefits for those too old to work. An insurance program implies spreading an unavoidable risk among those concerned. In this case the risk was economic insecurity in the form of destitution brought on by unemployment or old age. This application of the concept of insurance was a radical departure for the country, where self-help and mutual aid among family members and neighbors (extended to local government) were the accepted patterns. Need had been understood as an isolated, individual problem, carrying with it implications of character flaws such as laziness or poor management skills.[1]

These social norms were appropriate to an agricultural society but unfitted to an industrial age capable of economic disruptions as extensive as the Great Depression. Widespread unemployment and the loss of savings had destroyed people's ability to look after themselves and their dependents. Local governments were unable to generate the funds and the administration on the scale required.

Economic disruption put stresses on the social fabric that families and local welfare programs were incapable of combating.

The conditions of the 1930s made it clear that people could not rely solely on themselves or their neighbors. Industrialization created conditions with which traditional support systems could not cope. For instance, in 1932, 20 percent of the school children examined in New York City were diagnosed as suffering from malnutrition.[2] There were three states in 1933 in which approximately 25 percent of the population was on relief.[3] By 1934, 18 million people were on relief: one out of seven.[4] In that year, in thirty-nine states, one-tenth of the population was dependent upon public support.[5] In 1933 the rate of unemployment was 30 percent. It was the peak year of unemployment, with 13 million out of jobs.[6] In 1935 there were 10 million unemployed, and one-half of the elderly in 1935 were dependent upon others. Approximately 1 million of them were dependent on public support.[7] General health deteriorated. Although there were no serious epidemics in the 1930s, the death rate rose.[8] The suicide rate in 1932 reached a historical high of 21.4 per 100,000.[9]

In the face of such widespread misery and evidence of the malfunctioning of the economy, few could justify sole reliance on the self-help ethic. By 1935 the federal government had undertaken emergency relief, but it was not well suited to the long-term needs of those for whom society and the economic system could not directly provide income. Social Security was conceived as a more permanent solution. In a remarkably short period a Social Security program was formulated and became law. President Roosevelt, by executive order, created the Committee on Economic Security in June 1934. Social Security was researched, formulated, presented to Congress, hearings held, and final legislation adopted by August 14, 1935, little more than one year later.

The law encompassed pensions for the aged, unemployment insurance, federal support for public health, and aid for dependent children, the blind, and other handicapped people. It rested on the concept of entitlement—that every citizen included was a valued member of society to whom benefits were due as a right. Inclusion, however, rested upon being at one time or another a participant in the industrial system. It was not until 1939 that spouses and children were included. The final act covered 22 million working men, less than half of the persons gainfully employed. It did not cover agriculture or domestic work, where blacks and other minorities were most likely to find work at that time.[10]

This is a remarkable program, conceived and worked out as it was during a devastating economic decline. It is even more remarkable how limited it was in scope compared to other programs advocated at the time. The Townsend movement, the advocacy of social workers, the American Federation of Labor (AFL) and the National Joint Action Committee for Genuine Social Security, and the National Association for the Advancement of Colored People were all groups supportive of capitalism as an ideology with no wish to replace it with a different economic system. Revealing other sides of American sentiment were Huey Long and the Reverend Charles Edward Coughlin, who attacked capitalists directly and advocated major changes in the distribution of wealth. Surprisingly, considering the extent of the suffering in the Great Depression, radical ideology made little headway. There were Socialist and Communist parties, but they never constituted more than a political fringe. The Townsend movement and Huey Long were politically the most dangerous to Roosevelt's aspirations for a second term. Dr. Francis E. Townsend was a private citizen who was so moved by the needs of the elderly that he was inspired to develop a plan to lift them out of poverty and simultaneously solve the country's economic depression.

At the time, very few companies had voluntary pension programs. It was mostly public utilities and railroads who did. Few of them were vested, and coverage was limited even in the industries where plans existed. Because of the high failure rate of business, employee turnover, and unemployment, private pensions were inadequate. The average payout was $50 a month. This is a useful benchmark against which to compare state programs, which were $10–$15, or the $30 a month most often recommended for their replacement under a Social Security program. Only a few states had pensions. In all cases, families had to prove need in order for the elderly to become eligible. Even in these states there were many eligible who were unable to benefit because the states lacked sufficient resources.[11]

Townsend advocated a pension of $200 per month to all over the age of sixty, an enormous sum in those days. The recipients had an important task. They would specialize in consumption! They would be required to quit their jobs and spend the full $200 monthly in order to be eligible. It was a pay-as-you-go plan, to be financed by a 2 percent tax on the gross amount of all commercial and financial transactions. In this way Townsend expected to make room for younger people in the work force and to stimulate lagging demand. It was an enormously attractive idea for older people and their beleaguered families. Townsend claimed 20 million supporters in 1935 when he testified before the House Ways and Means Committee.[12] Four thousand five hundred and fifty clubs were formed to push the plan.[13]

Congressmen were appalled by Dr. Townsend's popularity. First, his plan was simplistic and economically unsound. At the hearings, questions were raised about increased velocity of circulation of money, inflation, how to ensure that the full amount would be spent, and what would constitute a transaction.

The political dangers were even more serious. The demographics were changing and affecting politics. The elderly were becoming a larger percentage of the population. They were 3.9 percent of the population in preindustrial 1860, 5.4 percent in 1930.[14] Life expectancy was lengthening. In 1900 it was 47.88 years for males; in 1929 it was 57.71 years.[15] In 1935 there were 7,583,000 Americans over the age of sixty-five.[16] More of them were seeking work, those who had work worked longer, and there were more of them.

In some states, because of the Townsend organizations, economic security for the aged became the pivotal political issue in congressional elections. Candidates who embraced the plan were serious threats to incumbents. Daniel S.

Sanders, in *The Impact of Reform Movements on Social Policy Change,* concluded that the popularity of the movement was so great that "the pressure exerted by the Townsend Movement in 1934—an election year . . . forced the inclusion of old-age insurance as a political necessity."[17]

Francis Perkins, secretary of labor at the time, writing in 1963, agrees: "Without the Townsend plan it is possible that the old-age insurance system would not have received the attention it did in the hands of Congress."[18] Sanders contends that it was "the threat of more extreme measures . . . [which] weakened the opposition of conservative elements to further liberalization and extensions of Social Security."[19]

Huey Long's threat was not only addressed to the Congress, to which he submitted radical programs for change, but struck directly at the presidency. He meant to run in 1936. Long, in his autobiography, *Every Man a King,* said that he foresaw the Depression. He attributed it principally to a lack of purchasing power because of the amassing of wealth in the hands of the richest 1 percent of the population.

The wealth of the land was being tied up in the hands of a few men. The people were not buying because they had nothing with which to buy. The big business interests were not selling, because there was nobody to sell to.

One percent of the people could not eat any more than any other one percent; they could not wear much more than any other one percent. So, in 1929, when the fortune-holders of America grew powerful enough that one percent of the people owned practically nothing, not even enough to pay their debts, a collapse was at hand.[20]

His remedy was redistribution of wealth. Unlike Townsend, his plan involved a major alteration of the economic system. Forrest Davis, in *Huey Long,* gives this summary of his Share-the-Wealth program:

1. A homestead allowance of $6,000;

2. A family income, guaranteed, of $2,000 at the bottom; not more than $1,800,000 at the top;

3. Regulation of hours of labor, up or down, to balance industrial surpluses, to be held until needed by the people;

4. Old age pensions to all poor persons over 60;

5. Purchase and storage by the Government of agricultural surpluses, to be held until needed by the people;

6. Immediate cash payment of veterans' bonus;

7. Universal, free education to all persons qualified by aptitude;

8. Drastic taxation of incomes and inheritances.

Now when Huey and the experts took to figuring how they might provide homesteads for families in three-room, walk-up, cold-water flats in New York's lower east side, they were forced to elevate their sights to the whole problem of decent, modern housing for the masses. That led to the stubborn question of what should be done in the power age

with cities built for a railroad age. The matter of removing stranded city populations to
the country, for so-called subsistence farming, led to the thought of decentralizing industry. And, when they came to consider what expedients the state, guaranteeing a family
wage, would be put to in supplying work to justify the wage, they entered upon the
exciting prospect of magnificent, Continent-changing public works.

Wherever they turned, they ran smack dab into the categorical necessity of a gigantic,
comprehensive "plan." A "plan," which, the more it emerged, the more it implied the
corollary of one, guiding will—a dictatorship.[21]

Long mixed his populist appeal with red-neck Louisiana speech, biblical injunctions, and references to Abe Lincoln, William Jennings Bryan, Daniel Web-
ster, and Teddy Roosevelt.[22]

He won attention throughout the United States, sometimes seriously, sometimes not. But Huey Long was very serious. He mixed a sense of mission with
calculated demagoguery, and as governor of Louisiana he governed with the
authority, capriciousness, and cupidity of the archetypical dictator. He extended
the size and role of the state government. He developed political control through
patronage, and he extended state government so there would be plenty of patronage to spread around.[23]

His expansion of public works to make jobs was taken up later in the New
Deal.[24] He supported Roosevelt in the 1932 election because he saw in his election
rhetoric promises of redistribution of income. In his autobiography he quotes
Roosevelt's Atlanta speech that for him was so persuasive.

The millions who are in want will not stand by silently forever while the things to satisfy
their needs are within easy reach.

Many of those whose primary solicitude is confined to the welfare of what they call
capital have failed to read the lessons of the last few years and have been moved less by
calm analysis of the needs of the Nation as a whole than by a blind determination to
preserve their own special stakes in the economic disorder.

We may build more factories but the fact remains that we have enough now to supply
all our domestic needs and more, if they are used. No; our basic trouble was not an
insufficiency of capital; it was in insufficient distribution of buying power coupled with
an oversufficient speculation in production.[25]

In office, Roosevelt proved much more cautious, and Long, who called himself
a leftist,[26] found Roosevelt elusive and uncooperative. He became a formidable
political enemy, and his threats to run for the presidency in 1936 were taken as
a serious political challenge.[27] It put pressure on Roosevelt to have economic
security legislation in place before the 1936 election and helped to propel him
toward accepting dramatically new roles for the federal government.

As it turned out, Huey Long was assassinated in September 1935, just a month
after passage of the Social Security Act.

The troubled times spewed forth Father Coughlin, a Catholic priest whom the
Church repudiated as its spokesman. He was antiwealth, anti-union, and anti-

Semitic. In 1935 he claimed 2 million followers. Their financial support made him a radio personality able to afford the air time to broadcast his views nationally. His League for Social Justice[28] was another pressure on traditional government and business to accept moderate change to forestall more dangerous assaults. But little pressure came from the communists, who were not dangerous in and of themselves. They were far more dangerous politically when used by others to provoke fear. Socialists, too, had limited appeal.

Townsend and Huey Long were politically important, and there were other voices as well. Social workers were also advocates for those in need.[29] They did not attack the system ideologically; their approach was humanistic. They were interested in Social Security as a device to restore to respectability those whom the economy had rejected. The medium they advocated was an income maintenance formula shorn of the debasing means test commonly used. It required an expanded role for the federal government in organizing and supervising programs. Their experience was that local programs tended to be inadequate and discriminatory in the interests of local politicians.[30]

Social workers went further still. They recognized that self-respect and skills were both perishable and dependent upon employment in the American culture. They therefore urged the federal government to undertake the provision of public jobs when the private sector fell short. This is nothing less than job entitlement, anathema to capitalists who connect such programs to higher taxes and lower profits.

Harry Hopkins, head of the Federal Emergency Relief Administration under Roosevelt, was a social worker. He was brought from New York, where he had directed the state's work/welfare program when Roosevelt was governor there. He brought to Washington the point of view of the social workers and first-hand knowledge of the unemployment and impoverishment of previously independent and self-respecting citizens. His position was high enough to make the views he espoused listened to.[31]

The National Joint Action Committee for Genuine Social Security was a broad-based coalition of organizations. It included labor groups, veterans' organizations, city councils, the Socialist party, the Communist party, clubs and fraternal organizations, and church groups. They were a visible and credible group in that they represented a broad swath of Americans willing to put aside other differences to unite behind this goal. They held a conference in Washington in January 1935 called the National Congress for Unemployment and Social Insurance, to bring to the attention of Congress the plight of the unemployed, the aged, and the veterans. It was headed by Herbert Benjamin, who had been an active advocate of Social Security for many years and had published on the subject.

Benjamin criticized the proposed Social Security tax that would be imposed on workers as well as employers. His point was that it would reduce purchasing power at a time when business was already seriously depressed by inadequate demand. He wanted funds to come from corporate capital accumulations. Business had underutilized savings that he thought should be tapped. There is a flavor of Keynesianism here. He wished government to intervene via the tax system to unfreeze unused savings in order to bolster total spending.

Samuel Gompers and organized labor were initially cool to plans to extend economic security universally. They preferred to bring pensions to the bargaining table. By the time hearings were held in 1935, they supported Social Security.[32] William Green of the AFL viewed the United States as a national market[33] and favored a national system of unemployment compensation with uniform benefits nationwide. Fearing that such a system would be declared unconstitutional,[34] he wished to see grants-in-aid to the states to finance the system. He argued that employee contributions to unemployment insurance would be double tax paid by labor, first as workers and then as consumers. He looked upon it as a reduction in wages. Green did accept contributions by workers to their old age pensions on the grounds that while workers were not responsible for unemployment, neither were employers responsible for the aging process. A nice distinction!

Some testimony from labor's ranks was more radical. O. J. Hall of the Local Action Committee for Workers, Philadelphia AFL, asked instead of unemployment insurance a redistribution of income through more progressive income and inheritance taxes.[35]

Presumably big business did not need to express itself in public. Its executives were the capitalists in the capitalist industrial society and its position was editorialized in newspapers with mass circulation.[36] Wall Street registered its concerns in the traditional way. In August 1934, a five-point fall in stock prices followed a brief mention by President Roosevelt that he planned to introduce Social Security legislation in the fall session of Congress.[37] The National Association of Manufacturers (NAM) testified on behalf of business, expressing the fear that firms already marginal would go under and, because of the additional payroll taxes, capital intensive industries would have a competitive edge over those that were labor intensive. James A. Emery, speaking for the NAM, argued that payroll taxes would lead to more unemployment as tax-free capital was substituted for labor.[38] Some businessmen did testify on behalf of Social Security, but their arguments were humanitarian rather than economic.

Thus, neither business nor unions took a leading role in shaping the philosophy or content of the Social Security program.

Rereading Charles H. Houston's testimony for the NAACP on the Social Security Act shows how times have changed, at least in rhetoric. He made no argument for civil rights. He requested only that where states had separate programs the federal government should require "equitable distribution between white and colored citizens."[39] He placed on the record that occupations omitted from coverage in the proposed law were those in which blacks were more than proportionately represented. Most blacks were either sharecroppers without wages or domestics who were not covered. No congressman answered his charges.

Progress toward enacting a program had to wait until Roosevelt judged the timing to be politically suitable. Business and Wall Street were skittish, and the economy was having such difficulties that he avoided the repercussions until mid-1934, when populist pressures could no longer be dealt with by rhetoric alone.

In the development and passage of Social Security legislation Roosevelt reveals himself as a patrician protecting little people, as an ideological and fiscal conservative protecting old values, as a realist, as a charismatic personality and a consummate politician and, as such, an innovator and pragmatist within the conservative framework.

Roosevelt's 1932 campaign speech in Atlanta, quoted above, gives the impression that he was a populist candidate, antibusiness and anti–Wall Street.[40] He was a master of rhetoric and political expertise, and much can be explained in that light. He knew his audience and geared his words to gain their support at the polls.

The impression one gets in the first Roosevelt administration is concern and sensitivity to the hapless victims of the Depression, but no great willingness to extend federal powers and responsibilities on their behalf. He used his best rhetoric to convey to Congress on January 4, 1935, that he was a protector of old values and that change would be "through tested liberal traditions, through processes which retain all the deep essentials of that republican form of representative government first given to a troubled world by the U.S."[41]

In that same address, the "profit motive" was nothing more nefarious than "the right by work to earn a decent livelihood for ourselves and our families,"[42] conservative words to a basically conservative Congress, from a basically conservative president.

Although he was elected in 1932, and the Democratic platform endorsed Social Security, he was slow to act. An awareness of the need did not mean a rush to action. His political realism and his distance from actual misery precluded that course of action. That is not to say that he found Social Security contrary to his personal philosophy. Ordinary people's well-being and dignity were part of his conservative values, and new approaches to meet extraordinary difficulties can be fitted within the conservative framework. He set about confronting the most extreme expressions of opposition, those couched in ideological terms:

A few timid people who fear progress will try to give you new names for what we are doing. Sometimes they will call it "Fascism," sometimes "Communism," sometimes "Regimentation," sometimes "Socialism." But in so doing, they are really trying to make very complex and theoretical something that is really very simple and very practical. I believe that what we are doing today is a necessary fulfillment of old and tested American ideals.[43]

Again, in an extemporaneous speech at the Subsistence Homes Exhibition, April 24, 1934, he said, "When people talk to you about the word 'revolution' in this country you tell them that they have one letter too many in that word. I say it's 'evolution.' "[44]

While there was opposition to economic security, there was popular support as well. There were tensions and countertensions at play from his own conservatism and the more dramatic programs being proposed by Townsend, Huey Long, and others. To these tensions and countertensions were added his own sense of noblesse oblige, which is expressed as a liberal creed in 1934:

We are compelled to employ the active interest of the Nation as a whole, through government in order to encourage a greater security for each individual who composes it. . . . If our Constitution tells us our Federal Government was established among other things "to promote the general welfare," it is our plain duty to provide for that security upon which welfare depends.[45]

There seems to be no evidence of a deliberate policy of encroachment on state powers by the federal sector. Nor is there evidence of an eagerness to see government more involved in the economic process. Indeed, while the rhetoric was expressed in ideological terms, presentation of an actual bill was held back. Business conditions were poor in 1934. Edwin E. Witte, executive director of the council on economic security which was established by Roosevelt to develop a Social Security program, reported:

In the summer of 1934 the Administration was very concerned about the downward trend in industrial production. The suggestions of a comprehensive social security program were considered, particularly by Treasury Department officials, to be alarming to business, and many people closely connected with the committee were at this stage anxious to allay these fears. The technical board in its preliminary report strongly suggested the advisability of timing the entire program so as to have the coming into effect of its various parts geared to industrial recovery. This was accepted by the committee as a good idea and accounts for the provisions in its proposals designed to have them come into effect only very slowly. The jitteriness over the conditions of business and the desire not to retard recovery also were factors in postponing the National Economic Conference and of any further pronouncement of the Administration's intentions until the middle of November.[46]

The growing popularity of the Townsend Movement, Huey Long, and others brought forward political considerations. On June 29, 1934, the Committee on Economic Security was brought into existence by executive decree. To the extent necessary, the federal government would take on a new role in its relation with the states and in the economy. The federal government would provide income maintenance to industrial workers and a measure of stability to aggregate demand. The government would not interfere in the way business functioned except to reduce the risks.

Roosevelt felt no need to go as far as other programs competing for the public ear. He seems not to have been concerned about Americans' loyalty or with fear of potential revolution. Howard Zinn, in his introductory essay for *New Deal Thought,* emphasized the manipulative aspects of Roosevelt's programs. He believes that Roosevelt concerned himself primarily with the middle class, giving them only enough to disarm dissatisfaction, and completely ignoring the needs of the powerless.[47] This is a cogent observation. Roosevelt was concerned about alleviating the effects of the Depression, not changing the power structure or redistributing wealth, and his first goal was to win the presidency in 1936. In this context, it is not surprising to find in his "Message Recommending Legislation on Economic Security" to the House Ways and Means Committee in January 1935 his concern for sound financial management. Protection of the credit structure of the nation emphatically came first.

For instance, he asked for a tax credit system controlled by the Treasury rather than grants-in-aid. He wished to forestall pressure from the states that would push the federal government further into welfare programs. Otherwise, "with all compensation having its source in federal grants there would be great and constant pressures for larger grants exceeding the money raised by the tax, with a consequent confusion of compensation and relief."[48] He cautioned the states that "to arouse hopes of benefits which cannot be fulfilled is invariably bad social and government policy."[49]

Three principles should be observed in legislation on this subject . . . except for the money necessary to initiate it, [it] should be self-sustaining, in the sense that funds for the payment of insurance benefits should not come from the proceeds of general taxation. Second, excepting in old age insurance, actual management should be left to the States subject to standards established by the Federal Government. Third, sound financial management of the funds and reserves and protection of the credit structure of the Nation should be assured by retaining Federal control over all funds through trustees in the Treasury of the United States.[50]

So strongly did Roosevelt feel about the solvency of the system that Witte tells this story:

On the afternoon of January 16 [1935], after the President had already notified Congress that he would, on the next day, submit a special message dealing with social security, and after press stories on the message and the committee's report had already been given out at the White House, the President discovered a feature in the old age insurance part of the program which he did not like. This was the aspect that a large deficit (to be met from general governmental revenues) would develop in the old age insurance system after 1965, as was stated clearly in the press releases which were prepared by Mr. Fitzgerald of the Department of Labor. The President thereupon sent for Secretary Perkins, who, in turn asked me to come over after the President had indicated that he could not support such a program. When I arrived, the President was still under the impression that there must be a mistake somewhere in the tables which appeared in our report. When advised that the tables were correct, the President insisted that the program must be changed. He suggested that this table be left out of the report and that the committee, instead of definitely recommending the particular tax rates and benefit schedules incorporated in the original bill, merely present these as one plan for meeting the problem which Congress might or might not adopt. . . . [The report] was not filed in final form until the morning of January 17, although it bears the date of January 15, 1935.[51]

This spontaneous reaction, revealed in private and not for effect, clearly indicates Roosevelt's personal financial conservatism, as well as his desire to placate Congress. It also reveals his determination that the general lines of the program not founder for lack of support.

Lester Seligman, in *New Deal Mosaic,* puts Roosevelt's political design this way:

Roosevelt's political conception seemed to be to use government to restore the stakes in the economy (and in society) of every economic group. He articulated a concept of the concert of interests, a consensus built to heal breaches rather than to unleash social indignation.[52]

I believe that this is a sound assessment, except that it is too all-inclusive. To describe Roosevelt only as a conciliator and a traditionalist is to underrate the force of his personality, his belief in the power of his personal charm, and his political ambitions for a second term.[53]

All of these elements can be observed in the manner in which the president handled the political problems involved in the passage of Social Security through Congress. He had experienced political reversals already in Congress and was concerned how Social Security would fare. The content of the program was novel, and he had reason to believe that Congress was not yet convinced. The House Ways and Means Committee had divided on party lines, with the Republicans accepting only the principle of assistance and rejecting pensions.[54] Careful political strategy was called for. It was for this reason that Roosevelt preferred to give Congress options, as long as the principles prevailed.[55]

He was equally pragmatic in ensuring its success. According to Barbara Blumberg, in *The New Deal and the Unemployed,* the emergency relief programs had survived the machinations of local politicians by associating the federal success with their own. Federal administrators took care to give credit to local politicians. Roosevelt wished this program to do the same as far as possible and within prudent limits wanted as much state involvement as possible. He seemed never to be committed to a policy for its own sake. Traditionalism was tempered with pragmatism. It worked, therefore it was a good idea.

This is not to say that he was not fully committed to the program when it became politically feasible and rewarding. When congressional leaders suggested dropping the old age insurance provisions, he insisted that all parts of the bill be retained.[56] He was determined to make his program secure. One reason, he said, that he favored financing unemployment insurance with a payroll tax rather than general funds was because "with those taxes in there, no damn politician can ever scrap my social security program."[57]

The Committee on Economic Security finished its studies, unanimously approved its recommendations, and sent its report to Congress on January 17, 1935. The House Ways and Means Committee and the Senate Finance Committee held separate hearings on the bill during January and February.

The election of 1934 had returned a substantial Democratic majority to Congress, but they were still open to such diverse pressures as business, the Townsend movement, and Huey Long. They were still a conservative group and assertive in their traditional independence from the presidency. Congress sifted out of the bill those recommendations that were politically unpalatable, either because they made the program too complicated to carry out or because they were too "socialist."

Congress was more interested in ideology and less in economics than was the Committee on Economic Security. They rejected wide-ranging, coordinated programs for supporting purchasing power and maintaining job skills. Congress stripped the unemployment insurance program of tie-ins with public jobs, shared work, and income maintenance at or near full-pay levels. The representatives accepted that industrial workers needed some institutionalized support, but the government was not to be the employer of last resort.

In general, Congress wished not to disturb the power structure or to enlarge the government's role in the factory or the marketplace. Congress rejected the option of investing in the private sector. Any surplus funds in the trust funds were to be invested exclusively in government securities. They had no intention of making government a partner of business. The structure of the economy was inviolate. There was to be no taint of socialism in the ordering of the economy or changes in the social order. Congress kept benefits as low as possible. They wanted to prevent privation, but they did not envision making possible a healthy, active, leisure class of older people living on government checks. The legislators wished the elderly still to depend on their own savings and contributions from their families. They did not wish to disturb what they perceived as the traditional role of the family in society and the responsibility of individuals to look after themselves.[58]

Roosevelt read the Congress' fiscal conservatism correctly. The legislature minimized the financial involvement of the federal government. They eliminated federal contributions in the old age insurance program except for administrative expenses, and originally set it up as a fully funded system, that is, the contributions into the trust fund would accrue to support that generation's benefits. It was not until 1939 that it went pay-as-you-go, with present workers financing with their payroll taxes the benefits of the retirees. This finally settled the sticky question of where the funds for the first group would come from since there was not time for them to contribute enough funds to cover their benefits. Future financial problems arising from demographic changes were postponed for later Congresses.[59]

Congress emphasized the insurance aspects of the program so that workers would recognize their stake in the program. They did, however, retain the welfare aspect suggested by the Committee on Economic Security. Regardless of the smallness of the workers' contribution to the fund, no workers otherwise eligible would get less than $10 a month. Contributions were made compulsory, and the option of voluntary additional contributions by workers and by the self-employed was cut out of the act. These are all contrary to common understanding of the insurance concept. The program was really a mixture of welfare and insurance, but Congress, like Roosevelt, wished the Social Security program to appear to be as mainstream as possible.

The House Ways and Means Committee accompanied the revised bill to Congress with this recommendation:

It makes a beginning toward economic security which has been long overdue. This beginning is made along lines which are in accord with our American institutions and traditions. It is not class legislation, but a measure which will benefit the entire public. While humanely providing for those in distress, it does not proceed upon the destructive theory that citizens should look to the Government for everything. On the contrary, it seeks to reduce dependency and to encourage thrift and self-support.[60]

"Economic Security" emerged from Congress as "Social Security." Dealing with the economic consequences of industrialization and capitalism was transmuted into dealing with the most glaring social consequences of poverty. The large issues of social justice and equity were not considered.

The Social Security Act basically maintained the status quo. Its provisions were based on the assumption that the household was a family unit whose head was male and upon whom the other members of the family were dependent. It continued the accustomed focus of government on the male, white, Protestant majority, and for the most part shut out women, blacks, and other minorities.

The act was formulated to improve the environment of business by reducing some of the risks in "an army of the unemployed," but in no way altered managerial prerogatives or the power structure.

There was no redistribution of income between social groups, but there was redistribution within the working class from the young to the old and from single workers to families (by the time its benefits were paid out).[61] The payroll taxes for Social Security were made national in scope so that there would be no states that could benefit by being tax-free. Incidence of the tax falls on consumers to the extent that the employers' contributions can be passed along in higher prices. The burden of the higher prices is not evenly distributed. Those receiving the lowest benefits are those at the lowest income levels who must spend all they earn. They cannot avoid any of the pass-along. Those with incomes large enough for saving or with income from property or securities have sheltered funds to that extent.[62]

Payroll taxes are regressive taxes in that they increase as income increases only up to the amount that is capped. Thereafter, regardless of income, the tax is the same. They are progressive in that incremental tax increases do not yield benefits proportionately as large.

Since coverage is dependent upon being part of the labor force, the poverty population, made up mostly of unskilled and secularly unemployed, has been largely excluded from its benefits.[63]

Of all the ideas that fired the imaginations in the 1930s, of all the options possible, Congress and Roosevelt chose the ones that fit most closely their traditional and narrow image of America. In so doing they initiated the very thing they hoped to avoid. The government more and more has become an active partner in the social and economic life of the nation.

NOTES

1. Bruno Stein, *Social Security and Pensions in Transition* (New York: The Free Press, 1980), p. 32.

2. Barbara Blumberg, *The New Deal and the Unemployed* (Lewisburg, Pa.: Bucknell University Press, 1979), p. 28.

3. Daniel S. Sanders, *The Impact of Reform Movements on Social Policy Change* (Fairlawn, N.J.: R. E. Burnick, 1973), p. 50.

4. Ibid., p. 47.

5. Ibid.

6. Ibid., p. 44.

7. U.S. Congress, Committee on Finance, *Senate Reports,* Report 628 accompanying Social Security Bill HR 7260, 74th Cong., 1st sess., 1935.

8. Ibid., p. 21.

9. *Statistical Abstract of the United States, 1940* (Washington, D.C.: Government Printing Office, 1941), Table No. 94.

10. Blumberg, p. 87.

11. Karl De Schweinitz, *People and Process in Social Security* (Westport, Conn.: Greenwood Press, 1948), p. 10.

12. U.S. Congress, House, Committee on Ways and Means, *Economic Security,* Hearings before the House Committee on Ways and Means on HR 4120, 74th Cong., 1st sess., January 21, 1935–February 12, 1935, p. 752.

13. Sanders, p. 55.

14. Ibid., p. 30.

15. Ibid., p. 37.

16. Twentieth Century Fund, *The Townsend Crusade; an Impartial Review of the Townsend Movement and the Probable Effects of the Townsend Plan* (New York: Committee on Old Age Security of the Twentieth Century Fund, 1936), p. 10.

17. Sanders, p. 136.

18. Edwin E. Witte, *Development of the Social Security Act* (Madison: University of Wisconsin Press, 1963), p. vi.

19. Sanders, p. 137.

20. Huey P. Long, *Every Man a King* (Chicago: Quadrangle Books, 1933. Reprint. Chicago: Quadrangle Paperback, 1964), p. 290.

21. Forrest Davis, *Huey Long* (New York: Dodge Publishing, 1935), pp. 276–77.

22. Long, p. 295.

23. T. Harry Williams, *Huey Long* (New York: Alfred A. Knopf, 1969), p. 16.

24. Ibid., p. 17.

25. Long, p. 298.

26. Williams, *Huey Long*, p. 639.

27. Ibid., p. 640.

28. Raymond Gram Swing, *Fore-runners of American Fascism* (Freeport, N.Y.: Books for Libraries Press, 1935), p. 56.

29. Blumberg, p. 28.

30. Ibid., p. 40.

31. Daniel S. Sanders, in *The Impact of Reform Movements on Social Policy Change*, plays down the work of social work *organizations*. "In the main, AASW (American Association of Social Workers) and other social work organizations had no major political thrust in the push for social security policy changes. . . . in the main social work's contribution was more evident in providing the necessary expertise in formulating proposals for changes in Social Security policies in progress" (p. 153).

32. Ibid., p. 131.

33. U.S. Congress, House, *Economic Security*, p. 387.

34. Ibid., p. 388.

35. Ibid.

36. Blumberg, p. 29.

37. Witte, p. 17.

38. U.S. Congress, Senate, Committee on Finance, *Economic Security,* Hearings before the Senate Committee on Finance on HR 7260, 74th Cong., 1st sess., January 22, 1935–February 20, 1935, p. 91.

39. U.S. Congress, House, *Economic Security*, p. 798.

40. Long, p. 298.

41. U.S. President, Address to Congress, January 4, 1935, *House Miscellaneous Documents*, Vol. 9927, No. 1 (Washington, D.C.: Government Printing Office), p. 1.

42. Ibid.

43. *The Public Papers and Addresses of Franklin Delano Roosevelt: 1934, the Advance of Recovery and Reform* (New York: Russell and Russell, 1969), p. 317.

44. Ibid., Document 64, p. 195.

45. Ibid., Document 102, p. 291.

46. Witte, p. 66.

47. Howard Zinn, ed., *New Deal Thought*, American Heritage Series, No. 70 (Indianapolis: Bobbs-Merrill Co., 1966), p. xxv.

48. U.S. President, Address to Congress, January 4, 1935, No. 1, p. 15.

49. Ibid., p. 17.

50. Ibid., p. vii.

51. Witte, p. 74.

52. Lester G. Seligman and Elmer E. Cornwell, Jr., *New Deal Mosaic* (Eugene: University of Oregon Books, 1965), p. xv.

53. Barbara Blumberg in her study of the Works Progress Administration in New York, *The New Deal and the Unemployed,* calls Roosevelt a "progressive." She sees his support of WPA as a movement toward job entitlement. Once conditions improved, public opinion returned to a negative view of aid for the able-bodied and because his view was more advanced she justifies the label "progressive."

54. Witte, p. 741.

55. Ibid., pp. 74, 94.

56. Ibid., p. 95.

57. Charles McKinley and Robert W. Frase, *Launching Social Security 1935–1937* (Madison: University of Wisconsin Press, 1970), p. 17.

58. Stein, pp. 42, 229.

59. Ibid., p. 42.

60. U.S. Congress, House, Committee on Ways and Means, *Report to Accompany Social Security Bill*, 74th Cong., 1st sess., April 5, 1935, *House Miscellaneous Documents*, Vol. 9887 (Washington: Government Printing Office), p. 16.

61. Rita Ricardo Campbell, *Social Security: Promise and Reality* (Stanford, Calif.: Hoover Institution Press, 1977), p. 71.

62. Ibid., p. xvi.

63. Stein, p. 59.

BIBLIOGRAPHY

Blumberg, Barbara. *The New Deal and the Unemployed*. Lewisburg, Pa.: Bucknell University Press, 1979.

Booth, Philip. *Social Security in America*. Ann Arbor: Institute of Industrial Relations, Unversity of Michigan, 1973.

Burns, Eveline M. *Toward Social Security*. New York: McGraw Hill, 1936.

Campbell, Rita Ricardo. *Social Security: Promise and Reality*. Stanford, Calif.: Hoover Institution Press, 1977.

Davis, Forrest. *Huey Long*. New York: Dodge Publishing Co., 1935.

DeSchweinitz, Karl. *People and Process in Social Security*. Westport, Conn.: Greenwood Press, 1948. Reprint. Westport, Conn.: Greenwood Press, 1970.

Kirkland, Edward C. *A History of American Economic Life*. Rev. ed. New York: F. S. Crofts and Co., 1946.

Long, Huey P. *Every Man a King*. Chicago: Quadrangle Books, 1933. Reprint. Chicago: Quadrangle Paperback, 1964.

McKinley, Charles, and Robert W. Frase. *Launching Social Security 1935–1937*. Madison: University of Wisconsin Press, 1970.

The Public Papers and Addresses of Franklin Delano Roosevelt: 1934, the Advance of Recovery and Reform. New York: Russell and Russell, 1969.

Sanders, Daniel S. *The Impact of Reform Movements on Social Policy Change: The Case of Social Insurance*. Fairlawn, N.J.: R. E. Burnick, 1973.

Seligman, Lester G., and Elmer E. Cornwell, Jr. *New Deal Mosaic*. Eugene: University of Oregon Books, 1965.

Smith, Alfred E. *The Citizen and His Government*. New York: Harper and Brothers, 1935.

————*Up to Now: An Autobiography*. New York: Viking Press, 1929.

Statistical Abstract of the United States, 1940. Washington D.C.: Government Printing Office, 1941.

Stein, Bruno. *Social Security and Pensions in Transition*. New York: The Free Press, 1980.

Swing, Raymond Gram. *Fore-runners of American Fascism*. Freeport, N.Y.: Books for Libraries Press, 1935.

Tugwell, Rexford G. *Roosevelt's Revolution, The First Year: A Personal Perspective*. New York: Macmillan, 1977.

Twentieth Century Fund. *The Townsend Crusade, an Impartial Review of the Townsend Movement and the Probable Effects of the Townsend Plan*. New York: Committee on Old Age Security of the Twentieth Century Fund, 1936.

U.S. Congress. *Conference Report of House and Senate on Social Security Bill, Report*

1744 To Accompany Social Security Bill, 74th Cong., 1st sess., April 5, 1935, HR 7260. Washington, D.C.: Government Printing Office, 1935.

U.S. Congress, House, Committee on Ways and Means. *Economic Security.* Hearings before the House Committee on Ways and Means on HR 4120, 74th Cong., 1st sess., January 21, 1935–February 12, 1935. Washington, D.C.: Government Printing Office, 1935.

———.*Report to Accompany Social Security Bill,* 74th Cong., 1st sess., April 5, 1935, HR 7260. Washington, D.C.: Government Printing Office, 1935.

U.S. Congress, Senate, Committee on Finance. *Economic Security.* Hearings before the Senate Committee on Finance on HR 7260, 74th Cong., 1st sess., January 22, 1935–February 20, 1935. Washington, D.C.: Government Printing Office, 1935.

———.*Senate Reports,* Report 628 accompanying Social Security Bill HR 7260, 74th Cong., 1st sess., 1935. Washington, D.C.: Government Printing Office, 1935.

U.S. President, Address to Congress, January 4, 1935. *House Miscellaneous Documents,* Vol. 9227. Washington, D.C.: Government Printing Office, 1935.

———. Committee on Economic Security, *Security.* Washington, D.C.: Government Printing Office, December 1934.

———. Committee on Economic Security, *Social Security in America, The Factual Background of the Social Security Act as Summarized from Staff Reports to the Committee on Economic Security.* Washington, D.C.: Government Printing Office, 1937.

———. Message recommending legislation on economic security to the House Committee on Ways and Means, January 17, 1935. *House Miscellaneous Documents,* Vol. 9927. Washington, D.C.: Government Printing Office, 1935.

Williams, T. Harry. *Huey Long.* New York: Alfred A. Knopf, 1969.

———. *Huey P. Long.* London: Clarendon Press, 1967.

Witte, Edwin E. *Development of the Social Security Act.* Madison: University of Wisconsin Press, 1963.

Zinn, Howard, ed. *New Deal Thought.* American Heritage Series, No. 70. Indianapolis: Bobbs-Merrill Co., 1966.

22

Madame Secretary and Mr. President: Frances Perkins and Franklin Roosevelt

Barbara Schindler

Social theory and political action shaped the public life of Frances Perkins. Her social philosophies, developed during the Progressive period, provided the impetus for social legislation during the administration of Al Smith as governor of New York and her long association with Franklin Delano Roosevelt. Her political acumen, honed to a fine edge under the guidance of Al Smith, enabled her to survive in a long public service career—seven years with the Smith administration in New York State and sixteen years with Franklin Roosevelt. Although her relationship with the press and sometimes the public was not completely satisfactory, her position with her mentors was never in doubt.

Until Al Smith's crushing defeat in the presidential election in 1928, he was the dominant political person in Perkins' life. Smith's appointment of Perkins to the State Industrial Commission in 1920 was a daring move for the times. He paid little attention to criticism concerning the appointment because he had observed her administrative talents. He also knew her agile mind and her efforts on behalf of social legislation while she worked for the Consumers' League and the Factory Investigating Commission. A vast new area of involvement in the problems of labor was opened to her with her association with the Smith administration. She established lines of communication between labor and management during disputes, she fought to extend workmen's compensation, and she vigorously enforced safety codes for industries. Perkins was unsuccessful, however, in her efforts to pass an eight-hour work day law for women. Smith gave her a great deal of latitude in working out the problems in the department. One critic observed, "Under the demands of her job Miss Perkins had been growing year by year in mastery of the subject of labor law, to the point where she had few rivals anywhere in the country."[1] Franklin Roosevelt, the newly elected governor of New York, was well aware of Frances Perkins' competence. She was not only retained in Roosevelt's administration but promoted from chairman of the Industrial Board to state industrial commissioner.[2]

In contrasting the differences between the position as state industrial commissioner and the one which she held under Governor Smith, she stated: "My old position was a judicial one, the new one is purely executive. The State Industrial Board is in reality a court for the settling of disputes between employer and employee and as such its decisions are reviewable only by the Appellate Division of the Supreme Court or the Court of Appeals. In my new position I am the head of the Labor Department of the State and hold a position in the Governor's Cabinet."[3] Perkins viewed the Labor Department as a service agency, as well as a policing organization. She felt that the Labor Department should be the source of impartial advice, assistance, and leadership to people in all walks of life—workers, employers, industrialists.[4]

The first year of Roosevelt's governorship continued the programs started in the Smith administration. With the exit of Belle Moskowitz from the official scene, the banner of social reformer was passed on to Perkins. In the short time between inauguration and the pinch of depression, Perkins' Labor Department made progress in labor legislation and social justice programs. Administrative practices in the labor, welfare, and health departments were improved. By 1930, beset by demands for unemployment insurance, public works, and free public employment agencies Perkins and Roosevelt responded.[5]

Precursors of New Deal philosophy were evident in Perkins' view concerning public works and unemployment insurance. By the middle of 1930, industry in New York State began to feel the effects of the stock market crash. Factory employment dropped steadily month by month—a total decline of 18 percent.[6] Perkins contended that when private industry was in a condition of temporary depression, the state had the power to institute programs of public works. Unfortunately, according to Perkins, public works undertaken at a time when the country was in a financial morass were not as effective as a system of public works that could go into effect at the slightest hint of an economic disturbance. Public works could revive an economy by keeping up the purchasing power of the wage earner and so gradually create a demand for manufactured goods, and this, in turn, could start the machinery of industry.[7] Another method of stimulating the economy during periods of temporary unemployment was the use of industrial or unemployment insurance. Governor Roosevelt asked Perkins to go to England to study their system of unemployment insurance.[8] In her battle to combat rising unemployment, Perkins recommended the establishment of free public employment offices which would benefit not only blue-collar workers but also white-collar workers by acting as a central clearing agency for available jobs.[9] Even before the stock market crash and the subsequent rise in unemployment, Perkins, with Roosevelt's blessing, began to revamp the state's public employment service.[10]

The election of 1932 proved to be an overwhelming victory for Franklin Delano

Roosevelt. He wished to appoint as secretary of labor a person in whose ability and integrity he had the utmost trust—Frances Perkins. He hesitated in her appointment, however, because organized labor and industrialists alike opposed her, both for her views and her gender. William Green, president of the American Federation of Labor (AFL), pointed out to Roosevelt that ''about eighty percent of labor is masculine and that with the head of the Children's Bureau a woman, and with the head of the Women's Bureau a woman, the appointment of another woman as Labor Secretary would put the Department of Labor almost completely under feminine control.''[11] The business community regarded her as an adversary because of her vigorous efforts, while state industrial commissioner of New York, to gain compliance by employers with safety regulations and compensation laws.

Despite these objections, President Roosevelt continued to press Perkins to accept the appointment. In February 1933, when Roosevelt first offered to appoint her, she refused since she was not a ''bona fide labor person.''[12] Pressed again to accept the appointment, Perkins agreed to become the new labor secretary if Roosevelt, in turn, would agree to pursue the following programs: immediate federal aid to the states for unemployment relief; an extensive program of public works; establishment by federal law of minimum wages, maximum hours, unemployment insurance, and old age insurance; abolition of child labor; and the improvement of the federal employment service.[13] Armed with Roosevelt's assurances that her suggested programs would be implemented, she agreed to accept the position of secretary of labor.

Frances Perkins, a legacy of Governor Smith's administration, had been accepted and nurtured by Governor Roosevelt. Bypassing the traditional union-affiliated person for the position of secretary of labor, Roosevelt chose her. Although it has been argued that this choice was influenced by Mrs. Roosevelt's desire to place a woman in the cabinet, Perkins' list of accomplishments as state industrial commissioner speaks for her.[14] Another reason that Roosevelt chose her as labor secretary, in lieu of a union man, was his fear of too close an association with the unions. Some union leaders expected Roosevelt to reward organized labor for its support during elections by appointing a union man as secretary of labor.[15] Since the administration was viewed as pro-labor, a capitulation to labor leaders' demands for political rewards would have rendered the Conciliation Service, as well as other services of the department, ineffective.

The relationship between the new labor secretary and Roosevelt was unique among cabinet officials. He placed great importance on her unwavering loyalty and on her personal relationship to the first family. Roosevelt paid little attention to a Gallup poll ranking her ninth in the field of ten cabinet officers where those surveyed responded to the question, ''Do you think that they are doing their jobs well?''[16] Her close relationship with the president was illustrated during the 1940 Democratic Convention when Roosevelt sought her advice concerning the vice presidential nominee. Still undecided, Roosevelt asked her opinion about

Henry Wallace. Getting a positive response, he announced Wallace as his choice. She acted as the courier to relay the information to Harry Hopkins, who then made it public.[17]

The new secretary believed that education and conciliation, in their broadest terms, should be the goals of the Department of Labor. During the strikes of the late 1930s, she was criticized by the press and the public for the department's lack of aggressive action. Despite this barrage of criticism, she steadfastly continued to advocate education and conciliation as the primary aims of the department and refused to interfere except in these areas.[18] She saw collective bargaining as an educational force—an exchange of information between two opposing groups. Her advocacy of collective bargaining to open lines of communication between labor and management, the establishment of ethical codes of conduct in business, and her concern for individual rights and freedoms were reflected in the legislation of the New Deal.

In his first inaugural address, Franklin Roosevelt stated: "This nation asks for action and action now. . . . We must act, and act quickly." With this resolution ringing in the air, Roosevelt set forth on a frenzy of activity resulting in fifteen major laws being passed by Congress within a span of a hundred days. This record beginning with the recalling of the Seventy-third Congress on March 9, 1933, and ending with its adjournment on June 15 was unequalled in American history. The New Deal was not a plan with form or content—it expressed a new attitude, not a preconceived program. Experimental, trial-and-error, pragmatic are all terms used to describe the New Deal. Improvising from one step to the next was characteristic of Roosevelt's program. Assuming that there was no direction, guidance, or historical precedent would be a mistake. From the populist movement, the New Dealers drew a bevy of ideas for regulating agriculture. From their experience in the settlement houses arose a concern for the aged and indigent. The Brain Trust above all believed that the "rugged individualism" of Herbert Hoover and the New Freedom concept of Woodrow Wilson no longer could be usefully applied to the economy. They believed in the cooperation of big business and government to rebuild the economy.[19]

President Roosevelt's message to Congress on March 21, 1933, signaled the beginning of the relief and recovery programs. He stated that "it is essential to our recovery program that measures be immediately enacted aimed at unemployment relief."[20] He suggested three types of legislation. First, he recommended the enrollment of workers by the federal government for such employment as could be quickly started and would not interfere with normal employment. This recommendation foreshadowed the Civilian Conservation Corps (CCC). The second type revolved around grants to states for relief work. The Federal Emergency Relief Act brought this idea to fruition. Last, legislation was needed for a broad public works, labor-creating program. This was accomplished by the Civil Works Administration (CWA), the National Recovery Administration (NRA), and the Works Progress Administration (WPA).[21] The hand of Frances Perkins guided the formulation of many of the bills that attempted to meet the immediate needs of the country.

The idea of the Civilian Conservation Corps originated with Franklin Roosevelt. As governor of New York State, Roosevelt had hired 10,000 unemployed men to work on reforestation, and now he wished to enlarge the program to include the entire nation. Frances Perkins and Louis Howe were entrusted with the details. They devised a plan whereby four departments in the executive branch would each have responsibility for a portion of the CCC. The Department of Labor would expand the services of the U.S. Employment Service to recruit men. The army, under the control of the War Department, would run the camps. The Departments of Agriculture and Interior would organize the work projects. Arthur M. Schlesinger, Jr., called the Corps one of the most fortunate of New Deal inventions. Over 2.5 million men enlisted; and of all the forest planting, public and private, in the history of the nation, more than half was done by the Civilian Conservation Corps.[22]

The Civilian Conservation Corps, despite its success, provided relief only to a small segment of the population—unmarried men between the ages of eighteen and twenty-five. There existed an urgent need for direct relief which was consistent with the president's March 21 address to Congress. The Depression in the United States contained the ingredients for revolution. Perkins was among those who recognized this. She saw the necessity for immediate relief measures in order "to see that our brothers should not starve."[23] Harry Hopkins, a former New York State colleague, found a receptive audience in Perkins when he broached his plan to her for immediate appropriation by the federal government of grants-in-aid to the states for unemployment relief. She made an appointment for Hopkins with the president and the result was the establishment of the Federal Emergency Relief Administration (FERA). Perkins considered the FERA "the first step in the economic pump priming that was to break the back of the depression."[24]

The broad public works, labor-creating program put forth by Roosevelt was consistent with the programs that Perkins had long advocated. She felt that a public works program would restore the purchasing power of the individual, which would be the heart of the recovery program.[25] Many, liberals and conservatives alike, felt that although the FERA was successful, a work-relief program was called for as a necessary step in the direction of building self-respect in the individual.[26] The Civil Works Program, later replaced by the Public Works Administration established under Title II of the National Industrial Recovery Act (NIRA), directly attacked the problems of unemployment. Perkins, because of her advocacy of public works, became labor's watchdog over the public works bills passed.

During the first hundred days, Perkins and other cabinet members clamored for consideration of various plans to stimulate the economy. Perkins got wind of two such plans, one developed by Rexford Tugwell and Hugh Johnson, and the other by Senator Robert Wagner and Meyer Jacobstein. She discovered that both plans rested on suspending the effects of the antitrust laws in return for voluntary agreement by industries for fair competition, minimum wage levels, and maximum hours. Perkins and Henry Wallace were instrumental in getting the two groups together.[27] She felt that since wages and hours controls were involved, William Green should be consulted. The result of his inclusion was the addition of Section 7A, which gave labor the right to organize and bargain collectively.[28] All of these considerations were embodied in Title I of the NIRA. During the development of the recovery bill, Roosevelt asked Perkins to see that a public works bill was included in it. Title II of the NIRA was the culmination of the work of her department on behalf of a public works program.[29]

While relief and recovery measures were being enacted to help revive the economy, Perkins and other policy makers of Roosevelt's administration were interested in measures to prevent another depression. Perkins' concern about labor's voice in industry, her distress about unemployment, and the need for old age pensions formed the basis of numerous reform New Deal labor measures. The National Labor Relations Act, the Fair Labor Standards Act (FLSA; also known as the Wage and Hour Law), and the Social Security Act became an integral part of economic life after "the New Deal" became a phrase in the history books.

The most obvious labor development of the New Deal era was the growth of union organization and the expansion of collective bargaining.[30] Perkins saw that a committee representing a group of workers could bargain more effectively with employers about salary and working conditions than an individual representing his own interests.[31] In her concern for the worker's right to organize and to bargain collectively, she supported William Green's efforts to include Section 7A, "labor's Magna Carta," in the National Industrial Recovery Act.[32] Although Perkins did not have a direct hand in the formation of the National Labor Relations Act (NLRA), she was given the task of acting as a watchdog over the National Labor Relations Board (NLRB). The bill was originally formulated to take care of the inequities of Section 7A of the National Industrial Recovery Act. After the Supreme Court declared Title I of the act unconstitutional, the NLRA served to replace Section 7A. Perkins assumed that the administration of the act would be placed in the Department of Labor. Over her protests, a separate agency was created to administer the NLRB. She argued that it would be wise to concentrate in the Department of Labor all problems concerned with labor. The Conciliation Service of the Department of Labor was a growing concern, and this would be the logical place for the NLRB.[33]

Although Frances Perkins warily described the National Labor Relations Act as "very interesting," she feared its effects upon organized labor and the reaction of labor leaders to it.[34] This fear stemmed from the consent-election provision whereby labor unions were asked to prove that they represented the majority of workers. However, after organized labor urged the passage of the bill, Perkins gave it her wholehearted support.[35] The National Labor Relations Act, by encouraging large-scale unionization, became extremely important in the labor history of the United States.[36]

The idea of social insurance had been in Perkins' mind for fifteen years, but implementation of the idea became the major project for the Department of Labor for the two years after 1933.[37] To investigate the possibility of social insurance, the president appointed the Committee on Economic Security with Frances Perkins as its chairman. Perkins felt that the best opportunity for passage of a bill of social insurance was at a time when the economy was beginning to regenerate itself but when memories of the Depression still remained fresh.[38] Although Roosevelt pressed for "cradle to grave" coverage, Perkins felt that it was necessary to get some experience and machinery for the most pressing problems. She stated that "the political climate was not right for such a universal approach."[39] As the Social Security Act finally read, it not only included the social insurance advocated by Perkins, but a relief program embodying old age assistance, assistance for crippled children, assistance for crippled and handicapped persons, and continuation of emergency assistance to the unemployed then in operation.[40] Perkins viewed the Social Security bill as perhaps the "most useful and fundamental single piece of federal legislation in the interest of wage earners in the United States."[41]

The last major New Deal legislation enacted was the Fair Labor Standards Act. Roosevelt feared that workers would not have minimum wage and maximum hours protection if the NRA was declared unconstitutional. Perkins responded to his fears by stating: "I've got two bills which will do everything you and I think important under NRA. I have them locked up in the lower left hand drawer of my desk against an emergency." One of Perkins' bills became the Walsh-Healy Public Contracts Act, passed in 1935, which determined rates and hours on public contracts. The other bill was similar to the Black-Connery bill that had been replaced by the NRA. Even though the groundwork for minimum wage and maximum hours had been laid first by the NRA and then by the Walsh-Healy Public Contracts Act, the passage of New Deal legislation through Congress was becoming more difficult. Opponents of this legislation included not only manufacturers, but conservative officials of the AFL who feared that federal regulation of hours and wages would make it unnecessary for employees to join unions. The Fair Labor Standards Act was introduced May 22, 1937, but it was not passed until June 14, 1938, a far cry from the rapid passage of early New Deal legislation. With the passage of this act the reform movement ended.[42]

In the fall of 1937 employment started to decline again. This downhill trend continued until the winter of 1939, when employment steadily began to rise. Perkins publicly declared that the recession was a "regular adjustment in a period of recovery and that no one was to blame for it."[43] In *The Roosevelt I Knew*, she subsequently placed the blame on Congress and others who followed a policy of retrenchment on public works expenditures.[44] There is no doubt that by 1938 the New Deal began to sputter. The recession of 1937–1938 did not seem to engender the fear that was apparent in the depression years of the early thirties.

Many of the New Deal reforms helped to alleviate some of the suffering of the recession, and the sense of urgency was gone.[45]

Midway through Frances Perkins' tenure in office world events called for an abrupt change in the emphasis of the Department of Labor. Throughout the thirties rumblings of war had been apparent with the aggressive actions of Germany in Europe, Italy in Ethiopia, and Japan in Manchuria. Roosevelt considered Germany's invasion of Poland as the beginning of the war years. Although the United States attempted to avoid physical involvement in the European war, this country found it necessary to provide defense material for our allies, the English. The primary concern of the Department of Labor from 1939 to 1945 centered on production for the war effort. This emphasis on fast and efficient production strained the relationships between labor and industry and between labor and the American public. Now labor, armed with the power to organize and to strike, became a giant—an enfant terrible. Frances Perkins, influential in creating strong unions, was called upon to control the actions of organized labor, and she felt alternately compelled to defend and to admonish.

Under a government sympathetic to the growth of organized labor, union membership grew at a rapid rate after 1933. This increase in unionization strained labor-management relations. Strikes usually occurred at this time when employers refused to grant full recognition to newly organized unions.[46] In addition, the jurisdictional disputes between the American Federation of Labor and the Congress of Industrial Organizations resulted in strikes. Perkins felt that the split prevented agreements on labor policies, labor legislation, and free interchange of information between labor and the Department of Labor.[47] Many times she called for a truce between the two warring organizations, both in her press releases and in the messages she wrote for the president.[48]

The American public grew increasingly concerned that strikes would seriously hamper defense production. Union support throughout the country, according to a Gallup poll, had slipped from 76 percent in 1936 to 67 percent in 1941.[49] This basis of support was to erode further during the war. The Bureau of Labor Statistics announced that strikes during the first seven months of 1941 cost 15,750,000 man days, five times more than in the corresponding period of the year before and 44 percent above the average during the corresponding months of the five-year period from 1935 through 1939.[50] Congressional efforts to pass antistrike legislation met resistance from the Roosevelt administration. In Perkins' opinion the right to strike should not have been abridged under any circumstances. She felt that the mediation and conciliation machinery of the federal government could settle industrial disputes.[51] The continued rise in the number of strikes culminated in the first anti-labor measure approved by the House and Senate in a generation. The War Labor Disputes Act (Smith-Connally bill) passed Congress in 1943 over the veto of President Roosevelt. Essentially, the bill gave the president the power to take over plants, mines, and other means of production if the war effort was impeded or delayed by such interruptions.[52]

With the increase of tension in the country over strikes in the vital industries of coal and steel, Frances Perkins felt compelled to act as a defender for the unions. In order to provide a forum for labor and management to meet, she persuaded the president to create the National Defense Mediation Board. She hoped that an agency that facilitated discussion between organized labor, management, and government could avert harmful strikes in defense industries.[53] Organized labor made a no-strike pledge for the duration of the war that was kept at the rate of 99 percent. Perkins believed that increase in war production was linked to the unions' observance of the no-strike pledge.[54]

Frances Perkins admonished organized labor on several occasions to refrain from striking and thereby upsetting the defense effort. In her annual report for 1941, she warned organized labor that they faced government regulations unless they abandoned excessive methods of picketing, boycotts, and stoppages of work due to jurisdictional disputes. Perkins pointed out that organized labor faced the possibility of government regulations like other American insititutions unless they adopted sound, intelligent economic, social, political, and moral practices.[55]

Perkins fought a continuous battle to keep labor-related agencies within the jurisdiction of the Department of Labor. Her first great disappointment came when the National Labor Relations Board was created in 1935 as a separate agency. As new agencies were created during the war she tried to have them incorporated within the Department of Labor, but was often thwarted in this attempt. The U.S. Employment Service, Selective Service, the Mediation Board, and the entire series of disparate federal training programs were not incorporated in the Department of Labor. Perkins' critics felt that the attrition of agencies from the Department of Labor was repudiation by the administration of her ability to administer them.

Since most of her goals had been accomplished during Roosevelt's first two terms, Perkins was willing to resign from office at the beginning of his third term. Demands for Perkins' ouster as a first step toward ending walk-outs and strikes were heard throughout the war.[56] Rumors concerning Roosevelt's plans to replace her and to reorganize the Department of Labor were also heard.[57] Perkins wished to resign after the 1944 election. This time Roosevelt accepted her resignation, to take effect on Inauguration Day. Inauguration Day came, but Roosevelt had not named a successor. When Perkins pressed Roosevelt, who was already exhausted and ill, he begged her to stay. With these words he acknowleged her long years of service with him: "Frances, you have done awful well, I know what you have been through. I know what you have accomplished. Thank you."[58] In reaction to Roosevelt's grateful acknowledgment, she wrote; "It was all the reward that I could ever have asked—to know that he recognized the storms and trials I had faced in developing our program, to know that he appreciated the program and thought well of it, and that he was grateful."[59]

Roosevelt insured Frances Perkins' place in history by appointing her as the first female cabinet member. Perkins and Harold Ickes were the only original cabinet appointees to serve with Roosevelt through his entire administration. Upon the death of Franklin Roosevelt on Friday, April 12, 1945, Perkins submitted her resignation. As one of Roosevelt's "inner cabinet" her mark upon legislation during the New Deal was unmistakable. Roosevelt retained her as a cabinet member during the war years despite her critics because his dependence on her loyalty and honesty transcended his need for a labor troubleshooter during this time.

NOTES

1. Matthew and Hannah Josephson, *Al Smith, Hero of the Cities* (Boston: Houghton Mifflin Co., 1969), p. 342.

2. Frances Perkins, *The Roosevelt I Knew* (New York: Viking Press, 1946), p. 48; *New York Times,* December 27, 1928, pp. 1, 8.

3. *New York Times,* January 13, 1929, pp. 3, 5.

4. *New York Times,* January 15, 1929, p. 20.

5. Perkins, *Roosevelt,* pp. 91–93; Arthur M. Schlesinger, Jr., *The Crisis of the Old Order* (Boston: Houghton Mifflin Co., 1956), p. 391.

6. Frances Perkins, "Unemployment," *The Women's Journal* 15 (November 30, 1930): 9

7. Frances Perkins, *People at Work* (New York: Charles Scribner and Sons, 1912), p. 117.

8. Ibid., p. 120.

9. Perkins, "Unemployment," p. 10.

10. Perkins, *Roosevelt,* pp. 92–93.

11. *New York Times,* December 18, 1932, p. 5.

12. Jerry Klutz and Herbert Asbury, "The Woman Nobody Knows," *Collier's* 114 (August 5, 1944): 50.

13. Perkins, *Roosevelt,* p. 152.

14. Benjamin Stolberg, "Madame Secretary, A Study in Bewilderment," *Saturday Evening Post* 213 (July 27, 1940): 9–14.

15. Harold Ickes, *The Secret Diary of Harold L. Ickes,* 2 vols. (New York: Simon and Schuster, 1954), 2:55–56.

16. Josephson and Josephson, *Al Smith,* p. 410.

17. Ickes, *Secret Diary,* 2:55–56.

18. Perkins, *People at Work,* p. 37.

19. *New York Times,* March 5, 1933, pp. 1, 3; Arthur M. Schlesinger, Jr., *The Coming of the New Deal* (Boston: Houghton Mifflin Co., 1959), pp. 20–21. William E. Leuchtenburg, *Franklin D. Roosevelt and the New Deal* (New York: Harper and Row, 1963), pp. 33, 34, 61; Hubert Humphrey, *The Political Philosophy of the New Deal* (Baton Rouge: Louisiana State University Press, 1970), p. 18; Howard Zinn, ed., *New Deal Thought* (Indianapolis: Bobbs-Merrill Co. 1966), p. xviii.

20. *New York Times,* March 22, 1933, p. 2.

21. Ibid.

22. Schlesinger, *The Coming of the New Deal,* pp. 338–340; Perkins, *Roosevelt,* p. 177; Leuchtenburg, *Franklin Roosevelt and the New Deal,* p. 40.

23. Perkins, *Roosevelt,* p. 182; Schelsinger, *The Coming of the New Deal* p. 275; Perkins, *People at Work,* p. 128.

24. Perkins, *Roosevelt,* pp. 184–185.

25. Perkins, *People at Work,* p. 178.

26. Schlesinger, *The Coming of the New Deal,* p. 275.

27. Perkins, *Roosevelt,* pp. 198–199.

28. Stolberg, "Madame Secretary," p. 79.

29. Perkins, *Roosevelt,* pp. 271–72.

30. Edgar Shor, "The Role of the Secretary of Labor," Ph.D. dissertation, University of Chicago, 1954, quoted in James Russell Anderson, "The New Deal Career of Frances Perkins," Ph.D dissertation, Case-Western Reserve University, 1968, p. 250.

31. Perkins, *People at Work,* pp. 148–149.

32. Perkins, *Roosevelt,* pp. 199–200; Stolberg, "Madame Secretary," p. 79.

33. Perkins, *Roosevelt,* pp. 242–243; *New York Times,* March 13, 1935, p. 12.

34. Schlesinger, *The Coming of the New Deal,* p. 401.

35. Stolberg, "Madame Secretary," p. 65; Perkins, *Roosevelt,* p. 243; C. K. Mc-Farland, *Roosevelt, Lewis and the New Deal, 1933–1940* (Fort Worth: Texas Christian University Press, 1970), pp. 31–32.

36. Perkins, *Roosevelt,* p. 245.

37. Ibid., p. 288.

38. F. Perkins to F. Roosevelt, April 17, 1934, Roosevelt MSS, Franklin D. Roosevelt Library, Hyde Park, N.Y., Official file 121 A, Unemployment Insurance File, quoted in Anderson, "The New Deal Career of Frances Perkins," p. 233.

39. Perkins, *Roosevelt,* pp. 282–283.

40. Zinn, *New Deal Thought,* p. 275; Perkins, *Roosevelt,* p. 287.

41. Zinn, *New Deal Thought,* p. 280.

42. Perkins, *Roosevelt,* p. 249; McFarland, *Roosevelt, Lewis and the New Deal,* pp. 36–37; Perkins, *Roosevelt,* p. 263. FLSA provided for increases from twenty-five to thirty to forty cents hourly over a period of seven years. Maximum hours were set at forty-four, with the provision that they should go to forty-two and then to forty over a three-year period. McFarland, *Roosevelt, Lewis and the New Deal,* p. 114.

43. New York Times, December 23, 1937, p. 4; June 22, 1939, p. 17.

44 Perkins, *Roosevelt,* p. 227.

45. Zinn, *New Deal Thought,* p. xviii.

46. Phillip Taft, *Organized Labor in American History* (New York: Harper and Row, 1964), p. 435.

47. Perkins, *Roosevelt,* p. 310.

48. *New York Times,* January 1, 1938, p. 8; February 26, 1939, p. 1.

49. *New York Times,* June 13, 1941, p. 12.

50. *New York Times,* August 27, 1941, p. 10.

51. *New York Times,* December 28, 1940, p. 6.

52. Taft, *Organized Labor in American History,* p. 557; U.S., *Statutes at Large,* Vol. 57, pt. 1 (1943), "War Labor Disputes Act," 1944, pp. 164–165.

53. Perkins, *Roosevelt,* p. 364; U.S. Department of Labor, *Twenty-Ninth Annual Report of the Secretary of Labor for the Fiscal Year Ended June 30, 1941* (Washington, D.C.: Government Printing Office, 1942), p. 4.

54. Frances Perkins, "Labor's Great War Record," *American Federationist* 50 (December 1943): 17–19.

55. *New York Times,* January 18, 1943, p. 37.

56. *New York Times,* February 26, 1942, p. 11.

57. *New York Times,* November 25, 1940, p. 1; November 27, 1942, p. 1.

58. Perkins, *Roosevelt*, p. 394.
59. Ibid.

BIBLIOGRAPHY

Anderson, James Russell. "The New Deal Career of Frances Perkins." Ph.D. dissertation, Case-Western Reserve University, 1968.

Humphrey, Hubert. *The Political Philosophy of the New Deal*. Baton Rouge: Louisiana State University Press, 1970.

Ickes, Harold. *The Secret Diary of Harold L. Ickes*. 2 vols. New York: Simon and Schuster, 1954.

Josephson, Matthew, and Hannah Josephson. *Al Smith, Hero of the Cities*. Boston: Houghton Mifflin Co., 1969.

Klutz, Jerry, and Herbert Asbury. "The Woman Nobody Knows." *Collier's* 114 (August 5, 1944).

Leuchtenburg, William E. *Franklin D. Roosevelt and the New Deal*. New York: Harper and Row, 1963.

McFarland, C. K. *Roosevelt, Lewis and the New Deal, 1933–1940*. Fort Worth: Texas Christian University Press, 1970.

New York Times, January 13, 1929–November 27, 1942.

Perkins, Frances. "Labor's Great War Record." *American Federationists* 50 (December 1943): 17–19.

———. *People at Work*. New York: Charles Scribner and Sons, 1912.

———. *The Roosevelt I Knew*. New York: Viking Press, 1946.

———. "Unemployment Insurance." *The Survey* 67 (November 1, 1931): 117–19.

Schlesinger, Arthur M., Jr., *The Coming of the New Deal*. Boston: Houghton Mifflin Co., 1959.

———. *The Crisis of the Old Order*. Boston: Houghton Mifflin Co., 1956.

Shor, Edgar. "The Role of the Secretary of Labor." Ph.D. dissertation, University of Chicago, 1954.

Stolberg, Benjamin. "Madam Secretary, A Study in Bewilderment." *Saturday Evening Post* 213 (July 27, 1940): 9–14.

Taft, Philip. *Organized Labor in American History*. New York: Harper and Row, 1964.

U.S. Department of Labor. *Twenty-Ninth Annual Report of the Secretary of Labor for the Fiscal Year Ended June 30, 1941*. Washington, D.C.: Government Printing Office, 1942.

U.S. "War Labor Disputes Act." *Statutes at Large,* 57 (1944), pp. 164–65.

Zinn, Howard, ed. *New Deal Thought*. Indianapolis: Bobbs-Merrill Co., 1966.

23

FDR's Personal Relations with Washington Correspondents during the Rise of Interpretative Journalism

Betty Houchin Winfield

The New Deal era in which Roosevelt interacted with the Washington journalists was also the era of interpretative journalism. Press historian Edwin Emery has called interpretative journalism "the most important press development of the 1930s and 1940s." Objectivity, the ideal of sticking to a factual account of what had been said or done, was now challenged by a new concept of reporting. The news emphasized the "why" and "how" to put the New Deal changes and events into a proper context.[1]

Washington correspondents wrote straight, "objective" news stories as well as interpretative pieces. Many journalists who covered the capital scene also wrote political columns, examining the background, the motivations, and the probable consequences of governmental acts. This was a golden era for interpretative columnists.[2] Nor was interpretation confined to newspapers. Author John Gunther's "Inside" books were best sellers. News magazines like *Time* and *Newsweek,* entirely interpretative, grew in circulation.

FDR wanted public understanding and support for his new programs and, recognizing the need to educate the American public, used newspapers as his major vehicles. As the public wanted to know about the vast governmental changes taking place, the correspondents had to have background information and explanations for their news stories and columns.

The journalist and the president had to get along with each other as well as possible, for they needed each other in order to perform their jobs. While it would be impossible to make a strict causal relationship between interpretative journalism and FDR's personal relations with reporters and columnists, these conditions do raise several questions:

1. How did FDR respond to interpretative journalism?
2. What were some of those personal relationships between FDR and the correspondents?
3. Was there any connection between the personal relations and interpretative journalism?

Franklin D. Roosevelt wanted a press channel for his viewpoint. Just before his first press conference, FDR's soon-to-be press secretary, Steve Early, confided to correspondent Raymond Clapper that he and the president wished ''to make the White House assignment an important one and not a watchdog affair.''[3]

Yet, even as Roosevelt acknowledged interpretative journalism and said that the press associations had got away from it pretty well, he lamented that most individual papers were demanding interpretative stories. The day after the Democratic party's smashing congressional victory in 1934, Roosevelt and the correspondents had a lively exchange over the conflict. The president said: ''It must be hell to have to interpret. It was a mistake for newspapers to go over into that field in news stories.'' They were losing the public confidence in the news. FDR stressed, give them the facts and nothing else.[4]

When Marvin McIntyre suggested that the president give the boys a few more leads, Roosevelt retorted: ''By God, I give them all the leads I can think of. I don't want to get into the dissertation stage.'' When a correspondent noted, ''Of course, Mr. President, our job is always finding out what you are going to do,'' FDR answered, ''about two-thirds of the time I do not know.''[5]

While Roosevelt might say that he did not know what he was going to do, the correspondents continued to discuss his options. And Roosevelt did his part. He had numerous background sessions on the budget and new programs. He planned the press conference explanations carefully, and he interacted personally with the Washington correspondents.

Roosevelt's friendly relationship with the press was not merely contrived. Members of his family and some of his closest friends were journalists. His wife Eleanor was a newspaper columnist and newspaper guild member. His only daughter Anna married *Chicago Tribune* correspondent John Boettiger. They both held editorial positions on the *Seattle Post-Intelligencer* after 1936. Old newspaper friends were on the White House secretarial staff: Louis Howe, Marvin McIntyre, William Hassett, and press secretary Steve Early.[6]

Also, Roosevelt enjoyed his ''beloved wolves'' at the press conference meetings; there was a climate of congeniality during this era. FDR and the correspondents had a clublike atmosphere at the press conferences; it was a place to have fun and see the president and other journalists. As the correspondents filed into Roosevelt's office, he teased the newsmen with the camaraderie of someone who knew their lifestyles and secrets. With the president's friendly encouragement, they kept up a repartee about the journalists' baseball team, their clothes, and their late night activities.[7]

Roosevelt's press conference humor could in a subtle way stop the flow of information and potential interpretation. The dunce hat was one well-known example. At his June 29, 1937, press conference, in a reference to a dunce hat, the president stopped the persistent questioning of *New York Times* reporter Bob Post about a possible third term.[8] Until the 1940 Democratic National Convention, whenever there was a third term query, FDR and the correspondents would refer to the dunce hat club.[9]

The president's relations with the Washington correspondents extended beyond the press conferences. Whenever a death or illness occurred in a reporter's family, the Roosevelts sent flowers and Mrs. Roosevelt would make a personal call.[10] And FDR would give letters of introduction to newly assigned correspondents.[11] For example, when the *New York Times* sent Charles Hurd to the *Times'* London bureau in 1937, the president gave the correspondent letters of introduction and invited the Hurds for tea to discuss the political and living situations. The Hurds kept FDR's letters of introduction as souvenirs. Several months later Hurd was admonished by the gruff Scottish telephone voice of British Labour party leader Arthur Murray, who rasped: "Hurd, this is Murray. Where the hell have you been? Franklin has written three times asking about you."[12]

The president held annual parties for all Washington correspondents and their spouses or sweethearts.[13] Rather than following the Hoover tradition of merely mingling, he invited journalists to state dinners, receptions, and other important White House functions as guests. Hurd remembered they were made to feel like friends, like equals, like statemen.[14]

The president attended the press functions, too: the National Press Club dinners and the White House Correspondents' Association banquets and the functions of the Gridiron, a select group of one hundred male Washington correspondents.[15] FDR openly complained about the Gridiron's forceful needling in the skits and the formality of a white tie dinner requirement and would refer to the group as the "stuffed, oops . . . I mean stiff shirt club."[16]

Rather than the Gridiron's formality and needling, the president preferred a playful club where he could relax in the frolic. A prime example was the J. Russell Young School of Expression, named after well-known Civilian Conservation Corps (CCC) and service club speaker and beloved elderly correspondent J. Russell Young.[17] The initiates had to prove that they too could earn "the silver tongue" with their speeches.[18] The president enjoyed being a graduate and having as the student body regularly assigned White House press corps members and "carefully screened outsiders." They held annual dinner convocations, complete with a daisy chain parade, class songs, reunions, a tree planting, and "try-outs" for diplomas.[19]

Attending the school of expression was an inside group, a small elite of reporters, numbering from eight to thirty-one, who covered the White House at all times. These insiders, representing the wire services and high circulation newspapers, followed the president on trips and usually spent eight to ten hours a day in their own White House quarters.[20] FDR called them by their first names, knew their little jokes, even swam and picnicked with them.[21] Two, Ernest K. Lindley *(New York Herald-Tribune* and later the *Washington Post)* and Frederick A. Storm (United Press), and their wives celebrated the Christmas Day evening meal with the Roosevelts.[22]

These White House intimates were often invited along with dignitaries to small, informal Sunday suppers, a tradition carried over from the president's Albany days. The journalists and others were made to feel like neighbors invited in for potluck. Mrs. Roosevelt scrambled eggs, and daughter Anna would see that everyone had enough to eat.[23]

Besides camaraderie, these early informal functions were valuable to reporters, as the president launched into anecdotes and stories that gave them background on the events of the day.[24] *Times* correspondent Hurd recalled that the no-direct-quotes but background-only pieces made up a large part of the dispatches. Hurd said, "Covering Roosevelt was somewhat like being assigned to the City Hospital; one never knew when something important would turn up. We always had to count on the unexpected and prepare for it."[25]

Informal functions gave the correspondents an unofficial press conference. For example, when FDR vacationed at Campobello Island, June 30, 1933, during the London Economic Conference, he gave the journalists a clear forecast of a "bombshell message" as he played cut-in bridge. Hurd recalled that

the President pushed back his wheel chair. Out came tumbling all of Roosevelt's resentment against the debtor nations' refusal to pay their obligations . . . and out came his firm statement that this was not the time for currency stabilization.

This was a major story. Although the president labeled the evening "off the record," FDR obviously wanted the story released without attribution to himself. When asked how to attribute the story, Roosevelt said: "How you handle anything you write is up to you. But isn't a Campobello dateline a pretty good hedge?"[26]

Together the correspondents reconstructed the account. When Hurd's dispatch appeared on the *Times* front page the next morning, the lead sentence read, "President Roosevelt will not obligate the United States at this time to any form of stabilization of the dollar, it was learned on high authority."[27] Within twenty-four hours, unofficially spoken words helped doom an international conference. The president had taken no formal action and had issued no formal statement. The correspondents issued the story his way, with his interpretation.

Charles Hurd wrote that these "little White Houses" became a special force in the conduct of the president's office. Away from his official residence, the "trial balloon" could be used with the cooperation of the press for actions that would be awkward or impossible within the limits of Washington's more formal procedure.[28]

Even with the inside group, the formal procedure meant following outwardly a policy of no exclusive interviews.[29] All questions were to be taken care of at the press conference.[30] Both Early and Roosevelt said they remembered Hoover's difficulties that came out of playing favorites. Nevertheless, bits of information, sometimes in exclusive form, were quietly given to reporters for interpretation—given to those reporters with whom Roosevelt had a close relationship.[31]

Columnist Raymond Clapper was one of those reporters. He sometimes served as a conduit for the president.[32] For example, Press Secretary Early once asked Clapper to do an article on Joe Davies, who was greatly disappointed when he was not named ambassador to England in 1937.[33] At his press briefing, Early praised Clapper's column as accurately representing the attitude of the administration.[34]

Washington columnists Joseph Alsop and Robert Kinter, "The Capital Parade," also received exclusive information. Their 1940 foreign policy monograph, *The American White Paper,* had the help of the White House and was contigent upon the approval of the president.[35] After three drafts, Secretary Early reported to FDR that "by correcting, eliminating and inserting, Joe Alsop has much improved his previous drafts and has given the final manuscript a fairer and much better balance."[36] The president's effort fooled at least one reviewer. Professor R. B. Mowat stressed in *The Fortnightly,* "This is not an official, white paper, but the work of two young Washington journalists who are obviously extremely well-informed and who have made a careful documentation of Mr. Roosevelt's policy."[37]

New York Times columnist Anne O'Hare McCormick had yearly "background conversations" with the president. FDR would set forth his philosophy to Mrs. McCormick during "tea and comprehensive talks."[38] During the New Deal era, she wrote, without quotations, what the president "foresees," "feels," and "thinks."[39] Her skill and revealing interviews won her the 1937 Pulitzer Prize for her general correspondence.

New York Times bureau chief Arthur Krock referred to McCormick's methods in a February 1937 exclusive interview request.[40] Roosevelt granted the interview, a channel he might have needed during the Supreme Court packing plan furor. Both Press Secretary Steve Early and Assistant Press Secretary William Hassett edited the article. Early wrote, "I have taken the liberty of making a few pencilled notations and also suggesting two insets and an "add." "[41] Krock incorporated the insets and adds into the *New York Times* front-page article, published on February 28, 1937.[42]

Although the Washington correspondents had not openly complained about the New York-based McCormick background sessions, they were most upset about Washington-based Krock's exclusive interview. The journalists vented their anger.[43] At the press conference two days later, Fred Essary of the *Baltimore Sun* immediately brought up the topic of favoritism. Roosevelt answered: "Fred, off the record, Steve laid his head on the block and so did I. It won't happen again."[44]

And it did not happen again, at least with the Washington-based correspondents. McCormick continued her yearly "conversation" with FDR. Yet, White House correspondents, competing with each other and "under the gun" from their editors, did not have any further exclusive interviews with the president.[45]

Roosevelt continued to use D.C. outsiders like George Creel, World War I chairman of the Committee on Public Information, as helpmates. Creel not only interviewed FDR for pro-Roosevelt articles for *Collier's Magazine* but allowed the president to dictate the exact wording for articles in 1933, 1935, and 1936.[46] FDR's ability to give his viewpoint directly to the country's second largest circulation magazine gave him yet another informational channel during those days of interpretative journalism.[47]

Roosevelt carefully followed these communication efforts and those of journalists. He read at least six newspapers daily.[48] And he reacted, sometimes with anger, anger especially concerning what he called erroneous budget stories and those personal stories that appeared to have been written from an "insider's" viewpoint.

One such insider who incurred FDR's anger was Ernest K. Lindley, Roosevelt's close friend and biographer.[49] Lindley was a prime example of a journalist who was caught in an era of professional change. Lindley, who said he was writing straight news in those days, recalled being in conflict with the president many times. In the midst of the August 1937 pressures following the Supreme Court Reform bill defeat and the unconfirmed appointment of Hugo Black, Lindley and others interpreted New York boss Ed Flynn's social visit to Hyde Park as proof of FDR's intercession in the heated New York mayoral race. Roosevelt was so furious that he spent forty minutes verbally abusing Lindley at his Hyde Park press conference. Finally, the president said, in reference to interpretative journalism: "Remember Ernest, this has happened before. 'It is reported,' or 'it is assumed.' I appreciate your difficulties but what the hell can you do when there isn't any news." Lindley did not respond.[50]

Roosevelt's most continuing battles over interpretative journalism were with *New York Times* bureau chief Arthur Krock. The *Times* commanded most of the president's early morning newspaper skimming.[51] FDR carefully followed major *Times* columnist and bureau chief Krock,[52] the most influential columnist of the era. Although he helped frame the *Times'* questions, Krock seldom attended Roosevelt's press conferences. When the president asked about his absences, Krock replied: "I lose my objectivity when I'm close to you and watch you in action. You charm me so much that when I go back to write comment on the proceedings, I can't keep it in balance."[53]

By 1934 Krock constantly incurred Roosevelt's wrath over his too detailed accounts, as with the Lewis Douglas resignation as budget director,[54] or his reference to Donald Richberg as "an assistant President,"[55] or his interpretation of the faltering world disarmament conference. The latter so infuriated the president that he complained to *Times* publisher Arthur Ochs.[56]

The fact that the *New York Times* had interpreted was especially onerous. Roosevelt wrote, "The *Times* is so widely accepted because of its general fairness that interpretive articles such as the ones that Mr. Krock writes are accepted as statements of fact."[57] Krock retorted, "I am not conscious of having done any more or less than my duty in what I have written about the administration; certainly there has been no unfriendly motive on my part."[58]

Krock and the president continued using each other. Roosevelt was the foremost news source. And Krock was hungry for information. During an August 1936 Hyde Park visit, Krock listened to FDR outline his "great design" for dissipating the gathering war clouds. Krock informed secretary Missy LeHand that he would report the proposal if it would not be denied. LeHand's return message was that Krock emphasize only "a small committee."[59] Krock had a definite scoop.

After the *Times* page one article appeared, other correspondents insisted that Roosevelt call the article a fabrication. FDR refused to comment. The "trial balloon," a gauge of the direction of the national and international winds, showed little support. Henry Wallace then refuted the story. Krock knew he had been used and was furious.[60] FDR's timing was wrong. The Krock article had been the test. Roosevelt even wrote Ambassador Dodd, "That story by Arthur Krock was not wholly crazy . . . a useful agreement might result."[61]

Krock often accused the administration of more manipulation, ruthlessness, and subtlety in suppressing legitimate information and eliminating sources than any other. Steve Early would retort that Krock's accusations were like the proud mother who stood watching the parade and declared when she saw her son's company passing by, "Everybody is out of step, except my son, John."[62]

Roosevelt continued to react to those journalists who were so independent and so out of step. And in a couple of instances, FDR's response became as well known as a Roosevelt punishment. Best known was the World War II incident involving John O'Donnell of the hostile New York *Daily News*. By 1942 the war was going badly and Roosevelt was under pressure. The *Daily News* remained isolationist. O'Donnell's column, "Capital Stuff," appeared especially critical. The president erupted in exasperation at his December 18, 1942, press conference over O'Donnell's satire on war censorship and handed correspondent Earl Godwin the German Iron Cross to give to the absent O'Donnell as a symbol of his aid to the enemy.[63]

The O'Donnell incident was unusual. For the most part, the president and the journalists had extremely pleasant personal contacts. Roosevelt not only invited the correspondents to his home and gave them inside information, but he charmed them with his jesting and his confidence. The working press tends to judge presidents as men. For the most part, Roosevelt gained their respect as a man.[64]

Good personal relations *can* lead to favorable news stories. Roosevelt discussed the background of many confidential policies in detail before publication. With background information, he could reinforce his own viewpoint, define exactly what was news, and use the press as a conduit. He could easily float a trial balloon and then deny it, as he did with Krock's summit meeting story. His method of personal relations would work if he happened to be the only news source. Roosevelt's methods were useful because no two versions of an event by different observers can be exactly alike, no two judgments about the exact nature of a political controversy are necessarily similar. Political change is usually described in subjective terms, as impressions rather than as analyses.[65]

Arthur Krock saw Roosevelt's numerous small, private hospitalities to the press as a way to gain the reporters' high regard. This would "impel many of them to give him and his plans the best of it when there is a best that can be given without violence to the facts."[66] If a correspondent had been swimming with the president, had dined at his table, had been charmed while playing a hand of bridge, then the reporter would probably be very careful about his choice of words concerning his admired friend, the president.

FDR maintained the lodgelike atmosphere with his en masse press relations. The White House correspondents were an exclusive fraternal club—as clublike as FDR's Hasty Pudding Club at Harvard. Mostly men, white men, the fraternity had the president as its senior member. Indeed, Roosevelt liked to refer to clubs, a fun-loving good club like the J. Russell Young School of Expression, an uncomfortable bad club like the "stiff shirt club."

Like a club, the White House correspondents had a set of rules. Members of this lodgelike organization expected to be treated equally, with no special favors, no exclusive interviews. A dog-eat-dog competition existed among those capital journalists. Roosevelt made their lives a little happier and their work a little easier by using the press conferences for giving information to the group en masse. The correspondents during the New Deal era were under great pressure from their editors to get new information. They were judged day by day by the production rate of their principal rivals.[67] Arthur Krock set the example. He was the formidable rival. When Roosevelt gave him an exclusive interview after submitting the sensational Supreme Court packing bill, it was almost more than the correspondents could stomach. The president realized his "mistake." He did not give any more exclusive interviews to individual White House correspondents.

Franklin D. Roosevelt the man was indeed a foremost publicist. He had remarkable journalistic skills. His personal relations enabled him to use his talents during the change to interpretative journalism. He knew what would make the kind of lively article to fit *Collier's Magazine*. He made sure that a foreign policy paper, the Alsop-Kinter White Paper, was carefully edited. He could release information as a dramatic "bombshell," as with the Campobello article, and point out how to write about the doomed economic conference. Some correspondents wrote for the president with pleasure. For at least part of the time, Clapper, Lindley, Creel, and McCormick functioned as administrative "mouthpieces." FDR had such proficiency that he could even get an unwilling participant like Arthur Krock to float a trial balloon.

Yet, the administration often felt that Arthur Krock was clearly out of step with their desires, as the Steve Early anecdote indicated. Krock tried to give his interpretation even though he knew he would incur the president's wrath. He made an abortive attempt to protect himself when he was given exclusive information, as with the president's peace-seeking efforts. Nevertheless, Krock knew the rules of FDR's game with the press. When he asked for an exclusive interview, he willingly let the press secretary check over the piece.

When the president's warm relations did not work, he had methods of punishment. He complained about inaccuracy and unfairness, as with the Krock and Lindley stories. His most extreme action involved John O'Donnell and the Iron Cross. Yet, this Roosevelt outburst was unusual and dramatic and did not fit the good press relations aspect of the Roosevelt myth. Instead, Franklin D. Roosevelt, the man, usually relied upon his personality and his humor to express his viewpoints, to influence that change in American journalism, that era of interpretative journalism of the 1930s and the 1940s.

NOTES

This chapter is part of a larger study on Franklin D. Roosevelt's news management tactics, *FDR and News: Master Publicist and the Press,* forthcoming.

1. Edwin Emery, *The Press and America* (Englewood Cliffs, N.J.: Prentice-Hall, 1972), p. 562.

2. Leo C. Rosten, *The Washington Correspondents* (New York: Harcourt, Brace and Co., 1937), p. 70. Edward Folliard, *Washington Herald* and *Washington Post,* President of the White House Correspondents Association in 1945, interview at his home in Washington, D.C., June 3, 1976; Richard L. Strout, *Christian Science Monitor* and the *New Republic,* interview at the *Monitor* office in Washington, D.C., June 2, 1976; Robert S. Allen, *Philadelphia Record* and columnist of the "Washington Merry-Go-Round" with Drew Pearson, interview at the National Press Club in Washington, D.C., June 8, 1976.

3. Raymond Clapper to Bob Bender, March 1, 1933, Raymond Clapper Personal File, #8, Letters, 1933, Manuscript Collection, Library of Congress, Washington, D.C. (hereafter cited as LofC).

4. Frankin D. Roosevelt, Press Conference 156, November 7, 1934, *Complete Presidential Press Conferences of Franklin D. Roosevelt,* 25 vols. (New York: Da Capo Press, 1972), 4:166.

5. Ibid., p. 167.

6. See Arthur M. Schlesinger, Jr., *The Age of Roosevelt,* Vol. 2, *The Coming of the New Deal,* p. 15. Louis Howe covered Albany for the *New York Herald* and until his death in 1936 was secretary to the president. Marvin McIntyre had had newspaper experience in Kentucky and had been in public relations for the Navy Department during the Wilson administration and was Roosevelt's appointments secretary. William Hassett had newspaper experience at the *Washington Post,* the Associated Press, and the *Philadelphia Public Ledger* and was appointments secretary after McIntyre's death in 1943. Stephen Early had been with the Associated Press, United Press, and Paramount Newsreel Company as its Washington editor until his appointment as the president's press secretary.

7. Press Conference 115, April 25, 1934, Press Conference 109, March 27, 1934, *Complete Press Conferences,* 3:262.

8. Press Conference 377, June 29, 1937, ibid., 9:466.

9. Press Conference 660, July 12, 1940, ibid., 16:34–35.

10. Charles Hurd, *When the New Deal Was Young and Gay* (New York: Hawthorn Books, 1965), p. 241; Delbert Clark, *Washington Dateline* (New York: Frederick A. Stoh Co., 1941), p. 87.

11. Steve Early to William Bullitt, no date, Box 1, William Bullitt Folder, OF36, Press, Franklin D. Roosevelt Library, Hyde Park, N.Y. (hereafter cited as FDRL). Letter concerned Mr. and Mrs. John O'Donnell (Doris Fleeson) and their trip to France and Germany.

12. Hurd, *When the New Deal Was Young and Gay,* pp. 243, 244. Colonel Arthur Murray was a prominent member of the British Labour party. He served as parliamentary

undersecretary to Sir Edward Grey at the Foreign Ministry and had been an assistant military attaché in Washington D.C., in 1917, 1918, and 1919. See Explanatory Notes in Elliott Roosevelt, ed., *F.D.R.: His Personal Letters,* 4 vols. (New York: Duell, Sloan and Pearce, 1947–1950), 3:198.

13. *Washington Post,* June 4, 1933. Found in Raymond Clapper Reference File 110, Censorship, 1934–1936; Clapper Diary, June 3, 1933, 1933 File, #5, LofC.

14. Hurd, *When the New Deal Was Young and Gay,* p. 241.

15. Leo C. Rosten, "President Roosevelt and the Washington Correspondents," *Public Opinion Quarterly* 1 (January 1937): 40; F. B. Marbut, *News from the Capital: The Story of Washington Reporting* (Carbondale: Southern Illinois Press, 1971), p. 173; Ruth Finney Allen, Interview, Washington, D.C., June 8, 1976; Mrs. Roosevelt entertained the female correspondents and the Gridiron widows at the White House the same evening.

16. A. Merriman Smith, *Thank You, Mr. President* (New York: Harper, 1946), pp. 277–78.

17. Ruth Finney Allen, Interview, Washington, D.C., June 8, 1976. Young was considered an "insider." Note that correspondents in press conferences in 1934 and 1935 tease Young about his inspirational talks to the CCC and the Kiwanis. Press Conference 162, December 4, 1934, *Complete Press Conferences,* 5:259; Press Conference 253, November 26, 1935, ibid., 6:318.

18. Ernest K. Lindley, Interview, Washington, D.C., June 4, 1976.

19. J. Russell Young to Steve Early, April 8, 1941, January 28, 1942; February 6, 1942, January 18, 1945, Early Collection, J. Russell Young Folder, FDRL; Clapper Reference File, 1940 Folder, Box 9, #5, LofC.

20. Hurd, *When the New Deal Was Young and Gay,* p. 266. During World War II only representatives of the three largest press associations, Associated Press, United Press, and International News Service, covered the president's trips, and no advance announcement was given as to departure or destination.

21. Raymond Clapper, "Why Reporters Like Roosevelt," *Review of Reviews* 89 (June 1934): 16.

22. Ernest K. Lindley, Interview, Washington, D.C., June 4, 1976.

23. Kenneth G. Crawford to Betty H. Winfield, May 18, 1976; Hurd, *When the New Deal Was Young and Gay,* p. 211; Henry F. Pringle, "The President" in Don Whapton, ed., *The Roosevelt Omnibus* (New York: A. A. Knopf, 1934), p. 57. After eating, the party would adjourn to the second floor to see a popular movie and the newsreels of the day.

24. John Herrick, "With Reporters at the Summer White House," *Literary Digest* 116 (August 12, 1933): 5. FDR would discuss such topics as the Treasury Department's refinancing program and the Justice Department's plan to curb racketeering and kidnapping.

25. Hurd, *When the New Deal Was Young and Gay,* p. 267. Ruth Finney Allen, Scripps-Howard Newspaper Alliance, Interview at her home, Washington, D.C., June 8, 1976; Lindley, Interview, Washington, D.C., June 4, 1976.

26. Hurd, *When the New Deal Was Young and Gay,* pp. 168–70.

27. Ibid., pp. 170–71. Information was based upon the *New York Times,* July 1, 1933. See also Frank Freidel, *Franklin D. Roosevelt,* Vol. 4 *Launching the New Deal* (Boston: Little, Brown and Co., 1973), p. 480. The Associated Press story that followed attributed the statement directly to the president.

28. Hurd, *When the New Deal Was Young and Gay,* p. 163.

29. Marvin McIntyre Confidential Memorandum to Steve Early, April 3, 1933, OF36, Folder 1933, Box 1, FDRL; M. A. LeHand to Arthur Krock, May 3, 1933, PPF, Box 82, FDRL.

30. Early Memo to J. C. Dunn, State Department, October 5, 1933, OF36, Box 1, FDRL.

31. Grace G. Tully, *F.D.R., My Boss* (New York: Charles Scrubner Sons, 1949), p. 151. Not even White House stationery was allowed. Arthur S. Draper to William McHenry Howe, July 18, 1933; Rudolphe de Zappe to *Literary Digest*, July 14, 1933, OF36, 1933, Box 1, FDRL.

32. Raymond Clapper Diaries, May 15, 1933, Box 5, 1933, Manuscript Collection, LofC. Clapper also asked for and saw a preview of FDR's 1933 Geneva Disarmament message, and Steve Early gave him exclusive background information on the Supreme Court packing proposal. See Diaries, February 2, 1937, Box 8, #1, 1937, LofC.

33. Ibid., December 21, 1937, LofC.

34. Ibid., January 12, 1938, LofC; "Clapper Gives a Truer Picture," Early Memorandum to the President, June 4, 1934, OF36, Press, 1934, Box 1, FDRL.

35. "The Capital Parade" was syndicated by the North American Newspaper Alliance. Alsop was Mrs. Roosevelt's second cousin, and his mother was in the Roosevelt wedding. Alsop and Kinter to Steve Early, February 21, 1940, President's Folder 24, FDRL. Early Memorandum to Franklin D. Roosevelt, March 23, 1940, President's Folder #24, FDRL.

36. Early Memorandum to Franklin D. Roosevelt, March 25, 1940, President's Folder #24, FDRL.

37. R. B. Mowat, "The White Paper," *Fortnightly* 154 (July 1, 1940): 43.

38. Marguerite LeHand telegram to Anne O'Hare McCormick, May 26, 1936, Selected Documents of Anne O'Hare McCormick, FDRL; her column was "Still a Little Left of Center," June 21, 1936, in Anne O'Hare McCormick, *The World at Home, Selections from the Writings of Anne O'Hare McCormick,* ed. Marion Turner Sheehan (New York: A. Knopf, 1956), pp. 278–88; Anne O'Hare McCormick telegram to Marguerite LeHand, July 12, 1937, arranging for talk on July 13, 1937; Anne O'Hare McCormick to Franklin D. Roosevelt, July 28, 1937; Marguerite LeHand telegram to Anne O'Hare McCormick, August 2, 1937, arranging for talk on August 3, 1937, Selected Documents, FDRL. Her article was "An Unchanging Roosevelt Drives On," in McCormick, *The World at Home,* pp. 300–320; Anne O'Hare McCormick to Franklin D. Roosevelt, October 13, 1938, Selected Documents, FDRL; article appeared as "As He Sees Himself," October 16, 1933, in McCormick, *The World at Home,* pp. 311–21.

39. McCormick, *The World at Home,* pp. 183–95.

40. Arthur Krock to Steve Early, February 16, 1937, Early Collection, Krock file, FDRL. Early to Krock, February 16, 1937. Krock had asked for an exclusive interview right after the president was inaugurated. Arthur Krock to Marguerite LeHand, May 2, 1933, PPF, Press, Box 82, FDRL; Marvin McIntyre Conference Memorandum to Steve Early, April 3, 1933, OF36, FDRL.

41. Steve Early to Arthur Krock, February 24, 1937; William Hassett Memorandum to Early, February 24, 1937; Stephen T. Early Papers, Krock file, FDRL.

42. Krock to Early, February 26, 1937, Stephen T. Early Papers, Arthur Krock file, FDRL; *New York Times,* February 28, 1937, p. 1.

43. Arthur Krock to Steve Early, March 1, 1937, Early Papers, Arthur Krock file, FDRL.

44. Press Conference 349, March 2, 1937, *Complete Press Conferences,* 9:190–91.

45. Hurd, *When the New Deal Was Young and Gay,* p. 230, contends that Roosevelt did not have exclusions, and if writers gained exclusive information, they received it from outside sources. This is somewhat puzzling as Hurd was from the *New York Times,* as were Krock and Anne O'Hare McCormick. George Creel became the Washington editor for *Collier's* during Roosevelt's second term, and he no longer received exclusive interviews either.

46. George Creel, *Rebel at Large: Recollections of Fifty Crowded Years* (New York: G. P. Putnam's Sons, 1947), pp. 271–74, 290–93; George Creel, "What Roosevelt Intends to Do," *Collier's Magazine* 91 (March 11, 1933): 7–9, 34, 36; "The Amateur Touch," *Collier's Magazine* 96 (August 3, 1935): 12–13, 34; "Looking Ahead with Roosevelt," *Collier's Magazine* 96 (September 7, 1935): 7–8, 45–46; "Roosevelt's Plan and Purposes," *Collier's Magazine* 98 (December 26, 1936): 7–9, 33, 49.

47. Creel recounted that among the reasons that the White House doors were open to him was because of his connection with *Collier's. Rebel at Large,* p. 295. *Collier's* circulation in 1936 was 2.4 million, just behind *Saturday Evening Post.* N. W. Ayer and Sons, *Directory of Newspapers and Periodicals* (Philadelphia: N. W. Ayer and Sons, 1936), p. 1188.

48. Early wrote that FDR read "about six newspapers, independent and Republican in policy. . . . He receives afternoon newspapers during the office hours of the day and gets the afternoon editions in his room, usually before dinner in the evening." Steve Early to Allen L. Appleton, March 4, 1935, PPD 82, FDRL. See also Tully, *F.D.R. My Boss,* pp. 76–77.

49. Franklin D. Roosevelt Memorandum to Steve Early, October 19, 1939, Early collection, E. K. Lindley folder, #10, plus clipping, FDRL. Once, Ernest K. Lindley's column referred to FDR's pro-English bias right after the repeal of the embargo acts when England and France had declared war on Germany. At Roosevelt's request, Early talked to Lindley, and the correspondent ran a twenty-three inch retraction on November 3. Lindley had been doing a column for the *Washington Post* since 1938 and also worked for *Newsweek.* Clark, in *Washington Dateline,* p. 195, referred to Lindley's dissatisfaction with the anti–New Deal attitude of the *New York Herald-Tribune* where he had previously worked.

50. Press Conference 389, August 9, 1937, *Complete Press Conferences,* 10:109–39.

51. Rosten, *The Washington Correspondents,* p. 94; Freidel, *Franklin D. Roosevelt,* 4:274–75.

52. Elliot Roosevelt, *F.D.R.: His Personal Letters,* Elliot Roosevelt wrote that Krock "was one of the best informal correspondents in Washington." 3:744.

53. Arthur Krock, *Memoirs: Sixty Years on the Firing Line* (New York: Funk and Wagnalls, 1968), p. 180.

54. Ibid., pp. 159–60.

55. Schlesinger, *The Age of Roosevelt,* 2:546. Footnote 5, p. 636, Franklin D. Roosevelt Memorandum to Steve Early, November 3, 1934, FDRL.

56. Franklin D. Roosevelt to Adolph S. Ochs, November 26, 1934, PPF29, FDRL.

57. Ibid.

58. Arthur Krock to Stephen Early, December 26, 1934, Early Papers, Arthur Krock Folder, #9, FDRL.

59. Krock, *Memoirs,* p. 183.

60. Ibid., p. 184; Clapper Diary, September 10, 1936 Folder, LofC. Clapper substantiates the Krock story from Joe Alsop.

61. Franklin Roosevelt to William E. Dodd, January 9, 1937, Elliot Roosevelt, ed., *F.D.R: His Personal Letters,* 3:648–49.

62. Steve Early to Arthur Krock, October 13, 1939, Krock to Early, October 16, 1939, Early to Krock, October 17, 1939, Early Collection, Krock Folder, #9, FDRL.

63. Press Conference 869, December 18, 1942, *The Complete Press Conferences,* 20:307, 309. The press conference transcript includes an addendum with the excerpt of O'Donnell's "Capital Stuff" column, *Washington Times-Herald,* December 16, 1942.

64. Clapper, "Why Reporters Like Roosevelt," p. 16. FDR may have had their sympathy because of his pleas for the forgotten man. Reporters considered themselves among the "underdogs."

65. Leo C. Rosten, "Political Leadership and the Press" in Leonard White, ed., *The Future of Government in the United States* (Chicago: University of Chicago Press, 1948), pp. 91–92.

66. Krock, Speech before the National Republican Club, January 26, 1935.

67. Clark, *Washington Dateline,* p. 24. Clark wrote in 1941 that if the correspondents were "scooped" by a rival, the method to follow was to obtain an official denial; then the correspondents had alibis for the home office. If the correspondent can "quote" the denial, then absolution is his until it happens again. More often than not, the story was likely to be one that the official had rather not see in print. Since technical denials are not considered "dishonorable" and they are not hard to obtain, Clark noted that it is a frequent practice to distort the story while angling for a denial to ensure obtaining one.

FDR

THE MAN, THE MYTH, THE ERA
1882 - 1945
CENTENNIAL CONFERENCE
HOFSTRA UNIVERSITY
MARCH 4 - 6, 1982

President Franklin D. Roosevelt at his Hyde Park Estate on July 4, 1937.
Franklin D. Roosevelt Library • Hyde Park, New York.
Reproduction rights reserved by United Press International.

FRANKLIN D. ROOSEVELT
THE MAN, THE MYTH, THE ERA
1882-1945

HOFSTRA UNIVERSITY
HEMPSTEAD, NEW YORK 11550

Conference Director:
Herbert D. Rosenbaum
Chairman of Conference Committee:
Harold A. Klein
Conference Coordinators:
Natalie Datlof
Alexej Ugrinsky

HOFSTRA UNIVERSITY CONFERENCE COMMITTEE

Bruce Adkinson, Associate Provost
Meyer Barash, Sociology
Herman A. Berliner, Associate Provost
Michael J. D'Innocenzo, History
Bernard J. Firestone, Political Science
Paul F. Harper, Political Science
David Kadane, Law
Mark L. Landis, Political Science
William F. Levantrosser, Political Science

Harvey J. Levin, Economics
Rhoda Nathan, English
Mary Anne Raywid, Foundations of Education
Ronald H. Silverman, Law
Robert Sobel, History/New College
Linton S. Thorn, History
John E. Ullmann, Management
Harold L. Wattel, Economics
Jacob Weissman, Economics

UNIVERSITY CENTER FOR CULTURAL & INTERCULTURAL STUDIES

HOFSTRA UNIVERSITY
HEMPSTEAD, NEW YORK 11550

Joseph G. Astman, Director
University Center for Cultural & Intercultural Studies

COVER DESIGN: George Muller, Hofstra University
                Winner of FDR Poster Contest

FRANKLIN D. ROOSEVELT
THE MAN, THE MYTH, THE ERA
1882-1945

THE GENEROUS PATRONS OF THIS CONFERENCE ARE:

ARA Services, Inc.
Philadelphia, PA

Mary W. Harriman Foundation
New York, NY
William Rich III, Vice President

Hofstra University Political Affairs Club
Mitchell Savader, President

Hofstra University Student Senate
Craig Heller, President

Suozzi, English and Cianciulli, P.C.
Mineola, NY

NATIONAL HONORARY COMMITTEE

John B. Anderson
George R. Ariyoshi
Isaac Asimov
Howard H. Baker, Jr.
Abraham D. Beame
Harry Belafonte
Ralph Bellamy
Jonathan Bingham
James MacGregor Burns
Hugh L. Carey
Jimmy Carter
Winston S. Churchill, M.P.
Harlan Cleveland
Mario Cuomo
Alphonse D'Amato
Margaret Truman Daniel
Bette Davis
John Eisenhower
William R. Emerson
Gerald R. Ford
Douglas Fraser
Frank Freidel
Mark O. Hatfield
Anna Rosenberg Hoffman
Harold M. Ickes
Henry M. Jackson
Jacob K. Javits
Barbara C. Jordan
Vernon Jordan, Jr.
Nancy Landon Kassebaum
Edward M. Kennedy

Lane Kirkland
Louis W. Koenig
Peter Kovler
Joseph P. Lash
David Laventhol
William E. Leuchtenburg
John V. Lindsay
Jan Hendrik Lubbers
Archibald MacLeish
William Manchester
Charles McC. Mathias, Jr.
George McGovern
Patrick Moynihan
Robert M. Morgenthau
Bill Moyers
Edmund S. Muskie
Richard Ottinger
Basil A. Paterson
Claiborne Pell
Esther Peterson
James Reston
James Rowe
Bayard Rustin
Eric Severeid
Arthur Schlesinger, Jr.
William L. Shirer
Adlai E. Stevenson, III
Cyrus Vance
Robert F. Wagner
Sidney R. Yates

COOPERATING INSTITUTIONS AND COLLECTORS

Division of Museum Services
Nassau County Department of Recreation and Parks
Syosset, NY
Edward J. Smits, Director

Eleanor Roosevelt Institute
New York, NY
Justine Wise Polier, Chair

Franklin D. Roosevelt Library and Museum
Hyde Park, NY
William R. Emerson, Director
Marguerite Hubbard, Curator
Frances Seeber, Archivist of Documents

Franklin Delano Roosevelt National Centennial Committee
Chicago, IL
Peter Kovler, President

Franklin D. Roosevelt Warm Springs Memorial Commission
Warm Springs, GA

Nassau County Office of Cultural Development
Roslyn, NY
Marcia E. O'Brien, Director

Nassau Library System
Uniondale, NY
Andrew Geddes, Director

The New York State Franklin D. Roosevelt Centennial Commission*
Arthur M. Schlesinger, Jr., President
Frederica Goodman, Director

The New York Times
New York, NY

Newsweek
New York, NY

Smithsonian Institution
Washington, D.C.
Susan Hamilton, Curator

Suffolk Cooperative Library System
Bellport, NY
Philip Levering, Director

Time
New York, NY

U.S. Merchant Marine Academy
Kings Point, NY

Vincent Pepi & Associates
Melville, NY

Patrick Doherty
Mineola, NY

Jerry Lowell Granat

Edward Novick
White Plains, NY

*For information on continuing events of the Franklin D. Roosevelt Commission contact:

Frederica Goodman, Director
New York State Franklin D. Roosevelt Centennial Commission
4 Burnett Boulevard
Poughkeepsie, NY 12603
(914) 473-8151

FRANKLIN DELANO ROOSEVELT, THE MAN, THE MYTH, THE ERA - 1882-1945

With this conference commemorating the centennial of Franklin D. Roosevelt's birth Hofstra University's Center for Cultural and Intercultural Studies inaugurates its Presidential series, whose intent it is to examine the lives and times of the Chief Executives of the American government.

While such a series might have commenced with the beginnings of the American constitutional experience, it is a happy accident that it starts with the life and times of Roosevelt, the initiator of the present-day relationship between our polity and our society. Our conference is not merely a celebration of the life and work of a famous and powerful man. Universities owe more to society and to scholarship than that. We hope also to present a thoughtful and fair rendering of the many disputed questions and unresolved controversies of the Roosevelt era which have survived until the present day.

Our hope that the Conference would be attended by the Governor of the State of New York, the successor in the office held from 1929 to 1933 by Franklin D. Roosevelt, was fulfilled when the Hon. Hugh M. Carey accepted our invitation to open the conference officially. We are honored to have him in at the launching.

One feature of this meeting is its topical arrangement. We felt constrained not to impose a fixed or pre-designed set of topics on our contributors. Instead, we chose to let interested scholars select their own favorite questions and answers. While we paid a price in incompleteness and possible partiality of questions addressed and omitted, we gained the advantages associated with a more spontaneously determined selection, which we take to be interest and topical currency. At another time, another set of scholars would have chosen to write about questions other than those presented here. We were happy to discover that the work of our twenty-seven authors fell easily and without strain into the eight panels you will find in the program. That approach worked well even when we invited papers on Eleanor Roosevelt. The six scholars' work fits nicely into the two panels devoted to the life and work of the First Lady.

The presence of two writers from abroad calls for mention. Professor David K. Adams of the University of Keele, Newcastle-under-Lyme, England, is a frequent visitor and resident in the U.S. He has written widely on the subject of his choice and other topics. Senior Scientific Assistant Vladimir Pechatnov of the Moscow Institute for the U.S. and Canada at the Academy of Sciences of the USSR, our other guest, is the author of a recent volume in which the subject of his paper here is a feature. He is well-known in the U.S. and has been a visitor, among other places, at the FDR Library at Hyde Park. We welcome them both.

Our second aim was to attract scholars of the first rank whose published works have earned them great reputations for the energy and sagacity of their historical and political analyses. There are many such people and while we called upon a number of these, we discovered that busy lives and heavy work schedules are difficult to reconcile with personal appearances. The participation of Arthur M. Schlesinger, Jr. and Frank B. Freidel, in our Keynote Panel on Friday morning is therefore one of the notable events of the conference. The moderator is Prof. Louis W. Koenig of N.Y.U., himself a distinguished scholar of the American Presidency. A special asset of that meeting will be its aegis: The University's Student Senate accepted the financial responsibility for it, and our Political Affairs Club assumed its general management.

As important as the two first elements was our concern to bring to the conference some of the governmental and intellectual leaders of the time who were in large part responsible for the shape and content of the New Deal itself, and who could share their memories of having worked under Roosevelt and with him. We are fortunate to have six men of consequence with us to constitute our "New Dealers" panel on Thursday evening. The names of some of them were and continue to be household words among those who know and remember recent history. Together with our three faculty members, they promise an interesting evening.

One of the most able eyewitnesses of the Roosevelt era to be present among us is the speaker at the Friday evening banquet. He is Senator Jennings Randolph of West Virginia, one of only two members of Congress from the Roosevelt era. Representative - and former Senator - Claude Pepper from Florida, could not be with us. A man of our own time, Senator Randolph began his legislative career with his election to the House of Representatives, where he remained until 1946, and resumed it in 1958, when he was elected to the U.S. Senate to fill a portion of an unexpired term, and where he still serves with distinction. The title of his talk is "Franklin Roosevelt: Man of Action."

No one who visits Hofstra and the Roosevelt Conference should fail to attend our three gallery exhibits. The generosity of the Directors of the Roosevelt Library and Museum at Hyde Park is responsible for the Filderman Gallery exhibit on the ninth floor of our Library The many items from Hyde Park which include books from their general collection, volumes from FDR's own personal collections, pictures, cartoons, sculptures, and documents from the archives contribute an element of weight and significance to our conference difficult to overestimate. Dr. William Emerson, the Director of the Library, Mrs. Frances Seeber, the Supervising Archivist and Mrs. Marguerite Hubbard, the Curator of the museum, are all respon sible in different, and generous ways for those loans. The arrangements there, including most of the cataloguing, are the work of three creative staff members of the Filderman Gallery: Mrs. Marguerite Regan, Assistant to the Dean for Special Collections, Mrs. Nancy Herb, her Assistant and Mrs. Ann Rubino, Volunteer Assistant.

Roosevelt's significance as a person in popular myth and legend, and as a campaigner and leader in great battles, domestic and foreign is well reflected in the Calkins Gallery exhibit of the private collection of Edward Novick, D.D.S., of White Plains. His offer to lend us a portion of his objects was far and away the most generous and attractive of all of the offers we had. We show it with pleasure and invite you to enjoy it. The glass cases in which it is displayed are on loan from the Division of Museum Services of the Nassau County Department of Recreation and Parks in Syosset. Its Director, Mr. Edward Smits, is among our most loyal alumni.

A timely addition to our event is the exhibit of World War II Propaganda Posters in the Emily Lowe Gallery collected and arranged by the Director, Miss Gail Gelburd. The show is instructive, attractive and interesting. By concentrating on World War II the posters compensate in part, at least, for the relatively low profile of the war in our conference.

Professor Meyer Barash of our Sociology Department was responsible for selecting three leading motion pictures of and about the age of Roosevelt with which to stimulate widesprea interest on this campus in the days prior to the Conference itself.

While this event is primarily a conference on scholars and therefore internal to the life of the University, its subject as well as the manner of presenting it are by way of inviting and involving the community in which we live. Roosevelt was the President of us all and this conference is properly a civic occasion as well as an opportunity for academic study. We believe to have arranged things so that this object will be promoted as well.

Like its predecessors, this conference is the work of many hands, heads and hearts. If we have failed in our attempt to acknowledge our indebtedness to all who have helped, we ask their pardon and thank them herewith. A particular expression of gratitude is owed to Professor Joseph G. Astman, Director of the University Center for Cultural & Intercultural Studies. His steady encouragement, ingenious intervention and helpful leadership enabled us to do our work and make our plans with confidence.

How well this commemoration of Franklin D. Roosevelt's birth will have achieved its various aims must, perforce, be judged by others. We trust that the great subjects about which we will have contended will have been fairly treated, that truth and memory will have been honored, that the just claims of our civic culture will have been served and that the love of learning will have been advanced as well.

Herbert D. Rosenbaum
Professor, Political Science
Director, FDR Conference

Wednesday, March 3, 1982   David Filderman Gallery, Department of Special Collections
                                  Hofstra University Library - 9th floor

Pre-Conference Event   The Hofstra University Alumni College Senate will honor
                                  Mr. George Williams, Class of '39.
8:00 P.M.   Executive Director of the American Judicature Society
                                  Chicago, IL
                                  Address: "Hofstra in the Days of FDR"

                                  Advance Showing of FDR Exhibit
                                  Reception

Thursday, March 4, 1982

9:00 - 11:00 A.M.   Registration David Filderman Gallery
                                                Dept. of Special Collections
                                                Hofstra University Library - 9th Floor

11:00   Greetings from the Hofstra University Community
                                  Prof. Herbert D. Rosenbaum
                                  Director, FDR Conference

                                  Mr. Harold A. Klein
                                  Director, University Relations
                                  Chairman, Conference Committee

                                  Dr. James M. Shuart
                                  President

                                  Opening Remarks:

                                  The Honorable Hugh L. Carey
                                  Governor of the State of New York

                                  Opening Address: Dr. William R. Emerson, Director
                                                     Franklin D. Roosevelt Library
                                                     National Archives and Records Service
                                                     Hyde Park, NY

                                  "Some Musings about an FDR Exhibit"

                                  Opening and Reception

                                  Exhibit: "Franklin D. Roosevelt: The Man, The Myth, The Era"

12:00   Lunch

1:00   PANEL I - FDR THE POLITICIAN   Dining Rooms ABC
                                                                        Student Center
                                  Moderator: Prof. Bernard Bellush
                                             Professor Emeritus of History
                                             The City College/CUNY, New York, NY

                                  "Upton Sinclair and Franklin D. Roosevelt"
                                  Prof. Abraham Blinderman
                                  C.W. Post Center/LIU, Greenvale, NY

Thursday, March 4, 1982 (cont'd.)   Dining Rooms ABC, Student Center

1:00   "Frank Hague and Franklin D. Roosevelt: The Hudson Dictator
                              and the Country Democrat"
                              Prof. John Kincaid
                              North Texas State University, Denton, TX

                              "FDR's First Hurrah: The 'Blue-Eyed Billy' Sheehan Affair"
                              Mr. Nathan Miller
                              Chevy Chase, MD

                              "FDR and the Democratic Party"
                              Vladimir O. Pechatnov, Senior Scientific Assistant
                              Institute for the U.S. and Canada
                              Academy of Sciences of the USSR
                              Moscow, USSR

                              Discussant: Prof. Mark Landis
                                          Dept. of Political Science
                                          Hofstra University

3:00   Coffee Break

3:15   PANEL II - ROOSEVELT'S RESPONSE TO HITLER AND THE
                                        REFUGEE PROBLEM

                              Moderator: Prof. Bernard J. Firestone
                                         Dept. of Political Science
                                         Hofstra University

                              "FDR and Palestine: The Role of Special Agents"
                              Mr. Matthew W. Coulter
                              Carbondale, IL

                              "The Prescience of a Statesman: FDR's Assessment of
                              Adolf Hitler before the World War -- 1933-1941"
                              Prof. William E. Kinsella, Jr.
                              Northern Virginia Community College, Annandale, VA

                              "Franklin D. Roosevelt and Refuge for Victims of Nazism,
                              1933 to 1941"
                              Prof. Sheldon Neuringer
                              Warren Wilson College, Swannanoa, NC

5:00   Opening and Reception   Emily Lowe Gallery

                              Exhibit: "Art and Psychological Warfare: World War II Poster

6:00   Dinner

7:30   Opening and Reception   Calkins Gallery

                              Exhibit: "FDR Memorabilia from the Edward Novick Collection"

                              Special Address: Dr. Edward Novick
                                                White Plains, NY

                              "A Piece of My Life"

Thursday, March 4, 1982 (cont'd.)   Dining Rooms ABC, Student Center

8:30 P.M.   NEW DEALER'S ROUNDTABLE

Prof. Herbert D. Rosenbaum
Conference Director
Dept. of Political Science

Introductions

Mr. Charles F. Brown, LL.B.
Santa Maria, CA
Civilian Conservation Corps (1933 - 1934)
Current: National Association of Civilian Conservation Corps Alumni,
          Regional President, Southwest Region
          Computer Specialist Global Position System with OAO Corp,
          Vandenburg AFB, CA

Dr. Marion Clawson
Washington, D.C.
U.S. Department of Agriculture, Bureau of Agricultural Economics, Washington, D.C. and
    Berkeley, CA (1929-1947)
Current: Author, Editor

Prof. Thomas I. Emerson, LL.D.
Yale Law School
New Haven, CT
NRA (1933-1934), NLRB (1934-1940), Social Security Board (1936-1937), OPA (1941-1945)
Current: Professor of Law, Yale Law School, Author

Mr. Leon H. Keyserling, LL.B.
Washington, D.C.
Secretary and Assistant to U.S. Senator Robert F. Wagner (1933-1937), U.S. Housing
    Authority (1937-1942), Federal Public Housing Authority (1942), National Housing
    Agency (1942-1946), President's Council of Economic Advisors, Vice-Chairman (1946-1949),
    Chairman (1949-1953)
Current: Author and Economist

Mr. James H. Rowe, Jr., LL.B.
Washington, D.C.
National Emergency Council (1934), RFC (1935), Dept. of Labor (1935-1936), Secretary to
    President (1938), Administrative Assistant to the President (1939-1941), Assistant
    Attorney General, Department of Justice (1941-1943)
Current: Private law practice
          Franklin Roosevelt Memorial Commission, Roosevelt-Campobello International Park
          Commission

Mr. Joseph C. Swidler, J.D.
Washington, D.C.
U.S. Department of Interior (1933), Legal Department, TVA (1933-1957), WPB (1942)
Current: Private law practice, Member: National Regulatory Research Institute, Gas Research
          Institute, National Academy Public Administration

Hofstra University Discussants:

Prof. Ronald Silverman   Prof. Robert Sobel   Prof. Jacob Weissman
School of Law   Teaching Fellow   Dept. of Economics
                                New College

Friday, March 5, 1982   John Cranford Adams Playhouse
                                             South Campus

9:00 A.M.   Registration

10:00   Keynote Panel
                            Sponsored by the Hofstra University Political Affairs Club
                            and the Hofstra University Student Senate

                            Greetings: Mitchell Savader
                                        President, Political Affairs Club
                                        Hofstra University

                            THE LEGACY OF FDR

                            Moderator: Prof. Louis W. Koenig
                                       Dept. of Political Science
                                       New York University, New York, NY

                            Professor Frank Freidel

                            Bullitt Professor of American History
                            University of Washington
                            Seattle, WA

                            Professor Arthur M. Schlesinger, Jr.

                            Albert Schweitzer Chair of the Humanities
                            The Graduate Center/CUNY
                            New York, NY
                            Chairman, New York State Franklin Roosevelt
                            Centennial Commission

12:00   Lunch

                            Visit to FDR Exhibits: Calkins Gallery
                                                          Filderman Gallery
                                                          Lowe Gallery

2:00   PANEL III - THE NEW DEAL RE-EXAMINED

                            Moderator: Prof. Michael D'Innocenzo
                                       Dept. of History
                                       Hofstra University

                            "The New Deal and the Vital Center: A Continuing
                            Struggle for Liberalism"
                            Prof. David K. Adams
                            University of Keele, Newcastle-under-Lyme, England

                            "The Paradox of the New Deal: Political Success and
                            Economic Failure"
                            Prof. Raymond S. Franklin
                            Queens College/CUNY, Flushing, NY

Friday, March 5, 1982 (cont'd.)

2:00 P.M.	"The New Deal and the Economic Role of Government" Prof. Daniel R. Fusfeld University of Michigan, Ann Arbor, MI

"Roosevelt, the Brains Trust, and the Origins of the New Deal"
Prof. Eliot A. Rosen
Rutgers University, Newark, NJ

Discussant: Prof. Basil Rauch
                 Professor Emeritus of History
                 Barnard College/Columbia University
                 New York, NY

3:45   Coffee Break

4:00   PANEL IV - FOREIGN POLICY:
                                  FDR'S BREAK WITH ISOLATIONISM

Moderator: Prof. William F. Levantrosser
                 Dept. of Political Science
                 Hofstra University

"The First Link: Toward the End of Isolation"
Mr. Joseph Cardello
West Hempstead, NY

"The Anti-Colonial Views of Franklin D. Roosevelt, 1941-1945"
Prof. John J. Sbrega
Tidewater Community College, Virginia Beach, VA

"Franklin D. Roosevelt and Naval Rearmament, 1932-1938"
Prof. John C. Walter
Smith College, Northampton, MA

Discussant: Dr. Leon C. Martel
                 New York, NY

6:00 P.M.   Cash Bar   Main Dining Room, Student Center, North Campus

7:00   Banquet

Guest of Honor

Honorable Jennings Randolph
United States Senator from West Virginia

U.S. House of Representatives, 1932 - 1946
U.S. Senate, 1958 -

Address

"Franklin Roosevelt: Man of Action"

Friday, March 5, 1982 (cont'd.)   Main Dining Room, Student Center, North Campus

8:30 P.M.   New Deal Musicale

                                       Carmel Ferrer   — Soprano
                                       Maryann Cincinnati   — Mezzo-Soprano
                                       Terrence Moore   — Tenor
                                       Curtis Davenport   — Base

                                       Edgar Dittemore, Ph.D.— Piano
                                                                Director, University Chorus
                                                                Dept. of Music, Hofstra University

9:00   Film   Student Center Theater, North Campus

                                       "Eleanor and Franklin"

                                       Part I — "The Early Years"
                                       Part II — "The Rise to Leadership"

                                       Contributed by the Suffolk Cooperative Library System
                                       Bellport, NY

Saturday, March 6, 1982   Dining Rooms ABC, Student Center, North Campus

8:00 A.M.   Registration

                                      Continental Breakfast

                                      Greetings: Mr. Harold A. Klein
                                                  Director, University Relations
                                                  Chairman, Conference Committee

9:00   PANEL V — FDR AND THE MODERN PRESIDENCY

                                      Moderator: Dr. R. Gordon Hoxie
                                                 President and Chief Executive Officer
                                                 Center for the Study of the Presidency
                                                 New York, NY

                                      "The Franklin D. Roosevelt Presidency,
                                      Louis D. Brandeis and Felix Frankfurter"
                                      Mr. Leonard Baker
                                      Washington, D.C.

                                      "Franklin D. Roosevelt and the Modern
                                      American Presidency"
                                      Prof. Morton J. Frisch
                                      Northern Illinois University, De Kalb, IL

                                      "Franklin D. Roosevelt's Administrative Contributions
                                      to the Presidency"
                                      Prof. A. J. Wann
                                      University of Utah, Salt Lake City, UT

Saturday, March 6, 1982 (cont'd.)   Dining Rooms ABC, Student Center, North Campus

10:45 A.M.   Coffee Break

11:00   PANEL VI - ELEANOR AND FRANKLIN ROOSEVELT AS A TEAM

                               Moderator: Hon. Judge Justine Wise Polier
                                          Chair, Board of Directors
                                          Eleanor Roosevelt Foundation
                                          New York, NY

                               "Some Dimensions of the Role Relationship between
                               Eleanor Roosevelt and Franklin Roosevelt"
                               Dr. Mildred Abramowitz
                               Roslyn, NY

                               "Eleanor Roosevelt and 'My Day': The White House Years"
                               Prof. Maurine Beasley
                               University of Maryland, College Park, MD

                               "The Contributions of Eleanor and Franklin Roosevelt
                               to the Development of International Protection for
                               Human Rights"
                               Prof. M. Glen Johnson
                               Vassar College, Poughkeepsie, NY

12:30   Lunch

                               Visit to FDR Exhibits: Calkins Gallery
                                                          Filderman Gallery
                                                          Lowe Gallery

2:00   PANEL VII - ELEANOR ROOSEVELT AS SOCIAL ACTIVIST

                               Moderator: Mrs. Margaret Partridge
                                          Site Manager
                                          Roosevelt Vanderbilt National Historic Site
                                          Hyde Park, NY

                               "Molly Dewson: The Roosevelts' Aid to the End"
                               Prof. Gloria J. Barron
                               Framingham State College, Framingham, MA

                               "The Character of Social Feminism in the 30's:
                               Eleanor Roosevelt and Her Associates in the New Deal"
                               Prof. Ann Davis
                               Vassar College, Poughkeepsie, NY

                               "Eleanor Roosevelt, Narcissa Cox Vanderlip and
                               The New York State League of Women Voters"
                               Ms. Hilda R. Watrous, Historian
                               League of Women Voters of New York State
                               Liverpool, NY

3:30   Coffee Break

3:45 P.M.   PANEL VIII - INSTITUTIONS AND POLICIES OF THE NEW DEAL

Moderator: Prof. Jacob Weissman
                Dept. of Economics
                Hofstra University

"FDR and the OPA: The Origins and Operation of One
War Agency"
Prof. Geofrey T. Mills
SUNY/Geneseo, Geneseo, NY

"An Examination of the Major Influences on the Content
and Timing of the Social Security Legislation, 1935"
Prof. Lottie Tartell
Hofstra University

"Madame Secretary and Mr. President: Frances Perkins
and Franklin D. Roosevelt"
Prof. Barbara Schindler
University of Oklahoma, Norman, OK

"FDR's Personal Relations with Washington Correspondents
during the Rise of Interpretative Journalism"
Prof. Betty Houchin Winfield
Washington State University, Pullman, WA

6:00   Wine and Cheese Reception

7:00   Film   Multi-Purpose Room
                                                                  Student Center, North Campus

"Eleanor and Franklin" - Part III - "The White House Years"

Contributed by the Suffolk Cooperative Library System
Bellport, NY

GREETINGS

"Have a conference worthy of the man and the programs you are celebrating..."

Richard Demuth

"...I wish you well on your project.."

Prof. Robert A. Divine
University of Texas, Austin

"...Je vous souhaite un vif succès lors de votre grand Conférence... et je
vous prie de croire, Cher Monsieur le Président, à mes sentiments les
meilleurs et les plus dévoués.

Pierre Mendes France
Paris, France

"...and I wish you success with your worthwhile venture"

Prof. Hans Gatzke
History - Yale University

"Best wishes for a successful conference"

Anna Rosenberg Hoffman

"I applaud the meaningful way that Hofstra has chosen to honor an outstanding
American. With all my good wishes for the success of your endeavors."

Lady Bird Johnson

".....Good luck on your conference..."

Joseph P. Lash

"...All good wishes.."

Prof. William E. Leuchtenburg
Columbia University

"...all best wishes for the success of the symposium.."

Prof. Arthus S. Link
Princeton

"...In keeping with FDR's unique ability to inspire hope, I hope a result of
your sessions will be a rekindling of that flame. For as FDR said: 'The only
limit to our realization of tomorrow will be our doubts of today.' With every
good wish for a successful conference and best wishes to you all..."

Warren J. Magnuson (U.S. Senate)

"...Due to Dillon's age (91 years) and poor health he must send his regrets... He
wishes you great success in your comparing notes and in the sharing of personal
recollections... how rich and rewarding all this will be. May it be a truly great
Conference."

Joanne Wirt Meyer
(Mrs. Dillon S. Meyer)

"...my best wishes for this great occasion in the life of the American people"

Prof. Z. Naidenov
Sofia, Bulgaria

"My fondest hopes for a most successful Conference..."

Sylvia Porter

"...I regret not attending...and I hope it will be a memorable occasion."

Robert Nathan

The President sends you his kind regard and best wishes and, again, an expression
of his appreciation for your thoughtfulness in asking him to be a part of the
Conference at Hofstra University.

Gregory J. Newell
Special Assistant to President Reagan

".... I would...like to wish you especially good fortune in the program's certain
success, and I will be most interested in reading...materials from it."

James Roosevelt

"I congratulate you on your efforts and hope you will have a successful Conference.

Franklin D. Roosevelt, Jr.

"I wish you good cheer on the program you've planned for the FDR Centennial"

Vermont Royster
(Wall Street Journal)

".... My schedule does not allow me to attend. Best wishes for a successful
discussion."

Bayard Rustin

" With all good wishes for a successful Conference "

Walter S. Salant
Senior Fellow Emeritus
Brookings Institution

"I wish for you a most successful Conference.

Elmer B. Staats

"I hope your Conference on Franklin Delano Roosevelt is a great success. His
friendship meant so much to Britain during the darl years of World War II. The
Queen greatly appreciated your kind invitation to become a member of the Conference
Honorary Committee."

Philip Thompson
Private Secretary to the Queen, Windsor Castle

CREDIT for the success of the Conference goes to more people than can be named on
     this program, but those below deserve a special vote of thanks:

HOFSTRA UNIVERSITY OFFICERS: James M. Shuart, President
                              Sanford S. Hammer, Acting Provost
                              Robert C. Vogt, Dean, HCLAS
                              Peter D'Albert, Special Assistant to the President

ARA Slater: Harry Martin, Director, Dining Services
             Jackie Baxter, Banquet Manager

CALKINS GALLERY: Donald Booth, Director

DAVID FILDERMAN GALLERY: Department of Special Collections
                          Marguerite Regan, Assistant to the Dean of Library Services
                          Nancy Herb
                          Anne Rubino

DEPARTMENT OF FINE ARTS: James J. Gaboda, Chairman
                          Beverly Zakharian, Instructor

DEPARTMENT OF MUSIC: Albert Tepper, Chairman
                      Edgar Dittemore
                      Raymond Vun Kannon

DEPARTMENT OF POLITICAL SCIENCE: Paul F. Harper, Chairman
                                  Marilyn Shepherd, Senior Executive Secretary

EMILY LOWE GALLERY: Gail Gelburd, Director

HOFSTRA UNIVERSITY LIBRARY: Charles R. Andrews, Dean

OFFICE OF THE SECRETARY: Robert D. Noble, Secretary
                          Frances B. Jacobsen, Assistant to the Secretary
                          Stella Sinicki, Supervisor, Special Secretarial Services

                          Jack Ruegamer, Graphic Artist
                          Doris Brown & Staff

OFFICE OF UNIV. RELATIONS: James Merritt, Asst. Director
                            Eve Glasser, Editor/Writer
                            M.F. Klerk, Admin. Asst.

TECHNICAL AND MEDIA SERVICES: Albert Nowicki & Staff

HOFSTRA UNIVERSITY POLITICAL AFFAIRS CLUB

Mitchell Savader, President
Constantine Sirigos, Vice-President
Robert Roday, Treasurer
Paul Siegle, Secretary
Connie Fratianni, Co-op

Bryan Rothenberg   Stephen Weddell
Pamela Stevens   Scott Olds
Martin Azarian   Beth Ritter
Lisa Nasoff   Bill Docalovich
Dawn Guarini   Kathy Stuart
Richard Schulsohn   Jon Kaimen
Cathy Cahill   Therese Chorun
Maria Gagliardo   Sandy Mullin
Robert Baer   John Trotta

UNIVERSITY CENTER FOR CULTURAL & INTERCULTURAL STUDIES

HOFSTRA UNIVERSITY
HEMPSTEAD, NEW YORK 11550

STAFF: Marilyn Seidman, Conference Secretary
         Conference Assistants: Kai Karttunen
                                 Nel Panzeca
                                 Stuart Weber

CONFERENCES AT HOFSTRA UNIVERSITY

George Sand Centennial - November 1976	Vol. I - available
Heinrich von Kleist Bicentennial - November 1977	Vol. II - available
The Chinese Woman - December 1977	
George Sand: Her Life, Her Works, Her Influence - April 1978	Vol. III - 1982
William Cullen Bryant and His America - October 1978	Vol. IV - 1982
The Trotsky-Stalin Conflict and Russia in the 1920's - March 1979	Vol. V
Albert Einstein Centennial - November 1979	Vol. VI
Renaissance Venice Symposium - March 1980	Vol. VII
Sean O'Casey - March 1980	
Walt Whitman - April 1980	Vol. VIII
Nineteenth Century Women Writers - November 1980	Vol. IX
Fedor Dostoevski - April 1981	Vol. X
Gotthold Ephraim Lessing - November 1981	Vol. XI
Franklin Delano Roosevelt: The Man, The Myth, The Era - March 4-6, 1982	Vol. XII
Johann Wolfgang von Goethe - April 1-3, 1982	Vol. XIII
Twentieth Century Women Writers - November 4-7, 1982	Vol. XIV
Harry S. Truman: The Man from Missouri - April 14-16, 1983	Vol. XV
Romanticism in the Old and the New World - Celebrating Washington Irving, Stendhal, and Vasilii Andreevich Zhukovskii -- 1783 - 1983 -- October 13-16	Vol. XVI
Espectador Universal: Jose Ortega y Gasset - November 10-12, 1983	Vol. XVII
Dwight D. Eisenhower - March 1984	Vol. XVIII
George Orwell - October 1984	Vol. XIX
Eighteenth Century Women Writers - November 1984	Vol. XX

"Calls for Papers" -- available upon request

Name Index

Subject Index

About the Contributors

DAVID K. ADAMS is Professor of American Studies and Director of the David Bruce Centre for American Studies at the University of Keele in the U.K. With principal research interests in the area of the New Deal and in twentieth-century U.S. foreign policy, he is the author of *America in the Twentieth Century*, *An Atlas of North American Affairs*, *Franklin D. Roosevelt and the New Deal*, and editor of *British Foreign Office Documents from the Confidential Prints*. He is also chairman of British-American Associates of London.

LEONARD BAKER won the 1979 Pulitzer Prize for Biography for *Day of Sorrow and Pain: Leo Baeck and the Berlin Jews*. Another of his biographies, *John Marshall: A Life in Law*, was described by *Newsweek* as "an impressive achievement . . . may well be the definitive work." Mr. Baker is also the author of five other earlier books, among them *Back to Back: The Duel Between FDR and the Supreme Court* ("worldly, savory, and altogether delightful—*American Historical Review*).   Born in Pittsburgh in 1931, Baker was educated at the University of Pittsburgh and at Columbia University. He was a reporter for the *St. Louis Globe-Democrat* and for *Newsday*. He is also the author of *Roosevelt and Pearl Harbor*, and *The Johnson Eclipse*. He died November 1984.

GLORIA J. BARRON is Professor of History at Framingham State College in Massachusetts, where she was formerly Chairman of the History Department. Her specialties are American political and diplomatic history. She has been concerned primarily with twentieth-century developments and particularly with the administration of Franklin D. Roosevelt. She is the author of *Leadership in Crisis: FDR and the Path to Intervention*, which focuses on presidential diplomatic initiatives and leadership of public opinion from 1939 through 1941.

MAURINE BEASLEY is Associate Professor of Journalism at the University of Maryland, College Park. She is a former staff writer for the *Washington Post* and holds a Ph.D. in American civilization from George Washington University. She is the editor of *The White House Press Conferences of Eleanor Roosevelt* and the author of *Eleanor Roosevelt and the Media: A Public Quest for Self-Fulfillment*.

JOSEPH CARDELLO is currently Executive Director of the Long Island Political Action Committee. He was Assistant Professor of History at Hofstra University from 1973 to 1980, and then worked as speech writer and issues advisor to Congressman Thomas J. Downey. He maintains an active research interest in American history from the New Deal to the present. This is his first publication in a scholarly format.

MATTHEW W. COULTER is Instructor of History and Political Science at Hibbing Community College in Hibbing, Minnesota. He has delivered several conference papers on twentieth-century international politics and previously published an article on the Franklin D. Roosevelt administration which appeared in *Mid-America*.

ANN DAVIS is an Assistant Professor of Economics at Marist College in Poughkeepsie, New York, where she has served for six years, following appointments at Vassar College and the University of Massachusetts in Boston. She has participated in numerous conferences and seminars on Eleanor Roosevelt. Her current research is in the area of women's labor force participation and the influence of means tested programs and labor market conditions. She resides in Poughkeepsie with her husband and two children.

RAYMOND S. FRANKLIN is Professor of Economics and Director of Labor Studies at Queens College and Professor of Sociology at the Graduate Center, CUNY. He is coauthor of *Political Economy of Racism* and author of *American Capitalism: Two Visions*. His current work is concerned with affluent workers and the limits of liberal growth strategies.

FRANK FREIDEL is an acknowledged leader among American historians and the author, editor, coauthor, and coeditor of many books, series, and articles. Foremost among his many works are the four masterly volumes of the yet-to-be-completed biography of Franklin Delano Roosevelt, many standard works of narrative and interpretive history, and works of reference, such as the *Official Papers of Presidents Roosevelt, Truman, Eisenhower, Kennedy and Johnson*.

   Dr. Freidel has taught History at Shurtleff College at Alton, Illinois, in 1941, and has held positions at the University of Maryland, Pennsylvania State University, Vassar College, the University of Illinois, Stanford University, and

Oxford University. Since 1955 he has been at Harvard University, where he became the Charles Warren Professor of American History in 1972.

He has been accorded honorary degrees at Oxford, Harvard, and Roosevelt University and has served as president of the Organization of American Historians, of the New England Historical Association, and the New England History Teachers Association.

MORTON J. FRISCH is Professor of Political Science at Northern Illinois University and has served as Fulbright Professor of Political Science at the University of Stockholm and Senior Scholar in Residence at the White Burkett Miller Center of Public Affairs at the University of Virginia. He is author of *Franklin D. Roosevelt: The Contribution of the New Deal to American Political Thought and Practice*, editor of the *Selected Writings and Speeches of Alexander Hamilton*, and coeditor of *American Political Thought: The Philosophic Dimension of American Statesmanship*.

DANIEL R. FUSFELD is Professor of Economics at the University of Michigan. He is the author of *The Economic Thought of Franklin D. Roosevelt and the Origins of the New Deal*. His more recent works include *The Age of the Economist, Economics: Principles of Political Economy*, and *The Political Economy of the Urban Ghetto* (with Timothy Bates).

JOHN KINCAID is Associate Professor of Political Science at North Texas State University and editor of *Publius: The Journal of Federalism*. He is currently on leave, serving as Director of Research of the U.S. Advisory Commission on Intergovernmental Relations. He is the editor of *Political Culture, Public Policy, and the American States* and has written extensively on federalism and intergovernmental relations and aspects of political theory.

WILLIAM E. KINSELLA, JR., is Professor of History at Northern Virginia Community College, and previously held appointments at John Carroll University and Georgetown University. He is the author of *Leadership in Isolation: FDR and the Origins of the Second World War*.

NATHAN MILLER is a Washington writer and author of several books including, *F. D. R.: An Intimate History* and *The Roosevelt Chronicle*, a history of all branches of the Roosevelt family. His most recent book is *Secret Warriors: The Hidden History of American Espionage*.

GEOFREY T. MILLS is Assistant Dean, School of Business, University of Northern Iowa in Cedar Falls. He is the author of a doctoral dissertation titled *The Political Economy of Price Administration, 1941–1946*, and has written widely on the OPA and has made presentations to many scholarly panels on this and related subjects. He has taught Economics and Finance at the State University of New York in Geneseo, at St. Bonaventure, and at the University of Illinois.

SHELDON NEURINGER is a member of the Department of History and Political Science at Warren Wilson College, Swannanoa, N.C. His principal scholarly interests are in the fields of ethnicity, immigration policy, and Holocaust studies. He is the author of *American Jewry and United States Immigration Policy, 1881 to 1952*.

VLADIMIR O. PECHATNOV is a Professor at the Academy of Sciences of the USSR, and a student of American political life in the Institute of the U.S.A. and Canada, in Moscow. He has been a researcher at the FDR Library in Hyde Park, New York, and has twice attended the Presidential Conferences at Hofstra University.

ELLIOT A. ROSEN is Professor of History at Rutgers, the State University of New Jersey, Newark. He assisted Raymond Moley in the preparation of *The First New Deal*, a study of the Moley-Roosevelt relationship in the creation of the New Deal, and he is the author of *Hoover, Roosevelt, and the Brain Trust*. Currently, as the recipient of a National Endowment for the Humanities fellowship, he is undertaking a study of the New Deal and its opposition.

JOHN J. SBREGA is Assistant Dean of Academic Affairs at the Community College of Rhode Island. His principal research interest lies in Anglo-American diplomacy during the war against Japan. He has written extensively in professional journals. In addition, he is the author of *Anglo-American Relations and Colonialism in East Aisa, 1941–1945*, editor of *The War Aganist Japan: An Annotated Bibliography*, and coeditor of *The American Experience: Documents and Notes*.

BARBARA SCHINDLER, Ph.D., is Executive Director of the Democratic party of Oklahoma. She has studied and written extensively about Franklin Roosevelt and was a recipient in 1986 of a National Endowment for the Humanities fellowship to study the Roosevelt era. Her current interests and research deal with campaign management and election strategies. In conjunction with her employment, she is a frequent guest lecturer at universities, partisan political organizations, labor union meetings, and churches.

LOTTIE TARTELL has been Adjunct Associate Professor, Department of Economics, Hofstra University, for twenty-three years, and was a member of the faculty of the Academy of Aeronautics for several years. Her specialization is in Consumer Economics with primary interest in the role of government in consumer affairs.

JOHN C. WALTER is Associate Professor of Afro-American Studies and American History at Smith College. He concentrates mostly on modern American history and has published numerous papers on the New Deal and on the Jazz Age. His articles have appeared in *Franklin D. Roosevelt, His Life and Times: An Encyclopedic View* (1985) and *The Chiefs of Naval Operations* (1980). He has recently completed a book-length manuscript on the politics of Tammany, 1920–1970.

A. J. WANN is Professor of Political Science at the University of Utah, where he was Chairman of the Department of Political Science, 1968–1974. He was previously a faculty member at Ohio State University, the University of Illinois, and the University of Wisconsin. A longtime student of the American presidency, he is author of *The President as Chief Administrator* and coauthor of *The Philosophy and Policies of Woodrow Wilson*.

BETTY HOUCHIN WINFIELD is an Associate Professor of Communications at Washington State University. She is author of *FDR: Master Publicist and the News Media* (forthcoming), and coauthor of *The Edward R. Murrow Heritage: A Challenge for the Future* and articles on news source dependency and presidential news management.

About the Editors

HERBERT D. ROSENBAUM is Professor of Political Science at Hofstra University, and was formerly Chairman of the Political Science Department there. He is the author of *A First Book in Politics and Government* (1972).

ELIZABETH BARTELME is Star Adjunct Professor of English at Hofstra University. She was formerly Senior Editor at Macmillan and Doubleday in New York.

Hofstra University's
Cultural and Intercultural Studies
Coordinating Editor, Alexej Ugrinsky

Walt Whitman: Here and Now
(*Editor: Joann P. Krieg*)

Harry S. Truman: The Man from Independence
(*Editor: William F. Levantrosser*)

Nineteenth-Century Women Writers of the English-Speaking World
(*Editor: Rhoda B. Nathan*)

Lessing and the Enlightenment
(*Editor: Alexej Ugrinsky*)

Dostoevski and the Human Condition After a Century
(*Editors: Alexej Ugrinsky, Frank S. Lambasa, and Valija K. Ozolins*)

The Old and New World Romanticism of Washington Irving
(*Editor: Stanley Brodwin*)

Einstein and the Humanities
(*Editor: Dennis P. Ryan*)

Women as Mediatrix
(*Editor: Avriel Goldberger*)

Dwight D. Eisenhower: Soldier, President, Statesman
(*Editor: Joann P. Krieg*)

Goethe in the Twentieth Century
(*Editor: Alexej Ugrinsky*)

The Stendhal Bicentennial Papers
(*Editor: Avriel Goldberger*)

George Orwell
(*Editors: Courtney T. Wemyss and Alexej Ugrinsky*)